UNDERSTANDING SHADOWS

If you have a home computer with Internet access you may:
- request an item to be placed on hold.
- renew an item that is not overdue or on hold.
- view titles and due dates checked out on your card.
- view and/or pay your outstanding fines online ($1 & over).

To view your patron record from your home computer click on Patchogue-Medford Library's homepage: **www.pmlib.org**

UNDERSTANDING SHADOWS

The Corrupt Use of Intelligence

BY

MICHAEL QUILLIGAN

CLARITY PRESS, INC.

© 2013 Michael Quilligan

ISBN: 978-0-9853353-9-7
EBOOK: 978-0-9860362-8-6

In-house editor: Diana G. Collier
Cover: R. Jordan P. Santos

ALL RIGHTS RESERVED: Except for purposes of review, this book may not be copied, or stored in any information retrieval system, in whole or in part, without permission in writing from the publishers.

Library of Congress Cataloging-in-Publication Data

Quilligan, Michael.
  Understanding shadows : the corrupt use of intelligenece / by Michael Quilligan.
     pages cm
  Includes bibliographical references and index.
  ISBN 978-0-9853353-9-7 (alk. paper) -- ISBN 978-0-9853353-8-6 (ebook)
  1. Intelligence service--Moral and ethical aspects--Case studies. 2. Espionage--Moral and ethical aspects--Case studies. I. Title.

JF1525.I6Q55 2013
172'.4--dc23

2013022555

Clarity Press, Inc.
Ste. 469, 3277 Roswell Rd. NE
Atlanta, GA. 30305 , USA
http://www.claritypress.com

For Nelleke

TABLE OF CONTENTS

Foreword by Olivier Schmidt / 9

Chapter 1
SLOUCHING TOWARDS JERUSALEM / 15

Chapter 2
'LONDONISTAN' / 59

Chapter 3
THE ITCHING PALM / 111

Chapter 4
SEEING THINGS INVISIBLE / 153

Chapter 5
UNDERSTANDING SHADOWS / 202

Chapter 6
WITHOUT GRACE OR FAVOR / 238

Chapter 7
THE BUTCHER'S APRON / 278

Index / 336

FOREWORD

Mike Quilligan and I are no strangers to Clarity Press readers, particularly those interested in intelligence services, their activities and what we tend to call "Parapolitics": the real use of power as opposed to the publicly-acknowledged use of power. That, of course, covers intelligence, assassination, corruption, media manipulation and all forms of major scandals, whence the subject matter of this book: *Understanding Shadows: The Corrupt Use of Intelligence*. Our previous Clarity book – *The Intelligence Files: Today's Secrets, Tomorrow's Scandals* – clearly acknowledged Mike's contribution.

> Michael F. Quilligan has worked extensively with the ADI [the French Association for the Right to Information] and *Intelligence* [the ADI-published journal], particularly on British and Irish affairs and, in this vein, is responsible for [the chapters] "Losing a Spy Elite - The Chinook Crash and Operation Madronna," and "'Bloody Sunday' – The Search for the Truth Continues...." Using *Intelligence* material and his own work, he also wrote [the chapters] "'Son of Star Wars' – Alive & Well... in Norway," "The Sinking of the 'Kursk'," "Today Pinochet, Tomorrow Kissinger?," "New Europe's Old Belgium – Murder, 'Passive Corruption' and the Pink Ballet," and "Bull's 'Super Cannon' & Moyle's 'Suicide'."

If the 15 chapters of that 2005 book were presented as "bringing up-to-date" the series of the best and most important *parapolitical* stories of the late 1990s and early 2000s, then *Understanding Shadows* is its thoroughly qualified successor; these are the scandals that are far from "over and done" and that "just keep on giving."

Why has the deadly June 1967 Israeli attack against the *USS Liberty* never been publicly investigated in the US? Why, until quite recently, were all Arabs killed by Israeli military or Mossad death squads referred to without question as "terrorists" by the international press? The many innocent victims of Israel's low-intensity war of attrition against all those it considers enemies is the subject of Chapter 1, "Slouching Towards Jerusalem."

And London's own 9/11, which entailed four 7 July 2005 jihadist bombings that killed several dozen persons? Couldn't it have been prevented by British intelligence which had supposedly been watching certain of the perpetrators but somehow decided they were not that dangerous or weren't "going into action" in the near future, even though similar attacks had taken place in 2004 in Madrid on public transportation systems? This major "miscalculation" is thoroughly documented in Chapter 2, "Londonistan," a term French intelligence likes to use to shame its cross-Channel colleagues.

Following a long and honorable liberation struggle against a brutal racist regime, it's difficult to believe what the ANC and South Africa have become under President Jacob Zuma, addressed in Chapter 3, "The Itching Palm," revealing an unmitigated series of corruption scandals, dissolved investigative police services and sabotaged official inquiries. It's a sad but well-documented tale, helped along by major Western corporations trying to win huge lucrative contracts.

And do you still believe in Saddam Hussein's "weapons of mass destruction" (WMD) that British Prime Minister Tony Blair claimed could be deployed in "45 minutes"? Blair and the British Iraq war machine are the subject of Chapter 4, "Seeing Things Invisible." The Bush regime's "Office of Special Projects" in the Pentagon, the US-UK "band of liars" and "media fellow travellers" have brought us the modern world's most unwanted and unnecessary war which has destabilized the entire Middle East and aligned the Islamic world against the US, the UK and the Western world in general, and still no blame has been discerned neither in London, nor in Washington.

Although the Bush-Blair fraudulent allegation, "Saddam Hussein's WMDs," is one of the modern world's major scandals, it's still second to the JFK assassination conspiracy which still hasn't been "solved," according to worldwide public opinion. But interest has been concentrated on the actual assassination and following official and unofficial investigations, where Chapter 5, "Understanding Shadows," concentrates on the period before that; that is, on who Lee Harvey Oswald was and what he was doing before the assassination, besides working for the CIA from 1958 up until...

In an era where the term "non-state" is derogatory, as in "non-state terrorism," one of the West's favourite "non-states," the Vatican, has done amazingly well at "keeping below the radar" in the international press, despite the long-enduring and widespread sexual abuse of young people and its cover-up, and direct Vatican association with financial organized crime and extreme-right political plots both in Italy and internationally. Chapter 6, "Without Grace or Favor," documents much of this activity by major figures such as Paul Marcinkus, Michele Sindona and Licio Gelli.

And then there's Mike Quilligan's specialty, "The Troubles" in Northern Ireland, thoroughly covered in Chapter 7, "The Butcher's Apron," and for which British Prime Minister David Cameroun has just done a great publicity job by recognizing that British agents "were not foreign" to the 1989 assassination of Belfast solicitor Patrick Finucane... but there will be

Foreword by Olivier Schmidt

no public inquiry. The major topics are the British re-arming of loyalist death squads and getting them and the Royal Ulster Constabulary (RUC) to carry out Britain's war in Northern Ireland against the IRA and the nationalist population. The British Army's Force Research Unit (FRU) and the SAS were central in this murderous effort.

Current history has its mainstream chroniclers and the corporate media to let you know what you should think has been happening, but here – based on extensive documentation and research work – you will learn what is actually behind the glossy print and public façade of these major events.

Olivier Schmidt
Author & *Intelligence* Editor
Paris, May 2013

UNDERSTANDING SHADOWS

THE CORRUPT USE OF INTELLIGENCE

CHAPTER ONE

SLOUCHING TOWARDS JERUSALEM

"What shocks and worries me is the narrow-mindedness and the short-sightedness of our military leaders. They seem to presume that the State of Israel may, or even must, behave in the realm of international relations according to the laws of the jungle—the long chain of false incidents and hostilities we have invented, and so many clashes we have provoked."
Former Israeli Prime Minister, Moshe Sharett

The Blood-Stained Sea

It's Memorial Day 2012 in America. One of the keynote speakers at the annual ceremony which took place at the Veterans Museum & Memorial Center in San Diego, California, to remember US Armed Forces personnel who have died in military conflicts since the Civil War, was John McCain, Republican Senator for Arizona. During the course of his speech McCain was interrupted by political activist, James Morris, who wanted to ask the former US Navy officer and Vietnam War PoW, about the attack on the *USS Liberty* in June 1967 by Israeli Air Force (IAF) fighter aircraft and naval torpedo vessels. The attack had killed 34 US crew members and wounded 170. Morris, wearing a black 'PoW/MiA' tee-shirt, was quickly silenced by security personnel and escorted from the site, while the audience, who obviously didn't give a damn about this or any other war crimes carried out by the IDF during the Six Day War, shouted "take him down." On stage Sen. McCain, who ran against Barack Obama in 2008, summoned the courage to call Mr. Morris "a jerk." Some people laughed loudly, or chuckled quietly, like another failed presidential candidate, former Massachusetts governor, Mitt Romney, who shared the podium with his Republican Party colleague.

The mainstream media reported the interruption, highlighting McCain's response, but ignored the point that Morris was trying to make - the official cover-up of Israel's cowardly attack on a US vessel by successive Democrat and Republican administrations since Lyndon Baines Johnson's presidency. The incident has generated more official paperwork than most: official US Naval and Joint Chief of Staff inquiries, CIA

Intelligence memoranda, Senate Foreign Affairs testimony, a House Armed Services Committee investigation, and a National Security Agency (NSA) History Report. Despite (or because of) the slow release of classified records generated by judicious use of the Freedom of Information Act (FOIA), which applies to federal agencies but not to the NSA, a clear understanding of the event has been deliberately obscured by official confusion and unanswered questions remain.

The joint services Israel Defense Forces (IDF) attack on the *USS Liberty*, a Belmont-class US technical research vessel tasked by the NSA to carry out SIGINT operations and monitor areas of conflict communications, took place in international waters in the Mediterranean, north of the Sinai Peninsula and about twenty-five nautical miles northwest of the Egyptian coastal city of el-Arish, on 8 July 1967, during the Six Day War, as a result of which the state of Israel more than doubled in size, capturing the Golan Heights, the West Bank and East Jerusalem, the Gaza Strip and Sinai. The *USS Liberty* was a converted 441-foot, former World War II cargo vessel, with a maximum speed of 11.5 knots and a distinctive profile. It was unlikely to have been mistaken by highly-trained and properly briefed IAF pilots for the *el Quseir* a 38-year old, 220-foot Egyptian coastal transport, as was later claimed in Tel Aviv.

The attack, on the third day of the conflict, commenced at 2pm and lasted almost two hours, according to the testimony of survivors, during which IAF Mirage IIIC. single-seat jet fighters heavily strafed the vessel from bow to stern with amour-piercing ordnance, while one of five torpedoes launched from three high-speed attack boats struck the *Liberty* on the starboard side, blowing a 40-foot hole in the forward cargo hold which housed much of the high-tech research equipment. Twenty-five servicemen died in that explosion, which effectively crippled the *Liberty*. The Israeli gunboats then circled, repeatedly firing on the ship's firefighters before the stricken vessel was eventually escorted to Valletta, in Malta, by units of the US Sixth Fleet, where shipyard workers patched up hundreds of gaping holes in the superstructure. The Israeli regime's explanation for the attack was an implausible mix of mistaken identity by IAF pilots, a plotting error aboard the torpedo vessels which convinced them the *Liberty*, which was cruising at 5 knots, was actually traveling at almost 30 knots (the speed of a US Navy Iowa-class fast battleship) while a lack of communications during shift change between officers at IDF command and control meant the *Liberty* remained tagged as a real and present threat. The US administration, and senior Pentagon staff officers had no choice but to publicly accept the Israeli explanation. However US Secretary of State, Dean Rusk, who had served both JFK and LBJ from 1961 to 1969, made an effort to put the record straight, claiming in his memoir, *As I Saw It*, that he was "never satisfied with the Israeli explanation. Their sustained attack to disable and sink *Liberty* precluded an assault by accident or some trigger-happy local commander. Through diplomatic channels we refused to accept their explanation. I didn't believe them then, and I don't believe them to this day. The attack was outrageous."

Despite the private outrage the Pentagon immediately classified the incident. Survivors were threatened with court-martial or prison if they revealed "classified information" about the attack, and the dead were buried in a communal grave in Arlington National Cemetery. In May 1968 Israel paid $3,323, 500 to the families of those who died, and 10 months later a further $3,566,457 to the wounded and maimed. Finally , on 18 December 1980, the Likud administration, headed by Menachem Begin, paid $6 million to the US Government as settlement for the final NSA bill, less than one-third the cost for damage to the vessel and the *Liberty*'s SIGINT equipment

So why did Israel try to take out *USS Liberty*. In his critical and humane account of the incident one of the survivors, James Ennes, claims Israeli aircraft made several reconnaissance flights prior to the attack, jammed *Liberty*'s radio equipment during the assault, ignored the obvious and prominently displayed US flag, and later machine-gunned the ship's empty life-rafts which had been launched in the event of the ship having to be abandoned.

The attack on the *Liberty*, armed with only four deck-mounted, Browning .50 caliber heavy machine-guns, which were totally inadequate against the IDF's coordinated assault, was a deliberate war crime. It wasn't a misguided, error-prone, friendly-fire incident undertaken in the "fog of war." The only fog surrounding this incident is the deliberate, and well-managed US cover-up. The author, James Bamford, in *Body of Secrets*, rejects Israel's claim that the attack was "an accident" pointing out that the US spy ship was observed by an IAF Nord Noratlas 2501 reconnaissance aircraft flying at 4000 feet, and *the Liberty*'s identification 'GTR-5' (General Technical Research) - the cover designation for the NSA's fleet - was "reported back to Israeli naval headquarters." Bamford suggests that Israel wanted to prevent the *Liberty* eavesdropping on the deliberate execution, on shore nearby, of Egyptian prisoners of war.

Based on testimony from dozens of IDF service personnel who admitted killing POWs collated by Israeli military historian, Aryeh Yitzhaki, Bramford describes how the Israeli soldiers turned El-Arish "into a slaughterhouse, systematically butchering their prisoners. In the shadow of El Arish mosque they lined up about sixty unarmed Egyptian prisoners, hands tied behind their backs, and then opened fire with machine guns until the pale desert sand turned red. Then they forced other prisoners to bury the victims in mass graves." Nearby, another group of Israeli soldiers "gunned down thirty more prisoners and then ordered some Bedouins to bury them with sand." Bamford also quotes Israeli journalist, Gabi Bron, who witnessed about 150 Egyptian POWs sitting on the ground in the airport area of El Arish, crowded together with their hands behind their heads, who were then ordered to dig pits before Israeli Army police shot them dead. According to Yitzhaki, as many as 1000 Egyptian PoWs were killed in cold blood in occupied Sinai, including at least 400 in El Arish. One war crime carried out to prevent the disclosure of another.

Despite suggestions the *Liberty* attack might have been to prevent Washington learning of Israel's intention to seize and annex the Golan Heights from Syria, the Zionist regime, headed by Prime Minister Levi Eshkol, a former member of the paramilitary Haganah high command during the 1948 Arab-Israeli War, wasn't concerned about postwar condemnation of the confiscation of Arab lands. Following Eshkol's death from a heart attack while in office in February 1969, and the brief two-week premiership of Yigal Allon, Golda Meir took charge, and immediately dismissed suggestions that the occupied territories should be returned. To whom? As far as she was concerned there was nobody to return them to, telling journalists on 15 June 1969, "there was no such thing as Palestinians, they never existed." Golda Meir was saying nothing new; the "best man in government" as she was described by Israel's first prime minister, David Ben Gurion, was simply repeating what successive prime ministers had been saying since Ben Gurion, who assured fellow Zionists in 1948 that the Palestinians forced from their villages would never return to their homes, telling them "the old will die and the young will forget."

Ben Gurion, whose suggestion for a 'Central Institute for Coordination' following Israel's declaration of independence in May 1948, led to the founding of Mossad, had a brutally concise understanding of the displaced Palestinian response to what Israel was determined to achieve by force of arms. He is quoted in Nahum Goldmann's *Le Paraddoxe Juif* (The Jewish Paradox) candidly admitting he would never have signed a peace agreement with Israel if he was an Arab leader: "Is it normal, we have taken their country. It is true God promised it to us, but how could that interest them? Our God is not theirs. There has been Anti-Semitism, the Nazis, Hitler, Auschwitz, but was that their fault? They see but one thing; we have come and we have stolen their country. Why would they accept that?"

Profound changes took place, not only in the Middle East but also at CIA HQ, Langley, after the Six Day War. For all the wrong reasons. According to US Foreign Service political counselor at the US Embassy in Cairo from 1965 to 1967, Richard Bordeaux Parker, the Six Day War was "a turning point" in Washington's relationship with Tel Aviv. Up until then "we had avoided being a major arms supplier to Israel, afterwards the security of Israel became one of our strategic objectives." Mr. Parker, who later served as ambassador to Algeria, Lebanon and Morocco, was less than forthcoming with the 'actualite'. According to Mitchell Geoffrey Bard, executive director of the American Israeli Cooperative Enterprise (AICE) - which claims to be a non-profit, 'non-partisan' organization established in 1993 to strengthen the US-Israeli relationship "by emphasizing the fundamentals of the alliance" - the US had been providing arms indirectly to Israel via West Germany since 1962 under the terms of a secret agreement signed two years earlier. The deal involved $80 million worth of weapons, including M48 Patton tanks delivered in 1965, and A-4E Skyhawk attack aircraft in 1968. By June 1967 Israel was becoming the largest recipient of direct US economic and military assistance since WWII (until overtaken by Iraq in 2003) and the multi-million dollar package in the mid-1960s was used by Israel to consolidate its conquest of lands confiscated during the six-day conflict.

In his excellent account of Israel's clandestine nuclear capability at Dimona, Seymour Hersh writes that Walworth Barbour, the US ambassador to Israel, spent much of the time during the Six Day War in the IDF war room, and there was "no pretense of objectivity in his reporting to Washington: his views and those of the Israeli leadership were identical." Hersh refers to a declassified cable on file at the LBJ Library in which Barbour reported that hours after the incident Israel did not intend to admit responsibility, adding "urge strongly that we too avoid publicity. [*Liberty*'s] proximity to scene could feed Arab suspicions of US-Israel collusion (...) Israelis obviously shocked by error and tender sincere apologies." Things were also different at Langley after the war, according to Hersh, who quotes a senior intelligence officer describing the "big change" that took place: "All of a sudden a lot of people were saying the Israelis were wonderful (...) Israeli intelligence became untouchable, and the professional suspicions you should have about another intelligence service—even a friendly one—disappeared." The Pulitzer Prize-winning investigative journalist writes that this was "especially true" during the Nixon administration, when the president and his national security advisor, Henry Kissinger, "became renowned inside the CIA for preferring Mossad's intelligence assessments on the Middle East to those supplied by the Agency."

With such powerful political and covert friends in Washington, and sycophantic European governments willing to turn a blind eye and a deaf ear to Israel's biblical response to Palestinian resistance, it is not surprising that the various elements of Israel's intelligence apparatus, Mossad, Shit Bet (better known by the acronym 'Shabak') and the Military Intelligence Directorate (Aman), have continued to carry out acts of terror with impunity at home and abroad.

"War is a Cowardly Escape from the Problems of Peace."
(Thomas Mann)

In the foreword to Livia Rokach's monograph, Noam Chomsky describes Moshe Sharett's diary as a "major documentary source" which remains "outside official history" and which reaches no more than a tiny audience "unsatisfied by conventional doctrine." Indeed, Sharett, who served as prime minister from 1953 to 1955, between David Ben Gurion's two terms in office, had numerous examples on which to base his analysis, set against a background in the late 1940s of Zionist terror, carried out by militant organizations like Irgun Tzvai-Leumi, whose members included the founder of Likud and the country's sixth prime minister, Menachem Begin, and the Stern Gang, led by another future prime minister, Yitzhak Shamir.

Both organizations operated in the British Mandate of Palestine with a ruthlessness which has characterized the Zionist response to any perceived threat ever since, including the assassination of Walter Guinness, in Cairo on 6 November 1944, while the Dublin-born businessman and former British Army officer, who had fought during the 1914-1918 Great War at Gallipoli and Passchendaele, was serving as Britain's minister of state for the Middle East. There was a clear political motive behind that attack, namely to highlight British imperialist rule and 'Ha-Yishuv', the presence of thousands of Jewish settlers in Palestine since the 1880s. Taking the war abroad, to the streets of a foreign capital city, also maximized publicity in the international media for a struggle which the British Government had tried to pass off as an internal 'law and order' conflict. The Irgun bombing, on 22 July 1946, of the King David Hotel in Jerusalem, which housed the Mandate Secretariat and British military headquarters, killing ninety-one people of various nationalities and injuring dozens more, quickly put paid to that nonsense. The Zionists now turned their ruthless attention to the real enemy - the Palestinians.

On 9 April 1948 the combined forces of Irgun and the Stern Gang massacred 254 Arab civilians in Deir Yassin, a village 18 miles outside the UN-mandated borders "which the Zionist leaders pretended to have accepted in the partition plan" according to British historian, David Gilmour, who quotes Jacques de Reynier of the International Red Cross (IRC) describing how "the wretched survivors were publicly paraded through Jerusalem in order to spread terror among other sections of the [Arab] population." The terror was "astutely fostered by the Jews" and the Arabs, "driven by fear, left their homes to find shelter among their kindred; first isolated farms, then villages and in the end whole towns were evacuated," while the Hungarian author, Arthur Koestler called the Deir Yassin bloodbath "the psychologically decisive factor in this spectacular exodus."

The commander of paramilitary Haganah (which later formed the core of the IDF), Moshe Dayan, spread the fear through the Arab-populated towns of Haifa, where thousands were forced to flee by sea to Lydda and nearby Ramle. Three months after Deir Yassin, both towns were captured by Israeli fighters, and 30,000 Palestinian Arabs "either fled or were herded on to the road to Ramallah," according to journalist, David Kimich, in a contemporary report in the semi-official Zionist newspaper, the *Palestine Post* (now the Rupert Murdoch-owned *Jerusalem Post*). However, one of Israel's so-called "new historians" Professor Benny Morris, in his comprehensive and detailed study of the plight of the Palestinian refugees, published by Cambridge University, puts the number of displaced Palestinians at between 50,000 and 70,000, based on the populations of both towns before they were captured, all of whom were expelled, except some old and ill residents, and a few Arabs required for manual labor.

Both towns were located in an area designated as part of the Arab lands following the 1947 UN resolution for the approximately 50/50 partition of Palestine - which wasn't really worth the paper it was written on, and actually provided Zionist forces with an expansionist blueprint to satisfy their rapacious desire for land which could be defended and safely colonized. Within a year Israel had enlarged its share by 78 percent, annexing over fifty percent more of the territory allocated by the UN, and the Zionist writ ran from the Lebanese border, to the Egyptian-controlled Sinai Peninsula, with the exception of a strip of land now known as Gaza, and the border-crossing at Rafah, while West Bank lands were also seized, and Jerusalem, designated an international zone, was occupied. This was the second stage of the conquest and colonization of Arab Palestine. The third stage would follow after the Six Day War.

Meanwhile there was still killing to be done. Low intensity warfare and 'mopping-up' operations, such as the massacre at Qibya, a village in the West Bank, which began at 9.30pm on 14 October 1953, carried out by members of IDF Special Forces Unit 101, headed by yet another future prime minister, Ariel Sharon, and a company of paratroopers, on the orders of Ben Gurion. An estimated sixty-nine Palestinian Arabs, two thirds of them women and children, were killed, many while hiding in houses, a school and a mosque later blown up by the Israelis. The massacre was in retaliation for the deaths of three Jewish settlers by an improvised explosive device earlier in the month, and although the Qibya villagers had nothing to do with that attack "the orders were utterly clear, Qibya was to be an example for everyone," Sharon wrote in his autobiography, *Warrior*. He also claimed the victims had hidden in the "cellars and back rooms of the big stone houses" and had kept quite while the buildings were searched by paratroopers before being demolished. However, a report by UN observer, Major General Vagn Bennike, the Danish chief of staff of the UN Truce Supervision Organization, designated *UN Doc S/PV630* and dated 27 October 1953, reached a different conclusion—many bodies were sprawled lying near bullet-riddled doorways, or sprawled across the thresholds, "indicating that the inhabitants had been forced by heavy fire to stay inside until their homes were blown up over them."

In his diary, four days after the slaughter of the innocent, Moshe Sharett writes that he condemned the Qibya killings during a Cabinet meeting, telling his colleagues that it had

> exposed us in front of the whole world as a gang of blood-suckers, capable of mass massacres regardless, it seems, of whether their actions may lead us to war. I warned that this stain will stick to us and will not be washed away for many years to come (...) It was decided that a communiqué on Kibya [the Hebrew spelling] will be published and Ben Gurion was to write it. I insisted on including an expression of regret. Ben Gurion insisted on excluding any responsibility of the army [claiming that]

the civilians of the border areas, enraged by the constant murders, have taken justice into their own hands. After all [Ben Gurion said] the border settlements are full of arms and the settlers are ex-soldiers (...) I said that no one in the world would believe such a story and we shall only expose ourselves as liars. But I couldn't seriously demand that the communiqué explicitly affirm the army's responsibility because this would have made it impossible to condemn the act and we will have ended up approving this monstrous bloodbath.

Ben Gurion's version of events was broadcast on Israeli radio the following day, telling listeners that many of the border settlers were Jewish refugees from Arab countries and from Nazi concentration camps who had been the target of "murderous attacks for many years and had shown great restraint." When they demanded protection the Israeli Government had given them weapons and trained them to protect themselves, but armed forces from Transjordan continued their criminal acts until some of the border settlers "lost their patience and after the murder of a mother and her two children in Yahud," they attacked Qibya, which he described as "one of the centers of the murderous gangs." He went on to express the Cabinet's regret for the shedding of innocent blood, before claiming that "responsibility for the atrocity" rests with the Transjordan Government which, for many years, "tolerated and thus encouraged attacks of murder and robbery by armed powers in its country against the citizens of Israel," and ended his litany of lies by stating that Israel "strongly rejects that ridiculous and fantastic version [of IDF responsibility] as if 600 soldiers participated [in the operation] against Qibya. We had conducted a thorough check and found out that not even the smallest army unit was missing from its base on the night of the attack on Qibya."

Necessary Lies and Delusions

Until the *Liberty* incident American domestic law-makers and senior Department of Foreign Affairs officials had cultivated the myth of the US role as 'honest broker' in Middle East affairs. During the Suez crisis in 1956 the US, the USSR and the UN had forced Britain, France and Israel to withdraw from Egypt, which stymied Israel's expansionist policy for more than a decade. When the opportunity to seize more land arose through conflict in 1967 the Israelis were determined not to be pushed back behind the 1948 peacetime borders. While the attack on the *USS Liberty*, and the publicly accepted apology, stymied official condemnation of the murders of Egyptian PoWs by US lawmakers, it also served as a warning to Washington not to repeat the 'folly' of Suez. This time around land seized would remain under Zionist control. Tel Aviv knew that Washington knew that Israel had the determination and the means to defend the spoils of war if necessary.

The role of honest broker demands transparency. Yet by 1967 successive US administrations since the Eisenhower era had 'signed-up' to the unwritten and unspoken policy of 'strategic ambiguity,' neither confirming nor denying that Israel was a nuclear power. This proverbial 'three wise monkeys' approach to the Zionist state's nuclear ambitions had facilitated the transfer of weapons-grade uranium, dual-use technology and classified data to Israel for more than a decade, according to a top-secret Government Accounting Office (GAO) 1978 report, *Nuclear Diversion in the US: 13 Years of Contradiction and Confusion,* finally released on 6 May 2010 by the (renamed) Government Accountability Office at UN headquarters in New York during the 2010 Review Conference of the Treaty on the Non-Proliferation of Nuclear Weapons.

The 62-page GAO report covered a ten year period from 1957 to 1967, and confirmed that the US law enforcement agencies failed to carry out a proper and credible investigation into security lapses at the Nuclear Materials and Equipment Corporation (NUMEC) plant at Apollo, Pennsylvania. Suspicions had been raised about the unaccountable loss of over 200 pounds of highly-enriched uranium-235 (U-235), following an audit by the Atomic Energy Commission (AEC) the Washington-based agency which regulated the entire scope of the nuclear industry, including scientific research and technology, which had been under civilian authority since 1946.

NUMEC was founded in 1957 by the Ohio-born, John Hopkins University-educated chemist, Zalman Mordecai Shapiro, with the aim of developing new conversion process methods for the production of nuclear fuel for utility power reactors. A life-long Zionist, he was a procurement agent for the Israeli Defense Ministry in the US, and a senior member of the Zionist Organization of America (ZOA), an influential group among the Jewish Diaspora founded in 1896 and "dedicated to the creation of a Jewish state in Palestine."

NUMEC's initial funding was organized by US citizen, David Lowenthal, who had fought with the Haganah during the 1948 Arab-Israeli War alongside Meir Amit, a protégé of Moshe Dayan who headed Aman in 1961, and two years later was appointed head of Mossad until 1968, the only Israeli ever to be in charge of both civilian and military intelligence organizations simultaneously. Several of NUMEC's directors also held "leadership positions" in the ZOA, according to Grant Smith, journalist and director of the Washington-based Institute for Research: Middle Eastern Policy (IRmep). In 1966 Shapiro incorporated an Israeli company called Isotopes and Radiation Enterprises Limited (ISORAD) to manage a range of research projects which involved "exposing agricultural products to radiation to kill micro-organisms and extend the shelf-life of fruit and vegetables." Shapiro's business partner in this venture was Ernest David Bergmann, who chaired Israel's Atomic Energy Commission (IAEC) from 1954 to 1966, an organization Smith describes as "the primary cover for Israel's clandestine nuclear weapons program."

Following AEC suspicions and an 'unsatisfactory' FBI investigation into the clandestine activities of Shapiro, the GAO had been asked to focus on three specific allegations: that U-235 had been "illegally diverted to Israel by NUMEC management" (enough to produce "dozens of nuclear weapons" according to Smith); that the CIA (laughingly described in the mainstream media as the world's nuclear proliferation 'watchdog') was involved; and that the LBJ administration acquiesced, in 1965, in the subterfuge and the subsequent cover-up of the 'Apollo affair.'

The AEC and the Department of Energy (DoE) cooperated with the GAO, but the FBI and the CIA "continually denied necessary reports and documentation" and FBI director, J Edgar Hoover, refused to allow FBI Special Agents who had been involved in the flawed investigation to be directly interviewed by GAO staffers. Although the GAO report is critical of the FBI's "on-again off-again approach to investigating NUMEC" the bureau was sufficiently concerned about the "security risks" posed by Shapiro to ask the DoE to consider terminating his security clearance and the transfer of sensitive materials to NUMEC. When the FBI's request was ignored the bureau shelved its investigation, and according to the GAO, "until the summer of 1977, the only publicized Government view on the NUMEC incident was that there was no evidence to indicate that a diversion of nuclear materials had occurred." The report described as "seriously flawed" the DoE's nuclear safety procedures which, prior to 1967, tracked the movement of materials such as uranium by monetary value rather than mass. NUMEC had claimed that during a "labor dispute" in 1964 key records covering the period of U-235 diversion were "unaccountably lost" and when NUMEC paid a $1.1 million fine two years later for the missing uranium, the DoE closed the file.

The subterfuge continued, however, and it is inconceivable that Langley was so blind-sided by such silliness as to believe that a visit to NUMEC's Philadelphia plant on 10 September 1968 by Israeli "thermo electric generator specialists" was for any reason other than a damage-limitation mission to assess the work in progress on the Zionist 'A Bomb'. The delegation included Avraham Hermoni, technical director of the nuclear bomb project, based at the Israeli embassy in Washington, and station chief of an organization which would later become known as Lekem; senior Shabak official (and later director of the organization from 1981 to 1986) Avraham Shalom Ben-Dor; and Rafi Eitan, long-time Mossad and Lekem operative who would later 'handle' Jonathan Pollard's espionage activities in the US. In their visa applications both Ben-Dor and Eitan listed themselves as "chemists with the Israeli Defense Ministry." When they returned to Tel Aviv, according to authors Raviv and Melman, they reported that Israel "still enjoyed the benefit of any doubt and would get away with its uranium procurement."

The Israelis certainly covered their tracks well. Grant Smith has dug deep, and concluded that there is "no single smoking gun" to show conclusively that Shapiro and NUMEC diverted U-235 to Israel, but there are "many smoking shell-casings." The former CIA chef-of-station in Tel Aviv in the mid-1960s, John Hadden, was under no illusion as to whether or not NUMEC was a clandestine Israeli intelligence operation, which provided its startup capital, while Jewish historian and writer on nuclear issues, Avner Cohen, has claimed that in 1958 Israeli PM Ben Gurion had arranged with US businessman, philanthropist and Democratic Party fundraiser, Abraham Feinberg, to secretly coordinate funding for Israel's nuclear weapons program among the wealthy Jewish Diaspora in the US. Feinberg had been a major contributor to Harry S. Truman's successful April 1945 whistle-stop presidential campaign, and had "opened doors in Congress" for leaders of the Israeli lobby in Washington, including Isaiah Kenen, the founder of the American Israel Public Affairs Committee (AIPAC). Seymour Hersh believes there is no question that Feinberg "enjoyed the greatest presidential access and influence" over a twenty year period which included the LBJ administration. Documentation at the Johnson Library and Museum in Austin, Texas, confirms that "even the most senior members of the National Security Council (NSC) understood that any issue raised by Feinberg had to be answered" and this, presumably, included the White House response to the assault on the *USS Liberty*. Other willing contributors to Feinberg's clandestine fundraising efforts, according to Israeli investigative journalist, Michael Karpin, included Canadian beverage magnate, Samuel Bronfman, founder of Distillers Corporation Limited, and several members of the Rothschild banking family.

The Problems of Peace

If war is an "escape from the problems of peace," as Thomas Mann suggests, Israel's unforgiving use of terror is certainly that, and while the securocrats might claim the bloodshed had paid dividends in many unexpected ways, it has not enhanced Israel's sense of security. Following the *USS Liberty* sinking, Israel's response to the Palestinians' outrage at the loss of land and seizure of property was to "strike at the nerve-centers of the Arab terrorists" using letter-bombs and car-bombs. Mossad assassins gunned down Palestinian leaders and intellectuals in the capitals of Europe in retaliation for acts of aggression – state-sponsored terror which only served to embed the spirit of resistance in the next generation of Palestinians. Refugee camps - poorly-constructed, over-crowded impoverished slums - were targeted by the IDF. On 21 March 1968, following Operation *Inferno* and a major gun battle with the Palestinian Al- Fatah Movement and Jordanian Army units near the Allenby Bridge border crossing, more than 175 buildings were destroyed and hundreds of Palestinians taken prisoner at the Karameh refugee camp, where the political and military headquarters of the Al-Fatah, led by Yasser Arafat, the largest faction within the Palestinian Liberation Organization (PLO) multi-party confederation, was based. Although the combined PLO/Jordanian

Army fatalities were close to 300 compared to the IDF losses of 32 Paras and members of the 7th Brigade, as well as armored vehicles, including four tanks, and two aircraft, it was a psychological victory for the PLO, because it helped establish their claim to Palestinian statehood. In response to Israeli aggression Jordan's King Hussein proclaimed "we are all fedayeen now," and before the smoke had cleared from the battlefield Fatah had replaced the fighters killed or captured.

Over the next 18 months the IDF focused on the threat from across the Suez Canal. The Defense Ministry, headed by 1967 War veteran and former Chief of Staff, Moshe Dayan, a member of the inner-circle 'Ministers Committee on Security Affairs,' still regarded Egypt under President Gamal Nasser as the most dangerous of the Arab nations. The USSR had replaced much of the Egyptian Armed Forces (EAF) stock destroyed during what is locally described as *an-Naksah* (the Set Back). The IDF, determined to underline its military superiority and encouraged by Washington (which now officially regarded Israel as a proxy ally in the Cold War), launched Operation *Boxer,* in July 1969. Over an eight day period, a successful, three-phase IAF aerial assault took place against SAM2-batteries and the Fan Song radar site near Port Said and the Gebel Ataka radar station, while missile strikes and bombings targeted Egyptian ground forces. On 19 July 1969, elements of the IDF's General Reconnaissance Staff 'Sayeret Matkal' unit and 'Shayetet 13' naval commandos destroyed an Egyptian ELINT station and early warning radar site at Al Jazeera Al Khadraa, a small island fortress built by the British during WWII, about 2 miles south of the city of Suez. Less than two months later, on 9 September, IDF land and naval forces, using captured Arab hardware, launched Operation *Raviv* across the canal. In the ensuing 10 hour battle, the EAF suffered 200-300 casualties, including a senior Soviet Army officer serving as a consultant, the destruction of a radar site at Ras Safrana and a dozen military outposts. The raid led to a purge of senior staff within the EAF, including the dismissal of the army's chief of staff, General Ahmad Ismail Ali, and the commander in chief of the Navy, Vice-Admiral Fouad Abu Zikry. Both officers were recalled when Anwar Sadat succeeded Nasser the following year, with Ismail being appointed head of the country's powerful General Intelligence Service (GIS). The year 1969 ended with Operation *Rooster* - the capture of an Egyptian P-12 *Yenisei* 'VHF radar system, manufactured by the Soviet Union in the mid-1950s, which was sited on a beach at Ras-Arab, by the IDF Nahal Brigade's 50th battalion and IAF US-manufactured F-4 Phantom and A-4 Skyhawk ground attack aircraft, French-manufactured Aerospatiale SA 321 Super Felon three-engine, heavy-lift helicopters, and Sikorsky CH-53 Jolly Green Giants, originally developed for use by the US Marine Corps in the mid-1960s.

The low-intensity 'war of attrition' against Egypt had a psychological as well as a military objective. The campaign against the largest army in the Arab world, in terms of manpower and equipment, resulting in several 'defeats' in successive raids across the Suez, served as a warning to other Arab states, damaged (through association) the military prestige of the USSR, undermined the Politburo's expansionist plans for the region at the

Slouching Towards Jerusalem

height of the Cold War, and embedded Israel as a reliable ally of the US and the western Europeans.

In Jordan 'Black September' emerged from the ashes of Karameh and the factional feuds within the Palestinian Diaspora after King Hussein expelled the refugees, in September 1970, and closed the camps following an unsuccessful attempt by the Popular Front for the Liberation of Palestine (PFLP), headed by George Habash, to challenge the Hashemite monarch's authority. The PFLP had seized 80 guests at the International Hotel in Amman, in June 1970, and hijacked three commercial airliners en route to New York - Pan Am Boeing 747 from Brussels, TWA flight 741 from Frankfurt and a Swiss Air Douglas DC-8 from Zurich - on 6 September. The planes were diverted to a former British RAF airbase, Dawson's Field, at Az-Zarqa, northeast of the capital Amman, where they were subsequently destroyed in front of the world's media five days later, after the passengers had been released. Hussein declared martial law, deployed his forces into Palestinian-controlled areas of the country, and over a 10 month period, until July 1971, killed or captured thousands of Palestinians.

Black September was not a breakaway Fatah faction. It was the *nom de guerre* of a specialist unit, formed following the Jordanian turmoil when the PLO was "unable to realize its military and political potential," according to Arafat's deputy intelligence chief, Salah Khalaf, later assassinated on the streets of Tunis, in January 1991. On 5/6 September 1972, eight members of Black September targeted the Israeli team during the Summer Olympics in Munich. Eleven members of the squad, five Black September gunmen, and a West German police officer died in a badly-managed and poorly-executed hostage-release operation at Furstenfeldbruck NATO airbase, near the Bavarian capital. Three Palestinians were captured, and later released by the West German authorities following the hijacking of a Lufthansa airliner. Israel's response was codenamed *Wrath of God,* signed-off by Prime Minister, Golda Meir, and carried out by Mossad, which reports directly to the prime minister's office. As former agent, Victor Ostrovsky, put it, Mossad's uninhibited operations carried out on the orders of successive prime ministers by a "ruthless group of highly-trained assassins, spies and saboteurs" hunting down and eliminating alleged 'enemies' of Israel "have turned the Zionist dream into a nightmare."

Golda Meir, once described by *Ha'aretz,* the country's oldest, Tel Aviv-based, daily newspaper, as the "grey-bunned grandmother of the Jewish people" signed death warrants for alleged members of Black September prominent on a list compiled by Mossad, including the organization's Beirut-based operations officer, Muhammad Yusif al-Najjar, and Al Hassan Salameh, known as the 'Red Prince' who, Mossad claimed, was based in East Berlin when he masterminded the Munich massacre. However, there were others on the death list, Palestinians linked to the political struggle but not connected with Black September, and if the horrors of the Third Reich death camps provided emotional cover for the terror inflicted on populated Palestinian villages in the late 1940s, the deaths of eleven Israelis at Munich was exploited by Mossad to eliminate these "troublesome bystanders."

The first post-Munich operation took place in Rome, on 16 October 1973, when Mossad agents gunned down the PLO's local representative, Abdel Wa'il Zwaiter, while he waited for an elevator in his apartment building. American author Aaron Klein believes that the 38-year-old waiter's death was an error, the result of "un-collaborated and improperly cross-referenced" intelligence.

Mossad's second victim was the PLO's representative in France, Dr Mahmoud Hamshari, who was fatally wounded, on 8 December, when a bomb hidden in the receiver of his desk telephone in his Paris apartment was detonated by remote signal when he answered a call. Hamshari died in hospital one month later. Fatah's representative in Cyprus, Hussein Al-Bashir, died in his second-floor room in Nicosia's Olympic Hotel, when a bomb hidden beneath his bed was detonated by remote control, on 24 January 1973. Just over two months later, on 6 April, Professor Basil al-Kubaissi, a member of the law faculty at the American University in Beirut, was shot dead by two Mossad gunmen while returning to his Paris apartment. Those who could not be reached by Mossad death squads - Kamal Nasser, Yusif al-Najjer and Kamal Adwen - were reached by IDF Special Forces and died, three days later, during an attack on the PFLP's six-storey headquarters in downtown Beirut, while in Paris, on 28 June, Algerian-born, Mohammad Boudia, died when a shrapnel-packed bomb exploded beneath the front seat of his car.

One killing attracted more international attention than most of the others - and became known as the 'Lillehammer fiasco' - when six Mossad operatives, two women, Marianne Gladnikoff and Sylvia Rafael, and four male colleagues, were arrested by Norwegian police following the murder of Moroccan waiter, Ahmed Bouchiki, who was shot repeatedly while walking with his pregnant wife near the city center on the evening of 21 July 1973. The arrested assassins claimed he had been mistakenly identified as Ali Salameh, to whom he bore no physical resemblance. In statements to Norway's Police Surveillance Agency (POT) officers, they revealed embarrassing details about Mossad's clandestine network, leading to the recall and debriefing of *kidon* units, the closing down of safe houses across Europe, warning of informants and changing of all contact details, including dead-letter drops and secret phone numbers. The Mossad agents were charged with second-degree murder, and each received five year jail sentences. The leader of the death squad, Michael Harari, was fired following an internal inquiry, while the intended target, Ali Salameh would die six years later, killed by a car-bomb in Beirut in an operation masterminded by Rafi Eitan.

It is difficult to determine how many of those whom Mossad assassinated by bullet and bomb were directly linked to Black September terror, and how many were simply Palestinian political activists, only making a propaganda nuisance of themselves, but worthy of elimination as far as a vengeful Zionist regime was concerned. The full truth about *Wrath of God* is buried beneath layers of unaccountable speculation, disinformation and lies. Even the numbers on Mossad's death-list ranges from twenty, according to Simon Reeve, to "about thirty-five" according to ex-Mossad agent, Ostrovsky. Authors like Gordon Thomas, Dan Raviv and Yossi Melman, accept without question that those on Mossad's death list were Black September activists linked to Munich and deserved to die, while Aaron Klein believes most of those killed were "minor Palestinian figures who happened to be wandering unprotected around Europe." While Israeli security officials, and press statements invariably described the dead as responsible for Munich, the PLO contributed to the myth-making by claiming the victims were important individuals, and so "the image of the Mossad as capable of delivering death at will grew and grew." A senior Mossad source, quoted by Klein, explained that another objective of the clandestine campaign was to "deter future acts of terrorism" - as far as Israel's security and intelligence apparatus was concerned "one dead PLO operative was a good as another" and when information implicating individuals was obtained "we didn't inspect it with a magnifying glass."

This type of slipshod approach to intelligence gathering and basic covert methodology left the whole clandestine network open to abuse by informants with an alternative agenda, as well as exposing agents to personal risk. Men like Baruch Cohen, one of Mossad's senior and more experienced officers and a veteran of the Six Day War, who had been a member of Shabak for ten years, working undercover in Gaza before transferring to the foreign intelligence service. In 1970, under diplomatic cover, using the name 'Moshe Hanan Yishai' and posing as an Israeli businessman, he had been posted to the Israeli Embassy in Brussels, and tasked with tracking PLO political activists and sympathizers. According to reports in the Israeli media, including the now-defunct journal, *Monitin,* and the Hebrew-language, evening newspaper, *Maariv,* Cohen had been photographed in combat fatigues in an IDF coffee-table book, published in 1970 to mark 1,000 days since the 1967 War (which might explain why he was posted overseas). The photograph showed Cohen alongside Zadok Ophir, another Brussels-based Mossad agent, who had been shot and wounded while sitting with Cohen in a Brussels café, waiting to meet an ex-con Moroccan informer, Muhammad Rabah, who had written to the Israeli Embassy while serving time in a Belgian prison, offering information about the PLO's network in Europe. His cover compromised after this incident, Cohen was moved to Spain, and died outside a Madrid cafe on the Gran Via, on 23 January 1973, gunned down by a Fatah recruit, a Palestinian medical student, whom Cohen was attempting to cultivate as an informant

Baruch Cohen's death was avoidable. After the Brussels incident he should have been recalled, but Mossad managers in Tel Aviv were beginning to believe their own propaganda, reading press-cuttings about the organization's competence and invincibility, and the unfortunate agent was allowed to continue traveling throughout Europe, meeting with agency contacts and informants. There were several opportunities during the two years prior to his death for Fatah to have killed him, but he had been allowed to live long enough for Fatah to track and identify Mossad's network of agents throughout the Netherlands, Belgium, France and Spain. Just two months before his death, in November 1972, Khodr Kanou, a Syrian journalist suspected of being a Mossad informant, died in the doorway of his apartment in Paris, and two months after Cohen's death, on 12 March 1973, en elderly Jewish businessman, Simha Gilzer, was killed in Cyprus. This war of the wolves, waged on the streets of several European cities, sometimes in the shadows, sometimes in broad daylight on crowded thoroughfares, had also spread fear among pro-Palestinian sympathizers, often naive members of solidarity committees, and undermined the willingness of 'non-combatants' to get directly involved in 'offensive tasks' such as facilitating the letter-bomb campaign which had fatally injured Dr Ami Shachori at the Israeli Embassy on Palace Green in London, on 19 September 1972, when he opened a package addressed to the "agricultural counselor." The device, in a manila envelope, had passed through the consulate's post-room and the British postal service's sorting office in Earls Court where diplomatic mail was regularly screened, and was one of dozens of similar packages posted in Amsterdam to Israeli embassies and consulates worldwide.

Israeli casualties made headlines, but the relationship between accredited diplomats and Mossad was hardly mentioned or even hinted at, and while it has never been shown that men like Simha Gilzer, for example, had any intelligence connections, the relationship between the foreign intelligence agency and the Jewish Diaspora worldwide accommodates such allegations. The Palestinians were roundly condemned by host-country ministers of state, but Israel was seldom rebuked for its part in the tit-for-tat killings. For many European nations, occupied during WWII, their policy towards Israel is a mixture of guilt and redemption for the fate of European Jewry during that period, and the Zionist regime is never slow to exploit this vacuous approach to the Middle East conflict and the "question of Palestine" by playing the Holocaust card.

"I will show you fear in a handful of dust" (T.S. Eliot)

Mossad's assassination campaign in the 1970s was a singular application of terror targeting individual Europe-based Palestinians, not dissimilar to the KGB's Cold War murders of Soviet dissidents. Efficient remorseless executions, by whatever means necessary. Despite the propaganda, attacks on Israeli interests abroad were planned in Beirut or Damascus, not in the capitals of Europe. Eliminating Palestinian political sympathizers silenced the voices of dissent raised in protest against ultra-orthodox settler practices in the occupied areas, and IDF military operations which facilitated colonial expansion.

Soviet-manufactured, WWII-vintage, self-propelled, inaccurate and indiscriminate Katyusha rockets, home-made, improvised explosive devices (IEDs), AK-47 assault rifles and portable, unguided RPG-7 anti-tank ordnance, was the Palestinian arsenal against the formidable, sophisticated, and lethal array of military equipment, from small arms to artillery, tanks and armored fighting vehicles, anti-tank rockets and missiles, from SMAWs, to *Popeye* AGMs, IAI Kfir all-weather, multi-role combat aircraft (a locally-modified version of the French-manufactured Dassualt Mirage fighters used during the 1967 War), a range of fast, off-shore assault watercraft, all supported by sophisticated remote, ground-based and aerial weapons systems, fire-control and tracking radar, air defense systems and optronics. In addition there is a huge arsenal of Soviet and Warsaw Pact-manufactured equipment captured from Arab armies and Palestinian resistance groups, some of which Israel provided to Central and Latin American death-squads and dictators, while acting as the Reagan administration's proxy arms supplier in the early 1980s. According to former Canadian diplomat and UC Berkley professor, Peter Dale Scott, the covert role of ex-IDF personnel, men like Colonel Yair Klein, in training members of CIA-endorsed military and drug cartel alliances in Colombia, drew a comment from a member of the Israeli Knesset, who described Israel as "the dirty work contractor for the US administration (...) acting as an accomplice and arm of the United States."

Outgunned on the battlefield, it was only a matter of time before Palestinian and Islamic militants resorted to what journalist Robert Fisk describes as the "fearful, unstoppable instrument of mass destruction" - the suicide bomber. There was nothing new about the concept of self-sacrifice in battle, but it was a an unexpected development in the Middle East, having no traditional basis in Islam, according to Harvard Law School professor Noah Feldman, who points out in his *New York Times* article, entitled *Islam, Terror and the Second Nuclear Age,* that as a technique it was also "totally absent from the successful Afghan jihad against the Soviet Union." One explanation for this, of course, was that the Afghan mujihadeen were well-armed by the CIA, MI6 and Pakistan's Inter-Services Intelligence (ISI) agencies, well-financed by the US, Saudi Arabia and other interested parties, and had access to ECHELON-generated intelligence. Feldman states that the suicide bomber "became a tool of modern terrorist warfare only in 1983, when Shiite militants blew up the US Marine base in Lebanon." Israel had, in fact, experienced a suicide attack more than a decade earlier, in May 1972, when three members of the Japanese Red Army (JRA) recruited and trained specifically for the task by the PFLP at a camp in Lebanon's Bequa Valley, arrived on an Air France flight from Rome, and launched a gun and grenade attack in the arrivals hall of Lod International Airport, 12 miles southeast of Tel Aviv city center, firing indiscriminately at passengers and staff, and killing 26 people. Two of the 'kamikazi' attackers were among the dead, the third gunman was wounded by security personnel, and served a 13 year prison sentence before being released in 1985 as part of a prisoner exchange deal with the PLO/PFLP.

To some degree the Lod Airport massacre was the brutal consequence of the failure of those within the civil intelligence community responsible for security at high-value, infrastructure sites, including Shabak's Protective Security Department (PSD). The PFLP had recognized and exploited the weakness, and in terms of the war being waged in the early 1970s it was regarded by Israel's enemies as a "successful operation."

The IDF's intelligence directorate, known as Aman, came in for criticism the following year for failing to monitor the Soviet re-arming of Egypt, and the pressure being brought to bear on President Anwar El Sadat by the senior echelons of the Egyptian Army to take back what had been lost in 1967 after Israel refused to negotiate the return of Sinai, or the Golan Heights to Syria. President Sadat had succeeded Gamal Nasser in October 1970, and the following year purged the political and military establishments of the most ardent 'Nasserists' in his administration. Sadat's "corrective revolution" also included a crackdown and imprisonment of political opponents including militant socialists, liberals and Islamists, and the promotion of a more nationalist society. In a letter to UN Special Envoy, Swedish diplomat, Gunnar Jarring, he also endorsed peace proposals, outlined in UN Security Council Resolution 242, which referred to the "inadmissibility of the acquisition of territory by war and the need to work for a just and lasting peace in the Middle East in which every state in the area can live in peace."

While there is no specific mention in the preamble to the plight of the stateless Palestinians, there was enough on offer which could have prevented the 1973 Yom Kippur War, had Israel and the US shown a willingness to accepted a UN-negotiated peace. But Tel Aviv and Washington were blind to the pressure on Sadat, and when diplomacy was rejected, the only option for Sadat was to retake Sinai by force. A coalition of willing Arab states, including Syria seeking to regain the Golan Heights, went to war with Israel, on 6 October 1973, with Egyptian forces successfully crossing the Suez Canal, destroying the massive, 100 miles long 'Ben Lev Line,' the supposedly impregnable defensive concrete and sand fortifications built by Israel on the canal's eastern coast at a cost of $300 million following the 1967 War. Egyptian amour and infantry penetrated about 10 miles into Sinai under cover of SAM batteries on the west bank before Israel managed to coordinate a response. Dug in beneath the SAM umbrella the Egyptians successful held the handful of sand gained, until a balance of sorts was reached when three IDF divisions, commanded by General Ariel Sharon, crossed Suez to the north of the Great Bitter Lake, and attempted to encircle the Egyptian Second Army. On the Golan Heights the war ended with the Israelis reclaiming the territory initially seized in a surprise Syrian attack, though both sides suffered heavy air and armor losses.

In total the Arab armies lost an estimated 20,000 dead and 35,000 wounded, while Israel's dead was estimated at 2,600, with 8,000 wounded and almost 300 captured, with 400 tanks and 102 aircraft destroyed, according to a declassified White House *Memorandum of Conversation*, dated 22 October 1973, between Prime Minister Meir, Defense Minister Moshe Dayan, the former Israeli ambassador, Yitzhak Rabin, IDF Staff of Staff, Lt. General David Elazar, the head of Aman, Major General Eliyahu Zeira and other senior IDF officials, and an American delegation representing the Nixon administration, which included Secretary of State, Henry Kissinger, and senior State Department and NSC staff. Having been briefed on Israel's progress and losses to Soviet SAM-7 missiles, and the quality of Egyptian and Syrian ground-forces and leadership, described as "significantly better" than in 1967, Kissinger expressed his and President Nixon's "admiration for the great military and political victory achieved," telling Meir "we're confident you'll be as successful in peace as in battle. Wherever you will be, you can count on us." Four days after the 45 minute military meeting at the secure 'Guest House' in Herzliya, the western suburb of Tel Aviv, and following the threat of Soviet intervention, a Kissinger-brokered ceasefire under the auspices of the UNSC was agreed.

When generals become politicians they also become aware of the political consequences of a rising body count for a few acres of sand. The three week conflict marked the end of conventional all-services warfare between Israel and its Arab neighbors, and when Egypt, Jordan and Israel signed UNSC Resolution 344 at a summit conference in Geneva in December 1973 calling for a "just and durable peace," the Israelis could now turn their attention to the Palestinian and Hezbollah threat. The Yom Kippur War was a military victory but a psychological defeat for Israel, and a report by Israeli Supreme Court president, Shimon Agranat, published in Tel Aviv in April 1974, criticized the complacency of the military and intelligence establishment, recommended the dismissal of the IDF and Aman leadership, and led to the resignation of Golda Meir and her cabinet. She was succeeded by Yitzhak Rabin, a Haganah veteran and former IDF general, who had been present, with David Ben Gurion, at a clandestine meeting in Haifa in 1942, when the momentous decision was taken to provide a homeland in Palestine for the survivors of the Nazi persecution and deportation of the Jewish citizens of occupied Europe. He was aware that it would lead to a bloody confrontation with the indigenous population, and probably the British, but could not have known, back then, that the manner of achieving this would determine the course of Israeli history from that day to this.

Yitzhak Rabin's first term as prime minister lasted from June 1974 to April 1977, and he was succeeded by Menachem Begin, who had led the Haganah breakaway Zionist faction, Irgun, from 1943 to 1948. Once denounced as a 'terrorist' by the British Government, he signed a peace treaty with Egypt in 1979, returning the demilitarized Sinai sands to the Sadat regime, and shared the Nobel Prize for Peace with the Egyptian president. He also signed-off on the June 1981 raid by eight IAF F-16s on the Osirak nuclear light-water reactor, about 12 miles southeast of Baghdad, which was viewed with suspicion by both Israel and, ironically, Iran, who shared the fear that Saddam Hussein was trying to develop a nuclear bomb. Iranian Phantom jets had attacked the complex in September 1980, but the French-built facility suffered little damage. Despite the site being monitored by the Vienna-based International Atomic Energy Authority (IAEA) the IAF raid was ordered when Israeli intelligence sources claimed that Osirak was a weapons-producing facility. Within minutes following the raid Mossad agents in the area confirmed that the reactor had been hit by several 2,000lb bombs. The Israeli Government, in an official statement, said "the atomic bombs which [Osirak] was capable of producing, whether from enriched uranium or plutonium, would be of Hiroshima size" and could have been a "mortal danger" to Israel. In January 1991, during Operation *Desert Storm*, the USAF later bombarded the site for days before the Pentagon announced that Osirak had been "severely downgraded."

Bolstered by these achievements and riding high in the popularity rating, Prime Minister Begin and his close advisers (including Defense Minister Arial Sharon) decided that the time was right to deal with the Palestinian threat. Begin believed that for the West Bank land of Judea and Samaria to be part of 'Greater Israel' the PLO had to be destroyed. He entrusted the task to Sharon, who had produced a plan in 1981 to destroy the PLO strongholds in Lebanon, force the Syrian expeditionary force out of the country, and put in power in Beirut the Christian Falange leader, Bashir Gemayel. In what Moshe Sharett had previously referred to as "false incidents and provoked clashes," for months Begin and Sharon had tried to provoke the Palestinians into confrontation to justify a large-scale IDF response. According to one of Britain's most experience Middle East specialists, *Observer* journalist and author, Patrick Seale, "five times between July 1981 and June 1982, Israel massed troops on the frontier - and five times called them back because the Palestinians refused to fight: In those eleven months, not a single shot was fired by Palestinians across Israel's northern border."

On 6 June 1982, Operation *Peace for Galilee* began when IDF forces crossed the border into southern Lebanon, after IAF aircraft had bombed West Beirut and long-range naval artillery had pounded the Palestinian refugee camps, causing hundreds of casualties. The pretext for the invasion was the attempted assassination of the Israeli ambassador to Britain, Shlomo Argov, who had been seriously wounded by gunmen 48 hours earlier as he left a banquet at the Doncaster Hotel in Park Lane, London. The would-be assassins were members of a breakaway PLO faction, the Fatah Revolutionary Council (FRC), headed by the hardline Palestinian nationalist, Abu Nidal.

There has never been a satisfactory explanation for the *raison d'etre* and timing of the attack on Argov. Some Israeli sources have suggested that the Syrian General Security Directorate (GSD) used Nidal's FRC in order to provoke the Israelis into destroying Arafat, whose presence in Lebanon was perceived as a threat to the Syrian dictator Hafez al-Assad.

Others have claimed Saddam Hussein's General Directorate of Intelligence (GDI), known locally as the Mukhabarat, was directly involved, while Arab sources, including Isam Sartawi, believe Mossad manipulated Abu Nidal in order to provoke the invasion. Seale refers to one of his "best Western intelligence sources" who claims that Mossad penetration agents had been instructed to mobilize the FRC into "providing the pretext" Israel needed, and the badly-planned attack on Argov - with no provision made for the hit team, which included one of Abu Nidal's distant cousins, Marwan al-Banna - was described by western intelligence analysts as "out of character" with the FRC leader's "cautious and carefully-planned" approach to operations, and "may have been an individual initiative." Ignored in the furor following the shooting was the fact that when two of the would-be assassins were later arrested in a London flat, the next target on their hit-list was the PLO representative in the UK, Nabil Ramlami, which suggests these men were not acting in the interests of the Palestinians.

Whoever was responsible for ordering the hit - and the GSD was the most likely paymaster - it mattered little to Begin, Sharon or the IDF Chief of Staff, Rafael Eitan, who was aware that Abu Nidal was Arafat's bitter enemy and brusquely dismissed questions when asked about the FRC's role in the attempted assassination. In Washington, Secretary of State, Alexander Haig, knew of Israel's plan to "reorder Lebanese internal politics" according to Mearsheimer and Walt, but had cautioned Begin and Sharon to respond only to 'internationally recognized provocation." The attempted assassination of Argov "fell far short of Haig's criterion." It had nothing to do with the situation along the Lebanon/Israel border, which had been relatively peaceful for almost a year apart from provocative IDF 'war games.' The CIA, the Pentagon's Defense Intelligence Agency (DIA), and State Department Middle East specialists knew that neither Ararfat or Fatah were involved in the London attack, but Haig should have been aware, as Shlomo Ben-Ami has pointed out, that Israeli politicians "are not especially sensitive to the nuances and understatements when he used unnecessarily ambiguous language in his conversation with Sharon."

None of this, of course, made any difference to the dead and maimed Palestinians. The war which had "started in deceit and with grand strategic designs," according to Ben-Ami, "ended in military disaster, political defeat and human disgrace." By mid-September the Palestinian refugee camps, Sabra and Shatila, were surrounded by IDF infantry and armor, who controlled all access points, prevented the inhabitants from leaving, and supervised the entry into the camps of the Phalangist militia. The pretext for the massacre of hundreds of Palestinian refugees was the assassination of Phalange Party leader, Bachir Gemayel, who died on 14 September with 26 others in a explosion at the party's headquarters in the Achrafieh district of eastern Beirut, just three weeks after succeeding Elias Sarkis as president of Lebanon. The attack was carried out by Habib Shartouni, a Maronite Christian and member of the Syrian Social Nationalist Party (SSNP) and not by the PLO, Fatah or any Palestinian-linked group. Nonetheless, an ANP report dated 15 September, claimed Defense Minister Sharon, had "tied the bombing to the Palestinians" claiming it symbolized the "murderous nature of the organization and its supporters." At 3.30am that day, only hours after Gemayel's assassination, a meeting was held between IDF CoS, Gen. Rafael Eitan, northern commander, Gen Amir Drori, and Phalangist officers in Beirut at which it was agreed that the Christian militiaman would hunt out the 'terrorists' in the refugee camps southwest of the city center, an impoverished district known locally as the "belt of misery."

On 16 September, at about 5.05pm Elia Hobeika, the Phalangist intelligence chief, who had been present at the massacre of Palestinians in the Tal Zaatar refugee camp in 1976, led his units into the Beirut camps, past IDF Paras stationed as close as 50 yards from the perimeters, and watched by Israeli soldiers on the roofs of the nearby seven-storey Kuwait Embassy, and several other buildings with a clear view over what was happening in both camps. At 11pm that evening, according to David Gilmour, the Phalangist leader told Gen. Drori that 300 civilians and terrorists had been killed. The message was immediately sent to Tel Aviv "where about twenty senior Israeli officers saw it." At 11.30am the following morning Gen. Drori ordered the militia to stop the killings, but they were allowed to remain in the camps for a further 24 hours, to bring in "two battalions of fresh troops." That afternoon "a new round of killings" began.

The official death toll, when the slaughter finally ended, was estimated at 650-700 men, women and children. But the unofficial death toll is as high as 1,700, many of whom had been taken prisoner and held at the Cite Sportieve Stadium, about 2 miles from Beirut Airport, before being taken away for 'interrogation' in Army transport and Phalangist vehicles, watched by IDF and Shabak personnel. Robert Fisk believes that as many as 1,000 of the 1,800 civilians reported missing after the Christian militia left the refugee camps, on 18 September, have been murdered and may be buried beneath the ruins of the stadium, which was demolished in 1982 and rebuilt as the multi-purpose Camille Chamoun Sports City Stadium in 1997. The invasion of Lebanon had cost the lives of 17,500 Palestinians and Lebanese, mostly civilians, five times the death toll of 9/11, yet as Fisk points out, there were no "stirring speeches about democracy or liberty or evil" for the innocent dead of Lebanon, in New York, Washington or the capitals of Europe. In the London-based daily, the *Independent*, on the 30th anniversary of the killings last year, the journalist observed that not a single European, US or Arab leader "has dared to visit the dank and grubby Sabra and Shatila mass graves, shaded by a few scruffy trees and faded photographs of the dead."

In December 1982, the UN General Assembly declared the massacre to be "an act of genocide," while an international commission into violations of international law by Israel, chaired by the former IRA Chief of Staff, Amnesty International co-founder, and Nobel Peace Prize recipient, Sean MacBride, a man with a profound understanding of the struggles of the oppressed, concluded in a 1983 report, entitled *Israel in Lebanon*, that Israel had committed "acts of aggression contrary to international law" and was "directly or indirectly responsible" for the Sabra and Shatila killings. In Israel, the President of the Supreme Court, Chief Justice Yitzkhak Kahan, chaired a four month investigation and published a report, on 8 February 1983, which concluded that Phalangist units were "directly responsible" for the massacre, and while no IDF personnel were involved, "no proper heed was taken" of reports describing what was happening in the refugee camps, and "no energetic and immediate action" was taken to restrain the Phalangists and "put a stop to the killings."

The three man commission, which included Yale and Georgetown University law graduate, former Israel Attorney General and Supreme Court Judge, Aharon Barak, and retired IDF Major General Yona Efrat, also found that Sharon had been negligent in protecting the civilian population of Beirut, and bore "personal responsibility for ignoring the danger of bloodshed and revenge" and for not taking "appropriate measures to prevent bloodshed" and recommended he be sacked from the Cabinet. The part played by Mossad was redacted from the published narrative, and remains under military censorship. Initially the ever-belligerent Sharon refused to resign. However, his tarnished profile became a political liability for Likud, and he reached a deal with Begin allowing him to step down as defense minister, but remain in Cabinet as minister without portfolio.

The Kahan Commission is the closest Israel has ever come to officially admitting some degree of responsibility for the inhuman treatment of the Palestinians. In contrast the only response from the EU was to join Israel, the United States, Canada, New Zealand and Australia among the 22 abstentions during the UNSC vote because of disagreement over the word 'massacre.' Sadly, the history of the Palestinian-Israeli conflict has also been reduced to semantics, not only in the mainstream media but also in international forums such as the UN: while the deaths of 11 Israeli sportsmen in Munich is generally referred to as a 'massacre', the deaths of hundreds of Palestinians in the impoverished refugee camps of Beirut appears not to have even merited being described as "ruthless and indiscriminate."

In June 2001 human rights lawyer and former Lebanese presidential candidate, Chibli Mallat, filed a case in Brussels against Ariel Sharon under a law allowing foreigners to be tried for crimes against humanity. Elia Hobeika, one of those named in the court documents, held a press conference and declared his willingness to testify against the former Israeli defense minister. Within days of his announcement, on 24 January 2002, Hobeika and two bodyguards were dead, killed by a car bomb outside his apartment on Rue Kamal Assad, in the southeast Beirut suburb of Hazmiyeh, when 22lbs of TNT in a parked Mercedes was detonated by remote control as Hobeika's blue Range Rover drove past. A bystander was also killed in the blast, six others were injured, and the 45-year-old former warlord's charred body was thrown more 50 feet from the wrecked SUV, and dozens of cars in the vicinity were also destroyed. The Lebanese Interior Minister, Elias Murr, blamed Mossad for the assassination. Although the neighborhood was a heavily-patrolled residential stronghold for senior Syrian intelligence officials close to the Presidential Palace and the Defense Ministry, Mossad had carried out similar assassinations in that fractured country. Black September's Ali Hassan Salameh was assassinated when a red Volkswagen containing a 50lb bomb, parked on Beirut's Rue Verdun, was detonated by remote control as Salameh's Chevrolet SUV passed at 3.35pm, on 22 January 1979. Four bodyguards in a second vehicle, and four bystanders going about their business, also died in the blast. Killing the 'Red Prince' concluded Operation *Bayonet* and revenge for Munich, but it also deprived the CIA of an important source, according to Gordon Thomas, who claims that during the 1970s Salameh, despite being top of Mossad's hit list, was also a regular visitor to CIA headquarters at Langley, meeting Deputy Director, Vernon Walters, and senior CIA officers in a "spacious office on the seventh floor." The CIA chief of station in Beirut, William Buckley, described Salameh as a "super informer" who provided the CIA with useful intelligence. Thomas also claims Salameh signed a "non-assassination guarantee" for all US diplomats in Lebanon, and after Mossad had taken its revenge the US ambassador, Hermann Eilts, described the Black September militant as having been "extraordinarily helpful, assisting with the security of American citizens and officials. I regard his assassination as a loss." The loss would be more keenly felt when William Buckley died in Hezbollah custody, on 3 June 1985.

Impatience with Suffering

By the mid-1980s the Palestinians in Gaza and the West Bank were left with no choice but to resist, by whatever means available, what Israeli Minister for Economy and Planning in the Alignment/Likud coalition government, Gad Yaacobi, described as a "creeping process of de facto annexation." The forceful relocation of the PLO to Tunis after the Lebanese War provided the opportunity for planned expansion, which began with a series of pogroms against the Arab inhabitants of small villages, who were burned out of their homes while the police stood idly by. The Hebrew press, according to Hebrew University Professor Israel Shahak, described the process as *Arabrein* meaning "clean of Arabs" - a retooling of the Nazi word *Judenrein* used during the Holocaust. In conversation with *Covert Action Information Bulletin* editor, Ellen Ray, during a US delegation visit to the West Bank and Gaza in February 1988, Prof. Shahak, also explained that a plan to transfer "all Palestinians from all the occupied territories" - proposed by IDF Gen. Rahaban Zahevi, and supported by several prominent members of the coalition Likud/Labor government - accompanied by a growing Zionist settler population and increasing Jewish economic integration, was a major factor of Palestinian resistance. The Irish statesman, Edmund Burke, had once observed that "a populace never rebels from passion but from impatience with suffering" and in the case of the occupied Palestinian territories, "founded on brute force, repression and fear, collaboration and treachery, beatings and torture chambers, and daily intimidation, humiliation and manipulation," according to Prof. Benny Morris, there was also an "all-pervading element of humiliation."

Other catalysts for the uprising included internment, deportations to North Africa, and collective punishment in the form of house demolitions - domestic properties that the IDF claimed were being used by militants as offices and bomb factories. The UNSC, Amnesty International, and the International Committee of the Red Cross (ICRC) condemned this "counter-insurgency tactic" - remarkably similar to the "collective responsibility" brutality used by the Gestapo against the Jewish inhabitants of occupied cities like Prague and Warsaw in the 1940s following partisan resistance - both on humanitarian grounds and as a flagrant breach of international law. But the official silence from Washington and the European capitals was deafening, and the Arab states were also growing weary of the Palestinian 'problem'. At the Arab summit in the Jordanian capital, Amman, in November 1987, delegates focused on the Iraq-Iran War, and the ongoing repression of the stateless Palestinians was ignored. During the civil rights unrest in the US in the 1960s Dr. Martin Luther King described the protests as "the voice of the unheard." In the context of the occupation of Gaza, the Palestinians were screaming.

They embarked on a campaign of civil disobedience, withholding payments for sub-standard services, boycotting the Israeli economy and taking strike action outside the occupied territories, refusing to collect the garbage in Haifa and Tel Aviv, downing tools on construction sites in Beersheba, Ramla and West Jerusalem. Stones and petrol bombs were the weapons of the rioting youths, while the well-armed IDF responded in the only way it knew how, with a disproportionate use of brute force. The western media referred to a "David and Goliath struggle," with the IDF representing the Philistine giant. Soldiers were filmed beating up women trying to protect their families and property, and stone-throwing children on the CS gas-drenched streets. The abnormal conditions in Gaza sustained the fury of the *Intifada*, and when footage of IDF brutality became a regular feature on western television news bulletins, even the cold-hearted Israeli coalition cabinet members knew the propaganda war was lost. There was even public criticism from Washington, low-key but something almost unheard of in the past.

The first *intifada*, which had begun in the overcrowded Jabalia refugee camp in autumn 1987, and spread to the West Bank and East Jerusalem, ended six years later with an estimated 2,250 Palestinians dead, and more than 120,000 interned in Ktzi'ot Prison, the largest detention facility covering 99 acres near Auja al-Hafir in the western Negev desert. The Swedish Branch of Save the Children estimated that "23,600 to 29,000 children required medical treatment for their beating injuries in the first two years of the intifada" nearly a third of whom were aged ten or under. This was the generation which would swell the ranks of Hamas, experienced intifadists for the struggle next time. At least 60 members of the IDF were among the estimated 165 Israelis who lost their lives, with 1,700 soldiers wounded. The uprising, and the depth of the spirit of resistance, had a profound effect on the former defense minister, Yitzhak Rabin, who succeeded Shamir as prime minister in July 1992. As IDF CoS during the Six Day War, his troops had captured the West Bank and during 25 years of occupation Rabin had condoned the use cruel and brutal treatment against the local population to quell dissent, and had inflicted as much punishment on the Palestinians as any IDF officer or politician. Robert Fisk writes of how, under his command and during his first term as prime minister, "Israeli soldiers were allowed to break the bones of Palestinians protesters, a practice that continued until an Israeli cameraman inconsiderately filmed Israeli soldiers snapping the legs of a Palestinian prisoner."

Rabin's militarist mindset predominated when he was appointed defense minister, and incorrectly assumed that the initial outbreak of violence at Jabila would end quickly. However, after 10 weeks of pitched battles between the rioters and the IDF, who were ill-equipped and ill-trained to deal with civil disorder, he told a February 1988 closed meeting of the Labor Party that 1,500,000 Palestinians cannot be controlled by force. He still ruled out political options being considered, according to journalists Karpin and Friedman, reminding his audience that mass expulsion had been previously used against the Jews, and "if we annex the territories and grant the Palestinians Israeli citizenship they will have between 25 and 30 seats in the Knesset. If we don't [grant them citizenship], we will be a racist state, not a Jewish one." Rabin was seriously considering some form of Palestinian self-rule. Four months later on ABC's *Nightline,* he announced his willingness to negotiate with Yasser Arafat if the PLO revoked the Palestinian National Covenant adopted in 1964, which described the state of Israel as "entirely illegal" and negated its right to exist. Rabin also wanted the PLO to adopt the UN Resolutions which called for negotiations "aimed at establishing a just and durable peace in the Middle East," and ending all "terrorist activity" including the ongoing and demoralizing campaign of civil unrest.

The collapse of Israel's National Unity government, in March 1990, left Yitzhak Shamir in charge but increasingly isolated at home and abroad as the IDF continued its wholly disproportionate response to the mass uprising in the occupied territories. The cost of trying to contain the intifada, the influx of tens of thousands Jews from Eastern Europe and the Soviet Union as hardline communist regimes collapsed, and the arrival of an estimated 14,300 Ethiopian Jews in a 36 hour, non-stop airlift involving IAF C-130 Hercules military transport aircraft and El Al cargo planes fleeing civil war, put a huge strain on the Israeli economy and military resources. Once again Tel Aviv turned to Washington with requests for increased aid, supported by the powerful Jewish Diaspora spearheaded by AIPAC. But the end of the 1991

Gulf War, with the defeat and isolation of Iraqi dictator, Saddam Hussein, had changed the geopolitical landscape of the Middle East. The US now had some powerful new Arab allies and political commitments in the region and, on 30 October 1991, a formal invitation to discuss the Palestinian question at a conference in Madrid was extended to Israel, Syria, Lebanon, Jordan and Palestinian representatives.

Israel's request for $10 billion in loan guarantees to help absorb the influx of immigrants was used as leverage to get the Likud government to send a delegation to Madrid, and although nothing concrete was achieved, the multinational forums, meeting of steering committees, working parties and bilateral discussions on issues such as water, the environment, economic development, arms control and refugees, eventually led to the Oslo Accords, and the assassination of Yitzak Rabin, who had succeed Shamir as prime minister following the June 1992 general election. The Labor Party leader had campaigned on the issue of long-term national security, which included an end to Shamir's settlement policy and on the need to "reformulate national priorities." Within months Rabin was on the White House lawn, shaking hands with President George Walker Bush, after reaching agreement on the withheld $10 billion loan package that many within Likud, including a former Sayeret Matkal team leader and Israeli ambassador to the UN from 1984 to 1988, Benjamin Netanyahu, believed were not even necessary and led to allegations among the hard-line Zionist wing of the party that Washington had conspired with Labor to bring about the defeat of Shamir.

Negotiations in Oslo were hosted by the Fafo Research Foundation, and initially focused on the economic conditions in Gaza and the West Bank, in particular the social impoverishment of the Palestinians. Both the Israeli and Palestinian negotiators acknowledged during opening exchanges that a large scale international aid program would be required to implement any agreement. Israeli Foreign Minister, Shimon Peres, proposed an international donors' conference, and by May 1993 there were two complementary economic drafts on the table, dealing with joint initiatives and cooperative work programs, and a proposed 'Marshall Plan' for the occupied territories and the Middle East in general, requiring the industrialized US, the EU and Japan to contribute to the post-peace agreement economic and social reconstruction. On 13 September 1993, President Bill Clinton hosted Israeli and Palestinian delegations, and a *Declaration of Principles* focusing on political and security arrangements, substantial international economic provisions, and bilateral cooperation on issues such as water, energy, finance, transport, communications and trade, was signed. Two weeks later, at an international donors' conference for the Palestinians in Washington, hosted by Secretary of State, Warren Christopher, $2 billion was pledged over five years, far less than originally estimated. Adding to the slow disbursement of financial and economic funds were conditions of strict transparency and accountability laid down by the donor countries. By 1994 the Palestinians were running out of patience and sporadic rioting led to a temporary closing of the border with Gaza, preventing Palestinian laborers and poorly-paid domestic workers from entering Israel, all of which contributed to the economic malaise and fuelled the unrest.

Prime Minister Rabin was also faced with the task of selling the vaguely-defined Oslo economic and social greements to a divided Israeli electorate amid a deteriorating security situation and an increasingly vociferous extra-parliamentary campaign by those who opposed Palestinian autonomy, led by a loose alliance of Zionist organizations. Likud, now led by the ambitious 'Bibi' Netanyahu, was a divided party. During the first debate in the Knesset on the Oslo package Netanyahu had accused Shimon Peres of being "worse than Chamberlain" and accused Rabin of agreeing to establish a "Palestinian bridgehead" that would eventually destroy Israel. But he backed away from calling for a national referendum when three members of Likud crossed the floor in the Knesset and voted with Labor, while several small-town Likud mayors, perhaps closer to grass-roots opinion than many of their parliamentary colleagues, also indicated support for cooperation and dialogue in an attempt to move on from the wreckage of the past. Netanyahu and like-minded Likud colleagues took their opposition to the streets, meeting with Ya'akov Novick and Meir Indor, 'Haredi' nationalists (the most conservative form of Orthodox Judaism) and representatives of Action Headquarters (AH), a coalition of Zionist hardliners that produced placards frequently seen at demonstrations calling Rabin a 'traitor.' Liaison between AH and Likud was the responsibility of Knesset members, Tsachi Hanegbi and Reuven Zadok, the head of the party's 'Operations Division.' Zadok described his contacts with AH, during which everything was coordinated "down to the smallest detail," to Karpin and Friedman. After each meeting Zadok would present a "work plan and budget to the Likud Executive. Bibi participated in and addressed all demonstrations we initiated with the Action Headquarters."

Netanyahu was photographed standing in front of a coffin painted with the slogan 'Rabin is murdering Zionism' at a demonstration in Ra'anana, on 4 March 1994. He spoke at a rally from the balcony of the Ron Hotel, in Jerusalem's Zion Square, on 2 July 1994, the day PLO chairman, Yasser Arafat, returned to the Gaza Strip, telling the estimated 100,000 crowd chanting "Rabin is a homo" and "Rabin is the son of a whore" that the "base murderer [Arafat] is now being carried along by the present Israeli government, which in its blindness, is allowing him to carry out the first stage of his plan: the destruction of the Jewish state." The Likud chairman was also present at a demonstration in Zion Square three months later where posters of Rabin dressed in an SS uniform were distributed. When a Hamas suicide bomber killed twenty-two people in a crowded bus on Dizengoff Street in Tel Aviv, on 19 October 1994, Netanyahu arrived at the scene of the carnage immediately after Rabin had left, and exploited the fear and suffering by holding an 'impromptu' news conference on site, claiming the PLO had carried out the attack, and telling press and television journalists that the prime minister had "chosen to prefer Arafat and the welfare of the residents of Gaza over the security of the residents of Israel."

The weekly Haredi magazine, *Hashavua*, published by Asher Zuckerman, was the hate-filled publication coordinating the campaign, in which Rabin was regularly called an "anti-Semite" and a "mentally-ill, alcoholic, pathological liar." The magazine published an interview with Ariel Sharon who described the Oslo peace accord as "graver" than the capitulation of Petain, and details of a conversation Zuckermnan had with Netanyahu, in which Bibi said the prime minister "had no reason to complain" when he was being called a murderer. An editorial, in August 1995, called for Rabin and Peres to be "placed before a firing squad," and on 3 November 1995, the day before Rabin's assassination, the magazine accused both men of being insane, or "flagrantly treasonous."

The fifth prime minister of Israel, Yitzhaz Rabin, died on the operating table of Tel Aviv's Ichilov Hospital of massive internal injuries shortly before 11.00pm on Saturday night, 3 November 1995, about 90 minutes after being shot in nearby King of Israel Square, where he had spoken at a mass rally of 100,000 from the City Hall stage, and sung the 'Song of Peace' standing alongside Foreign Minister Peres. As he walked to his car in the parking area he passed close to his assassin, Yigil Amir, who fired three shots from a semi-automatic pistol. Two of the hollow-point rounds hit Rabin in the chest, rupturing his spleen, shattering his spinal cord and severing several major arteries. The third shot wounded Rabin's bodyguard, Yoram Rubin. The gunman, a radical, right-wing, Orthodox Jew, was immediately overpowered by Shabak agents and taken into custody. He would later be found guilty and sentenced to life imprisonment.

At an emergency Cabinet meeting within hours of Rabin's death Shimon Peres was appointed as acting prime minister. He continued with efforts to implement the Oslo peace agreement but the momentum had been lost, a collective deflation of hope and optimism, similar in some respects to the mood in the US following the assassination of John Fitzgerald Kennedy in Dallas thirty two years earlier, almost to the day. In an election in 1996 Labor lost to Likud, and Netanhayu, who had exploited the Haredi opposition to Rabin while the Labor leader argued in favor of the Oslo agreement, successfully exploited his murder to became prime minister of the Jewish state.

Netanyahu was a former team leader with the IDF's elite Sayeret Matkal, who had crossed the Suez during the Six Day War. After the war, he returned to the US (where he had graduated from Cheltenham High School in Philadelphia in 1967) to study at the Massachusetts Institute of Technology (MIT) and at MIT's Sloan School of Management. He returned again to Israel in 1977, and after a brief career in the private sector, he headed the 'Yonatan Netanyahu Anti-Terror Institute' - called after his brother who died in 1976 at Entebbe Airport in Uganda during the successful IDF Special Forces operation to free 100 Israeli and Jewish passengers of the PFLP-hijacked Air France Flight 139 Airbus A300.

In 1982 the Israeli ambassador to the US (and fellow MIT graduate), Moshe Arens, appointed him deputy chief of mission at the Israeli Embassy on International Drive, Washington DC. Two years later he was appointed ambassador to the UN in New York when Arens returned to Tel Aviv to take up an appointment as minister for defense. In 1988 Netanyahu returned to Israel , joined Likud and was elected to the 12th Knesset in the November legislative elections. It was during Netanyahu's time in the US, prior to his election to the Knesset, that he was involved in a plot to illegally purchase US-manufactured, dual-use technology, for Israel's clandestine nuclear weapons program, according to declassified FBI documents released last July, which include details of an interview the FBI conducted with an indicted smuggler, Richard Kelly Smith, at the US Attorney General's office, in April 2002. Smith, an American citizen and former chief executive of California-based Milco International Incorporated, which also manufactured microchips for the US space administration, NASA, was charged with smuggling 800 dual-use Krytrons - small, gas-filled tubes which can be used as high-speed nuclear switches in detonation systems. The chips had been manufactured by the Massachusetts-based, EG&G Company, sold to Milco and shipped on to the Israeli Defense Ministry (IDM) through a front-company called Heli Trading in Israel. Heli Trading, owned by Arnon Milchan, a Hollywood-based Israeli film producer and an agent for the scientific liaison bureau, Lekem, was tasked with purchasing equipment and obtaining classified data for Israel's Dimona-based nuclear program. In a clandestine operation codenamed *Project Pinto* Milco dispatched the Krytron triggers to Israel in fifteen shipments between 1979 and 1983 without applying for a State Department 'Munitions Export License,' which was required because of Nuclear Suppliers Group (NSG) restrictions on the sale of dual-use technology. Netanyahu allegedly met the Milco president in Tel Aviv restaurants, at his home and elsewhere in the city. At the time Netanyahu was in contact with Heli Trading, as well as senior politicians and IDF staff, among them another future prime minister, Ariel Sharon.

After being questioned by the FBI in relation to breaches of nuclear proliferation legislation, Richard Kelly Smith and his wife fled the US in mid-1985, leaving behind their $500,000 Los Angeles home and forfeiting a $100,000 bail bond. He was eventually arrested in Malaga, Spain, on an Interpol 'Red Notice' warrant, in July 2001, and extradited to the US. The following year Smith was found guilty as charged, received a 40 month prison sentence and fined $20,000.

On 21 November 1985, three months after the Smiths had fled California, the FBI arrested Jonathan Pollard outside the Israeli Embassy in Washington, DC. The 31-year-old civilian intelligence analyst, who worked at the US Navy's top-secret Anti-Terrorist Alert Center (ATAC) in Suitland, Maryland, was later charged with spying for Israel, including passing classified material about the international eavesdropping activities of the National Security Agency (NSA) and details of the bugging methodology used against foreign embassies in the nation's capital to his Lekem handlers, Yosef Yagur and Aviem Sella, who had left the country within hours of

Pollard's arrest, on an El Al flight from New York to Tel Aviv. Pollard began a life sentence at the Federal Correction Complex in Butner, North Carolina, in March1987, where he was visited by Netanyahu for the first time in January 2002. Netanyahu found him an "especially intelligent man" and assured him that the government of Israel would act "in every possible way" to secure his release.

Vexed to Nightmare

Prime Minister Netanyahu's priority when he took office, in June 1996, for the first of two terms as premier, was the destruction of what he had called the Palestinian 'bridgehead', and with it the hopes and aspirations of the Oslo participants and their supporters among the Palestinian and Israeli populations. An early indication of the provocation he would use and exploit internationally was the opening of an exit in the Arab Quarter of Jerusalem for the Western (Wailing) Wall Tunnel, which the Israeli newspaper *Ha'aretz* likened to "throwing a burning match into an area filled with flammable material." For the ultra-orthodox Shas political party, the right-wing National Religious Party (NRP) which was linked to the settlers moving into the occupied lands, and Yisrael BaAliyah, a party representing the interests of Russian immigrants (which would merge with Likud in 2003) who between them held 26-seats in 120-seater Knesset, and whose support Netanyahu relied upon following the legislative elections, the opening of the access to the Via Dolorosa - close to the most sacred shrines of Islam, the Al-Aqsa Mosque and the Byzantine Dome of the Rock, from where the Prophet Muhammad is believed to have ascended to heaven - was an assertion of Israel's 'de facto sovereignty' over the divided and occupied city. In the riots which followed dozens of people, the majority of them Palestinians, died in clashes with the IDF and Jewish residents of Jerusalem. During a trip to Europe Netanyahu accused Yasser Arafat of exploiting the issue and waging a campaign of "deliberate disinformation." However, his Labor predecessor, Shimon Peres, accused him of deliberately provoking a confrontation, saying "nothing was urgent, it waited for 2,000 years, it could have waited for another year or so."

In an effort to advance the Oslo peace process the Clinton administration pledged an additional $1.2 billion in military aid to Israel, in return for implementation of an interim agreement on the West Bank and Gaza Strip. The agreement had included the slow withdrawal of Israeli troops, with the PLO to have full control of the occupied territories. It was renegotiated at a conference held at the Aspen Institute Wye River Center in Maryland, in autumn 1998, and almost ended in a complete failure and an embarrassing farce when Netanhayhu insisted on the release of the spy, Pollard, as a condition for his signature on a 'memorandum of understanding'. On 17 November 1998, the Knesset approved the Wye River Agreement by 75 votes to 19. Netanyahu suspended the agreement shortly afterwards following the deaths of two Israelis during a violent confrontation with a crowd of Palestinians. According to US negotiator, Dennis Ross, quoted in Mearsheimer and Walt's important book on the Israel lobby in the US, it was "hard to escape the conclusion that Bibi was seizing on this incident to avoid further implementation. This was unfortunate, because the Palestinians were working diligently to carry out most of their commitments under Wye, particularly in the area of making arrests and fighting terror."

Netanyahu's premiership ended due to well-documented allegations of corruption and influence-peddling which were under investigation by Israel Police Force (IPF) fraud squad involving Netanyahu, his wife Sara, and the personal retention of state gifts, including silverware, paintings, and a gold letter opener from US vice-president Al Gore, as well as services rendered by a private building contractor in return for political favors who later tried to bill the state for $100,000. After being beaten by Ehud Barak's Labor Party in the 1999 legislative elections, he temporarily retired from politics to spend more time with his lawyers.

Following the collapse of the Barak regime in 2000, Bibi returned to politics and built up support and momentum among the grassroots for a challenge to the leadership of Likud with high-profile, carefully-managed public appearances. He met with Russian President, Vladimir Putin, for example, during a visit to the Jewish Community Center in Moscow, in December 2000. He exploited the grief and anger in the US following 9/11 in an op-ed piece in the *Chicago Sun-Times*, in January 2002, calling on American 'power,' which had "destroyed the Taliban" to "act similarly against other terror regimes [including] Iran, Iraq, Yasser Arafat's dictatorship, Syria and a few others." In a speech to the US Senate, on 10 April 2002, he again reminded US lawmakers of the PLO threat: "If we do not immediately shut down the terror factories where Arafat is producing human bombs, it is only a matter of time before suicide bombers will terrorize your cities. If not destroyed this madness will strike in your buses, in your supermarkets, in your pizza parlors, in your cafes." Netanyahu played on America's fear and prejudices, and the Bush administration, now focused on Saddam Hussein's unproven and unprovable links to al Qaida, mindlessly danced to the Jewish organ-grinder's tune.

What became known as the 'second intifada' began in September 2000, during the premiership of Ariel Sharon, the former defense minister who was directly involved in the 1953 Qibya massacre and "shared responsibility" for Sabra and Shatila slaughter in 1982, and lasted five years. It was a broad and bloody escalation of the Al Aqsa Mosque riots, influenced by Israel's failure to implement its obligations agreed in Maryland and Oslo and the increasing presence, since the Madrid Conference in 1991, of Zionist settlers illegally living in the occupied territories. The previous May, Israel had finally withdrawn from the 'security zone' in southern Lebanon after an eight year, low-intensity conflict with Hezbollah in which the Iranian-backed militant Shi'a organization routinely attacked IDF convoys, used

IEDs and remote controlled culvert bombs, launched wire-guided, ground-to-ground, Russian-manufactured 9KII *Malyukta* missiles (obtained from the Syrian Armed Forces) against IDF tanks and amoured personnel carriers (APCs), occasionally attacked IDF outposts, and indiscriminately shelled border towns in northern Israel with platform-mounted and notoriously inaccurate *Katyusha* rockets. The IDF lost 260 personnel in the conflict, and the 2,500 strong South Lebanon Army (SLA), a breakaway militia from the regular Army of Free Lebanon (AFL) supporting the Israeli presence in south Lebanon, lost almost 25 percent of its fighters. The decision to retreat behind the border of northern Israel, as defined by various UN resolutions, and abandon the SLA to its fate was regarded as a victory in the Arab world for Hezbollah, and emboldened the PLO-backed resistance in Gaza and the West Bank.

The second intifada claimed the lives of more than 3,380 Palestinians, of whom 676 were children and 1,815 were bystanders not directly involved in the fighting, while 1,075 Israelis, including 118 children and 332 members of the IDF died. The fatalities also included 37 foreign citizens killed by the Palestinians, and 10 killed by the IDF, according to the human rights organization, B'TSELEM. Three of the IDF's foreign dead caught the attention, for a brief spell, of the media in Europe and the US that was dominated by, but growing increasingly weary of, the anonymous carnage in Iraq, with American soldiers being shipped home in body-bags without public ceremony, while the British paraded their dead through the flag-draped street of the small market town of Wootten Bassett, in Wiltshire, near RAF Lyneham, where C-130 Hercules repatriated service personnel killed in Blair's war in Iraq.

Alongside the thousands for Palestinians who died by bomb, bullet and shell fire, and whose deaths are remembered only by their families, are the deaths of Rachel Aliene Corrie, the 24-year-old American student from Washington State, crushed to death, on 16 March 2003, by an IDF armoured Caterpillar bulldozer in Rafah, the site of the border crossing with Egypt in southern Gaza; James Miller, a Welsh filmmaker shot dead by an IDF soldier at a refugee camp in Rafah, on 2 May 2003, despite being identified as 'Press,' while working on a documentary, *Death in Gaza*, for the American cable network HBO; and Tom Hurndall, a British freelance photographer, who died on 13 January 2004, eleven months after being shot, on 11 April 2003, by an IDF sniper while trying, with several other International Solidarity Movement (ISM) volunteers, to set up a peace camp to block IDF tank patrols near Rafah. Their deaths provided context and background which could not be easily dismissed as "collateral damage" by Israel's highly-efficient international propaganda machine. Unlike the Palestinian deaths, they were also the subject of judicial scrutiny. In the case of James Miller, an inquest jury at St. Pancras Coroner's Court in London, on 2 April 2006, returned a verdict of "unlawfully killed" by a "classic sniper shot." The London *Times* published testimony given by a former British Army officer and weapons instructor, Chris Cobb-Smith, who told coroner, Dr. Andrew Reid, that the filmmaker's death was "calculated and cold-blooded murder." The shots "were not fired by a soldier who was frightened, not fired by a soldier facing incoming fire - these were slow, deliberate, calculated and aimed shots. It was a soldier aiming and firing deliberately. He should not have been firing anywhere near a lit building, anywhere near where he knew there were women, children or foreign journalists." One week later the same court found that Hurndall had been "unlawfully killed" by the IDF sniper who had initially told a military tribunal in Israel that Hurndall was armed, then admitted he lied but was under orders from his commanding officer "to open fire even on unarmed people." In complete contrast to the British verdicts, last August the District Court in Haifa blamed Rachel Corrie for her own death while trying to prevent the demolition of Palestinian houses. Judge Oded Gershon ruled that she had risked her own life "by entering a place where there was daily live fire" and that she had "put herself in a dangerous situation" because the driver of the bulldozer couldn't see her, and she refused to move "like anyone of sound mind would. She found her death even after all of the IDF's efforts to move her from the place."

Only three deaths among tens of thousands but the killings of these silenced witnesses have helped expose the tragedy of Gaza, in a way, sadly, that the ongoing killings of significant numbers of innocent Palestinians have failed to do, and that is also the tragedy of this place.

In Washington the Palestinian-Israeli struggle was now regarded as part of the "great war for civilization" which was based, inter alia, on Saddam Hussein's non-existent WMD threat, oil, al-Qaida, and 'pay-back time' for several senior members of the neo-conservative influenced White House administration who had been prevented from getting the job done a decade earlier. There was almost an anaesthetized indifference to the plight of the Palestinians, who were widely depicted, following carnage on the streets of Israeli cities, as manic, one-dimensional, suicide bombers with no reference to the desperation, courage and self-sacrifice of the stateless men and women who strapped explosives to their bodies and boarded downtown buses in Haifa and Tel Aviv.

The cause of the Palestinians wasn't helped by well-publicized and shockingly brutal incidents, including the deaths of two IDF reservists who were arrested by the Palestinian Authority police in Ramallah, on 12 October 2000. The police barracks where the men were held was stormed by hundreds of Palestinians, following malicious rumors that Vadim Nurzhitz and Yossi Avrahami were part of an undercover elite Israeli assassination unit. The two men were beaten, repeatedly stabbed, and disemboweled, and their mutilated bodies dragged through the streets to Al-Manara Square where they were lynched. An impromptu 'victory celebration' was filmed by an Italian television crew and solicited worldwide condemnation. It was a most horrific incident, but it was also an inevitable consequence of the rage which had built up over years of IDF brutality, including the disproportionate responses to clashes with stone-throwing youths, which Fisk describes as "profoundly disturbing." Repeatedly in the Israeli media, he writes, "the beastialization and fear of Palestinians betrayed a total inability to grasp reality: you might think that Israel was under Palestinian occupation, that Israelis were being shot down in their dozens by Palestinian security forces, that Palestinian tanks and helicopters were blasting away at Israeli towns." Despite the physical impossibility of the task, the failure of the poorly-equipped PA police to protect their prisoners led to questions about Yasser Arafat's leadership, authority and willingness to implement what had been agreed, even among men like Amos Oz, Israeli journalist, award-winning author and prominent advocate of the two-state solution to the conflict. Oz was quoted in the London-based *Independent* as blaming the Palestinian leadership who "clearly did not want to sign an agreement at Camp David [September 1978 talks in the US involving Egyptian President Sadat, Israeli Premier Begin and brokered by President Jimmy Carter, but with no Palestinian representation]. Maybe Arafat prefers to be Che Guevara than Fidel Castro. If he becomes president of Palestine, he'll be the leader of a rough, Third World country and have to deal with sewage in Hebron, drugs in Gaza, and the corruption in his own government." Janet Aviad, a veteran leader of the Peace Now Movement, was quoted in the same article, expressing doubts about the "trustworthiness of our Palestinian friends" and being "shocked by the expressions of hatred for each other, on both sides." The disappointment among left-wing, mostly secular Israelis who supported a fair and lasting peace with the Palestinians was summed up by journalist, Lily Galilee, who wrote in *Ha'aretz*: "It is one thing to be thought of as a liberal and even a traitor. It is an entirely different matter to be considered a fool whom reality has slapped in the face."

The political assassination of Yasser Arafat was completed by President Bush, on 24 June 2004, during a major speech on the Middle East, in which he called for the creation of a Palestinian state by 2005, but only on condition that Arafat relinquish power before negotiations could begin, saying "peace requires a new and different Palestinian leadership." The Israeli regime, which had been calling for the isolation of Arafat for months, were "ecstatic" according to *Ha'aretz* journalist, Uzi Benziman, who added that Benjamin Netanyahu and Yisrael BaAliya co-founder, Natan Sharansky - in coalition with PM Sharon's Likud - both claimed to have played a part in convincing Bush to include the demand for Arafat's resignation in his speech, which had the desired effect of denigrating the two-state proposal into nothing more than a self-serving sound-bite. Meanwhile, across the Potomac from the White House the Pentagon sought to enlighten those officers who manned the Middle East desks with a screening of the 1966 film, *Battle of Algiers*. The in-house flyer for this event read "How to win [the] battle against terrorism and lose the war of ideas. Children shoot soldiers at point blank range. Women plant bombs in cafes. Sounds familiar? The French have a plan. It succeeds tactically, but fails strategically. To understand why, come to a rare showing of this film." The years in Iraq and Afghanistan, including the use of drones in over-the-horizon warfare, suggests that the men and women who attended the screening learned nothing at all, except to see no evil, and allow the IDF to get on with it.

The Degradation of Suffering

Waiting in the wings to replace the left-wing, strongly nationalist Fatah was the Palestinian Sunni Islamic resistance movement, Haraket al-Muqawamah al-Islamiyyah, (Hamas), founded in 1987 during the first intifada, which was growing stronger as Fatah weakened. The organization's affiliated military wing, the al-Qassam Brigades, were responsible for rocket and mortar attacks against Israeli settlements and IDF outposts, using a variety of outdated, unreliable, but still lethal ordnance, and suicide bombings in the major cities. Between 1989 and the start of the second intifada, in September 2000, the al-Qassam Brigades, sometimes alone and sometimes working with the Palestinian Islamic Jihad (PIJ), a small militant group with links to radical elements within Egyptian Muslim Brotherhood, carried out 25 suicide attacks, including the Dizengoff Street bus bombing, in Tel Aviv, on 19 October 1994, in which 22 people died; the Jerusalem bus bombings, in February and March 1996, which killed 45 people; and a 4 March attack on Tel Aviv's largest shopping mall in downtown Dizgenoff Street, killing 13 Israelis and injuring more than 130. The following year, on 30 July, two suicide bombers killed 16 people and injured almost 200 in Jerusalem's main outdoor fruit and vegetable Mahane Yehuda Market. These attacks were planned and carried out to cause the maximum physical and psychological damage, to impress on the hardcore religious groupings within Israeli society, those most opposed to any compromise or accommodation with the Palestinians, that nowhere was safe, that joyous celebrations could not be exempt from requital for the ongoing infliction of Palestinian suffering. The attack on the Dizgenoff Centre, for example, was deliberately planned to take place on the eve of the Jewish holiday, Purim, which commemorates their deliverance from the Persian Empire as recorded in the Old Testament's *Book of Esther.* The full text is read aloud publicly on the eve of Purim, and again the following morning. In 1996, however, attention focused on deliverance from the Palestinians, not the Persians.

Over a period of five years, from October 2000 to the Israeli withdrawal from Gaza and the West Bank in August 2005, there were more that 135 suicide bombings against civilian targets in the cities, but with fewer civilian casualties than might be expected considering the number of attacks, with the exception of three bus bombings in Jerusalem, Tel Aviv and Haifa, between November 2002 and March 2003 that claimed the lives of 51 passengers and passersby, and injured more than 230. During this five year period, suicide attacks carried out by Hamas militants, with or without the cooperation of the PIJ, decreased from 40 in 2001, to 9 in 2005. The PIJ began to act alone, while a militant Palestinian coalition based in the West Bank, calling itself the al-Aqsa Martyrs' Brigades, with alleged links to Fatah, carried out more than 20 attacks. Increased security on public transport in the major Israeli cities, and increased attacks on IDF targets rather than on civilians, were also factors in the decreasing death toll, while conscripted sons and daughters manning check-points and on patrol in the occupied territories began to feel the blunt of the Palestinians' rage.

The possibility of a civil war between Fatah and Hamas for control of the Gaza Strip was averted, despite brief clashes between often young, armed and undisciplined fighters from both organizations, when an 'armed truce' was agreed in the run-up to the January 2006 Palestinian legislative elections. Hamas won 74 of the 132 seat available, and with Fatah taking only 45 seats, and four smaller parties (who campaigned on a wide variety of issues including democratic reform, socio-economic progress, respect for human rights, peace and security, and the dismantling of the 430-miles long fencing and 26ft tall concrete 'apartheid wall', surrounded by a 200ft wide seclusion zone along the 1949 Armistice line dividing Israel and the Palestinian West Bank) winning the remainder, Hamas had a working majority to form a government. The victory, and the short-lived but bloody fratricidal conflict between both organizations which followed the election, claimed the lives of at least 250 militants and 98 civilians, according to several Israeli media sources, which described the conflict as a "religious war." Israel and the international political community, represented by the Madrid Quartet, had a vested interest in the defeat of Hamas, according to the daily *Yedioth Ahronoth* website, YnetNews, which stated, in an April 2007 editorial, that the "entire region would be much better off if Fatah were to win this war."

The New York-based nonpartisan, public think-tank on US foreign policy and international affairs, the Council on Foreign Relations (CFR), in a background briefing on Hamas, stated that while its known aversion to corruption "partly explains its defeat of Fatah" a large part of its estimated $70 million annual budget goes to supporting its "extensive social services network. In Gaza "Hamas pays for schools, healthcare centers, mosques, orphanages, soup kitchens and sporting facilities." The Israeli scholar, Reuven Paz, a former head of Shabak's research department, believes that 90 percent of Hamas' work is providing social, educational, health and cultural services, which the Palestinian Authority failed to do while in power. Hamas is funded by the Palestine Diaspora, several oil-rich Arab states, including Saudi Arabia, and Iran. However, since the organization's election victory foreign aid, previously available to the PA and channeled through the Madrid Quartet, ended, despite Hamas having responded to calls by representatives of the international community to end its militant campaign and "embrace the democratic process."

This is exactly what Hamas did, but a democratically-elected Hamas administration - following a fair and honest election - was obviously not what the Quartet envisaged, and the malicious ending of financial and material aid to the impoverished Gaza community represented all that is ugly and cruel about the manner which the Palestinians in Gaza are viewed and generally treated. On 19 February 2006, one day after Hamas, headed by Ismail Haniyeh, took charge in Gaza, the Israeli Government froze the payment of taxes and custom fees legally due to the new administration. Fewer than two months later EU officials followed the petulant and dishonest behavior of Likud Prime Minister, Ehud Olmert, a veteran of the IDF's Golani Brigade, and suspended direct aid, bringing Gaza and the civil administration to the verge of bankruptcy.

Having isolated Hamas financially in the non-Arab world, it was time for a display of Zionist anomie, just to remind First Minister Haniyeh that even for those citizens striving for peaceful co-existence in a democracy, life can be nasty, brutish and short. On 9 June 2006, an uneasy ceasefire ended when IDF artillery and gunboats off the coast fired a barrage of 76mm naval and 155mm artillery shells on a northern Gazan public beach near Beit Lahia, killing eight civilians, including seven members of the Ali Ghaliya family, injuring more than thirty, and effectively putting an end to a 16 month truce. The beach was packed with picnicking families, and when the ordnance exploded, body parts were scattered among the sand dunes. The Palestinian President, Mahmoud Abbas, in Ramallah, described the incident as a "bloody massacre" and called on the international community, the UN, the US, Russia and the EU to help "put an end to Israel's killing policy," while his political rival, Haniyeh, described the deaths as a "war crime" and asked Jordan and Egypt to intervene. In a statement the military wing of Hamas warned that "the earthquake in Zionist towns will start again and the aggressors will have no choice but to prepare their coffins or their luggage."

The eight shells which landed on Beit Lahia beach were the latest of over 6,000 fired into Gaza by Israel over an eight week period (an average of 100 shells per day). Initially the IDF denied responsibility and the Defense Ministry blamed the deaths on a discarded Palestinian land mine. However, after the New York-based Human Rights Watch (HRW) and the British *Guardian* newspaper highlighted obvious flaws in the Israeli report, and published an assessment by Marc Garlasco, a former Pentagon senior intelligence analyst specializing in battle damage analysis who had joined HRW , and examined shrapnel taken from the bodies of the victims, including three children under 10 years, the Ministry admitted "unexploded IDF ordnance" had caused the deaths, but claimed they might have been used by Hamas as IEDs.

Two weeks later, early on the morning of 24 June, an IDF commando raided a house near Rafah and kidnapped Dr Osama Muamar, and his brother Mustfa. The following day Palestinian fighters attacked a frontier post near the Kerem Shalom border crossing, killed two soldiers and abducted Corporal Gilad Shalit (who would be held for over five years until his release in a prisoner exchange deal in October 2011). Between 28 June and 26 November 2006 the IDF launched a huge and punishing ground and air offence, codenamed Operation *Summer Rains*, against the population of Gaza which involved several smaller military operations - including

Locked Garden, in Gaza City's historic Sajaiyeh neighborhood, home to 100,000 residents and several ancient structures, mosques and tombs, as well as the British Commonwealth War Cemetery, and *Autumn Clouds*, which concentrated on Beit Hanoun in the north of the Gaza Strip, which lasted six days and ended with the deaths of 60 Palestinians and a ceasefire. The five month offensive had claimed the lives of almost 400 Palestinians, including 277 combatants and 117 civilians, and 7 Israeli soldiers. It also destroyed much of Gaza's economic infrastructure, including the region's only electricity power plant, hit by at least nine AGMs. Water treatment plants were also damaged, resulting in contaminated drinking water, uncontrolled and untreated sewage, and polluted agricultural land. Israel justified its assault and collective punishment in a statement issued through its embassy in Washington DC, for the benefit of the Jewish Diaspora and its US Congressional House and Senate supporters, claiming it had "exhausted all diplomatic options" in seeking the return of Cpl. Shalit. Prime Minister Olmert (who would later be indicted and convicted of corruption while in office) took pride and personal responsibility for what amounted to crimes against humanity, saying "I want no one to sleep at night in Gaza."

Following a vote in the Knesset's security council, Israel declared the Gaza Strip a "hostile entity" on 19 September 2007, and imposed economic sanctions and a blockade. Military offensives continued, including Operation *Hot Winter* in response to a *Qassam* rocket salvo and the death of an IDF soldier. More than 120 Palestinians, including 54 civilians, among them women, children and several infants, died in the 4 day ground and air offensive, during which the IDF's Combat Engineering force inflicted further damage on Gaza's infrastructure. Olmert tried to justify the disproportionate use of force, and a killing ratio of almost 40-to-1, saying if there were no rocket attacks on Israel there would be no IDF attacks on Gaza. This self-serving explanation was repeated by the world's print and broadcast media, which conveniently failed to point out on this occasion, and many others, that Israel doesn't need a wayward *Qassam* to satisfy its perverse need to punish the Palestinians. By December 2008, and Israel's failure to lift the blockade agreed during an Egyptian brokered mediation process the previous June, Hamas announced it was ending a six month ceasefire, a belligerent but fatal error of judgment because it provided Israel with the opportunity to launch Operation *Cast Lead*, the biggest military offensive against the Palestinians since the 1967 Six Day War. It began on 27 December with an IAF Fighting Falcon F-16's assault, using infrared-guided AGMs, and AH-64 Saraph attack helicopters, supported by IDF artillery, and killed over 400 Palestinians within days. The second stage began on 3 January 2009, with a ground offensive involving more than 9,000 troops, supported by tanks and mobile artillery units, which destroyed "all viable targets" including factories, warehouses, homes and three UN-managed schools. By the time Israel declared a unilateral ceasefire, on 17 January 2009, twelve days after the UN Security Council had voted for an "immediate cessation," at least

1,330 Palestinians had died, 430 of whom were children, and 4,450 people, mostly civilians, were wounded, with thousands more homeless. On the Israeli side 10 IDF soldiers and sappers had been killed, and three civilians. Condemning what had happened as a "disproportionate use of force" does not even begin to describe the carnage left behind when the Israelis withdrew behind their security wall, reinforced military outposts and checkpoints.

Former South African Supreme Court judge, Richard Goldstone, headed a UN 'Fact Finding Mission' into the unequal struggle, and produced a report which accused both the IDF and Palestinian groups of "possible crimes against humanity." Those of the Palestinians were for firing rockets into Israel calculated to kill civilians, damage buildings and cause psychological trauma, and amounted to a "serious violation of human rights." The report was far harsher when dealing with Israel, stating that the blockade of Gaza constituted a violation of the country's obligations as an occupying power; that the response to the indiscriminate *Qassam* attacks, including the intimidation and targeting of the entire population of Gaza, was "a calculated aim" of the *Cast Lead* operation, designed to "humiliate and terrorize (...) radically diminish its local economic capacity, both to work and provide for itself, and to force upon it an ever increasing sense of dependency and vulnerability." In 11 out of 36 cases examined by the mission, Goldstone's report concluded that the IDF deliberately opened fire on civilians who were "trying to leave their homes and walk to a safer place, waving white flags." There was a deliberate missile strike against the Ibrahim al-Maqadna Mosque on the outskirts of Jabilyah, where hundreds of Muslims had gathered for evening prayer, which killed 15 people and wounded more than 40, while twenty one members of the al-Samouni family, including women and children, were killed when an IDF Boeing-manufactured AH-64 *Apache* attack helicopter fired a missile salvo into several houses in the Zeitoun district of Gaza City, and 35 people died when the UN-managed Al-Fakhura school in the Jabaliya refugee camp was hit by IDF mortar fire.

The report also accused Israel of the "systematically reckless" use of white phosphorous incendiary munitions in residential areas, specifically referring to an attack on the UN Relief and Works Agency compound in Gaza City, and the attacks on the Al Quds and Al Wafa hospitals, and accused the IDF of using Palestinians as human shields and torturing detainees. In conclusion the reports states that Israel was in "systematic and deliberate" violation of the *Fourth Geneva Convention,* and placed the blame on those in the coalition administration who had planned, ordered and managed the operation: Likud Prime Minister Ehud Olmert; Labor Defense Minister, Ehud Barak; IDF Chief of General Staff, Gavriel Ashkenazi; the head of Southern Command, Gen.Yoav Galant; IAF Commander-in-Chief Ido Nehoshtan; the head of Home Front Command who led the IDF's Gaza Division, Gen. Eyal Eizenberg; Navy Commander Vice-Admiral Eliezer Marom; and Yuval Diskin, the director of Shabak.

Ha'aretz journalist, Gideon Levy, described Israel's response to Goldstone's "bold, probing report" as "aggressive and blunt." Without even giving it a proper reading "Israel denounced Judge Richard Goldstone, a renowned international jurist - a self-proclaimed Zionist whose daughter spent twelve years in Israel - as an anti-Semite. What he had to say on Rwanda and Yugoslavia is applauded in Israel; what he wrote about Israel is considered treason."

The resignation of PM Olmert amid bribery and corruption allegations paved the way for the return of Benjamin Netanyahu, who had spent several years on the Knesset backbenches, biding his time, building up grassroots support, waiting for his chance to take charge and once again lash the Palestinians. Netanyahu's Likud cobbled together a right-wing, hard-line, Zionist coalition administration from several parties with one thing in common - Israeli supremacy on a range of issue. These included opposition to further unilateral withdrawal from the occupied territories, support for Jewish settlements in the West Bank, continued control of the Jordan Valley, and construction of the "separation barrier" to include more territory on the Israeli side.

In becoming prime minister for a second time, on 31 March 2009, having secured a vote of confidence in the Knesset by 69 to 45 for his Likud-led administration, Netanyahu also became the chief warden of the largest open-air prison in the world, on the eastern coast of the Mediterranean, 25 miles long and between 3.7 and 7.5 miles wide, with a total inmate, predominantly Sunni Muslim, population of 1.7 million most of whom are the descendents of refugees who fled to this place during the exodus following the Zionist terror in the 1940s.

Under a range of international legal conventions to which Israel is a signatory, no state is entitled to discriminate, on the bases of race, religion or nationality, between those over whom it exercises legal jurisdiction. Despite these international obligations the Netanyahu regime continues to be in breach of Article 76 of the *Fourth Geneva Convention* to safeguard the basic rights of people detained in the occupied territories, in its arrest procedures, transfer, and treatment of minors in Israeli military custody, and as a result Israel has been condemned in numerous reports by UN bodies such as the Committee on the Rights of the Child, the Committee Against Torture and the Human Rights Committee. The Geneva-based independent NGO, Defense for Children International (DCI), Palestine Section, published a report, *Bound Blindfolded and Convicted*, in April 2012, based on four years work in the occupied territories, and including 311 sworn affidavits taken from children between January 2008 and January 2012. The report found a systematic pattern of ill-treatment and abuse which begins during night-time raids on the family home, in villages close to points of friction, namely illegal Jewish settlements and roads used by the IDF and settlers. During the hours-long journeys to interrogation centers and transfers to prisons, "avoidable suffering" takes place in the army vehicles and during intermediate stops at settlements and military bases, including prolonged exposure to the elements, a lack of water and toilet facilities.

The discriminatory treatment of Palestinian children is no different to that suffered by their parents. It is but another aspect of the increasingly institutionalized racism which is the mark of Israeli society - certainly contradictory to the democracy which Israel claims to be. Palestinian children are prosecuted in military courts which deny bail applications in 85 percent of the cases, and have a conviction rate of 99.74 percent, while Jewish children are processed through Israel's juvenile system, their cases are heard by civilian judges, and they are generally released on bail.

This is how it is, and how it has been for 65 years, since 'Medinat Yisrael' was founded on the forced expulsion of Palestinians from their homes and villages and the illegal expropriation of their lands. Racism, discrimination and hatred, recently focused on the Christian minority in Israel, are not the hallmarks of a democratic state, despite Benjamin Netanyahu's bluster at the UN and other public forums, always ready to point an accusatory finger at the other side, claiming that "they started it" and Israel has justice on its side. Gideon Levy, who served with the IDF, would disagree. He had been a regular visitor to Gaza for almost three decades until banned, with other journalists, in 2006. In one of his *Twilight Zone* articles for *Ha'aretz* he explains how "nobody would have given any thought to the fate of the people of Gaza if they had not behaved violently. That is the bitter truth, but the first twenty years of the occupation passed quietly, and we did not lift a finger to end it. Instead, under cover of the quiet, we built an enormous criminal settlement enterprise" and when the Palestinians respond with whatever they have at their disposal, Israel deploys almost all of its enormous military resources against an entire population, "but the fact is that they [the Palestinians] did not start it, and justice is not with us."

Moshe Sharett believed that Western morality would not allow a Jewish state to behave according to "the laws of the jungle." However, this assumption has been shown to be naive and unrealistic, as Livia Rokach, the daughter of the General Zionist Party (GZP) Knesset member and Tel Aviv lord mayor, Israel Rokach, explains in her monograph based on the personal diary of the former prime minister: "In the final analysis the West, and in particular the US, let itself be frightened or blackmailed, into supporting Israel's megalomaniac ambitions, because of an objective relationship of complicity and because once pushed into the open this complicity proved capable of serving the cause of Western power politics in the region. Just as Zionism, based on the de-Palestinization and Judaisation of Palestine, was intrinsically racist and immoral, thus the West, in reality, had no use for a Jewish state in the Middle East which did not behave according to the laws of the jungle, and whose terrorism could not be relied upon as a major instrument for the oppression of the peoples of the region."

BIBLIOGRAPHY
Bamford, James. *Body of Secrets*. New York: Arrow, 2002.
Bard, Mitchell G. *The Water's Edge and Beyond*. Piscataway: Transaction Publishers, 1991.

Bard, Mitchell G. *Myths and Facts*. Chevy Chase: American-Israeli Cooperative Enterprise, 2006.
Ben-Ami, Shlomo. *Scars of War, Wounds of Peace*. London: Weidenfeld & Nicolson, 2005.
Black, Ian and Morris, Benny. *Israel's Secret Wars*. London: Warner Books, 1991.
Cohen, Avner. *Israel and the Bomb*. New York: Columbia University Press, 1998.
Corrie, Rachel. *Let Me Stand Alone*. London: Granta Books, 2008.
Davis, Leonard J. *Myths and Facts 1989*. Washington D.C: Near East Report, 1988.
Donovan, Robert J. *Israel's Fight for Survival*. New York: Signet Books, New American Library, 1967.
Doron, Meir & Gelman Joseph. *Confidential*. New York: Gefan Books, 2011.
Ennes Jr., James M. *Assault on the Liberty*. New York: Random House, 1979
Fisk, Robert. *The Great War for Civilization*. London: Fourth Estate, 2005.
Gilmour, David. *Dispossessed: the Ordeal of the Palestinians*. London: Sphere Books, 1982.
Gilmour, David. *Lebanon: The Fractured Country*. London: Sphere Books, 1984.
Hersh, Seymour. *The Samson Option*. London: Faber and Faber, 1991.
Hurndall, Jocelyn. *Defy the Stars*. London: Bloomsbury Publishing, 2007.
Klein, Aaron. *Striking Back*. New York: Random House, 2007.
Mearsheimer, John J. & Walt, Stephen M. *The Israel Lobby*. London: Penguin Books, 2007.
Morris, Benny: *Righteous Victims*. New York: Random House Inc., 2001.
Morris, Benny: *The Birth of the Palestinian Refugee Problem Revisited*. Cambridge: Cambridge University Press, 2004.
Ostrovsky, Victor & Hoy, Claire. *By Way of Deception*. New York: St. Martin's Paperbacks, 1990.
Raviv, Dan & Melman, Yossi. *Every Spy a Prince*. Boston: Houghton Mifflin Company, 1990.
Ray, Ellen & Schaap, William H. (eds). *Covert Action: the Roots of Terrorism*. Melbourne: Ocean Press, 2003
Reeve, Simon. *One Day in September*. London: Faber and Faber, 2000.
Rokach, Livia. *Israel's Sacred Terrorism*. Washington D.C: AAUG Press Association, 1986.
Rusk, Dean. *As I Saw It*. New York: W.W. Norton & Co., 1990.
Scott, Peter Dale. *Drugs Oil and War*. Lanham: Rowman & Littlefield Publishers, 2003.
Schmidt, Olivier (ed.). *The Intelligence Files*. Atlanta: Clarity Press, 2005.
Seale, Patrick. *Abu Nidal: A Gun for Hire*. London: Hutchinson, 1992.
Smith, Grant. *Divert*. Washington D.C: Institute of Research: Middle Eastern Policy (Irmep), 2012.
Thomas, Gordon. *Gideon's Spies*. New York: Thomas Dunne Books, 2005.

NEWSPAPERS, PERIODICALS, GOVERNMENT & NGO REPORTS, VIDEO

Arutz Sheva (www.israelnationalnews.com)
Chicago Sun-Times (www.suntimes.com)
Guardian (www.guardian.co.uk)
Haaretz (www.haaretz.co.il)
Independent (www.independent.co.uk)
Jerusalem Quarterly (www.jerusalmenquarterly.org)
Maclean's Magazine (www.thecanadianencyclopedia.com)
Maariv (www.nrg.co.il)
New York Review (www.nybooks.com)
Times (www.thetimes.co.uk)
Washington Post (www.washingtonpost.com)
Yedioth Ahronoth (www.ynetnews.com)
Advocacy Group Opinion (www.prnewswire.com)
American-Israeli Cooperative Enterprise/Jewish Virtual Library (www.jewishvirtuallibrary.org)
Benmelech, Efrain & Berrebi, Claude. *Human Capital and the Productivity of Suicide Bombers*, (www.economics.harvard.edu)
B'TSELEM:Israeli Information Center for Human Rights in the Occupied Territories (www.old.btselem.org/statistics/english/casualties.asp)
CIA, *World Fact Book* (www.cia.gov/library/publications.html)
Council on Foreign Relations (www.cfr.org)
Defence for Children International (www.defenceforchildren.org)
Government Accounting Office (GAO) 1978 Report: *Nuclear Diversion in the US: 13 Years of Contradiction and Confusion* (www.gao.gov)
International Middle East Media Center (www.imemc.org)
Institute for Intelligence and Special Operations (www.mossad.gov.il)
Institute for Research: Middle East Policy (www.IRmep.org)
Israel Police Force (www.police.gov.il)
Middle East Intelligence Bulletin (www.meforum.org)
Miller, James & Sarah Shah, Sarah. *Death in Gaza*. Warner Home Video, 2006.
Pontecorvo, Gillo (dir.) & Solinas, Franco. *The Battle of Algiers*, Argent Films, 2009.
Radio Islam (www.radioislam.org)
United Nations Conventions on the Rights of the Child/Torture/Human Rights (www.en.wikisource.org)
United Nations Documentation: Research Guide (www.un.org)
United Nations Fact Finding Mission into the Gaza Conflict (UNFFMGC) Report, 2009 (www2.ohchr.org)
United States Senate (www.senate.gov)

CHAPTER TWO

'LONDONISTAN'

> *"Take the so-called politics of fear—the constant reference to risks, from 'hoodies' on the street corners to international terrorism. Whatever the truth of these risks and the best ways of dealing with them, the politics of fear plays on an assumption that people cannot bear the uncertainties associated with them. Politics then become a question of who can better deliver an illusion of control."*
>
> **Former vicar Mark Vernon quoted in "God. Who Knows? BBC News, 4 December 2006**

The Bombs of Bloody Thursday

The terror that day, 7 July 2005, began on the London Underground at 8.50am, when three bombs exploded at three separate locations within 50 seconds. These were coordinated attacks which had required prior reconnaissance, familiarity with the London transport network, access to significant amounts of bomb-making equipment and chemicals, and the knowledge of how to put it all together, and make it work.

The first bomb exploded on train number 204 traveling between Liverpool Street and Aldgate on the Circle Line, eight minutes after leaving Kings Cross-St Pancras tube station. At the time of the explosion the third carriage, where the bomb had been detonated by 22-year-old Shehzad Tanweer, was about 100 yards along, in the tunnel from Liverpool Street station.

The second bomb exploded on another Circle Line westbound train, in the second carriage of train number 216, heading towards Paddington, moments after leaving Platform 4 at Edgeware Road station. This train had also left Kings Cross station eight minutes earlier. Seven people died when Mohammad Sidique Khan, aged 30, detonated the device. A report in the *Daily Telegraph* the following day quoted survivors describing how the blast ripped open the carriage "like a can opener." The casualties could have been considerably higher. At least three other crowded commuter trains were in the vicinity, one of which, an eastbound Circle Line train arriving at Platform 3 from Paddington, was passing the targeted train when the device was detonated.

The third bomb went off on the Piccadilly Line, on southbound train number 311, from Kings Cross-St Pancras and Russell Square, about one minute, and 500 yards, after leaving the station. The bomb, detonated at the rear of the first carriage by 19-year-old Germaine Lindsay, seriously damaged the front of the following carriage which was crammed with commuters, and killed 27 people.

The emergency services converged on the tube stations. Breaking news carried details on the mounting list of casualties, their injuries and footage of yellow-clad, fully-equipped paramedics heading underground. It was assumed the terror was over. Until 9.47am when a fourth bomb was detonated by the youngest of the four suicide bombers, 18-year-old Hasib Hussain, on the top deck of an double-decker No.30 bus traveling across town from Marble Arch to Hackney Wick, in Tavistock Square, near the headquarters of the British Medical Association (BMA). On BBC Radio5 witnesses spoke of seeing parts of the bus flying through the air. The location of the bomb meant that the front part of the vehicle remained intact. The driver and most of the passengers seated at the front on the top deck survived. However, fourteen people seated near the bomber died.

This bomb, like the other three, was a home-made, organic, peroxide-based device, packed into a rucksack. A photograph of the red double-decker AEC Routemaster, a familiar sight on the streets of London, blown apart - a twisted wreckage on a carpet of glass and incidental debris, partly hidden behind a blue tarpaulin screen - became an iconic image of the London bombings. It was a powerful image made all the more dramatic because of the familiarity of the target to Londoners and foreign visitors. Its 'message' was quickly exploited by the far-right, anti-immigrant British National Party (BNP) who distributed leaflets within days with a photo of the No. 10 bus and the slogan, "Maybe now its time to start listening to the BNP." Three years later, in the 2008 London mayoral election, six National Front (NF) and BNP candidates would secure 5.2 percent (almost 54,000) of the vote.

It took the deaths of 56 people, including the bombers, and terrible injuries to many of the 700 officially-listed casualties, to remind the British Prime Minister, Tony Blair, that all politics is local, even foreign policy decisions. Britain's former ambassador to Washington, Sir Christopher Meyer, who had supported the invasion of Iraq in March 2003, in an interview in the *Guardian* on 5 November 2005 delivered a damaging critique of Blair's blunt dismissal of the suggestion that supporting President George W. Bush was, as some commentators had claimed, to "settle old scores" with Saddam Hussein, and had exposed British citizens to terror at home. As Meyer put it, "there is plenty of evidence around at the moment that home-grown terrorism was partly radicalized and fuelled by what is going on in Iraq. There is no way we can credibly get up and say it has nothing to do with it. Don't tell me that being in Iraq has got nothing to do with it. Of course it does."

Within hours of the attacks the Labour Government's Home Secretary, Charles Clarke, described the four bombers as 'clean skins' - counter-terrorism jargon first used to explain the failure of the British authorities to identify IRA sleeper-cells based on the mainland during the Troubles. Many British newspapers and London-based foreign press agencies, even before all the dead were identified and figures for the final, grim body-count were released, carried reports which had little to do with the brutal reality of the situation. According to Nick Davies, in his excellent book, *Flat Earth News*, the *Independent on Sunday* blamed the attacks on "white mercenary terrorists" while the *Sunday Telegraph* claimed that a "foreign-based Islamic terrorist cell" was responsible, and the *Times* reported that the "London rush-hour bombers are alive and planning another attack." This was before the newspapers realized the bombers were British born, Muslim and dead. Fleet Street-based newspapers, in stories immediately after the attacks, identified "four different masterminds behind the plot" all of which were "directly contradicted" during the subsequent investigation by the Metropolitan Police, the West Yorkshire Police (WYP) and the intelligence and security services, MI5 and MI6.

One man with more experience than most is dealing with such threats, the former Scotland Yard Commissioner, John Stevens, told BBC News, on 10 July, before the bombers were identified, that those responsible were "almost certainly" British and "did not fit the caricature of [an] al-Qaida fanatic from some backward village in Algeria or Afghanistan." Stevens had been in charge of three external police inquiries into collusion between the British Army's Force Research Unit (FRU) and loyalist gunmen in the North of Ireland, and was regarded as one of the country's top police officers.

Stevens, of course, was correct. What is surprising is why so many newspapers go it so badly wrong in the beginning. They had, after all, published what Davies refers to as "terror error stories" following the New York and Washington attacks almost four years earlier, and although many of the stories had simply contributed to the climate of fear and had little basis in fact, they featured British-born, or British-based, radicalized Islamists.

One of these reports had involved three men from Leicester, in the English Midlands, who allegedly planned to hijack a helicopter and fly it into the US Embassy in Grosvenor Square, London, a prime target for jihadists. All were subsequently released and handed over to the UK Immigration Service. This story had its roots in another false threat when a Swedish citizen of Tunisian descent, Kerim Sadok Chatty, was arrested at Stockholm-Vasteras Airport, trying to board the Irish airline, Ryanair Flight 685 for London's Stanstead Airport, with a loaded pistol in his luggage. Anonymous intelligence sources quoted in the media claimed he was planning to hijack the plane and fly it into the US Embassy in the capital, using the rooftop eagle to identify the building. Mr. Chatty was known to the Swedish police. He had briefly attended a flight school in South Carolina, in the US in 1996, and became involved in Stockholm's criminal underworld when he returned to Sweden, serving time for possession of a Glock 9mm machine pistol. The *Times* newspaper reported that while in jail Mr. Chatty had met Oussama Kassir, whom the FBI alleged in a US indictment against another man, was a "hit man" for Osama bin Laden. Mr. Kassir was instrumental in Chatty's conversion to Islam, and although he was a devotee of the ultra-orthodox, Saudi-based Salafi school of Islam, the Swede had no interest in violence, and never planned to hijack the Ryanair Boeing 737-800. The Swedish National Police Board security service, SAPO, subsequently described the reports as "false information." Mr. Chatty, who had been traveling to a Muslim conference in Birmingham, was cleared of all terrorism-related charges. He was released on 30 September 2002, after spending one month in police custody when chief prosecutor, Thomas Haggstrom, said in a statement that "nothing in the investigation indicates that Chatty had intended to hijack and crash the plane into any target in Sweden or any other country."

There were other false terrorism-related tales brewed by imagination and fear. One involved a plot to blow up Manchester United's football ground at Old Trafford, involving eight locally-based men who were arrested and subsequently released without charge, but not before some UK media reports had carried gruesome reports of the horrific consequences of bombs exploding among a closely-packed crowd in excess of 50,000 at a home game. Another involved the arrest of six men in London who allegedly planned to carrying out a ricin attack on the Underground. No ricin was found, five of those detained were cleared of all criminal intent and released, and one individual was later convicted of "conspiracy to cause a public nuisance."

The Death of Democratic Islam

A decade earlier the French media first referred to the British capital as 'Londonistan' to describe the 500,000-strong Muslim community based in the Greater London area and the hardline London Imams at some inner-city mosques who called the faithful to weekly prayer and preached the way and duty of jihad. The perception across the English Channel was of a city offering refuge to Rachid Ramda, the Algerian-born alleged 'mastermind' of a series of bombings in Paris, carried out by the Armed Islamic Group (GIA). Other members of the organization had also fled to Britain after black-clad members of EPIGN, the parachute-trained squadron attached to the French Gendarmerie used in large scale anti-terrorist operations, shot dead Khaled Kelkal, a senior GIA operative. Kelkal had been responsible for bombs which had exploded at Saint-Michel station on 25 July 2005, killing eight people and injuring eighty, a bomb at the Arc de Triomphe less than a month later which wounded 17 people, an unexploded bomb found on the TGV high-speed rail-link near Lyon (where Kelkal had been reared since infancy and educated), a bomb which exploded in a Paris square, injuring four people on 3 September, and a car-bomb outside a Jewish school in Lyon four days later which injured 14 people. Kelkal's fingerprints were found on the unexploded device, he was tracked to Malval Forest near Lyon, where he died, armed with a pistol and attempting to resist arrest.

Why GIA decided to begin a campaign of random violence in France remains puzzling. Perhaps the no-warning attacks were intended to draw attention to France's role in the Algerian civil war, and the complicated relationship between the Algerian 'coupists' and the Balladur administration in Paris. If so, no one in London or Washington was listening.

The brutal conflict, which would eventually cost the lives of an estimated 200,000 people, began in December 1991 when the Islamic Salvation Front (FIS) - one of twenty political parties founded in 1989 after the National People's Assembly adopted an electoral system which allowed new political parties to contest both local and national elections - won 55 percent of the vote in local elections. In June 1991, the (military-backed collective presidency) High Council of State, headed by Mohamed Boudiaf, one of the founders of the Front de Liberation Nationale (FLN) that had secured Algerian independence from France in July 1962 (after eight years of armed conflict and 250,000 dead), announced parliamentary elections and changes to the electoral system, including restrictions on campaigning in mosques. The FIS called a general strike. The HCS declared a state of siege, and elections were postponed for several months. FIS leaders, Dr Abbassi Madani, a former FLN veteran of the War of Independence, who had studied for a doctorate in educational psychology in London from 1975 to 1979, and Ali Belhadj, were arrested and jailed on charges of threatening state security. In the first round of elections for the 600-seater National Peoples Assembly, in December 1991, the FIS won 188 seats outright, and were virtually certain to win an absolute majority in the second round. However, on 4 January 1992, President Chadli Bendjedid, under pressure from the Algerian Military Council, dissolved the NPA. Following his resignation a week later, the 5-member HCS took charge. Street gatherings were banned after Friday prayers, and following several days of violent clashes between FIS supporters and the heavily-armed security forces, a state of emergency was declared, the FIS was ordered to disband, and all 411 democratically-elected FIS-controlled local and regional authorities and councils were dissolved. Throughout this slow and seemingly irrevocable slide into civil conflict, Paris, London and Washington were silent. These "champions of democracy" were willing to sacrifice the political system they paid lip-service to, in order to prevent the rising tide of democratic, if uncompromising, Islam.

All armed conflicts have pivotal moments and the assassination of Mohamad Boudiaf, is one of those in modern Algerian history. He was shot dead, on 29 June 1992, by his bodyguard during a televised speech at the opening of a cultural centre at Annaba, the fourth largest city. It was Boudiaf's first trip outside the capital, Algiers, since becoming chairman of the HCS. His assassin was described as a "lone gunman with Islamist sympathies." However, many independent commentators, including Robert Fisk, believe Boudiaf was murdered by the military establishment, which had been responsible for the coup and his chairmanship of the HCS. In *The Great War for Civilization* Fisk writes: "Boudiaf concentrated his anger on two targets: the FIS, and the corruption [of the Algerian regime] which had driven so many Algerians to despair of the democracy they had been promised. The first of his targets would despise him. The second would kill him."

Part of the secret history of the Algerian civil war is the existence and influence of a corrupt network of Algerian Francophile military officers headed by General Larbi Belkheir, who, as Minister for the Interior in 1992, facilitated the military coup that deposed his friend, Chadli Bendjedid. Known as the *Francalgerie*, which is also the title of an important book by journalists, Lounis Aggoun and Jean-Baptiste Rivoire, this covert network signed-off on secret agreements, conducted parallel diplomacy, and shaped the economic, political and military relationship between Algiers and Paris. Belkheir would later be accused of ordering the assassination of Ali Mecili, a member of the Algerian Socialist Forces Front (FFS) in Paris in April 1987, and of complicity in torture while serving as Interior Minister, in a complaint filed on 5 December 2003 on behalf of political refugee, Abderrahmane El-Mahdi Mosbah, while Belkheir was staying at the Val-de-Grace hospital in Paris. The complaint was heard by French police four days later, leaving enough time for Belkheir to flee France.

Another malignant influence which shaped the conflict was the relationship, within the Algerian security service, Department du Renseignement et de la Securite (DRS), headed by Major General Mohamed Mediene, one of the junta officers who forced the cancellation of the second round of the 1991 general election, and a key member of a military cabal known as the 'eradicators' who advocated the harsh repression of the Islamists, and the reconstruction of Algeria along the lines of modern secular France, and a group were moderate officers known as the 'conciliators' who believed the state could only survive through a process of dialogue and compromise. According to historian Martin Stone, the conciliators had "considerable support among Algerians" including the two main political parties, the FLN and the FFS. Unfortunately for this group the powerful French Direction de la Surveillance du Territoire (DST) headed by Yves Bonnet, sided with the eradicators, and in the late 1980s moved to silence the opposition and neutralize all political dialogue. The murder of Ali Mecili, a close colleague of FFS leader Hocine Ait-Ahmed, by an assassin hired by the DRS, and carried out with the covert assistance of the DST, was a "prelude to the collaborative efforts between the two intelligence agencies" according to Aggoun and Rivoire, who also provide evidence, through extensive research and interviews, of several other incidents which prolonged the conflict.

On 24 October 1993, three employees of the French consulate in Algiers were kidnapped. Two days later GIA allegedly claimed responsibility in a faxed message to London, which also criticized attempts at "reconciliation and dialogue" and demanded, in exchange for the hostages, the release of one of its founders, Abdelhak Layada, who had been arrested in Morocco and extradited to Algeria the previous month. The abduction was a 'black flag' operation, designed to solidify French Government support for the Algerian coupists. The two journalists learned that Jean-Charles Marchiani, a former French foreign intelligence, Direction Generale de la Securite Exterieure (DGSE) counter-terrorism officer, who had moved into the private sector in 1970, and served as special adviser to Interior Minister, Charles Pasqua, from 1993 to 1995, "knew of the abduction and possibly even proposed it." For security reasons he also demanded from the Algerians that the operation "should not be entrusted to uncontrollable Islamists but to DRS agents." In return for cooperation with the French, the Algerian regime demanded the arrest of FIS activists who had fled to France, and produced an extradition-request list of 162 individuals. Eventually, French police arrested over 180 'suspected' Islamic terrorist and many were deported to Burkina Faso after the hostages were released, unharmed, on 30 October, with a warning, allegedly from GIA that "all foreigners should leave the country within a month."

The second incident was the hijacking of an Air France airline at Algiers Airport on 24 December 1994, which just happened to coincide with a meeting, organized under the patronage of the Community of Sant'Edidio in Rome, of the Algerian constitutional opposition, including the FLN, the FFS, and the Islamist FIS, to draft a platform to provide a solution to the conflict, which included a return to democratic practices, an independent investigation of human rights abuses following the coup and the repeal of the dissolution of the FIS. The initiative had the support of French President

Francois Mitterrand, Foreign Minister Alain Juppe, US President Bill Clinton and German Chancellor Helmut Kohl.

However, instead of dialogue, the hijackers executed three passengers, flew the plane to Marseille for refueling and threatened to fly it into the Eiffel Tower if their demands were not met. A brief stand-off at Marseilles ended when French Special Forces (GIGN) stormed the plane and killed the hijackers. The Algerian authorities blocked French efforts to investigate the incident, and having attempted to make sense of the "countless inconsistencies of this strange affair" Aggoun and Rivoire came to the conclusion, as did retired judge and former head of the French central anti-terror service, Alain Marsaud, that the hijacking was organized by the DRS. Robert Fisk notes that the surprising thing about the incident was not that it happened "but that the French national airline was still operating scheduled flights into a country where law and order had virtually disintegrated." Fisk also points out that no one bothered to ask if the hijackers seriously intended to fly into the Eiffel Tower, or more importantly in the light of events in the US seven years later, "whether their plan might in the future inspire other, more ambitious projects involving passenger airlines and tall buildings."

It was against this background, and a series of brutal massacres - including 4 May 1994 El Marsa Forest reprisal killings of 173 people who had been kidnapped by the security forces and the OJAL pro-government militia from villages in eastern Algeria following the recent deaths of 16 soldiers in a GIA ambush; the Berrouaghia Prison massacre, on 14 November 1994, in which 30 inmates were killed according to government sources, while 200 died according to the independent national daily newspaper *El Watan*; and the Serkadi Prison mutiny, between 21 and 23 February 1994 when the security forces killed between 96 and 110 inmates during an alleged attempted breakout—that the French authorities demanded the extradition of Rachid Ramda, who had lived in London for several years. Ramda wrote for *El Ansar*, described by the French Justice Ministry as the "official newspaper" of the GIA. Self-righteous articles in the French media accused Britain of providing a "safe-haven" for a wanted terrorist without considering the possibility of the covert role of the DRS, or the possibility of clandestine collusion with French agencies in the Algerian conflict.

There was no mention of Ali Touchent, the primary Paris bomber who was known to have worked for the DRS, according to Aggoun and Rivoire, who was allowed to "slip out of France." The attacks in summer 1995, systematically attributed to GIA in the media, undermined the recently-appointed French Prime Minister Alain Juppe's "nuanced position" on the Algerian civil war, and despite the fact that some French senior politicians who had headed the relevant ministries, and liaised with trusted officials in the DST and the DGSE, were aware of the 'dirty war' being waged by the

DRS, they were also aware - or perhaps 'fearful' would be a better word - that public condemnation could provoke further attacks in France.

Numerous intelligence agents confirmed this in interviews with Aggoun and Riviero, including Alain Marsaud, who told the journalists that if they "traced the hierarchy of the responsible groups, at some point they would encounter DRS agents." Some senior French officials, including Interior Minister Jean-Louis Debre, were aware that the Algerian regime and the DRS had crossed a line by targeting Parisians and visitors to the capital. However, despite suggesting at a press conference in mid-September 1995 that the military authorities in Algiers condoned the brutality of the DRS, the French Government was reluctant to publicly criticize the coupists, and continued to discreetly support the regime.

Eventually the British Conservative Government's Home Secretary, Michael Howard - a man "with something of the night about him" according to his Home Office colleague, Anne Widdecombe - ordered Rachid Ramda's arrest. He was taken into custody on 4 November 1995, and held at southeast London's 'Category' A Belmarsh Prison and various UK high-security facilities for over a decade without being formally charged with an offence while he challenged the French extradition request through the British courts. Eventually he was transferred to the Palais de Justice in Paris, in December 2005, after the 7/7 bombings changed public opinion in the UK.

Five months earlier, on 5 August, 2005, Prime Minister Blair had announced that Her Majesty's Government (HMG) would sign extradition agreements with Algeria, Egypt, Libya and Jordan, to ensure that Islamic jihadists could be returned to their home countries. Blair, of course, made no mention of the fact that the systematic torture of detainees was part of the custodial regime of these Arab states. "Chillingly" as Philippe Sands notes, the prime minister added, "should legal obstacles arise, we will legislate further, including, if necessary, amending the Human Rights Act in respect of the interpretation of the European Convention on Human Rights."

During his trial before the Cour d'assises in October 2007, Ramda denied knowing two of the Paris bombers, Ait Ali Belkacem and Boualem Bensaid (who were serving life sentences since 2002) despite his fingerprints on a Ffr. 38,000 Western Union money order sent to Belkacem, and wiretap 'evidence' of alleged conversations with both convicted bombers, which he denied existed and were not made available to the defense. He was convicted of "complicity in assassination in relation to a terrorist enterprise" and sentenced to life, with a recommendation that he serve a minimum of twenty-two years.

The British were right to be cautious despite the stern French demands for Ramda's extradition. In the mid-1990s there was growing body of evidence, including statements taken under oath, forensic reports and eyewitness testimony of collusion involving British security forces, in particular the British Army's FRU, with loyalist paramilitary organizations and freelance proxy assassins in Ireland. The preceding Tory administration had been careful about being linked to allegations of similar state collusion with some pretty horrendous events in Algeria and France. Against the backdrop of the slaughter of an estimated 1,000 civilians in the killing fields of Algeria, including 412 in four villages near the town of Relizane on the last day of December 1997, and at least 172 at Had Chekala and Remka five days later, evidence was beginning to emerge of state complicity. Two members of the Algerian security forces had fled to the UK and sought political asylum. In an interview with the *Guardian Weekly* on 16 November 1997, and the *Observer* on 11 January 1998, one of the men, identified only as 'Yussuf' who had spent 14 years with the Securite Militaire (renamed the DRS in 1990) claimed to have been ordered to take part in massacres and the torture of detainees, and that Algerian Special Forces, disguised as bearded Islamic fundamentalists in Arab clothing, "slaughtered entire families." He suggested that the European Union should send a human-rights mission to visit torture facilities in Algiers, including the basement of Chateauneuf barracks, a complex beneath the barracks at Ben Aknoun and a similar facility at Beni-Messous, two of four municipalities in the Bouzareah district of Algiers, as well as cells in the basement of the city's Central Police Headquarters.

Yussuf told journalists John Sweeney and Leonard Doyle that the "constant terror" in which civilians were living was orchestrated by two men, more powerful than the nominal president, General Liamine Zeroual. He identified them as the head of the DRS, Mohammad Mediane (codename 'Tewfik') and General Smain Lamari, the head of a sub-division of the DRS, the counter-intelligence agency DCE. He described the GIA in the mid-1990s as a "pure product" of the DCE after the organization had been infiltrated and turned by government agents, and claimed that the Paris bombings in 1995 were ordered by Gen. Smain, that the operation was run by Gen. Souames Mahmoud, head of the DRS at the Algerian Embassy in Paris, and carried out by two DRS agents who had flown in from Algiers. Yussef's testimony was supported by a former diplomat who also defected to Britain, Mohammed Larbi Zitout, deputy head at the Algerian Embassy in Tripoli. There was also a further interesting element to Yussuf's story, his claim that Algeria was hiding materials for President Saddam Hussein's nuclear, chemical and biological warfare program, and that intelligence agents from both countries were "collaborating" to defeat the UN sanctions against Iraq.

The Algerian civil war continued until February 2002, although a small, al-Qaida linked organization, called the Salafist Group for Preaching and Combat (GSPC), continued to carry out sporadic acts of violence against state interests. The Algerian generals were quietly feted in Washington for having defeated insurgent Islam, and as President George W. Bush, the neocons and the generals planned for war in Iraq, it was best to ignore, rather than address, allegations of Algerian covert practices to facilitate Saddam's WMD program. .

Legislation Not Fit for the Purpose

In the UK between 1974 and 1989 several amended versions of the Prevention of Terrorism Act (PTA) were passed by Parliament conferring emergency powers on Scotland Yard and the 42 regional police forces in England and Wales. The legislation worked alongside similar measures in the North of Ireland, and was primarily designed to curb the mainland activities of the Provisional IRA and the Irish National Liberation Army (INLA). The original PTA allowed for arrests without warrant and the detention for up to 7 days, without access to legal representation, of persons on "reasonable suspicion" that they were guilty of an offence, or otherwise "concerned in the commission, preparation or instigation of acts of terrorism." Provisions under the legislation included a 14-year prison sentence and an unlimited fine for persons "contributing, receiving or soliciting" financial support for acts of terror, and "exclusion orders" as an "expedient" to prevent acts of terror relating to the Troubles which rather bizarrely allowed the authorities to ban British citizens from the North of Ireland from entering certain parts of the UK. A form of internal exile, similar to the widely-condemned apartheid legislation in South Africa.

The PTA was first enacted in 1974 by Labour Home Secretary, Roy Jenkins, then rewritten in 1976, 1984 and 1989, in response to IRA attacks. In a climate where suspicion had replaced evidence, statements were altered by the police, confessions were obtained under duress (in several cases as a result of physical and psychological abuse) the PTA accommodated the benign complicity of the judiciary. It led to shameful miscarriages of justice, including that suffered by the Birmingham Six, the Guildford Four, six members of the Maguire family and several other individuals.

Except in cases of national security, where 'foreigners' could be deported by the Home Secretary - usually acting on the advice of an anonymous panel of legally well-versed civil servants, and following a perfunctory examination of the particular case in question, without hearing testimony from witnesses - the PTA worked well as far as the Home Office mandarins were concerned. However, in 1986, a Sikh separatist, Karamjit Singh Chahal, was arrested on suspicion of conspiring with others to assassinate the Indian Prime Minister, Rajiv Gandhi, during an official visit to the UK. The Cambridge University-educated eldest son of Prime Minister Indira Gandi had taken office following the assassination of his mother on 31 October 1984, who was shot dead by two of her Sikh bodyguards in the grounds of her official resident in New Delhi. The assassination was a consequence of Operation *Blue Star* four months earlier, when she had ordered the Indian Army to occupy Harmandir Sahib ('The Abode of God'), the most prominent Sikh gurdwara also known as the 'Golden Temple' in the Punjabi city of Amritsar, to prevent it being used by Sikh separatist militants. During the 72-hour military assault on the complex up to 8,000 Sikh fighters, Sikh pilgrims, civilians and Indian soldiers died

Within hours of Mrs. Gandhi's assassination riots erupted in predominantly Sikh areas of the city. Armed mobs swarmed into neighborhoods killing Sikh men women and children, ransacking and burning Sikh property. In other areas of Delhi individual Sikhs were attacked, some were lynched, others were doused with petrol and burnt alive. In the Punjab-based, English-language daily newspaper, the *Tribune*, the anti-Sikh terror was described the as a "pogrom" which lasted several days, and ended with an official death toll of 2,700 (the unofficial toll was much higher) and an estimated 50,000 people displaced.

This was also the conclusion reached by authors, Manoj Mitta and H.S Phoolka, in their book *When a Tree Shook Delhi*, based on court transcripts, hundreds of sworn affidavits and eye-witness accounts. They wrote that instead of defending innocent victims of the rampant violence, Delhi Police "cracked down" on Sikhs who were defending their properties and the lives of their families from attacks "by hooligans led by Congress leaders." The title of the book comes from a speech Rajiv Gandhi made less than three weeks after his mother's death, telling INC supporters at rally in mid- November: "Some riots took place in the country following the murder of Indiraji. We know the people were very angry and for a few days it seemed that India had been shaken. But, when a mighty tree falls, it is only natural that the earth around it does shake a little."

Describing the deaths of innocent Sikhs as a "natural response" to a political assassination marked Rajiv out for a similar fate by men like Karamjit Singh, according to the British authorities. However, attempts to deport Singh quietly failed and his appeal worked its way through the British judicial system eventually reaching the European Court of Human Rights (ECtHR) in Strasbourg. The ECtHR ruled that there was a risk of the plaintiff suffering inhumane and degrading treatment if deported to India, which would leave the UK in breach of Article 3 of the European Convention of Human Rights (ECHR). The court also ruled the British Government's continued detention of Karamjit Singh while he challenged the deportation order was a breach of Article 5 of the ECHR.

In response to the ECtHR ruling, Home Secretary Howard introduced the Special Immigration Appeals Commission (SIAC) in 1997, which Conservative politicians and Downing Street officials claimed would "strike a balance between national security and natural justice." SIAC is a court of record which hears cases partly in secret, to allow the British Security Service (MI5) and the Metropolitan Police Special Branch to present their argument for deportation, and partly in public session, where a 'special' advocate (who has been vetted by MI5 as a 'suitable' person to be allowed access to classified material) appointed by the Attorney General puts the case for the appellant. The special advocates cannot cross-examine intelligence officers, and cannot take instructions or communicate with their clients. The SIAC was designed with one objective: to prevent appellants using the judicial system to challenge the Home Secretary's decision to return foreign nationals to their homelands, even if they are likely to face torture and possible death at the hands of an oppressive regime. While trade, for example the $75 billion Al-Yahamah arms deal with Saudi Arabia, prevents the Foreign and Commonwealth Office (FCO) protesting about human rights abuses when the Riyadh regime lobbies the British Government for the return of their nationals, Amnesty International has criticized the SIAC's "shockingly low burden of proof" because evidence cannot be tested to the same standards as in a criminal trial.

In the decade following the Soviet retreat from Afghanistan, when the Afghan mujahideen and Arab jihadists from countries such as Saudi Arabia, Algeria, and Egypt turned their attention westward, the US remained complacent to the threat from groups which had been organized, trained, and armed by the CIA, MI6 and other intelligence agencies in the 1980s. In the US the threat was local, the enemy within were citizens who read William Luther Pierce's *The Turner Diaries* and 'safe havens' were in places like the Coeur d'Alene National Forest, in northern Idaho, and the backwoods of Colorado and Montana. The hatred that kindled had spawned white supremacist organizations like Aryan Nation and The Order, which carried out the 18 June 1984 machine-gun murder of Jewish radio talkshow host, Alan Berg, in Denver.

Pierce's book, written under the pseudonym 'Andrew MacDonald,' is set in the 1990s and tells the story of a neo-Nazi group which blows up the FBI headquarters in Washington after the 'Day of the Rope' in which 'traitorous' whites are hanged from lampposts. It was the favorite reading material of Timothy McVeigh, the 1991 *Desert Storm* veteran, executed at the Federal Correctional Facility, Terre Haute, Indiana, on 11 June 2001 for the truck-bomb destruction of the Alfred P. Murrah Federal Building in Oklahoma City on 9 April 1995, in which 168 people died and over 800 were injured. During his trial prosecutors described *The Turner Diaries* as a "blueprint" detailing the kind of bomb (a 5,000lbs mixture of ammonium nitrate and nitro methane) McVeigh used, and a passage from the book was found in his car after his arrest.

After Afghanistan and the satisfaction of contributing to the defeat of Soviet aggression, the US intelligence and security agencies paid scant attention to the patently obvious - that the enemy might also arrive from without. What was America expecting after 25 January 1993, when a lone Pakistani gunman, Aimal Kasi, opened fire with an AK-47 semi-automatic on Route 123 in Fairfax County on vehicles taking a left into the main entrance of CIA HQ, killing two agency employees? After a coalition of jihadist groups successfully bombed the World Trade Center in Lower Manhattan, using a 1336lb urea-nitrate-hydrogen gas-enhanced bomb packed into a yellow Ryder rental van, killing six and injuring over 1,000 people? Certainly not, as the official narrative, the discredited *9/11 Commission Report,* claims - that terror on a virtually unmanageable scale could be perpetrated by a group of well-funded young men from Saudi Arabia, a friendly state, in the US to enjoy the good life in Miami, drink beer in strip-clubs and learn to fly. Not that taking off mattered, and landing was never a consideration. Just how to navigate, fly below 1,300 feet and not avoid obstacles.

There had been no major nationwide terrorist alerts in the US during the Clinton presidency. The FBI treated the two local attacks as isolated incidents, while the CIA focused on the jihadist threat to American interests abroad, sometimes successfully, sometimes not. Nineteen Americans died when a truck-bomb exploded outside the US military's Khobar Towers housing facility near Dhahran, Saudi Arabia, on 25 June 1996. The attack, according to the Saudi interior minister, Prince Nayif, was probably carried out by individuals "motivated by bin Laden." Twelve Americans were among the 303 dead when the US embassies in Nairobi and Dar es Salaam were destroyed by car bombs in coordinated attacks on 7 August 1998, within three-weeks of Osama bin Laden's deputy, Ayman Zawahri, declaring "enough of words, it is time to take action against this iniquitous and faithless force [the United States] which has spread its troops through Egypt, Yemen and Saudi Arabia." At 11.18am on 12 October 2000, suicide bombers in a small craft approached the *USS Cole,* an Arleigh Burke-class, Aegis-equipped vertical-launch, guided missile destroyer, while it was on a routine refueling stop in Aden harbor. They detonated an estimated 500lbs of RDX (Composition C-4) explosives, killing 17 crew-members and seriously injuring 39 when a 40-by-40 foot gash ripped through the port side of the vessel. And then came the well-planned, low-tech, coordinated, hijacked commercial airlines attacks in the US itself. When compared with the billions of dollars spent on security, this was an extremely cheap, off-the-shelf operation, costing less than $300,000, according to a 13 January 2002 *New York Times* article, which estimated that the hijackers had brought about $40,000 into the country personally, and about $240,000 was sent to them by wire transfers.

The Days of the Preachers

In Britain, in an immediate response to the attacks on the prestige targets, the World Trade Center and the Pentagon, the Labour Government formally introduced the Anti-Terrorism Crime and Security Act 2001, which was rushed through Parliament and came into force on 14 December. The legislation, described by some commentators as "draconian" because it contained many measures not directly relating to terrorism, allowed the Home Secretary to certify and order the indefinite detention of non-British citizens suspected by MI5 or Scotland Yard Special Branch of being involved in "activities associated with terrorism," including charitable fundraising and possible recruitment.

One premises in particular was attracting the attention of the authorities, the modern, five-storey Finsbury Park mosque in the north-central London borough of Haringey, where uniformed police were a 24-hour presence since the US attacks, to protect worshippers from racist attacks. They were also there to keep an eye on the mosque's radical imam, Sheikh Abu Hamza al-Masri, whose preaching had increasingly infuriated the French after a global round-up of French suspects linked to the al-Qaida network, several of whom had regularly attended Friday prayers at the Finsbury Park mosque.

Abu Hamza was an Egyptian-born Sunni activist, who had studied civil engineering at Brighton Polytechnic on the south coast of England in the late 1970s before joining the jihadist struggle against the Soviet Army in Afghanistan. While there, he lost both hands, and his left eye while clearing Soviet landmines for the mujahideen, according to the Edinburgh-based daily newspaper, *The Scotsman*. A British citizen through marriage since 1981, he returned to the UK in the early 1990s via Yemen. By 1996 he was a figurehead among radicalized Muslims at the Finsbury Park mosque, where he openly supported the jihad through his 'Supporters of Sharia' movement. Abu Hamza's preaching, which was monitored by a DST informant, Reda Hassaine, an Algerian journalist who had fled to the UK, and his growing influence among British Muslims, were key considerations in French counter-terrorism experts constantly referring to the British capital in the local media as 'Londonistan'. In January 1999 Abu Hamza came to the attention of the wider public when five British Muslims were arrested in Yemen, among them the cleric's 17-year-old son, and his stepson from his second marriage, and accused of planning attacks against British interests in the capital, Sana'a. During their trial the prosecution claimed that the plot had been conceived in the Finsbury Park mosque, and that Abu Hamza had links with a local radical fundamentalist leader, Zayn-al-Abidin al-Muhdar, whose group, the Islamic Aden-Abyan Army, had kidnapped 16 Westerners in Yemen in late December 1998, and executed three British citizens and an Australian when Yemeni Special Forces tried to rescue the hostages. In March 1999, Abu Hamza was arrested by Special Branch officers at his four-bedroom council home in Shepherd's Bush, north London, in connection with the Yemen plot. He was held for several days under the provisions of the PTA, before being released when no incriminating evidence was found to justify further detention.

The French authorities' criticism of the British for allowing London to become a safe haven where terrorist attacks were planned and financed appeared justified when Djamel Beghel was arrested at Dubai International Airport on 28 July 2001 after arriving from Pakistan and preparing to transfer to a European flight. Charged with possession of a false French passport he confessed to the United Arab Emirates (UAE) authorities that he planned to bomb the US embassy in Paris. In a 13 October 2001 *Daily Telegraph* article. the DST informant Hassaine, who also provided background to the British Special Branch and MI5, claimed that Beghel had been recruited at Finsbury Park, and that those who attended after hours of prayer "celebrated the killing of innocent people in Algeria, they encouraged raising money for GIA, and there were classes in martial arts and combat." Hassaine also claimed that following the 9/11 attacks Abu Hamza told his followers that the deaths of over 3,000 were justified, claiming that "many people will be happy [because] America is a crazy superpower and what was done was done in self-defense."

The man who would later be called the "20th hijacker" also attended Finsbury Park mosque. Zacarias Moussaoui, born in St. Jean de Luc in the Basque region of southern France, was a student at South Bank University in London between 1993 and 1995, before graduating with an MA degree in international trade, financing and marketing. He lived in Brixton, south London, and according to the DST, regularly attended Brixton Mosque and the Islamic Cultural Centre, on Gresham Road, which follows the Sunni Islamic Salafiyyah tradition and is related to, but not synonymous with, the ultra-conservative Saudi Wahhabist movement. Moussaoui was proselytized by the radical Islamist Al-Muhajiroun (The Emigrants) organization which had been founded by Sheik Omar Bakri Mohammed and British-born solicitor, Anjem Choudary, in Mecca on 3 March 1983. After the organization was banned by the Saudi regime because of its hardline anti-western rhetoric, frequently focusing on the US 'occupation' of Muslim holy places, the Syrian-born Omar Bakri moved to London in January 1986 where he worked for the international pan-Islamic Sunni organization, Hizb ut-Tahir (The Party of Liberation) until 1996 when disagreements with the party's leadership led to his expulsion. He declared Al-Muhajiroun an independent organization, and continued as its emir until 2003. Under Bakri's spiritual guidance Al-Muhajiroun began leafleting followers at several of London's moderate mosques, including Brixton.

From the mid-1990s Moussaoui's association with radical Muslims, and his 'conversion' to jihad, was monitored by London-based, French-

Algerian DST agents. In the late 1990s Moussaoui attended the Khalden training camp in Afghanistan, described by Lawrence Wright in his compelling narrative, *The Looming Tower*, as the "entry point" for al-Qaida trainees from Yemen, Saudi Arabia, Sweden, Turkey and Chechnya. Each nationality had its own emir, and they "created cells that they could then transplant to their own or adopted countries." Several of the 9/11 hijackers attended the Khalden camp, as did Richard Colvin Reid, the Bromley, south London-born 'shoe bomber' who also attended Brixton mosque before moving on, like Moussaoui, to Friday prayers at Finsbury Park. In September 2000, Moussaoui travelled to Malaysia, and stayed with Yazid Sufaat, a Malaysian-born, California State University graduate with a degree in biochemistry. Sufaat had served with the Malaysian Army as a medical technician before joining Jemaah Islamiyah (Islamic Congregation) and setting up a company called Green Laboratory Medicine (GLM) in 1993 through which, according to the *9/11 Commission Report*, he later tried to weaponize anthrax for al-Qaida in a laboratory near Kandahar Airport in Afghanistan. Sufaat signed letters of employment, identifying Moussaoui as a representative of GLM, documents Moussaoui would later use to obtain a US visa in order to attend a three-month flight training course at Airman Flight School in spring 2001. He left without attempting solo flight and was arrested in Minnesota on immigration charges by FBI and INS agents on 16 August 2001. The charges were upgraded to conspiring to use hijacked aircraft to attack the WTC and Pentagon after 9/11, based on the itemized data on his laptop computer, including Boeing 747 flight manuals, a flight simulator program, and information about crop dusting, plus "elements of information" provided by the DST, and the DGSE, confirming Moussaoui's connections with the suicide hijackers, after the US Department of Justice (DoJ) agreed not to use the French material to "require or execute the death penalty" according to French Justice Minister, Dominique Perben. On 3 May 2006 Moussaoui was found guilty as charged, and the following day Federal Court Judge Leonie Brinkema sentenced him to six consecutive life sentences without the possibility of parole, saying it would deprive the defendant of "martyrdom in a great big bang of glory."

Another jailed jihadist who frequently attended Finsbury Park mosque was Jerome Courtailler, a former Roman Catholic son of a French butcher, born in the Alpine resort town of Bonneville, who converted to Islam in the mid-1990s before moving to London where he came under the influence of Al-Muhajiroun. He was arrested by the Dutch Police in Rotterdam on 13 September 2001, in possession of fake travel documents and a machine for printing credit cards. Extradited to France, he willingly co-operated with French magistrate, Jean-Louis Bruguier, who was conducting a background investigation into the August 1998 US embassy bombings in Kenya and Tanzania. Courtailler admitted attending a training camp in Khowst, Afghanistan in 1997 and 1998, where he met two "Anglo-looking Americans" but denied knowing Moussouri, despite attending Friday payers at Finsbury Park mosque during the same period.

After his arrest Abu Hanza quickly became a figure of hate in the British print media, and his physical appearance, including the distinctive hook prosthesis on his right hand, became an object of ridicule. He was nicknamed 'Captain Hook' (after the main antagonist in J.M. Barrie's *Peter Pan*) in some British tabloids. Amid calls for his deportation, the Murdoch-owned, largest-selling British daily in the mid-2000s, the *Sun*, ran a front-page headline, 'Sling Your Hook'. His case exposed the failings of the PTA, and as a result of a Law Lords ruling about indefinite detention in high-security facilities like Belmarsh, the Labour Home Secretary, David Blunkett, introduced 'control orders' a curfew-based, graduated-scaled technological 'prison without bars' using electronic tagging, electronic surveillance, and enforcing a ban on internet access and other forms of communication, as well as restrictions on social inter-change and association.

The measures were designed to work within the provisions of the ECHR, but because they were issued at the discretion of the Home Secretary, they infringed Article 5 of the Convention, which states that an individual cannot be deprived of liberty or freedom of movement without due process of law. In February 2003 Abu Hanza was dismissed from his position at Finsbury Park mosque by the Charity Commission which, as its name suggests, regulates the financial and taxable status of registered charities in England and Wales. He began holding weekly prayer services on the roadway outside the building until his arrest by Special Branch officers under Section 41 of the Terrorism Act 2000, on 26 August 2004, on terrorist-related charges, and five days later the US DoJ applied for his extradition.

In the mid-1990s, while Abu Hanza was based at Finsbury Park mosque, across town at the Four Feathers community centre, near Regent's Park in the north-western central London borough of Camden, another radical cleric, Abu Qatada al-Filistini, was attracting a following from members of the Egyptian and Algerian Muslim Diaspora, who had fled repressive and despotic Arab regimes in their homelands. Born in Bethlehem, in the West Bank in 1960, which was then under Jordanian occupation, Abu Qatada had arrived in the UK in September 1993 using a false UAE passport and seeking political asylum, claiming he had been the subject of religious persecution and torture by the Jordanian General Intelligence Directorate (GID), which worked closely with the CIA, MI6 and Mossad, monitoring seditious activity in the region and preserving a degree of political stability in Jordan. He was granted refugee status in June 1994, and quickly established himself as an influential figure whose religious views were taken seriously by a broad

Islamic movement willing to take up arms against repressive, undemocratic regimes, but he was not considered to be part of the international anti-western jihad, spearheaded and shaped by the principals known as al-Qaida. Certainly MI5 did not consider Abu Qatada a threat to the interests and security of the UK, and sought his help on several occasions in an effort to obtain some insight into the radicalization of mainly London-based Islamists. It was only after the 9/11 attacks that Abu Qatada would come to be regarded by MI5 as a 'dangerous influence' after copies of his sermons were found in the apartment at 54 Marienstrasse, Hamburg, where Mohamed Atta, the Egyptian-born hijacker/pilot of the American Airlines Flight 11, Boeing 767, which crashed into the WTC North Tower, had lived between 1998 and 2001.

Abu Qatada had been arrested by Special Branch officers in February 2001 and questioned by MI5 about his alleged connection with a German jihadist cell, and almost $200,000 found in his possession. Released without charge due to a lack of evidence (which would have secured a conviction had the legislation existed) he 'disappeared' shortly before new measures were introduced allowing the authorities to detain foreign terrorist suspects without charge or trial, leading to speculation in the media that he had been working for British intelligence as part of an arrangement to be allowed to remain in the UK. He was later tracked down to a council house in Acton, south London, and taken to Belmarsh, to begin a long legal battle to prevent deportation to Jordan. He was treated as a convicted felon in the British media. Spanish judge Baltasar Garzon described him as the "spiritual head of the mujahideen in Britain," while British journalist, Jason Burke, in his book, *Al-Qaeda: The True Story of Radical Islam*, states that Qatada had "acted as the in-house alim [Sharia legal scholar] to radical groups, particularly in Algeria, from his base in northwest London since 1994."

In the post 9/11 years the part played by radical Islamic clerics was subject to closer security by UK and US intelligence and security agencies, and attendance at the Four Feathers community centre was sufficient reason for an individual to be regarded as a 'person of interest' and placed on an international 'watch-list' without any collaborative evidence whatsoever.

In 2002 Martin Mubanga, a Zambian-born British citizen, was arrested by police in Lusaka by local police accompanied by US security officials, and interrogated by MI6 officers before being illegally transported to Guantanamo Bay, where he was held for 33 months. According to the CIA, Mubanga had been "influenced by Omar Uthman [Abu Qatada] while attending the Four Feathers mosque in London" and also "by Sheikh Faisal, who was encouraging all Muslims to go help their brothers in jihad in Afghanistan." Mubanga's Guantanamo file also states that during interrogation "he admitted to the following: he is an al-Qaida member, he fought against allied interests in Afghanistan and Bosnia; he would rejoin the fighting if he were released."

When Mubanga was transferred into UK custody in January 2005 he was released shortly after being briefly questioned by anti-terrorist detectives when British Home Office officials admitted there were "no grounds" to charge him or warrant his continued detention. Martin Mubanga denied the allegations made against him, and described how, prior to his 'admission', he had been subjected to physical abuse in Guantanamo, subjected to extreme degrees of heat and cold, and daubed with his own urine when he lost control of his bladder. With the help of UK human rights lawyer, Louise Christian, co-founder with Labour MP, Sadiq Khan, of the law firm, Christian Khan, Mubanga successfully sued HMG for the clandestine part Downing Street played in his wrongful incarceration. Documents released to the plaintiff during the case disclosed that following Mubanga's detention by the Zambian authorities, Prime Minister Blair's office had intervened to ensure he was rendered to Camp Delta rather than be allowed to return to the UK.

In 1997 Britain had a reputation as a 'safe haven' for international jihadist terror, and it was 'well-deserved' according to western intelligence analysts tasked with tracking the rise of militant Islam. The general consensus was that this 'accommodation,' which allowed militant groups from Algeria, Kashmir, Pakistan, Sri Lanka, Afghanistan, Yemen, Egypt, and Turkey, to raise funds, forge links, print and disseminate propaganda, and which began under the Tories in the early 1990s, was set to continue after Labour's landslide victory in May 1997, despite the Luxor massacre six months later when 62 tourists, including six Britons, died at Dier el-Bahri, trapped inside the mortuary Temple of Hatshepsut, the 18th-dynasty female pharaoh. The attack was carried out by an Islamist group called Jihad Talaat al-Fath, but planned and instigated, according to the Egyptian General Intelligence Service (GIS), by exiled leaders of al-Gama'a al-Islamiyya, several of whom were believed to be living in London. The newly-elected Labour Home Secretary, Jack Straw, in the wake of the Luxor killings, promised to "curb the activities of international terrorist organizations based in Britain."

Faced with similar criticism from the US after 9/11, Mr. Straw, now Foreign Secretary, blamed parliamentary opposition for allowing Britain to become a safe haven for Islamist movements by opposing legislation which would have facilitated deportation. He also blamed the judicial system, saying the UN Convention on Refugees "was never designed to allow people convicted of terrorist offences to be given asylum, but we have to face the fact that our courts have interpreted the convention in ways which have not been helpful," adding that as a result of the attacks in New York and Washington, "there is now a better understanding by the public and some politicians about the need to take tough and effective action against theses people and he had to do it." The pro-Conservative broadsheet, the *Daily Telegraph*, which is regarded as a sympathetic conduit for MI5, reported Straw's comments, and asked if the new resolve meant that "dissidents, militants and suspected terrorists living in London will be extradited or expelled from the country" a question, the newspaper claimed, "that Egypt and others want Britain to answer" - the others being the 'securocrats' in MI5.

Certainly, threat assessment analysts listening to the audio tapes of the preachers' bitter recriminations against undemocratic Arab regimes supported by the West, and reviewing material, including photographs and details of visitors, provided by MI5 'watchers' in static observation posts overlooking Finsbury Park and the Four Feathers mosques, should have been concerned. The radicalization of Richard Reid, who had been 'talent spotted' outside the Brixton mosque in 1997, and within five years was serving life without parole at ADX Florence, Colorado, convicted of eight counts of attempting on, 22 December 2001, to blow up American Airlines Flight 63, en route from Paris to Miami by using an explosive devices hidden in his shoes, was a case in point. It must have been impressed on MI5 just how easy it was for a man like Reid, a petty criminal in his early teens who graduated to crimes against persons and property, and served sentences at Feltham Young Offenders Institution in southwest London, and at Blundeston Prison in Suffolk before converting to Islam, to travel back and forth to training camps in Afghanistan, accumulate duplicated British passports from various overseas consulates, and pass through Israel El Al security at Ben Gurion International Airport, Tel Aviv, in July 2001 (part of his training was to move through high-security systems without attracting attention). After all this, Reid flew to Amsterdam where he lived for several months, returned to Pakistan to collect the PETN-explosive device then traveled to Paris where he eventually boarded the commercial American Airlines flight to Miami, where he ending up being tranquilized after being jumped on by fellow passengers when flight attendant, Hermis Moutardier, spotted him trying to light the fuse of his IED. The boy from Bromley, south London had come a long way, and part of that spiritual journey had been spent listening to Abu Hanza al-Masri at Finsbury Park mosque.

On 30 April 2003, two British Muslims, 22-year-old, Asif Muhammad Hanif from London and 27-year-old Omar Khan Sharif, from Derby, died following a a suicide bombing of 'Mike's Place' a bar in Tel Aviv, killing three people and injuring more than fifty. By now there should have been no doubt at Thames House, MI5's headquarters in central London, that British-born Muslim men were willing to die as 'shahids' in the jihad, spurred on by their outrage at UK complicity in the devastation of Muslim-populated countries. But even after the commuter train attacks in Spain, there was a misguided assumption among members of the Joint Terrorism Analysis

Centre (JTAC) at Thames House, including senior representatives of MI5 and MI6, the Defense Intelligence Staff, (DIS), the SIGINT agency, Government Communications Headquarters (GCHQ), Scotland Yard's Counter-Terrorist Command (CTC) and six relevant Government departments, that violent jihad and the use of suicide bombers would not happen in the UK. This is the only logical explanation for the JTAC's threat level reduction from 'Severe General' (an attack was highly likely) to 'Substantial' (an attack was a strong possibility) prior to 7 July 2005 bombings. There is no evidence that 'agent provocateurs' were involved in the attacks (as had happened on numerous occasions in the US). The British state had nothing to gain. All the legislation and security paraphernalia was in place. The flaw was hubris on the part of those responsible for the security of the state and the safety of its citizens.

The Cercanias Attacks

Residents of Madrid refer to the Thursday morning, 11 March 2004, bombings of the city's commuter train system as '11-M.' The coordinated attacks were carried out by an "al-Qaida inspired Islamist cell," according to the Spanish Judiciary report, but unlike similar incidents elsewhere, those who carried out these attacks were not suicide bombers, and one year after the most destructive terrorist incident in recent Spanish history, only one person had been convicted, a 16-year-old youth, 'El Gitanillo' (Little Gipsy) sentenced to 5 years in a juvenile detention center for stealing and transporting 22lbs of explosives used in the attacks. More than 70 people had been arrested in the course of the police investigation, all but 22 of whom were released on police bail. At least eight members of the cell escaped, and seven of the 'most wanted' perpetrators, including the alleged North African ringleaders, Sarhane ben Abdelmajid Fakhet, and Jamal Ahmidan, and the emir of the cell, Allekema Lamari, who had been released from a Spanish prison in 2002 after serving 5-years of a 14-year prison sentence for membership of an Algerian terrorist organization, later died in an apparent suicide explosion on 3 April 2004, following a shootout with the Spanish National Police Corps (NPC) urban counter-terrorism 'Grupo Especial de Operaciones' in Leganes, a suburb about 5 miles from Madrid city center.

The timeline of 11-M should have been of particular interest to MI5 analysts in London, although there is no indication in the official reports into the London transit bombings, that the British security service took any more than a cursory interest in the Madrid attacks, any more so than the agency took in the 5 December 2003 suicide bombing of a commuter train as it was leaving Yessentuki, in Stavropol Krai, Russia, killing 46 people and injuring 150, or a similar attack at Moscow's Avrozavodskaya metro station, at 08.40am on 6 February 2004, in which 41 people died and at least

120 were seriously hurt. Urban transit systems were particularly vulnerable, and as Madrid had shown, coordinated morning rush-hour attacks could cause a huge number of casualties, major economic consequences and severe psychological damage among those who were present.

According to the Spanish Judiciary's 'Audiencia Nacional' Criminal Chamber 21-month investigation, headed by Judge Juan del Olmo, the four targeted trains, run by the Spanish national rail company, Renfe, were traveling on the same line in the same direction (unlike the London attacks in which three lines were targeted) away from the UNESCO World Heritage site, Alcala de Henares, about 18 miles northwest of Madrid to the city's Atocha railway station, the primary rail terminal serving intercity and regional trains from the south and the high-speed AVE network. Thirteen home-made rucksack bombs had been placed on the trains which left Alcala de Heranes between 7.01am and 7.14am. Ten of the improvised devices exploded within three minutes, two were later defused by the bomb disposal TEDAX squad, and one was found in luggage recovered several hours later. Atocha CCTV security footage shows three explosions within one minute, 7.37/38am, on stationary train number 21431. Two bombs exploded in different carriages while train 21435 was pulling out of El Poze del Tio Raimundo station at 7.38am, another exploded at the same time on train 21713 at Sanata Eugenia station, and four more went off in four different carriages on Caale Tellex train 17305 about 700 yards from Atocha station.

The attacks took place three days before the Spanish general election and were widely regarded as a consequence of Spain's role in the Iraq War and the pro-Washington policies of the incumbent, right-wing Partido Popular (PP) of Prime Minister Jose Maria Aznar, who was subsequently defeated at the polls by the Spanish Socialist Workers Party (PSOE), headed by Jose Luis Zapatero.

Immediately after the attacks PM Anzar had personally contacted the editors of four of the country's leading newspapers, and blamed the Basque separatist group, Euskadi Ta Askatasuna (ETA) for the atrocity. The Spanish Foreign Minister, Ana Palacio, also implicated ETA, according to the BBC, saying there were "very strong clues" and "very strong precedents" to support that view. However, 24 hours before polling stations opened the Spanish Interior Minister, Angel Acebes Paniaqua, admitted that a stolen van found near the route of the trains contained detonators and recordings of Qur'anic verses, "possibly indicating militant Islamist involvement," while a previously unknown group called the Abu Hafs al-Masri Brigades issued a statement through a London-based Arab newspaper, claiming to have carried out the attack on "America's ally in the war against Islam" on behalf of al-Qaida.

The British Labour administration under Blair was America's 'closest' ally in what large parts of the Arab world perceived as "the war against Islam" - a fact that should not have been lost on the JTAC, as well as the vulnerability of the London underground transit system. They should have also taken into account the PSOE victory in Spain, and the new regime's first measure - complete Spanish military withdrawal from Iraq, and from political support for war. If it had worked in Spain why not in the UK? Certainly these developments were not lost on the suicidal jihadists who planned and carried out the attack the following year. Madrid was a warning, and it could not have been louder, but despite all the expertise available, nobody in authority in London appeared to be listening.

The Smell of Burning Plastic

History almost repeated itself, almost to the hour, on 21 July 2005, when four Muslim men attempted to replicate the bloody events of a fortnight earlier with a coordinated series of small explosions, causing panic and fear among commuters using the city's transit system. The IEDs were timed to explode at around 08.00 a.m. on trains at Warren Street tube station, at the intersection of Tottenham Court Road and Euston Street, at Shepherd's Bush on the Circle line and Oval in Kennington, on the Northern line, and a double-decker bus in Hackney. In each case the detonator caps fired, but the homemade bombs failed to explode, leaving only an acrid smell of burning plastic. The Metropolitan Police and the Home Office were reluctant to share information about the failed attacks and the type of explosives used. However, later that evening, the BBC's counter-insurgency expert, Mark Urban, quoted official sources claiming the devices were "put together in a way very similar to those used two weeks ago," so similar, in fact, "that they may have been part of the same batch." The following day CCTV footage identified four men wanted in connection with the attacks, and within a week, as a result of what senior counter-terrorism officers described as the "largest investigation and manhunt the Met ever mounted," all four were in police custody, including an Ethiopian-born, naturalized British citizen, Hamdi Adus Isaac, arrested at an apartment in Rome, after being tracked to Italy by his cell phone signal. According to Nafeez Ahmed's excellent independent analysis of the London bombings, when questioned by British and Italian police Isaac claimed the he and his accomplices "had not sought to kill anyone, not even themselves," the devices were "only supposed to make a bang," to cause terror "rather than mass casualties" and he described the operation as a "demonstrative action in response to the treatment of Muslims in Iraq and the UK."

The backpack bombs were meant to "convey to the public the state of fear in which one lives in countries afflicted by wars, including Iraq," according to his Italian lawyer, Antonietta Sonnessa. An Italian magistrate's report, referred to during the extradition process, described the bombs as a mix of flour, hair lotion, nails, nuts and bolts in plastic containers, attached to a "primitive device featuring a battery, which included a powder to act as a detonator once it had been manually attached to some electric wires." In the European arrest warrant for Isaac, British Home Office forensic scientists failed to competently identify the white powder found on the detonator of an abandoned IED, describing it as "TATP or HMTD." Although it was never shown conclusively that the primary explosive material was either TATP or HMDT (two very distinctive chemicals derived from hydrogen peroxide used in hair products) Nafeez Ahmed described the 'bomb' as a "lackluster sludge" of flour and hair lotion, in a plastic container with miscellaneous pieces of metal which "simply does not constitute a chemical explosive of any kind." The IEDs failed to detonate because they lacked a properly constituted secondary explosive content, either deliberately, which supports Isaac's explanation but which also fails to explain why the devices contained shrapnel if the intention was only to scare and not cause injury. Was it because the fugitive and his associates were incompetent bomb makers? Given the level of fear and apprehension among rush-hour commuters, even setting off a firecracker in the overcrowded London underground would have cause panic and injuries as people scrambled to escape what they would surely have assumed was a repeat of the attacks two weeks earlier.

Operation *Kratos*

Following the WTC and Pentagon attacks, Metropolitan Police Deputy Assistant Commissioner, Barbara Wilding, and a team of counter-terrorist specialist, traveled to Israel, Sri Lanka and Russia to consult with officers who had experienced having to deal with suicide attacks, and drew up a series of guidelines to be implemented in the UK in the event of similar situations. The result was Operation *Kratos*, a set of procedures developed by Wilding, an officer with 30 years experience who had served with the Kent Constabulary and the South Wales Police before transferring to the Met, and her immediate boss at Scotland Yard, Assistant Commissioner Sir David Veness, who had been with the Met since 1966. The *Kratos* 'shoot-to-kill' guidelines were based on two key findings, namely that the explosives used by suicide bombers were sensitive and likely to detonate by conventional firing at the chest of a suspect or by the use of non-lethal weapons, and that the bombers were likely to detonate their devices once they had been identified, therefore covert tactics must be devised and the would-be bomber incapacitated before given an opportunity to trigger the device. Some senior Government ministers and officials at the Home Office, were aware of the *Kratos* guidelines, but details were not published or discussed by MPs before being introduced.

However, in February 2005, the Home Office-funded Association of Chief Police Officers (ACPO) felt it necessary to redefine the parameters of *Kratos,* informing CPOs in charge of the 44 police forces in England and Wales, including Ian Blair over at Met HQ (New Scotland Yard) in Whitehall Place, now stipulating that members of specialist firearms units may open fire "only when absolutely necessary after traditional methods have tried and failed, or must, by the very nature of the circumstances, be unlikely to succeed if tried. To sum up, a police officer should not decide to open fire unless that officer is satisfied that nothing short of opening fire could protect the officer or another person from imminent danger to life or serious injury." Yet even these clearly defined guidelines were violated in the death of a 27-year-old Brazilian electrician, John Charles de Menezes, who was acting like thousands of other commuters when he was shot dead by SO19 police firearms officers on 22 July 2005, while sitting on a train waiting to depart Stockwell tube station in the London borough of Lambeth.

Perhaps it was fear. The fear of failure among Metropolitan Police officers that contributed in some degree to the death of Jean Charles de Menezes. The 18th century English essayist and biographer, Samuel Johnson, wrote that fear is "implanted in us as a preservation against evil" - in this case fear of a suicide bomber on a morning train - "but its duty, like that of other passions, is not to overbear reason but to assist it." Putting seven hollow-point bullets into the skull of an innocent man suggests fear extinguished reason, leaving not a consideration of innocence or shadow of doubt in the minds of two SO19 officers that the victim was a man of evil intent. In fact Jean Charles de Menezes was on his way to fix a broken fire alarm in Kilburn when he was gunned down in the carriage of a Northern Line train.

The controversy surrounding this particular death, only one among many, direct and indirect, in the 'war on terror' was the manner of Menezes's execution and the initial attempts made by Home Office officials to lie, and to blame the victim for his fate, suggesting that he was an illegal immigrant who should not have been in the UK in the first place. This was denied by his family and by Foreign Secretary, Jack Straw, who later admitted the slain electrician was living legally in the UK, having entered the country via the Republic of Ireland sometime after 23 April 2005, which allowed him to remain for three months under the terms of the 'Common Travel Area' agreement between the two countries to accommodate cross-border traffic between the Republic and the North of Ireland.

Jean Charles de Menezes was caught up in the nationwide hunt for the suspected Islamic jihadists who had attempted to bomb the London transit system the previous day. He was incorrectly identified as one of the suspects, Hamdi Isaac, by an undercover UK Special Forces (UKSF) Special Reconnaissance Regiment (SRR) soldier, seconded to the Met, as he left an apartment block on Scotia Road, Tulse Hill, south London, at 09.30am, an address which was under surveillance after being found in one of the unexploded rucksack bombs. Instead of making an arrest, the 'suspect' was followed by armed SRR officers, allowed to board a bus to Brixton tube station, which was actually closed that morning because of a security alert, make a cell phone call, then take another bus to Stockwell station, about two miles away.

The surveillance operation was under the command of Met Police Commander, Cressida Dick, who had allowed Menezes to travel across London for thirty minutes. She now ordered that he should be "detained as soon as possible" and not allowed board a train. Special Forces Command (SFC) SO19 officers took charge, followed Menezes into the station where he bought a newspaper, paid his fare using an electronic ticketing Oyster card, descended the escalator and crossed the platform to board the stationary train, sitting opposite the door. One of three surveillance officers who had followed him immediately blocked the door while two others pinned him to his seat and fired eleven rounds times within 30 seconds, hitting Menezes seven times in the head and once in the shoulder, using jacketed hollow-point (JHP) rounds, designed to expand and disintegrate when the intended target is hit in order to prevent further penetration and avoid collateral damage.

The SO19 firepower left Jean Charles de Menezes unrecognizable on the carriage floor. Nafeez Ahmed raises the point that even if the victim had been an armed suicide bomber, ready to detonate a device he was carrying, the manner of his death would not have prevented an explosion, and as such contravened the *Kratos* guidelines, which therefore "neither absolves or explains" the Brazilian's death. He quotes John Gardiner, Professor of Jurisprudence at Oxford University, and Visiting Professor at Yale Law School, who expressed alarm at the "Mossad style shooting of an innocent suspect," pointing out that whatever the self-adopted guidelines used by the police to arrest and search "there is no special police license to injure or kill." The police "need to rely on the same law as the rest of us" and the necessity and proportional use of force should be judged on the facts as they reasonably believed them to be. Prof. Gardiner added "it is no defense in law that the killing was authorized by a superior officer. A superior officer who orders an unauthorized killing is an accomplice."

Unfortunately, in the UK the legal culpability of the police in shoot-to-kill operations is often not worth the paper it's written on. In the North of Ireland during the Troubles three Royal Ulster Constabulary (RUC) officers involved in the murders of three unarmed and cooperative IRA members at a vehicle check point in the early 1980s were commended by Chief Justice Maurice Gibson for their "courage and determination in bringing the deceased men to justice, in this case the final court of justice." In the case of Jean Charles de Menezes, the Metropolitan Police immediately claimed his death was linked to the hunt for the fugitive bombers, the *Kratos* shoot-to-kill guidelines were revealed to the general public and MPs for the first time, and the Home Office defended the use of hollow-point 'dum-dum' bullets, saying "Chief officers can use whatever ammunition they consider appropriate for the operational circumstances."

'Taught History' Sources

It is not without good reason that the Troubles in Ireland - because they spanned three decades from the pre-fax era of the mid/late 1960s to the widespread use of the World Wide Web - are often referred to as a counter-insurgency laboratory where the British State refined the techniques and technology of political control. A standard technique, used since the 'glory days' of Empire, is the criminalization of the victims of state violence. The unarmed civilians who died on Bloody Sunday in Derry City, 1972, were initially described by Conservative and Unionist politicians and senior British Army officers as "nail and petrol bombers." This was proved to be completely untrue, but remained part of the official historical account until the 1972 Tribunal report into the killings by Lord Chief Justice Widgery was totally discredited when the Saville Inquiry report was published in mid-June 2010. Heather Brooke writes that Jean Charles de Menezes was variously described by senior police officers as "running away from the police, jumping a tube barrier, wearing unusually bulky clothes in hot weather, and ignoring shouted warnings from the police. All these proved completely untrue."

'Taught history' sources relating to Britain's colonial past and post-colonial security agenda are the official tribunals, judicial inquiries, and Parliamentary select committee hearings which dominate the public debate, often providing so much circumstantial data not necessarily pertaining to an incident that most daily print and broadcast media reports simply carry wire service copy of proceedings. In the UK, when police are involved in shooting incidents, or in controversial deaths of civilians, the Independent Police Complaints Commission (IPPC) investigates. In some cases the various inquiries can take precedence over regular procedures, such as the Hutton Inquiry which replaced a coroner's inquest into the controversial death of Ministry of Defense (MoD) WMD specialist, Dr David Kelly, in July 2003.

Media reports following the 7/7 bombings tried to put the bombings into some sort of historical context. Some papers described the attacks as the single deadliest act of terrorism in the UK since the December 1998 destruction of Pan Am Flight 103 over the Scottish town of Lockerbie in which 270 people died. The four suicide bombers who had carried out the first such attack in Britain, were identified from CCTV footage at Luton railway station, about 30 miles north of London, at 7.21am, and after arriving at Kings Cross-St Pancras tube station. This led to raids on six properties in Leeds by West Yorkshire Police, where "significant amounts of bomb-making materials" were found according to a WYP statement. Explosives were also found in a car in which the bombers had traveled south from Leeds, owned by Shehzad Tanweer and left parked at Luton railway station. On the morning of 7 July Abu Hamza was due to stand trial at the Old Bailey, and details of the court's schedule had been published several months earlier. This prompted speculation that the attacks were timed to coincide with the opening of the high-profile trial, which was immediately postponed for six months. Terrorist trials are a "traditional watch date" for security services, according to Nafeez Ahmed, who points out that the 9/11 attacks were on the same date as the conviction of Ramzi Yousef, five years earlier, for his part in the 1993 World Trade Center bombing. He also refers to Omar Bakri's threat of jihadist terror in London, referring to Abu Hanza's detention and forthcoming trial under new anti-terror legislation in a khutbah, in January 2005, in which he also denounced Britain as a "land of war." The speech, which Ahmed describes as the "most pristine example of advanced warning of an attack that intelligence services could ever hope for" was monitored by MI5, and reported in the *Times* and as such the opening day of Abu Hamza's trial "should have been a watch date."

This was the second time Omar Bakri had warned of a major terrorist incident in the UK. On 18 April 2004, in an interview with the Portuguese daily newspaper, *Publico*, he referred to a "well-organized group in London calling itself al-Qaida-Europe [who are] on the verge of launching a major operation." Following the Madrid attacks, Bakri repeated his warning in the Lisbon-based newspaper, talking about the "inevitability" of a large attack in the British capital, already being prepared by an independent group who were part of the al-Qaida franchise, describing them as "freelancers who are willing to launch operations similar to those by al-Qaida."

This is part of the public record, and it's MI5's job to monitor such public utterances and act accordingly. But there's no evidence that Bakri was questioned specifically about what he knew of "planned operations" prior to 7 July. The FBI appeared to take things a bit more seriously, with the New York-based *Newsweek* reporting online on 17 November 2004 that "fears of terror attacks have prompted FBI agents based in the US embassy in London to avoid traveling on London's popular underground railway (or tube) system" because Washington had 'evidence' of a possible attack. Given the 'special relationship' between the UK and the US, particularly in intelligence matters and the jihadist threat to the West, we must assume that the FBI shared its information with MI5 and New Scotland Yard, but there is no reference to FBI warnings in subsequent 7/7 reports into how this was handled, and who knew what and when. And if not, why not?

Several foreign intelligence agencies did warn their British counterparts that London was a likely target as Britain became more embroiled in the Iraq War. The Saudi General Intelligence Presidency (GIP) headed by Prince Abdul-Majeed bin Abdulaziz, a prominent member of the ruling House of Saud, had twice warned MI6 of an imminent strike on the London transit system to be carried out by four members still at large following the Operation *Crevice* raids on 30 April 2004. These were carried out after GCHQ had intercepted communications from an al-Qaida cell in Pakistan to militants in the UK who had fairly tenuous links to Omar Bakri's organization, al-Muhaliroun. An estimated 1,300lbs of ammonium nitrate fertilizer and chemicals were confiscated in raids on private property and a commercial storage facility in Hanwell, west London, and six men taken into custody would later be found guilty of conspiring to cause explosions likely to endanger life.

There was a second warning from the authorities in Riyadh in May 2005, this time referring to the attacks in Madrid and the 16 May 2003 Casablanca bombings, where 45 people died, including twelve Salafia Jihadia suicide bombers, in attacks on Western and Jewish targets. Coinciding with the second Saudi alert the CIA added its intelligence take, according to author, Naseef Ahmed, claiming a network controlled by al-Qaida's Abu Faraj al-Libbi, who had been linked to *Crevice,* was planning an attack on London's transit system, involving the "Finsbury division." This information came from a notebook al-Libbi tried to destroy after he was ambushed and captured by Pakistan's Inter Service Intelligence (ISI) on 2 May 2005 in Mardam, while riding pillion on a motorbike. The Fort Meade, Maryland-based National Security Agency (NSA) using the global ECHELON eavesdropping system, had intercepted a cell phone call al-Libbi made setting up a meeting that day in the 'city of hospitality' about 120 miles northwest of Islamabad.

Three days after the London attacks, Meir Dagan, the director of the Israeli intelligence agency, Mossad, in an interview published in the Berlin-based, broadsheet *Bild am Sonntag,* claimed Mossad's station in London, located in the country's embassy at 2 Palace Green in Kensington, had been alerted to an attack at 8.43am. on 7 July, seven minutes before the first bomb detonated on the Circle Line The warning of the imminent attack was the result of an investigation into an earlier bombing in Tel Aviv, according to the spy chief. This, presumably, was a reference to the suicide bombing of Mike's Place and the part played in that attack by two British Muslim men, and was Dagan's way of pointing out to the Brits that there are no 'clean skins' in the war on terror. Every Muslim male, as far as the Israelis are concerned, is a potential bomber and should be treated as such.

MI6 officers stationed under diplomatic cover at embassies abroad are the initial recipients of the intelligence obtained by their colleagues in the host countries, yet there is no mention of these 'concerns' in the top-secret MI6 assessment leaked while the final draft of the cross-party Intelligence and Security Committee (ISC) was being prepared for presentation to Prime Minister Blair in March 2006, and only one mention in the ISC's *Report into the London Terrorist Attacks on 7 July 2005*, published two months later. The MI6 assessment was among several classified documents leaked to the *Sunday Times* by dissident MI5 officers in order to highlight the lack of frontline resources, and to underline the need for a public inquiry into the behavior of ministers whom the agents believe withheld information from the public about what was known about the bombers prior to 7/7 and 21/7. This was quite an unusual development, given the fact that MI5 is traditionally opposed to any form of public scrutiny - one needs only to look at the disruptive behavior of the agency during the half-hearted attempts to get to the bottom of shoot-to-kill operations in the North of Ireland to understand the 'bullish' attitude of MI5 to what it considers 'outside interference' into how it carries out its mandate. The MI6 document was prepared by the director, John Scarlett, and submitted to the ISC's inquiry into the 'lessons learnt' from the 2005 attacks. He refers to himself, as the head of Her Majesty's Secret Intelligence Service, in the traditional, anonymous fashion as 'C' (a peculiarity dating back to a period, not too long ago, when the HMG refused even to admit the existence of MI6) and states: "On the events of July itself, and the question of whether intelligence was missed, C noted that SIS had previously been involved in an earlier investigation of one of the 21 July [suspects] in Pakistan. This had been at the Security Service's behest, and should be discussed with MI5."

Mr. Scarlett, former MI6 chief of station in Moscow and chairman of the Joint Intelligence Committee (JIC) who took responsibility for the 'sexed up' WMD dossier used by PM Blair to justify the invasion of Iraq, admits in his assessment that MI6 was "slow to react" to the potential threat:

> Summing up the position before July 2005, C noted that SIS were aware of the size of the target but equally conscious of what we did not know; we were thinly spread in North and East Africa; we were looking at new ways of increasing our reach; and we had sought funding to grow as fast as we thought feasible. Turning to the lessons learnt, C noted that SIS had understood the nature of the threat and that there was a great deal we did not know. SIS had developed strategies to meet this threat. The attacks had shown that our strategies were correct, but needed to be implemented more extensively and more quickly.

The rank stupidity of some of the statements made in this key paragraph should be of concern to those who assume that those who promote public fear are, on the other hand, capable of defending the public from the consequences. The document is written in narcissistic, repetitive, ambiguous jargon, and Scarlett seems to suggest that a budget increase wasn't immediately available, or that the Treasury disagreed with MI6's assessment of the costs of extending its reach as fast as the agency "thought feasible." Because of their colonial past Spain and France are capable of reaching into North and East Africa, and were willing to share their intelligence product with MI6. The London bombers were from Leeds and Aylesbury, they were coached in Pakistan, a member of the Commonwealth, and influenced by preachers in Finsbury and Regent Park mosques. There was no African connection to these attacks, but as far as C was concerned the only lesson to be drawn from the bloody events of 7 July was the lack of funding to extend MI6's global reach, and by implication that was the fault of the politicians. All this is explained in the past tense, as is the assertion that the agency knew the nature of the threat but there was a great deal MI6 did not know

As for MI5, it was the same old story - blame some other organization for their failures, in this case the Pakistani ISI. The Thames House submission to the ISC, *The July Bombings and the Agencies Response,* states that the ISI was responsible for the failure of the British agencies to apprehend at least one of twenty potential British jihadists "who had been subject of a low-level, short-term investigation concerning a visit he made to Pakistan after he was interviewed on departure from the UK. However, the Pakistani authorities assessed he was doing nothing of significance in a terrorist context" and MI5 stopped monitoring his movements when he returned to Britain.

In its report the nine-member ISC - which included two former Secretaries of State for Northern Ireland, Paul Murphy (chairman) and ex-British Army officer, and Tory MP, Michael Mates, as well as the former MI6 chief of station in Helsinki, Margaret Ramsay - refers to media speculation about prior warnings and says the ISC were "assured by the Agencies that there were no prior warning of the attacks that took place from any source, including from foreign intelligence services. We have looked in detail into claims that the Saudi Arabian authorities warned the British Agencies about the attacks. We found that some information was passed to the Agencies about possible terrorist planning for an attack in the UK. It was examined by the Agencies who concluded that the plan was not credible. That information has been given to us: it is materially different to what actually occurred on 7 July and clearly not relevant to these attacks."

However, the ISC found that MI5 failed to fully investigate Mohammed Sidique Khan, the man described as the "ringleader of the cell" who had come to the attention of the agency on five occasions between 2003 and 2005. He had traveled to Afghanistan in the late 1990s, and to Pakistan in 2003 and 2003, the second occasion with Shehzad Tanweer, who carried out the Aldergate station bombing. Khan and Tanweer were also identified "on the peripheries" of other surveillance operations in the UK. At that time, according to the ISC report, "their identities were unknown to the Security Service and there was no appreciation of their subsequent significance." MI5 officers were diverted to other anti-terrorist operations, and as a result "the chances of identifying attack planning" and possibly of preventing the 7 July attacks might have been greater "had different investigative decisions been taken by MI5 in 2003-05."

There was a "pattern of disagreements" and "failures of communication" between MI5 and Scotland Yard's anti-terrorist branch. In March 2005, four months before the attacks, senior police officers had concluded that "home grown terrorists" were likely to mount an attack. One SO13 officer actually predicted that London Underground would be targeted by bombers using explosives in rucksacks, similar to the 11-M attacks. However, the Madrid bombings were not suicide attacks, and a JIC assessment, also in March 2005, had concluded that suicide attacks "would not become the norm in Europe." MI5 went along with this analysis and director-general, Dame Manningham-Buller, told the committee that she had been "surprised" that the first major attack in the UK for years had been carried out by suicide bombers, and she described the JIC's assessment as a "reasonable judgment." Given the fact that Britain had already produced several 'home grown' Islamic jihadists prepared to carry out suicide attacks - the shoe-bomber Richard Reid, and the two men who attacked Mike's Place in Tel Aviv - the ISC was left with no choice but to express concern that MI5 had judged a suicide attack in the UK as "unlikely."

There was also criticism of the threat assessment level and alert status system, with the report stating that while it was "not unreasonable" to have reduced the threat level from "severe general to substantial" before the bombings, given that there was "no specific intelligence of [the] 7 July plot, nor of any other group with a current credible plot," there was concern it made little difference to the "preparedness and alertness" of MI5 and Scotland Yard, and raised questions about the "usefulness of a system in which changes can be made to threat levels with little or no practical effect." In order to avoid "inappropriate reassurances" in the absence of intelligence of a current plot, the terror alert system should be changed in order to "better inform the authorities and the public about the level of threat faced." One reason why there was a lack of "specific intelligence" was the failure of MI6 and MI5 to fully co-operate with the ISI when Khan and Tanweer had "sought meetings with al-Qaida figures" in Pakistan. A photograph of Khan, taken by MI5 watchers during a surveillance operation in the UK, had been circulated to foreign intelligence agencies and "foreign detaining authorities" but he had not been identified. This may explain why Manningham-Buller told the ISC that Khan was "not listed as a terrorist suspect."

According to a Home Office narrative, also published on 11 May, Khan, Tanweer, and Jermaine Lindsay, had traveled from Luton Station to King's Cross, London, where they met the youngest bomber, Hasib Hussain, who had not accompanied the other three when they visited London, on 28 June, to reconnoiter the routes they would take the following month, which suggested that he may have been a last minute recruit. The four were seen at King's Cross at 8.30am in a "happy, even euphoric" mood before splitting up. Khan, Tanweer and Lindsay headed for the three different targeted trains, while Hussain went to buy a 9v battery in a Boots store on the concourse of King's Cross, probably because the detonator of his IED had failed. He then went to a McDonalds fast-food restaurant, and almost an hour his companions had died in the blasts on the underground trains, he detonated his bomb on the top deck of the No.30 bus in Travistock Square. The four men were motivated by a "mixture of anger at the perceived injustices by the West against Muslims and a desire for martyrdom." The rucksack bombs were made from readily available materials, and the estimated cost of preparing and executing the attacks was less than $5,000.

Both the ISC and the Home Office narrative dismissed the 'fifth bomber' theory, who had allegedly left the UK shortly before the attacks, despite MI5's failure to account for the keys of the blue Nissan Micra later found at Luton Station car-park. Although these could have been thrown from the train en route to London and their loss is probably an insignificant detail, the Home Office report states that despite bomb-making instructions being available on Islamic websites, the volatile nature of the peroxide-based mixture made it likely that the group "would have had advice from someone with previous experience, given the careful handling required to ensure safety during the bomb-making process." The absence of the fifth bomber may explain why the 21/7 'wannabees' could only manage a mixture of unexplosive sludge when they attempted to repeat the slaughter, but neither the ISC or the Home Office narrative bothered to explore this possibility.

Two days after the ISC report and the Home Office narrative were published the recently appointed Labour Home Secretary, John Reid, told MPs that it had been difficult to defend the UK against acts of terrorism carried out by "ordinary British citizens with little known history of extremist views, far less violent intentions." He described three of the bombers as "apparently well-integrated" and claimed that their radicalization "to the extent that we know how and where it happened" was conducted "away from places with any obvious association with extremism."

As a former Defense Secretary, Dr Reid must have been aware of the role Pakistan had played as a destination for disaffected western Muslim males. He was probably not aware, however, when ruling out a parliamentary inquiry into the attacks, that MI5 had deliberately withheld evidence from the ISC to cover up intelligence failings prior to the bombings, and had failed to disclose details of covertly-recorded audio tapes of Sidique Khan talking about waging jihad in the UK, and leaving the country to avoid a police manhunt. He was also taped taking part in late night discussions about bomb-making with another jihadist cell also planning another attack, probably in London, which would have the most impact. A member of the ISC confirmed to the *Guardian* and *Sunday Times* that committee members, despite top secret security clearance, had not seen transcripts of MI5's recordings, but had accepted assurances from senior MI5 officers who had claimed that Khan was a peripheral figure and there was no reason to regard him as a serious threat. Conservative MPs tried, without much success, to raise the matter in the House of Commons, and both David Davis, who deals with internal affairs, and his colleague Patrick Mercer, who handles homeland security issues, narrowly avoided describing the ISC report as a "whitewash" which, in the time-worn tradition of British reports into the activities of MI6 and MI5, would have been the norm rather than the exception.

The ISC report is a bland document with no attempt to place the attacks in the context of the 'wider' picture, namely the war in Afghanistan and the illegal invasion of Iraq, or to the almost daily criminalization of large sections of the Muslim community in the country by frequent anonymous allegations in right-wing publications, and by politicians using public fear to rant against all they regarded as a "threat to the British way of life." One consequence of this reckless behavior was a raid on two homes in Forest Gate, east London, on 2 June 2006, by armed SO19 officers acting on what Metropolitan Police Assistant Commissioner, Andrew Hayman, described as "special intelligence" that Muslim terrorist were in possession of a chemical bomb. There were eleven people, two law-abiding Muslim families with children, living in the terrace houses on Landsdown Road, when more than 250 police officers, including specialized WMD teams in protective clothing, backed up by helicopters policing a 2,500ft 'no-fly' zone over the area, descended on the properties. In the resulting melee one man, Abdul Kahar, a postal worker, was shot and later arrested while receiving treatment at Royal London Hospital. His brother was also taken into custody and held at Paddington Green police station "on suspicion of the commission, preparation and instigation" of acts of terrorism. Nearby roads were closed for several days. The two houses were shrouded in plastic suspended from scaffolding while forensic officers in white boiler suits and masks searched the buildings. Footage of the work in progress was repeatedly shown on national and international news channels, often accompanied by warnings of the Muslim 'threat' by blatantly biased and often unqualified 'security experts.' After several days the operation ended. No chemicals or bomb-making equipment were found. The postman and his brother were released without charge on 9 June. The Metropolitan Police apologized, and agreed to pay almost $200,000 for repairs to the damage caused to the houses. In total, Operation *Volga*, based on a tip-off from an MI5 informant, had involved a four-weeks, round-the-clock HUMINT and SIGINT surveillance, and had cost $5 million. Solicitor Gareth Peirce, who was acting for the family of Jean Charles de Menezes, and the Kahar brothers, described the botched operation and the behavior of the police as being "as lawless as the Wild West."

Within days of the men's release Scotland Yard announced that Abdul Kahar was to be charged with downloading child pornography after indecent images were found on an external computer hard drive and a mobile phone confiscated during the raid. This development undermined public criticism of the raid, a suspected bomber was now a suspected sexual deviant, and the allegations remained in the public domain for almost 5 months until the Crown Prosecution Service (CPS) finally admitted that the embedded images could have been downloaded inadvertently on the back of other computer files, that all had been deleted, and in order to transfer the images to his Nokia cell phone the suspect would have had to have specialist knowledge and there was "no evidence that Mr. Kahar had possession of, or access to, equipment of the technical knowledge to do so." The IPCC held a quick and fairly cursory inquiry into the raid and concluded, on 3 August - the day the police announced Mr. Kahar was in custody on child porn charges - that the gunshot wound had been the result of an "accidental discharge." Six months later a second IPCC report upheld complaints about the treatment of the Forest Gate detainees while in police custody at Paddington Green, including the withholding of medication for several hours from Mr. Kahar. The report, however, ignored an important factor in the whole affair—how the Metropolitan Police had obtained and handled the bogus intelligence which led to the raid, leaving open the possibility that the same response to anonymous tip-offs would happen again, in the name of national security. Just another day in the 'war' on terror.

Truth Withheld is Truth Denied

One year after the 7/7 bombings the British Government continued to reject calls for an independent public inquiry, from relatives of the victims and opposition MPs in the Commons, and despite fresh claims from credible sources suggesting that MI5, Scotland Yard counter-terrorist analysts, and homeland security 'experts' had missed, or simply ignored, vital information about the suicide cell that "may have influenced" the course of events prior to carnage, and the consequences, including the death of Jean Charles de Menezes.

In an interview with the *Guardian*, on 24 June 2006, Michael Gilbertson, an IT consultant who had worked in the Islamic Iqra bookshop and at Hamara Youth Access Point (HYAP) in Beeston, West Yorkshire, claimed he had contacted local police at Holbeck station in October 2003 about anti-western propaganda videos, secure websites and encrypted emails he had produced for radical Muslim HYAP members, and was told to send copies of the material to West Yorkshire Police HQ in Wakefield. The package contained DVDs he had compiled for circulation by the bookshop, a list of names linked to jihadist websites, including Sidique Khan and Shehzad Tanweer, and a covering letter providing a contact number where he could be reached by anti-terrorist officers. The WYP never called back, and Mr. Gilbertson was only questioned for the first time by two Metropolitan Police Special Branch officers when he contacted Scotland Yard after the 7/7 attacks. West Yorkshire constabulary denied having withheld records showing that a tip-off had been received from Gilbertson, or whether it had been acted upon even if it had been received, and also refused to respond to a report that a tracking device had been found in Khan's Honda Civic after it was removed from his home in Dewsbury. The device had been hidden in the car by the Special Branch who were taking part in a surveillance operation aimed at suspected Muslim jihadists in West Yorkshire. This was part of the information withheld from the ISC prior to its May publication, and was not included in the Home Office narrative.

The Iraq War dominated the political landscape for several years, with British casualties increasing as the so-called "battle for hearts and minds" became just another tired cliché, and post-7/7 fears of repetitive jihadist terror increasing. In August 2006, less than a month after Stephen O'Doherty, a senior lawyer with the CPS Special Criminal Division (SCD) announced that despite "errors in planning and communication," the two SO19 officer had shot Mr. de Menezes because they "genuinely believed" he had been identified to them as a suicide bomber about to blow up the train, and that there was "insufficient evident to provide a realistic prospect of prosecution" against any individual police officer involved in Operation *Kratos* that day. Scotland Yard confirmed that Cmdr. Cressida Dick, the "fast-track" Oxford graduate, who had been in charge of the shoot-to-kill operation, had applied for promotion to the post of Deputy Assistant Commissioner of the Metropolitan Police. According to senior colleagues, Cmdr. Dick, who had previously headed the Thames Valley Police *black-on-black* drug-related, gun-crime investigations, had impressed members of the Metropolitan Police

Authority (MPA), the body responsible for decisions regarding promotion within the force, simply by playing the political game, keeping her head down and not getting involved in the public controversy surrounding the Stockwell station incident. The IIPC which produced a two-part Stockwell report, also found that the shooters had been cleared, although Cmdr. Dick had told the IPCC she had "not used a specific code word" which authorized the use of lethal force, and had wanted Mr. de Menezes arrested, not shot dead.

While the IIPC's *Stockwell 1* report listed some offences the commission considered had been carried out by police officers, the commission also noted that its "lower threshold" judgment was less than what a criminal prosecution required, while *Stockwell 2* which focused on the conduct of Met Police Commissioner Blair and Deputy Hayman, found that both senior officers had "made or concurred with inaccurate public statements" concerning the circumstances of the Brazilian electrician's death, including the suggestions that he had been "wearing clothing and behaving in a manner that aroused suspicion." The end result was the unanswered question - who had ordered de Menezes's death, if it wasn't the officer in charge of the operation?

A more accurate assessment of what took place that day was implied in the "open verdict" returned by an inquest jury on 12 December 2008, during which 70 witnesses, including 40 police officers were questioned by former High Court judge, and assistant deputy coroner for Inner South London, Sir Michael Wrights. A verdict of "unlawful killing" was ruled out, however, the open verdict option meant that the jury believed the death was suspicious, that the SO19 officers, when they opened fire, did not honestly believe the unfortunate Mr. de Menezes represented "an imminent mortal danger" to themselves and other passengers, and that they had used more force than was necessary. In reaching their verdict the jury basically found that the officers had lied. They had not identified themselves as armed police, de Menezes had stood up when he entered the carriage and not remained seated as the police claimed, and he had not moved towards an officer, identified as 'C12' before being shot.

The public controversy surrounding the London bombings, Forest Gate and the de Menezes killing took its toll among the senior echelons of Scotland Yard, with a series of resignations, none more farcical than that of Assistant Commissioner Bob Quick, who was photographed arriving at No. 10 Downing Street with a clearly visible Operation *Pathway* briefing paper market *SECRET* with details of a "joined-up intelligence-led investigation" involving MI5, Scotland Yard's CTC, and the Merseyside and Lancashire North-West Counter-Terrorism Unit (NWCTU), forcing the police to hurriedly carry out a series of daytime raids, on 8 April 2009, which were filmed by the public on cell phones and broadcast nationally. Within hours the 30-year police career of Mr. Quick was over, leaving only two of the six permanent positions at the top of the force in the frontline of the war on terror in the UK filled.

Operation *Pathway* turned into another major political embarrassment. Shortly after the arrests of eleven Pakistani nationals, Prime Minister Gordon Brown claimed on national television that the police were dealing with a "very big terrorist plot" and accused the Pakistan Government of not doing enough to tackle international terrorism. The Islamabad regime responded by pointing out that the issuing of visas to foreign nationals to enter the UK was the "sole responsibility of British diplomats serving overseas, not officials of the host nations." Things got worse when no evidence was found to warrant terrorism charges in the UK, and those arrested were deported after the FCO made a point of announcing that the HMG had received assurances they would not be tortured by the ISI or other elements of the Pakistani security forces. Under normal circumstances suspects are bundled into planes without publicity, not quite the fine art of rendition as carried out by the CIA, but close enough.

Dangerous Professionals

Survivors of the 7/7 attacks, and the relatives of those who died suddenly and slowly that day while minding their own business, have welcomed the support of the retired head of special operations at Scotland Yard, Andy Hayden, for a public inquiry into how Sidique Khan and the Leeds-based Islamist cell was allowed to plan and carry out the attacks on London's transit system despite being having been photographed, bugged and tailed from London to Yorkshire by MI5 officers following a meeting with suspects in another terror-related undercover operation.

In a second report, published in June 2009, the ISC had stated that MI5's assessment that Khan was not a "priority target" was "understandable and reasonable." Independent intelligence analysts criticized the ISC, pointing out that the committee heard evidence in secret, and hadn't explained how MI5 failed to identify Khan as a suspect known as 'Ibrahim' whose identity and potential threat had led MI5 to mount its covert HUMINT operation in the first place. The ISC report also returned to the question of warnings from foreign agencies, and dismissed the majority in a couple of heavily-redacted paragraphs, stating that the UK received hundreds of reports daily based on intelligence about threats or attacks, some of which are directly relevant to domestic situations or British interests abroad, but these warnings are "generally not specific and, in the absence of sufficient detail, there is often little our intelligence Agencies can do to follow up on them. "

On the specific question of the (redacted) Saudi warning, the ISC acknowledges some minor similarities between this intelligence and the events of 7/7 (redacted) "but nevertheless it differs substantially from what actually took place." Hayden's call for a inquiry coincided with the pre-publication serialization of his book, *The Terrorist Hunters*, in the *Times*, co-authored with the BBC journalist, Margaret Gilmore, in which he writes that despite two ISC reports "there has been no overview, no pulling together of each strand of review, no one can be sure if key issues have been missed." He describes the 7/7 attacks as a "bolt from nowhere" and states that when he was called to a top-secret Cabinet Office Briefing Room A (COBRA) civil contingencies committee meeting in a fortified, windowless room, fitted with video and audio links in Whitehall within an hour of the bombings, he had to admit he had no idea what was happening in the capital. He describes COBRA, first established by the Thatcher Government in 1980 to manage the Iranian Embassy siege, to enable the prime minister, senior cabinet members, the heads of MI5, MI6, Scotland Yard, the director of the SAS and key municipal officials to share information, as a "nonsensical system that drags people away from a serious job at hand to attend a crisis meeting," making it difficult to immediately respond to an emergency because it "blurs the lines between what's operational and should be left to the police and experts, and what's political." He claimed that political considerations tend to dominate the decision-making process "when we should have been focused on the operational response to the crisis." He accused some individuals of making decisions for their own good, rather than the good of the nation, including the Labour Transport Secretary, Alastair Darling, who was "on my case all the time" telling him that the underground system needed to be reopened, to which Hayden responded by asking "if he wanted to get traffic moving, or if he wanted crime scenes secure in order to obtain evidence to prosecute the terrorists."

A more grounded anti-terrorist strategy assessment was published by the London-based Royal United Services Institute (RUSI), the world's oldest security and defense think-tank, founded by the Duke of Wellington in 1831 to study naval and military science. Written by RUSI director, Professor Michael Clarke, and research analyst, Valentina Soria, the research paper *Terrorism in the UK: Confirming its Modus Operandi* focuses on the "significant terrorist plots" since 2001, analyses the "resolutely amateur tradecraft" of UK jihadists, and concludes that while the al-Qaida core remains an 'inspiration' for British jihadists, it was having "less direct involvement in terrorist planning" because of the wave of arrests across Europe following the Madrid and London attacks, and increased NATO operations in Afghanistan and the Pakistan border areas where al-Qaida had suffered considerable losses of key personnel and "may now be struggling to be relevant in the jihadi movement." Despite what the jihadists would regard as the 'success' of the London bombings, over the past eight-years most of the British plotters had left "a trail of forensic evidence behind" that has led some police professionals to predict that this period will seem like "the golden age of counter-terrorism, when we were both successful and lucky."

However, Prof. Clarke also warns that the success of MI5 and Special Branch operations, and the conviction rate - more than 90 percent since the London carnage - had turned the prisons into "universities of terror." Criminal trials had highlighted the shortcomings of UK-based jihadist cells, and many of those who failed to make viable explosive devices had left themselves exposed to MI5 infiltration and SIGINT operations. Intercept evidence had shown that UK jihadists "talk like terrorists operating in professional cell structures but do not normally act that way." Among the UK cells "face to face communication" was very prevalent because they were "chiefly self-help groups and act both as recruiters as well as planners." According to Clarke and Soria, for cells consisting of radicalized amateurs, "constant social reinforcement is necessary" which helps explain their "predilection for outward-bound training, even paint-balling sessions, which draws attention to their connections with each other and usually appears risible when used as prosecution evidence against them." The paper warns that while the tradecraft of UK jihadists is extremely variable "for the movement as a whole this is not a problem" because amateurs are as dangerous as professionals "if they are lucky and if there are enough amateurs plotting, some of them will be lucky [while] those who are not keep the security services stretched and public anxieties high." Referring to the difficulties of making viable IEDs which may have prevented an "unknown number of deaths and injuries" in the UK, the report states that while it is "theoretically possible" to learn to make a bomb from the Internet, it is "generally regarded as not feasible unless there is some tangible training and/or knowledge of chemical handling among bomb-makers."

The Liquid Bomb Plot

All the factors which contributed to the portmanteau 'Londonistan' and made US agencies fearful of the British jihadist 'amateurs' were present in the "most grave and terrorist conspiracy ever proven within this jurisdiction" according to Mr. Justice Henriques, presiding at Woolwich Crown Court, South London, on 14 September 2009, when he sentenced three British-born Muslims, Abdullah Ahmed Ali, Assad Sarwar and Tabvir Hussain, to a total of 108 years (life sentences with a minimum of 40, 36 and 32 years respectively to be served) for their part in a plot to detonate home-made liquid bombs on board seven trans-Atlantic flights bound for North American cities. The plot had reached "an advanced state in its development" and had only been prevented by the largest-ever counter-terrorism investigation carried out in the UK. Emails at the center of the retrial, which had been unavailable to the CPS in 2006, were now a "vital source of information" which established beyond question that the "funding, control, progress and scope of the conspiracy" was in Pakistan.

The MI5 investigation into the plot, codenamed Operation *Overt*, began in July 2006, less than a month after Abdullah Ali returned to the UK from one of several trips to Pakistan during the previous two years. Born in 1971, Ali was a City of London University engineering graduate radicalized by the anti-western rhetoric of Omar Bakri, who was based at Queen's Road mosque in Walthamstow, and also by an Islamist spiritual reformist organization, Tablighi Jamaat, founded in India in 1926, which despite its pacifist credentials has been flagged in several anti-terror investigations as an "unwitting recruiting agent for various Islamist militant groups." Ali worked for two London retail outlets and for the Hockney-based charity, the Islamic Medical Association (IMA). According to the CPS this was a cover which allowed him to travel to Afghanistan where he drove an ambulance in sprawling refugee camps. When MI5, with the co-operation of ISI, began to collate information on Ali's previous trips to the region in 2005 and 2006, accompanied by Assad Sarwar, they found he had been in contact with Rashid Raul, a Birmingham-born jihadist described as an al-Qaida 'fixer' who had fled to Pakistan in 2002 after West Midlands Police (WMP) had issued a warrant for his arrest in connection with the murder of his uncle.

Ali and Sarwar had attended "bomb-making master classes" on how to assemble hydrogen peroxide IEDs, conducted by Egyptian-born Abu Ubaida al-Masri, and the Metropolitan Police believed both men were in Pakistan on 7/7, and when an attempt was made to repeat the attacks a fortnight later. Despite a fairly comprehensive knowledge of counter-surveillance techniques - including the use of multiple SIM cards, using public phone-boxes to call Pakistan, and holding meetings in open spaces, such as Lloyd Park in Croydon, south London - intercepted emails between Ali and a recipient in Pakistan called 'Papa' whom MI5 believed was Rashid Raul, suggested that a major attack in the UK was being planned.

On 26 July 2006, MI5 broke into a flat owned by Ali's brother in Forest Road, Walthamstow, and planted bugs and surveillance cameras which recorded Ali (codenamed 'Lion Roar') and a third 'executive', Tanvir Hussain, drilling a hole in the bottom of a soft drink bottle in order to replace the contents with a liquid explosive mixture without breaking the seal. On 4 August Ali sent an email to Raul, stating "I've done my prep. All I have to do is sort out opening timetable and bookings. That should take a couple of days." Two days later MI5 followed Ali to an internet cafe where he copied details onto a USB flash drive of seven North American bound flights - including Air Canada flights to Toronto and Montreal, as well as two United Airlines (UA) flights to Chicago, and scheduled UA flights to San Francisco, New York and Washington - all of which were to leave the UK between 2.15pm and 4.50pm which meant, according to the CPS, that all the planes would have been in the air at the same time, making it impossible for any of the aircraft to be recalled once the first bomb had exploded. No date had been chosen to launch the multiple attacks, but the timetables related to travel between July and October 2006.

During the course of the joint Scotland Yard/MI5 investigation, the US Department of Homeland Security (DHS), the CIA and the FBI were regularly briefed on developments, and were becoming "increasingly edgy" according to Andy Hayman. The former DHS Secretary, Michael Chertoff, co-author of the US Patriot Act, described the liquid bomb plot as "being of a very substantial dimension, advanced, specific and sophisticated, and of a scale comparable to 9/11." Although Scotland Yard and MI5 wanted to continue the investigation to obtain more admissible evidence, rather than rely on covert intercept communications, Hayden believes that the Americans "lost their nerve" and President Bush ordered the arrest of Raul in Pakistan, which forced the Yard's CTC to arrest Ali and Sarwar in a car-park beside Waltham Forest Town Hall on 9 August. In a series of co-ordinated raids across London another twenty-four people were detained, five of whom (apart from the ringleaders) were later charged and convicted in connection with the plot. At Sarwar's home several suicide videos were found in a garage, and a list of alternative targets, described by the prosecution as "iconic and sensational" including nuclear power plants, oil and gas terminals, Canary Wharf, Liverpool Street railway station in central London, and the Bank of England. Planning for attacks on these targets, according to MI5 sources, was less advanced than the ambitious airlines targeting. An immediate consequence of the failed plot was enhanced security on flights between the UK and the US, with passengers only allowed to carry permitted liquids sealed and in transparent plastic bags.

Credit where it's due. Operation *Overt* was a well-managed, competently-handled investigation. However, MI5's peremptory attitude and its willingness to deceive in order to cover-up incompetence damages the public's perception and trust in an organization tasked with dealing with the jihadist threat. Indeed, it may have contributed to the Americans becoming increasingly nervous about allowing Operation *Overt* to proceed. This 'flaw' in MI5's character - reciprocated in almost every local and foreign intelligence agency globally, where lying to protect the national interest is the norm, and telling the truth, even to basic non-intrusive questions, is often the exception, even under oath - was highlighted during a three-day hearing, in May 2010, at the Royal Courts of Justice, in London, presided over by coroner, Lady Justice Heather Hallett, to decide the format of the inquests into the 52 victims of the 7/7 attacks, when Patrick O'Connor QC, counsel for four of the bereaved families and fifteen survivors stated that MI5 had deceived MPs by claiming, in 2006, that the four bombers had not been identified, and that the agency had demonstrated flaws in its assessment policy, co-operation with other agencies and record-keeping, adding "the last time MI5 was accused of deception, the ceiling seemed to fall in, as if MI5 was incapable of deception. They aren't and they deceived the ISC."

The 2009 ISC report had disclosed that both the Metropolitan Police and MI5 had information on file relating to Sidique Khan, which had been denied three years earlier, and Christopher Colhart QC, representing seven of the victims' families, suggested that the state may have breached its human rights obligation under the ECHR to protect the lives of citizens because no action had been taken, and had Khan and his accomplices been put under HUMINT and SIGINT surveillance prior to July 2005, "it may have been possible" to prevent the attacks.

Counsel for the Home Secretary and MI5, Neil Garnham QC, argued that investigating whether the Security Service could have prevented the atrocities was impossible because it would involved "handing over the keys" to Thames House, MI5's HQ. There was "no problem in providing highly sensitive intelligence material to the coroner on request" said Mr. Garnham, but the jurors could only be allowed access if they underwent "intrusive developed vetting" and neither the victims' relatives or their lawyers would be allowed to see it. When Lady Hallett confirmed that she had read many of the "conspiracy theories" on the internet, and asked if it was possible to restrict the intelligence data to that specifically related to the bombings, she was told by Mr. Granham that a "problem could arise" because the decision not to put the 7/7 bombers under surveillance would have to be placed in the context of other MI5 investigations taking place at the time. He also claimed that the ISC, a committee of MI5-vetted MPs and members of the House of Lords, was not "institutionally independent" because it was appointed by No.10 (the prime minister's residence in Downing Street) and was not "operationally independent" from the Home Office, MI5 and MI6. He added that MI5's role had already been "adequately investigated" and there was "overwhelming public interest" in not having "top secret MI5 documents revealed" during the inquests.

Giving evidence anonymously to the inquest, on 21 February 2011, a senior MI5 officer somewhat arrogantly rejected as "nonsensical and offensive" suggestions that MI5 bore any responsibility for the 52 deaths and hundreds of injuries, claiming that the agency had "no inkling" of the terror which struck the capital that day. 'Witness G' the acting chief of staff for MI5 boss, Jonathan Evans, told Lady Justice Hallett that the organization had no case to answer and he warned against the "benefits of hindsight and unreasonable expectations in a world of fragmentary intelligence" adding that it was "not feasible" for MI5 to do things seen in TV dramas.

Prompted by Hugo Keith QC, counsel to the inquest, Witness G - who had spent four months preparing his answers by reviewing what MI5 knew about the bombers prior to the attacks - said there were "no guarantees" in national security because MI5 "could not foil all the attacks all the time" and he agreed with Mr. Keith that there was "no significant intelligence failure." In July 2005 the MI5 officer, who was a senior manager in the department responsible for international counter-terrorism, and presumably was aware of warnings from agencies abroad, confirmed that MI5's budget to deal with the domestic jihadist threat had "increased dramatically" in the years prior to 7/7, but claimed there were concerns about the "somewhat limited" financial resources, which meant MI5 had to "prioritize ruthlessly" and could only "pin-down the crocodiles nearest the boat." Asked if lessons had been learnt from the follow-up to Operation *Crevice* which was "not quite as thorough as it might have been" the senior staff officer replied, "not just *Crevice*, I think we learned lessons from a number of operations between 2004 and mid-2005." He mentioned the number of jihadist threats facing the UK around the time of the London bombings, and described the foiled plot to bring down seven trans-Atlantic airliners in 2006 as the "most significant" faced by MI5 since 1945.

Despite the number of 'primary' investigative targets MI5 was trying to deal with, the workload was no excuse for the poor quality of how basic tasks were carried out, such as trying to identify Khan using a badly-copied and cropped surveillance photograph. In February 2004 several high-definition color photographs were taken of Khan and Shehzad Tanweer at Toddington Motorway Service station in Bedfordshire by MI5 agents who were following the Leeds-based suspects as they returned from a trip to West Sussex, on the south coast, where they had met several men who would be later convicted of the Operation *Crevice* plot.

The original, well-defined images which were shown to the inquest jury, revealed Khan's and Tanweer's faces in some detail, but the black-and-white copies sent to an al-Qaida 'super-grass,' Mohammed Junaid Babar - a US/Pakistan jihadist who had met Khan at a training camp in South Waziristan, and had agreed to work for the FBI after he was arrested in New York in 2004 - had been so incompetently cropped that only a photograph of Tanweer had been sent to Washington. Not surprisingly Babar, who served less than five years of a possible 70-year sentence after agreeing to work with the Bureau and testifying against the 21/7 plotters, was unable to identify the man known as 'Ibrahim' and MI5 had missed an opportunity to identify the 30-year-old 7/7 planner more than one year before the suicide attacks took place. Asked by inquest counsel why this had occurred, the MI5 witness replied: "I can only speculate here because we don't know exactly why. The judgment we formed was that the cropped photograph was probably of such poor quality it wasn't worth showing, but I don't have any contemporaneous documentation." Which is not exactly an answer to the question he was asked, but Mr. Keith didn't see fit to pursue the matter. It does say a lot about the senior officer's attitude, that he could not be bothered to look into the matter which was an important factor in the allegations of agency failure, and about the contempt that MI5 officers have for those who question their judgment, and competence. Witness G did admit that Khan's name had "cropped-up in at least seven separate pieces of intelligence" prior to 7/7, but MI5 software had failed to flag-up the connection, either because the name was "too common" or the data hadn't been properly collated. Asked if 'Khan' could now be flagged as a result of improved software, the MI5 officer said it would depend on "how unique the name was, software has improved, fuzzy searching is better than it was but still a long way from being perfect." The short answer, in other words, was "No."

The critical question of whether MI5 could have prevented 7/7 was the subject of a BBC 2 television documentary, *The Secret War on Terror*, by reporter Peter Taylor, a experienced veteran of the Troubles in Ireland. The program focused in some detail on Operation *Crevice*, and MI5's surveillance of another British-born jihadist, Omar Khyam, from a family with a tradition of serving in the Pakistan military and the ISI, who was born in Crawley, West Sussex, in 1981, attended meetings of al-Muhajiroun as a teenager, and had been instructed in bomb-making at the Malakand training camp in Pakistan in 2001. When he returned to Britain he became involved in recruiting and providing financial support for the resistance in Afghanistan, and planning a fertilizer-based bomb attack in London. At one stage, according to Taylor's report, Khyam met two 'UDMs' (unidentified males) whose Honda Civic was tailed 180 miles up the M1 to West Yorkshire on 2 February 2004, during which time the service station photograph was taken. The address of the two UDMs (later identified as Khan and Tanweer) were noted by MI5, but the agency failed to notify WYP Special Branch that they had followed two suspects associated with Khyam and the *Crevice* cell into their area of operations.

MI5 did share their information with the FBI in Washington. Special Agent, Art Cummings, who was in charge of the American end of *Crevice*, was communicating with his counterpart at the British Embassy on Massachusetts Avenue at least three times a day, "and knew exactly what was going on" because the FBI was concerned that elements of the *Crevice* cell might also be planning attacks in the US. Cummings later explained, in an interview with Taylor, that the "fact that the core [*Crevice*] group were talking to some people traveling outside their area (..) and that needed to be identified because if the operation goes down early, then you leave this bad spot that can come back and haunt you later."

Two days after the UDMs had been followed north, MI5 learned from electronic intercepts that Khyam had been asking a member of a Luton cell, whom he had met in Malakand, about a formula to make an explosive device based on ammonium nitrate fertilizer. At this point, according to Taylor, MI5 knew it was no longer dealing with a group facilitating jihad abroad "but with terrorists planning an attack in the UK." Despite this upgrade in the seriousness of the plot, MI5 still didn't tell WYP Special Branch about the two UDMs "on their patch" who might be involved in the plot, and when the police were finally provided with details of the Honda Civic registration and the suspects' addresses they were asked simply to "carry out checks" but not to "mobilize their experienced surveillance teams to keep a detailed watch on the two men." Only in June 2008, two months after members of the *Crevice* cell were arrested, did MI5 fully brief the regional Special Branch. The 'simple' answer - if anything is simple when dealing with MI5 at any level - to the question of why Khan and Tanweer hadn't been under surveillance earlier was because MI5 only proscribed tasks to Special Branch "within certain parameters and on a need-to-know basis" according to Taylor.

Not really good enough. MI5, the lead agency dealing with the domestic jihadist threat to the UK, had obviously learned nothing from The Troubles, when the lack of trust and co-operation between the Security Service, the Royal Ulster Constabulary (RUC) the RUC Special Branch (famously described as a "force within a force") and the British Army's Intelligence Corps, was exploited both by the Provisional IRA to wage its campaign, and by Ulster loyalist gunmen in various internecine power-struggles to maintain control of loyalist working-class areas in Belfast and other urban developments in the North of Ireland. Inter-agency trust has always been a problem for British agencies (including MI6 when it has to deal directly with Thames House), however, the relationship between MI5 and the regional police forces has improved since the establishment of specialist CTC units (merging fire-arms officers and Special Branch) throughout Britain. These were planned before 7/7, but their implementation and operational responsibilities were only fast-tracked following the London attacks.

After seven months the findings of the Rt. Honorable Lady Justice Hallett's inquest were read into the House of Commons record, on 9 May 2011, and the report was welcomed by the Home Secretary, Theresa May, who was "pleased that the coroner had made clear there is simply no evidence that the Security Service knew of, and therefore failed to prevent, the bombings of 7/7." Speaking at a press conference later that day, however, some relatives of the victims said they "did not recognize her assessment of MI5's role." The inquest had determined that the 52 victims had been unlawfully killed, that it was neither "right nor fair" to say more attention should have been paid to the ringleader Khan, and suggest, therefore, that the plot might have been uncovered in time to prevent the jihadist terror, and that there should be no public inquiry. In her remarks Lady Justice Hallett said she was not aware of having left "any reasonable stone unturned" and that the proceedings had gone "much further than simply recording the sad fact that 52 innocent members of the traveling public were unlawfully killed in a dreadful act of terrorism, we have unearthed material that has never previously seen the light of day." One reason that she could say they had unearthed new material, of course, was that five years earlier MI5 had failed to provide complete and accurate information to the ISC.

An Orwellian Response

MPs from all parties were fulsome in their praise for Lady Hallett's efforts. This was not a time to quibble over minor details like how MI5 conducts itself under pressure. There were more jihadist plots to deal with, real and imaginary, and while the behavior and heroism of members of the emergency services was rightly praised, no one bothered to point out, for the record, that incorrect analysis and wrong decisions on the part of MI5, in the first place, had resulted in fatal consequences and the need for the emergency services to be deployed on 7/7.

Instead, the Conservative/Liberal Democrat coalition decided to revise existing anti-terror legislation to implement a plan drawn up by MI5, MI6 and GCHQ in which details of every landline and cell-phone call, text messages, email traffic (including addresses of recipients) and websites visited will be stored in vast databases, to which the security and intelligence services and the police will have unrestricted access. Direct subscriber messages on social networking sites, such as Twitter and Facebook, will also be stored, as well as communications between players in online video games. The plan also allows for MI5 to be given 'real time' access to all SIGINT and digital records of those they have under surveillance, as well as the ability to reconstruct an individual's movements through the intelligence stored on the databases. The plan is a revised version of the former Labour Government's 'Intercept Modernisation Programme' which was shelved in November 2009 after consultation showed a lack of public support, and vociferous criticism (including self-righteous outbursts by Conservative politicians warning about Labour's "reckless" record on individual privacy) of the number of public bodies which could access the data. Apart from the intelligence, security and law enforcement agencies, the list included local councils and non-departmental pubic bodies. In total, at least 653 public sector organizations.

There are also well-founded concerns that techniques being deployed by MI5, Special Branch, the CTC, and the CPS to monitor students are leading to incidents of Islamophobia at universities throughout the country. One of the worrying examples of this trend was the arrest by CTC officers, in May 2008, of Nottingham University student, Rizwaan Sabir, who had downloaded an al-Qaida training manual as part of his dissertation research, and Hicham Yezza, a staff member of the NU's School of Modern Languages, and magazine editor, who was helping Sabir draft his PhD proposal.

Despite the training manual being available in the university's Hallward Library, from high street retailers Waterstone's and Blackwells, and online from Amazon, NU senior management called the CTC. Both men were detained and repeatedly questioned for six days, and although they were eventually released without charges, the non-existent jihadist threat is still listed in a Home Office online report, *Terrorist Plots in Great Britain: Uncovering the Truth*. According to documents posted on the 'academic whistleblowers' website 'Unileaks' in June 2011, NU security staff were told to keep contemporaneous accounts of Arab/Muslim-themed activity on campus. Students who protested were "routinely filmed," and both staff and students who spoke at demonstrations in support of Sabir and Yezza were logged by a little-known, Whitehall-based, counter terrorism unit, embedded in the Office for Security and Counter-Terrorism (OSCT), called the Research, Information and Communications (RIC) unit. Dr Rod Thornton, a lecturer on security issues at NU's department of Politics and International Relations (who had served as a British Army infantry sergeant in the North of Ireland in the early 1980s) was suspended in May 2011 after writing an article for a British International Students Association (BISA) conference publication, held at the University of Manchester two months earlier, in which he accused NU of "attempting to smear" Sabir and Yezza, stating that "untruth piled on untruth until a point was reached when the Home Office itself farcically comes to advertise the case as a major Islamist plot." Dozens of internationally-respected scholars, including the indomitable Noam Chomsky, called for Dr Thornton's "immediate reinstatement," describing the original arrests as "indicative of a growing tide of Islamophobia." Indeed, and among the peripheral casualties of this intolerance are people like Dr Thornton, who resigned his post at NU last March.

The hugely-prolific American author and political activist, the late Gore Vidal, once described himself as a "conspiracy analyst" not a conspiracy theorist. A crucial difference, sadly lost on mainstream media critics of those who bother to take a closer look at the "clash of civilizations" from the bottom up. The threat of domestic terror in the UK has not been politicized. Few, if any, MPs would not want jihadist violence tackled with all the resources of the law, although there are differences in detail of application, such as the length of time (currently 14-days) suspects can be detained, or the consequences of deportation/extradition to regimes who make no secret of the fact that torture is part of the brutal art of in-depth interrogation. Whatever the outcome of minor political differences on the periphery of the bigger picture, it is probably true to say that the majority of British citizens would welcome indefinite incarceration, or better still, deportation for "loud mouthed" clerics, and to hell with thinking about what happens when the plane touches down in Islamabad, Cairo, Algiers or JFK.

In the mainstream media the 'war against terror' is couched in breaking news, sound-bites, tired slogans and statistics which conceal more than they reveal, and lies. And the 15 minutes of attention the victims receive will be quietly deleted from the back-story if closer inspection reveals incompetence and/or gross stupidity on the part of those whose job it is to protect the public, but whose presence on the front line depends on the success of the terror. There is an obvious contradiction here, and in the end the only real losers - apart from the innocent victims of jihadist terror - are standing on the corners of the Arab street. Those in the West who believe the threat can be imperiously conquered, indeed that this war can be waged by drones, Special Forces ops, quiet assassinations, incarceration and torture, and it can still be won, should visit the ghettos and refugee camps in North Africa, the Middle East, southeast Asia or the Gulf states, and wait, with fear and trepidation, for the terror next time.

BIBLIOGRAPHY

Aggoun, Lounis and Rivoire, Jean-Baptiste. *Francalgerie*. Paris: La Decouverte, 2004.

Ahmed, Nafeez Mosaddeq. *The London Bombings*. London: Gerald Duckworth & Co. Ltd., 2006.

Burke, Jason. *Al Qaeda: The True Story of Radical Islam*. London: Penguin Books, 2004.

Cheurfi, Achour. *La Classe Politique Algerienne*. Paris: Casbah Editions, 2006.

Davies, Nick. *Flat Earth News*. London: Vintage Books, 2009.

Evans, Martin. *Algeria: France's Undeclared War*. Oxford: Oxford University Press, 2011.

Fisk, Robert. *The Great War for Civilization*. London: Fourth Estate, 2005.

Hayden, Andy and Gilmore, Margaret. *The Terrorist Hunters*. New York: Bantam Books, 2009.

Horne, Alistair. *A Savage War of Peace: Algeria 1954-1962* New York: NYRB Classics, 2006.

Kee, Robert. *Trial and Error*. London: Hamish Hamilton, 1987.

Martinez, Luis. *The Algerian Civil War 1990-1998*. London: Hurst & Co., 2000.
Mitta, Manoj and Phoolka, H.S. *When a Tree Shook Delhi*. New Delhi: Roli Books, 2007.
Mullin, Chris. *Error of Judgement*. London: Chatto & Windus, 1986.
Phillips, John and Evans, Martin. *Algeria: Anger of the Dispossessed*. New Haven: Yale University Press, 2007.
Roy, Arundhati. *Listening to Grasshoppers*. London: Penguin Books, 2010.
Sands, Philippe. *Lawless World*. London: Penguin Books, 2006.
Scheuer, Michael. *Through Our Enemies Eyes*. Washington D.C: Potomac Books, Inc. 2006.
Schmidt, Olivier (ed.) *The Intelligence Files*. Atlanta: Clarity Press, 2005.
Singular, Stephen. *Talked to Death*. New York: Berkley Books, 1987.
Stone, Martin. *The Agony of Algeria*. New York: Columbia University Press, 1998.
Suskind, Ron. *The One Percent Doctrine*. New York: Pocket Books, 2007.
United States Congress. *The 9/11 Commission Report*, (authorized edition). New York: Norton & Co., 2004.
Wright, Lawrence. *The Looming Tower*. London: Penguin Books, 2006.

NEWSPAPERS & MAGAZINES
El Watan (www.elwatan.com)
Guardian (www.guardian.co.uk)
Independent (www.independent.co.uk)
New York Times (www.nyt.com)
*Newsweek (*www.newsweek.com)
Observer (www.observer.guardian.co.uk)
Scotsman (www.scotsman.com)
Statewatch Online Magazine (www.statewatch.org)
Sunday Times (www.thesundaytimes.co.uk)
Times (www.thetimes.co.uk)

OFFICIAL REPORTS, NGOs & ONLINE SOURCES
Algeria Watch (www.algeria-watch.de/en/)
British Home Office *WMS (Written Ministerial Statement) 7/7 Inquest* (www.homeoffice.gov.uk)
British Security Service (www.mi5.gov.uk)
El Auto de Procesamiento por el 11-M (www.elmundo.es)
Independent Police Complaints Commission (IPPC) *Stockwell One 2007*. (www.ipcc.gov.uk)
Intelligence and Security Committee. *Report into the London Terrorist Attacks on 7 July 2005*. (www.tso.co.uk) 2007

Intelligence and Security Committee. *Could 7/7 Have Been Prevented?* (www.tso.co.uk) 2009

Pontecorvo, Gillo & Solinas, Franco. *The Battle of Algiers.* London: Argent Films 2009

Royal United Services Institute, *Terrorism in the UK; Confirming its Modus Operandi,* (www.rusi.org/journal) 2009

The Trial of Zacarias Moussaoui (www.law2.umkc.edu)

UK Statutes Database (www.legislation.co.uk)

Unileaks (Scienta Potentia Est) *The Case of the Terror Plot that Wasn't* (www.unileaks.org)

CHAPTER THREE

THE ITCHING PALM

"I see in the near future a crisis approaching that unnerves me and causes me to tremble for the safety of my country (...) Corporations have been enthroned, an era of corruption in high places will follow, and the money-power of the country will endeavor to prolong its reign by working upon the prejudices of the people until the wealth is aggregated in a few hands and the Republic is destroyed."
Unknown; often attributed to Abraham Lincoln

Daring to Speak Above a Whisper

Two initiatives took place in South Africa in late 2011 which, up to that point in time, summed up the political career of President Jacob Zuma, and the moral landscape in which men like Zuma have thrived, and which has turned the country into the "most unequal on the planet" according to former ANC parliamentarian, Andrew Feinstein.

The first was an announcement, at a press briefing in Cape Town on 27 October 2011, by the South African Justice Minister, Jeff Radebe, of the terms of reference for the long-awaited judicial inquiry into allegations of "corruption and impropriety" during the 1999 Strategic Defense Procurement (SDP) process. The multi-billion-rand arms deals involved several European manufacturers, most prominently, the UK-based BAE Systems. Radebe described the establishment of the three-member judicial commission, to be chaired by Supreme Court of Appeal Judge Willie Seriti, as a "watershed moment" in South Africa's history, which would "rid the nation of what has become an albatross" that has damaged the country's reputation. The commission, he claimed, would work "independently of everyone, including the executive."

Judge Seriti, who had been appointed by President Zuma to serve on the Judicial Service Commission (JSC) in 2009, chose a team of experienced advocates to analyze evidence, while the commission's secretary was to be another former member of the JSC, attorney Edward Mvuseni Ngubane. His appointment to such a key position has been somewhat controversial, according to local sources. He had been perceived (correctly or not) as supporting Western Cape Judge John Hlophe's alleged attempt to influence the Constitutional Court in Johannesburg in favor of President Zuma, who had challenged the legality of raids carried out by the disbanded Directorate of Special Operations (DSO) – an elite, multi-disciplined unit known as the 'Scorpions' - during an anti-corruption investigation.

The judicial commission was to be based in Johannesburg, with a budget of R40 million (approximately $5 million). Judge Seriti would have the power to issue search-and-seizure warrants, hold public hearings, and subpoena witnesses, including members of the ruling Executive; and failure to co-operate would be an offence punishable with a "substantial" fine or a prison term of one year. The inquiry is expected to be completed within two years, with the final report including recommendations (which are expected to be made public) going to President Zuma. However, interim reports also submitted every six months to Zuma, "will not necessarily be released," but in his statement to a generally-skeptical media which has covered the great arms swindle for more than a decade, Redebe was at pains to point out that the mere fact that President Zuma had initiated the commission indicated that he would take its recommendations seriously.

According to the six-point terms of reference, the Seriti Commission would examine, conclude, and make recommendations concerning the rationale of the SDP packages, addressing: whether the arms and equipment purchased "are underutilized or not unutilized at all"; whether job opportunities anticipated to flow from the deal have materialized, to what extent, and the steps that ought to be taken to realize them; whether "offsets anticipated" to flow from the deal have materialized, to what extent, and the steps that ought to be taken to realize them; whether anyone in or outside the Government "improperly influenced any of the contracts awarded," and, if so, whether legal proceedings should be instituted against them, and what would be the nature of such legal proceedings. The inquiry will also assess whether there is any basis for pursuing such people to recover any losses that the state might have suffered as a result of their conduct; whether any contract concluded after the procurement process is tainted by fraud or corruption that can be proved and that would justify its cancellation, and the ramifications of canceling such a contract.

There was what might best be described as a "mixed response" to Minister Radebe's announcement. Lawyer Paul Hoffman, who represented Terry Crawford-Browne, the anti-arms deal activist whose campaign is credited with forcing Zuma to launch the judicial inquiry, told the *Mail & Guardian* newspaper that the "route the president has chosen is to look tough on crime and corruption, but also to try and flush people out from many years ago who may be reluctant to come forward." However, Richard Young, who lodged corruption charges with the fraud squad relating to the arms deals, was more cautious in his initial assessment, telling the same newspaper that "nobody should get too excited just yet. Remember what happened with the Hefer Commission in Bloemfontein, whose terms of reference were changed several times, which meant that Hefer never had the wherewithal to really go after national intelligence documents."

Less than a month after the inquiry announcement, which to many outsiders may have seemed like the regime was finally coming to grips with the corrupt legacy of the SDP following a long and honorable campaign in the South Africa media, dozens of journalists wearing black and blowing plastic vuvuzelas (a long horn with a loud monotonous note, once used, in its traditional form, to summon distant villagers to attend community gatherings), gathered outside the Johannesburg headquarters of the ruling ANC to protest against President Zuma's second initiative, the passing of the Protection of State Information Bill (PSIB), which many felt was nothing more than a legal instrument designed to restrict and curtail the anti-corruption inquiry. There were also protests outside ANC offices in Pretoria, at Hecter Petersen Museum Square in Orlando West, Soweto, at Parliament buildings in Cape Town, and outside Durban City Hall.

The media dubbed the 22 November 2011 protests *Black Tuesday* to emphasize the connection with the *Black Wednesday* of 19 October 1977, when the ruling white minority National Party, headed by Prime Minister B. J. Vorster - who, as justice minister under his predecessor, PM Verwoerd, had managed, from a distance, the Rivonia trial in which Nelson Mandela was sentenced to life imprisonment - cracked down on the South African media. Vorster banned the daily *World* and *Sunday World* newspapers, as well as sanctioning 20 individuals and organizations in an effort to curtail criticism of the uncompromising and brutal system of racial segregation which had been on the statute books since 1948. These included anti apartheid activist Beyers Naude's Christian Institute, an ecumenical organization he founded in 1963 to promote reconciliation through interracial research and dialogue, and the Union of Black Journalists (UBJ.).

The PSIB proposes severe penalties (including prison sentences for up to twenty-five years, with no 'public interest' consideration) for journalists and other citizens found in possession of classified documents as well as "harboring state secrets," in effect treating them no differently than foreign spies. Intentionally accessing classified information carries a ten-year jail term, and there is no independent appeals mechanism for those who might wish to access information that may have been classified as 'SECRET' without justification. While there is a provision for what is described as a "mostly independent" committee to review decisions, (treasonous) citizens will have no direct access to it. Disclosing classified information, except in a limited and selective number of cases, which does not include investigative journalists, trade unions, NGOs or community leaders, is punishable by a fine or maximum five-year prison term. Last but by no means least, there is a 15-year jail term for the retention and disclosure of classified information that relates to the civilian, military and police intelligence agencies.

While there is equally repressive anti-media legislation in many countries, there is something sad and distasteful about the fact that a

Government, many of whose past and present members, as political and militant activists just over a decade earlier, had fought and died to achieve a just and equal society for all South Africans, should now embrace legislation which had been so repugnant in the past.

During the parliamentary debate several members of the ANC majority in the National Assembly described and condemned the *Black Tuesday* protests as a "distortion of facts" stating that the Government had no intention of "banning, torturing or murdering journalists" and that the only result of the protest was to "dilute the real history of *Black Wednesday* and insult the victims of apartheid's barbaric laws." However, two South African Nobel Prize recipients have strongly criticized the PSIB, claiming its sole purpose is to muzzle the media. Retired Anglican Bishop Desmond Tutu, one of the country's most indefatigable and eloquent anti-apartheid activists in the 1980s and a recipient of the Nobel Peace Prize in 1984 and the Presidential Medal of Freedom in 2009 (the highest civilian award in the US), has described the legislation as "insulting to all South Africans to be asked to stomach legislation that could be used to outlaw whistle-blowing and investigative journalism (...) and that makes the state answerable only to the state," Author Nadine Gordimer, Nobel Prize winner for Literature in 1991, said the legislation was taking South Africa "back to the years of minority rule." She described the bill on the *Times Live* website as "totally against" freedom, adding that the "corrupt practices and nepotism that they [ANC politicians] allow themselves is exposed if we have freedom of expression." The National Press Club publicly criticized the PSIB and, as was to be expected, voiced its support for the public protests that were organized by the Right2Know group. That group's spokesperson, Dale McKinley, told the Johannesburg-based *Mail & Guardian* weekly newspaper that the PSIB has the potential to "stymie the flow of information to ordinary citizens," adding that without information "we have no power and it will threaten our democracy." At the University of Witwatersrand School of Journalism, Professor Anton Harber said the restrictive legislation was a "huge setback in the push towards an open democracy."

A timely example of Prof. Harber's fears was a lawsuit filed by President Jacob Zuma's spokesman, Sathyandranath 'Mac' Maharaj, against the M&G and senior journalists, Sam Sole and Stefaans Brummer, preventing the publication of their detailed report linking him to the arms corruption scandals back in 1999. Their story, which was due to appear in the paper's 18 November 2011 edition, suggested that Maharaj had lied during a 'Section 28' inquiry into his involvement in corrupt practices by the DSO, the organized crime unit. The DSO had been disbanded in January 2009 by the former (interim) South African President, Kgalema Motlanthe, before being appointed deputy president by Mbeki's elected successor, Jacob Zuma.

Following threats of prosecution and on the advice of in-house lawyers, the newspaper published a heavily-redacted report, with large sections blocked out, making its point under the headline 'CENSORED: We Cannot Bring You This Story In Full Due to a Threat of Criminal Prosecution.'

The South African media had originally broken the story using 'leaked' classified documents, but under the PSIB journalists and editors will now face harsh prison sentences for similar practices. Although not directly connected to the PSIB, it is more than just a coincidence that 48 hours after the two-thirds ANC majority voted in favor of the repressive media legislation, (by 229 to 107 with two abstentions), McIntosh Polela, a spokesman for the Directorate for Priority Crime Investigation (DPCI), also known as the 'Hawks', confirmed that an investigator from within the unit had been appointed to look into alleged violations of 'Section 41 paragraph (6)' of the 1998 National Prosecution Authority (NPA) Act. Polela insisted there was "nothing out of the ordinary" for the DCPI to investigate allegations made against the *M&G* journalists by a senior ANC official "at this particular point in time" and denied that the DPCI had been directed to proceed by President Zuma, telling those still willing to believe the 'spin' that the Hawks "don't take instructions from Mr Zuma" or any other high-ranking official. All cases, according to Polela, are investigated at the discretion of the DPCI National Commissioner, Anwar Dramat. However, Johan Burger, director of the Institute of Security Studies (ISS) crime and justice program, described the DPCI investigation as an abuse of 'Section 17 (d)' of the 2008 South African Police Service Amendment Act, which directs the DCPI to investigate national priority offences only,

Apart from the NPA 'Section 28' inquiry, which related specifically to the dissemination of information, DPCI officers had been instructed to investigate allegations of theft, based on "certain suspicions" that the material in the possession of *M&G* journalists. Brummer and Sole, was "unlawfully obtained" while Maharaj's legal representatives, WDK Attorneys, considered the possibility of a civil suit on behalf of their client in pursuit of damages against the two *M&G* journalists.

Three opposition parties in the 400-seat National Assembly in Cape Town (elected every 5 years under a party-list, proportional representation system), criticized the DPCI's *M&G* investigation. Dianne Lohler Bernard, police spokesperson for the Democratic Alliance (67 seats) pointed out that a "mere detective" could establish how the *M&G* got the information, adding that Mac Maharaj "is on his own mission" and the DPCI should not be used by politicians "to fight their own battles." This was echoed by parliamentarian Mario Ambrosini, of the Inkatha Freedom Party (18 seats), who warned of the adverse effect on the freedom of the press "something that at times should override certain state interests." The United Democratic Movement (4 seats) leader, Bantu Holomisa, was more forthright than either of his colleagues, suggesting that Maharaj was using state resources to fight his personal battles. Maharaj, he said, " cost the country R12-million through the Hefer Commission, when he falsely accused the then head of the NPA, Bulelani Ngcuka, of being an apartheid spy. If the Hawks continue with this investigation they will be deviating from their mandate. They should, in fact, look into the allegations leveled against Maharaj."

The third largest newspaper in South Africa (in terms of circulation), the weekly *City Press*, with an estimated (predominantly Black) readership of 2.5 million, and a distribution network throughout neighboring Botswana, Leshoto, Namibia and Swaziland, published the unabridged text of a DSO 2003 interview with the "gaunt and bespectacled" Maharaj, on its front page on 27 November 2011, pointing out that confidentiality was a "moot point" because the information was already in the public domain, having been previously published in the newspaper in April 2007, in two articles under the headlines 'Mac Fights Back' and 'Inside the Maharaj Interrogation.'

These reports raised questions relating to Maharaj's propriety and honesty during his five years as transport minister, when he allegedly received 'kickbacks' from the French arms and defense electronics company, Thomson-CSF, which had been chosen by the German Frigate Consortium (GFC) to provide combat suites for the Valour-class patrol corvettes being sought by the South African Navy (SAN). One of the men involved in the procurement process for the Department of Defense was Chippy Shaik, whose brother, Schabir Shaik, was a director of African Defense Systems (ASD) which was bidding for SAN sub-contracts. Schabir Shaik was also the owner and sole director of a company called Nkobi Holdings, which went into joint venture with Thomson-CSF and tendered for various highly-lucrative infrastructure and security contracts, including the N3 highway (Johannesburg to Durban) and the N4 National Route. The Durban-born businessman was a close friend of Jacob Zuma, and had helped him financially through interest-free loans with no final repayment arrangements when JZ returned to South Africa from exile in Mozambique in 1990. He also helped Zuma secure the chairmanship of the ANC, where the future president cultivated a power-base which would eventually take him to the top of the political establishment.

Private Income Before Public Virtue

Mac Maharaj had left politics after the 1999 general election to spend more time with his bank account, joining the FirstRand Bank as the financial services provider's highest-paid, non-executive director. In August 2003 he was forced to resign, following allegations of corruption published six months earlier in the Johannesburg-based *Sunday Times*, the country's largest weekly newspaper with an audited circulation of over 500,000 and an estimated readership of 3.2 million. He left South Africa and joined the faculty of Bennington College, a private liberal arts co-educational school in Vermont, US. Four years is a long time in South African politics at the level at which JZ and Maharaj play the game, and in July 2011 Maharaj re-engaged, and was appointed Zuma's official spokesman. Having previously made no attempt to prevent *City Press* publishing allegations against him in April 2007, prior to the republication of much of the same material in November 2011, his attorney, Rudi Krause, then threatened *City Press* with criminal charges, including "unlawful possession of classified documentation" if the newspaper went ahead.

Before doing exactly that, *City Press* issued a statement pointing out that if President Zuma's 'spin doctor' had lied during his "secret interview" with the DSO in 2003, he could face a prison sentence of 15 years if prosecuted and found guilty of perverting the course of justice. Majarah's statements to the police, according to the newspaper, contradicted details of the "substantial payments" both he and his wife Zarina had received from Zuma's former 'financial adviser' and now convicted fraudster, Schabir Shaik, and contradicted allegations that they had "operated a network of foreign bank accounts" through which these payments from 'shell companies' were routed, while Maharaj served as transport minister and his department was involved "in awarding two lucrative tenders" from which Shaik benefited financially.

Shaik's eight month trial at Durban High Courtbefore Judge Hilary Squires, exposed the corrupt and fraudulent relationship between the accused and Jacob Zuma. Both men had a "discreet and profitable" business relationship, only visible, according to the prosecution, in several incomplete documents and transactions, dealing almost exclusively with the interest free loans to Zuma with no specific repayment date, which Shaik wrote off without explanation in 1999. On 30 May 2005, Shaik was found guilty on two counts of corruption for paying Zuma R-1.2 million and for soliciting a bribe from Thomson-CSF, and one count of fraud for writing off Zuma's debts. He was sentenced to 15 years for corruption and 3 years for fraud, to be served concurrently. Zuma resigned his parliamentary seat, but remained deputy ANC president, a political platform from which he resurrected his political career, eventually leading to his election by the National Assembly as President of the Republic of South Africa, following the 2009 general election. He is the most powerful and influential political leader in southern Africa, and despite his corrupt pedigree, a man with whom the US and Europe have no choice but to do business

On several occasions during conversations with the DSO, according to the first *City Press* report in 2007, Mr. and Mrs. Maharaj denied having bank accounts in Switzerland, or that they had received payments from Schabir Shaik, claiming that all the offshore-banked cash was earned by Zarina Maharaj, for her consultancy work for the Geneva-based International Trade Center, General Electric and Xerox, and that the family's Milsek Investment Trust (MIT) account was "dormant" despite two deposits of R-100,000 (one from Nkobi Holdings) which both claimed to know nothing about, where it came from, who used it or why.

In the second article the newspaper followed the money - more than US$200,000 paid into secret bank accounts in the British Virgin Islands, a tax haven in the Caribbean, and in France by Minderley Investments, an off-shore shell company set up by Shaik, and an undisclosed sum paid into a Swiss account opened by Zarina two days before the first deposit in 1996 and closed in April 2000. The period coincided with her husband's tenure as transport minister during which his department awarded the R-2.5 billion contract to upgrade the N3 highway to a consortium which included Shaik's Nkobi Holdings. Another R-265 million contract for credit card driver's licenses also benefited Nkobi, Thomson-CSF, and Denel (Pty) Ltd., the state-owned aerospace and defense conglomerate, based in Centurion, Gauteng, and established in 1991/92 under the Ministry of Public Enterprise when these manufacturing subsidiaries of the Armaments Corporation of South Africa (ARMSCOR) were set up in response to the UN mandated international arms embargo, in order that ARMSCOR could become the procurement agency for the South African National Defense Force (SANDF). On 21 November 2011 the *Sunday Times* disclosed details of a consultancy agreement between Thomson-CSF and Minderley Investments, which "confirmed secret payments" totaling Ffr1.2 million into a Swiss bank account held by Zarina Maharaj, two months before the first five-year driving licenses contract was awarded in March 1998.

DPCI press officer, McIntosh Polela, speaking to journalists after news of the Hawks inquiry was released, sounded like a man sinking up to his knees in quicksand while trying to convince a skeptical audience that the ground underfoot was rock solid. He admitted that the previously published articles in *City Press* will have an "impact on our investigation because the information will already be public knowledge" but ignored the fact that details of Mac Maharaj's mendacity and greed had been in the public domain for four years. He had asked *City Press* to provide the DPCI "with the story so that we can see if we are investigating something that is already in the public domain. We will make a decision [whether or not to prosecute] from these." Within hours *City Press* had provided the published reports to Polela, who, alternatively, could simply have gone to the corner and bought a copy of the paper from a local vendor.

Money Answereth All Things (Ecclesiastes 10:19)

The post-apartheid archives of several South African newspapers are now a limited resource, containing hundreds (possibly many more) of ground breaking, but now legally liable articles, politically damaging to the ANC, published over the past 15 years, based on leaked copies of classified internal reports, off-the-record briefings and material generated by the disbanded Scorpions. This material would not have seen the light of day had the PSIB been on the statute books. The reports include details of the 'hidden agenda' of the 1999 Strategic Defense Procurement (SDP) process in which R-30 billion was spent buying weapons systems and military hardware, helicopters and fighter aircraft from several foreign manufacturers, including BAE Systems and its Swedish partner SAAB, and upgrading existing stock at a time when tens of thousands of Black Africans (many of whom were, and probably still are, ANC supporters) were hungry and homeless, while the 'lucky ones' survived in corrugated iron shacks in the townships on the outskirts of the major cities, out of sight and out of mind, ignored by the rich and powerful.

In 1999 Patricia de Lille, MPP, a former journalist, Pan Africanist Congress of Azania (PAC) parliamentarian, and currently leader of the Independent Democrats (ID), which she formed in 2003, produced a file detailing allegations of bribery and corruption and calling on the National Assembly to investigate. According to Andrew Feinstein, the former ANC ranking member on the Finance Committee and chairman of the Public Accounts Committee (PAC) in the late 1990s, who also worked closely with the non-ANC chair of the cross-party Standing Committee on Public Accounts (SCOPA), the source of De Lille's report was Bheki Jacobs, a "small man with an animated bird-like face" who worked at the Africa Institute in Pretoria. Bheki told Feinsten he had been an ANC agent, trained and based in Moscow during many years in exile, and claimed that the arms deal had been plotted in the early 1990s during World Trade Center negotiations on the transition of power, when Joe Modise and Thabo Mbeki had, allegedly, been persuaded that the ANC "could access millions of dollars from arms companies if there was sufficient contractual reward for the companies once the ANC was in government."

That the ANC was seriously short of cash there is no doubt. After the 1994 non-racial general election, which the ANC won with a two-thirds majority, Joe Modise was appointed defense minister, and authorized the SAN to begin tendering for new vessels. In December that year, at the ANC's Annual Conference in Bloemfontein, the party's treasurer-general admitted that the organization was "struggling financially" because foreign funding had dried up, and no plans had been made to achieve financial self sufficiency. At this stage the arms deal option must have seemed an attractive and possibly the only long-term solution.

In 2000 the *M&G* obtained and published details of a leaked internal "affordable study" on the financial implications of the SDP which stated that an analysis of these risks "suggests that as the expenditure level increases these risks escalate significantly. In fact even expenditure of R-16.5 billion may create a situation in which the Government could be confronted by economic, fiscal and financial difficulties at some point." This was a clear indication, according to the newspaper, that the country could not afford the SDP package, and that finance minister, Trevor Manuel, was aware of this when he signed-off on the deal. By 2008 the DSO was in possession of documents from its own investigation and from the Serious Fraud Office (SFO) in London, which was investigating BAE's international business practices, showing that the British company, listed that year on the *Financial Times* (FT) index as the world's second-largest defense, security and aerospace manufacturer, had paid R-1.73 billion in bribes and 'commissions' to agents, including men like Fana Hlongwane, adviser to the late defense minister,

Joe Modise (who had died of cancer at his home in Pretoria on 26 November 2001), and Zimbabwean businessman, John Bredenkamp, in return for intervention to secure contracts for the London-based purveyor of military hardware.

In his excellent book, *The Arms Deal in Your Pocket*, Paul Holden describes the decision to pay R-15.3 billion to buy Swedish Gripen jet fighters and British Hawk trainers from BAE/SAAB as the "most scandalous element of the arms deal." The single-seat Hawk jet trainer aircraft cost twice as much as an Italian Aermacchi MB-339 trainer and light attack aircraft, and was favored by the SAAF, while in another rival bid the SADF had no need of SAAB's Gripen JAS-39 light-weight, single-engine, multi-role fighter. However, when Modise removed costs as a criterion, "the deal was signed, sealed and delivered." Competition for the lucrative arms contracts had intensified in 1998, according to Feinstein, and British Aerospace (which changed its title to BAE Systems in 1999 following the purchase of Marconi Electronic Systems and the naval shipbuilding subsidiary of GEC) made a "generous donation" of R-5 million to the MK [Umkhonto we Sizwe, the military wing of the ANC] Veterans Association, whose life president was MK's former chief of staff, Joe Modise. One of the bidders allegedly bought Modise millions of shares in Conlog, a local defense company likely to benefit from sub-contracts. Within weeks of leaving office in 1999 he was appointed chairman of the company. It was also alleged that Modise received between R-10 and R-35 million in cash from a variety of bidders for several of the arms contracts, while other key ANC officials were also recipients of off-the-books payments, and that the ANC received millions of rands from successful bidders which, Feinstein suggests, "was probably used in our 1999 election campaign."

There was no investigation into the alleged corrupt practices of Joe Modise by any of South Africa's 'white collar' law enforcement authority - the Directorate of Serious Economic Offences (DSEO), the Heath Special Investigative Unit (HSIU), nor the Public Protector, a constitutional body established to investigate public complaints of government lapses. Shortly before his death he was quickly made a decorated hero of the freedom struggle, a man to be honored for his part in the history of those times. The historian R.W. Johnson, former South African correspondent for the London *Sunday Times* and a fairly brutal critic of the ANC leadership, likened it to a mixture of Black nationalism and 1960s Marxism "striving to create a black bourgeoisie," and described President Mbeki as rushing to award Joe Modise the South Africa Grand Cross while he lay dying, adding that there were

> doubtless concerns in some quarters that Modise's death would bring to light some of the dirt surrounding the arms deal and the Hani assassination (...)There were many possibilities, but not many had bet on Modise being singled out to receive the nation's highest honor.

Modise was too ill to be shown the pictures of the award ceremony depicting ministers in vigil pose around the bed of Bra Joe—gangster, killer, car thief, bank robber, arms trader, military commander, police informer, businessman, Defense Minister, decorated national hero and bon viveur.

Johnson's column in *London Review of Books* was described as "often stacked with the superficial and the racist" by seventy-three writers, academics and cultural figures, in a letter published in the *Guardian* newspaper, on 21 July 2010, and however uncomfortable Johnson's death-bed scene reads to those who supported the ANC in their long struggle for justice and equality against a heartless apartheid regime inside Southern Africa - often in the face of unsympathetic and hostile rebuke from western Governments, in particular the Reagan administration in Washington and the Tories under Thatcher, who is on the record as describing Nelson Mandela and his ANC comrades as "terrorists" - it does raise the question of how we should now regard many of these men and women who have failed to live up to the values they set themselves.

In his book, *South Africa's Brave New World,* Johnson accuses Modise of ordering the murder of Chris Hani, the 51-year-old leader of the SACP, and Chief of Staff of Umkhonto we Sizwe (MK), the paramilitary wing of the ANC, who was shot dead in the driveway of his home in Dawn Park, a racially-mixed suburb of Boksburg, in Gauteng Province. At the time of his death in April 1993, Hani was regarded as the most popular ANC leader after Nelson Mandela, with significant support among former MK activists and the SACP's Young Communist League (YCL). His support for the negotiated end to apartheid was critical, and his age and popularity, had he lived, would have made him a strong candidate to succeed Mandela. "Everything points to Modise," Johnson writes, "he alone had a compelling motive to kill Hani, the seniority as MK commander to represent his decisions as those of the ANC and the necessary access to MK intelligence to play a role from the shadows." Modise was a protégé of Mbeki, and although Johnson reluctantly concedes that Mbeki may not have known of the 'plot' to kill Hani, he protected Modise in his rise to the top of the ANC, especially in relation to SDP corruption allegations. There's no doubt that Hani posed a threat to the political ambitions of both men. At the ANC's first National Executive Committee leadership elections in 1991, Hani challenged Mbeki for the ANC's deputy presidency. Many delegates disapproved of a divisive and sometimes bitter internal brouhaha because the ANC, with the whole world watching, wanted to project a more moderate image. Eventually a compromise candidate was agreed— Walter Sisulu, a member of the ANC since 1940, former Robben Islander, and Mandela's closest friend and political ally for almost a half century.

The simmering tensions within the ANC almost descended into anarchy during Hani's funeral, according to Andrew Feinstein, when gunfire was heard as the coffin was being lowered into the ground. A relatively unknown member of the ANC, Tokyo Sexwale, a close friend and neighbor of Hani, who was first on the scene in Dawn Park, and was photographed "weeping over the bloodied body of his friend and comrade" grabbed a microphone and ordered a ceasefire "with an authority that quelled the shooting." Sexwale later served almost four years as premier of Gauteng province. He was exonerated of being involved in a plot to depose Mbeki in 2001. When he was later refused a visa to enter the US to attend the New York Stock Exchange (NYSE) listing of Gold Fields, a mining company in which he had a 15 percent shareholding, it emerged during a threat of legal action that many leading ANC anti-apartheid activists, including Mandela, were originally on the US Immigration and Naturalization Service (INS) list, and on the post-9/11 Department of Homeland Security's list of global terrorists.

No direct connection between the ANC leadership and Chris Hani's assassination has ever been proved. Indeed R.W. Johnson's 700-page tome has been described by the *Guardian*'s local correspondent, David Beresford, as a "record of pretty well every piece of unsubstantiated gossip to have circulated in South Africa's rumor mills" and whose "defense against plagiarism is to list 1,500 footnotes, mostly newspaper references."

A Polish immigrant and member of the far-right Afrikaner Weerstandsbeweging (AWB), Janusz Walus, was arrested shortly after leaving the scene of the crime, still in possession of the Z88 pistol he had used to kill Hani that had been given to him by South African Conservative Party MP, Clive Derby-Lewis. A hit-list was discovered during a search of the MP's home which included the names of Mandela and Joe Slovo (whom Hani had succeeded as head of the SACP). Chris Hani was number three on the list, and the motive for his murder was part of a so-called "strategy of tension" by the extreme right to undermine negotiations between the ANC and the National Party for a peaceful transition to majority rule. Both Walus and Derby-Lewis were convicted of conspiracy to murder on 14 October 1993 by Witwatersrand Local Division of the Supreme Court, and sentenced to death. This was later commuted to life imprisonment when the Constitutional Court abolished the death penalty in June 1995, following the ANC's landslide victory in the previous year's general election. Both men applied for amnesty when they appeared before the Truth and Reconciliation Commission (TRC) claiming the assassination was a politically motivated act carried out on the orders of the Conservative Party. The application was rejected by the TRC which ruled, on 7 April 1999, that the men had not been ordered to kill Hani, and had failed to make a full disclosure of all relevant facts relating to the crime. A parole application was rejected by Cape High Court, on 17 March 2009. One assumes that if they had something more to say to secure their release, they'd have said it then. Joe Modise was a decade dead, and his mentor, Thabo Mbeki, was no longer a serious player in South African politics having been soundly trashed, politically, by Jacob Zuma.

Padraig O'Malley, in *Shades of Difference,* describes how Mac Maharaj, the former MK activist, who was imprisoned on Robben Island following the Little Rivonia sabotage trial, toiled in the stone quarry alongside Mandela, secretly transcribed Mandela's book, *Long Walk to Freedom,* and helped smuggle it out of the Table Bay-located prison, in 1976, had his contribution to the struggle forgotten and his political career destroyed, after falling out of favor with President Mbeki. O'Malley quotes Mac Maharaj:

> When you look at allegations of corruption, you find investigations are extremely selective. All things being equal, if you are perceived to be a friend of the President's or within his political circle, the less likely there is of being investigated by the Scorpions. In a certain sense corruption and abuse are two sides of the same coin. In the case of corruption, people in positions of power use their positions in a manner contrary to the statutory obligations prescribing the way in which that power can be used.

Times change. Mac Maharaj - once praised by Feinstein as having one of the sharpest analytical minds in politics, whose "words are always wise"- is back in town, once again a friend of the President and making sure it stays that way by unleashing the Hawks on *City Press* and other branches of the media who might revisit his past.

The Zuma Tapes

The DSO was an investigative unit of the National Prosecuting Authority (NPA), and its 530 staff were considered by many to be the best financial, forensic and intelligence specialists in the country. In June 2008 the ANC Government decided to merge the DSO with the South African Police's high-level crime unit, the Directorate of Priority Crime Investigations (DPCI) following a sustained campaign by ANC officials in the wake of the conviction of Zuma's friend and financial mentor, Schabir Shaik. The decision to put the Scorpions "under new management" came at a time when lawyers acting for President Zuma were preparing to request a permanent stay of prosecution on money-laundering, racketeering, corruption and graft charges at Pietermaritzburg High Court, before Judge Chris Nicholson.

The Scorpions' days had been numbered since officers from the unit served an indictment on the future president the previous December. Conviction on any one of the charges listed would have meant a mandatory prison term of more than 12 months, and the end of Zuma's political career. On 12 September, Judge Nicholson dismissed the corruption charges on procedural grounds, and suggested "willful interference" by the Government headed by Zuma's political rival, President Thabo Mbeki, who had appointed Zuma as deputy president in 1999. Zuma's appointment came as "something of a surprise" according to Feinstein, because Mangosuthu Buthelezi, founder of the Inkatha Freedom Party (IKP) had turned it down, and Zuma, a former ANC senior intelligence officer and party leader in KwaZulu-Natal, was "generally perceived" as a good replacement "who wouldn't harbor ambitions for the top position." Mbeki has made many decisions (and errors of judgment) in his political career, but he'll regret few more than the elevation of the man who would become his nemesis.

It was only a matter of time before the remaining charges were dropped by the NPA. At a press conference on 6 April 2009, the chief prosecutor and acting head of the NPA, Mokothedi Mpshe, referred to the political intervention which had tainted the prosecution. He accused Leonard McCarthy, former head of the DSO and former NPA boss, Bulelani Ngcuka, of manipulating the legal system, claiming that the "abuse of process" uncovered in taped conversations between the two men in which the timing of the charges to cause the most political damage to Zuma was discussed, was the reason why the charges were dropped. The decision was not based on the merits of the case, Mpshe explained, and did not "amount to an acquittal" but McCarty's conduct "offends one's sense of justice [and] it would be unfair as well as unjust to continue with the prosecution." Central to the misconduct was the timing of the NPA charges against Zuma, according to Mpshe, because any timing of the charging of an accused person which is not aimed at serving a legitimate purpose is "improper, irregular and an abuse of process. It is not so much the prosecution itself that is tainted, but the legal process."

Transcripts of the Zuma SIGINT tapes had been leaked to Zuma's lawyer, Michael Hulley, by a former SAPS Criminal Intelligence boss, Mulangi Mphego, according to two sources quoted in the *M&G,* on 21 May 2010. Mphego, who had authorized the bugging of McCarthy, had traveled to KwaZulu-Natal where Zuma was staying at the home of "long time associate" Erwin Ullbricht, while his legal team was preparing to appeal his corruption case to the Constitutional Court, and played the encrypted recordings, which required "highly sophisticated and restricted software" provided by Mphego. A third unnamed source, who had "senior level insight into police intelligence," told the newspaper that only Mphego could authorize access to the code used to protect the decryption keys on the recording. During the KwaZulu-Natal meeting arrangements were made to make the tapes and the decryption software available to Hulley.

At the press conference Mbshe told journalists that there was no "conclusive evidence" that Thabo Mbeki had attempted to manipulate the legal system for political ends while in office. He had also quoted from the monitored conversations (which took place just prior to the ANC's Polokwane Conference in December 2007, where Zuma was elected leader of the party) in which McCarthy and Ngcuka, using codenames such as 'Ouboet' for former SAPS boss and Interpol President, Jackie Selebi, and referred to Zuma as 'Oujan' and Mbeki as 'Number One' and the 'Fellow' while discussing the timing of recharging Zuma. The following day the leadership of the ANC and its alliance partners, the ANC Youth League, the South African Communist

Party (SACP) and the Congress of South African Trade Unions (COSATU) accompanied Jacob Zuma to the High Court in Durban where the charges against him were officially struck off. Some of those who were there that day would later regret their unconditional support for Zuma when he moved to take control of the investigative agencies by promoting his own people into positions of authority, and to compromise press freedom in November 2011.

An investigation into the leaked recordings was conducted by the former Inspector General of Intelligence, Zolile Ngcakani, and his report was presented to the parliamentary standing committee on such matters before his retirement in December 2009. The report is still "being considered" but various media sources have suggested that while the "finger of suspicion" points to senior South African Police Service (SAPS) officials, no single individual had been blamed for the breach of security.

It later emerged, following an analysis of transcripts and sworn testimony in several high-profile criminal trials over a five-year period between 2004 and 2009, that key members of the Scorpions had been deliberately targeted in a joint SAPS/National Intelligence Agency (NIA) operation, codenamed *Destroy Lucifer*, which seriously undermined organized criminal investigations, including the NPA's abandoned prosecution of Zuma. According to the *M&G* which collated and analyzed the data, the SAPS/NIA operation was launched in 2000 to covertly monitor the NPA to discover what evidence the DSO had on suspended National Police Commissioner, Jackie Selebi, who had been under investigation on corruption, fraud and racketeering charges. Selebi was accused by the NPA of allegedly receiving $170,000 from convicted criminal, Glenn Agliotti. He was also accused of failing to take action against a Chinese drug trafficking cartel in the Western Cape, headed by Mrs. 'Mommy' Chen, following a "massive drug bust" of the sedative Mandrax, known as Quaaludes in the US and 'buttons' in South Africa, where it is usually crushed and smoked in a pipe with a mixture of tobacco and cheap, low-grade marijuana. Because of its price, about $2.50 a hit, it is the recreational drug of choice among South Africa's low-income communities. Mommy Chen's Mandrax was hidden among boxes of tiles, and Agliotti was the source, according to the NPA.

Operation *Destroy Lucifer* was also used to compromise the former Cape Town-based DSO investigator, Ivor Powell, when NPA acting head, Mokothedi Mpshe, ordered an investigation into McCarthy, Powell and other NPA officials following leaks to the *M&G* and *City Press* about SAPS failure to move against Cape criminals, including Igshaan Davids. On 22 January 2008 Powell was arrested allegedly while driving under the influence of alcohol. According to the *M&G* the DSO man had been set up by a registered crime intelligence informer, Franklin Gray, who had earlier that day attended a meeting between Powell and Davids, where Powell was attempting to recruit Davids as a HUMINT source to obtain information about crime networks linking Western Cape and Guateng drug and abalone syndicates.

The damage done by SAPS to serious crime investigation practices was revealed in the case of Philip du Toit, an expert in electronic surveillance and a registered NPA source, despite two arrests in connection with abalone smuggling, a profitable business, managed by syndicates who also trafficked in drugs.

Du Toit had access to the same organized crime networks as Davids, and had also succeeded in getting close to the mysterious Stanley Lau, a Chinese criminal mastermind wanted by the authorities in Beijing since 2003 for narcotics trafficking, including the 10,000lbs Mandrax shipment to South Africa. This was precisely why the NPA had recruited du Toit. However, his cover was blown when he was arrested at his home by SAPS in September 2007, and charged with abalone smuggling. One of those involved in the raid was SAPS liaison officer for *Destroy Lucifer* in the Western Cape, which gave rise to suggestions that the raid was not about edible sea snails trafficking, but was a hunt for surveillance tapes implicating former Cape Town mayor, Helen Zille, leader of the parliamentary opposition, Democratic Alliance (DA) in the illegal SIGINT spying on councilor, Badih Chaaban, a member of the Africa Muslim Party (AMP) who was allegedly involved in corrupt business practices in the city when the ANC ran the council, and in an attempt with ANC councilors to topple the Zille-led DA coalition. There were also rumors about the existence of another set of tapes that could seriously embarrass the former ANC Western Cape premier, Ebrahim Rasool, a veteran of the anti-apartheid struggle since the mid-1970s, who was fired by the party's National Executive Council in July 2008, three months before the NEC 'retired' President Thabo Mbeki, following a report which inferred Mbeki's "improper interference" in the NPA's prosecution of Jacob Zuma.

The ANC in the Western Cape was divided into two main factions, according to Feinstein - the Africanists, headed by the province's General Secretary, Mcedesi Skwatcha, and James Ngculu, both National Assembly and NEC members, and a non-racial grouping around the provincial leader, Rasool, who were involved "in a battle [which was] as much about control of the province as ideological differences or race" and which "blighted the ANC in the Western Cape." It was Zuma's followers in the Western Cape Legislature in 2007 who supported the opposition-instigated inquiry into Mbeki-supporting Rasool, when Mbeki's supporters began to highlight Zuma's well-known crimes and misdemeanors because it suited the incumbent president to move against his former deputy. The bitter struggle between the two men was marked by "intemperate language [and] verbal indiscipline" such as the "notorious outburst" by the ANC Youth League leader, Julies Malema, at a rally in Thaba Nchu, a town in Free State Province on 16 June 2008, when he told the Youth Day rally: "We are prepared to die for Zuma. We are prepared to take-up arms and kill for Zuma." As Feinstein observes, even if this was "hyperbolic passion" or a threat to those threatening to prosecute Zuma for corruption, it was nevertheless "remarkable in a country,

The Itching Palm

ravaged by violent crime and recent attacks against immigrants that Jacob Zuma, sitting behind Malema on the stage that day, chose not to dampen or criticize in any way the remarks or sentiments of his most vocal supporter." A few days later the COSATU leader, a former uranium plant clerk at Vaal Reefs gold mine, and a member of the National Union of Miners (NUM) who led the Anglo Gold strike in 1987, stated that COSATU's rank and file were also prepared to die and kill for Zuma.

In the Western Cape, and other provinces where the power struggle dominated the politics of the day, dozens of local, regional and provincial meetings were frequently disrupted by verbal abuse, mayhem and serious violence, which culminated in a near-fatal stabbing at a party meeting in Worcester, the largest town in Western Cape's interior region. There were political purges across South Africa after Mbeki's resignation. It was "a season of political cannibalism in which nobody was safe" according to former ANC and SACP leader, Phillip Dexter, quoted in the Johannesburg-based, *Business Day* newspaper, on 3 December 2008. And while all this was taking place at the national and provincial level, two DSO agents, who attempted to salvage the Du Toit operation after he was "outed and deregistered" by the NPA, were "temporarily arrested" and warned not to get involved in the case by SAPS officers in Atlantis, a 'community' town established by the apartheid regime to house Cape Town's racially-restricted and ethnically-diverse Colored population.

For No Good Reason

The case of Jacob 'Jackie' Sello Selebi illustrates the tragedy of the "beloved country" under a corrupt regime. Like many of his comrades he had lived in exile in Zambia during the anti-apartheid struggle in the 1980s, was appointed to the ANC National Executive in 1987, and took responsibility for the repatriation of the exiles after 'Madiba' Mandela's release from Robben Island, the isolated prison used, initially by Dutch colonists, for political prisoners in the 17th century.

Elected to the National Assembly in June 1994, he served as ambassador to the United Nations for three years before his appointment in 1998 as director of the Ministry of Foreign Affairs. Two years later he was appointed SAPS national commissioner, and was elected vice-president of the international law enforcement organization, Interpol, (Africa region) in 2002, and two years later became president of the world's second largest intergovernmental organization, (after the UN), with 190 member states. During his four-year tenure he served as chair of the Anti-Landmine Conference in Oslo, chair of the Justice, Crime Preservation and Security Commission, and chair of the 54th session of the UN's Human Rights Commission. Selebi was a powerful, influential and internationally respected figure in South Africa and abroad. His webpage on *Who's Who (Southern Africa)* includes related profiles of South Africa presidents Mbeki and Zuma, EU Human Rights Foundation member and Constitutional Court trustee, Vusi Pikoli, former NPA boss Menzi Sinelane, former Director of Public Prosecutions (DPP), Mokothedi Mpshe, murdered business tycoon, Brett Kebble, and convicted felon, Glenn Agliotti.

But despite his public achievements he was also an arrogant man, an individual full of his own sense of achievement who responded to concern about the rising crime rate which had taken South Africa close to the top of the world's violent crime list with a dismissive comment, "what's all the fuss about crime" and he reportedly had called a female SAPS officer a "chimpanzee" after she failed to recognize him when he walked into a police station shortly after being appointed national commissioner.

He was personally ordered to take an "extended leave of absence" by Mbeki on 12 January 2008. He resigned as Interpol president the following day, after being accused of corruption, racketeering and fraud by the NPA in connection with receiving payments totaling R-1.2 million ($157,000) over a five-year period from Agliotti (whom Selebi once described as a close friend), from slain mining magnate Kebble, and from former Hyundai (SA) chief executive, Billy Rautenbach, "in return for favors." After several delays, which Judge Meyer Joffe warned would "tarnish the country's judicial system," the trial began in October 2009 and soon ran into procedural difficulties. It resumed six months later in the South Guateng High Court in Johannesburg following a failed attempt by the State Security Ministry to prevent a former chairman of the National Intelligence Coordinating Committee (NICC) from testifying about a 2005 draft intelligence document containing a reference to several allegedly "untoward payments" Selebi received from Brett Kebble, who was shot dead by unknown gunmen in Melrose, an affluent tree-lined suburb of Johannesburg, on 27 September 2005. The low velocity rounds which killed Kebble, who had strong business and political ties with Jacob Zuma and the ANC Youth League, required a specially-adapted pistol mainly used by bodyguards and state security officers to prevent bullets passing through targets and causing collateral damage to hostages or innocent bystanders. On 27 October 2008, the NPA deputy director produced a report which concluded that Kebble's death was a "self-assisted suicide" and provided a list of fifty witnesses whom the prosecution claimed would prove that Agliotti, and Kebble's former business partner, John Stratton, were involved in the plot. The list included nineteen police and forensic witnesses, two paramedics who attended the crime scene within minutes, three IT specialists, a sushi restaurant staff member and several residents of Melrose.

Also on the list was a self-confessed drug dealer, who admitted hiring the gunmen, but the shooters' names were not included. The NPA admitted, however, that "precisely when, where and in what manner the common purpose was formed is, at present, unknown to the state." Although the Northern Cape High Court Judge never actually ruled that Kebble's death was an assisted suicide, he did grant indemnity from prosecution to three Johannesburg underworld figures, who were involved, implying that he believed them. They later "spoke candidly" to an *Eyewitness News* journalist, as did Glenn Agliotti, who also testified for the prosecution in return for immunity for offences relating to the case at Selebi's trial when it resumed, without further interference, on 8 April 2010.

From the witness box Agliotti told the court he had given small amounts (R-5,000 to 10,000) in "cash stuffed envelopes" to the accused since 2000, shortly after he met Selebi, who had asked him for money to pay medical bills. Later payments were worth R-120,000 and R-200,000. He also said that the two men became friends, and would meet, with their wives, at Sandton City, an up-market shopping center in Johannesburg: "When the accused and I met, I enjoyed shopping and so did he. Him being my friend, I would instruct shop attendants to put all the clothes on my account. For the accused wife's birthday I wanted to buy her a Louis Vatton handbag from Sandton, a red patent one [that] cost 10,000 rand." He also claimed to have acted as a go-between for Selebi and Brett Kebble, who wanted the SAPS commissioner to stop an investigation into alleged "accounting discrepancies" amounting to R-2 billion-worth of Randgold Resources shares.

Lawyers acting for Selebi argued that the charges were part of a "politically-motivated conspiracy" orchestrated by the NPA because their client was a close ally of former President Mbeki, a bitter rival of Jacob Zuma, who had claimed in his defense against corruption charges that he had been the victim of a similar plot, orchestrated by Mbeki's supporters. On 2 July 2010, Jackie Selebi was found guilty of corruption, and sentenced to 15 years. In his summary the judge, a former director of the South Africa Judicial Institute (SAJI), described the defendant as a man of "low moral fiber" who had shown "complete contempt for the truth." Selebi was released on R-20,000 (US$2,745) bail pending appeal, but the sentence was upheld by the Supreme Court of Appeal, on 2 December 2011.

Yet, despite the evidence of Jackie Selebi's guilt, and the 15 year sentence which reflected the grave nature of the offences, a sentence supported after due consideration by senior figures at the highest level of the South African judicial system, there are still those holding influential positions in South African society who believe the whole affair has been a travesty and a grave injustice. Men like Mosibudi Mangena, President of the Azanian People's Organization (AZAPO) and the former Minister for Science and Technology in the Mbeki Cabinet (until Mbeki's resignation in 2008) who called on President Zuma to show mercy and pardon the former police chief for his crimes on health grounds. In an op-ed piece also carried by the *Pretoria News* shortly after the Supreme Court of Appeal upheld Selebi's conviction, a former South African diplomat, Abbey Makoe, had blamed former President Mbeki for removing Selebi from his position as Director of Foreign Affairs after just 17 months, and putting him in charge of the police, and ultimately, "on the road to perdition." However, Dr Greg Mills, director of the South Africa Institute of International Affairs (SAIIA), believes that

Mbeki came under pressure from Foreign Minister Nkosazana Dlamini-Zuma, (ex-wife of Jacob Zuma) whose "management style and attitude" had led to a falling out with Selebi.

Mangena's plea for clemency was supported by Isaac Mpho Mogotsi, executive director of the Centre for Economic Diplomacy in Africa (CEDIA) in a feature article posted, on 7 February 2012, on the on-line news source, *Politicsweb*, describing Selebi as a "truly great diplomat" who alongside Mandela and Mbeki was in the forefront of South Africa's "re-integration into the fold of community of nations following the end of the apartheid era." However, while Selebi was arguably the country's "most successful multilateral diplomat so far" and despite suggesting a character flaw which made Selebi seems like as "a bad accident waiting to happen," Mogotsi quotes from Thomas Carlyle's *On Heroes, Hero-Worship and the Heroic in History* to explain Selebi's behavior, providing in some respects an epitaph for his career: "Their heroism lay in their creative energy in the face of difficulties, not in their moral perfection."

And therein lies the dilemma for South Africa. Simply quoting from a 19th century Scottish Calvinist preacher and essayist does not excuse Selebi's behavior, nor those of his compatriots in times of war and peace. Men like Jacob Zuma, who appears never to have let his conscience get in the way of doing what was wrong. Power corrupts? It's a well-worn cliché but it's all we have to explain why these men changed, changed utterly. All we have to explain the greed and avarice of men who lived in exile for years and risked freedom and their lives in a morally-justified armed struggle against the pervasive evils of apartheid. Who took power after the ANC's landslide victory in June 1994, and then went for the fast buck.

The Man from MI6

Patricia De Lille wasn't the only parliamentarian to suggest that the end of the DSO was the "final excuse" not to investigate ANC corruption in high places. Administrative changes in other areas of law enforcement also hampered investigations. The NPA, for example, was unable to respond to a request from German prosecutors in 2007, asking for assistance in their investigation into alleged corrupt business practices involving ThyssenKrupp, the Düsseldorf-based company that supplied South Africa with four corvettes, because the documents were held by the Justice Ministry, and the NPA request for a copy of the German letter was ignored by the then Justice Minister. When Brigitte Mabandla briefly replaced him the following year the NPA refilled its request and was told that the letter had been returned to Germany for clarification. The manipulated chaos and disruption which De Lille had warned about was illustrated during hearings of the cross-party (but ANC dominated) Select Committee on Public Accounts (SCOPA) which was hurriedly examining new evidence relating to the estimated $4.5 billion SDP purchases when the committee was told by the NPA's Mokothedi Mpshe, that he had only learned about the German request for assistance from newspaper reports. It was later reported that the German prosecutors had abandoned their investigation "because of the lack of co-operation from their South African counterparts."

SCOPA was anxious to get as much work done as possible before interim President Kgalema Motlanthe (who had succeeded Mbeki the previous September) announced the date of the forthcoming general election, which meant automatic dissolution of the current committee. Opposition MPs believed that the SDP inquiry would be shelved by a post-election, ANC-controlled, SCOPA, and their pessimism proved correct. But not before the outgoing committee received submissions from private individuals whose offers to testify in person were turned down by ANC committee members. The offer of a former secretary for defense to provide information on the Defense Ministry's procurement procedures was rejected by Don Gumede, MP, who told the ex-civil servant that there was "nothing new in what he had to say," while Vincent Smith, MP, told lawyer and author, Paul Holden, a former member of the Center for Constitutional Rights, that the information he had to offer should be sent to the NPA, not SCOPA. Instead Mr. Holden went home, and decided to include the information in his excellent book, *The Arms Deal in your Pocket*. Richard Young, an arms dealer turned whistle-blower, also offered information about the extensive rewriting of a report into the arms procurement process, including the offset agreements which are alleged to be the prime sources of corruption, and involve the Department of Trade and Industry (DTI) which deals with the civilian National Participation Program (NIPP) and ARMSCOR, which handles the Defense Industrial Participation Program (DIPP). He was told by Mr. Smith that SCOPA had already carried out a "thorough investigation in that aspect of the affair a few years ago."

This may be a reference to the two-part investigation into false accounting by ARMSCOR carried out by CIEX, a UK-based assets recovery agency, which was initially contacted by senior ANC politicians in 1997 to investigate corruption linked to arms procurement under the previous apartheid regime, and two years later, according to CIEX officials, the agency was "officially tasked by the President" to do "almost precisely the same thing." Perhaps the late 1990s seemed like a good time for Mr. Mbeki and his ANC colleagues to check out ARMSCOR to learn some lessons in the fine art of corrupt business practices, including how not to get caught. Despite the wealth of economics degrees available there's no third-level textbook that teaches this sort of thing, but it could be learned by studying the ARMSCOR files, see how the professionals got the job done.

CIEX was founded by former MI6 agent, Michael Oatley, who headed secret talks with Sinn Fein's Martin McGuinness which paved the way for the IRA's ceasefire and a settlement of the conflict in the North of Ireland. Oatley, with his connections in the underbelly of British intelligence, knew that corrupt ARMSCOR officials had provided the fire-power for loyalist gunmen who had been used as proxy assassins by British Military Intelligence and the Security Service, MI5, to almost destroy the peace process, and the ex-MI6 man took his job very seriously. CIEX is an arcane reference to CX reports, MI6's weekly intelligence summaries, routed to senior members of the British Cabinet responsible for the Foreign and Commonwealth Office (FCO), the Ministry of Defense (MoD) and other relevant ministries, as well as the Joint Intelligence Committee (JIC). CX reports were also available to corporate 'liaison officers' who "rewrite them as memos for restricted internal distribution." Not surprisingly defense manufacturers are the most important recipients, although many of the multinationals in the arms trade have their own independent economic intelligence sources and specialists, who often produce more accurate (and unredacted) data than MI6, which is subject to the Official Secrets Act with regard to what it can pass on to 'outsiders.' Stephen Dorril, in his book on MI6, refers to an interview a former MI6 officer, New Zealand-born, Richard Tomlinson, gave to the UK financial newspaper, *Sunday Business,* in November 1998, where he claimed that MI6 helped BAE Systems win a controversial deal in 1993 to supply Indonesia with twenty-four Hawk trainer jets for almost $800 million "by supplying details of a competing bid from French aircraft manufacturer, Dassault." Similar CX intelligence summaries were provided to help the company secure a $2.5 billion defense package for Malaysia, which included Tornado jets fighters and Hawk trainers, a deal that was partly financed by the secretive defense division of the London-based Midland Bank Plc.

It's safe to assume that BAE received CX summaries when the ANC's SDP 'wish-list' was drawn up by Joe Modise and his advisers/agents. Indeed, Michael Oatley was the agency's African specialist who also served in the Middle East, and had worked for another intelligence-linked consultancy, Kroll Associates, before setting up CIEX, which quickly "cornered a lucrative market in providing a restricted confidential service in strategic advice and intelligence for a small group of very substantial customers" and may have had a hand in writing-up the original briefing reports on the state of South Africa's Armed Forces, on which the CX hardcopy reports later provided to BAE were based. Former members of Her Majesty's Secret Intelligence Service, when they leave Vauxhall Bridge HQ in central London for the private sector, never stray too far from the reservation.

In part one of his report on ARMSCOR, Oatley examines allegations of how more than R-26.1 billion was siphoned from public funds through several illegal transactions - money that should have been spent on housing, health and education. One specific payment of R-3.2 to Bankorp, one of the banks that later formed Amalgamated Banks of South Africa (ABSA), was investigated after an official commission of inquiry, chaired by Judge William Heath, had found the payment "irregular" but did not recommend that the banks or its investors be made to repay the funds. Judge Heath was a member of the apartheid National Party who had served on the bench in the former homeland of Ciskei. He came across as a "rather grey accountant" according to Feinstein, but was, in fact, one of the country's post-1994 "leading crusaders against corruption" and his Special Investigation Unit (SIU) had built up a "tenacious reputation" for getting the job done. When the unit claimed to have uncovered "significant evidence" of corruption surrounding the SDP, the ANC hierarchy successfully moved to exclude Judge Heath from having anything to do with the SDP.

Apart from the ABSA cash, there was also between R-3 to R-6 billion paid to Sanlam & Rembrandt, major investors in Bankorp, and "up to R-5.5 billion" to the French/German aerospace manufacturer, Aerospatiale/ DaimlerChrysler AG, all of which could still be recovered, according to CIEX. Thabo Mbeki, deputy president at the time CIEX began its forensic examination of the money trail, and his colleagues, the former finance minister, Trevor Manuel, and the former labor minister, Tito Mboweni, were all aware of the possibilities of recovering the cash which had been looted from state coffers, but did nothing. When CIEX's formal contract was suspended, on 31 December 1998, the assets recovery bureau was "informally tasked" - without remuneration - to continue its investigation into ABSA/ARMSCOR payment and bond issues "with the assurance that the contract could be revived" after the June 1999 general election. CIEX went on, in good faith, to discover that ARMSCOR had siphoned off a further R-14,4 billion using Luxembourg bank accounts, managed through the South African embassy in Paris. Other schemes include one in which US suppliers and South African government officials, between 1987 and 1993, "collaborated to defraud" the Government "by ordering large items of expensive equipment which were paid for but not delivered." Legal opinion, obtained by CIEX, supported the assets recovery option, and the report suggested that Swiss, German and French banks, which were sympathetic to the apartheid regime, could be subpoenaed.

When Thabo Mbeki succeeded Nelson Mandela as South Africa's second post-apartheid president, following the June election, the formal contract with CIEX was not renewed, and the various strands of the corruption inquiries "which began at official expense and continued at our own expense and which offered considerable political and financial rewards to the [post-apartheid] Government, according to Oatley, were "left hanging in the air."

Billy Masetlha, ANC NEC member and former head of the Pretoria-based National Intelligence Agency (NIA) formed in 1994 with responsibility for domestic and counter-intelligence, was one of the co-signatories of the CIEX report. He was sacked by Mbeki, and the report remained TOP SECRET until advocate, Paul Hoffman, head of the Institute for Accountability in South Africa (IASA), obtained a copy in October 2010, and submitted it to the State Public Protector's office, one of the 'Chapter 9 Institutions' established under the South African Constitution, with a mandate to "guard democracy" and investigate, on the basis of a public complaint or on its own initiative, any level of government (national provincial or local,) any public office bearer, or any state-owned corporation or enterprise. The SPP incumbent, lawyer and former Law Reform Commissioner, Thulisile Madonsela, admitted that previous ANC administrations had done nothing to retrieve the looted funds, but claimed her office did not have the resources "to investigate the extent of the plundering" and pursue the matter. Some time later came a more considered response, with SPP spokesperson, Oupa Segalwe, saying that Ms. Madonsela had the legal discretion not to pursue any case "older that two years" under the Public Protector Act (PPA) and had concluded that the end result of an investigation "does not merit the resources required."

This, of course, is a wholly feeble excuse for all that has happened since ARMSCOR, the ABSA and other local and foreign firms and financial institutions named in the CIEX report made off with the cash. No investigation into corruption could simply draw a line in the sand, in June 1994, and ignore the corrupt opportunities and malevolent practices which the ANC's arms procurement program provided. Several of the most serious allegation made in the CIEX report had been supported in a 113-page study back in 2006, *Apartheid Grand Corruption: Assessing the scale of Crimes of Profit in South Africa from 1976 to 1994,* by Hennie van Vuuren, head of the Institute for Security Studies (ISS) corruption and governance department, and submitted to the National Anti-Corruption Forum (NACF) The ISS report called for "serious action to be taken against those who had looted state coffers" and according to Van Vuuren, it should have been up to the NPA "but they have failed at prosecuting apartheid [economic] crimes as if they never happened." The same charge could be made against the SPO, and when Van Vuuren suggested that Ms. Madonsela should have referred the case to the NPA and asked the National Assembly for extra resources to pursue the matter "rather than wish it away," one wonders what he saw as the difference between apartheid and post-apartheid crimes of profit and which merited further investigation, and which deserved to be covered-up and ignored.

Interim President Kgalema Motlanthe's decision, on 29 January 2009, to finally enact the South African Police Service Amendment Bill, and the National Prosecuting Authority (NPA) Amendment Bill , and officially disband the multidiscipline DSO Scorpions "marked a dark day in our short democratic history" according to Dianne Kohler-Barnard, spokesperson for the Democratic Alliance (DA). The legislation transferred investigative power to SAPS, and gave an ANC-dominated ministerial committee the authority to decide what criminal behavior the replacement specialist unit, the Directorate for Priority Crime Investigation (DPCI), should focus on. With several corruption scandals still dominating the political agenda, there were justifiable concerns among independent political and judicial analysts that political expediency had played a part in Motlanthe's timing and decision in order to salvage the political careers of allegedly corrupt politicians prior to the 22 April general election, including the career of Jacob Zuma. These concerns were underlined by reports circulating among the political establishment, and referred to in the media, that Zuma's former lawyer would be appointed the new DPP. However, the decision was welcomed by the ANC, which continued to propagate the myth that senior party officials had nothing to do with all of this, and by COSATU, which had campaigned for several years to have the DSO disbanded. COSATU spokesperson, Patrick Craven, claimed that the unit had evolved into an "elite, unaccountable force" which had been "redirected from the fight against organized crime to political campaigns against individuals" and had "undermined the legal rights of those they were investigating."

The next move to keep a lid on things was made by NPA director Menzi Simelane, who ordered the Asset Forfeiture Bureau (AFB) headed by the deputy director of national prosecutions, Willie Hofmeyr, not to proceed against Fana Hlongwane, former adviser to the late Joe Modise, who had, allegedly, accepted off-the-books payments from BAE, and whose greed had also benefited Mbeki and Zuma. During the course of its investigation the DSO had carried out raids on multiple premises used by BAE and Hlongwane in December 2008, and confiscated files which confirmed that the British company had paid over R-1 billion in undeclared fees and commissions. Shortly after he had been appointed to take charge of the NPA by President Zuma, in December 2009 - despite a statutory commission, headed by senior ANC member, Frene Ginwala, describing him as "unfit" for the job because of his interference in the investigation of Jackie Selebi - Simelane visited the NPA officers in Cape Town to be briefed on the ongoing Hlongwane investigation. This included requests from the authorities in Liechtenstein (that landlocked central European principality with an ambiguous banking system) who had frozen two suspicious bank accounts containing R-35 million registered to Hlongwane. In early 2008 a Liechtenstein judge wrote to the NPA stating that it was suspected that the accounts were "linked with active and passive bribery and corruption [by BAE] using a system of international representation" and that a local court order relating to one of the accounts was due to expire on 14 March "unless renewed by a South African court."

Two weeks before the expiration date the AFB obtained an "extra-territorial application preservation order" under South Africa's asset-forfeiture legislation, authorizing the attachments of assets suspected of being the proceeds of crime. Under the law this has to be followed, within 90-days, by a final forfeiture application - a three month period to allow the registered owner of the account to contest the application. On 9 March, in the presence of Hofmeyr and two of Hlongwane's legal representatives, the newly appointed NPA boss "all but instructed the lawyers" to make representations on their client's behalf "as to why the matter should not be pursued." According to an unidentified *M&G* source (not authorized to speak to the media) the representation was submitted the following day, and within hours Simelane had ordered Hofmeyr to drop the case. The NPA later issued a statement saying that the primary reason for Simelane's instruction was "that there was no indication of criminal conduct on the part of Mr. Fana Hlongwane at this point. Criminal conduct will be determined by a police investigation and that is a police matter." However, informed legal opinion in South Africa has since been proved correct in suggesting that this development marked the end of the road for one of the "most politically corrosive" of the arms deals investigations.

The ANC under Zuma went on to secure 279 seats in the 400-seater National Assembly, just under 70 percent of the total vote cast in the April 2009 general election. The party's nearest rival, the Democratic Alliance (DA) under Helen Zille, won 50 seats, while a "coalition of the wounded," the Congress of the People (COPE) - founded by former ANC members following the 52nd ANC National Conference at Polokwane, on 18 December 2007, at which Jacob Zuma was elected President of the ANC, beating Thabo Mbeki by 2329 votes to 1505 – won 30 seats

If power corrupts, by this point in time the ANC was eminently corruptible. And one man who had seen this coming but was unable to do anything about it, was Andrew Feinstein, the ranking ANC member of the parliamentary Public Accounts Committee (PAC) who realized corruption was a "huge political issue" when he read the Auditor-General's interim report into the arms procurement program in September 2000, which he describes as a "litany of irregularities, including "conflicts of interest among key decision makers" in awarding contracts to BAE and SAAB, the GFC, a naval sub-contract to a French company "at a substantial increase in costs" over a local company tender, failure to consider staff requirements to operate the high-tech systems purchased and "inadequate offset guarantees."

Feinstein was subjected to vicious and openly hostile denouncements by President Mbeki's inner circle. The first pressure to prevent any further investigation into how the primary hardware contracts, and the sub-contracts, had been secured by the winning tenders, came from ANC chief whip, Tony Vengeni, who began "intimidating" ANC committee members called to a meeting before senior officials, while other ANC parliamentarians were called into Mbeki's office and told "who they could and could not investigate." One senior party member told Feinstein that some of the funds had been used to finance election campaigns and an investigation would embarrass the ANC. "The situation was out of control," he writes, "I was being bullied into accepting the leadership's line and if I didn't it would be clear that I was a traitor with an agenda of my own." Vengeni, who would later serve four months of a four year sentence for accepting bribes from a German company, sacked Feinstein as head of the ANC delegation on the PAC, and told the remaining members that the ANC "from the president down, will now exercise political control."

The final PAC report into corruption was a complete whitewash, concluding there was "no evidence of irregularities" on the part of senior officials and ministers in relation the the SDP. Feinstein resigned from the ANC in 2001, later explaining that the decision to upgrade the defense forces capabilities had cost 10 percent of the country's GDP, and came at a time when the country had no external or internal enemies, but massive social problems, including high unemployment, a failing educational system, millions still living in poverty in overcrowded townships with totally inadequate health and sanitary conditions, and a health service unable to cope with the HIV/AIDS pandemic.

The Money Trail

In London things were becoming increasingly uncomfortable for Britain's senior arms-sales personnel when Andrew Feinstein arrived in town. For almost thirty years a department within the Ministry of Defense (MoD), the Defense Export Services Organization (DESO), founded in the mid-1960s, had promoted the commercial interests of arms manufacturers based in the UK. Apart from promoting exports, the taxpayer-funded DESO was supposed to 'police' the trade to ensure ethical business practices. However, this hived-off entity, traditionally headed by executives from the arms companies, instead diligently fended-off attempts to deal with corruption until the mid-1990s when the Paris-based Organization for Economic Co-operation and Development (OECD) urged member states to tackle overseas bribery, and three years later adopted a binding, anti-corrupting convention, which was signed by Britain in 1998. By this time many of the UK's arms manufacturers, including BAE, had been privatized under the Conservative administration of Prime Minister, Margaret Thatcher, but the DESO was still lobbying for business abroad on behalf of the privatized companies, including massive government-to-government contacts, particularly the Al-Yamamah ('The Dove') arms deal with Saudi Arabia, brokered by Mrs. Thatcher during a visit to Riyadh in the early 1980s. More than 450 civil servants were employed at the DESO under the Tories (and later under Labour) of whom one-third worked specifically on the 'Saudi Armed Forces project' across Britain and the Middle East. Instead of honoring the OECD agreement British officials simply put more distance between HMG and the arms manufacturers, rewriting a 1977 directive stating that DESO and MoD officials would no longer authorize, discuss or correspond about commission payments, merely "consider and advise."

In the mid-1990s, while the OECD was drafting "transparency in business" legislation, BAE began to consider its options to deceive, according to a cache of internal memoranda dating from the period obtained by the Centre for Investigative Journalism (based at City University, London) and Swedish television journalists investigating the SAAB sale of Gripen jets to the SADF as part of a joint R-60 billion arms deal with BAE. The first memo provided details of the company's payments to marketing consultants, middle-men, and fixers helping to facilitate arms sales worldwide. In 1995, at least 225 'brass-plate advisers' were paid an estimated R-275 (US$40) million, while 74 'confidential advisers' received another R-230 (US$35) million. The second memo considered the fine art of deception in all its complexities, stating "it has been suggested that in order to increase security and confidentiality of marketing advisers' payments, consideration should be given to the possibility of making these payments through a company set up for the purpose and given a name which has no connection with BAE. For the purpose of this note the company is called JBL (Joe Bloggs Ltd)."

There were three options of illegality for consideration. The first was for BAE business units to continue to manage the network but pay its 'back-handers' through JBL; however, this was rejected as "too risky" after due deliberation because the "wide circulation in BAE would continue" and while the arrangement might "deter casual observers" it would still be "obvious to anyone investigating." The second option was to transfer liaison with the motley crew of fast-buck merchants from the business units to BAE's Farnborough offices, in Hampshire, but this was rejected as being "too transparent if investigated." The chosen alternative was incorporating an off-shore company "with sufficient expert directors to be credible" to administer the slush fund derived from levies imposed on BAE business units, and transferred from Farnborough "in round block numbers." The advantage included the off-shore storage of files and all paperwork relating to the system, while business units would know virtually nothing, apart from the "sales levy" paid to Farnborough, and optimism that the "arrangements can be justified if investigated and would be difficult to penetrate anyway." There was also a separate memo on how much business units, like SAAB, should raise the price of their products in order to facilitate the slush-fund levy, and the solution was "percentage enhancement increases" covered in BAE company records as "HQ management charges etc."

The secret fund was originally managed from BAE's Marketing Services Division at Warwick House, in Farnborough, and was headed by Hugh Dickinson, who was also responsible for liaison with MI6. BAE, under chief executive and later chairman Sir Richard Evans (educated at the Royal Masonic School in Bushley, Herefordshire, who had joined the company as 'contracts officer' in 1969, and worked his way up through the ranks of management) decided to move all covert paperwork to Switzerland. This was not "illegal per se" but according to the UK's Serious Fraud Office (SFO), when it finally began to take an interest in how BAE did business abroad, it was maintained "in such conditions of secrecy" that there was "legitimate suspicion concerning the real purpose" of the payments.

BAE set up a front company called Novelmight Ltd, and rented offices on the sixth floor of a building at 48 Route des Acacias, in Geneva. Security included CCTV surveillance, and an encrypted fax and telecom system, and specialists were regularly brought in from the UK to sweep the premises for bugs. Just before the Blair administration signed the OECD convention "filing cabinets and safes containing agent details were loaded into a van and driven by trusted staff from Farnborough to Geneva" according to documentation obtained by the SFO, and the *Guardian* newspaper, which successfully defended its persistent coverage of Britain's secretive arms trade when challenged by Conservative Minister of State for Procurement, Jonathan Aitken. Aitken resigned from the Tory Cabinet in 1995 after allegations that a weekend at the Ritz Hotel in Paris had been paid for by Lebanese businessman, Mohammed Said Ayas, a close business associate of Prince Mohammed, son of King Fahd of Saudi Arabia. Aitken's crusade to "cut out the cancer of bent and twisted journalism (...) with the simple sword of truth and the trusty shield of British fair play" ended in the Old Bailey when his libel action against the newspaper and Granada Television collapsed amid further lies and ignominy, in June 1997.

He was eventually charged with perjury and perverting the course of justice, found guilty and sentenced to 18 months in 1999, the same year that BAE de-registered Novelmight in the UK, and re-registered the shell company in Road Town, the capital of the British Virgin Islands, taking advantage of banking anonymity. BAE payments were handled by Swiss lawyers, Cyril Abecassis and Rene Merkt, who also set up parallel offshore companies for agents to receive payment via Swiss bank accounts. Files relating to these arrangement were kept under lock and key in BAE's Geneva office, which had been discretely acquired through the Swiss branch of BAE's bankers, Lloyds TSB, and when necessary Hugh Dickinson, or his deputy, Julia Aldridge, traveled to Switzerland to represent the company at signings. The purpose of using these 'cut outs' was to maintain secrecy and ensure that the hiring of agents and 'middlemen' to act for BAE took place outside UK jurisdiction and EU banking scrutiny which Switzerland, a non-EU country, provided, apart from traditional banking anonymity for 'legitimate' account holders.

In February 1998, according to a US Department of Justice (DoJ) charge sheet, BAE "engaged Uniglobe Aktiengesellschaft, a trust company in Vaduz, Liechtenstein to create Red Diamond Trading Ltd," incorporated in the British Virgin Islands. Although not a BAE subsidiary, Uniglobe structured the shell company so that it could not operate "without BAE's written agreement," and it was used to channel payments, via Red Diamond-registered accounts in London, Geneva and New York, to agents in Chile, the Czech Republic, Tanzania, South Africa, Romania and Qatar, and to pay BAE consultants in the UK, using Lloyds TSB's online 'Lloydslink' to move cash through the bogus company's accounts to various recipients. There were approximately 350 covert agreements with 299 brokers, structured to "circumvent the normal payments reviews." In the nine years of its existence Red Diamond made over 1,000 covert payments to brokers and advisers, including Fana Hlongwane, who helped BAE secure its massive share of the SDP contracts.

The SFO investigation had also followed the money which passed through Red Diamond accounts and in documentation, dated 26 June 2006, submitted with a "mutual legal assistant request" to the DSO, the SFO claimed to have "reasonable cause to believe" that four senior BAE executives - former chairman Sir Dick Evans, the chief executive, Mike Turner, head of marketing, Mike Rouse, and deputy head at Fairnborough sales division, Julia Aldridge - had committed "offences of corruption" involving payments totaling $140 million passing through off-shore, secretive accounts, most of which went to BAE's network of agents in Southern Africa, including Tanzanian middleman, Sailesh Vithlani, and his business partner, Tanil Somaiya.

The Tanzanian anti-corruption bureau had proved more receptive than their South African counterparts in cooperating with the SFO's investigation into the sale of an unnecessary $40 million radar system to one of the world's poorest counties. The decision to use Vithlani, a British passport holder and covert controller of the Panama-registered Envers Trading Corporation, was signed off by Dick Evans. BAE paid $12 million 'commission' into a Swiss account, through Red Diamond and a Tanzanian-registered agency called Merlin International Ltd., yet another shell company whose majority share-holder was Sailesh Vithlani. According to Tanil Somaiya, who was interviewed by SFO officers in Dar es Salaam, BAE made "stage payments" through the Red Diamond network to Merlin's account as the radar equipment was being delivered, and under a second secret agreement the British company paid 30 percent of the radar contract price into a Swiss account controlled by Vithlani. The Tanzanian deal was pushed through the British Parliament by the former Prime Minister, Tony Blair, another unworthy example of the unethical dimension of the Labour administration's foreign policy, which would culminate in the decision to ride shotgun alongside US President, George W. Bush, to force regime change in Iraq in 2003.

After the 9/11 attacks on the World Trade Center and the Pentagon, the US State Department began to take a serious look at BAE following a crackdown on terrorist funding and the transfer of suspicious funds through the world's banking system, under the Foreign Corrupt Practices Act, specifically the financial 'black holes' in the Caribbean. An added incentive for the American authorities was the use of US technology in the BAE and SAAB aircraft, in breach of the US Arms Export Control Act, which is intended to control arms sales using US manufactured technology and prevent bribery by requiring brokers involved in sales to report fees paid. The DoJ investigation into BAE was cheered on, from a distance, by the chief executives of several US defense manufacturers, who had watched BAE's rise up the league table of world arms manufacturers with a mixture of suspicion and envy. Why the Clinton administration, and the State Department under Foreign Secretaries, Christopher Warren and Madeleine Albright, failed to take a closer look at BAE's corrupt practices, which were at the expense of Lockheed Martin, Boeing and others in the US with millions invested in the deadly business, remains an interesting and unanswered question. US technology was in the British aircraft years before the low-tech attacks in New York and Washington, which could not have taken place or succeeded "without the complicity or complete failure of US agencies," according to a former senior Treasury official during the Reagan presidency, and *Wall Street Journal* associate editor, Paul Craig Roberts.

The anti-apartheid struggle was also a Marxist-based revolution, seeking equality for all, and the South African Communist Party (SACP) is an integral partner in the tripartite alliance, with the ANC and COSATU. Many of the cadre became (and remain) influential in forming post-apartheid attitudes, including the murdered Chris Hani, former Housing Minister, Joe Slovo, the incumbent Minister of Higher Education and Training, Bonginkosi 'Blade'Nzimande, and Zuma's personal spokesperson, Mac Maharaj.

Issues which the ANC inherited included ARMSCOR's role in arming Iraq during war with Iran in the 1980s. The Iraqis became interested in buying from South Africa in 1984 when Saddam Hussein's procurement chief, General Neguib Thanoon, traveled to an isolated shooting range outside Johannesburg to watch the SADF's 4th Infantry Training Brigade test-fire Canadian engineer Gerald Bull's 155mm field howitzer, called the G5. The G5 had been manufactured by ARMSCOR since 1981 under license from SRC Composites Ltd., a Belfast-based front company which had bought the local Learfan production plant. By 1984 Armscor had improved the design, including a hardened steel, 45-caliber gun barrel which gave the G5, using Bull's base-bleed munitions (a method used to reduce drag to the vacuum using a small gas generator to increase pressure at the shell's base) an increased range of almost 25 miles, at least 5 miles farther than any artillery piece in the Pentagon's inventory. Mossad was certainly interested, and eliminated the problem by eliminating Gerry Bull in the darkened hallway on the sixth floor of a Brussels apartment block on 22 March 1990, using a silenced Colt 7.65 pistol and shooting him five times in the head, neck and upper spine in a seven-second burst of gunfire.

The Central Intelligence Agency (CIA) would have been wholly negligent to ignore South Africa in the 1980s or when the major shift in global political authority began to take shape in the early 1990s. The CIA may be many things but it is neither deaf nor stupid, and Langley was aware of BAE's sales 'strategy' in securing SDP contracts. According to a Wikileaks-released US diplomatic cable entitled *Zuma Advisor Threatened to Expose Political Skeletons*, dated 10 September 2008 (two months before corruption charges were dropped against Jacob Zuma by Judge Chris Nicholson) posted from Pretoria to the State Department, and routed to several relevant recipients in Washington, including the National Security Council (NSC) and the Pentagon, with copies also going to US consuls in Durban and Cape Town, the CIA (under lame diplomatic cover as 'political officers' at the embassy in Pretoria) had cultivated a key political informant and personal friend of President Zuma who provided information on ANC politics. The name of the informant was Mo Shaik, the brother of convicted fraudster, Zuma's business partner and fundraiser, Schabir Shaik..

Mo Shaik was a trusted comrade. He had been in charge of ANC security at the Conference for a Democratic South Africa (CODESA), the negotiations between the ANC and the National Party to determine an interim constitutional transition of power, held in the early 1990s in a hanger-like structure at the World Trade Centre near Johannesburg International Airport (to facilitate exiled ANC leaders). Shortly after Thabo Mbeki's visit to

Germany as deputy to President Mandela, the tender for naval frigates was reopened despite the South African Navy deciding that the ships they wanted should be built by the Spanish military shipbuilder, Empresa Nacional Bazan, and Mo Shaik was appointed South African Consul General in Hamburg, headquarters of the GFC. Within months of the successful completion of the SDP business in Germany, Shaik was appointed ambassador to Algiers and in October 2009, he became head of the South African Secret Service (SASS) – an agency which performed intelligence tasks at the request of the incumbent South African president, including monitoring foreign investigations which could damage the country's economic interests, at home or abroad.

The US confidential cable records several meetings between Shaik and an unidentified female US political officer (PolOff) and mentions that "as usual" Shaik expects "respect and gratitude" for the information he provided, including "motivations and strategies of the Zuma camp" and plans for Zuma's legal team to subpoena several of the country's most influential people if he lost the appeal to have the corruption charges against him re-examined. The list included the suspended National Police Commission, Jackie Selebi, former DPP Vusi Pikoli, chief prosecutor Mokothedi Mpshe, and former National Assembly speaker, Frene Ginwala, all of whom were regarded by Zuma as loyal to incumbent President Mbeki, and had planned, according to Shaik, to challenge Zuma's eligibility to stand for election at Pokokwane "by leveling corruption charges against him."

Mo Shaik was a busy man. Apart from the Americans he met with other foreign government representatives "within a limited diplomatic circle" including the Australian High Commissioner on at least one occasion, and the Norwegians. He used to meet with the French but "cut then off after a French diplomat insulted him immediately before the Pokokwane conference." In a second US classified 'dipcomm' dated 4 June 2009, dealing with a cabinet reshuffle under Zuma, Shaik described the appointments of various government officials - including Collins Chabane, as "minister in the presidency for performance monitoring," Ayanda Dlodlo, as deputy minister of public service and administration, Mandisi Mpahlwa, as envoy to Moscow, and Lindiwe Zulu, as adviser at the Foreign Ministry - as "concessions to keep them quiet."

Third World Procedures

Just over a decade earlier, in October 1998, it was business as usual among the shell companies. BAE agreed to a bogus contract with another British Virgin Island-registered entity, Arstow Commercial Corporation (ACC) which listed among its executives an unassuming banker and economist, Dr Ian Hugh Thurston, chief financial adviser to the PM, Margaret Thatcher, and her son Mark, since the late 1970s. Thurston, who lived quietly in a large, two-storey house in Jersey, one of the Channel Islands, worked for British and Commonwealth Shipping in the mid-1950s, as economic adviser to business consultants Bidir, Hamlyn & Fry, served on the board of Citibank, and in 1993 became a director of the merchant bank, Lazard Brothers & Co. (Jersey) Ltd. He had set up many tax shelters for the Thatcher family, and once boasted, in a *Jersey Evening Post* article, in August 1973, of knowing "some of the Gnomes of Zurich."

The BAE/ACC contract promised a commission of 1.5 percent of the sale of Hawk trainers and SAAB Gripen fighters as part of South Africa's Strategic Defense Procurement (SDP) package. In April 1999, the contract was substituted by another, with the same commission percentage, but with Red Diamond replacing BAE as the principal. Five months later, in the finals stages of the SDP negotiations, ACC signed a contract with another company called Westunity Ltd., which promised to "provide the services of [recently resigned adviser to Defense Minister Joe Modise] Fana Hlongwane, who will use his best efforts to promote the reputation and sale of the product in the territory." A contract was also signed between Westunity and Hlongwane, in which the latter agreed to "promote the sales" of Westunity products in South Africa. Cash transfers from Arstow's accounts to Hlonwane through Westunity and a Hong Kong-based company began almost immediately, with $200,000 paid, in October 1999, shortly before the arms contracts were signed, and $1.2 million transferred in May 2000, after the contracts were signed. By July 2001 Arstow had transferred almost $10 million to several of Hloagwane's shell companies. The convoluted payment system to Hlongwane and others, originating with Red Diamond and moving through several off-shore accounts, amounted to $200 million in respect of the BAE and SAAB sales to South Africa alone, according to SFO investigator, Gary Murphy, who stated in a sworn affidavit included with the SFO request to the DSO for assistance: "I suspect that a primary reason behind the inception of Red Diamond was to ensure that corrupt payments could be made, and it would be more difficult for law enforcement agencies to penetrate the system."

In order to facilitate the sale of the Gripen fighter jet, SAAB has admitted setting up the South African National Industrial Participation (SANIP) company to manage the enormous offset obligations expected to be generated by the Gripen (and Hawk) deal, and to handle negotiations with Fana Hlongwane, one of the main 'movers and shakers', with Chippy Shaik, on the Armaments Acquisition Council (AAC) the body tasked with overseeing the bids, according to Feinstein. At least $5 million was paid through SANIP to Hlongwane by BAE, who ran SANIP for SAAB, committing him to deliver outcomes on offsets on which he had no bona fide influence. The SANIP contract with Hlogwane, dated August 2003, agreed to pay a 'success fee' of $4.5 million, if the South African Government confirmed, in writing, that BAE had secured its first offset projection, namely achieving investments of $300 million and exports of $2 billion by April the following year. Despite issues around deadlines, from the available documentation it appears that this money was paid, and Hlongwane was promised a further $7.5 million if the government certified that BAE had achieved its final offset/export milestone by April 2011. It is not known if this amount has been paid.

Fana Hlongwane had no obvious business experience, certainly not in the international arms trade, and SFO officials who seized BAE documentation at various stages of their investigation, and questioned senior BAE executives, could find little evidence of Hlongwane's input. It is unclear why he was regarded as a "person of influence" to deal with the offset requirements, other than to make sure the relevant senior politicians and ACC officials engaged in the required off-the-books accounting to produce the approvals required by BAE. BAE also paid Hlongwane an extra $1 million, through SANIP, for a report on the government's Black Economic Empowerment program, launched to address the business and economic inequalities, under the iniquitous apartheid system, of the previously disadvantaged majority of South Africa's non-white citizens.

The only explanation on BAE's books for this was a brief report referring to the choice of a strategic Black Economic Empowerment partner, which came to nothing at all. BAE had tried to claim that its relationship with Hlongwane began in 2003, in an attempt to conceal its involvement with Joe Modise's adviser on the ACC during the negotiations phase of the Hawk and Gripen deal. However, SFO sworn affidavits from officials involved state that BAE, on 2 December 1999, the day before the contract was signed, approved a payment of $4.4 million to Huderfield Enterprises, another covert company set up by BAE's South Africa agent, Richard Charter, alongside his overt consultancy, Osprey Aviation, and that $200,000 had been paid to Arstow, on 5 October 1999, after the ANC Defense Ministry announced the procurement of the BAE/SAAB aircraft. Both these payments were approved by "extraordinary ex-committee procedures" attended by only a handful of BAE's most senior executives, according to the *M&G* newspaper.

The decision to disband the DSO, and effectively shut down the arms deal investigation, leaving many unanswered questions, not least why Kayswell Services, one of the targets of DSO raids on BAE offices and commercial premises linked to the SDP corruption allegations, was paid more that $60 million to act as consultant. Kayswell Services was headed by John Bredenkamp, a former financial adviser to Zimbabwean dictator, Robert Mugabe, and according to an affidavit sworn by former BAE executive in South Africa supporting the DSO raids, Bredenkamp "contributed nothing" towards the selection of BAE/SAAB as preferred bidder for the South Africa Air Force contract, that Bredenkamp told him "key decision makers had to be identified" in order that they could be "financially incentivized" to make the right decision, and had boasted "we can get Chippy Shaik." There was also talk among British officials of "Third World procedures" required to win the SDP contract, which DSO and SFO investigators assumed was a reference to bribery, although neither agency ever got the opportunity to conclusively prove that the secret Red Diamond arrangements were designed to facilitate the payment by Hlongwane and Bredenkamp to senior ANC politicians and officials to influence the decision making procedures, and to disguise delayed rewards to Hlogwane himself for influence exercised in the late 1990s.

It is reasonable to assume that when SFO made its request for assistance through the NPA the agency had no idea how widespread and institutionalized corruption was among senior ANC officials. The US DoJ may have been aware of the SFO's difficulties but felt no obligation to share information after waiting for six months, and getting no response from the British Home Office to a request for assistance in the DoJ's investigation of the illegal $2.5 million paid via Washington-based banks to Prince Bandar bin Sultan, the Saudi ambassador to the US, from 1983 to 2005, which were connected to the al-Yamamah deal, worth an envious $80 billion.

Achtung Chippy!

On 19 June 2006, prosecutors in Düsseldorf publicly announced an investigation into corruption allegations against ThyssenKrupp AG, with an early morning raid on the company's head offices in Essen. The company's tax records had shown that an estimated $25 million had been paid in 'commissions' to South African politicians to secure a share of the SDP largesse. TyssenKrupp was part of the GFC and had chosen Thomson-CSF to provide the combat suites for the four SAS Spionkop (F147) Valour class frigates the CSF had been contracted to build for the South African Navy, after Thabo Mbeki had visited Germany as Mandela's deputy and "trusted comrade" Chippy Shaik was appointed Cousul General in Hamburg, in 1997. The German company (unlike BAE) kept records of several meetings with Chippy Shaik prior to $3 million being paid into the account of Ian Pearce, CEO of a Mbeki-approved company called Futuristic Business Solutions (FBS), as an alternative cash channel to Shabir Shaik's African Defense Systems (ADS). Chippy Shaik wasn't there to negotiate, simply to ensure that arrangements already agreed between South African officials and TyssenKrupp sales executives during several meetings while he was in town, were honored. As Feinstein points out, if FBS was an "approved channel" the question remains whether Chippy Shaik was "soliciting money for himself alone or other entities as well."

In late 2007 the indefatigable Democratic Alliance (DA) leader, Patricia de Lille, stood up in the National Assembly and announced that she had evidence of three payments, each roughly $50,000, paid by ThyssenKrupp, on 29 January 1999, into accounts with Credit Suisse First Boston (CSFB) bank, linked to the ANC, the Nelson Mandela Children's Fund (NCF) and a charity associated with Mr. Mandela's second wife, Graca Machel. All three alleged recipients have denied any knowledge of the payments which came to light when SFO investigators raided the London office of ThyssenKrupp's South African agent, Tony Georgiadis, and the banking authorities in Switzerland were subsequently asked to provide details of accounts linked to him at the CSFB.

There is no evidence, and there has never been any suggestion, that Nelson Mandela, either during his term as president or subsequently, had any knowledge of the rampant corruption raging through the ranks of his senior ministers, their advisers, and a shabby crew of middlemen and hustlers, although in all honesty it's difficult to see how he could have remained in ignorance of the seeping contamination of greed that had infected the higher ranks of the ANC, every bit as damaging to the health of the nation as a virus, and as difficult to detect and combat because of the necessary lies, deceit and convenient lapses of memory of once honorable men.

Germany was one of the countries to sign and ratify the OECD's Anti-Bribery Convention, and there is no evidence to suggest that members of the Bundestag - whether in office as part of the Christian Democratic Union (CDU) Chancellor Helmut Kohl's administration in the mid-1990s, or on the backbenches - had lobbied on behalf of the GFC, unlike UK Conservative and Labour politicians who had a symbiotic relationship with BAE. What was good for BAE was good for Britain. And if kickbacks secured contracts and jobs for British workers, well, that was the "Third World way" of doing business, even at the expense of deprived, undernourished, poorly educated and impoverished indigenous peoples in Africa or elsewhere. After all, if their own political representatives didn't care, why should British ministers, of whatever political persuasion, lose sleep over such crass inequality.

This indifference didn't rest well with the OECD. In its 2008 annual report, signed-off on by the chairman of the OECD's anti-bribery international working party, Professor Mark Pieth, the Paris-based agency publicly criticized Britain for failing to deal with corrupt business practices, and depicted the Labour administration under Blair as morally bankrupt, having spent years making promises about passing anti-corruption legislation when it had no intention of doing so because the ministers that mattered, and the constituency MPs from regions where BAE and other heavy industry entities of the arms industry employed thousands of potential Labour voters, wanted nothing to do with reforms that would inconvenience how contracts were secured, or undermine re-election prospects next time.

The language in the 75-page report reflects Prof. Pieth's belief that nothing had changed in the UK since the signing of the OECD anti-bribery convention a decade earlier, and the fact the OECD has no power to make Britain change, only shaming the country into making good on its international obligations. The report refers to the al-Yamamah deal between BAE and the Saudis, brokered by Thatcher during a visit to Riyadh in the 1980s, and political interference when the SFO tried to investigate allegations that members of the Saudi royal family had received hundreds of millions in secret payments. The report also states that taking into account 10 years of duplicity and lies, the "fundamental touchstone" of Britain's good intentions will be HMG making good on promises to reform the wholly inadequate anti-corruption legislation, and turn it into an "effective instrument for corporate discipline." The OECD's criticism of Britain fell on deaf ears in London. It had been expected, although not in the blunt terms in which it was expressed, which were described as being "outside the boundaries of normal diplomatic language" by economic analysts. The previous November, the Solicitor General for England and Wales, and Labour Party MP, Vera Baird, had refused an invitation to attend a meeting in Rome, hosted by the Italian Prime Minister, Romano Prodi, to 'celebrate' the OECD's 10 year anti-bribery treaty. A keynote speaker at the event was US assistant attorney general and head of the DoJ's Criminal Division, Alice S. Fisher, who was in charge of the BAE/Saudi investigation. She told delegates that 37 countries were now part of the "mutual legal assistance co-operation agreement" which was vital to tackle a multi-layered international corruption investigation, and she thanked several countries for recent cooperation, including France, Germany and Italy. The UK wasn't mentioned, an indication that the 'special relationship' was a little tarnished, at least at this level.

The DoJ had continued its investigation after PM Tony Blair halted the SFO's inquiry into the Saudi deal, when Riyadh had threatened to withhold intelligence on Islamist jihadists, and 'warned' that anti-terrorist non-cooperation could result in further deaths of the streets of London - a "veiled reference," according to media commentators and security officials, to the July 2005 carnage in London in which 52 people died in four suicide bombings. Blair, not for the first time in his political career, hadn't the moral courage to deal with this type of bullying and ordered Attorney General Lord Goldsmith to close down the al-Yamamah investigation, claiming the decision was taken for "national security reasons."

After six months of waiting for the British Home Office to respond to a request for mutual legal assistance in its widening investigation, Alice Fisher finally ran out of patience and arranged for a key British witness, businessman Peter Gardiner, to secretly leave Britain on 20 August 2007. He traveled to Paris where he met two FBI agents who accompanied him to Washington. Gardiner, who had agreed to testify (apparently without pressure), had copies of hundreds of invoices detailing illegal BAE payments to senior members of the House of Saud, including Prince Bandar, who had received about $1.5 billion in 'commissions' for brokering arms deals for BAE worth more than twenty times that amount.

The British Foreign Office lodged a formal protest through its embassy in Washington when the Home Office learned of Gardiner's presence in the city as a witness for the DoJ. AAG Fisher was warned that his testimony was "contrary to international protocols" - as if such a baseless threat would be heeded by the independently-minded Fisher, a Bush appointee who had managed high-profile Criminal Division prosecutions in areas such as counterterrorism and corporate fraud. What was contrary to the UK's anti-bribery treaty obligations was the Home Office's continued refusal to assist the DoJ, which had requested more than one million standard A4 pages of documentation seized from BAE, the company's bankers Lloyds TRS, and subpoenaed from the DESO (at a time when the 'policing' agency was headed by former BAE executive Alan Garwood) during the SFO investigation. Prince Bandar had been paid in installments of $240 million over a ten-year period. The money moved through two Saudi US embassy accounts, one for official embassy use, and one for personal use, such as the operating expenses of Bandar's private, four-engine, wide-body, long-range Airbus A340, the 'standard variant' (as opposed to the stretched version) commercial airliner with a seating capacity of 375 passengers. According to the DoJ there was "no distinction between the accounts of the embassy or official government accounts (...) and the accounts of the [Saudi] royal family." Prince Bandar resigned in June 2005 for "personal reasons." NBC reported his resignation, claiming health reasons and "problems with overuse of antidepressants" but made no mention of the DoJ's BAE investigation, which may have been the cause of his depression in the first place.

Attention abroad to the ever-widening BAE corruption scandal, with investigations in Sweden, Austria, the Czech Republic and Tanzania, finally made the National Assembly in the legislative capital, Cape Town, sit up and take notice. It wasn't only the ANC that was being damaged by the allegations of corporate and personal greed, the key institutions of democracy were being compromised by the corrupted. In 2006 NA members commissioned a panel of political and constitutional experts, chaired by Pregs Govander, and including Chancellor Frederick van Zyle Slabbert, of Stellenbosch University, and political analysts, Sipho Seepe and Judith February, to assess the NA's performance and the damage to the legislature. When the panel finally reported after two years assessing almost a decade of greed, lies and high-level deceit, it recommended that MPs should "revisit the arms deal and take such steps that are necessary, including a debate on the adoption of a resolution calling for the appointment of such a judicial commission of inquiry into the arms deal." The report also highlighted the Government's weak oversight procedures, failure to adequately consult the public on issues of national interest and the failure of certain members of the NA "to adhere to high moral standards." Unfortunately this type of report, despite the good intentions and high academic qualifications of those involved, given the climate of avarice that prevailed in South Africa at the time it was regarded by many as not worth the paper it was written on. However, its publication was welcomed by NA speaker, Gwen Mahlangu-Nkabinde, who indicated that a decision to implement its recommendations would have be taken by "the next generation of politicians" after the April 2009 general election.

As expected, the 'next generation' is headed by Jacob Zuma, and one of the changes made by the new administration was to replace Gwen Mahlangu-Nkabinde by Max Sisulu, son of Walter and Albertina Sisulu, comrades of Mandela when the going was tough, and former chief whip in the mid-1990s during the Mandela administration. The passage of the PSIB, the prohibitive censorious press legislation, which is a real and present threat to democracy in South Africa, was largely facilitated by four men who were moved into positions of influence after the 2009 election. The most prominent member of this 'Gang of Four' is the Minister for State Security, Siyabonga Cwele, a medical doctor from Port Shepstone on the south coast of President Zuma's home province of KwaZulu-Natal, whose unconditional loyalty to the ANC, and handling of the 'Browse Mole' affair (which could have seriously damaged Zuma's political career and his presidential aspirations) were factors in Zuma's refusal to sack him after his estranged wife since 2005, Sheryl Cwele, a former health service executive within the Hibiscus Coast municipality, was convicted of international drug trafficking, on 5 May 2011.

Siyabonga Cwele had been chairman of the multi-party, parliamentary Joint Standing Committee on Intelligence (JSCI) when the DSO's 18-page, *Special Browse Mole Consolidation Report* was leaked to the press in 2007. The TOP SECRET document, written by Scorpion senior investigator, Ivor Powell, claimed that Zuma, while ANC deputy president, was involved in a conspiracy to topple his boss, President Thabo Mbeki. The plot was apparently "driven by left-wing groups," including the SACP, COSATU and the ANC Youth League, while the President of Angola, Jose Eduardo dos Santos (who has been in office since September 1979) and the deposed and murdered Libyan leader, Muammar Gadaffi, were alleged to be supporting and funding Zuma's cause. At a press briefing Dr Cwele stated that the DSO had no mandate to collect political intelligence, and claimed the organization had "fallen prey to information peddlers." The JSCI declared that the report had no formal status and that investigators should dismiss it as the "work of sinister forces."

Dr. Cwele has been a member of the ANC's Kwa-Zulu Natal executive for more than twenty years, and apart from his friendship with Zuma, he is also a close friend and colleague of SAPS National Commissioner, General Bheki Cele, who was suspended in October 2011 following charges of corruption. Cwele and Cele worked together in setting up the ANC party structure in Kwa-Zulu Natal in the late 1980s and early 1990s during a period of intense and bloody conflict with the Inkatha Freedom Party. Cele had been appointed SAPS commissioner in July 2009, replacing Jackie Selebi, who had been suspended the previous January. As Minister for State Security, Siyabonga Cwele is responsible for the powerful State Security Agency (SSA), set up in 2009 and incorporating the previously-separate National Intelligence Agency (NIA), the South African Secret Service (SASS), the South African National Academy of Intelligence (SANAI), the National Communications Centre (NCC) and COMSEC (South Africa). Based at the Musanda Complex, on Delmas Road in Pretoria, the SSA, with responsibility for civilian intelligence operations, will be the primary agency overseeing the enforcement of the PSIB

Dennis Dlomo, special adviser to Cwele on intelligence and national security matters, worked closely with his boss on the 'PSIB Project.' He is a former political detainee, held under the apartheid regime's Internal Security Act (ISA) in the late 1980s while deputy president of the Student

Representative Council at the University of Durban-Westville, established in 1972 and one of the few universities to admit non-whites. Dlomo was also a member of the ANC and United Democratic Front (UDF) activist network, which was controlled and influenced by Mo Shaik, the former SASS boss who was a senior operative in the ANC's counter-intelligence structure at the time. According to *City Press*, Dennis Dlomo was part of the Natal Indian Congress 'cabal' inside the UDF which dominated the UDF's political leadership through control of access to foreign funding and key ANC leaders in exile, including Jacob Zuma, and his good buddy, Mac Maharaj.

For several years Dlomo worked for the former Minister for Intelligence, Joe Nhlanhla (who died, aged 71, in a comatose state in Milpark Hospital, Johannesburg, on 2 July 2008) before becoming deputy coordinator of the National Intelligence Coordinating Committee (NICC) in 2003, and two years later was seconded to the African Union (AU) based in the Ethiopian capital, Addis Ababa. The AU was established in July 2002, and consists of fifty-four African nations, with the exception of Morocco, and Dlomo served for five years as executive secretary of the AU's Committee of Intelligence and Security Services (CISSA) before returning to South Africa in 2010 to take up his current post

The third member of the quartet is Luwellyn Landers, MP, a former deputy minister in the apartheid administration under Pieter Willem Botha, in the 1980s, who was one of several Labor Party MPs to join the ANC in September 1993. In 2011, before the PSIB went before the National Assembly, he was appointed chairperson of the parliamentary Justice Committee, having previously served as co-chair of the Ethics Committee, where he was criticized for not acting against MPs accused of corruption. He was also one of eight ANC members of the 12-strong, cross-party JSCI. During the 22 November PSIB debate, Landers accused critics of the bill of wanting the 1982 National Party's repressive media legislation to remain on the statute books. He claimed the PSIB compared favorably with the Council of Europe's Convention on Access to Documents, regarding the release of documents in the public interest upon application, and the 1985 Canadian Security of Information Act (CSIA), where a security establishment employer is permitted to publish within the required whistle-blowing requisites of the country's Official Secrets Act (OSA). Landers also described the Right2Know campaign - whose members include solicitors, journalists and ordinary citizens concerned about the potential abuse of a free press - as the "Right2Lie campaign."

And finally there's Cecil Burgess, a lawyer whose political career began with Patricia deLille's newly-formed Independent Democrats in 2004 (which merged with the DA in August 2010) and within a year had left to join the ANC. Since then he has served as chairperson of the JSCI and as chairperson of the Joint Standing Committee on State Security (JSCSS) since 2009, a position of some authority and power, reserved solely for MPs trusted by the ANC leadership who are sworn to secrecy because of access to sensitive state information. In this capacity Burgess was appointed in

2010, by Minister Cwele, to co-chair an ad-hoc internal ANC committee to facilitate the successful passage of the PSIB through Parliament.

Indeed, a "terrible beauty" (the words used by Irish poet, WB Yeats. to describe the outcome of another revolution. at another time and in another place) was born in South Africa when Nelson Mandela walked free from Victor Venster Prison and led the ANC into the country's first multi-racial election in which the ANC secured 62.65 percent of the popular vote, and 252 seats of the 400-seats in National Assembly.

These were the glory days, with the de facto end of the old apartheid regime, *Black Wednesday* legislation and other cruel and claustrophobic repressive laws. But the hopes and aspirations that underlined the sacrifices made during the "long walk to freedom" have been overshadowed by the greed of politicians who have lined their pockets with the cash that should have been used to better the lives of millions of citizens, the majority of whom are ANC supporters.

In an editorial in the *M&G,* on 9 May 2013, Archbishop Emeritus, Desmond Tutu, a lifelong friend and comrade of Nelson Mandela, claimed that South Africa was now "the most unequal society in the world." He described the ANC as a "good freedom-fighting unit" which had led the people in the struggle against oppression, but had failed to "make the transition to becoming a political party." He identified corruption, unaccountability and weaknesses in the constitution as key issues that should be tackled, and criticized the ANC support for Zimbabwe at international forums, including the UN, despite the deterioration of Zimbabwe's economy, democracy and basic human rights. The 1994 Nobel Peace Prize winner will no longer vote for the ANC, and has expressed the hope that in future the South African people will elect a government based on its policies "rather than emotional attachment to the liberation movement."

BIBLIOGRAPHY
Benson, Mary. *Nelson Mandela*. London: Penguin Books, 1986.
Brooke, Heather. *The Silent State*. London: Windmill Books, 2011.
Crawford-Browne, Terry. *Eye on the Money*. Johannesburg:, Random House Struik, 2007.
Dorril, Stephen. *MI6*. New York. The Free Press, 2000.
Feinstein, Andrew *After the Party*. London: Verso, 2009.
Gevisser, Mark. *A Legacy of Liberation*. Basingstoke: Palgrave Macmillan, 2009.
Holden, Paul. *The Arms Deal in Your Pocket*. Johannesburg:Jonathan Ball (reprint edition), 2008.
Halloran, Paul & Hollingsworth, Mark. *Thatcher's Gold*. London: Simon & Schuster, 1995.
Johnson, RW. *South Africa's Brave New World* London:Penguin Books, 2010.
Mills, Greg. *The Wired Model*. Cape Town: Tafelberg Publishers, 2000.
Pakenham, Thomas. *The Boer War*. London: Abacus, 1992.

Schmidt, Olivier (ed). *The Intelligence Files.* Atlanta: Clarity Press, 2005.
Timmerman, Kenneth R. *The Death Lobby.* London: Bantam Books, 1992.
Wiener, Mandy. *Killing Kebble: An Underworld Exposed.* London: Pan Macmillan, 2011.

NEWSPAPERS, NGOs, ONLINE SOURCES
Cape Times (www.capetimes.co.za)
City Press (www.citypress.co.za)
Mail & Guardian (www.mg.co.za)
Pretoria News (www.iol.co.za/pretoria-news)
Sunday Independent (www.timeslive.co.za)
Sunday Times (www.timeslive.co.za)
The Citizen (www.citizen.co.za)
Campaign Against Arms Trade (www.caat.org)
Independent American Journalism (www.newsmax.com)
www.ever-fasternews.com
www.politicsweb.co.za
www.sa.indymedia.org
www.whoswhosa.co.za

CHAPTER FOUR

SEEING THINGS INVISIBLE

> *"What difference does it make to the dead, the orphans and the homeless, whether the mad destruction is wrought under the name of totalitarianism or the holy name of liberty and democracy."*
> **Mahatma Gandhi**
> *Non Violence in Peace & War*

An Imperious Decision

Tony Blair's enthusiasm for war in Iraq may have come as a surprise to a large number of elected members of the Labour Party in the House of Commons, but not to the neoconservatives within the Bush administration in Washington and their colleagues who emerged from the long grass after eight barren Clinton years. The British prime minister was not content to be part of the so-called "coalition of the willing" bandwagon, but was up there in the driver's seat riding shotgun alongside the Texan. And he brought his own payload of deceit, lies and "sexed-up" intelligence, using the pretext of a real and present danger from a non-existent WMD arsenal to justify ordering British troops abroad to die in the Basra desert. The lonely death of Ministry of Defence (MoD) weapons inspector, Dr. David Kelly, was an unfortunate distraction from the business of war.

Britain's military history, for those who have suffered the harsh impact of imperial aggression, is a bloodthirsty narrative of colonial campaigns conducted for all the wrong reasons. This was the case in Iraq. Initially both Blair and Bush flagged-up the threat to the region of Saddam Hussein's alleged biological, chemical and nuclear weapons arsenal. When this threat became increasingly unlikely, "regime change" became the mantra in London and Washington. And while few in the West would dispute the need to remove from power men like Saddam Hussein, neither Tony Blair nor George W. Bush had a political mandate, nor a moral or international legal right to do so. Twelve years had passed since US President, George Herbert Walker Bush, on 17 February 1991, declared victory over Iraq as a result of Operation *Desert Storm* which had forced Iraqi troops out of Kuwait. In this case Saddam was clearly seen as the aggressor, and although access to Middle East oil was a factor in the decision to go to war, there was both a valid international legal argument related to aggression, and a real and convincing threat to Saudi Arabia from a military force that both the UK and the US had helped to create during the 1980s, when the Iraqi dictator waged war against Iran from September 1980 to August 1988, the longest conventional war between nations of the 20th century.

The Iraqi war machine prior to the invasion of Kuwait was still one of the most formidable in the Middle East, thanks to the greed of European and US businesses and bankers who sold everything necessary to wage a campaign of aggression, including fighter aircraft, armored vehicles, tanks and missiles. The West had filled a vacuum created when the Soviet Union announced an arms embargo on sales to Iraq in the mid-1980s, and while western governments and intelligence services turned a blind eye to the conventional arms buildup, and in some cases facilitated sales to boost their own economies, Saddam's procurement agents scoured Europe to purchase the tools, equipment and know-how necessary to manufacture WMDs. Nonetheless, in May 1990, four months before the invasion of Kuwait, the Assistant Secretary of State for Near Eastern and South Asian Affairs in the Bush administration, John Hubert Kelly, told the US Congress that Saddam Hussein was a "force for moderation." Two months later the US ambassador to Baghdad, April Glaspie, a respected Arabist and the first woman to be appointed ambassador to an Arab country, made the biggest error of judgment of her diplomatic career. Tasked with "broadening the cultural and commercial ties" between the US and Iraq, she failed to notice the obvious threat of an Iraqi troop build-up on the border with Kuwait. Ambassador Glaspie had her first meeting with Saddam Hussein and his Deputy Prime Minister, Tariq Aziz, on 25 July 1990, and in a diplomatic memo to the State Department later that day, released by Wikileaks in August 2011, she told the Iraqi leader that Washington did not have an opinion on the "disagreement" between Iraq and Kuwait, and did not have an opinion on Arab-Arab conflicts in general.

The Iraqi Republican Guard armored and motorized infantry divisions crossed into Kuwait shortly after midnight on 2 August 1990, supported by a squadron of US/Canada-manufactured Bell 412 multi-purpose helicopters, and Soviet Mil-M1 gunships and transport aircraft which had been sold to Iraq in the 1970s, prior to the downfall of the Pahlavi dynasty in Iran, which had been in power for more than 50 years, helped in no small measure by an MI6/CIA coup d'etat in 1953, codenamed Operation *Ajax*, which overthrew the democratically-elected regime of the Prime Minister, Mohammad Mosaddegh, the first time the US, using the CIA, had openly acted in the interests of western conglomerates and overthrown an elected civilian government.

Seven months of cruel occupation followed the invasion of Kuwait. Hundreds of thousands fled, human rights were systematically and brutally violated, the country's coffers were looted and, perhaps for the first time, western politicians, heads buried in the sands of Arabia for years, learned the true nature of the despot they had helped create in Baghdad.

Saddam Hussein needed victories after the Kuwaiti debacle following the UN-mandated Operation *Desert Storm*. The opportunity to do just that was presented to him by President Bush, Sr., who encouraged the mainly Shia Arabs in the southern Iraqi Tigris-Euphrates marshlands to "take matters into their hands" during a *Voice of America* radio broadcast, on 15 February 1991, calling on them to force Saddam to "step aside," then comply with UN resolutions and "rejoin the family of peace-loving nations." In retrospect, the advice given to Bush to go ahead with this "address to the Iraqi people" and encourage revolt among the disaffected masses was the result of wishful thinking among CIA strategists who assumed - following the retreat from Kuwait - that Saddam was vulnerable and his Revolutionary Guards demoralized and "not up to the fight."

Langley should have known better. Its agents and Washington's diplomats (often one and the same) had been close-up and personal with Saddam for years, and should have been aware that men like the Iraqi dictator are at their most dangerous when 'wounded'. Three years earlier, even with the war with Iran going badly, Saddam had launched a genocidal poison gas attack on the Kurdish population of Halabja, in the Kurdish region of northern Iraq, in which 3,500 to 5,000 men woman and children died, and up to 10,000 were injured. Iranian freelance photographer, Kaveh Golestan, (who would later die in Kifri, on 2 April 2003, while working for the BBC) took the first published photographs of the Halabja attack, and described the scene to *Financial Times* journalist, Guy Dinmore: "It was life frozen. Life had stopped, like watching a film and suddenly it hangs on one frame. It was a new kind of death to me. You went into a room, a kitchen and you saw the body of a woman holding a knife where she had been cutting a carrot (...) The aftermath was worse. Victims were still being brought in. Some villagers came in our chopper. They had 15 or 16 beautiful children, begging us to take them to hospital. So all the press sat there and we were each handed a child to carry. As we took off, fluid came out of my little girl's mouth and she died in my arms."

According to Human Rights Watch (HRW) in a March 1991 newsletter, despite the international outcry over Halabja, little was heard in the US about Saddam Hussein's "brutal treatment of his own people" until the invasion of Kuwait. "Even now, virtually no mention is made of the many other times the Iraqi Government has gassed its large Kurdish minority," the publication states, adding that tens of thousands were killed during chemical and conventional bombardments from spring 1987 to fall 1988, "part of a long-standing campaign that destroyed almost every Kurdish village in Iraq."

The post-Kuwait uprising began in Sa'ad Square in the southern Shia city of Basra, on 1 March 1991, when the commander of a retreating column of tanks fired a shell into a huge mural of Saddam in military uniform next to the Ba'ath Party headquarters. A crowd gathered, the Ba'ath Party building was stormed, the residence of the governor and several police stations were attacked. The offices of the security service, Jihaz Al-Mukhabarat Al-A'ma, were ransacked and Directorate IV files, dealing with internal opposition and dissent, were destroyed. Within days unrest had spread to other cities across the south. On 4 March, fighting erupted in the north, where Kurdish rebels took control of several cities while NATO aircraft enforced a no-fly zone. However, the high-altitude fighters proved useless against low-flying helicopter gun-ships and heavy artillery, while the rebels had little more than a few captured tanks, artillery, rocket-propelled grenades and small arms which quickly proved ineffective against the force deployed by Baghdad. In the south most of the fighting was between demoralized Shia deserters from the Iraqi Army, mostly unwilling conscripts who had been in the forefront of the Kuwaiti occupation, and the elite Republican Guard.

Having encouraged the uprising Washington and London betrayed the rebels, and watched idly and silent while the superior firepower of the Revolutionary Guard slaughtered the opposition. The rebels retreated from Basra, and the other cities swept up in the revolt, into the swamps of Hamar, Amara and Howeiza, where they were given sanctuary by the Marsh Arabs. After consulting with his military commanders Saddam ordered the marsh lands drained, a counter-insurgency strategy which one of the best western Middle East analysts, the London *Independent* correspondent, Robert Fisk, described as far worse than Israel's campaign of "political assassinations and property destruction." Hundreds of dams were constructed to block the flow of water from the Euphrates and Tigris rivers into the marshes. Eventually most of the marsh land was drained, and the resistance was broken.

In the Kurdish north, the overwhelming force deployed by Saddam crushed the opposition within a month. According to a New York-headquartered, non-governmental, Human Rights Watch (HRW) report, the Revolutionary Guard, in their attempt to retake the region's capital, Erbil, and other occupied cities such as Silemani, Kelar, Helebce and Ranye, and consolidate control, "killed thousands who opposed them whether a rebel or a civilian by firing indiscriminately into the opposing areas; executing them on the streets, in homes and in hospitals; rounding up suspects, especially young men, during house-to-house searches, and arresting them with or without charge or shooting them en masse, and using helicopters to attack those who try to free the cities."

Even if Saddam Hussein was a cruel and vicious dictator who deserved to be removed from power, the manner in which it was eventually carried out was equally egregious. Blair and Bush cared not a damn for the Kurds, the Marsh Arabs, or the thousands imprisoned, tortured and murdered, systematically, in cities and towns which have never made headlines. The invasion of March 2003 had little or nothing to do with human rights abuses, however grave. The slaughter of the innocent was a convenient backdrop, and a distraction from the neoconservatives true agenda. There was no mention of human rights after their first bombs and cruise missiles fell on Baghdad.

A former member of the Pentagon's Office of Special Plans (OSP) tasked with finding, or creating, a pretext to invade Iraq, retired USAF Lieutenant Colonel, Karen Kwiatkowski, believes there were three main reasons why the neo-conservatives felt it necessary to topple Saddam and replace him with a friendly pro-US regime. In a May 2004 interview with the free 'alternative' tabloid, *LA Weekly*, she explained that - despite the deaths of almost 500,000 children - one of the reasons was that "sanctions and containment were working and everybody pretty much knew it." This meant that many multinational companies were preparing to do business with Baghdad once the UN lifted sanctions, but it was unlikely that US or UK companies would benefit if Saddam remained in power. The second reason was the Pentagon's military presence in the region. Washington was "dissatisfied" with Saudi Arabia, and was "looking for alternative strategic locations" beyond Kuwait and Qatar "to secure the energy lines of communication," and the third was the switch made by Saddam in the 'Food for Oil' program "from the dollar to the euro." The Iraqi leader began selling oil for euros in November 2000, a decision which could cause "massive, almost glacial shifts in confidence in the dollar" once sanctions were lifted, with sales from the country with the world's second-largest oil reserves supporting the euro. Less than two months after the invasion one of the first executive orders Bush signed, in May 2003, "switched trading on Iraq's oil back to the dollar" according to Kwiatkowski, who had served in various branches of the security and intelligence apparatus, including the National Security Agency (NSA). She left the OSP in February 2003, and resigned from the USAF the following month.

The OSP had been set up by Paul Wolfowitz and Douglas Feith, in June 2002, under the watchful eye of Secretary of Defense, Donald Rumsfeld, to "stovepipe" raw intelligence to senior officials in the Bush administration. In a series of articles for various publications and websites, Kwiatkowski continued to expose the "corrupting influence" of the OSP on intelligence analysts, describing in an article entitled *The New Pentagon Papers*, published by *Salon* in March 2004, how a former aide to Vice-President Dick Cheney, retired Naval officer, Captain William Luti, headed a group of officers who turned the OSP into a censorship and disinformation unit within the Pentagon's Near East and South Asia (NESA) directorate: "I witnessed neo-conservative agenda bearers within the OSP usurp measured and carefully considered assessments, and through suppression and distortion of intelligence analysis promulgate what were in fact falsehoods in both Congress and the executive office of the president."

There was, of course, the outsider's analysis of the momentum to war. In the *London Review of Books* in May 2004, Stephen Holmes, research director at the Centre for Law and Security at New York University School of Law, wrote that various motives, promoted by various people at different times, contributed to the decision " to frighten any group or state that might feel emboldened to replicate 11 September; to offer solace to American voters traumatized by 11 September by letting them see US military supremacy in action; to show that the US was still responding aggressively to 11 September even after running out of targets in Afghanistan; to finish a job that George H. W. Bush had left undone; to avenge Saddam's attempt to assassinate the first President Bush; to field-test [Secretary of Defense] Rumsfeld's proposals for military reform; to reduce US dependency on the Saudis by securing some leverage over Iraqi oil supplies; to allow the US to evacuate troops from Saudi Arabia, thereby removing a point of anti-American rage; to make sure that Saddam could not acquire the capacity for nuclear blackmail after France, Germany and other countries dismantled the UN embargo."

Is this, then, what it was all about? Financial, commercial, psychological and military interests, as well as settling old scores. Were these the reasons why the neoconservatives were banging the drums of war so deafeningly? Nothing to do with human rights? But also nothing to do with oil, the dollar, regional or even global domination? Nothing to do with appeasing an increasingly belligerent Israel? And while the Bush administration exploited the 9/11 attacks and dishonored the dead with lies about links between Saddam Hussein and Osama bin Laden, in London Prime Minister Blair and his friends in the intelligence community had work to do.

The former director of the Westminster Foundation for Democracy (WFD), Professor of European Studies at Oxford University, and regular *Guardian* columnist, Timothy Garton-Ash - described by author Robin Ramsay, the former editor of the defunct (and sadly missed) journal, *Lobster*, as one of those figures "who bridge the gap between academia and the Foreign Office/MI6" - claimed that the British were "duped" into believing "that if they could not find a case for war that would win a majority in the House of Commons, and be (just about} acceptable in international law, Britain would face the unimaginable; leaving America in the lurch." As Ramsay pointed out, this shows the "level of delusion" among some of Britain's foreign policy intellectuals: "The reality is that Britain could leave America in the lurch the way a flea might leave an elephant in the lurch. And why is it unimaginable not to support the US? Edward Heath [Tory PM in the 1970s] declined to support the US in the 1973 Arab-Israeli war. Harold Wilson [Labour PM from March 1974 to April 1976] refused to send troops to fight with the US in Vietnam."

In *Web of Deceit,* Mark Curtis writes that "open defiance of the UN is a permanent feature of British foreign policy" noting that in the final 25 years of the Cold War, Britain vetoed twice as many Security Council resolutions as the Soviet Union, twenty-seven "mainly in support of racist regimes in South Africa and Rhodesia" compared to thirteen, adding that he was unable to find any mention of this fact in mainstream political culture "which continues to promote the myth of Britain's enduring support for the UN." In launching the invasion of Iraq with the US, and defying the UN, British leaders (and their US counterparts, "could hardly have displayed more open contempt for international law" according to Curtis, a former research fellow at the Royal Institute of International Affairs (RIIA), with Blair speciously suggesting, in evidence to the House of Commons Foreign Affairs Committee, in 2002, that "lawful and legitimate are not necessarily the same thing." Foreign Secretary, Jack Straw, described a UN Security Council resolution authorizing the use of force as "desirable," while Defense Secretary, Geoff Hoon, stated it was for the UK to determine "whether or not force will be used."

A former MI6 agent, Sir Thomas Brimlow, who served in Moscow under diplomatic cover on several occasions from the 1940s to the mid-1960s, claimed in the bi-monthly, peer-reviewed journal, *International Affairs*, in July 1992, that Britain's ability to make friends and "get others to do our fighting for us" was a "quality which most disquiets the Soviets." It was all part of what British politicians of whatever political persuasion like to describe as the "special relationship" with the US - a phrase first coined by Winston Churchill in 1946. This economic, cultural and military symbiosis between the UK and the US is not an partnership of equals, as successive British prime ministers like to imply, but while Britain lacks military muscle, it serves Washington's interests in the international arena to "win or extract the co-operation of Great Britain," according to Brimelow.

Cold War analysts were not the only people to notice Britain's ability to win friends and potential military allies. Former CIA officer, Michael Scheuer, has pointed out that in 1996, eleven years before US Navy Seals finally caught up with him in the Pakistan city of Abbottabad on 1 May 2011, Osama bin Laden, in an interview with the magazine, *Nida'ul Islam* ('Call of Islam'), stated that alongside the US, "Britain bears the greatest enmity towards the Islamic world." In a June 2000 speech he accused Britain of destroying the Caliphate system, creating the Kashmiri and Palestinian problems, supporting an arms embargo on Bosnian Muslims, starving Iraqi children and enforcing the no-fly zone over northern Iraq. The Labour Government had also amended prevention of terror legislation (a legacy of the 'Troubles' in the North of Ireland) in early 2001, making it easier to charge and convict individuals of conspiring to incite terror, which *Guardian* columnist, Faisal Bodi, described as "reshaping the landscape in which opposition groups can operate," including those opposed to the Algerian and other despotic regimes in the Arab world. Twenty-one mainly Islamic organizations were banned, and several leading members who had been on MI5's watch-list were arrested, earning Britain "the scorn of Islamists, Muslim governments, and the Arab League," according to Scheuer. The Saudi Arabian daily newspaper, *Al-Watan*, owned by businessman, Bandar bin Khalid, a member of the House of Saud, posted online the official government response on 2 March 2001, accusing the Blair administration of passing legislation that shows "the word Islam has come to be synonymous with terror."

At 3.09 p.m. on 9/11/2001, just six hours after the low-tech attacks on America's symbols of free-market capitalism and military power, Blair declared that the conflict was not between the US and terrorism "but between the democratic world and terrorism" and that Britain will not rest "until this evil is driven from the world." For the Islamic and Arab world, and those who had criticized Britain's anti-terror legislation, this was virtually a declaration of war against Islam in general, which by implication, was both undemocratic and evil. On 12 September, President Bush described the attacks as an "act of war" and within two days had obtained $40 billion from Congress "to provide resources to address the terrorist attacks, and the consequences." The following day Bush promised that America would "lead the world to victory" over terrorism and described the conflict as the "first war of the 21st century." In response Taliban leaders, including Mullah Mohammed Omar and his deputy and the Taliban Movement's co-founder Abdul Ghani Baradar, called on Muslims to wage 'jihad' against America if Afghanistan was attacked. On 22 September Bush ordered US sanctions, whichi had been imposed on Pakistan and India following their 1998 nuclear tests, to be lifted, and within ten days NATO, for the first time since its founding, invoked its mutual defense clause, and the World Health Association (WHA) warned world governments to take seriously the risk of a WMD attack by a terrorist group. This was a response to a series of anthrax attacks which began one week after the Pentagon and WTC destruction and death, when anthrax spores were mailed to several media organizations, including the *New York Post*, the *National Enquirer*, ABC and CBS News, and the offices of two US Democratic Senators, Patrick Leahy and Tom Daschle. Five people died, 17 others were infected, dozens of buildings were contaminated and people, who had never paused in their daily routing to consider death in any form, were being warned of several exotic ways to die. Suddenly, life as a postal worker, a personal secretary or a mail-room gopher was a dangerous occupation. The FBI later admitted that the source was domestic but not before fear had been exploited and focused on the overseas threat of weapons of mass destruction in the hands of Muslim jihadists.

Three days after the WMD warning, under the codename Operation *Enduring Freedom*, the US and the UK began air and missile attacks against Taliban and al-Qaida targets in Afghanistan, despite the Taliban, on 5 October 2001, offering to put Osama bin Laden on trial in an Afghan court, or have him tried in another country, if the US provided "solid evidence" of his guilt, an offer, described by the *Guardian* newspaper as a "clear sign" that the Taliban was willing to co-operate with NATO's mission to hunt down the al-Qaida leader.

The object of Washington's assault was three-fold - destroy al-Qaida training camps, remove the Taliban and create a pro-western regime in Kabul. As far as the Bush administration was concerned there was no difference between terrorist organizations and the governments that allegedly supported them, or allowed them to operate within their borders. On 12 November 2001,

Taliban forces abandoned the capital Kabul, which was occupied by Northern Alliance fighters, and a fortnight later US Marines landed by helicopter at Forward Operating Base (FOB) Rhino, in the Registan Desert about 100 miles southwest of the city of Kandahar, the traditional seat of power of the Pashtun people, and the last Taliban stronghold. From Camp Rhino the USMC 26thMarine Expeditionary Unit advanced to capture and secure Kandahar International Airport, and by 6 December, the city was occupied. The UN Security Council moved laboriously to legitimize the conflict, and under Resolution 1386 established the NATO-led International Security Assistance Force (ISAF).

With Afghanistan 'secure' Bush and Blair turned their attention to Iraq, and by early 2002 the prospect of invading Iraq to deal with the threat of WMD-armed terrorists "had become the world's single biggest story" according to award-winning *Guardian* investigative journalist, Nick Davies. The story began with ""cautious estimates from intelligence experts who happened to be wrong." The reports were then "picked up and exaggerated" by politicians in London and Washington, by Iraqi exiles who had vested interests in regime change, and by pundits "who genuinely knew nothing at all about Iraqi weapons." As an example of the mass deception in the UK, Davies refers to a study of British broadcast news reports in the buildup to the invasion, conducted by Professor Justin Lewis of Cardiff University, which found that "86 percent of them assumed that Iraq had these weapons [WMDs] and only 14 percent of them registered any doubt at all about their existence." In the US, according to media analysts Rampton and Strauber, an opinion poll carried out in October 2002 by the Washington DC-based Pew Research Center found that 66 percent of the those asked believed that Saddam Hussein was involved in the 9/11 attacks, while 79 percent believed that Iraq already possessed or was close to possessing nuclear weapons. Many of those polled supported war with Iraq because they believed it would reduce the threat of terrorism. When this was broken down, pollsters found that 25 percent of the war's supporters "related to their perception of Hussein or the nature of his regime," describing him as "evil" and "a madman who represses his own people," while sixty percent gave a reason "related to their concerns stemming from 9/11."

While Bush and the neoconservative cabal in Washington focused on alleged links between Saddam Hussein and al-Qaida, the hawks in the Blair Cabinet, with all the high-rise commercial centers in London still standing, went with the threat of Iraq's alleged WMDs. In Washington the neoconservatives openly welcomed Ahmed Chalabi, head of the Iraqi National Congress (INC), an artificial opposition established by the locally-located Rendon Group, a PR and propaganda firm headed by John Rendon, the former election campaign consultant to Democratic presidential candidates Michael Dukakis and Jimmy Carter, who described himself in a 1998 speech at the National Security Conference (NSC) as an "information warrior and a perception manager," and was described by the author, James Bamford, in his 2006 award-winning *Rolling Stone* article as "the man who sold the war." Ahmed Chalabi, who was once referred to by supporters in the neoliberal magazine, *The New Republic* (which supported the war in its early stages) as the "George Washington of Iraq" - a political, military and moral insult to the commander-in-chief of the Continental Army who defeated the forces of King George III in the American Revolutionary War - was the conduit who provided much of the false information on Saddam's non-existent WMD arsenal and alleged ties with al-Qaida on which various agencies within the US intelligence community based its assessment of the Iraqi dictator's ability to wage war and threaten the West.

The British relied on their own band of liars to make the case for war, and the Labour PM played a dishonorable and devious role in the pre-invasion deception. President Bush may have had the military might of the US at his disposal, and this, no doubt, impressed Blair and his ministers on several visits to Washington, but Blair had a finely-tuned sense of political know-how, honed in the back-stabbing world of British Labour Party politics of the 1980s and mid-1990s. He knew how to make friends, pacify enemies and influence the right people, and by the time George Bush stole the US presidential election from Al Gore in 2000 (aided and abetted by the US Supreme Court 7-2 ruling, on 12 December, that the Florida recount of 70,000 ballots rejected by voting machine counters was unconstitutional) the right honorable MP from Sedgefield was already a wily and consummate performer on the world stage, ready to do business with men like Putin and Bush, on his own terms. His brand of diplomacy 'blindsided' the Foreign and Commonwealth Office (FCO), according to a *Guardian* editorial, on 7 November 2005, citing a speech he made in 1999 against the background of the Balkans conflict, long before the 'war on terror' came to dominate world politics and the relationships between nations, in which he had justified the "violation of state sovereignty to prevent genocide." Apart from the discredited claims about the 'threat' to the UK from Iraq's non-existent WMDs, this question about the violation of sovereignty, with or without a UN mandate, was one of the key arguments deployed by Downing Street to support the violent and illegal demise of Saddam Hussein's regime.

Sir Christopher Meyer, the British ambassador to Washington from 1997 to February 2003, provides an interesting insider's account of the interaction between Blair and Bush in his book, *DC Confidential*. Meyer supported the war, and was the confidant of senior figures in the Bush administration, holding regular private meetings with Vice President Dick Cheney, his aide Lewis Libby, Defense Secretary Donald Rumsfeld, and Bush's political adviser, Karl Rove. He describes the invasion of Iraq as a "political war" but is critical of how it was prosecuted. Meyer participated in crucial meetings at the Oval Office, had access to transcripts of Blair/Bush telephone conversations and Downing Street position papers, and was in the unusual position (for an outsider) of being trusted by the Beltway neoconservatives who shaped US foreign policy. Meyer describes Blair as an "impatient man" who liked "the vision thing" and paid less attention to the "ballast behind the ideas" that many of the pre-war issues demanded. He also reveals that when the FCO raised questions about the legality of going to war, the mandarins of King Charles Street were marginalized by Downing Street. In the 18 months before the March 2003 invasion Meyer dealt almost exclusively with the PM's office, and could not recall any telephone conversations with the FCO during that time.

In April 2002, the President and the Prime Minister met at Bush's Prairie Chapel Ranch, seven miles north of the town of Crawford, in McLennan County, Texas, and Blair signed up to regime change in Iraq. Two months later the Cabinet Office, a department in Whitehall which facilitates the decision-making process and hosts 'miscellaneous' units of Government, including the Joint Intelligence Committee (JIC), issued a summary of the Crawford meeting stating that Britain would support military action in Iraq as long as the Palestinian question was "quiescent" and that "all the options to eliminate Iraq's WMD through UN weapons inspectors" were exhausted. In the end neither of these pre-conditions were met, and in retrospect the summary's attempt to claim the high moral ground for the UK proved only to be a useful indicator for where the deceivers should focus their deception.

Damned Lies

In the House of Commons, on 24 September 2002, Tony Blair stood to address MPs on the issues raised in *Iraq's Weapons of Mass Destruction: The Assessment of the British Government* report. Parliament had been recalled for the occasion, the debating chamber was crammed. The document, signed-off on by the JIC's director, John Scarlett, contained a number of wholly inaccurate claims, unaccredited to protect sources, that Baghdad possessed chemical and biological, and had "revived" its nuclear weapons program. There were two specific allegations, one of which was recycled by President Bush in his State of the Union address, on 28 January 2003, that "Saddam Hussein had recently sought significant qualities of uranium from Africa" and the claim made in the foreword, personally written by Mr. Blair, that the document discloses that Saddam Hussein's military planning "allows for some of the WMD to be ready within 45 minutes of an order to use them." This was headline fodder for the following days' tabloids, exactly the type of audience that Blair's director of communications, Alistair Campbell, himself a former *Daily Mirror* journalist and founder of the Coalition Information Centre (CIC), wanted to reach, and which both Labour and Conservative MPs would have difficulty ignoring. Campbell was correct. Rupert Murdoch's *Sun* newspaper, which had supported Labour in the previous general elections, carried the headline "Brits 45 Mins from Doom" while the *Star* went with "Mad Saddam Ready to Attack: 45 Minutes from a Chemical War." The work of the Iraq Survey Group (IRG) would later prove that all the allegations made in the report, which became known as the 'September dossier' were false. The sole purpose, as Major General Michael Laurie, director of the Defence Intelligence Staff (DIS) who was involved in the document's production would later admit, in a 2011 letter to the Iraq Inquiry chairman, Sir John Chilcot, was "precisely to make a case for war, rather than setting out the available intelligence, and that to make the best of the sparse and inconclusive intelligence the wording was developed with care."

The genesis of the September dossier dates back to late July 2002, two months before MPs returned to Westminster, when PM Blair chaired a meeting of the 'war cabinet' in Downing Street, attended by his close political colleagues, Defence Secretary, Geoff Hoon, Foreign Secretary, Jack Straw, the Attorney General, Lord Goldsmith, MI6 director, Sir Richard Dearlove, the Chief of the Defence Staff, Sir Michael Boyce, David Manning, and Alistair Campbell. Not surprisingly the only topic on the agenda was "how to make the case for war" to Parliament and the public. A fortnight earlier, at a press conference in Washington, on 8 July, President Bush stated that it remained the policy of his administration "to have regime change [in Iraq] and that hasn't changed, and we'll use all tools at our disposal to do so." According to a confidential memo of the London meeting, published in the *Sunday Times,* on 1 May 2005, the MI6 boss acknowledged that Bush wanted to get rid of the Iraqi dictator by military action "justified by the conjunction of terrorism and WMD," that the "intelligence facts are being fixed around the policy" and that the NSC "had no patience with the UN route."

Four of the decision-makers at this meeting were lawyers - Tony Blair has a second class honors degree in jurisprudence from Oxford University, Jack Shaw qualified as a barrister at Inn of Court School of Law and had practiced criminal law from 1971 to 1974, Geoff Hoon read law at Jesus College, Cambridge, and Peter Goldsmith also read law at Cambridge and University College, London, while David Manning was an experienced diplomat having served in Poland, India, Paris and Moscow, and as ambassador to Israel from 1995 to 1998, before being appointed Blair's foreign policy adviser, and later replacing Christopher Meyer as ambassador to Washington. These men were fully aware of the illegality of un-mandated war. The only individual 'off message' was Admiral Sir Michael Boyce, who was skeptical of the Pentagon's claims about Saddam Hussein's links with al-Qaida, and the existence of his WMD stockpile. Within months Admiral Boyce, an experienced submariner who had served with the Royal Navy since 1961, was replaced by the more compliant General Michael Walker. His departure followed unconfirmed reports of a "difficult relationship" with Defense Secretary Hoon, with Boyce on one occasion contradicting Hoon's claim that chemical protection suits and gas masks found by coalition forces proved that the Iraqi Army intended to use chemical weapons. When CDS Boyce pointed out that the suits could also have been used for defense protection rather than for offensive purposes, Hoon retracted his claim. Boyce was also critical of the legal advice given by Attorney General Goldsmith, claiming he was not assured of full legal cover to avoid prosecution for war crimes at the International Criminal Court in The Hague. Although Boyce believed the war was "legally and morally justified," in an interview with the *Observer*, on 1 May 2005, he claimed to have warned Lord Goldsmith, after learning that the legal implications of un-mandated military action prior to the invasion contained none of the "top cover caveats," that if British soldiers were jailed for war crimes, "some others would go down" also. Asked if this meant PM Blair and the Attorney General, he replied "too bloody right."

The September dossier, one of two 'dodgy' documents produced by HMG prior to the invasion, which proved that when it comes to fooling most of the people all of the time, the British are past masters at the fine art of deception. The second file, a Downing Street briefing document, entitled *Iraq: Its Infrastructure of Concealment, Deception and Intimidation,* was issued to journalists on 3 February 2003. This one, known as the 'February dossier', was the product of Alistair Campbell's CIC unit, and purported to be an "updated intelligence assessment" of Iraq's WMD threat. Both of these documents were the basis of the argument used by Tony Blair to persuade 412 Labour and Conservative MPs to support the use of force to achieve regime change in Iraq. Eighty-five Labour 'rebels', the Liberal Democrats, and representatives of the Scottish and Welsh parties, were among 149 parliamentarians who weren't fooled by Blair's bluster, and opposed the war.

Within weeks of the February dossier's publication, Cambridge University international humanitarian law lecturer, Dr Glen Rangwala, disclosed on ITN's *Channel 4 News* that much of the briefing document - referred to by US Secretary of State Colin Powell during a press conference at the UN in New York as a "fine paper (...) which describes in exquisite details Iraqi deception activities" - had been plagiarized, lifted verbatim (including grammatical errors) from un-attributed sources, the most important being an article, entitled *Iraq's Security and Intelligence Network: A Guide & Analysis*, written by Ibrahim al-Marashi, a research associate at the Center for Nonproliferation Studies at the Monterey Institute of International Studies (MIIS) in California, and published in the quarterly, *Middle East Review of International Affairs.* According to Lib-Dem MP, Norman Baker, the CIC staff member responsible for lifting the *MERIA* article, was Paul Hamill, the CIC's "head of story development" and there was some rewriting done to make the downloaded document seem more "intelligence sourced and threatening." Mr. al-Marashi appeared before the House of Commons, cross-party, Foreign Affairs Select Committee (FASC), on 19 June 2003, telling the eleven MPs, appointed to monitor policy, administration and expenditure at the FCO (which was nominally responsible for the CIC) that he was "quite shocked to see it end up in this dossier. That was not my intent, to have it support such an argument to provide evidence necessary to go to war."

CIC staffers also lifted three articles from *Jane's Intelligence Review*, a monthly publication dealing with international security-related issues and arms proliferation, one by Ken Gause and two by Sean Boyne, an author and analyst opposed to the seemingly-inevitable war with Iraq. MI6, was not involved in the CIC briefing document because the agency's Middle East analysts privately disagreed with PM Blair's public position on Iraq's WMD threat and other aspects of the disinformation campaign. On 5 February, two days after the CIC release and only hours before Colin Powell was scheduled to speak at the UN prior to a crucial Security Council vote, MI6 leaked a three-week-old, classified DIS report to the BBC's defense correspondent, Andrew Gilligan, which explicitly contradicted one of the main charges against Saddam Hussein - that he had cultivated contacts with al-Qaida. The report had been sent to Blair and other senior members of the Cabinet, including Straw and Hoon, stating that Osama bin Laden's aims "are in ideological conflict with present day Iraq" and he [bin Laden] regarded the ruling Ba'ath Party as an "apostate regime." In his BBC report, Gilligan described the leak as "unprecedented" and a "shot across the politicians' bows" but it made no difference to Downing Street. Responding to the leak in a BBC Radio 4 interview, Jack Straw claimed that the Iraqi regime "appeared to be allowing a permissive environment in which al-Qaida is able to operate," adding that HMG had "some evidence of links between al-Qaida and various people in Iraq" and while the extent of these alleged links was unknown, it made no difference because the Iraqi regime "have been up to their necks in the pursuit of terrorism generally."

Saddam Hussein also went on the record, denying the existence of WMD, telling the retired, anti-war Labour MP (and former government minister) Tony Benn, in a Channel 4 interview; "These weapons do not come in small pills that you can hide in your pocket. These are weapons of mass destruction and it is easy to work out if Iraq has them or not." He also denied any connection with al-Qaida, saying, "if we had a relationship, and we believed in that relationship, we wouldn't be ashamed to admit it."

Meanwhile, in New York, Colin Powell went ahead with his duplicitous presentation, trying to sell the war to the UN and secure a second Security Council resolution mandating the use of force against the so-called WMD-hoarding, al-Qaida-connected Iraqi dictator. In his speech, Powell described a compound in north-eastern Iraq, run by the Islamic jihadist group, Ansar al-Islam, as a "terrorist chemicals and poisons factory." When reporter Luke Harding, of the London *Observer*, visited the site he found a "dilapidated collection of concrete outbuildings at the foot of a grassy sloping hill. Behind the barbed wire, and a courtyard strewn with broken rocket parts, are a few empty concrete houses. There is a bakery. There is no sign of chemical weapons anywhere - only the smell of paraffin and vegetable ghee used for cooking. In the kitchen, I discovered some chopped up tomatoes but not much else. The cook had left his Kalashnikov propped neatly against the wall."

Harding, one of a group of journalists invited by the Islamist group into the region, described Ansar al-Islam in his article on 9 February 2003, as a "brutal bunch" who had killed more than 800 opposition Kurdish fighters "but posed no real threat to Washington or London." He described the invitation to himself and other journalists to visit the site as a "doomed attempt to prevent an American missile strike once the war with Iraq kicks in." Powell had actually identified Khurmal, a small town about 2 miles from the dilapidated compound, as the site of the WMD factory. On the first weekend of the war Khurmal was bombed by US cruise missiles, and 45 villagers were killed, a brutal price to pay for what Harding described as Powell's "cheap hyperbole."

MI6 was not the source of another fabricated lie - that Saddam's procurement network had been active in Africa, attempting on several occasions to purchase yellow-cake uranium from the landlocked western state of Niger - made by President Bush in his January 2003 State of the Union address. The Italian military intelligence service, SISMI, acted as a conduit for forged documents supporting the unfounded allegation, which was included in an October 2002, 90-page US *National Intelligence Estimate* (NIE) and eventually found its way into Bush's speech to the nation

As a result of Bush's mendacity the yellow-cake allegation was included in a review of British intelligence relating to Iraq's WMD program. The five-member committee, chaired by Lord Butler of Brockwell, published its report on 14 July 2004, and claimed that there was sufficient intelligence to make a "well-founded judgment" that Iraq was seeking to obtain uranium illegally from Niger, and also the Democratic Republic of Congo, and referred to a 1999 visit by Iraqi officials to Niger, before stating that the British Government had intelligence from several different sources "indicating that this visit was for the purpose of acquiring uranium. Since uranium constitutes almost three-quarters of Niger's exports, the intelligence was credible." Without actually naming the CIA, the Butler report found that a "foreign intelligence agency" produced "seriously flawed" information on Saddam Hussein's WMD program, that Iraq was no greater a threat than other countries to the UK, and that the lack of success by the United Nations Monitoring, Verification and Inspection Commission (UNMOVIC) in finding WMDs should have prompted a "re-think" on the part of PM Blair, and senior ministers, whose language in the months prior to the invasion left the impression there was "fuller and firmer intelligence" to justify the deployment and inevitable deaths of British troops. The committee's handling of the yellow-cake/Africa connection attracted the most controversy. The criticism of the panel - Sir John Chilcot, a career diplomat and senior civil servant; a former Chief of the Defence Staff, Field Marshal Peter Inge; Labour MP, Ann Taylor, chair of the Commons Intelligence and Security Committee (ISC), who supported the invasion, and was involved in the preparation of the September dossier, and another voice for war, the Tory MP, and former Minister for State for Northern Ireland (1992-1993) Michael Mates, among others - was well-deserved. In their excellent book, *The Best War Ever*, Rampton and Stauber point out the committee's report offers no details of the alleged African shopping spree, not even an approximate date when this might have happened, thus giving no way to access its credibility. The British have also declined to share any information about this intelligence [possibly because none exists], even with the International Atomic Energy Agency (IAEA), which was responsible for prewar monitoring of Iraq's nuclear capability. In any case, the Congo's uranium mine was flooded and sealed several decades ago, which means that Iraq would not have been able to obtain uranium there even if it tried.

In the London *Evening Standard,* on 17 July 2004, University of Sussex professor of Theoretical Physics, and an expert in the field of nuclear proliferation and its consequences, Norman Dombey, stated that the Butler committee's data on the Niger issue was "incomplete" and described its conclusion - that the Iraqi procurement of yellow-cake was "credible" because three-quarters of the country's exports in 1999 was uranium - as "irrelevant since France controls Niger's uranium mines." He also pointed out that Iraq already had uranium in its main nuclear site, the gutted Tuwaitha research facility, heavily bombed in the 1991 Gulf War, which was far more than the country needed for any "conceivable" nuclear weapons program, adding

> nuclear weapons are difficult and expensive to build not because uranium is scarce, but because it is difficult and expensive to enrich U235 from 0.7% to the 90% needed for a bomb. Enrichment plants are large, use a lot of electricity and are almost impossible to conceal. Neither British security services [a reference to the foreign and domestic agencies, MI6 and MI5] nor the CIA seriously thought Iraq had a functioning enrichment plant that would have justified all the noise about nuclear weapons we heard before the war. When I read of the supposed Iraqi purchase of uranium from Niger, I thought it smelt distinctly fishy. It was a gigantic red herring.

Three days earlier a front-page report in the same newspaper, under the headline "Whitewash (Part Two)" stated that Butler had thrown Blair a "lifebelt" by claiming Iraq had tried to purchase uranium. The first 'whitewash' was the 2003 judicial inquiry into the death of Dr. David Kelly, chaired by a former Lord Chief Justice of Northern Ireland, Baron Brian Hutton.

The Lonely Death of David Kelly

The body of Dr. David Kelly, the MoD's highly-qualified WMD

inspector, was found at around 8.30am, on 17 July 2003, at Harrowdown Hill, one mile north of the Oxfordshire village of Southmoor. Two days before his death he gave evidence to the Foreign Affairs Select Committee (FASC) investigating the lack of evidence supporting "the alleged 45 minutes WMD threat to the UK," and had effectively "signed his own death warrant" according to Lib-Dem MP, Norman Baker. The decision to order Dr. Kelly to appear before the committee of MPs - after he had been 'outed' as the source of Andrew Gilligan's BBC report that the September dossier had been sexed-up to include the WMD threat Blair had used in the Commons to justify war - was taken by Defense Secretary Hoon during a Downing Street meeting attended by the PM. It was taken against the wishes of the Permanent Under Secretary of State at the MoD, Sir Kevin Tebbit, who had tried to protect the MoD scientist from the political and media fallout following Gilligan's report. Suggestions by unidentified Whitehall sources in some press reports that Dr. Kelly had been driven to suicide by the harsh treatment he received during questioning by MPs were described as a "worrying myth" by the political columnist of the *Guardian*, Simon Hoggart, who wrote in his 17 July 2003 report on the committee's proceedings that when Dr. Kelly left the committee room "he pushed past me [and] he was smiling."

The inquiry into Kelly's death lasted 110 hours, over a 22-day period, and took testimony from 74 witnesses. Its 750-page report, with 18 appendices, was published on 28 January 2004, although most of the material, including transcripts of conversations, copies of letters and emails, were posted online during the course of the inquiry. Lord Hutton concluded that Dr. Kelly had left his home with the intention of killing himself, and having taken an overdose of painkillers prescribed for his wife's arthritis, cut his left wrist with a gardening knife, and had bled to death where his body was found.

The report mildly rebuked the MoD for its treatment of Dr. Kelly, but found that the September dossier had not been sexed-up but correctly represented the "available intelligence" although the JIC, chaired by John Scarlett, who had signed-off on the dossier (and was later rewarded for his loyalty by being appointed director-general of MI6) may have been "subconsciously influenced" by Blair's Cabinet. In reaching this conclusion the Hutton Inquiry had to dismiss or discredit testimony from several witnesses, including FCO senior diplomat, David Broucher, who appeared late on Thursday afternoon, 21 August 2003. Broucher had met Dr. Kelly in February 2003, and during the course of a conversation about WMDs and his work in Iraq, Dr. Kelly had told him that he had assured his Iraqi sources that there would be no war if they cooperated with UNMOVIC, and that a war would put him in an "ambiguous moral position." When he asked what would happen if Iraq was invaded, Dr. Kelly had replied, "I will probably be found dead in the woods." Mr. Blair and his senior ministers were almost completely exonerated by Lord Hutton despite the 'presentation' changes made by Alistair Campbell to the September dossier, Blair's misleading performance in the House of Commons, and the Downing Street decision to 'out' Dr. Kelly.

In general the British media was both surprised and angry at the findings of the Hutton Inquiry, and the word 'whitewash' was frequently used in headlines and by commentators. Even the introverted, Tory-supporting tabloid, the *Daily Express,* headlined its report "Hutton's whitewash leaves questions unanswered." A similar line was taken by the *Daily Mail,* asking in its editorial "Does this verdict, my lord, serve the real interests of truth?" while the *Independent* produced an almost completely blank front-page, with WHITEWASH? in blood-red capitals above the fold. If truth is indeed the first casualty of war, as former Californian governor, Senator Hiram Johnson, stated in 1917 while opposing US involvement in the Great War, then David Kelly was a close second in this one. His death, however, was quickly forgotten - except in the *Daily Mail* which has carried on a campaign to have an official inquest -when cruise missiles rained down on Baghdad one month after publication, and British troops set off to "fight the good fight," occupy the southern city of Basra, and secure the surrounding desert landscape.

Interest was regenerated in 2007 by Norman Baker, who resigned as Lib-Dem spokesman for Environment, Health and Rural Affairs, to carry out an 18-month investigation, which culminated in the publication of *The Strange Death of David Kelly.* As accidental death or natural causes had been ruled out, Baker began with the premise that Dr. Kelly had either committed suicide, as Hutton concluded, or he had been murdered and his body dumped in Harrowdown Wood. Based on the criticism of several prominent doctors that the medical evidence cited in the Hutton report - an overdose of the painkiller, coproxamol, and the severing of an ulnar artery - could not have caused Dr. Kelly's death, that the pills found in the victim's stomach were less than a third needed for a fatal overdose, on the lack of blood where the body was found (as the two paramedics who first arrived on the scene later testified) and the fact that no fingerprints at all were found on the blunt-edged pruning knife that Kelly had allegedly used to slash his wrist, Baker concluded that the WMD inspector had been 'suicided' and bled-out elsewhere, before his body was dumped where it had been found.

Pursuing the theory that "suicide can be staged to cover murderers' tracks" Baker referred to the unexplained, and still unsolved, killing of American journalist, Danny Casolaro, who was found naked, with his wrists slashed, in a bath at the Shearton Inn, Martinsburg, West Virginia, on 10 August 1991. In the absence of any visible signs of violence the local police investigation concluded that Casolaro had committed suicide. At the time of his death he was investigating the 'Inslaw affair' and allegations of inter-government corruption involving the US intelligence agencies and the FBI, linked to the development of a software package called *Prosecutor's Management Information System* (PROMIS). A former CIA forensic pathologist, Dr. Christopher Green, who discovered that Bulgarian dissident and BBC journalist, Georgi Markov, had been poisoned by risin delivered into his system by a pellet fired from an adapted umbrella while crossing Waterloo Bridge in London, on 7 September 1978, participated in Casolaro's autopsy. He believed the victim was incapacitated, stripped, placed in the bath and his left wrist slashed "precisely in the same manner as Dr. Kelly," according to Baker. The former *Washington Post* White House correspondent, and investigative journalist, Sterling Seagrave, claimed a group of professional assassins, not connected with the CIA, had been commissioned by the Pentagon to carry out 'wet operations' and had murdered Casolaro, and suggested to Baker that the MoD scientist "might also have fallen victim to these shadowy killers."

This 'conspiracy theory' may not be as far-fetched as it seems. In 1992, despite the official verdict of suicide, the US House of Representatives published a report on the Inslaw affair and concluded that, "based on the evidence collected by the committee, it appears the path followed by Danny Casolaro in pursuing his investigation into the Inslaw matter brought him into contact with a number of dangerous individuals associated with organized crime and the world of covert intelligence operations. The suspicious circumstances have led some law enforcement professionals and others to believe that his death may not have been suicide. As long as the possibility exists that Danny Casolaro died as a result of his investigation into the Inslaw matter, it is imperative that further investigation be conducted."

Norman Baker concluded, however, that the 'shadowy killers' of David Kelly were closer to home. Referring to a claim made by respected US microbiologist and UN weapons inspector, Dr Richard Spertzel, that his slain colleague was "on an Iraqi hit list," the MP suggests various possible motives for the scientist's death, before putting forward his "most plausible explanation" - that a London-based Iraqi exile group may have organized the killing as an act of revenge or to prevent Dr. Kelly undermining the exiles' western power base, with the key question being whether the actions of the Iraqi group were "self-generated, and subsequently covered up by the Government, or whether a tiny cabal within the British establishment commissioned the assassins to undertake this." He also suggests that senior officers within the local Thames Valley Police (TVP) were aware of the plot to kill the scientist, but had failed to act in time to prevent the murder. Within hours of the body being found a decision was taken by senior intelligence and security personnel to cover up the incident by making Dr. Kelly's death look like suicide in order to prevent diplomatic turmoil with the US and Britain's EU partners who opposed the invasion, and domestic political consequences for the Labour Government and the parliamentary party, many of whom now enthusiastically supported the war.

Mr. Baker is by no means alone in challenging the official account of Dr. Kelly's death, and those who agree with the MP cannot easily be dismissed as "conspiracy junkies." They include a campaigning group of senior medical personnel, headed by former assistant coroner, Dr. Michael Powers,

QC, who were forced to take legal action to secure the release of the medical evidence after Lord Hutton's unprecedented 70-year ban on the publication of the post-mortem records and all additional medical data. There was no coroner's inquest into Dr. Kelly's death, which is standard practice for all suspicious deaths in the UK, because the Labour MP, Baron Falconer, serving as Lord Chancellor in the Blair administration, with responsibility for the "efficient functioning of the courts" ruled in 2003 that the independent legal forum to assess all the evidence to determine how and why he died would be replaced by the Hutton inquiry.

US Air Force officer, Mai Pederson, who had met David Kelly when she worked as a translator for UNMOVIC in 1998, has challenged Lord Hutton's conclusion that there was "no third party involvement," claiming that an injury to Dr Kelly's right elbow made it difficult for him to carry out even relatively minor tasks, and his right hand grip was so weak he would have been unable to hold a knife and severe the ulnar artery on his left wrist, buried deep in the tissue below the small finger. Pederson, whose official duties included classified intelligence assessments, had been interviewed by TVP officers over a two-day period in New York after the 59-year-old scientist's body was found, and had explained her reservations about the published reports, but her statement was never given to the Hutton committee. The former TVP Chief Constable, Michael Page, testified that it "contained nothing of relevance." The police have implied, according to a *Daily Mail* interview with Ma Pederson on 31 August 2008, that she refused permission for her statement to be submitted to the Hutton Inquiry, when in fact she had stipulated that if it was "deemed relevant" to the coroner's inquest, she was willing for the police "to reveal the information on a non-attributable basis."

One of the last people that David Kelly was in contact with - by email at 11.18am on 18 July, about four hours before he left home for the final time - was former *New York Times* journalist, Judith Miller, who had contacted Kelly after he had appeared 'in camera' before the ISC two days earlier, stating that she had heard (probably from her connections in the US intelligence world, as Baker suggests) that things had gone well for him. Dr. Kelly replied that he was waiting a few days before making a judgment, because "many dark actors" were playing games. Baker speculates that these 'dark actors' were Blair, Hoon and Campbell, who were using him to discredit the BBC. As the MP points out, Dr. Kelly's measured approach "does not suggest an emotional churning that might be associated with someone about to commit suicide just a few hours later." Judith Miller would later suffer the consequences of her own reporting on Saddam Hussein's WMD program, spending almost three months in jail in 2005 for contempt of court after she refused to testify before a Federal Grand Jury investigating a leak which named Valerie Plame as an undercover CIA agent. In fact her source had been Lewis 'Scooter' Libby, chief of staff to VP Dick Cheney, whom she had met on 8 July 2003, two days after Plame's husband, former US ambassador, Joseph Wilson, had published an *op-ed* piece in the *NYT*, entitled *What I Didn't Find in Africa*, accusing the Bush administration of "twisting" intelligence about the alleged procurement of yellow cake from Niger to justify war in Iraq. In the final two paragraphs, Wilson, who had entered the US Foreign Service in 1978 and was Deputy Chief of Mission in Baghdad to US ambassador, April Glaspie, prior to the invasion of Kuwait, wrote:

> I was convinced before the war that the threat of weapons of mass destruction in the hands of Saddam Hussein required a vigorous and sustained international response to disarm him. Iraq possessed and had used chemical weapons; it had an active biological weapons program and quite possibly a nuclear research program - all of which were in violation of United Nations resolutions. Having encountered Mr Hussein and his thugs in the run-up to the Persian Gulf War of 1991, I was only too aware of the dangers he posed. But were these dangers the same ones the administration told us about? We have to find out. America's foreign policy depends on the sanctity of its information. For this reason, questioning the selective use of intelligence to justify the war in Iraq is neither idle sniping nor 'revisionist history', as Mr. Bush has suggested. The act of war is the last option of a democracy, taken when there is a grave threat to our national security. More than 200 American soldiers have lost their lives in Iraq already. We have a duty to ensure that their sacrifice came for the right reasons.

Miller was released on 29 September 2005, and disclosed her source before the grand jury. She subsequently testified against Libby, who had been indicted on two counts of perjury, two counts of making false statement to federal investigators and one count of obstruction of justice. He was found guilty of all but one indictment, sentenced by District of Columbia Federal Judge Reggie B. Walton, to 30 months imprisonment, fined $25,000, and then pardoned by President Bush after his appeal failed and before he ever saw the inside of a prison cell.

Before a Shot Is Fired

There was considerable popular opposition in the UK to what had become known as 'Blair's War.' Peaceful protest on the streets of London attracted around one million people, while several prominent politicians also expressed anti-war views, including Foreign Secretary Straw's predecessor, the late Robin Cook. In an article in the *Guardian*, on 12 July 2004, Cook disclosed that he had been assured by JIC chairman, John Scarlett, during a February 2003 briefing, that the 'threat' weapons in question were "only battlefield ones." When Cook suggested that, in his opinion, Saddam had no long-range WMDs, Scarlett "readily agreed," but when he asked why the JIC believed the Iraqis would not use battlefield chemical weapons against British troops, Scarlett "surprised me by claiming that, in order to evade detection by the UN inspectors, Saddam had taken apart the shells and dispersed them - with the result that it would be difficult to deploy them under attack. Not only did Saddam have no weapons of mass destruction in the real meaning of that phrase, neither did he have usable battlefield weapons."

Mr. Cook, who had served as Foreign Secretary from 1997 to 2001, and was Leader of the House of Commons from June 2001 to 17 March 2003, subsequently put these points to Blair, twelve days before he resigned as Speaker. Blair confirmed what Scarlett had told him- that the battlefield weapons had been disassembled and stored separately, adding, "I was therefore mystified a year later to hear him say that he had never understood that the intelligence agencies did not believe Saddam had long-range weapons of mass destruction." He accused Blair of showing a "surprising lack of interest as to what the threat actually was," given that he was justifying war to the nation "on the grounds that the Iraqi dictator was a serious threat to British interests." As a result the British people had been asked to accept that from September 2002 to March 2003, Blair had been allowed to think that Saddam had long-range chemical weapons, while MI6, the DIS and the JIC assessed he had only battlefield weapons. Mr. Cook characterized this as representing "the most extraordinary failure of communication in the history of the British intelligence agencies."

And there were individuals who put their freedom and their livelihood on the line in an attempt to prevent the subsequent slaughter of Iraqi civilians and British troops. People like Katharine Teresa Gun, a 29-year-old Mandarin linguist at the British Government's SIGINT/ELINT agency, GCHQ, based at Cheltenham, who was charged, on 13 November 2003, with a breach of Section 1 of the *Official Secrets Act* (1998), namely the disclosure of classified information, documents or other articles relating to security or intelligence. In Gun's case the document in question was a *Top Secret/COMINT//X1* email she received, at 12.06am on 31 January 2003, from the NSA's deputy Chief of Staff (Regional Targets), Frank Koza, explaining that the NSA was "mounting a surge" particularly directed at the UN Security Council (UNSC) members, Angola, Cameroon, Chile, Bulgaria and Guinea, whose votes were crucial to the US and the UK for the UNSC to mandate the use of force to secure regime change in Iraq. Koza also emphasized the need to "pay attention to existing non-UNSC members UN-related and domestic communications" for anything useful that could give US policy makers "an edge in obtaining results favorable to US goals or to head off surprises." Explaining that the Fort Meade-based NSA already had "special UN-related diplomatic coverage" from non-sitting UNSC members in place, Koza also asked for support from GCHQ analysts "who might have similar more indirect access to valuable information from accesses in your product lines." In other words, the NSA was asking GCHQ, whose 'product' is the covert monitoring of telephone and computer communications, to spy on UNSC delegations, a clandestine task totally illegal under the UN Charter.

The fact that this memo was sent at all indicates how corrosive the Washington neo-cons influence was in the pre-war days. Presumably a copy of the memo, with a similar request for UNSC 'product' was sent to other members of the UKUSA/ECHELON global monitoring community- Australia's Defense Signals Directorate, (DSD) headquartered at Russell Offices complex in Canberra, which operates monitoring facilities at Kojarena, in Western Australia, and at Shoal Bay, near Darwin, in the Northern Territory; the Communications Security Establishment (CSE) in Canada which operates the country's SIGINT collection base at CFS (Canadian Forces Station) Leitrim, in Ottawa, Ontario, with regional intercept facilities at CFS Alert at Nunavut, CFS Gander in Newfoundland, and CFS Barret in British Colombia; and New Zealand's Government Communications Security Bureau (GCSB), which operates a satellite communications listening and intercept station in the Waihopai Valley, on the South Island, and a radio communications intercept facility at Tangimoana.

On-duty officers at these facilities were recipients of Frank Koza's memo, yet only Katharine Gun had the courage to act on this blatantly illegal disregard for UN protocols, and leaked the email to the *Observer*, doing so "without regrets and with a clear conscience" hoping to prevent an illegal war. In a BBC2 *Newsnight* interview, on 25 February 2003, she explained that what the NSA was asking was "both legally and morally wrong." She also admitted not raising the matter with an external staff counselor because she "honestly didn't think it would have had any practical effect." Several hours earlier the now ex-GCHQ linguist had appeared at the Old Bailey before the Recorder of London, Judge Michael Hyam, and within 30 minutes was told that she was free to go after prosecutor, Mark Elison, told the court there was "no longer sufficient evidence for a realistic prospect of conviction." This was another lie, this time to prevent the disclosure of classified documents relating to Attorney General, Lord Goldsmith's advice to PM Blair about the legality, or otherwise, of the Iraq war, which Ms Gun's legal team, headed by solicitor, James Welch, had requested the previous day.

Two points are worth noting in this brief but telling footnote to the complex and disingenuous history of Blair's War, but important nonetheless. Under the OSA only the Attorney General has the authority to make the final decision on whether or nor to proceed with prosecution, and all that is needed to secure a conviction under the secrecy legislation is for the prosecution to demonstrate that the defendant's action was covered by the terms of the OSA. Ms Gun's actions were covered, she had breached Section 1 of the Act and admitted doing so. The truth was far more dangerous for Mr. Blair. Ms Gun planned to argue that she had leaked the NSA email in order to save British and Iraqi lives in a war which she opposed, and the Old Bailey jury might have returned a verdict of not guilty, damaging both the use of draconian legislation in such circumstances, and Downing Street's argument that war was the only option to secure regime change in Baghdad. This, in turn, might have raised questions about the single-minded drive to war in Washington, not that the Beltway neocons would have noticed, or even cared.

There was a precedent for the AG Goldsmith's concern about the juridical response to Katharine Gun's moral dilemma, which she briefly mentioned on the day of the court case, telling journalists how she was "baffled that in the 21st century we as human beings are still dropping bombs on each other as a means to resolve issues."

Killing to make a point and lying about it had also bothered Clive Ponting, a senior civil servant at the MoD, almost two decades earlier, in relation to the sinking of the Argentinean light cruiser, *ARA General Belgrano*, during the South Atlantic *Guerra de las Malvinas*, at 3.57pm on 2 May 1982, by the British nuclear-powered, hunter-killer submarine, *HMS Conqueror*, with the loss of 323 lives, just over half the total of Argentinean military service personnel deaths in the 73-day conflict. Ponting had been charged under Section 2 of the 1911 OSA, after admitting to sending two documents to Labour MP Tam Dalyell, in July 1984, about the sinking of the Argentinean warship, which revealed that the vessel had been sighted on 30 April by *HMS Conqueror*, a day earlier than officially reported, and was sailing away from the British-declared 200 nautical miles total exclusion zone. Under international law an exclusion zone is for the benefit of neutral vessels, and the location and bearing of hostile vessels does not make them immune from attack. What bothered Ponting was the lies and what he regarded as the "unnecessary loss of life." Fourteen hours earlier the Peruvian President, Fernando Belaunde, proposed a comprehensive peace plan; however, during a live television debate on BBC1 in May 1983, British prime minister, Margaret Thatcher, claimed she was unaware of the Peruvian peace proposal, and that the Argentinean vessel - a Brooklyn-class CL-46, built by the New York Shipbuilding Corporation in 1935, and originally named *USS Phoenix*, which had survived the 1941 Pearl Harbor attack and served in the Pacific before being sold to the Argentinean Navy in 1951 - was a threat to the British naval blockade off the Malvinas. Mrs. Thatcher was correct, and under the Geneva Convention which regulates how humans should go about killing each other legally, the sinking of *ARA Belgrano* was not a war crime. The vessel was involved in a pincher movement according to SIGINT intercepts disclosed by former British naval intelligence officer, David Thorp, who headed the SIGINT team on board the amphibious warship *HMS Intrepid*, during the conflict, and the legality of the sinking is no longer a matter of dispute in Buenos Aires or London. But with public support for the war declining, Thatcher needed a victory, and the vessel's sinking earned headlines in the UK, the most gung-ho being 'GOTCHA' in the *Sun*, the Tory-supporting, biggest-selling daily tabloid.

Ponting's lawyer put forward a "public interest" defense, claiming the disclosure of classified documents to an MP was covered by parliamentary privilege. He expected to be jailed, as did most of Whitehall's political commentators, but despite Mr. Justice McCowan's opinion during his summing up, that the "public interest is what the Government of the day says it is," followed by his rhetorical question to the vetted jury of eight men and four women, "Can it then be in the interests of the State to go against the policy of the Government of the day?" it took less than three hours, directly after lunch, for the jury to return an unanimous "not guilty" verdict. The British Government responded by tightening UK secrecy legislation, resulting in the 1989 OSA, under which Katharine Gun had been charged, The last thing the Blair administration wanted was another acquittal, and the legal and legislative consequences that would bring.

On 20 March 2003, three days after Lord Goldsmith's written parliamentary answer on the legality of using force in Iraq, in which he claimed authority existed in a combination of UNSC Resolutions adopted under Chapter VII of the UN Charter, Elizabeth Wilmshurst, a fellow at the Royal Institute of International Affairs (RIIA) and Professor of International Law at University College, London (UCL), resigned from her position as deputy legal adviser at the FCO after the Attorney General reversed her legal opinion, submitted in a classified memo, on 10 March, that the invasion was illegal without a second UNSC resolution. Goldsmith now claimed that the use of force was covered by Resolution 678, which had been adopted in November 1990, authorizing military action if Saddam failed to unconditionally withdraw his troops from Kuwait to pre-1 August 1990 positions, the day before the invasion. This was followed by Resolution 687, in April 1991, that set out the ceasefire conditions after Operation *Desert Storm*, included an obligation on Saddam Hussein to remove or destroy all biological and chemical weapons, and ballistic missiles with a range greater than 80 miles, but crucially, according to Goldsmith, it did not terminate the authority to use force as stated in Resolution 678. The UNSC had determined that Iraq was in breach of 687 because it had not fully complied with its obligation to disarm, and had given Baghdad a "final opportunity to comply" or face "serious consequences." This exercise in legal semantics was based on the false assumption, itself based on disinformation promoted by Iraqi exiled opposition and intelligence abuse, that somewhere in the deserts of Iraq there were concealed WMDs, and that Saddam had the means of delivery.

Wilmshurst's resignation letter was released by FCO to the BBC under the *Freedom of Information Act* (FIA) two years later. In it she stated her opposition to the use of force without a second UNSC resolution "to revive the authorization given in SRC 678." What is of interest is the FCO's attempt to manipulate the message, redacting the passage, later obtained by Channel 4 News, in which she writes: "My views accord with the advice that has been given consistently in this office before and after the adoption of UN security council resolution 1441 and with what the attorney general gave us to understand was his view prior to his letter of 7 March. (The view expressed in that letter has of course changed again into what is now the official line.)" She went on to explain to her boss at the FCO, senior Legal Advisor Michael

Wood, that she could not, in conscience, go along with advice within the FCO, or given to the public or Parliament "which asserts the legitimacy of military action without a resolution, particularly since an unlawful use of force on such a scale amounts to the crime of aggression; nor can I agree with such action in circumstances which are so detrimental to the international order and the rule of law."

The full extent of how Blair and his senior armchair warriors in the Cabinet manipulated the legal justification for war and put political pressure on Lord Goldsmith to "tow the party line" was revealed in *Lawless World* by Philippe Sands, a colleague of Elizabeth Wilmshurst's at the International Law department at UCL, whose letter of resignation was released by the FCO shortly before the book's publication in March 2005. Mr. Sands, an acknowledged expert in the coercive abuse of international law by supposedly law-abiding, democratic administrations, accused President Bush and PM Blair of "conspiring to invade Iraq" and was the first to refer to the five-page Blair/Bush memo, dated 31 January 2003. It was written by Blair's chief foreign policy adviser, David Manning, and provided a contemporaneous account of a two-hour meeting at the Oval Office between both men during which Bush made it clear to Blair that he was determined to invade Iraq without a second UNSC resolution, even if the arms inspectors failed to find unconventional weapons of mass destruction, and that the "start date for the military campaign was now penciled in for 10 March" when the bombing would begin. The President is paraphrased as saying that the US would put its full weight behind efforts to get another UNSC resolution and would "twist arms or even threaten" but even if that failed - which, of course, it did despite Colin Powell's best lying efforts five days later in New York- "military action would follow anyway." Prime Minister Blair responds, saying, "if anything went wrong with the military campaign, or if Saddam increased the stakes by burning the oil wells, killing children or fermenting internal divisions within Iraq, a second resolution would give us international cover, especially with the Arabs." Bush didn't give a damn about Arab opinion, especially with his friends, the Saudis, onside, but nonetheless suggested three ways Iraq might be provoked into a military confrontation: bringing out a defector to "give a public presentation" about Saddam's WMDs, assassinating the Iraqi dictator, or flying a U2 reconnaissance aircraft painted in UN colors, with USAF fighter cover, over Iraq so that, if fired upon, it would be in breach of UN resolutions. The two men envisaged a quick victory on the battlefield, with the planned air campaign wiping out Iraq's command and control centers, and decimating the Revolutionary Guard, while the conscripted Iraqi Army could be expected to "fold very quickly." All of which would result in a complicated but manageable transition to a new Iraqi administration.

At this meeting, Mr. Bush was flanked by his national security adviser, Condoleezza Rice, her senior aide, Daniel Fried, and the White House chief of staff, Andrew Card, while Blair, apart from Manning, was joined by two members of the Downing Street 'inner circle', Matthew

Rycroft and Jonathan Powell. On the subject of post-invasion planning the Manning memo states that "Condi Rice says a great deal of work was now at hand" that the Pentagon would deploy a "planning cell" to Iraq directly after operations, and that detailed planning had already been done "on supplying the Iraqi people with food and medicine." He also suggested it was "unlikely there would be internecine warfare between the different religious and ethnic groups" - an opinion with which Mr. Blair agreed. Sadly, for the tens of thousands of Iraqi civilians who would die in the blitzkrieg and the eight-year occupation, all of the above turned out to be wishful thinking. Condoleezza Rice acknowledges this in her detailed, but also highly-selective, memoir, *No Higher Honor*, where she claims she tried but failed to get a "workable plan" for the maintenance of law and order in Baghdad after the fall of Saddam on the President's agenda, but Bush "wasn't interested in this issue."

Occupation and Aftermath

Tony Blair was a man for all clichés. In Belfast, during the long-drawn-out, patience-sapping peace negotiations, he spoke about feeling the "hand of history on his shoulder." However, in Iraq he was an the wrong side of history, and there were no polished one-liners to explain why it was all allowed to go so badly wrong from the beginning.

British forces were given the responsibility of taking and occupying Iraq's second largest city and main port, Basra, located along the Shatt al-Arab waterway, and the southern provinces bordering Kuwait to the south and Iran to the east, which included the oilfields at Rymayalh. From March to May 2003 some of the heaviest fighting took place on the outskirts of the city. After the largest tank battle involving British forces, including the 7th Armored Brigade, since the North African WW2 campaign the city was captured on 6 April, and the Parachute Regiment was deployed to clear the 'old quarter' of fedayeen fighters and small groups of irregular Iraqi forces. For Blair that was about as good as it got. Several highly-classified memos, sent over a two month period after the March 2003 invasion by John Sawers, his personal envoy in Baghdad, to David Manning, to Downing Street chief of staff, Jonathan Powell, to Blair's private secretary on foreign affairs, Matthew Rycroft, and to the Chief of the General Staff (CGS) at the MoD, Sir Michael Walker, confirm that the senior echelons of the political and military decision making establishment were fully briefed of the "disastrous mishandling" of the occupation, mainly the result of a "series of failures by US forces" according to Sawers.

The memos, obtained by the *New York Times* chief military correspondent, Michael Gordon - the first journalist to write about Saddam Hussein's alleged nuclear weapons program in the *NYT* in August 2002, in an inflammatory article entitled, 'US Says Hussein Intensifies Quest for A-Bomb Parts,' and who was embedded with US Land Forces commanded by General Tommy Franks during the first phase of the war - are referred to in his 2006 book, *Cobra II: The Inside Story of the Invasion and Occupation of Iraq*, (written in collaboration with retired Marine Corps Lieutenant-General Bernard Trainor) and blame the descent into anarchy on bad political and military decision-making in Washington. They expose the inability of the Blair administration to influence events on the ground in Iraq, despite the much-vaunted UK/US 'special relationship.'

In a memo written on 11 May 2003, four days after Sawers arrived in Baghdad, unambiguously headed 'Iraq: What's Going Wrong,' the experienced FCO senior diplomat and Arabist (who had worked on behalf of MI6 in Yemen and Syria in the early part of his career and served as ambassador to Egypt from 2001 to 2003) described the deceptively named Office of Reconstruction and Humanitarian Assistance (ORHA), the first US civilian administration in Iraq, headed by retired US Gen. Jay Garner, as an "unbelievable mess" with Garner and his well-meaning team of "60-year-old retired generals" out of their depth. According to Sawers (who is currently head of MI6) the only senior US official "offering any direction" was Garner's British deputy, Major-General Tim Cross, a veteran of the Troubles in Ireland, the 1991 Gulf War, and three tours of duty in the Balkans. On 12 May, Garner was replaced by Paul Bremer, who reported primarily to Secretary of Defense Donald Rumsfeld. Very little changed, however, and in a memo dated 25 June, Blair's man in Baghdad concluded that situation had "continued to deteriorate."

Referring to security matters, Sawers believed that a "big part of the problem is the US Third Infantry Division. They fought a magnificent war but now just want to go home. Unlike more mobile US units they are sticking to their heavy vehicles and are not inclined to learn new techniques. Our Para's company at the embassy witnessed a US tank respond to (harmless) Kalashnikov fire into the air from a block of residential flats by firing three tank rounds into the building." He concluded by stating "frankly, the 3rd Inf. Div need to go home" and suggested that the military slack might be taken up by British troops, "at least one battalion with a mandate to deploy into the streets could still make an impact." The suggestion was supported by GCS Gen. Walker, but rejected by Mr. Blair and his civilian Downing Street advisers.

Bechtel Corporation, the main US civilian contractor, awarded the reconstruction contract - which was hopelessly underestimated to be worth $680 million - through USAID in April 2003 by President Bush, had been slow to tackle the reconnection of basic services, according to Sawers, with "dire consequences," leaving at least 40 percent of Baghdad's sewage pouring into the River Tigris untreated. OHRA also failed to take into account the fear among Iraqi civilians that officials of Saddam's Ba'ath Party might be re-appointed to "quite senior positions in the trade and health ministries" while thousands of party members "who held relatively junior posts" were sacked.

Mr. Sawers' views were supported in a memo dated mid-July 2003 by Maj-Gen. Albert Whitley, the most senior British officer serving with US

Land Forces, who warned his military bosses back at the MoD in Whitehall that the US/UK coalition was "in danger of losing the peace." He blamed Gen. Franks, who had taken credit for the swift fall of Baghdad but showed little interest in post-war responsibilities: "I am sure Franks did not want to take ownership of Phase IV" - the occupation and reconstruction of the country - and there was a failure [in Washington, London and Baghdad] to "anticipate the extent of the backlash or the mood of Iraqi society." Both Whitley and Sawers agreed that – despite the dissolution of the Iraq Army, the aggressive de-Baathification policy, the destruction of government buildings and cultural artifacts, and the exacerbations of the Sunni-Shia discord - one of the biggest mistakes made in Washington was the decision, signed-off on by Rumsfeld and Franks, to withdraw several thousand US troops after the invasion, leaving the country with insufficient military capacity to ensure security. Once again London failed to respond to this warning, and the security vacuum was quickly occupied by various rebel militias, and campaign-experienced al-Qaida fighters, creating a situation from which the country has still not managed to recover.

The fracture which runs through the official narrative of Blair's War, including the Butler, Hutton and ISC reports, and the incomplete Chilcot Inquiry, is that it was an illegal enterprise under international law from the beginning. And everything that follows is criminal behavior, sanctioned, if not tacitly approved, at the highest level of government, including the deaths of civilians and coalition military personnel, Iraqi soldiers and insurgents, and the abuse and torture suffered in prisons and detention centers. This is Blair's legacy.

The history of the British Empire, since the legitimate use of force against the Third Reich, has been a litany of appalling noncombatant abuse. In Malaysia in the late 1940s, the 12-year 'Emergency' included widespread and indiscriminate bombing, and the resettlement of hundreds of thousands in 'fortified' villages. It was here that Gen. Frank Kitson refined his counter-insurgency techniques which were later used in the North of Ireland. The emergency in Kenya in the early 1950s included Nazi-style concentration camps, resettlement, torture and execution. An estimated 150,000 African men, women and children died in that brutal, anti-colonial struggle. In 1953, Winston Churchill deployed the Black Watch Regiment to British Guyana to remove from power the democratically-elected People's Progressive Party (PPP) and its leader, Cheddi Jagan, after Washington and the CIA warned that Jagan was a "crypto-communist whose election would facilitate Soviet influence in the region." In October 1956, Britain invaded Egypt to force regime change after President Nasser moved to nationalize the Suez Canal. From 1957 to 1959, Britain deployed the RAF and the SAS in Oman to support the repressive regime of Sultan Said bin Taimur against the Omani Liberation Army (OLA). In the mid-1960s, according to declassified documents available at the Public Records Office in Kew, Britain supplied warplanes, arms and intelligence to the centralized, military-dominated Suharto regime in Indonesia that were used in anti-communist operations which resulted in an estimated one million deaths, and in the invasion and occupation of East Timor, which resulted in at least 100,000 deaths, according to the Commission for Reception, Truth and Reconciliation 2006 report, *The Profile of Human Rights*. In 1968, Britain began the secret and forceful removal of 1500 indigenous inhabitants of the Chaos Islands in the central Indian Ocean before handing over the largest, depopulated Diego Garcia, to the Pentagon. The tropical coral atoll was used by the USAF as a staging post for B-1, B-2 and B-52 bombers to attack targets in Afghanistan after 9/11 and in operations against Iraq, as part of Rumsfeld's "shock and awe" overture in March 2003.

British Army overt and covert abuses in Ireland between 1970 and the mid-1990s have been well-documented by human rights organizations and the European Court, which begs the question why those who supported the war, including the majority of Labour and Tory MPs and (for the most part) the mainstream media, believed Blair's rhetoric that the occupation of Iraq would be any different.

It was business as usual for the MoD. Incredibly, the Army's training manuals used prior to the invasion failed to explain that the five interrogation techniques, used against Republican prisoners in Ireland and banned since the early 1970s, were also illegal under the Geneva Convention, and had been condemned in a ruling against the British Government and the MoD by the European Court of Human Rights (ECtHR) in 1977. As a result of MoD 'negligence' Iraqi detainees were subjected to "serious, gratuitous violence," including Baha Mousa, a receptionist at the Haithan Hotel in Basra, who was hooded, severely assaulted, and died within 36 hours after being taken into custody by members of the 1st Battalion Queen's Lancashire Regiment (QLR), on 14 September 2003. A post-mortem examination found that the 26-year-old, widowed father of two young children, had suffered at least 93 injuries, including fractured ribs, all of which contributed to his death. Seven British soldiers, including six members of the QLR, were tried on war crimes charges under the International Criminal Court Act (ICCA) 2001, relating to the ill-treatment of Mousa and nine other men detained with him during the counter-insurgency operation. One man, Corporal Donald Payne, pleaded guilty to charges of inhumane treatment shortly after the court martial began, at the Military Court Centre at Bulford Camp on Salisbury Plain, Wiltshire, on 18 September 2006. He was jailed for 12 months and dishonorably discharged from the British Army. His six co-accused, including the officer in charge, Colonel Jorge Mendoca, and Major Michael Peebles of the Intelligence Corps, were cleared of "negligently performing a duty." Four others were also cleared of charges ranging from common assault to inhumane treatment. The British Defence Secretary, Des Browne, admitted in the House of Commons to "substantial breaches" of Articles 1 (right to life) and 2 (prohibition on torture) of the European Convention of Human Rights (ECHR). Four months later the MoD announced a $2.5 million compensation package for the family of Baha Mousa and the eight surviving detainees

In February 2006, a video taken from an upper story of a building in the town of Al-Amarah was posted on the Internet showing a group of British soldiers beating several Iraqi teenagers who had been part of a crowd protesting outside the British military compound. The footage was downloaded and broadcast by the mainstream international media, with MoD sources expressing concern for the safety of British troops in the region after repeated transmissions, while some commentators and politicians argued it would "damage the favorable reputation" of British troops, and worried about comparisons with the reputation of the feared and hated US military following the Fallujah killings, on 28 April 2003, when 82nd Airborne soldiers, billeted inside a local school, opened fire on unarmed civilians protesting against the military presence, killing 17 and wounding at least 70. The Pentagon claimed the soldiers had responded to "effective fire" from the crowd, who had simply wanted their school back. Two days later, however, the 82nd Airborne was withdrawn, and replaced by the 2nd Troop/Fox 3rd Armored Cavalry Regiment, and a decision was also taken at command level not to reoccupy the schoolhouse.

The following month, US helicopters attacked a wedding party at Mukaradeeb, a small village near the Syrian border, killing 42 people, including 13 children. The deputy CoS of US operations, Brigadier Gen. Mark Kimmitt, claimed the Americans had operated "within our rules of engagement" after taking ground fire, while USMC Major Gen. 'Mad Dog' Mattis, claimed there was no evidence of a wedding, and while there may have been some kind of celebration, "bad people have celebrations, too." This glib and demeaning explanation for the massacre was contradicted by *Associated Press* (AP) footage of the scene, filmed the following day, showing brightly-colored bedding and bunting, pots and pans, and fragments of musical instruments scattered around a bombed-out tent. Just three months before the Al-Amarah incident, in the western city of Haditha, on 18 November 2005, a group of US Marines murdered 24 unarmed Iraqi men women and children, several of whom were shot multiple times at close range, allegedly in retaliation for an improvised explosive device (IED) attack on a Marine convoy. This incident is well-documented, with several reports and online commentators, including the George Polk Award-winning investigative journalist and author, Robert Parry, comparing it to the mass murder at My Lai, in South Vietnam in March 1968.

The Royal Military Police (RMP) carried out an investigation into the Al-Amarah beatings, however, the MoD's prosecuting authority found there was "insufficient evidence to justify court martial proceedings" as a result of a "more or less obvious closing of ranks" - which Justice Ronald McKinnon had also noted in the Baha Mousa case. Attorney General Goldsmith claimed to be "deeply troubled" about military procedures, and testifying before a Parliamentary Committee on Human Rights, on 27 June 2007, he called for an inquiry into how illegal torture techniques were still being used by British troops in Iraq, and expressed "grave concern" that these interrogation tools were approved at brigade level. Goldsmith's resignation came into effect that day, as did that of his boss, Tony Blair, leaving behind several abuse cases which he had ignored while in office. Solicitor Phil Shiner, of the Birmingham-based Public Interest Lawyers (PIL), which has handled up to 40 cases representing the families of Iraqis allegedly killed, tortured or abused by British troops, had criticized Goldsmith during his post-invasion/pre-resignation four years in office for ignoring a London High Court ruling in December 2004, which confirmed that British troops in Iraq were bound by the UK's Human Rights Act, which guaranteed the right to life and prohibits inhumane treatment of prisoners.

Mr. Shiner and his colleagues are currently representing the families of twenty Iraqis allegedly murdered by British troops after being taken into custody following the 'Battle of Danny Boy' which took place at Al Amara in Maysan Province, north of Basra, on 14 May 2004. During the three-hour gun-battle between members of the Mahdi Army, a paramilitary force loyal to Shia cleric, Muqtada al-Sadr, and soldiers from the Argyll and Sutherland Highlanders and the Ist Battalion, Princess of Wales Royal Regiment, 28 Iraqis were killed. Those who had witnessed the fighting claimed that Iraqi prisoners taken during the battle were later tortured and murdered, and that the 'war crimes' were covered-up by an inadequate RMP investigation. On 25 November 2009, the former Minister of State for the Armed Forces, Bob Ainsworth, announced an official inquiry into the incident, to be chaired by retired High Court judge, Sir Thayne Forbes, and a team of retired British civilian police detectives traveled to Iraq to investigate the allegations. The MoD denies that twenty insurgents were captured, but admits that twenty bodies were removed from the battlefield for identification before being returned to their families.

Testimony, in what is known as the Al-Sweady Inquiry (after one of the victims, 19-year-old, Hamid al-Sweady), began in mid-March 2013. This is expected to be a long drawn out affair, with the MoD slowly trawling through hundreds of thousands of 'relevant' documents, including all the emails sent from Basra theatre-of-operations base to the Permanent Joint Headquarters (PJHQ) at Northwood, in Eastbury, north London, where all UK overseas military operations are planned and controlled. On the evidence of how previous inquiries directly involving the MoD have been conducted there are likely to be several legal attempts to exclude anything that remotely suggests national security interests or culpability, as well as attempts to control the conditions ('in camera' or behind screens) in which 200 military witnesses - former and serving members of the Army - will be expected to testify, and immunity from prosecution will be granted to those who might implicate themselves during testimony. The inquiry Is also expected to hear evidence, in London and Beirut, from 60 Iraqi civilians, and is not expected to publish its findings before the end of 2014.

The prosecution of British troops for alleged war crimes had been a concern for the retired Chief of Defence Staff Lord Boyce, and the former

British Land Forces commander, and Chief of the General Staff (CGS), Gen. Sir Michael Jackson. The latter is quoted in Philippe Sands' book as telling Peter Hennessy, professor of contemporary history at Queen Mary College, London, that he had recently spent a good deal of time in the Balkans "making sure Milosevic was put behind bars, I have no intention of ending up in the next cell to him in The Hague."

Indeed, shooting people dead without legal cover has always been a concern for Gen. Jackson. While the GCS was planning the course of Blair's War he was summoned, on 15 October 2003, to the Bloody Sunday Inquiry which was investigating the killings of 14 unarmed civil rights demonstrators in Derry City on 30 January 1972. The inquiry was sitting at Methodist Central Hall Westminster, taking evidence from former paratroopers under Jaackson's command. He was asked to explain his handwritten 'shot list' drawn up shortly after the killings, detailing where each soldier had been standing when he fired and the location of each of the victims. Every target on Jackson's list was identified as either a gunman or a bomber and every detail had, during the course of the inquiry, been shown to be incorrect. Jackson had been a captain, and was second-in-command of the 1st Battalion, Parachute Regiment, in Derry in 1972. He told Lord Saville that he had simply followed orders from senior officers, it had been a long day, the list was compiled in the early hours, and the inaccuracies were a result of fatigue.

The Chilcot Inquiry

John Gordon Brown, the son of a Presbyterian Church of Scotland minister, succeeded Tony Blair as Prime Minister and leader of the Labour Party, on 27 June 2007. Brown had served as Chancellor of the Exchequer for more than a decade, and while committed to regime change in Iraq, he was careful to maintain a low profile publicly from the more vociferous approach of his predecessor, and members of the No. 10 'war cabinet'. In a speech shortly before he took charge, Brown said he would "learn the lessons" from the mistakes made in Iraq, a less than subtle criticism of how the campaign was conducted. Brown wasted no time in seeking some form of moral redemption from a foreign policy decision over which he had no real influence, and on 15 June 2009, two months after British troops ended combat operations, the Iraq Inquiry was announced. Blair's War had lasted six years, claimed the lives of 179 UK military personnel, and cost almost 10 billion pounds.

The inquiry chairman was career diplomat Sir John Chilcot, a veteran of the Hutton Inquiry, and the members, personally chosen by Mr. Brown, were Sir Lawrence Freedman, Professor of War Studies at King's College, London, the official historian of the Falklands War, and a former foreign policy advisor to Mr. Blair; Sir Roderic Lyne, a former Private Secretary to Tory PM John Major in the early 1990s, and British ambassador to Russia (under Putin) from 2000 to 2004; Kenya-born Baroness Usha Prashar, an independent member of the House of Lords and former chairperson of the Judicial Appointments Commission; and Oxford University historian, Sir Martin Gilbert, the official biographer of Winston Churchill, who supported the invasion of Iraq, comparing Blair and Bush favorably to Churchill and Roosevelt in a December 2004 article in the *Observer*, with a provision that any accurate assessment of both men "must wait, perhaps a decade or longer, until the record can be scrutinized."

In his opening statement, on 24 November 2009, Sir John said the inquiry was "not seeking to apportion blame" but would make criticism if justified while seeking "to get to the heart of the matter." Given the past record of previous official inquiries, in particular those involving the MoD, MI6 and the Security Services, MI5, it was easy to be skeptical about what the Iraq Inquiry might achieve. PM Brown originally wanted proceedings to be held 'in camera' with the public and press excluded. However, following criticism which challenged the credibility of the exercise before it had even got off the ground, Sir John wrote to Brown insisting it was "essential to hold as much of the proceedings of the Inquiry as possible in public, consistent with the need to protect national security and to ensure and enable complete candor in the oral and written evidence." To satisfy the defense and intelligence establishment, Downing Street published a "protocol of agreement" with the inquiry, on 29 October 2009, which excluded from the public domain all 'sensitive' back-channel, hard-copy and electronic information on which crucial decisions were made.

Britain is not called the "secret State" without good reason, with a "shocking and farcical lack of transparency at all levels of government" according to journalist, Heather Brooke. Not available to the press or public during civil or criminal court proceedings, is any information classified under the "normal and established principles" of state secrecy, determined on the grounds of Public Interest Immunity (PII) certificates, which are essentially 'gagging orders' allowing government ministers to protect what they, or senior civil servants (unelected mandarins who stalk the corridors of power in Whitehall) regard as 'secret' – ranging from the genuine classified material to career-damaging information and lies

Excluded from the Chilcot Inquiry was information not only relating to national security, defense and international relations, and the economic interests of the UK, but also:

- information which might endanger the life of, or cause serious harm to an individual;
- commercially sensitive data;
- anything which might be in breach of legal professional privilege regarded as prejudicial to the position of HMG in relation to ongoing legal proceedings;
- breach of rules in legal proceedings in England and Wales under Section 17 of the Regulation of Investigatory Powers Act (2000);
- specific information sought for release regarded as possibly

prejudicial to ongoing statutory inquiries or criminal investigations in breach of:
- the Data Protection Act (1998), or in breach of the all-encompassing official secrecy legislation and "in-house" principles regarding disclosure of HUMINT or SIGINT product by MI6, MI5, GCHQ,
- the "third party rule" (in this case anything from the CIA, the NSA, Mossad or the French DGSE) of non-disclosure, or
- commitments under secret protocols with these agencies governing the release of sensitive information.

So what was left to talk about? Very little which hadn't already been disclosed.

The Iraq Inquiry generated few surprising headlines during fourteen months of oral testimony. There were no smoking WMDs. Reading through the testimony of the key players in the decision-making process prior to the March 2003 invasion, one gets the impression that for many HMG employees, from Blair and others who supported the use of force, what was at stake was how their actions would be perceived in the official narrative of a wholly unlawful breach of international law, and its consequences..

The Iraqi people had been the victims of ill-conceived UN sanctions, the oil-for-food and medicines needed by a deprived population had benefited the Iraqi dictator, his extended family, senior Ba'ath Party officials and the higher echelons of the military and intelligence establishment. Those who had opposed the war had no reason to embellish their views. History had borne out their concerns - there was no WMD arsenal, no delivery system ready to fulfill the 45 minutes warning, the country's civil infrastructure was destroyed, and more than 150,000 (and counting) Iraqi civilians, including insurgents, had been killed, according to the web-based Iraq Body Count (IBC) project, which uses English and Arab language media reports and NGO figures to compile its ongoing toll, and is the most-often quoted source in the mainstream media.

The IBC, however, has been criticized for grossly under-reporting, even by non-partisan sources, including one of the world's oldest scientific medical journals, the London-based, peer-reviewed weekly, the *Lancet*. In a survey sponsored by the Baltimore (US)-based Johns Hopkins Bloomberg School of Public Health's Center for International Emergency Disaster and Refugee Studies (CIEDRS), and Baghdad-based Al-Mustansiriya University's Department of Community Medicine (DCM), published on 29 October 2004, the *Lancet* estimated 98,000 excess Iraqi deaths, using a 95 percent 'confidence interval'- a type of interval estimate of a population parameter used by statisticians to indicate the reliability of an estimate - from the March 2003 invasion and subsequent occupation up to the date of publication, which the authors, L. Roberts, Phd and Dr. G. Burnham, MD, described as a "conservative estimate."

On 11 October 2006, the *Lancet* published a second survey, by the same authors, using the same methodology, and estimated 654,965 deaths since March 2003, a huge figure representing 2.5 percent of the population. In a *Washington Post* article, on the same day the *Lancet* report was published, the newspaper wrote that the survey was carried out between 20 May and 10 July that year by eight Iraqi physicians, who visited 1,849 "randomly selected households that had an average of seven members each" one of whom was asked about deaths during a 14-month period before the invasion and the subsequent three years of war and occupation. The interviewers asked for deaths certificates 87 percent of the time, and when they did, "more than 90 percent of households produced certificates."

As might be expected, the *Lancet* was criticized by journalists in many well-established newspapers and magazines who expressed disbelief at the figures quoted, by government officials in Washington and London, and by the IBC, whose figures some researchers, and historian Neta Crawford, regard as a "baseline for mortality" and that the actual death toll is "underestimated by several factors." Debarati Guha Sapir, the director Brussels-based Centre for Research on the Epidemiology of Disasters (CRED), at the Catholic University of Leuven (CUL), accused the *Lancet* of publishing "inflated figures that discredit the process of estimating death counts," while the International Committee of the Red Cross (ICRC), published a paper by the experienced demographer, Beth Osborn Daponte, which concluded that the most reliable information to date is that produced by the IBC and the World Health Organization's Iraq Family Health Survey (IFHS), published in the Massachusetts Medical Society's peer-reviewed *New England Journal of Medicine* (NEJM) on 9 January 2009, which surveyed 9,345 households in 2007 and 2007 and estimated 151,000 deaths for the same period as the *Lancet*'s second survey. JHPSH, the US sponsors of the *Lancet*'s second survey, published a review of the *2006 Iraq Mortality Study,* on 23 February 2009, which criticized researchers in the field for using data collection forms different to those originally agreed, and suspended Dr. Burnham from serving as principal investigator on future human subject research. However, the organization stood by the data, stating that while some minor errors in transcription were detected, "they were not at variables that affected the study's primary mortality analysis or causes of death." The review concluded that the data files used in the second survey, which had been available to outside researchers and which JHPSH had provided upon request, had "accurately reflect the information collected in the original field surveys."

The first witness to appear before the Chilcot Inquiry, on 24 November 2009, was Sir Peter Ricketts, chairman of the JIC in 2000/2001, who told the panel that two years before the invasion, and prior to the 9/11 attacks, there was serious talk among senior Bush officials in Washington that the three elements of the "containment strategy" - sanctions on oil exports for anything other than essential foodstuffs and medicines, 'no-fly' zones over north and south Iraq, and the possibility of Saddam allowing weapons inspectors to carry out their UNSC mandate - were "in trouble" and regime change was being considered as an option. He added that supporting the UN approach had remained HMG's policy until late November 2001 or early 2002 when President Bush's state of the union address identified Iraq as one of the three "axis of evil" countries. Appearing the same day was Sir William Patey, a 'graduate' of the British Government's 'school for spies', the Middle East Centre for Arabic Studies (MECAB) in Chemlane, a Christian area in the Mount Lebanon Governorate of Lebanon, and who headed the FCO's Middle East Department in 2001 until his appointment as ambassador to Sudan the following year. He told the inquiry that the FCO was "aware of these drumbeats from Washington" and while it was initially discussed - as might be expected, indeed, it would have been totally incongruous had the Arabists at the FCO totally ignored the 'chatter' - the policy was to keep a healthy distance: "We didn't think Saddam was a good thing, and it would be great if he went" said Patey, "but we didn't have an explicit policy for trying to get rid of him."

The following day, two senior FCO officials were questioned about Iraq's WMD profile. Both men said they believed the country's nuclear program had been dismantled and there was no evidence, from the available MI6 reports, that the Iraqi dictator was trying to provide chemical or biological weapons to terrorists. Sir William Ehrman, the director of international security, mentioned that ministers in Blair's inner circle were repeatedly warned about the limits of intelligence, and that a report, dated 10 March 2003, indicated that chemical weapons "might have remained disassembled and Saddam hadn't yet ordered their assembly." There was also a suggestion that Iraq "might lack warheads capable of effective dispersal of agents," yet despite the sporadic intelligence, Blair continued to describe the 'invisible' WMD program as "active, detailed and authorized" when it was anything but conclusive. Ehrman, however, said the intelligence warnings made no difference to the case for war Blair had made in the House of Commons, because it didn't "invalidate the point about the programs he had, it was more about use," and he defended the decision to go to war, saying Saddam had "flouted" various UN resolutions.

Tim Dowse, head of the FCO's Counter-Proliferation Unit from 2001 to 2003, said that Iraq was not seen as a main concern in the region in 2001, and even after the 9/11 attacks, "we concluded that Iraq actually stepped further back. They did not want to be associated with Al-Qaida. They weren't natural allies." Asked if Blair's 45-minute deployment warning referred to WMDs capable of striking other nations, Dowse replied that it was never said "it was for use in a ballistic missile in that way." However, as Sir Lawrence Freedman pointed out, the FCO "didn't say it wasn't." Neither the JIC or MI6 had explained to Downing Street that the 45-minute assembly claim was a speculative reference to short-range missile deployment only, although ministers later claimed they never bothered to seek further clarification about the weapons supposedly covered by the ambiguous warning.

The list of potential witnesses, mostly senior mandarins and politicians directly involved in the 'ownership' of information and the decision-making process, provoked criticism that the inquiry was not being "aggressive enough in seeking the truth," and was deliberately ignoring the views of lower-ranking civil servants who had argued that there were alternatives to regime change by force. Carne Ross, the FCO's 'Iraq expert' who had worked at the British diplomatic mission to the UN from 1999 to June 2002, and later resigned over the decision to invade, compared the inquiry to a "fireside chat at a Pall Mall club." Ross spoke out in the *Guardian* on 24 November 2009, after the former UK ambassador in Washington, Christopher Meyer, told the inquiry that the sanctions policy had "run its course" by 2002, a bland statement which ignored the deaths of an estimated 500,000 Iraqi children, five years and younger, as a result of UNSC Resolution 661. Ross pointed out that mid-level FCO staffers, who had spent all their time focusing on Iraq, were of the view that despite the child mortality rate, sanctions "had been effective in stopping Saddam rearming, and several of us believed a lot more could have been done to stop Iraq's illegal oil sales." He wondered why Chilcot and his panel were not "digging below the surface" and why Blair and the Downing Street 'hawks' did not consider the alternative: "Were there meetings to consider the alternatives, or were the Brits just swept along with the Americans?"

On the evidence so far it appeared that those who opposed the war simply resigned, and some, like Katherine Gun, had risked jail to make her point. One man who almost resigned in 2002, but decided to stayed on to complete his five years as UK ambassador to the UN was Sir Jeremy Greenstock, who eventually left New York in mid-2003 to work alongside Paul Bremer in Baghdad, trying to put together what the FCO described as a "credible" Coalition Provisional Authority (CPA). Bremer had his own way of doing things, however. He moved in, ruled by decree, retained veto power over CPA proposals, threw out all the Iraqi social programs, privatized much of the country's infrastructure and natural resources, and disbanded the Iraqi Army, a decision widely criticized with fueling Iraqi insurgency against American occupation. Large sums of money - an estimated $8.8bn - went missing under Bremer's leadership, pilfered in transit from the US, stolen from the Iraqi Central Bank, and in salaries to 'ghost' employees of firms doing 'phantom' work. One example, highlighted in an article entitled 'So, Mr. Bremer, where did all the money go?' published in the *Guardian*, on 7 July 2005, referred to almost $3.5m, billed on just one oil pipeline repair contract, for "personnel not in the field performing work" and what was described as "other improper charges."

Greenstock ignored all this. He told the inquiry that he considered the invasion "legal but of questionable legitimacy." In his opinion this was because there is no supreme court to arbitrate in international law and "it is up to a nation state to make decisions as to whether to adhere to the judgments of the International Court of Justice" however, because Iraq was not a member of the IJC "that did not come into our considerations." He also blamed "belligerent noises" in Washington for the failure to get UNSC backing for the invasion, claiming that HMG's attempt to obtain a consensus had had only a slim chance of success, "made slimmer by the recognition by anyone else following events closely that the United States was not proactively supportive" of the British effort, and that the Bush administration was preparing for conflict,"whatever the UK decided to do."

However, Blair's foreign policy adviser, Sir David Manning, deflated Greenstock's self-serving testimony when he told the inquiry that 11 months before the Iraq invasion, during a visit to Bush's ranch in Crawford, Blair said he would be prepared to go to war along with the US "whatever the outcome" of efforts at the UN. At the time Blair had been warned by AG Goldsmith that military force to achieve regime change in Iraq was unlawful and in breach of the UN Charter. Manning suggested that Blair had resisted efforts to go to war back in late 2001when Bush had claimed there might be evidence linking Saddam Hussein to the attacks in New York and Washington, and Blair had warned that only "compelling" evidence could justify military action. By the time Blair went to Texas, according to Manning, "he was very conscious that Iraq would be on the agenda."

Philippe Sands QC, was critical of the inquiry's handling of Manning, in particular its failure to question him about leaked correspondence which Sands had submitted to the committee. In one of the confidential memos, one month before Blair's visit to Washington, Manning assured NSC adviser, Condoleezza Rice, that the PM would not budge in support for regime change, but had to manage the press, Parliament and public opinion "which is very different from anything in the US." This suggests that Blair and his Downing Street advisers were more concerned with how to sell the war to the British people and their parliamentary representatives than with obtaining legal cover at the UN.

The second document was a letter from Ambassador Meyer to Manning, dated 17 March 2002, following Sunday lunch with the US Deputy Defense Secretary, Paul Wolfowitz, who was described in the 1 November 2004 issue of *The New Yorker*, as a "major architect of President Bush's Iraq policy and its most hawkish advocate," whose "formidable intellect" Meyer admired. Having discussed how the French could be handled if they opposed the war, Meyer and Wolfowitz "went through the need to wrongfoot Saddam on the inspectors and the UN security council resolution and the critical importance of the Middle East peace plan. If all this could be accomplished skillfully, we were fairly confident that a number of countries could come on board." Meyer also refers to the letter in his book, *DC Confidential*, adding that Wolfowitz was "noncommittal," and was more interested in "reminding the world of Saddam's savage barbarism." He was also less attracted to fermenting a military coup in Iraq "than replacing the regime with a democratic alternative." Prof. Sands was "pretty shocked" by the line of questioning the inquiry followed, and expressed his "surprise and disappointment by the failure to press Manning on any issues."

Several of those who testified appeared to cultivate the impression that publicly and in Parliament prior to the invasion, Blair and his diplomats were desperately trying to persuade the Americans to go down the UN route. Privately it seemed that Blair, at least, was already 'on board' with Bush and the posse of hawks at the White House. Edward Chapin, director of Middle East and North Africa policy at the FCO, told the inquiry that the British effort had "foundered on a blind spot" in Washington, where senior officials assumed "everyone would be grateful and there would be dancing on the streets" when the US arrived and that "we shouldn't worry so much about the aftermath because it was all going to be sweetness and light." This was the picture painted by Iraqi National Congress (INC) leader, Ahmed Chalabi, because it was exactly what the Beltway neocons wanted Chalabi to say. Chapin told the inquiry that the British had told the Americans that the INC had very little credibility in Iraq, and FCO officials were "dismayed" by the Bush administration's failure to take the post-war planning issue seriously, "despite personal appeals" from Blair to Bush.

The former JIC chairman, Sir John Scarlett, told the inquiry, on 8 December 2009, that there was "no conscious intention" to manipulate information about Iraq's WMDs, and while he denied he had been put under pressure to "firm up the September 2002 dossier" and the claim that the weapons could be used within 45 minutes and were a threat to the UK, it would have been better to have made it clear this referred to battlefield munitions not missiles. He wasn't asked about a claim, made a week earlier by an ex-Grenadier Guards officer, the Tory MP Adam Holloway, a former member of the Commons Defence Select Committee, in a report, published by the Wiltshire-based, centre-right think-tank, First Defence, entitled, *The Failure of British Political and Military Leadership,* that the 45 minutes threat came about because MI6 was "squeezing its agents" to back up the case that Saddam had WMDs. Holloway, who served in the 1991 Gulf War, and worked as an investigative journalist with ITN and the *Sunday Times* after leaving the British Army, wrote, "The provenance of this information was never questioned in detail until after the Iraq invasion, when it became apparent that something was wrong. In the end it turned out that the information was not credible, it had originated from an émigré taxi driver on the Iraq-Jordanian border, who had remembered an overheard conversation in the back of his cab two years earlier." An MI6 intelligence analysts had flagged up the claim as "demonstrably untrue" yet despite this "glaring factual inaccuracy" the HUMINT report was "characterized as reliable."

In contrast to Scarlett's second thoughts about the 45 minutes threat, Blair's former communications chief, Alastair Campbell, gave a belligerent five-hour performance, telling the committee he defended "every single word" of the discredited September dossier, and that Britain "should be proud of its role" in the overthrow of Saddam Hussein. He said Scarlett was 100 percent in charge of the process of drawing up the dossier, and he had not asked him to "beef up any of the judgments he had made." Scarlett had told him that the dossier "needed a bit of presentational support" because it was going to be presented by Blair to MPs, that there were "massive global expectations" around it, and "that is what I gave him." He was dismissive about the WMD 45 minutes claim, saying it had been given "iconic status" in the media, and that the failure to make it clear that this was a reference to battlefield missiles, not ICBMs, was "not a big point." Responding to persistent questioning by committee member, Sir Roderic Lyne, he disclosed that Blair had privately reassured Bush "in quite a lot of notes" during the 12-month period prior to the invasion. The substance of the correspondence was not shared with the Cabinet, but it amounted to the PM telling the President: "We share the analysis, we share the concern, we are going to be with you in making sure that Saddam Hussein faces up to his obligations and that Iraq is disarmed," and if that cannot be done diplomatically "it is to be done militarily, Britain will be there."

The testimony of two senior Army officers focused on inadequate pre-war preparations and post-war planning. Lt. Gen. Sir Frederick Viggers, a veteran of the Gulf War and the ethnic conflict in the Balkans, said more training was needed to deal with the "complexities of mounting an invasion," and that the operation suffered from a lack of direction and a clear idea of what to expect. Lt. Gen. Sir Graeme Lamb, commander of the multinational forces in south-east Iraq from July to December 2003, and senior British military adviser between September 2006 and July 2007, told the inquiry that working with Paul Bremer and the CPA was like "dancing with a broken doll. It was a lot of effort and your partner wasn't giving you much in return." During his time in Iraq, disorder following the invasion had turned from "insurgency on steroids" to serious sectarian conflict, and few lessons had been learnt from the experience.

The regional coordinator for southern Iraq, Sir Hilary Synott, a former Royal Navy submariner who joined the FCO in 1973, and served as High Commissioner to Pakistan from 2000 to 2003 before being posted to Iraq to replace the Danish ambassador, Ole Wohlers Olsen, had complained of the lack of support from the CPA for reconstruction in the south. He described Basra as a "bloody mess" without secure communications with London. He had to set up a free Yahoo email account to send confidential dispatches back to the FCO. Meanwhile, the "top-end" of the Ba'ath Party were still driving around Baghdad in SUVs with black-tinted windows, and 150,000 'criminals' released from prison shortly before the invasion were also "on the loose and tooled up." Synott retired in 2005, and later wrote a book about his experience in Iraq, neatly summed up in the title *Bad Days in Basra.*

The current head of MI6, Sir John Sawers, who was Blair's special envoy to Iraq from May to July 2003, surprised some of the committee when he suggested that Britain - by which he meant Mr. Blair and the Downing

Street 'hawks' -might have had second thoughts about the "entire project" had they been aware of the scale of armed opposition to the presence of foreign troops. He claimed that "very few observers" foresaw that Iraq would attract al-Qaida fighters and "Shia extremists backed by Iran." He wasn't asked why the MoD highly-paid intelligence analysts, and Blair's neocon cabal, expected the Iraq people to passively accept military occupation by troops from western nations taking orders from politicians with no knowledge of even the basic history or culture of the country, an ignorance which had been a hallmark of US foreign policy and the "savage wars of peace" since the early 19th century. The British experience of invasion, occupation and suppression dated back even further, to the invasion of Ireland in 1169. Despite being part of the "forces of occupation" Sawers said he did not believe the war had caused "lasting damage" to Britain's reputation in Muslim countries, adding that the people of Iraq had "benefited enormously" since March 2003. He didn't elaborate, nor was he asked to, but he admitted that the former Egyptian president, Hosni Mubarak, got it right when he warned that the invasion would "unleash a hundred Bin Ladens." This is no evidence, anecdotal or otherwise, to support Sawers' assertion about Britain's reputation among Muslims, and his suggestion to Chilcot is yet another example of ignorance shielding criminality and predation.

When the former Defence Secretary, Geoff Hoon, took the stand he blamed the Chancellor of the Exchequer, Gordon Brown, for forcing MoD planners to cut their budget, which prevented them ordering basic military hardware for troops deployed to Iraq. This meant that Basra-based service personnel had to rely on Snatch Land Rovers, designed for use in the urban environment of the North of Ireland during the Troubles, and which were vulnerable to roadside IEDs. Hoon admitted that the purchase of "urgent operational equipment" had been approved five months before the invasion, but distribution problems meant that many soldiers were left without enhanced combat body armor. What was available went to "front-line troops" while others were considered "low priority," despite also being targeted by insurgents. There was a shortage of desert combat fatigues, "so quite a lot of soldiers went into action in green combats," while others did not have the right boots.

Tony Blair spent six hours, on 29 January 2010, explaining to the Iraq Inquiry why he had no regrets about removing Saddam Hussein from power, saying the slain Iraqi dictator "threatened not just the region but the world." He argued that the world was more secure and that Iraq has replaced the "certainty of suppression" with the "uncertainty of democratic politics." During cross examination he denied there was a "covert deal" with President Bush at Crawford to invade, whatever the outcome at the UN; and asserted that a UNSC resolution was "preferable but not legally necessary;" that the basis for the war was Iraq's breach of UN disarmament resolutions; and that he stood "without doubt" by the claims about Saddam's chemical weapons capability. When asked about sending 40.000 troops to disarm Saddam of weapons he did not possess Blair claimed that the Iraqi leader would have reassembled and used WMDs "because he had the intent and ability to do so." He displayed all the rhetorical skills and guile which had brought him to power in 1997 and he had used during his ten years as premier, easily handling the five-strong inquiry team's questions. He conceded that postwar planning had been a failure, and admitted there were "some disagreements" with Washington on the reconstruction issue. He was "shocked and angered" by US torture of Iraqi prisoners in Abu Ghraib , and had protested to the Bush administration when US troops "went in too hard in Falluja," but made no mention of incidents involving British soldiers, which also alienated the civilian population, including the arrest in mid-September 2005, by local Iraqi police, of two SAS operatives carrying heavy weapons, large amounts of ammunition and driving around Basra in a "booby-trapped car," wearing wigs and dressed as Arabs. Their freedom from Jamiat Police Station was "negotiated" by the locally-based Coldstream Guards, supported by ten tanks and helicopter gunships. Iraqi parliamentarian, Fattah al-Shaykh, who spoke to Al-Jazeera just before the assault on the jail, suggested that the explosives-laden car was intended to be detonated in a central Basra marketplace. The ensuing carnage would be blamed on al-Qaida or Shia insurgents supported by Iran.

Asked finally by Inquiry chairman, Sir John Chilcot, if he had "any regrets," Blair ignored the families and relatives of dead British service personnel in the public gallery, saying he did not regret removing Saddam Hussein from power, "insofar as I think he was a monster." As he left the chamber there were shouts of "liar" and "murderer" from some of those present. The leader of the Scottish National Party (SNP) at Westminster, Angus Robertson, summed up what many felt about Blair's performance, telling BBC News "no matter how skillfully he ducked or dived today, Tony Blair's legacy will forever be that of an illegal, immoral Iraq war" with no regret for his dubious decisions and the "worst foreign policy disaster in modern times."

Despite criticism that the inquiry was "too narrow," during the course of 2010 the committee continued to take testimony from senior British government officials, former Labour ministers, diplomats and retired military officers. An exception was 82-year-old Hans Blix, the former head of UNMOVIC between 1999 and 2003, who gave evidence for three hours, on 27 July, before heading off for several print and broadcasting media interviews. He told the inquiry that before UNMOVIC was forced to pull out of Iraq, his team found some "prohibited items," such as missiles beyond the permitted range capability, missile engines, and a "stash of undeclared documents," but these were "fragments" and "not very important" in the bigger picture.

"We carried out about six inspections per day over a long period of time. All in all, we carried out about 700 inspections at 500 different sites and in no case did we find any weapons of mass destruction." Although Iraq had failed to comply with some of its disarmament obligations, the retired Swedish diplomat added that it was "very hard for them to declare any weapons when they did not have any." He believed Saddam Hussein had "unilaterally" destroyed his WMDs in the 1990s after the Gulf War, described the CIA's claim about yellow-cake procurement from Niger as "flawed" and accused UK intelligence of "over-interpreting" HUMINT to "bolster the case" for war. He described the military momentum in early March 2003 as "almost unstoppable" but was adamant that had UNMOVIC been allowed to conduct more inspections, the US/UK intelligence on Iraq's alleged WMDs would have been "undermined" and the invasion harder to justify. He criticized the decision-making process on both sides of the Atlantic that led to war, saying the existing UNSC resolutions did not contain the authority needed. His "firm view" was that the Iraq war was illegal, and suggested that ex-AG Goldsmith, who advised Blair and Lord Boyce at the MoD, had "wriggled about" because he "very much doubted they [UNSC resolutions] were legally adequate."

The final scheduled public hearing took place on 30 July, and from 26 September to 1 October, four members of the committee traveled to Baghdad and Basra on a five-day, fact-finding mission to hear the "Iraqi perspective" and view the consequences of Britain's six-year occupation. In Baghdad's heavily-guarded 'Green Zone' private talks were held with the former PM Ayad Allawi, deputy Foreign Minister, Labeed Abbawi, Planning Minister Ali Baban, the leader of the INC, Ahmed Chalabi, and senior officials from the UN, the European Union and the World Bank. In mid-November Sir John Chilcot and another panel member made a brief visit to Northern Iraq to meet senior officials of the Kurdish regional government, before announcing that several witnesses, including Tony Blair, would be recalled to clarify some significant details following the inquiry's analysis of the evidence given 'in camera' during the summer recess.

Prior to Mr. Blair's second appearance Sir John criticized retired Cabinet Secretary, Gus O'Donnell, for refusing to release "key extracts" from the correspondence between Blair and Bush before to the invasion. Lord O'Donnell said the material "represented particularly privileged channels of communication, the preservation of which is strongly in the public interest" - another example of the Orwellian use of language in British politics, where the "need for secrecy" is disingenuously used to protect the public interest and conceal the private follies of public representatives. In his 1946 essay on *Politics and the English language,* George Orwell criticized the "ugly and inaccurate" use of English political prose, in order to "make lies sound truthful and murder respectable" and to obscure and distort reality, and he described political speech and writing in post-colonial Britain as the "defense of the indefensible" consisting largely of "euphemism, question-begging and sheer cloudy vagueness." This about sums up much of the rhetoric surrounding Blair's War, from 'dodgy' dossiers to 'dodgy' legal advice, none of which is ever likely to be tested at the ICC in The Hague.

As expected from a highly-skilled politician, Mr. Blair - now referred to in some sections of the media as a "deeply-religious man" who had converted to Roman Catholicism following his resignation as prime minister - used his second appearance before the Iraq Inquiry to tidy up some loose ends. After saying his refusal to apologize for his decisions during his first appearance had been "misinterpreted" he indicated that he regretted "deeply and profoundly the loss of life" to shouts of "too late" from the public gallery. He warned of the influence of the "looming and coming challenge" from Iran in the region which he described as "negative, destabilizing and supportive of terrorist groups." He claimed Tehran was "doing everything it can to impede progress in the Middle East peace process" while ignoring the threat of a nuclear-armed Israel to its Arab neighbors. He finally acknowledged "things invisible" which he had previously referred to as Saddam Hussein's WMD "arsenal" and later, when no weapons were found, a "program" which could be reactivated, although no military or procurement documentation was found to support even this allegation. He also claimed that after 9/11, "everything changed" because of the risk that terrorists could get hold of chemical or biological weapons. He wasn't asked to explain why, after almost a decade since the Twin Towers and Pentagon attacks, there was no evidence to support this contentious claim, and he wasn't questioned about Bush's unfounded allegations of Baghdad's link with al-Qaida, the 'source' of the WMDs that worried Blair, while, in reality, there was a greater danger of Osama bin Laden procuring WMD capability from the Saudis' connection with rogue Pakistani nuclear or biological scientists and engineers, who had been part of Dr. A. Q. Khan's WMD procurement network in the late 1970s and 1980s.

Despite two Downing Street staffers expressing embarrassment, in published testimony, at attempts by Alastair Campbell, on Blair's instructions, to blame the French President, Jacques Chirac, for blocking a second UNSC resolution mandating the use of force, the former PM repeated this allegation, and criticized Hans Blix's evidence, saying there no point in giving the Iraqi dictator more time so that extra UNMOVIC inspections could be conducted. What was needed was a "change of attitude" but he failed to explain what he meant by this, and wasn't asked. He was forced to concede that he was wrong to claim at both public and private meetings in early 2003 that the UN had authorized the use of force when Lord Goldsmith was saying the opposite, but pointed out that the former AG "later fell into line" and provided legal cover for the war. After 18 months of public and private hearings Sir John Chilcot's plan to release a report by December 2011 was delayed for six months, partly due to a dispute with the Government over the release of secrets documents. In a statement on Remembrance Day, 11 November 2011, the committee mentioned the need to negotiate the declassification of a "significant volume of currently classified material" with the Tory/Lib-Dem coalition administration "to enable this to be quoted in, or published, alongside the inquiry's report."

War was not the only option. Mr. Blair could have chosen diplomacy over the wanton destruction of a sovereign state. He could have shown some of the patience he had displayed in the face of Unionist intransigence during the peace process in the North of Ireland, and allowed more time for the UNMOVIC inspectors to do their job—at the end of which, surely, the *casus belli* would have been proved untrue. The shift in Blair's rationale for war corresponded with that in Washington, from the non-existent WMD threat, to regime change and providing "western democracy and freedom" for twenty-five million Iraqis. He described this in testimony to the Iraq Inquiry as "different ways of expressing the same proposition."

    The diplomatic strategy "always came second to the military planning" according to Philippe Sands, even when Blair and Bush had "no hard evidence of the existence of weapons of mass destruction." The British PM also chose to "ignore the advice of those who warned him there would be internecine warfare if there was no strategy lined up for a replacement regime once Saddam Hussein had been toppled." Mr. Blair deliberately misled the House of Commons on 15 January 2003, when he spoke about the "legitimate" use of force, and he lied to MPs, the press and the public about the inconclusive nature of the available intelligence. He blatantly exaggerated the 45 minutes threat to the UK of Iraq's WMD/ICBMs, and lied when he blamed French President Chirac for the failure to secure a second UNSC resolution. He marginalized Attorney General Goldsmith, eventually forcing him to provide "legal cover" for his commitment to the blunt use of force. He deliberately concealed his intentions, discussed in several 'notes' to President Bush prior to the invasion, from the majority of his Cabinet colleagues. He also must share responsibility for the postwar reconstruction fiasco, and not simply blame lack of planning in Washington DC, the Iraqi Shia insurgents, and Iranian interference for the failure, a decade later, to improve the civil infrastructure after 14 years of debilitating economic sanctions and war. US multinational companies, Bechtel and Halliburton, with executive links to the Bush administration, received profit-guaranteed, fixed-fee contracts worth billions to reconstruct water-treatment plants, the sewage system, highways and the electricity network, but left the country without completing many of their contracted tasks. And Mr. Blair also endangered the lives of British citizens, ignoring the advice of senior domestic intelligence officials, including the head of MI5, Eliza Manningham-Buller, who was "as explicit as possible" with her warning of the increased threat of domestic terror as a consequence of the war. The 7 July 2005 suicide bombers, whose coordinated attacks on the London transit system killed 52 people and injured hundreds, blamed their cruel and brutal act of violence on British foreign policy decisions from Afghanistan to the invasion of Iraq.

    The official inquiry into Blair's War, expected to report in mid-2012, has been delayed for at least 12 months, and chairman, Sir John Chilcot, is not expected to contact those who will be criticized – for comment before publication - until mid-2013. The report, which is expected to be more than one million words, may not be available to MPs until summer 2014, with a more digestible summary, for those who prefer a more compact narrative, likely to be published earlier that year. In a letter to Conservative Prime

Minister David Cameron, on 16 July 2012, Sir John complained that the effort to deliver "a balanced, fair and accurate" narrative within the agreed time-scale had been undermined by senior Whitehall officials who refused to allow the publication of documents on which the report's conclusions are based, relating to a number of "particularly important categories of evidence including the treatment of discussions in the cabinet and cabinet committees and the UK position in discussions between the prime minister and heads of states or government of other nations."

Among the classified material Chilcot wants to include are intelligence reports and assessments provided by MI5, MI6 and GCHQ, the deliberations of the JIC, and the private correspondence between PM Blair and President Bush, which will show that Blair was committed, in principle, to supporting the US-manufactured war in Iraq long before he argued for regime change in Parliament and in public. The senior Whitehall officials Chilcot referred to include Cabinet Secretary, Sir Jeremy Heywood, and his predecessor, Lord O'Donnell, who have argued that publication of the Blair/Bush correspondence could damage "future candor" between world leaders and Britain's relations with the US. Chilcot has repeatedly explained that protocols in place will protect national security, international security and the personal security of individuals, but "they are not there to prevent embarrassment." He is also on record as saying that Blair's claim that MI6 established "beyond doubt" that Saddam Hussein had WMDs was "not possible to make on the basis of intelligence."

Anthony Charles Blair was on the right side of history in Ireland. But what he helped to achieve in Belfast, with the signing of the 1998 peace agreement, has been completely overshadowed by his "almost evangelical commitment" to war in Iraq. He had shown an aptitude for peace-making, and might well have achieved more in the Middle East had he remained on this course. Instead, he will be remembered, and despised by many, for the bloody war he waged alongside George W. Bush to disarm and defeat Saddam Hussein.

BIBLIOGRAPHY

Baker, Norman. *The Strange Death of David Kelly*. London: Methuen, 2007.
Baxter, Jenny and Dowling, Malcolm (editors). *The Day that Shook the World*. Sidney: ABC Books, 2001.
Brooke, Heather. *The Silent State*. London: Windmill Books, 2011.
Campbell, Julieann. *Setting the Truth Free*. Dublin: Liberties Press, 2012.
Curtis, Mark. *Web of Deceit*. London: Vintage, 2003.
Davies, Nick. *Flat Earth News*. London: Vintage, 2009.
Fisk, Robert. *The Great War for Civilization*. London: Fourth Estate, 2005.
Gordon, Michael and Trainor, Bernard. *Cobra II*. London: Atlantic Books, 2007.
Makiya, Kanan. Cruelty and Silence. London: Jonathan Cape Ltd., 1993.
Meyer, Christopher. *DC Confidential*. London: Weidenfeld & Nicolson, 2005.

Moorehouse, Geoffrey. *The Diplomats: Foreign Office Today.* London: Jonathan Cape Ltd., 1977.
Norton-Taylor, Richard. *The Ponting Affair.* London: Cecil Woolf Publishers, 1985.
Orwell, George. *Shooting the Elephant and other Essays*, London: Penguin Classics, 2003.
Rampton, Sheldon and Stauber, John. *Weapons of Mass Deception.* London: Constable & Robinson Ltd., 2003.
Rampton, Sheldon Rampton and Stauber, John. *The Best War Ever.* New York: Penguin Books, 2005.
Rice, Condoleezza. *No Higher Honor.* New York: Simon & Schuster Ltd, 2011.
Sands, Philippe. *Lawless World.* London: Allen Lane, 2005.
Scheuer, Michael. *Through Our Enemies' Eyes.* Washington D.C., Potomac Books, 2006.
Shawcross, William. *The Shah's Last Ride*. London: Chatto & Windus, 1989.
Synott, Hilary. *Bad Days in Basra.* London: IB Tauris & Co., 2008.
Timmerman, Kenneth R. *The Death Lobby.* New York: Bantam Books, 1992.

NEWSPAPERS & MAGAZINES
Al-Watan (www.alwatan.com.sa)
LA Weekly (www.laweekly.com)
London Review of Books (www.lbr.co.uk)
Daily Mail (www.dailymail.co.uk)
Guardian (www.guardian.co.uk)
Jane's Intelligence Weekly (www.janes.com)
Lancet (www.elsevier.com)
Lobster (ed. Robin Ramsay) Hull, UK.(www.lobster-magazine.co.uk)
Middle East Review of International Affairs (www.meria.idc.ac.il)
New England Journal of Medicine (www.nejm.org)
New York Review (www.nybooks.com)
New York Times (www.nyt.com)
New Yorker (www.newyorker.com)
Observer (www.observer.guardian.co.uk)
Rolling Stone (www.rollingstone.com)
Salon (www.salon.com)
Washington Post (www.washingtonpost.com)

NGOs & ONLINE SOURCES
BBC News (www.bbc.co.uk/news)
Centre for Research and Epidemiology of Disasters (www.cred.be)
Common Dreams (www.commondreams.org)
Crawford, Netta. *Assessing the Human Death Toll of the Post-9/11Wars*, (www.costsofwar.org)
First Defence Policy Group (www.firstdefence.info)
House of Commons Foreign Affairs Select Committee (www.parliament.uk)

House of Representatives Judiciary Committee Report. *The Inslaw Affair.* (www.w2.eff.org/legal/cases/INSLAW/inslaw_hr.report)
Human Rights Watch (www.hrw.org)
Hutton Inquiry (www.the-hutton-inquiry.org.uk)
International Committee of the Red Cross (www.icrc.org)
Iraq Body Count Project (www.iraqbodycount.org)
Iraq Inquiry (www.iraqinquiry.co.uk)
Johns Hopkins Bloomberg School of Public Health (www.jhsph.edu)
Morbidity and Mortality among Iraqi Children from 1990 through 1998 (www.casi.org.uk)
Parry, Robert. *Consortium News* (www.consortiumnews.com)
PR Watch -- The Center for Media and Democracy (www.prwatch.org)
Wiley Online Library, *International Affairs*, (www.eu.wiley.com)

CHAPTER FIVE
UNDERSTANDING SHADOWS

"If we are on the outside, we assume a conspiracy
is the perfect working out of a scheme.
Silent nameless men with unadorned hearts.
A conspiracy is everything that ordinary life is not.
It's the inside game, cold, sure, undistracted, forever closed to us.
We are the flawed ones, the innocents, trying to make
some rough sense of the daily jostle.
Conspirators have a logic and a daring beyond our reach.
All conspiracies are the same taut story of men
who find coherence in some criminal act."
Don DeLillo, *Libra*

The Flawed Ones

This is an account of the curious journey Lee Harvey Oswald, his Russian-born wife, Marina, and their four months old daughter, made in June 1962 from Bjelorusskaja Station in central Moscow to Rotterdam in the Netherlands, and from there to Hoboken, New Jersey, under the watchful eyes of the world's most powerful intelligence organizations, at the height of the Cold War in Europe, where nervous, armed stand-offs were almost a daily occurrence in places like the divided city of Berlin. The actual journey took approximately 13 days, yet it remains one of the lesser known episodes in the life of the alleged assassin of John Fitzgerald Kennedy, the 35th President of the United States.

Out of the thousands of well-sourced books, articles, and academic papers forensically examining (almost) all aspects of Oswald's life - and some of the research done and represented in JFK assassination literature is the best in the business - all we have to go on regarding the journey is Marina Oswald's unreliable testimony before the Warren Commission, her account to a friend, sometime US intelligence asset and author, Priscilla McMillan, an analysis of Oswald's notebook (his 'historic diary') and various brief references in dozens of published reports.

Following the fatal shooting of John Kennedy at 12.30pm on Friday 22 November 1963, as his motorcade cruised past the Texas School Book Depository on Dealey Plaza in downtown Dallas, his death at Parkland General Hospital, approximately 45 minutes later, and the charging of Oswald in connection with the President's death, at 1.30am the following morning, it was already 8.30am in the Netherlands, and several Dutch national newspapers were on the streets carrying detailed reports of events in the life of his alleged assassin. They included Oswald's military service record, his defection to the USSR at a particularly sensitive and dangerous period in US-USSR relations, and his detention by the Dallas Police Department (DPD) in connection with the death of the President. It had been a very public execution carried out in front of millions of witnesses present in Dealy Plaza and watching the nationwide television coverage, which nonetheless created a labyrinth of deceit and lies, and generated a cover-up of such immense proportions that even Plato - who refers to those in authority (in his dialogue on justice and order) "contriving some magnificent myth that would in itself carry conviction to our whole community" - would have been proud.

The ingredients were already in the mix, and the timeline is interesting. In the Netherlands those who had read or listened to the early coverage of Kennedy's death had already been given what the authorities hoped would be the definitive account of how he died, and who was responsible - three shots fired by a single shooter called Oswald. Only a select and secretive few - members of the CIA based at the US Embassy in The Hague, the powerful Soviet foreign intelligence agency, KGB, and its military intelligence counterpart, GRU, the Dutch internal security service, Binnenlandse Veiligheidsdienst (BVD), and the foreign intelligence agency, (since disbanded) Buitenland Inlichtingendienst (BID) - had ever heard of Lee Harvey Oswald, and probably couldn't quite recall all the details. That would come later when they looked back over case files for June 1962, and remembered that Oswald, his wife and daughter, had spent just over 24 hours in the country before taking the Holland-America Line's *SS Maasdam* to the US.

The Oswalds were in town to collect tourist-class tickets for the one-way, trans-Atlantic voyage, a scheduled sailing via Cobh, in the Republic of Ireland, which departed from Rotterdam on 4 June 1962. The family had stayed in a self-contained, six-room apartment at 250 Mathenesserlaan, an anonymous, red-brick, rowhouse provided by the CIA, set back from the tree-lined tram route in an affluent district of Rotterdam. The apartment, on the first floor of the spacious three-storey premises, was part of a long-term lease, paid for by a cut-out 'third party' through a local housing agency. It was bugged by the CIA in order to monitor the couples' private moments to determine if there was an active Soviet intelligence interest in Oswald's return to the US. An understandable concern. Indeed, Langley would have been negligent if that possibility had not been considered. His wife was a former member of the Komsomol, the Communist Party youth movement, and was the niece of one of Minsk's prominent citizens, Lieutenant Colonel Ilya Prusakova, a member of the secretive MVD, the security service of the Ministry of Internal Affairs, based at KGB HQ in Minsk, where Oswald had found employment at the Gorizont Electronics Factory, producing radio, television, military and space electronic components, and where he met and married a young pharmacology student, Marina Nikolayevna Prusakova.

Mr. Oswald Goes to Moscow

Lee Harvey Oswald was still only 23-years-old in June 1962, when he left the USSR, but in terms of experience he had already lived a lifetime. He had been born in New Orleans in October 1939, and educated in Texas, Louisiana and New York, before joining the US Marine Corps (USMC) on 24 October 1956, six days after his 17th birthday, at the USMC Recruit Depot, San Diego, California. After eleven months training in the US, including eight weeks at the Naval Air Technical Training Center in Jacksonville Florida, he was posted to Marine Control Squadron No.1 at the Atsugi Naval Air Facility in Japan, the CIA's main station of operations in the Far East where the top-secret, Lockheed TR-1, U-2, all-weather reconnaissance aircraft was based.

After a thirteen-month tour of duty in Japan, Oswald returned to the US in November 1958, and was assigned to Marine Air Control Squadron 9, based at Santa Ana, California. On 25 February 1959, Oswald passed a USMC proficiency test in the Russian language, and the following month he applied to join the Albert Schweitzer College, in Switzerland. On 11 September 1959, after requesting a hardship discharge in order to support his mother, Oswald was released from the USMC, and within 10 days began his long journey into exile - his so-called 'defection' to the USSR.

He sailed from New Orleans on board the *SS Marion Lykes* bound for Le Havre in France on 20 September 1959, and transferred to the 51,000 ton French liner *Liberté* shortly before midnight on 8 October for the relatively short trip across the English Channel. He passed through HM Customs at Southampton, then travelled by train to Waterloo Station in central London, arriving in the British capital late in the evening of 9 October 1959.

Oswald's passport contains a stamp confirming that he left Heathrow Airport, London, on 10 October 1959, and also contains a stamp confirming his arrival at Helsinki-Vantaa Airport, Finland, on the same day. There was only one direct commercial flight leaving Heathrow for Helsinki on that date, a FinnAir flight which left London in mid-afternoon and arrived at Helsinki at 11.35pm (local time). The airport, built for the 1952 Olympic Games, is located about 11 miles north of the city center. According to the register at the Hotel Torni in central Helsinki, Lee Harvey Oswald checked in before midnight, on 10 October. The Warren Commission established that it would have been impossible for Oswald to clear customs at Helsinki Airport, and manage to reach Hotel Torni, presumably by taxi, and register within 25 minutes. This led to speculation that US intelligence assisted the ex-marine to complete this leg of his journey. However, according to Chris Mills, who researched the journey and published his findings in the British 'parapolitical' magazine, *Lobster,* the British Airways (BA) flight timetable, for 10 October 1959, confirms that there were two other commercial flights, one leaving Heathrow for Helsinki via Copenhagen at 8.05am, and the other leaving at 8.50am for Helsinki via Stockholm. Taking into account the BST/CET time difference, the planes arrived in the Finnish capital at 5.05pm and 5.50pm, allowing Oswald plenty of time to clear Finnish customs, reach Hotel Torni and register well before midnight. Mills points out that passenger lists for all flights leaving Heathrow for Helsinki that day have since been destroyed, but they would have been available to the Warren Commission in 1964 "had anyone taken the trouble to look."

Within the confirmed time-line there is no reason not to believe that Oswald's rather strange and unnecessary route from New Orleans to Helsinki could not have been achieved using scheduled commercial transport, either by sea or air. The important question is, who paid for the trip? Oswald's basic wage would not have covered the travel and hotel costs, and why travel via France and the UK when more direct (Paris to Helsinki), and less expensive routes were available? One explanation might be found among the company Oswald kept during the trans-Atlantic voyage from New Orleans to Le Havre. Unfortunately, the FBI, the primary investigating authority for the Warren Commission, or independent investigators working for the 1979 House Select Committee on Assassinations (HSCA) never bothered to try and find out if Oswald had traveled alone.

In testimony to the Warren Commission CIA director, John McCone, stated that, based on his personal knowledge and "detailed inquiries [of the agency's records] he caused to be made," the conclusion was reached that Oswald "was not an agent, employee, or informant" of the CIA, and the organization had "never contacted him, interviewed him, talked with him, or received or solicited any reports or information from him, or communicated with him directly or in any other manner." McCone emphasized that he was speaking only for the CIA, and was keen to distance Langley from any other US agency that might have had an intelligence interest in Oswald's presence in the USSR. When McCone gave his assurances to the Warren Commission about Oswald he relied on a "key briefing" provided by his Deputy Director of Plans, Richard Helms, who in 1963 was "responsible for the CIA's activities with agents and informers" and who had sworn, in 1964, according to the author, Anthony Summers, that there were no CIA records on Oswald, nor had any agency employee "even contemplated" having contact with the alleged assassin.

The former senior editor at *Philadelphia* magazine, and House Select Committee on Assassinations (HSCA) investigator, Gaeton Fonzi, who died in Florida in August 2012, was convinced that Kennedy had died as a result of a conspiracy, He "considered it impossible" according to colleagues, that the CIA had no contact with Oswald, and believed that McCone had been deceived by Helms, who had "deliberately" kept his boss in the dark about the "existence of certain covert operations." It does not take a major leap of faith to suggest that Helm had also lied to McCone about Oswald's connection with the agency prior to the latter's testimony before the Warren Commission.

McCone sent Oswald's military records to the commission, but not his restricted CIA '201' file held by the Counter Intelligence/Special Investigations Group, according to Hood College (Maryland) Professor Gerald McKnight, who claims that this highly-secretive branch "may have had a special interest in the former Marine, PFC Lee Harvey Oswald." Indeed, Oswald's behavior suggests that he was what's known in the trade as a 'dangle' - someone sent over by one side during the Cold War to see how the other side reacted, to see if he was either welcomed as a propaganda 'coup', briefly detained and expelled, or incarcerated and shot-up with truth seeking serums available to both CIA and the KGB interrogators. Temple University Professor, Joan Mellen, believes that Oswald was part of the James Jesus Angleton's 'false defector program' (FDP). The CIA's head of counterintelligence operation, from 1954 to 1975, was a controversial, sometimes paranoid, figure, but was highly-regarded in the trade by his US and British colleagues. Based on declassified documents released under the *JFK Records Collection Act*, and interviews conducted for her book, *A Farewell to Justice*, Prof. Mellen states that Angleton was the "mastermind" of the FDP, that sent spies, including Oswald, into Soviet Union. In a talk at the 92nd Street Y in New York, on 28 January 2008, she mentioned an "inadvertently redacted" reference in a CIA document to a FBI "65" espionage file for an individual called Michael Jelisavcic, the manager of American Express in Moscow, one of Angleton's agents through whom Oswald communicated back to the CIA. Prof. Mellen - who has written for a variety of publications, including the *New York Times*, the *Los Angeles Times*, and the *Philadelphia Inquirer* - has also described Angleton's FDP as "among the CIA's most closely-guarded secrets, a secret necessary to preserve the fiction of the Warren Commission" - that Lee Harvey Oswald, acting alone, had been responsible for the assassination of John Kennedy.

Whatever the 'false' defector's reception in Moscow, a file was opened and maintained at KGB HQ. If released and allowed to remain, the 'visitor' was kept under HUMINT and SIGINT surveillance. Informers and 'agents in place' (in this case, in the US) were contacted, and usually 'reliable' sources were questioned. Dangles were a nuisance, they distracted attention and occupied resources, but, in general, they were little more than that.

There may, however, have been another element to Oswald's mission. Because of his military background, language skills, and familiarity with late-1950s high-tech radar and surveillance electronics, there was a possibility -

admittedly a long shot taking into account the paranoid nature of relations between Moscow and Washington - that Oswald might find employment with one of the state-owned companies involved in the development of Soviet 'Sputnik' technology, an added bonus for the CIA and perhaps for the Office of Naval Intelligence (ONI), the oldest continuously-reporting American intelligence agency, whose mission is to "seek out and report" on developments in other nations, and the organization whose clandestine activities McCone didn't want associated with Langley. Unfortunately for Oswald's spymaster, he ended up 'quarantined' in Minsk, an unproductive agent who became even more difficult to handle following his marriage.

American consul, John McVickar, was on duty at the US Embassy in Moscow when Oswald entered his office shortly after 11am on 31 October 1959, to loudly renounce his American citizenship. McVickar told the Warren Commission that Oswald had entered the Soviet Union through Helsinki, which was not the normal route for American citizens wishing to visit the USSR, but an ideal location to obtain a quick entry visa. The usefulness of the Soviet Embassy in Helsinki was common knowledge among foreign intelligence personnel and diplomats working in Moscow, and those in the US dealing with Soviet affairs, but it was not common knowledge among ordinary citizens. Three of the most commonly used Helsinki travel agencies were investigated by the Warren Commission, and the normal visa processing time was between seven and fourteen days. It took Oswald two days to obtain his visitor's visa. According to a confidential telegram from the US embassy in Moscow, to the State Department in Washington, dated 31 October 1959, Oswald entered the Soviet Union from Helsinki on 15 October, and the following day had applied for Soviet citizenship by letter to the Supreme Soviet. Detail's of Oswald's 'defection' was filed by UPI Moscow-based correspondent, Aline Mosby, and published in the *Washington Post* on 1 November 1959. She was one of only two journalists who succeeded in getting an interview with Oswald. The other was Priscilla Johnson, who would later play a significant part in the dissemination of information about the ex-Marine and his family following the assassination of JFK.

After his visit to the US Embassy Oswald returned to Room 233, Hotel Metropol, in central Moscow, and spent the next three weeks waiting while Soviet officials assessed what he had told them during repeated interviews by the KGB, seeking to discover whether the former Marine was a genuine defector from capitalism, willing to share what he learned while serving in the US and Japan, or whether he was being used, perhaps even unwittingly, by US intelligence agencies.

Although Oswald's Soviet citizenship application was rejected, he was allowed to remain in the country. He was issued with a 'stateless person' identity card, and given 5,000 rubles by a branch of the MVD. In January 1960 he was moved to Minsk, the capital of the Byelorussian SSR, one of fifteen constituent Soviet republics. According to Oswald's 'historic diary', written after after leaving the USSR and found among his personal effects in

Dallas after his death, "after a certain time [and] after the Russians had assured themselves that I was really a naive American and believed in Communism, they arranged for me to receive a certain amount of money each month."

Oswald was given a flat with a balcony overlooking the River Svislach, described as a "one-room apartment with kitchen, bathroom and separate entrance" - something which the average Soviet worker could only aspire to. He worked as an assembler at Gorizont. His wages and his MVD allowance allowed him to pursue a lifestyle beyond the reach of the ordinary Soviet citizen in the 1960s. According to his diary he was "living big." He had a large record collection and enjoyed classical music. His favorite composers were Tchaikovsky, Grieg, Rimsky-Korsakov and Schumann. His favorite opera was Tchaikovsky's *Queen of Spades,* based on the Alexander Pushkin short story, and he saw the 1960 film adaptation, directed by Roman Tikhomirov, "four or five times" during frequent visits to the cinema. He often shopped at the GUM (state department store) in Minsk. He listened to the *Voice of America* broadcasts, transmitted on short-wave from the US Coast Guard cutter, *USCGC Courier*, whose target audience was Russia and its Warsaw Pact allies, and he had sex with at least two women, Inna Tachina and Nellya Korbinka, before he met Marina.

Is this relevant? It was to Norman Mailer, who regressed from muted criticism of the Warren Commission's shortcomings to concluding that this 'straight' American male was the lone assassin, armed with an Italian-manufactured, bolt-action, Carcano 6.5mm infantry rifle, who had accurately fired the two shots in 1.66 seconds, at a range of 150 feet from a concealed sniper's nest on the sixth floor of the TSBD, that mortally wounded 'Lancer' - something not achieved later by FBI marksmen in less-stressful circumstances. A third shot missed, fragmented when it hit the south-kerb on Main Street, and slightly wounded spectator James Tague, who was standing several hundred feet further on from the TSBD waiting for the motorcade to pass.

Three years before his turgid account, *Oswald's Tale*, was published, in a wonderfully-titled, *Footfalls in the Crypt*, review of Oliver Stone's 189-minute, $40 million film, *JFK*, published by *Vanity Fair* in February 1992, Mailer suggested that there were "too many theories and too much contradictory evidence" for an accurate file to be made about the assassination. Mailer averred that a tragedy of such dimensions is comparable to the "whole force of Greek drama" in which Americans - presumably those who still remember where they were that day - repeatedly live with "the mystery, the awe, the horror, and the knowledge that a huge and hideous event" took place in Dallas.

Mailer, one of America's most distinguished authors, also refers to the "inflamed ragtag of assassination buffs" working in "relative solitude for decades" in the "private, inspired and isolated hope" that they might one day uncover the mystery. And although he describes that task as a "fantasy," pointing out that "to the degree that the murder of JFK was a conspiracy, so could one assume that the most salient evidence and the most inconvenient witnesses have been removed long go," this is a review by a man still sympathetic to the task, referring to the public execution of Kennedy as a mystery, not a homicide case, properly investigated and closed. When he set out to search for the soul of the assassin in his 828-page book, he began "with a prejudice in favor of the conspiracy theorists." He relied on his own 30 years experience as a "self-confessed conspiratorialist," and ended the journey after convincing himself that every insight he gained into the mind of Lee Harvey Oswald "suggests the solitary nature of the deed" and concludes that Oswald killed Kennedy simply because it was "the largest opportunity he had ever been offered." Mailer came to accept that Oswald was too unstable to be a 'regular' CIA or KGB agent, but enough of a psychopath to be an assassin. The night before he carried out the deed, according to Mailer, Oswald the assassin "reached a zone of serenity that some men attain before combat, when anxiety is deep enough to feel like quiet exhalation."

Apart from the twenty-six volumes of *Hearings and Exhibits* accompanying the Warren Commission report, Mailer's main sources are Pricilla Johnson McMillan's, *Lee and Marina*, from which he quotes scores of passages "for which he paid a modest sum," according to Thomas Powers in the *New York Times* in April 1995; *Legend*, by Edward Jay Epstein, who suggests a wider conspiracy without actually placing Oswald in the center of it; and *Case Closed*, by Wall Street lawyer, Gerald Posner, that had been widely discussed at the 1993 'Assassination Symposium on Kennedy,' held at the Hyatt Hotel in Dallas, at which Mailer was the keynote speaker. The ballistics work in Posner's book troubled Mailer, who described it as "both tendentious and mind-numbingly technical" and not the type of information usually taught at law school. It had Mailer wondering "whether there weren't organizations within the US Government that wanted their version of the story told." According to Texas-based *NameBase Newsline*, journalist, Steve Badrich, who covered the symposium, Mailer conceded that Posner's book might have cleared the "thicket of assassination research" of some of its "sillier and more fragile growths" but he criticized the lawyer for "cutting the same bloody corners" as the conspiracy theorists he [Posner] mocks, and then "ignoring the same problems he should be examining."

Posner was also accused of "false quotation syndrome" by Martin Cannon, a writer with *Prevailing Winds Magazine*, founded in the mid-1990s by the Santa Barbara-based Center for the Preservation of Modern History (CPMH), who says Posner either misrepresented those he supposedly interviewed, such as the autopsist at Bethesda Naval Hospital, Dr. James Humes, or misrepresented those he had not spoken to, such as Dr. Thornton Boswell (Humes colleague at Bethesda) and James Tague, an eyewitness and the third man hit on Dealey Plaza, who told the Warren Commission that he had not been struck by the first shot fired - testimony at odds with the Commission's basic premise because it suggests another rifle using different ammunition was involved, and therefore a second assassin. In his book Posner claims Tague "changed his mind" after a series of interviews, and this is important because Tague's alleged revised testimony is vital to Posner's conclusion that Oswald acted alone. Tague hadn't changed his mind, according to Cannon. He told so-called "assassination buffs" Harold Weisberg and Walt Brown, as well as medical expert, Dr Gary Aquilar (who double-checked Posner's claimed interview subjects), that the lawyer hadn't spoken to him at all.

Posner's book hit the bookshelves in 1993 with a full-page ad in *The New Yorker* proclaiming 'One Man, One Gun, One Inescapable Conclusion' and buoyed by fulsome praise from, amongst others, the *New York Times*, who saw it as a vindication of the newspaper's shamefully blinkered acceptance of the Warren Commission's conclusions. The book was part of a determined effort by one of America's 'Big Six' publishers, Random House, to rehabilitate the single assassin theory, to shore-up the findings of the Warren Commission on the 30th anniversary of the assassination, and respond to Oliver Stone's genuinely sincere account of the guns at Dallas. Referring to the genesis of the book, Posner wrote that Random House didn't care if he wrote a book that concluded that the assassination was a conspiracy or the work of a lone assassin "so long as my work was supported by credible evidence." However, Posner's editor at Random House, Robert D. Loomis, in an interview in *Publishers' Weekly* on 3 April 1993, suggested a different agenda, saying "All the conspiracies have undermined the public's belief in Government. They believe that everybody's in cahoots, that we have murderers in the CIA. That's what has been accepted, and that, to me, is a crime."

There and Back Again

Oswald was kept under close surveillance by the MVD. Apparently the agency didn't regard the ex-Marine as a genuine traitor but he was of interest because of his technical knowledge of the CIA's Lockheed-manufactured U-2, and the agency's high-altitude surveillance program which monitored the Soviet's inter-continental ballistic missile arsenal. Flights of the single-engine, *Dragon Lady*, spy plane - the single most important US high-tech intelligence asset - across the USSR originated at Atsugi Naval Air Station in Japan, where PFC Oswald had worked as a radio operator using sophisticated equipment to track the aircraft for up to 70,000 feet before losing radar contact, and had often communicated with the pilots during their flights and when they returned to base. While CIA officers at Atsugi often used Lysergic Acid Diethylamide (LSD) to interrogate suspected spies and drug dealers, and where the agency "most likely" recruited Oswald to serve as a double-agent in the Soviet Union and later "in a world of mystifying intrigues that ended in epic tragedy" according to author Douglas Valentine, the "misfit marine" was not a MK-UTLRA-programmed patsy or 'Manchurian Candidate' spy.

Oswald had knowledge of the secret radio frequencies, call signs and codes as well as the location and radar capability of every unit on the

US West Coast, but apparently none of this information was disclosed to the Soviets. On 5 January 1960, a U-2 spy plane piloted by Francis Gary Powers was shot down over the USSR, and the incident fuelled unfounded speculation among 'hawks' in the US intelligence community that information provided by Oswald might have helped the Soviets target the plane. This, however, is highly unlikely. All the vital tactical information, according to Oswald's former commander at Atsugi, John Donovan, was changed following Oswald's defection. After Gary Powers fell to earth the Kremlin made no attempt to exploit Oswald's presence, nor was there any back-channel chatter to suggest he had anything at all to do with bringing down the Operation *Grand Slam* Soviet over-flight, from the US base in Peshawar, Pakistan, to Bode in Norway, which was tasked with photographing ICBM sites in Sverdlovsk and Plesetsk, and the plutonium processing facility at Mayak.

Working at the GRT was as close to Sputnik technology that Oswald was likely to get, and just over a year after moving to Minsk he wrote to the US embassy in Moscow saying he wished to return to the US. The following month at a dance at the Trade Union Palace in Minsk, he was introduced to Marina Prusakova, who worked at the city's Third Clinical Hospital. Marina claimed they met during a social evening at the Medical Institute on 4 March 1961. She had been invited by a medical student, referred to as 'Sasha P', and one of his friends introduced her to Oswald.

After a whirlwind romance, Lee Harvey Oswald and Marina Prusakova, with the permission of her aunt and uncle, were married, on 30 April 1961, at the local ZAGs (records) office where they were both registered. Within a month, according to Marina's account to the Warren Commission, Oswald told her he wanted to return to the United States. He arranged to retrieve his passport, which he had left on John McVickar's desk at the US Embassy after his defection in October 1959, while in July 1961 Marina submitted an application to the American Embassy in Moscow for an entry visa to the US, and a request for an exit visa to the USSR Ministry of Foreign Affairs. By the New Year 1962, she had been officially granted permission to enter the US, and five months later she obtained her exit visa. On 15 February 1962, she gave birth to her first child, a daughter, and less than four months later, on 2 June, the Oswald family left Moscow by train for Rotterdam, on the first part of their journey to America.

According to Assistant Professor John Newman, faculty member at the University of Maryland, specializing in Sino-Soviet and US-East Asian studies, Oswald's clearance procedures for departure from Minsk included an interview with a senior MVD official - perhaps Marina's uncle, but this is not mentioned - before an exit visa was stamped on his passport. The family then traveled to Moscow, on 24 May 1962, where the US Embassy renewed his passport, adding the birth of his daughter, June, and providing Marina with a US entry visa. Two days later Marina's passport was stamped by the Soviet authorities.

Prof. Newman states that Oswald borrowed $435.71 from the US State Department, and on 2 June, the family "boarded a train for Holland, which passed through Minsk that night, crossed the Russian border at Brest, and transited Poland and Germany. On June 3, Oswald's passport was stamped at the Oldenzaal Station, in the Netherlands. On June 4 1962, the Oswalds' steamship tickets were delivered to them in Rotterdam. On June 6, they departed on the *SS Maasdam*, a Holland-American Line ship, bound for New York." Prof. Newman's account is based almost totally on the largely discredited Warren Commission report, which also refers to US ambassador Thompson's comments, in *Volume XXVI*, that the Soviet's treatment of Marina was "noteworthy" because it was "unusual for the Russians to allow the baby to leave."

Anthony Summers claims that before leaving the Soviet Union "both Lee and Marina talked with Captain Alexis Davison," the US embassy doctor and assistant Air Attaché, who was the CIA's contact with GRU Colonel Oleg Penkovsky, a double agent for western intelligence, later convicted for treason in 1963, executed and cremated. The Oswalds left the Soviet Union by train on 1 June, according to Summers. Marina's passport was stamped at Helmstedt, "one of the most strictly-monitored checkpoints" into the West, while her husband's wasn't. The only explanation given for this 'omission' is that Oswald carried an American passport, although given the suspicious nature of the relations between the Warsaw Pact and the West, this fact alone (and the East German transit visa) should have merited far closer scrutiny. Summers refers to Oswald's diary, and a hand-drawn map of cross-country train connections at Helmstedt, and suggests that Oswald "may have stopped over in West Berlin, briefly and without Marina" before "continuing his journey west by other means."

Until the collapse of the Warsaw Pact in the late 1980s, Helmstedt was the major border crossing between West Germany and the GDR, with the main rail and autobahn routes across the GDR to West Berlin beginning at the Helmstedt-Marienborn crossing, officially known to Washington's military and intelligence establishment as 'Checkpoint Alpha'. Official NATO military traffic to West Berlin was only allowed to use this rail and road link. Having raised the issue, Summers explains that Oswald had "no known reason for the diversion" before pointing out that the divided German city had "long served as an intelligence crossroads, and as a haven for operatives coming in from the cold." It is worth noting that the hand-drawn 'plan' of Helmstedt station's rail links is not something which could be copied from a book but, more likely, sketched from details provided by an individual. And once again suspicion falls on staff at the US embassy in Moscow.

Perhaps Oswald's CIA handlers had thought, at some point after Oswald's repatriation request, of switching trains and sending him to Berlin, but this would have been fraught with danger at an extremely tense time. Less than nine months earlier, on 13 August 1961, the construction of the Berlin Wall between the allied-controlled West Berlin and the German

Democratic Republic (GDR) began, and it had already become a bloody symbol of the Cold War. The GDR called it the "anti-fascist protection barrier" while West German politicians called it the "wall of shame." It was built slightly inside the GDR and building had commenced when workmen made the roads impassable and erected about ninety miles of barbed wire fencing around the US, British, and French controlled western sectors of the city. The first concrete blocks were laid 48 hours later, under the watchful eyes of NVA and KdA border security, with specific orders signed by GDR State Council chairman, Walter Ulbricht, to shoot anyone attempting to defect. The CIA, and their British counterpart, MI6, were busy on the ground in West Berlin, and had been underground, beneath East Berlin, in a joint eavesdropping operation to monitor Soviet landline communications, known as Operation *Gold* at Langley, and Operation *Stopwatch* at MI6 headquarters in central London. It was a more ambitious and complex covert operation than *Silver* - the successful MI6 monitoring (from a shop selling Scottish tweed clothing) of Soviet military chatter in Vienna - but it was only after the arrest of Rotterdam-born MI6/KGB double agent, George Blake, did the allied intelligence agencies realize that the Berlin SIGINT operation was a long-compromised embarrassment. Blake was found guilty of treason and sentenced to 42 years following a secret trial at the Old Bailey in London in May 1961 - one year for each of the British spies he allegedly betrayed.

Oswald's diary is not always precise, but the errors are excusable. For example, on one page is the address of the Dutch embassy in Moscow, and the name 'Van Hattun'. All diplomatic business, included transit visas, was handled at consular level in the non-descript building, and G.J. van Hattum was the delegation's legal attaché in 1962. Other members of staff included Senior Consul, Dr G Vixseboxse, 1st. Secretary, P.G. Bolak, and Consul (2nd class) N.J. Scheele. The Dutch followed the British and US practice of posting intelligence operatives abroad under diplomatic cover, and for this reason it is likely that either Bolak or Scheele (or both) were members of the Dutch foreign intelligence service, BID, closely liaising with the CIA and MI6. Dutch Foreign Ministry employee records are scarce on detail, but it would have been a breach of basic tradecraft if Oswald had been given the name of a BID contact agent by his CIA handler. Amd it is safe to assume that whatever Van Hattum knew or learned would have found its way to his BID colleagues. Moscow was Van Hattum's first diplomatic posting. He went on to serve as Dutch ambassador in Havana, Washington DC, and Oslo.

Even the experienced investigative journalist, Summers, got it wrong the first time in *Conspiracy* (published in 1980) when he wrote that "when the Oswalds arrived in Amsterdam they stayed not in a hotel but at an establishment recommended by the US Embassy in Moscow" and that they only stayed one night. He mentioned one of the "nagging inconsistencies" of the journey - Marina's initial claim that they had stayed three nights at a "boarding house" or "private apartment." However, in the 1998 edition of the book, *Not In Your Lifetime,* Summers, who by then had access to Oswald's diary, immediately recognized another significant inconsistency - that the industrial port city Rotterdam, not Amsterdam, was the couple's Dutch destination.

Norman Mailer differs in his narrative, claiming that the Oswalds "left Moscow by train on May 30, 1962, and traveled through Poland, Germany, and Holland. In Holland they boarded the *SS Maasdam* for the US and arrived in New York on June 13, 1962." Mailer also refers to a report by FBI agents, Anatole Boguslav and Wallace Heitman, headed, *An Investigation of the Assassination of President Kennedy*, which states, on page 31, that an FBI investigation of Oswald "had been instituted on May 31, 1962" so that the bureau would be notified of his re-entry to the US by Immigration authorities. The purpose of this low-key inquiry was "to determine if Oswald had been recruited by a Soviet intelligence service."

Marina's Story

Marina Oswald has never been the most reliable source of information, and her account of the journey to the Warren Commission is riddled with inconsistencies. Some are errors of geography, encouraged perhaps, but certainly not corrected by the CIA or the Secret Service, and some are honest mistakes, made by a young, recently-widowed stranger in a strange land.

Following the assassination and arrest of her husband in connection with the death of Dallas Police Department (DPD) officer, J.D. Tippit, she was held in Secret Service protective custody at the Inn of the Six Flags in Fort Worth, Texas, until she completed her testimony before the Warren Commission. During the first fortnight of what turned out to be a three month restrictive regime, according to McKnight, "she was under intense government pressure." Texas industrialist, Jack Crichton, the 1964 Republican candidate for the Lone Star State, who was heavily involved in a local Cold War initiative called 'Know Your Enemy' to defend the American way of life against the Communist threat, suggested that Ilya Mamantov, a member of the Russian community in Dallas, work as a translator for Marina during initial questioning by DPD and the Secret Service. Crichton was a former member of the CIA's predecessor, the Office of Strategic Services (OSS), and as part of the "readiness (better dead than red) program" he maintained HUMINT surveillance of the Russian community in Dallas, working closely with the local police. Russ Baker, investigative journalist and author of the excellent book on the Bush dynasty, *Family of Secrets*, claims Mamantov's work "was far from literal translations of [Marina's] Russian words and had the effect of implicating her husband in Kennedy's death." It also had the effect of focusing attention away from Rotterdam, and however flawed her testimony - and Mamantov's deliberately disingenuous translation - her narrative remains the official, on-the-record account of the leaving of Moscow.

The commission had been appointed by President Lyndon Baines Johnson, on 29 November 1963, under the chairmanship of Chief Justice

Earl Warren. The commission was asked to "satisfy itself that the truth is known as far as it can be discovered and to report its findings and conclusions to him [the President], to the American people and to the world." On 23 November 1964, one year and a day after JFK had been murdered in Dallas, the Warren Commission published its findings, in twenty-six closely-printed volumes, and concluded that Lee Harvey Oswald was the lone assassin, who had planned and carried out the killing.

Warren Commission *Exhibit 994* is an English translation of Marina Oswald's narrative of life with Lee, and the journey from the USSR to America.

> In the middle of May [1962] I received my Soviet exit visa. We went first to Moscow to put our documents in their final form, i.e., to obtain a foreign passport for myself, to exchange some money (to get dollars for rubles) and to buy a ticket. In Moscow we stayed several days in the Hotel Ostankino and then transferred to the [Hotel] Berlin because it was closer to the center of town.
>
> The last days in the USSR were spent in a frantic rush There was a lot to be done and it took up a lot of time. Basically Lee took care of the packing, since I was occupied with June. We had saved a little money and in addition we had money from the sale of our furniture and some other things. This we exchanged for dollars but of course it was not enough to buy a ticket and get a start in the United States. So Lee borrowed some money from the American Embassy.
>
> From Moscow we took the train to Warsaw, Berlin and Amsterdam. Holland, that small and cozy country, pleased me most of all. We went through Holland on a Sunday. The bells were ringing in the churches and people were going to church. It was sunny and everything was very quiet. It seemed the people here had never known trouble, and everything was like a fairytale, with lots of glass and light. Holland is a very, very clean country, surely the cleanest country in the world.
>
> We lived in an apartment in Amsterdam for three days, and our landlady was so neat that we were afraid to lie down on the sheets for fear of getting them dirty (...) In Amsterdam we bought a ticket on a boat for New York. It was already June, but in Holland it was still cold. We wore our overcoats. On June 13 we arrived in New York. Rain was falling. It was rather cold...

The former United States Solicitor General, and general counsel for the inquiry, J. Lee Rankin, then asked her how much time the couple had spent in Amsterdam on the way to the United States?

> Mrs. Oswald: "Two or three days, it seems to me."
> Mr. Rankin: "What did you do there?"
> Mrs. Oswald: "Walked around the city, did some sightseeing."
> Mr. Rankin: "Did anybody visit you there?"
> Mrs. Oswald: "No."
> Mr. Rankin: "Did you visit anyone?"
> Mrs. Oswald: "No."
> Mr. Rankin: "What hotel did you stay in?"
> Mrs. Oswald: "We didn't stop at a hotel. We stopped at a place where they rent apartments. The address was given to us in the American Embassy."
> Mr. Rankin: "Do you recall what you paid in the way of rent?"
> Mrs. Oswald: "No, Lee paid it. I don't know."
> Mr. Rankin: "How did your husband spend his time when he was aboard the ship?"
> Mrs. Oswald: "I was somewhat upset because he was a little ashamed to walk around with me, because I wasn't dressed as well as the other girls, Basically I stayed in my cabin while Lee went to the movies and they have different games there. I don't know what my husband did there..."

At the beginning of her testimony Marina was asked by Mr. Rankin: "Do you recall the date you arrived in the United States with your husband, Lee Harvey Oswald?"

> Mrs. Oswald: "On the 13th of June 1962, I am not quite certain as to the year, 61 or 62, I think 62."
> Mr. Rankin: "How did you come to this country?"
> Mrs. Oswald: "From Moscow, via Poland Germany and Holland. We came to Amsterdam by train. And from Amsterdam to New York by ship and New York to Dallas by air."
> Mr. Rankin: "Do you recall the name of the ship on which you came?"
> Mrs. Oswald: "I think it was the *SS Rotterdam* but I am not sure."
> Mr. Rankin: "What time of day did you arrive in New York?"
> Mrs. Oswald: "It was about noon, or 1pm, thereabouts. It is hard to remember the exact time."

She was then asked if the couple had received any financial assistance for the trip to Texas. She replied that Lee had got money from his brother, Robert, for the final stage of the journey from New York to Dallas, "but the money for the trip from the Soviet Union to New York was given to us by the American Embassy in Moscow."

Marina Oswald's account of her journey, leaving her homeland for the first and last time, is so unemotional it could have been scripted by someone else. This was a dangerous and tense period in central Europe, yet there is no mention of being afraid of being stopped at the Polish or East German frontiers and asked awkward questions by nervous border guards. The KGB had obviously arranged a smooth passage westward. On the GDR border with West Germany the CIA took over, until the odd couple's totally uneventful trans-European rail journey, which might even be described as "boring and forgettable," ended at Central Station, Rotterdam.

A Witting Asset

Priscilla Johnson McMillan, was a freelance journalist, a fluent Russian speaker with a masters degree from Harvard in Soviet studies, and her dual biography, *Marina and Lee,* published in 1977 - in time to be considered by the HSCA - provides a more concise time-frame, particularly of the hours spent in Rotterdam.

McMillan was an accredited Moscow-based correspondent, working for the North American Newspaper Alliance (NANA) when Oswald arrived in the Soviet capital seeking political asylum, and she was 'encouraged' by US consul, John McVickar, to talk to the ex-marine, reminding her, according to Summers, that there was a "thin line somewhere between her duty as a correspondent and as an American." She interviewed him at the Hotel Metropol, and her two-column story, published in the Washington DC-based, *Evening Star,* in November 1959, was the first time the American public learned of his defection. It also contributed to his 'legend' as an ex-marine at odds with the capitalist system seeking a new life in the USSR, which had, seemingly, failed to convince the Soviets that they were dealing with the genuine article.

In its final report, published in 1979, the HSCA concluded that McMillan did not have a "clandestine relationship" with the CIA, but among declassified CIA files released in 1975 she is listed as a "witting collaborator 01 code A1" which means, according to James diEugenio and Lisa Pease, former editors of the Los Angeles-based *Probe* magazine, "not only was she working with the agency, she knew she was working with the agency." And, in a memo dated 11 December 1962, the CIA's Soviet Russia Branch chief, Donald Jameson, wrote that McMillan "can be encouraged to write pretty much the articles we want."

And her account of the leaving of Moscow should be read as "pretty much" what the CIA wanted. Before their departure the Oswalds stayed in the Hotel Ostankino, them moved to the city center Hotel Berlin. They visited the US embassy several times, Marina got her American visa, and the embassy suggested a hotel where they could spend a "cheap and comfortable night in Rotterdam" and "either Oswald or the embassy made the reservation." Since they were to cross Europe in the grip of the Cold War, they had to visit the Polish, East Germany, West Germany and Dutch embassies to apply for and obtain transit visas, all of which they managed to do within 5 working days, an extraordinary achievement, difficult if not impossible to achieve even in these days of insincere perestroika. Their last night in Moscow, 31 May 1962, was spent partying in the apartment of Yury and Galka Belyankin, who had been friends of Marina in Minsk. From Moscow to Brest, and on to Warsaw where they "changed a few dollars into zlotys and bought beer" before continuing their journey across Poland to East Germany and Berlin. Here Marina woke briefly and noticed East Berlin was dark and the Western section was "brightly lit." The next morning they were in Holland, and to Marina each village seemed "prettier than the last" and "entire families were walking to church." When they arrived in Rotterdam they went directly to the boarding house recommended by the embassy. The landlady provided lunch. Then they went window-shopping, drank Coca Cola, and "the next morning, June 4, 1962, they boarded the *SS Maasdam* bound from Rotterdam to New York."

Based on archived Nederlands Spoorwegen (NS) material, the Sovetsky Zheleznye Dorogi (SZLD) trans-European *Moscow Express* steamed out of Bjeloruisskaja Terminal on Friday 1 June 1962 at 4.10pm, traveled via Minsk and Brest to arrive in Warsaw the following afternoon at 1.15pm, then continued on schedule across Poland via Poznan, crossing into East Germany at Frankfurt-aan-Oder at 8.37pm and arriving in East Berlin at 10.04pm. Via Magdeburg the train crossed the GDR border into West Germany at Helmstedt, and traveled via Hannover and Osnabreuk to reach Oldenzal, in the Netherlands, at 8.12am. Through Holland, via Hengelo at 8.30am to Amersfoort. Here the train split, one section going via Utrecht at 10.14am heading for Amsterdam, while the second section traveled to Rotterdam, arriving at Central Station at 11.22am, where the Oswalds' embarked. The train then continued on to the Hook of Holland, a seaport on the North Sea coast, administered by the municipality of Rotterdam.

For obvious reasons, during the contagiously paranoid Cold War era, passengers traveling from Moscow to western European destinations were not allowed to leave the train in transit and go walk about in Warsaw or East Berlin. In the unlikely event that Oswald, or his handlers, had even considered changing trains for some hair-brained adventure in Berlin, Helmstedt was the first opportunity to legally do so.

In the early 1960s the Moscow to Hook of Holland journey was a regular and efficient service by Soviet standards, sometimes with full accommodation (including sleeping compartments, dining facilities and regular (classless) seating for up to 300 passengers, the majority of whom were Communist Party apparatchiks, Soviet military personnel, front-office diplomatic staff and the usual traveling contingent of KGB domestic division agents, who strolled through the carriages after scheduled stops, keeping a close eye on west-bound passengers with transit-only visas, especially during scheduled stops in Warsaw and East Berlin. There was no such thing as a one-hour (or less) entry/exit visa, as some accounts have suggested.

Professor McKnight writes that the Warren Commission, in its final report, "spent more than thirty pages of tedious detail on the legal intricacies and financial arrangements involved in the State Department's efforts to return Oswald and his family to the United States" and describes it as a "classic example of the report's telling too much about too little." This response might be exactly what the CIA wanted to achieve, using the Warren Commission as a more than willing conduit and collaborator. The less known about time spent in Rotterdam the better. The CIA could not be accused of lying when the agency denied having anything to do with Oswald after he returned to the US, and nobody though of asking if contact had been made outside American jurisdiction, in Rotterdam for example, or even on board the *Maasdam*, during its trans-Atlantic voyage

Former US Republican senator, Richard Schweiker, a member of a US Senate Select Committee, chaired by Democrat Senator Frank Church, and established in the wake of the Watergate affair to investigate allegations of illegal CIA and FBI intelligence-gathering operations, issued a statement in September 1975, calling on the committee to reopen the investigation into JFK's assassination, citing the suppression of evidence, and the role played by US intelligence agencies. "We don't know what happened," Schweiker said in his statement, "but we do know that Oswald had intelligence connections. Everywhere you look with him, there are the fingerprints of intelligence." Among the questions Schweiker wanted answered was how the ex-marine could afford the $1,500 trip to Moscow in 1959, when he only had $203 in his bank account, how he managed to get a visa in two weeks when it normally took six, how did he travel from London to Helsinki, when there was no commercial flight scheduled, and why did the CIA not question or debrief him when he returned from the USSR?

Two of these 'unresolved' questions can be answered. There were three commercial flights scheduled from London's Heathrow to Helsinki, two of which would have landed Oswald in the Finnish capital with time to spare. And the CIA did debrief their agent when he returned, but did so in a 'friendly neighborhood' outside US jurisdiction.

Spy v Spy in the Lowlands

In post-WW2 Holland, from the remains of a savagely disseminated and hugely discredited internal security apparatus, a new counter-insurgency ethos began to emerge once the treacherous legacy of informants and pro-Nazi sympathizers had been confronted and eradicated. Some of the Third Reich's most willing collaborators were agents of the Dutch state who had changed uniform and worked under new management, enforcing a different set of brutally inhumane principles after the shameful flight of the Dutch monarchy to Canada.

By the early 1950s, however, the BVD, under director L. Einthoven, a close friend of CIA director, Allan Dulles, had faced up to the legacy of its contaminated past, and evolved into an efficient internal security agency. The evolution had been a painful but rewarding experience for Einthoven, a former Rotterdam Police Commissioner who had been appointed head of the Bureau van Nationale Veiligheid (BNV) - the Office of National Security - following liberation in May 1945, to absorb the London-based intelligence agents and the Dutch-based resistance groups, and take charge of all the data on spies, saboteurs and collaborators that the separate groups had collated. The BNV was set up as a temporary organization, according to Dutch historian, Dick Engelen, and tasked with clearing up "the remnants of the German intelligence and security services," hunting down and arresting agents and collaborators of the Abwehr, the Gestapo and the Sicherheitsdienst, to be tried and punished by the Extraordinary Administration of Justice, while a small unit called Bureau B, initially established to monitor the orderly return to pre-war democracy, was later used to "observe political parties and groups on the extreme left and extreme right." Less than a year later, in April 1946, the BNV was replaced by the Centrale Veiligheidsdienst (CVD). This domestic security service was modeled on the British agency, MI5, and was intended to be a small, efficient, pro-active organisation working closely with the police to uncover plans by alleged communist activists and sympathizers to infiltrate the established political order. A card-index system was created (similar to MI5's 'A Division' Registry) and people suspected of 'extreme left' affiliations, or Dutch Communist Party (CPN) membership, were excluded from civil service employment, and from companies in the private sector considered 'security sensitive'. Cold War paranoia hung over the Lowlands, in the Netherlands as well as Belgium, where NATO had established its headquarters in the capital, Brussels, and its central military command, Supreme Headquarters Allied Powers Europe (SHAPE) at Casteau, in the French-speaking Walloon region of the country near the city of Mons. In 1954 Washington rejected the USSR's application to join the newly-formed organization to preserve peace in Europe, convincing its 'partners' - all of whom were dependent on Marshall Plan largesse to rebuild their economies - that it was a "sinister endeavor" to prevent or restrict the build-up of NATO forces in Europe. The CVD also compiled a 'Top Secret' list of persons to be arrested and interned in the event of war or serious civil unrest.

In August 1949, the CVD was renamed the Binnenlandse Veiligheids-dienst (BVD), and in the following decade the organization grew from 196 employees to 596, an expansion only made possible by subsidies from the CIA, which Dulles offered to Einthoven, to be used against the KGB and the GRU in Holland. In 1950 Langley provided 'special equipment' worth $25,000, including bugging devices and D/F (direction and frequency) units to be used to monitor and locate clandestine radio broadcasts. The financial support was also used to purchase cars, weapons and to pay staff. By the early 1960s at least sixty-five BVD agents - approximately 10 percent of the entire workforce - were being paid directly from the CIA's budget. This material and financial support was specifically intended for 'Project A' - monitoring daily activity at the Soviet Embassy in The Hague, while premises used by trade-mission personnel in Amsterdam and Rotterdam, the offices of the Soviet state airline, Aeroflot, and state shipping line, Morflot, staff-members of the news agencies ITAR-TASS and RIA-Novosti, and the Amtorg Trading Corporation, all used by the KGB and the GRU as commercial cover for agents abroad, were under HUMINT and (at permanent locations) SIGINT surveillance, and the 'product' was shared with CIA station personnel at the US Embassy in the Dutch capital, and routed to Langley. Both Einthoven and Dulles retired in 1961 (with the former CIA chief later serving on the Warren Commission). J.S. Sunnighe Damste, who succeeded Einthoven, gradually reduced the BVD's dependence on Langley's technical and financial assistance, but with the Soviet threat still large over Western Europe the BVD remained, until at least the late 1960s, an 'appendage' of the CIA.

Thanks to the Warren Commission it is not difficult to be suspicious about so many matters that still demand consideration, before and after the assassination of John Kennedy, and about almost every decision made in relation to Lee Harvey Oswald - even the timing of his recall from the USSR. After his recent marriage to Marina Prusakova, was Langley afraid of Oswald 'going native', having doubts perhaps that Oswald was still 'one of ours' and deciding to repatriate him by taking the long way home, allowing just enough time in Rotterdam for a debriefing before the boat sailed? Who signed-off on that? There was a better way to do this if the objective of the exercise was to get Oswald and his family safely out of the USSR. There had to be some good reason why the most efficient, straightforward, and safest exit wasn't considered. By plane, from Moscow to Heathrow and on to LaGuardia, in New York. No need to bother the Poles, the GDR authorities, the West Germans or the Dutch.

Or maybe not. Diplomatic relations between the Soviet Union and the Netherlands had been seriously damaged by a major intelligence-related incident, part and parcel of the Cold War's clandestine, spy-versus-spy world of shadows. Meanwhile, Oswald's techno intelligence-gathering mission in the USSR had been unproductive, and his marriage raised doubts about his loyalty if he remained in Minsk. His request to be repatriated had provided an opportunity. He was now a pawn at Langley's disposal, and a decision was taken to run him through the Netherlands, hoping to flush out the KGB/GRU in Rotterdam, one of the Pentagon's main European ports of entry for military hardware heading for West Berlin.

Vladimir Yefimovich Semichastny was chairman of the KGB, from November 1961 to April 1967, and the head of the First (Foreign Intelligence) Directorate (FID) was Aleksandr Mikhailovich Sakharovsky, a melancholic but competent bureaucrat who had personally welcomed home Vilyam Genrikhovich Fisher, the British-born KGB spy, based in New York, arrested by the FBI, indicted, convicted and sentenced to 45 years by a New York Federal Court in October 1957 for conspiring to obtain and transmit classified US military information to Moscow Central. He had served less than five years in Atlanta State Penitentiary, Georgia, before being exchanged, in February 1962, for the CIA's U-2 pilot, Gary Powers. The First Directorate's 'Department 5' was responsible for clandestine HUMINT tasks in the Benelux countries, while 'Department 16' was responsible for SIGINT operations. In Holland these operations were headed by the KGB resident (chief of station) at the Soviet embassy. The residency included D5 staff dealing with political, economic and military strategic intelligence, and D16 line managers handling counter-intelligence and security with SIGINT operational technical officers, coordinating radio communications with HUMINT surveillance teams of two to four agents, depending on the nature and mobility of the target.

Among the enormous pressures of the job as FID chief, during these Cold War years, was to avoid failure at least to such a degree so as not to embarrass the Foreign Ministry, the International Department of the Central Committee, or the Presidium of the Supreme Soviet, headed by the unpredictable president, Nikita Khrushchev. And Sakharovsky, - whose "first hand experience of the outside world was limited to Romania and other parts of eastern Europe" according to Mitrokhin's smuggled archives - had already embarrassed his bosses with his handling of what became known among intelligence professionals as the 'Schiphol incident.'

This began on 7 October 1961, when Soviet chemist, Aleksej Goloeb, who was visiting the Benelux with his wife as part of a trade delegation, requested political asylum in Amsterdam. He also told the Dutch authorities that his wife was being held against her will at the Soviet trade delegation offices in the city, although she had issued a statement saying she wasn't seeking asylum and wanted to return to Moscow. Two days later an Aeroflot Tupalov Tu-104 landed at Schiphol, and Mrs. Goloeb was escorted to the plane by the Soviet ambassador, Panteleimon Ponomarenko, and at least eleven staff from the residency in The Hague. Within hours the Dutch Foreign Minister, Joseph Luns, declared Anatoli Popov, 2nd Secretary at the embassy, and Sergei Shibayev, head of the trade mission in Amsterdam, *persona non grata* for "hindering attempts" by the Royal Military Constabulary at Schiphol to "speak privately" with Mrs. Goloeb, and both men were ordered to leave the country within 48 hours. When Soviet Foreign Minister, Andrei Gromyko, refused to apologize for the incident, ambassador Ponomarenko was the next to go. The Kremlin responded immediately by ordering the Dutch ambassador, Henri Albert Helb, an experienced diplomat who had previously served in Belgrade in the early 1950s, to leave the USSR, and for the next 18 months neither country had diplomatic representation at ambassadorial level, until Luns and Gromyko met at the United Nations in New York in September 1963, and normal diplomatic service was resumed.

Aleksej Goloeb was questioned by the BVD, and the agency initially assumed he was an ICBM specialist, involved in the development of the P-36 series of heavyweight missiles. The CIA was called in, but the men from Langley warned their Dutch counterparts that Goloeb was a fake. When it emerged during questioning that the 'suspicious' asylum seeker had been involved in cancer research, the BVD also lost interest. He was passed over to the BID, who discovered that the facility where he worked had a defense technology and pharmaceutical research division. Langley resumed interest, and a team of specialists from the agency's TSS Chemicals Division, working on a covert 'mind control' program with the US Army Chemical Corps, based at Fort Detrick, designated MK-ULTRA (launched in 1955 but not revealed to the American public until the Rockefeller Report was published in 1975) studying the use of LSD and other hallucinogens, was dispatched from Maryland to question the Russian chemist. It was an unproductive journey. Nothing useful was learned from these sessions, although this assumption is based on the fact that Goloeb remained in Holland, and went to work at a biochemical and biophysics laboratory in Delft. While presenting the finding of the Rockefeller Report, CIA director Admiral Stansfield Turner, revealed that all operational records on MK-ULTRA projects, including (presumably) the interrogation of Aleksej Goloeb, were destroyed in 1973 on the orders of his predecessor, Richard Helms, the only CIA director ever convicted of lying to the US Congress about CIA activity. Within months the BVD learned from monitored Soviet embassy landline communications that Goloeb wanted to return home. On 27 March 1962, he flew back to Moscow and at a press conference he claimed that the Dutch and the Americans had tried to force him to reveal information about Soviet scientific, industrial and military capabilities and potential. Goloeb was a chemist, and he knew nothing to interest the CIA. He had to put a brave face on his 'defection' and once he said what he was instructed to say he disappeared. Another disposable pawn in the covert intelligence wars, whose Lowlands adventure, nothing more than a storm in a test tube, doesn't even merit a mention in Vasili Mitrokhin's archive.

Serving Clandestine Interests Only

There is no overt redeeming factor in the decision to have the Oswalds travel across Cold War Europe to spend time in a country where the political climate with regard to anything to do with the USSR was close to freezing. If we are to believe the official KGB version of events, nobody at KGB HQ Moscow Central was really interested in the ex-marine, and nobody bothered to "discretely accompany" the Oswalds out of the USSR. This was claimed by Major Yuri Ivanovoch Nosenko, a KGB officer who had worked on US affairs at the organization's Second Chief Directorate in Moscow. In 1962, while part of a diplomatic delegation to Geneva, he had contacted the CIA after an altercation with a prostitute, and offered his services. Two years later Nosenko was a part of a KGB security detail attached to a Soviet delegation attending disarmament talks in Geneva. On 24 January 1964, less than two months after the murder of JFK, he contacted the US embassy from a payphone in the lobby of his hotel, claiming he needed to defect immediately because his role as a double-agent had been discovered and he was being recalled to Moscow.

Within 3 days two senior CIA agents, Peter Bagley, recently promoted to Chief of Intelligence for the Soviet Bloc Division, and George Kisvalter, were sitting with Nosenko at a CIA safe house in the Geneva suburbs, listening to the Ukrainian-born spy claiming he had personally monitored the Oswald defection case, and denying any KGB role in Oswald's defection and subsequent repatriation to the US, or in the assassination of the American president.

Bagley in particular was skeptical of Nosenko, and had recently circulated an internal 12-page CIA memo warning that Nosenko might still be under Soviet control, despite the fact that the KGB officer had warned the CIA that the KGB had blackmailed and recruited a homosexual clerk in the British naval attaché's office in Moscow in the early 1950s, a tip which led directly to the arrest, in September 1962, of John Vassall, who had been supplying Moscow Central with classified Admiralty material for almost a decade.

Nosenko also told the US State Department the location of 42 tiny listening devices which had been embedded in the walls in the US Embassy in Moscow when it was built in 1952. The microphones remained undetected for 12 years, despite "fairly regular" anti-bugging electronic sweeps by US security officers. Although US diplomats were aware of the possibility of undiscovered bugs in the building and took the standard precautions, general conversation, not regarded as sensitive, was part of the KGB's SIGINT product. From this Moscow Central would have learned about US international priorities, interests and concerns, and, presumably, the KGB knew that Oswald had threatened to reveal information about Atsugi and the U-2 flights when he visited the office of US consul, John McVickar, in October 1959, shortly after he had crossed the Finnish/USSR border.

So Nosenko had a track record of providing reliable information. Bagley believed, however, that the KGB knew both operations - the bugs and the Vassall affair - had already been compromised by the defection of Anatoli Golitsyn, a KGB officer who had worked in the US/UK department of the First Chief Directorate, the branch that carried out hostile espionage operations, and later processed reports from KGB agents inside NATO HQ in Brussels. In 1961 Golitsyn, using the identity Klimov, was working at the KGB Embassy in Helsinki, when he turned up on the doorstop of the home of the CIA chief of station in the Finnish capital with a batch of classified NATO documentation, and announced that he wanted to defect, with his wife and child, to the United States. Golitsyn was regarded as a bona fide defector, based on information he supplied which could be checked against what the CIA already knew about the Soviet Embassy in Helsinki. He warned of KGB penetration among the UKUSA Agreement countries, including Canada, New Zealand and Australia, who exclusively shared SIGINT data.

During his interrogation by Bagley and Kisvalter, Nosenko claimed he had joined the KGB in 1953 as a member of the Second Chief Directorate responsible for the surveillance and recruitment of foreigners visiting or working in Moscow, and by 1962, as deputy chief of the Seventh Department, he was in charge of operations against US tourists. He told Kisvalter (who had been born in St Petersburg) that the KGB had not even taken the trouble to question Oswald because he was considered "unstable." When he visited the US Embassy in Moscow in 1962 to arrange for his passage to the US for himself and his family, Oswald had also claimed that he had never been questioned by the KGB about his work at Atsugi Base, or the CIA's U-2 flights which originated in Japan.

Neither Oswald nor Nosenko were being honest. CIA sources, almost without exception, believe the KGB would have questioned Oswald simply because he was an ex-marine, even without the offer to provide information on Atsugi and the U-2. A former CIA career officer, Harry Rositzke, in a 1977 *Reader's Digest Press* publication called *The CIA's Secret Operations* states that the KGB "favored targets" are junior employees of the US Government, both male and female, and "Marine guards in the embassies, enlisted men in the armed forces." KGB agents worldwide, according to Rositzke, were actually encouraged to "cultivate" such contacts. The idea that Oswald wasn't a "person of interest" while he was living in Moscow or Minsk, is simply untrue, and is contrary to everything that is known about how the KGB handled defectors. Agent Bagley was also dismissive of Nosenko's statements about Oswald and the KGB's lack of interest, writing in his report: "Could this be true? Could we all be wrong in what we've heard about rigid Soviet security precautions and about their strict procedures and disciplines? Of course not."

The KGB, according to Nosenko, only allowed Oswald to remain in the Soviet Union after his suicide attempt, but regarded him as "too unstable" to be taken on as an agent. In his diary Oswald claims he slashed his left wrist in his hotel room at 7pm on 21 October 1959, after being told by Moscow Police that he must leave the country by 8pm that evening because his visa had expired. He was found by his (official state travel agency) Intourist guide, Rimma Shirokova, and taken to the Botkin Hospital at Khodynka, north-west of Moscow where, according to the hospital's records (later released by the Russian authorities) the patient – who refused to speak Russian – spent a week recovering from his self-inflicted wound. Three days after being discharged Oswald marched into the US Embassy, handed his passport to John McVickar, and renounced his American citizenship.

After being called in to examine the file following the assassination of JFK, Nosenko concluded that the only Soviet intelligence link had been Marina Oswald's uncle, the MVD officer, who asked his niece to persuade her husband not to spread anti-Soviet propaganda on his return to the US. He described Marina Oswald as stupid, uneducated, and had "anti-Soviet characteristics," and the KGB was "perfectly content" to see the couple leave the USSR. Bagley and Kisvalter reported back to Angleton. The two agents summarized their encounter with Nosenko: "The thrust of the Source's account was that neither Oswald nor his wife had at any time been of any interest whatsoever to Soviet authorities, that there had not ever been thought given to recruiting either of them as agents and that, in fact, the Soviets were glad to get rid of them both."

Angleton, nicknamed 'Kingfisher' by colleagues, was a close friend of Kim Philby, the senior MI6 spy suspected of being a KGB mole inside the British Secret Intelligence Service, suspicions that were confirmed by Anatoly Golitsyn. Confirmation of Philby's duplicity (he was probably one of the KGB's most productive agents in the West) caused Angleton to develop what his critics have described as "acute clinical paranoia." Kingfisher became a mole-hunter, and Golitsyn fed that anxiety, at one stage claiming the British Labour Party Prime Minister, Harold Wilson, was a KGB agent. Golitsyn also warned that the KGB would try to discredit his information.

With two defectors on their hands, both claiming to be a more accurate and trustworthy source on the clandestine work of the KGB in the USSR and the West than the other, the CIA was caught in a dilemma which it 'solved' by locking-up Nosenko, who repeatedly failed lie detector tests. Angleton didn't order Nosenko's detention, but he did not object when David Murphy, then head of the CIA's Soviet/Russia Division, ordered the Ukrainian to be held in solitary confinement "under brutal conditions for almost five years" according to the author, David Wise, "much of the time in a twelve-by-twelve foot windowless concrete cell in a house deep in the woods at The Farm, the CIA's training base. Despite the horrendous treatment of Nosenko, he never changed his story."

In 1968, an internal inquiry conducted by several experienced CIA Soviet Division veterans, including Benjamin Pepper, who had served in Berlin in the mid-1950s and Mexico City in the early 1960s, concluded that Nosenko was a genuine defector. He was released from CIA custody in March 1969, put on the agency's payroll and given a new identity as compensation for the inhumane treatment he had been subjected to – simply because his version of Oswald's USSR and JFK's assassination was "off message" and didn't fit with the CIA's "corporate view" of events, according to the agency's former Middle East case officer, Robert Baer.

Bugs in the Brickwork

The clandestine world of spy agencies was described as a "wilderness of mirrors" by author David Martin. However, an important 'tool' to understanding the nature of espionage is basic common sense, and common sense suggests that the KGB, as sophisticated as any secret intelligence organization in the business, and more capable than most, would not have passed up on an opportunity of using Oswald to monitor his reception in the West.

The KGB was fully aware of Oswald's comings and goings at the red-brick US Embassy in central Moscow. After being tipped-off by Golitsyn in the early 1960s, security men at the embassy broke into the walls of the 50-year old building and found more than 40 microphones, planted 8-to-10 inches inside the brickwork. The bugs were estimated to be at least 12 years old, dating back to Stalin's era, but still operational. The US, according to one National Security Agency (NSA) official, had been using the "most up-to-date methods" to detect "sophisticated bugs," unfortunately, the Soviets had "an old system of crystal sets" buried in the building. A declassified State Department memorandum, dated 2 October 1964, into the damage done to US security, makes uncomfortable reading, and is an important piece of the Oswald puzzle. An NSA assessment, the assessment of the State Department's security experts, and information which the CIA acquired from a defector, makes it virtually certain, according to the SD memo, that "extensive quantities of classified information were compromised as a result of the Soviet microphone operation." All the more embarrassing for Washington since it was just over a decade since the 'Great Seal Bug' affair - the bugging of the residential study of the American ambassador using a passive cavity resonator, connected to a small quarter-wavelength antenna, and activated by a correct frequency radio signal sent by an external transmitter. The bug had been embedded in the carved wooden plaque of the Great Seal of the United States, and presented by the All-Union Pioneer Organization to the US ambassador, Averill Harriman, on 4 August 1945, as a "gesture of friendship" for aid and assistance during World War II, and which hung on the wall above the ambassador's desk for seven years until it was discovered during the tenure of Ambassador George Keegan, after a British SIGINT specialist monitoring Soviet radio traffic accidentally overheard American conversations on an open channel while the KGB's 16D (Communications Intercept) was beaming radio signals at the ambassador's residence.

The KGB may have been suspicious of Oswald – despite (or perhaps because of) his overly-dramatic visit to the US Embassy in October 1959 - but it is unlikely the organization knew of his clandestine connection to Michael Jelisavcic, the local manager of American Express, who acted as Angleton's FDP conduit. Michael Jelisavcic was born in the small town of Raska, in the Serbian region of Yugoslavia, in 1912. He served as a junior diplomat with Royal Yugoslavia Foreign Ministry in the 1930s before escaping to South Africa shortly before German, Italian and Hungarian forces invaded the country, on 6 April 1941. In the early 1950s he moved to the US, graduated from Columbia University in 1956, and then worked for ten years as a 'businessman' in Moscow. At some stage between his arrival in the US and his departure for the USSR he was recruited by the CIA, presumably in return for US citizenship which he obtained in 1958. Jelisavcic conducted business on behalf of American Express from Room 384 at Moscow's Hotel Metropol. Built in the art noveau style just before the 1917 Russian

Revolution, "Room 233 Hotel Metropol" was the address given by Oswald to John McVickar when he called at the US Embassy on Saturday, 31 October 1959, just after 11am, wearing a dark suit, white shirt and tie, and white gloves, to surrender his passport, loudly renounce his American citizenship, and formally submit, in a handwritten note, his defection to the Soviet Union.

Rotterdam Sojourn

When Oswald arrived in Rotterdam on 3 June 1962, Jelisavicic's name, his Hotel Metropol address and telephone number were in his address book. Initially the scrawled reference "K-4200, 384, 1-2 Dinner Room 384, Jelisavcic" was assumed by JFK researchers to refer to a Rotterdam establishment. However, Dutch author, Perry Vermuelen, tidied up this loose end, pointing out that in the late 1950s the letter 'K' and the number '9' were interchangeable in the Soviet telephone system, and that this was the number of Jelisavcic's office at the Hotel Metropol. The Warren Commission, as Belgium journalist, Filip Coppens pointed out in the magazine, *Fourth Decade*, two decades ago, described the 'Dutch period' as "difficult and inexplicable" and refers to an "important CIA officer" who may have been involved with Oswald on another occasion, and who was living in the Netherlands in mid-June 1962, but took the matter no further.

The Warren Commission deliberately made no honest effort to explain the Dutch period. Even simple errors, such as the 6 June departure date for the *Maasdam* were allowed to stand in the official report, and have been quoted in numerous books and articles since. A phone call to the Holland-America Line head office in Rotterdam would have cleared up this discrepancy, or a memo to the State Department, which had requested the Travelers Aid Society (TAS) to send a case-worker to meet the Oswalds when the ship docked at Hoboken, N.J. on 13 June. TAS representative, Spas Theodore Raikin, told the Warren Commission that Oswald had tried to avoid him, but later accepted the society's help, and the family passed through customs and immigration without incident. Not mentioned "but surely relevant" according to Peter Dale Scott, was the fact that Spas Raikin was a "revanchist Bulgarian émigré" and general secretary of the American Friends of the Anti-Bolshevik Bloc of Nations, a group supported by US intelligence and part of the shadowy anti-Communist network which later became known as the World Anti-Communist League (WACL). According to Oswald's public legend, he was an ex-marine who breached the US Internal Security Act (1950). If he had been a genuine defector, G-men personally dispatched by FBI director, J. Edgar Hoover, would have been waiting to arrest the "pro-Commie traitor."

One of the notes in Oswald's address book - "Holl-tram n.11 left to right"- suggests, as some writers have claimed, that the family took a tram to Mathenesserlaan when they finally arrived in Rotterdam. However, after a 42 hour train journey, with a wife, a two-month-old baby daughter, and seven

Understanding Shadows

pieces of luggage, it would have been far easier, efficient, and not much more expensive to simply take a taxi across town from Central Station, a journey which would have taken less than 10 minutes on a quiet Sunday morning. There was just over 24 hours before the SS *Maasdam* departed, and debriefing Oswald was a priority. Although there were at least a dozen CIA agents based under diplomatic cover at the embassy in The Hague during this period (where the US ambassador, John S Rice, appointed by President Kennedy in 1961, was mid-way through his final diplomatic appointment) or working out of the American Consulate in Amsterdam, only one of Angleton's 'boys' would have been required to carry out this task that Sunday afternoon.

Fifty years and possibly hundreds of CIA whistleblowers later, surely someone would have talked? Why? Maybe nobody had anything to say, and Angleton chose his agents well. The heavy lifting in Rotterdam, keeping the safe-house safe was done by the CIA's salaried BVD employees, working on Project A. Those men and women deployed on HUMINT duty would have known nothing about Lee Harvey Oswald. He was just another subject to be closely observed and safeguarded. Unlike their Soviet counterparts' brash display at Schiphol, the CIA preferred to remain in the shadows, operating on a tight, need-to-know basis. There is no reason to believe more than half-a-dozen officers, including chiefs-of-station in Moscow and The Hague, knew about the Oswalds. And nothing extraordinary happened in Rotterdam, except the top secret debriefing of an unproductive agent.

Oswald understood shadows, and went about his business as instructed. In his notebook he had the address of the American Express Travel Service office at 92 Meent, near Rotterdam City Hall, and the name of a clerk employed there in 1962, a certain Mr. de Booy. He may have visited the office on Monday, 4 June, taking Tram 11 from outside 250 Mathenesserlaan, (which may explain the notebook entry) but none of the staff remember Oswald, according to a co-worker called Scheffer, when questioned by Dutch journalist, Daan Dijksman. This in itself is not significant, however, it does confirm that the CIA, or at least Angleton's counterintelligence division, used American Express as legitimate cover when placing agents overseas. The company was a permanent presence in the USSR and several Warsaw Pact allies, including East Berlin, the "destination of choice" for several US ex-servicemen during the early 1960s, including US Army Sergeant, Ernie Fletcher, who defected in 1959, Sgt. Joseph Dutkanicz and Pvt. Vladimr Sloboda, who followed him over in spring 1960, and US Air Force Sgt. Jones, who crossed two months later, according to declassified USAF Intelligence Information Report (No. 1430233), dated 9 August 1960.

Moscow Central watched the house on Mathenesserlaan from a distance. KGB and GRU agents were thick on the ground in Rotterdam, which had developed, in the 15 years since the end of WW2, into the largest seaport in Europe and NATO's most important logistics hub. The weekly current affairs magazine, *Time*, once described the KGB as the best intelligence-gathering organization in the world. This was an assessment based on years of endeavor, and while the KGB shared such endearing qualities as a ruthless, cruel and mean regard for humanity with other agencies in the great game, what made the KBG so good at its job was patience. The agency patiently allowed Oswald and the CIA to run out of patience in Minsk. Left him to work, without prospects, in a non-sensitive radio factory. Book-learned ideology was never going to sustain his belief in the Soviet system. Angleton and the CIA counterintelligence 'hawks' had monitored Oswald's reception in the USSR. The KGB watched closely, while the CIA recalled and debriefed its agent, and went through all the repatriation nonsense to satisfy the defection legend, and learned the location of the CIA 'safe house' in Rotterdam, the identities of those who came and went, and perhaps Oswald's contact, de Booy, at the American Express office downtown

From noon on Monday, 4 July 1962, passengers began to arrive at South Head pier in Rotterdam for the 3pm sailing of the SS *Maasdam*. The Oswalds, traveling tourist class, had cabin 473. There was a total of 350 passengers, and a crew of almost 300. On 6 June, the date the Warren Commission claims the voyage began, the vessel was actually off the south coast of Ireland, according to the *Positions of Ships* list published in *Het Parool* newspaper, and President John Kennedy was putting the final touches to a speech he was due to make later that day at West Point Academy.

Foundations of Sand

At a conference in Havana in March 2002, a declassified CIA document distributed to delegates boasts of the CIA's ability to place stories about the 17-19 April 1961 Bay of Pigs invasion of Cuba by CIA-trained and armed exiles "directly on international wire services." The documentation was attached to the Taylor Commission's report into the US role in the bloody failure of the three-day invasion. Although a section on the wire services distributed to delegates was redacted, according to former National Security Archive employee, Jon Elliston, who obtained complete copies of the files under the Freedom of Information Act for his book an the CIA's psy-ops war on Cuba, the document states that the placing of news stories on the wire services was the "most effective" way to reach the Cuban people. Elliston added, "one radio report on United Press International, for example, will be repeated on nearly every radio station and most of the newspapers in the Caribbean area." Because of this, the document continues, "military planners should be aware of Headquarters' capability of placing items directly on the wire service tickers."

Former *Washington Post* journalist, Carl Bernstein, while researching the CIA's manipulation of the media, found that most of the reporting staff in major news organizations were "bona-fide journalists when they began undertaking tasks for the Agency." The use of journalists was scaled down when William Colby took charge of the CIA in September 1973, and CIA operatives were "taught to make noises like reporters" when placed on the staff of some major newspapers and broadcasting outfits, then told to resign and become stringers or freelancers "thus enabling Colby to assure concerned editors that members of their staffs were not CIA employees." Two months later, at a meeting with editors and staff of the *New York Times* and the *Washington Star*, Colby admitted that about three dozen American newsmen were still "on the CIA payroll" including five who worked for "general circulation news organization." Three years later, an unpublished report by the US House Permanent Select Committee on Intelligence, chaired by retired New York 1st District Democratic Congressman, Otis Pike, stated that at least fifteen news organizations still provided cover for CIA operatives.

Wes Gallagher, Associated Press general manager from 1962 to 1976, took "vigorous exception" to the notion that AP might have aided the agency, telling Bernstein that he went to Colby when it was first disclosed that reporters worked for the CIA and tried to find out names: "All he would say was that no full-time staff member of the Associated Press was employed by the agency. We talked to [CIA director from January 1976 to January 1977] Bush. He said the same thing." However, according to Bernstein, CIA officials said they were able to make "cover arrangements through someone in the upper management levels" of AP, whom they refused to identify.

Apart from the speed of their publication, what is extraordinary about the first reports of Lee Harvey Oswald's alleged role in the murder of John Kennedy in the early editions of the international press, on Saturday, 23 November 1963, is the amount of detailed background information concerning the designated assassin. Too much, and far too soon not to arouse suspicion. Newspaper production in the early 1960s was a labor intensive process which could proceed only as fast as editors, reporters, typesetters and letterpress equipment allowed. Wire service photographs, sent over telephone landlines, took approximately eight minutes to arrive, one at a time on revolving cylinders, while 'hot metal' page design involved type-written reports or transmitted wire service material having to be locked, line by line, into a metal 'type chase'. It would have taken any time from 30 minutes to 2 hours, using acid, to carry out the corrosive etching process necessary to produce photographic images on a printed page. Only after the edition was "made-up and locked-up" could the printing process begin.

Leroy Fletcher Prouty, a former senior USAF officer who carried out overt Cold War missions rescuing Nazi intelligence officers in the Balkans at the request of the Office of Strategic Services, (OSS) the predecessor of the CIA, in 1944, and served as special operations chief for the Joint Chiefs of Staff during the Kennedy era, in charge of a global logistics support network for CIA clandestine operations, was in New Zealand at the time of the JFK assassination - Friday afternoon, 12.30pm, 22 November in Dallas, Saturday morning 6.30am in New Zealand - and mentions purchasing the "first paper available" while having breakfast with a member of Congress from Ohio, the morning edition of the *Christchurch Star*, which already had a detailed account of Lee Harvey Oswald's alleged role in the murder of the President on its front page, and on page three, a "fine studio portrait" of the 'assassin' wearing a dark business suit, white shirt and tie.

Instant communication has been possible, ever since Thomas Edison and Elisha Gray invented the land-bound, multiple, telegraph message traffic system. Alexander Graham Bell patented the telephone, and Guglielmo Marconi, had worked out how to get the message across oceans. While most of the world's quality broadsheets would have had more than enough archived material available to cover the assassination story, what makes uncomfortable reading is the detailed content of the front-page reports on Oswald - information obtained, edited and transmitted, with photographs of Oswald, of the weapon allegedly used, and of the TSBD building on Dealey Plaza where the alleged sniper had hidden, as if, as Prouty suggests, "those in charge of the murder had prepared the patsy and all of that intimate information beforehand."

Oswald was arrested at the Texas Theatre in the Oak Cliff district of Dallas, shortly after 1.40pm on 22 November, for "acting suspiciously," and taken to DPD headquarters. After several hours questioning he was initially charged, at 7.10pm, with the murder of patrol-car officer, J.D. Tippit, who had been shot earlier that afternoon on East 10th Street, about 45 minutes after the assassination of John Kennedy and just over a mile from Dealey Plaza. Later that evening, the head of DPD Homicide, Captain J.W. Fritz, who had recognized Oswald's name as that of the TSBD employee who had gone missing after the Dealey Plaza shootings, and Assistant District Attorney, William Alexander, decided there was enough evidence to charge him with killing the President. Shortly after 1.30am the following morning he was brought from his holding cell and charged by Judge David Johnson, that he "did voluntarily and with malice aforethought kill John F. Kennedy by shooting him with a gun." By this time several editions of the *Christchurch Star* were on the street, running the Oswald story from reports provided by the Associated Press (AP) and United Press International (UPI) with photographs wired to Australia, then routed to Auckland and finally to Christchurch. As Prouty correctly summarizes in his book on the plot to kill the President, "there is no way one can believe that these press agencies had in their files, ready and on call, all the detailed information that was so quickly poured out in those first hours after the assassination."

The "detailed information" on Oswald, taking up about one-fifth of the broadsheet's front page, is contained in a three-column, left-hand corner report, beneath a picture of the TSBD, with an arrow pointing at the sixth floor window of the 'sniper's nest' and the headline, 'Arrested Man Lived in Russia'. The report refers to the detention of a man employed at the building where a rifle was found after the assassination, who is quoted by UPI as telling the police after his arrest at the Texas Theatre, "Well, it's all over now." The AP named the man as Lee H. Oswald, aged 24, who had defected to the Soviet Union in 1959, following his discharge from the US Marine Corps, and returned to America in 1962 with a Russian wife and child. While in the Soviet Union he had worked in a Minsk factory, and had later been identified as chairman of a 'Fair Play for Cuba Committee'. The photograph of the well-groomed 'assassin', on page 3, was credited to Radio Pictures but was, in fact, a personal photograph taken by a professional photographer in Minsk shortly before Oswald's wedding to Marina in April 1961. How this photograph was obtained and packaged along with the rest of the material has never been explained, but the information in this concise report contains all the basic ingredients for the cover-up to follow. The CIA had succesfully used one of the basic rules of covert deception - using the foreign media to place a story before bringing it home.

In the Netherlands the first report of an "attack on President Kennedy" was received by the UPI office in The Hague at 7.35pm, filed four minutes after the actual shooting took place on Dealey Plaza by UPI's Washington correspondent, Merriman Smith. Approximately 30 minutes later, after emergency vascular treatment by Dr Malcolm Perry in Trauma Room 1 at nearby Parkland Memorial Hospital, just west of Oak Lawn, the President was confirmed dead. At 1.33pm acting White House press secretary, Malcolm Kilduff, told journalist waiting in the nurses classroom at the hospital that the President had died of a "gunshot wound to the brain" at approximately 1:00pm CT (Central Time). It was now 8.33pm in Holland. At 1.30am the following morning in Dallas, Oswald was charged with Kennedy's murder, 8 hours after the first Saturday, 23 November 1963, edition of *De Telegraaf* had sold out on the streets of Amsterdam. On its front page, directly beneath a photograph of Lyndon Baines Johnson being sworn in as 36th President of the United States by Judge Sarah Hughes, in the presidential suite of a Boeing 707, there's an un-attributed 'telephoto' of Oswald, bruised and bleeding around his left eye, in handcuffs outside the Texas Theatre following his arrest, and the headline 'Sensationele arrestatie in een bioscoop' ('Sensational arrest in a cinema').The article states that Oswald, chairman of the 'Eerlijk Spel voor Cuba' (Fair Play for Cuba) committee, had shot DPD officer Tippit, and was being held as a suspect in Kennedy's assassination. What makes this piece both interesting and suspect is the rare photograph, and the fact that Dallas Police had no idea who the suspect actually was.

Another morning newspaper, *De Volkskrant,* was more subdued in its presentation, with only a brief mention in its front page of Oswald being questioned by police officers in connection with the Dealey Plaze shootings, while the *Algemeen Handlesblad* carried three front-page photos, one of Marina Oswald, holding the couples' one-month-old second child, standing just behind their 18-months-old daughter, June, next to Oswald's mother. The caption identifies both women as wife and mother of the alleged assassin, and (wrongly) states that the couple had one child. Directly beneath this photograph there's another of a Dallas police officer holding up the weapon that the sniper allegedly used, and beneath a headline 'Oswald woonde drie jaar in Sowjet-Unie' ('Oswald lived for three years in the Soviet Union') there's that Minsk studio portrait, and an almost verbatim account of the suspect's background to that published in the *Christchurch Star*. It is worth noting that besides the seven hour time difference between Dallas and Amsterdam, there was also the time consuming task of translating copy into Dutch before the papers could be "made-up and locked-up."

Consider what is now known about Kennedy's political agenda before his death: his intention to withdraw from Vietnam "1,000 US military personnel by the end of 1963" and the bulk of 16,500 military 'advisers' by the end of 1965, according to *National Security Action Memorandum No. 263*, dated 11 October 1963; plans to close 52 domestic and 22 overseas military bases by the mid-1960s, announced by Secretary of Defense, Robert McNamara, on 30 March 1963; his refusal to support a second CIA-proposed Bay of Pigs operation, and attempts to open 'back channel' dialogue with the Havana regime, using French journalist Jean Daniel, Fidel Castro's aide Rene Vallejo, and US journalist and diplomat, William Attwood, according to Catholic theologian, peace activist and author, Professor James Douglass; and convincing efforts by the White House administration, headed by Attorney General, Robert Kennedy, to beak the venal and murderous influence of the Mafia on the US economy. In this context, it is difficult to argue against the conclusion that an unsolved homicide in downtown Dallas was a key event in post-1945 US history,

Lancer's Lost Legacy

Consider the Sixties and subsequent decades without the post-Kennedy Vietnam War, the blinkered 'domino theory' policies of Lyndon Baines Johnson, leading to an upgrade of US involvement in South East Asia, with 550,000 American soldiers inside Vietnam and neighboring Cambodia by 1968, being killed at a rate of 1,000 per month; the madness of Richard Nixon and his Cold War 'eminence grise', Henry Kissinger (who signed-off on that other, almost forgotten 9/11, in Santiago ten years after Kennedy was slain) and the terrible consequences of the Reagan years on the peoples of Central America, and appreciate what was lost that afternoon when the motorcade turned onto Dealey Plaza, and into the cross-hairs of several snipers. The conspiracy-based perspective is now a "scientifically-based fact," accordng to G. Robert Blakey, chief counsul of the HSCA, whose 1978 report, which somewhat reluctantly conceded the likelihood of more than one gunman, probably acting on behalf of organized crime. That's where the case rests, officially. And even among the most diligent assassination buffs there is a grudging acceptance that the whole truth is probably buried forever. The murder of the 35th President has passed into myth.

In 1966, two years after the publication of the Warren Commission report, which concluded that Oswald, acting alone, had changed the course of US history, the New York lawyer, Mark Lane, published the first major critical assessment of the report, *Rush to Judgment*, described as "the book that started it all." In fact Lane had "started it all" within four weeks of the assassination when he published an in-depth article in the independent, 'left-wing' New York-based weekly newspaper, *Guardian*, on 19 December 1963, questioning - from the perspective of a defense attorney - the official statements in Dallas and Washington about the murders of Kennedy and Tippit; the statements of witnesses who claimed to have seen the alleged assassin at the 6th floor window of the TSBD; the paraffin tests which, according to Lane, indicated that Oswald had not recently fired a gun; the original identification of the weapon used, a German bolt-action Mauser rifle, later changed to an Italian Mannlicher-Carcano; the confusion about the wounds among doctors at Parkland Hospital and the role of the US media; recycling foreign press reports; and the FBI in 'convicting' Oswald of the crime before his guilt was proved.

Lane's perspective worried the CIA. In 1966 Langley sent a damage-limitation memo, *Dispatch Document 1035-960*, to "Chiefs-of-Stations and certain bases" which revealed the agency's "concern at speculation" about who might be responsible for Kennedy's death. The CIA's CoS in The Hague was one of the recipients of the document which was intended to "provide material for countering and discrediting the aims of the conspiracy theorists" so as to "inhibit circulation of such claims in other countries." In order to achieve this, agents were told to "discuss the publicity problems with friendly elite contacts (especially politicians and editors)" to emphasize that the Warren Commission "made as thorough an investigation as humanly possible" and that "parts of the conspiracy talk appears to be generated by Communist propagandists." Back then Langley still believed that "open-minded foreign readers should still be impressed by the care, thoroughness, objectivity and speed with which the Commission worked" and recommended that book reviewers, in order to discredit forthcoming publications, "might be encouraged to add to their accounts the idea that, checking back with the [Warren] Report itself, they found it far superior to the work of the critics." The CIA had 'agents of influence' in the Dutch media. At least a dozen 'elite' contacts were named during hearings of the House of Representatives Permanent Select Committee on Intelligence, in July 1982.

The agency's perspective since the mid-1960s has never changed. In the early 1990s there was a coordinated effort to discredit Oliver Stone's *JFK* with dozens of hostile articles in US prestigious mainstream publications, ranging from *Time* and *Newsweek* to the *Wall Street Journal*, the *New York Times* and the *Washington Post*, by prominent journalists, many of whom hadn't written about Kennedy's death since the Warren Report was published. The destructive energy devoted to the task of discrediting the project was not directed at Stone as a film-maker, but at criticizing his political judgment. What also scared the political and intelligence establishment within the Beltway was the fact that Stone had $40 million to defend his position. For the first time some serious money had been invested in considering the view from the grassy knoll, from which thirty-five of those spectators present in Dealy Plaza that afternoon testified to hearing at least one shot fired from the direction of the small, sloping hill next to the TSBD, located to the front and right of the President's limousine.

And so we remain, victims of that dramatic and efficient 20th century crime, of those fatal seconds in Dealey Plaza, There's a dispute over the timing of the shots, from 4.9 seconds to 11.2 seconds - depends on when you start counting! - when *gunmen fired four shots* at John Fitzgerald Kennedy. The first, second and fourth from the rear of the presidential motorcade. The third, the fatal shot, from the direction of the grassy knoll.

In a reaction to the cover-up in 1964, the English philosopher and Nobel Prize winner, Bertrand Russell, wrote, "there has never been a more subversive, a more conspiratorial, unpatriotic or endangering course for the security of the United States, and the world, than the attempt by the United States Government to hide the murderer of its recent President." This assessment is as valid today as it was almost fifty years ago when folk singer, Phil Ochs, sang about the "bullets of the false revenge" cutting down JFK. The assassination has become a "magnificent myth" but for the majority of Americans, the official account of what happened that afternoon in Dallas fails to carry conviction.

BIBLIOGRAPHY

Andrew, Christopher and Mitrokhin, Vasili. *The Sword And The Shield.* New York: Basic Books, 1999.
Baer, Robert. *See No Evil.* New York: Arrow Books, 2002.
Barron, John. *KGB: The Secret Work of Soviet Agents.* London: Corgi Books, 1975.
Baker, Russ. *Family of Secrets.* New York: Bloomsbury Press, 2009.
Black, David. *ACID: A New Secret History of LSD.* London: Vision Paperbacks, 2001.
Buchanan, Thomas G. *Wie Vermoordden Kennedy?* Amsterdam: Uitgeverij Contact, 1964.
Corson, William and Crowley, Robert. *The New KGB.* New York: William Morrow & Co., 1985
de Graff, Bob and Wiebes, Cees. *Villa Maarheeze.* Den Haag: SDU Uitgevers, 1998.
DeLillo, Don. *Libra.* London: Penguin Books, 1988.
DiEugenio James and Pease Lisa (editors). *The Assassinations.* Los Angeles: Feral House, 2003.
Douglass, James W. *JFK and the Unspeakable.* New York: Orbis Books, 2008.
Elliston, Jon. *Psywar on Cuba.* Mellbourne: Ocean Press, 1998.
Engelen, D. *Gesciedenis van de Binnenlandse Veiligheidsdienst.* Den Haag: Sdu Uitgeverij, 1995.
Fonzi, Gaeton. *The Last Investigation.* New York: Thunder's Mouth Press, 1994.
Joesten, Joachim. *De Waarheid over de Moord op Kennedy.* Utrecht: Bruna &

Zoon, 1966.
Kuijk, Otto and van Veen, Bart. *Kennedy: President voor ons allen.* Amsterdam: Van Holkema & Warendorf N.V. 1964.
Lane, Mark. *Rush To Judgment.* New York: Thunder's Mouth Press, 1992.
Lane, Mark. *Plausible Denial.* London: Plexus, 1992.
Lifton, David. *Best Evidence.* New York: Carroll & Graf, 1980.
Mailer, Norman. *Oswald's Tale.* New York: Random House, 1995.
McKnight, Gerard D. *Breach of Trust.* Kansas: University Press of Kansas, 2005.
Newman, John. *Oswald and the CIA.* New York: Carroll & Graf Publishers, 1995.
New York Times (edited). *The Witnesses.* New York: Bantam Books, 1964.
Ranelagh, John.*The Agency.* London: Weidenfeld & Nicolson, 1986.
Scott, Peter Dale. *Deep Politics and the Death of JFK.* Berkeley: University of California Press, 1993.
Smith, Matthew. *Say Goodbye to America.* Edinburgh: Mainstream Publishing, 2001.
Stone, Oliver and Sklar, Zachary. *JFK: The Book of the Film* New York: Applause Books, 1992.
Summers, Anthony. *Conspiracy.* New York: Paragon House, 1989.
Summers, Anthony. *Not In Your Lifetime.* New York: Marlow & Company, 1998.
Valentine, Douglas. *The Strength of the Wolf.* London: Verso 2004.
Vermeulen, Perry. *Lee Harvey Oswald:* Eindhoven: De Boekenmakers, 2008.
Wise, David. *Nightmover.* New York: HarperCollins, 1995.

NEWSPAPERS & MAGAZINES
Christchurch Star, 23 November 1963 (www.christchurchcitylibraries.com)
De Volkskrant - 28 March 1962 & 23 November 1963 - (www.volkskrant.nl)
Fourth Decade Magazine, Volume 2, No.1, November 1994.
Het Parool - 7 June 1963 & 23 November 1963 - (www.parool.nl)
NRC Handelsbad - 28 March 1962 & 23 November 1963 - (www.nrc.nl)

ONLINE ARCHIVES & OTHER SOURCES
BA Archives & Museum Collection. (www.culture24.org.uk/am4677)
Dutch Biographical data (www.biografischportaal.nl/en/personen)
Dutch Historical data (www.historici.nl/zoek/en/)
NL Diplomatic List 1962, Foreign Affairs Library, Den Haag.
Ochs, Phil. *I Ain't Marching Anymore.* New York: Electra Records, 1965.
US National Archives (www.archives.gov/research/jfk/warren-commission-report/index.html)
US National Archives (www.archives.gov/research/jfk/select-committe-report/)

CHAPTER SIX
WITHOUT GRACE OR FAVOR

"I am surrounded by priests who repeat incessantly that their kingdom is not of this world, and yet they lay their hands on everything they can get."
Napoleon Bonaparte

In spring 2010, six months before recently-retired Pope Benedict XVI was due to visit Great Britain, Richard Dawkins, the English ethnologist, evolutionary biologist and author of *The God Delusion,* and the late Anglo-American journalist and author, Christopher Hitchens, whose book, *God is Not Great,* was described in an *Irish Independent* review as "the *Das Kapital* of a tolerant if exasperated atheism,"commissioned barrister Geoffrey Robertson and solicitor Mark Stephens to draw up a case for "crimes against humanity" using the same legal principles that led to the arrest of the former Chilean dictator, General Augusto Pinochet, during his visit to the UK in 1989. They were instructed to ask the Crown Prosecution Service (CPS) to initiate legal proceedings against the Bishop of Rome for his alleged cover-up of clerical sexual abuse of children in Ireland, Germany, the Netherlands, the US, Canada and Belgium.

Dawkins, the former chair of the Simonyi Professorship for the Public Understanding of Science at Oxford from 1995 to 2008, who has been referred to as "Darwin's rottweiler," and Hitchens, who died in Texas in April 2011, less than four years after becoming an American citizen, and was listed in *Forbes* in 2009 as one of the twenty-five "most influential liberals in the US media," threatened to launch their own civil action in the UK against Benedict if the CPS refused to act, or refer the case to the International Criminal Court (ICCt) in The Hague, which was established in July 2002 as a permanent tribunal to prosecute individuals for genocide and crimes against humanity.

Appetites of Lust and Destruction

Joseph Aloisius Ratzinger, a native of Bavaria, southern Germany, and the former Archbishop of Munich and Freising, was the ninth German

Pope, and the 265th successor of Saint Paul the Apostle to head the Roman Catholic Church. He was chosen on 19 April 2005 in the usual secretive fashion, on the fourth ballot of the papal conclave, following the death of John Paul II, the second-longest serving Pontiff in Vatican history.

During the 1980s and 1990s his predecessor, had promoted strong, orthodox Catholic values, such as opposition to artificial contraception and the ordination of women. John Paul II also supported the anti-Communist Polish trade union, 'Solidarnosc', and publicly criticized Latin American Catholics and clergy who opposed repressive right-wing regimes, ordering them to "stay out of politics." At that time, Cardinal Ratzinger was in charge of the Vatican's Congregation for the Doctrine of the Faith (CDF). The CDF is the oldest of the nine congregations of the Roman Curia, the administrative apparatus of the Holy See, which had initiated the Roman Inquisition, found Galileo Galilei "vehemently suspected of heresy" in 1633, and prosecuted individuals, including many women for 'crimes' ranging from sorcery, immorality, witchcraft, and blasphemy. The CDF is responsible for dealing with all matters to promote and safeguard the faith and morals of the Catholic world, according to the Vatican's 'Apostolic Constitution'. It also undertakes the investigation of *delicta graviora*, those grievous 'transgressions' against the Eucharist and the sanctity of the Sacrament of Penance on the road to salvation by priests and nuns, as well as by senior members of the clergy accused of, or directly involved in, the physical and sexual abuse of children, and the attempted cover-up of the "sins of the Fathers."

The CDF under Ratzinger argued that the "good of the universal Church" should be given priority over allegations of rape and sodomy, and the defrocking of pedophile priests. Dawkins once described Benedict as a man "whose first instincts when his priests are caught with their pants down is to cover-up the scandal and damn the young victims to silence," while Hitchens claimed the former Pope was "not above or outside the law" and argued that the "institutionalized concealment of child rape is a crime under any law and demands not private ceremonies of repentance or church-funded pay-offs, but justice and punishment."

There was a certain degree of naive optimism expressed by solicitor Stephens that some form of legal action could be taken against Benedict XVI, based on the argument that the Vatican was not actually a state under international law, not recognized as such by the United Nations, does not have borders that are policed, and that its relations, at least with the UK, were not of a "full diplomatic nature." However, nothing happened. The CPS dismissed the brief, and the Bishop of Rome came and went without much of a fuss. Those victims who tried to call attention to his complicity in the cover-up of appalling crimes were marginalized and confined to the fringes of public gatherings, unseen, unheard, and generally ignored by the mainstream media.

However, the allegations of widespread clerical sexual abuse exposed fault-lines within the higher echelons of the Curia, on 9 May, when Cardinal Christoph Schonborn became involved. Schonborn, the Archbishop of Vienna a member of the Dominican Order, who had obtained a Licentiate of Sacred Theology, a graduate degree with ecclesiastical authority within the Catholic Church in 1971, and later studied in the medieval city of Regensburg, under Joseph Ratzinger, accused the former Vatican Secretary of State, the Italian Cardinal Angelo Sodano, currently Dean of the College of Cardinals and a close aide of Benedict, of covering up past scandals and impeding and investigation into sex abuse allegations against his predecessor in Vienna, Cardinal Hans Hermann Groer. Sodano had previously dismissed detailed allegations of the predatory and brutal sexual and physical abuse of children in several European countries and in the US as "petty gossip." According to Schonborn, the statement caused "massive damage" to the victims and the Church. His remarks, just reported by 'Kathpress' the Austrian Catholic news agency, were "without precedent" and a sign of "nervous tension" among members of the hierarchy, according to biographer Andrea Tornielli, author of *Benedicto XVI: El Custodio de la Fe*.

The allegations against Cardinal Groer were made in 1995 by a former seminary student who claimed that the head of the Austrian RCC had abused him repeatedly in the early 1970s. Several other former students and monks then came forward and made similar allegations. As a result Groer retired as Archbishop of Vienna in September 1995, and moved to Roggendorf monastery where he served as abbot until 1998, when he relinquished all ecclesiastical duties and privileges at the request of Pope John Paul II.

Hans Hermann Groer died in March 2003 without admitting any wrongdoing, while his accomplishments in promoting priestly and monastic vocations were praised by his successor, Cardinal Schonborn, during requiem Mass in St Stephen's Cathedral. The service was attended by several of the Vatican's 'heavy hitters' including the conservative Archbishop of Cologne and member of the Congregation of Bishops, Cardinal Joachim Meisner, and Cardinal Franz Konig, founder of the Vienna-based Pro Oriente, an organization established in 1964 and mandated to improve relations between the Roman Catholic Church, Eastern Orthodox and Oriental Orthodox Churches.

Austrian investigative journalist, Hubertus Czernin, in his 1998 book, *Das Buch Groer*, accused the Cardinal of abusing more than 2000 young men between 1950 and 1990, making him one of the Catholic Church's most persistent sexual deviants. Schonborn claims that efforts to instigate an inquiry into many of these allegations, by Joseph Ratzinger, were blocked by Sodano and his boss, John Paul II, and attempts were made to cover-up the scandal by offering 'hush money' to several of the surviving victims who were prepared to testify against Groer. One of those was 54-year-old, Michael Tfirst, who claims to have reported abuse to senior church officials from 1970 onwards and was offered $5000 in 2004 under a contract that obliged him not to repeat the allegations. "There is no doubt that Ratzinger knew all the details of reports on abuse within the Church" according to Tfirst, and there is "no doubt that John Paul II, his superior, took part in a massive and systematic cover-up."

Schonborn wasn't alone in his criticism of the Curia's influential 'fixer', Angelo Sodano, who had served as papal nuncio to Chile and arranged for the country's military dictator, General Pinochet, to meet John Paul II publicly during the 'traveling' Pope's visit to the country in 1987. Despite protests by several Chilean clergy, the following year Sodano was promoted to Secretary of the Council for the Public Affairs of the Church (the equivalent of foreign minister), and by 1990, to the post of Secretary of State. Sodano was now the most powerful man in the Vatican after the Pope, and used his influence, according to several US Catholic publications, to persuade John Paul II not to investigate allegations against the Mexican-born priest, Father Marcial Maciel Degollado, founder of the conservative Legion of Christ in Mexico in 1941, the religious wing of the apostolic lay movement, Regnum Christi. Under Maciel's leadership the Legion of Christ established a network of schools and universities across Mexico, and later expanded with seminaries in Spain, Latin America, Ireland and the US. By 2003 the Legion of Christ would claim management over 150 prep schools worldwide, eleven universities, 2373 seminarians, and 889 priests working in 22 countries.

As a result Maciel's stature rose in the Vatican, according to *Vows of Silence* authors, Jason Berry and Gerald Renner. However, the Mexican priest - the grand-nephew of Bishop Rafael Guizar Valencia - had been expelled from two seminaries "for reasons that have never been explained" and only became a priest "when one of his uncles ordained him after private studies," was also a serial abuser of dozens of under-age seminarians and fathered six children - two of whom he was later accused of abusing - by several wives/mistresses. Eventually Maciel's crimes could no longer be ignored, despite his influence with senior Curia members during the reign of John Paul II. In 2006, less than a year after he was elected, Pope Benedict ordered Maciel, who had resigned a general director of the Legion of Christ in January 2005, to spend the remainder of his life in prayer and penance. Just over two years after Maciel died, on 30 January 2008, in Jacksonville, Florida, the organization which he founded finally issued a carefully-worded, 'apologetic' communiqué on its website, acknowledging as factual the "reprehensible actions" of Fr. Marcial Maciel, "including the sexual abuse of minor seminarians."

The Vatican had been well aware of Maciel's grievous, culpable behavior since the late 1970s, according to a series of articles published in the *Hartford Courant* in 1997 by Berry and Renner, who spoke with nine former seminarians who were victims of sexual abuse perpetrated by the priest. However, sociologist and author, Fernando Gonzalez, claims it was far earlier than that, two decades earlier in fact, when Maciel's former personal secretary accused him of drug abuse and financial mismanagement. At that time he was suspended by the Vatican for two years while a cursory investigation took place. It rejected the allegations and reinstated the priest in 1959. "From that moment on, he was completely protected by all the high offices in the Vatican," Gonzalez told the *New York Times* in a 2 May 2010 report on Vatican politics which highlighted the Maciel affair.

One of Maciel's most powerful Curia friends was Cardinal Sodano, who attended lavish meals at the Legion of Christ headquarters on the Via Aurelia in Rome, according to Glenn Favreau, a lawyer acting for abused seminarians. Favreau, a former deacon in the order who had previously worked at the Legion's HQ, told the *New York Times* that it was "very clear that Angelo Sodano was going to do everything in his power to protect not just Maciel but the Legion of Christ."

Maciel's successor was the Mexican priest, Fr. Alvaro Concuera, one of the founders of the Legion's 'Instituto Irlandes' in Mexico City, and the congregation's language academy 'Dublin Oak' in Ireland, who had been rector of the seminary in Rome before taking charge of the "congregation of the pontifical right," in January 2005. He was a friend of John Paul II's personal secretary, Monsignor Stanislaw Dziwisz, who was a "major gatekeeper of the information to the Pope," according to Favreau, and the Polish prelate - currently Archbishop of Krakow - frequently sent postcards to Fr. Concuera when he was traveling abroad with the Pope.

None of this, however, explains why nothing was done about Maciel until it was far too late, and the former Pontiff, while he was in charge of the CDF, bears some responsibility for this. In 1998 Ratzinger had met two former Mexican seminarians who traveled to the Vatican to present a case detailing decades of sexual abuse by Maciel. One of those who tried to bring the allegations of abuse to Ratzinger's attention that year was Mexican priest, Fr. Alberto Athie Gallo, who has since accused the Vatican of allowing Maciel to "lead a double life for decades." Gallo told the *New York Times* that the allegations of sexual abuse were "tolerated" by the Holy See for years, saying "in this sense I think the Holy See cannot get to the bottom of this matter. It would have to criticize itself as an authority."

Indeed, and there is no record of Ratzinger, a product of parochial, uncomplicated, village-based Catholicism, expressing sympathy or concern for Maciel's victims, whose ages ranged from 10-to-16 years when they were repeatedly abused from the early 1940s to the 1960s. However, the head of the CDF was well aware of the financial and criminal consequences of the sexual abuse allegations, especially in the US. In 2005 he formally asked President George W. Bush to "declare the Pontiff immune from liability" in a lawsuit that accused Pope John Paul II of conspiring to cover-up the abuse of three boys by a seminarian in Texas. In September 2005, the US Department of Justice (DoJ) instructed that the lawsuit should be dismissed because Pope John Paul II, as head of the Vatican City State, "enjoys immunity from prosecution." In fact, this walled enclave of 110 acres was only established on 11 February 1929 by the Lateran Treaty, signed by Cardinal Pietro Gasparri, on behalf of Pope Pius XI, as head of the Holy See, the Episcopal jurisdiction of the Catholic Church of Rome, and by the Italian fascist Prime Minister, Benito Mussolini, on behalf of the Italian monarch, Victor Emmanuel III. The Treaty sought to end the political dispute, *la questione romana*, between the Italian Government and the Papacy, which had lasted since 1861, when Rome was declared the capital of Italy following the capture of the 'eternal city' by the Italian Army, commanded by Raffaele Cadorna, finally ending the sovereignty of the Papal States, which dated back to 754.

Despite Mussolini's anti-Catholic rhetoric and his distrust of the power and influence of successive Popes over the world's Catholic community, it was politically expedient for 'Il Duce' to sign-off on the Vatican's sovereignty. The move was widely welcomed by western Christian denominations - in the UK, for example, by both the Catholic, London-based, international weekly, *The Tablet*, and the Whig (Church of England/ Constitutional monarchist) daily newspaper, the *Morning Post*, an openly anti-Semitic publication which frequently denounced international Jewry for causing unrest among Christian nations. *The Post's* articles formed the basis of a book, *The Cause of World Unrest*, which might be described as a "more polished," contemporary English version of *The Protocols of Elders of Zion*, the anti-Semitic Russian diatribe, published in Moscow in 1903, purporting to describe a Jewish conspiracy to achieve global financial and cultural domination.

There were dissidents, of course, a minority within the Catholic Church, men like Fr. Ernesto Buonaiuti, a key figure in the Italian Modernist movement, who publicly criticized Mussolini and his fascist paramilitary 'lancieri', who believed, according to author Francis Stoner Saunders, that the Lateran compromise would result in fascism making an *instrumentum regni* of the Church. Buonaiuti's alleged call, according to a report by Italian police, Chief Superintendent Epifanio Penetta, for "someone to kill Mussolini" brought an Irish woman, Violet Gibson, to the steps of the Campidoglio, outside the Fascist Party headquarters at Palazzo Littorio in Rome, where, on 7 April 1926, using an unreliable, French military service, Lebel Modele 8mm revolver, she narrowly failed to assassinate Il Duce and, possibly, change the course of European history

Although several Catholic nations quickly recognized the Vatican as a sovereign state, the United Nations, at its inception, refused membership. However, in April 1964, the Holy See was granted permanent 'observer status' and the right to attend all sessions of the General Assembly, the Security Council, and the Economic and Social Council. Papal representatives have spoken and voted at UN conferences in New York and Geneva, opposing abortion, the use of artificial contraception (a major factor in the HIV/AIDs pandemic in Africa and other Catholic dominated regions) and homosexuality. This has involved the UN in "blatant discrimination on grounds of religion," according to Geoffrey Robertson. This UN status has encouraged the Vatican to claim immunity from prosecution as a sovereign state, which Mr. Robertson believes, "could be challenged successfully" at the European Court of Human Rights (ECtHR). In return for observer status, the Vatican became a signatory to a range of 'standard' common-sense and humanitarian

UN treaties related to nuclear weapons proliferation, the rights of refugees, health and the environment. Notably, it is also signatory to the Optional Protocol on the Convention on the Rights of the Child, on the involvement of Children in Armed Conflict, on the Sale of Children, Child Prostitution and Child Pornography adopted by the General Assembly in March 2000, which became operative two years later. Article 2 of the protocol defines child pornography as "any representation, by whatever means, of a child engaged in real or simulated explicit sexual activities or any representation of the sexual parts of a child for primarily sexual purposes," and defines a child as "any human being under the age of 18" except in countries where a lower age of majority is now part of the legal system.

Cardinal Ratzinger's back-channel access to the White House in 2005 was facilitated by the president's younger brother, Neil Bush, who was co-founder with Ratzinger, in 1999, of a little-known Swiss ecumenical organization, the Geneva-based, Foundation for Inter-religious and Intercultural Research and Dialogue (FIIRD), established to "promote ecumenical understanding and publish original religious texts." Charter members of the FIIRD board at the organization's inauguration were well-known, international establishment religious/political figures; the former chief rabbi of France, Rene Samuel Sirat, two prominent Muslims, Prince Hassan of Jordan and the late Prince Sadruddin Aga Khan, the director of the Institute of the History of the Reformation (IHR), Olivier Fatio, and the FIIRD president, Greek Orthodox leader, Metropolitan Damaskinos. All except Neil Bush and his US/Swiss business partner, Jamal Daniel. Prior to the founding of FIIRD neither man had any public connection to any prominent religious institution.

Ratzinger himself would benefit from the DoJ's legal opinion when he was accused, in documents filed in April 2010 in the US District Court in Milwaukee, of covering up the sexual abuse of plaintiff 'John Doe 16' by Fr. Lawrence Murphy, director of Milwaukee's St. John's School for the Deaf. The accused had worked at the school from July 1950 to May 1974. Despite multiple allegations of sexual abuse against him, reported to the Milwaukee Police Department (MPD) and investigated by St. Francis Police Department, no charges were filed. He was, however, removed as director of the school, but remained as fundraiser and alumni director, placed on temporary sick leave and relocated to Boulder Junction, Wisconsin, in the Diocese of Superior. In July 1980, the Bishop of Superior, in Douglas County, informed the Archdiocese of Milwaukee that this sexual predator was assisting in pastoral work in three parishes in the diocese. Murphy remained active in Superior until 1993, when Milwaukee Archbishop, Rembert Weakland, reinstated restrictions on the predatory cleric after meeting several of his victims. In December that year Murphy admitted having abused up to 200 pupils at the residential school for almost 25 years, deliberately targeting boys with hearing parents who couldn't sign, in order to isolate them. He also claimed he was trying to "cleanse" his victims of their homosexual tendencies "by taking their sins upon himself."

The case was referred to the CDF in Rome but after two years canonical consideration, the testimony of victims, and a series of articles in the *Milwaukee Sentinel,* which had covered the case since the mid-1970s, the institution, headed by Ratzinger at the time, decided not to laicize (secularize) Murphy, and he remained "restricted in ministry" until his death in August 1998. The Milwaukee lawsuit, and the accusations that the Vatican had known about child sexual abuse committed by clergy for centuries, and had deliberately "covered up that abuse and thereby perpetuated the abuse" was dismissed in February 2012.

Centuries of Abuse

In his book, *The Case of the Pope,* Geoffrey Robinson QC, - who has exposed corruption, hypocrisy and government cover-ups in a series of high-profile trials in the UK, the British Commonwealth, and before the ECtHR since the early 1970s - reveals "three stunning, shameful and incontrovertible facts" about the "governance of the Catholic Church" since Joseph Aloisius Ratzinger became Archbishop of Munich and Freising in 1977, then CDF Prefect in 1981, and Pope in 2005. The British barrister claims that "tens of thousands, perhaps even a hundred thousand children and teenagers, mainly boys, have been sexually abused by the clergy and most have been caused serious and long-term psychological damage" and, as in the case of Lawrence Murphy, "thousands of clergy, known to be guilty of very grave crimes, have not been defrocked. They have been harbored by the church, moved to other parishes or countries and protected from identification and from temporal punishment - usually a prison sentence - under Canon Law protocols that offer them forgiveness in this world as well as the next." Robinson also argues that the Holy See, which he describes as a "pseudo-state," has established a foreign law jurisdiction in other friendly states "pursuant to which, in utter secrecy, it has dealt with sex abusers in a manner incompatible with, and in some respects contrary to, the law of the nation in which it operates, and has withheld the evidence of their guilt from law enforcement authorities."

These figures may be shocking, but the abuse of minors is almost a tradition within the Catholic Church, even outlasting many more honorable acts of grace and favor over hundreds of years. The Holy See hierarchy's tolerance of the wanton and widespread debauchery was publicly criticized in the 2nd century by the philosopher, Athenagoras of Athens, a convert to Christianity in the Eastern Orthodox Church. He described degenerate members as "enemies of Christianity" in *Apology for the Christians,* a 177AD plea for tolerance and justice to Roman Emperor Marcus Aurelius. The Council of Elvira in southern Spain, in the first quarter of the 4th century, recorded eighty-one Canons - the legal code of the Catholic Church - dealing with the conduct and discipline of members of the hierarchy in particular, and the Christian community in general, the most important of which, in the context of the current sexual abuse crisis, is number thirty-three - imposing a vow of celibacy on all who minister at the alter.

In *Liber Gomorrhianus*, written around 1051 AD, the prior of the Hermitage of the Holy Cross in Serra Sant'Abbondio, Petrus Damiani, called on Pope Leo IX to take "swift and decisive action against sodomites" within the Church, clerics who "administer the sacrament of penance through confession to those they have just sodomized."

In 1145, the French Cistercian abbot, Bernard of Clairvaux, wrote to one of his disciples, Bernardo da Pisa, the first Cistercian monk to be elected Pope, taking the name Eugenius III, warning of the practices of predatory, sex-crazed clergy, according to Italian cleric, Luigi Marinelli, accredited author of *Shroud of Secrecy*, an anonymously published account of corruption within the Vatican: "You cannot be the last person to know about disorder in your house. Raise your hand to the guilty, since a lack of punishment breeds recklessness that opens the door to all kinds of excess. Your brothers, the Cardinals, must learn by your example not to keep young, long-haired boys and seductive men in their midst."

The 12th century legal textbook of Canon Law, *Decretum Gratiani*, compiled by the Bologna jurist, Gratian, a monk of the Camaldolese order at the Holy Hermitage monastery in the Tuscan Apennines, recommended that members of the clergy found guilty of sexual abuse should be subjected to the same harsh penalties as lay members of the congregation, ranging from the death penalty for crimes against children, to excommunication for sexual association with consenting male or female adults. Parts of this *Concordantia Discordantium Canonum* retained its legal status until the early part of the 20th century when it was revised and re-titled *Codex Iuris Canonici*, in 1917, during the papacy of one of Joseph Ratzinger's predecessors, Pope Benedict XV.

There have, of course, been many distractions for the Roman Catholic Church since the 2nd century. Power to be consolidated, crusades to be preached, those condemned as 'heretics' to be subjected to the harshest of punishments, such as the 20,000 Albigensians at Bezier, slaughtered "in a wonderful manner" following a military campaign in the 13th century, led by the Dominicans, known within ecclesiastical circles as the 'Black Friars', and sparing "neither dignity nor sex nor age," according to the monk, Arnold du Citeaux, in a letter to his commander-in-chief, Pope Innocent III. There were witch-hunts between 1480 and 1750 in which an estimated 40,000 to 60,000 practitioners of Wicca were executed in Europe and North America. There were Jews to be condemned for usury and other 'ungodly practices', and repressive ideologies, including Fascism and National Socialism to be tolerated and tacitly supported. On the other hand, Agrarianism and other peasant utopian 'threatening' ideologies were to be resisted at all costs well into the 20th century, even if this meant murder, such as the 24 May 1980 assassination of the Archbishop of San Salvador, Monsignor Oscar Romero, shot dead by members of a death squad led by Major Roberto

D'Aubuisson, as he raised that chalice during mass in the hospital chapel 'La Divina Providencia'. The Vatican condemned the killing from a distance, but repeatedly failed to criticize the regime, headed by Jose Napoleon Duarte, which had carried out the injustices and massacres of civilians that Romero had frequently mentioned and condemned in sermons throughout the country. After all, for the Vatican there was more important business elsewhere. The Polish trade union, *Solidarnosc*, had emerged from the Gdansk Shipyard and was on the march, the first major internal challenge to a Warsaw Pact communist regime, and the Polish Pope John Paul II, was looking East.

Blaming the Bishops

Apologists for the Vatican's self-serving indifference to the physical and psychological damage suffered by the victims of abuse have argued that the Curia is not responsible for the chastisement of predatory priests. What happens to individual priests at diocese level is the responsibility of the bishops, and in the US, Ireland and elsewhere it was the bishops who transferred degenerate clergy, known to be guilty of the rape of children, from parish to parish, a practice which enormously perpetuated the cycle of abuse. However, from a study of Irish 'abuse literature' -those shocking accounts of victims permanently damaged by the betrayal of trust - it becomes apparent that in many cases, even had Irish bishops reported allegations of abuse to the civil authorities, little would have been done because of the intrusive role of the Catholic Church in the daily life, and within the political establishment. of the Irish Republic since the early 1920s. The Ferns Commission, set up to identify allegations and the lack of accountability of bishops in the County Wexford diocese prior to 2002, presented its report to the Irish Government on 25 October 2005, and it was released online the following day. The commission, headed by retired Supreme Court Judge, Dr. Helen Buckley, examined in detail more than 100 allegations made against twenty-two priests, and the nature of the response by the local hierarchy, and concluded that the Rev. Donal Herlihy, appointed Bishop of Ferns in 1964, had knowingly failed to exclude unsuitable candidates from the priesthood, failed to ensure that those against whom allegations of abuse were made were denied access to children, and had failed to report allegations of abuse to the civil authorities, the Garda Siochana. Following Herlihy's death in 1983, his successor, Bishop Brendan Comiskey, continued these practices until 1990, when he was left with no choice but to report allegations of abuse to the Irish police, a force which, prior to 1990, had repeatedly failed to properly investigate allegations of sexual abuse against minors involving 'men of the cloth' even when complaints were made.

In his excellent account of how the Ferns bishops handled abuse allegations, Tom Mooney, former editor of the *Wexford Echo,* relates one incident involving the parish priest of Monageer village, Fr. James Grennan, chairman of the board of management of the local primary school, who was accused by ten young, pre-confirmation girls of putting his hands under their skirts and forcing them to touch his genitals. Fr. Grennan denied the allegations, and his superior, Bishop Comiskey, believed him and dismissed the allegations as "mischievous." On 20 June 1988, the day of confirmation, Bishop Comiskey and Fr. Grennan attended Monageer Church. As they walked together up the centre aisle at least two families whose children were abused "stood up and abruptly left" while other parishioners were "visibly upset" by the appearance of the two men together, an image, according to Tom Mooney, "perceptively interpreted" by Irish author, Colm Toibin, lecturer in Irish Letters at New Jersey's Princeton University, who described how "Bishop Comiskey and Fr. Grennan stood proudly on the alter waiting for the ten little liars to come up and be confirmed."

Following a 3-part Radio Telefis Eireann (RTE) program in 1999, which exposed decades of ritual sexual and physical abuse in the Reformatory and Industrial Schools system, the Irish Government established a Commission of Inquiry into Child Abuse (CICA), headed by Justice Sean Ryan, to investigate all forms of abuse in the sixty residential industrial schools in the country, which were financed and inadequately supervised by the Department of Education, and managed and staffed by the Catholic Church. Several of these bleak Victorian-age institutions, such as St. Joseph's Industrial School in Letterfrack, County Galway, which was opened in 1887, were run by the Irish lay teaching order, the Congregation of Christian Brothers.

Two examples, from hundreds, will suffice to illustrate what was happening in these institutions throughout the country. At Letterfrack, where 147 children died of abuse and neglect in the care of the Christian Brothers before the school was closed in 1974, Peter Tyrrell suffered appalling brutality at the hands of the regime in the 1920s and 1930s, wrote about his "stolen childhood and life destroyed" in *Founded on Fear*, and later committing suicide by burning himself to death on Hamstead Heath, London, in 1967, while at Artane Industrial School, in Dublin, established in 1870, Patrick Touher, in *Fear of the Collar*, recounts eight years in the 1950s when he was the victim of a regime which demanded "absolute obedience, absolute submission" and involved "continuous labor, never-ending hunger, malicious cruelty and sexual assault."

There were similar institutions managed by various congregations of Catholic nuns, such as St. Michael's Industrial School for Junior Boys, run by the Sisters of Mercy in Cappoquin, in County Waterford, where Paddy Doyle, a four-year-old orphan, was 'sentenced' to seven years in 1955, because a suitable, adult guardian could not be found, and, from 1922 to 1996, the international Magdalene Asylums, known in the Irish Republic as the Magdalene Laundries, for those often described as "fallen women" and being of "poor moral character." Irish courts routinely sent young girls convicted of petty crimes to the Magdalene Laundries, keeping these harsh and inhumane facilities stocked with submissive workers, while State-controlled institutes, public and private sector organizations, and the country's defense forces, offered 'lucrative contracts' for laundry services, without any attempt to find out how the 'penitents' were treated. It wasn't until 1993 that the horrors of the Irish Magdalene asylums became known when nuns in Dublin sold part of their convent to a real-estate developer and the remains of 155 women were found buried in unmarked graves on the property. Having tried and failed to get the Irish Government to fully investigate the Magdalene Laundries, an advocacy group, Justice for Magdalene's, presented a report to the UN Committee Against Torture, outlining the conditions in which thousands of women in Ireland were forced to live and work, claiming their treatment amounted to human rights violations. On 6 June 2011, the UN committee called on the Dublin Government to "investigate allegations that for decades women and girls sent to Catholic laundries were tortured."

On 6 February 2013, an interdepartmental committee published an official 1,000 page report into ten Magdalene laundries run by four congregations, and found that 10,012 women had spent time in the laundries since 1922. Their average age was 23.8 years, the youngest was 9, and the oldest was 80, and some 2,124 (26.5 percent of the total) were referrals made or facilitated by the State. Other reasons included foster parent rejection, physical or mental disability, homelessness and family placement. More than one third stayed for less than 3 months, while 61 prcent stayed for less than a year yet more than 7 percent stayed for 10 years or longer. Some women were incarcerated for minor offences, such as petty theft or vagrancy, and despite only a small number being there for prostitution, many of the women who were sent to the laundries became known as 'Maggies' – a Dublin slang term for prostitute.

While the report also found "little evidence of sexual or physical abuse" many young girls found themselves alone in a "harsh and physically demanding work environment," and the laundries were "lonely and frightening" places for many of the inmates. Despite suggestions that the institutions were highly profitable, the committee, surprisingly, found "no evidence of profiteering" by the nuns who ran the laundries, and that most operated on a "subsistence or close to break-even" basis. The Irish Prime Minister, Enda Kenny, refused to apologize for the State's shameless complicity, for more than 70 years, in the incarceration, and often brutal treatment, of vulnerable young girls and women, while claiming, as late as May 2011, to "know nothing" about conditions in the laundries - the position taken by Sean Aylward, the former general secretary of the Irish Department of Justice, when he spoke, in Geneva to the UN Committee Against Torture.

"Ireland's Holocaust"

Far worse - if such appalling treatment can, or should, be measured by degrees of suffering - was the litany of physical, emotional and sexual abuse at the Reformatory and Industrial Schools investigated by Justice

Ryan, which included beatings, rape, oral sex, and public floggings of naked children. The damage done to generations of Irish youth has been accurately described in publications such as the *Belfast Telegraph*, and the Toronto-based, *National Post*, as "Ireland's Holocaust," while the London-based *Guardian*, in an article entitled "An abuse too far by the Catholic Church," described the Ryan Report as the "stuff of nightmares" and left columnist and associate editor, Madeleine Bunting, wondering how long she could continue "to feel part of this church." Indeed, chapter six of the report, published in five volumes on 20 May 2009, in a heart-breaking and shameful indictment of the Irish Catholic Church at every level.

The Ryan Commission concluded that children at the Reformatory and Industrial Schools lived in a climate of fear, created by "pervasive, excessive and arbitrary punishment," not knowing where "the next beating was coming from." Children who tried to escape were hunted down by the Garda Siochana and other temporal authorities, and returned to the institutions where, in many cases, they were severely beaten and publicly humiliated, including having their heads shaved - a well-documented ritual punishment used on Nazi collaborators in liberated European countries following WWII. Severe corporal punishment was "an option of first resort" and "prolonged excessive beatings with implements intended to cause maximum pain" were tolerated and "rarely challenged" by school management or the Department of Education, which adopted a "deferential and submissive attitude" towards the congregations. Similar punitive and brutal practices took place in the female institutions, where corporal punishment was "often administered in a way calculated to increase anguish and humiliation."

In the male institutions sexual abuse was endemic and extended from "improper touching and fondling to rape with violence" while the perpetrators, who were able to "operate undetected for long periods," were at the core of the institutions. The response of the religious authorities when confronted with irrefutable evidence of sexual abuse, was to "transfer the offender to another location where, in many instances, he was free to abuse again," without any consideration given to the safety of the children. Documents obtained by the commission revealed that, despite claims by the congregations that the recidivist nature of sexual offending was not understood, sexual abusers were often "long-term offenders who repeatedly abused children wherever they were working." The superiors of the congregations, and the Irish Church authorities outside the institutions, were aware of the "propensity for abusers to re-abuse." However, the risk of re-offending was calculated "in terms of the potential scandal and bad publicity should the abuse be disclosed [and] the danger to children was not taken into account." This conclusion alone is universal, not simply a practice of the Irish Catholic Church. It was, in fact, the unspoken but effective Vatican policy for decades when confronted with reports of sexual abuse worldwide. There may be administrative distance between the realms of bishops and the Holy See, but those who managed Church affairs at local level, the bishops and their parish priests, instinctively knew what was required of them, and acted accordingly.

In the female institutions, although sexual abuse was not systemic, many girls were the victims of "predatory sexual abuse" by male employees, visitors, or in outside placements. Allegations of sexual abuse were "generally taken seriously by the Sisters" and lay-staff were dismissed without being reported to the Church or civil authorities. However, the nuns' attitude towards sex made it "difficult for them to deal with such cases candidly and openly" while the victims of sexual assault felt shame and fear of punishment for lying if they reported abuse.

Physical neglect was also endemic. Children were frequently hungry, and witnesses told the commission of scavenging for food from waste bins and animal feed. Smaller boys were intimidated and bullied at meal times which were inadequately supervised, and malnourishment was a serious problem in institutions like the Magdalene asylums. Clothing was inadequate, accommodation was "cold, spartan and bleak," and sanitary conditions were primitive in the male institutions. The standard of education was inferior to that among similar age groups in the national school system, particularly in female institutions where girls were removed from class to perform domestic chores, or work in the laundries. Academic education was not a priority, and although the institutions were mandated to provide basic industrial training to enable "young adults to take up positions of employment" once released, the industrial training afforded by all schools was such that "served the needs of the institution rather than the needs of the child."

What Justice Ryan describes as "disturbing" was the evidence of the level of "emotional abuse the disadvantaged, neglected and abandoned children were subjected to" by religious and lay staff in institutions. Apart from constant criticism and verbal abuse, witnesses spoke of "humiliating practices" such as underwear inspections, and private matters, such as bodily functions and personal hygiene, being used as "opportunities for degradation," particularly in female institutions where "personal and family denigration was widespread." There was, and in some cases still is, long-term psychological damage among former victims of the institutions who witnessed the abuse of co-residents, seeing other children, including siblings, being beaten, hearing their cries, and in some cases being "forced to participate in beatings" which had a "powerful and distressing effect."

Apart from the Reformatory and Industrial Schools inquiry, the Confidential Committee of the Ryan Commission also heard evidence in relation to 161 primary and secondary schools, Children's Homes, foster care, hospitals, and services for children within special needs hostels and other residential settings, all run by various religious orders of priests, nuns and lay congregations, and heard from witnesses who told of abuse and neglect "in some instances up to the year 2000." Once again the predatory nature of sexual abuse was a common feature, including the "selection and grooming of socially disadvantaged and vulnerable children" particularly in special needs services where "children with impairments of sight, hearing and learning were particularly vulnerable to sexual abuse." And once again there was an absence of supervision by external authorities, which allowed the abuse to continue even when children were placed with unsuitable foster parents, according to witnesses.

The final chapter of Judge Ryan's report contains a series of strongly-worded recommendations based on late 20th-century knowledge and progress in relation to how vulnerable and socially-deprived children should be cared for in state institutions, and on the known predatory and recidivist nature of pederasts, pedophiles and sexual sadists. A memorial to the victims was also proposed, a permanent public acknowledgement and formal recognition for the pain they suffered, with the following words: "On behalf of the State and of all the citizens of the State, the Government wishes to make a sincere and long overdue apology to the victims of childhood abuse, for our collective failure to intervene, to detect their pain, to come to their rescue."

Although it will never be possible to determine the number of Irish children who passed through the industrial school system and, deprived of a proper education, emerged as physical, sexual and psychologically-abused young adults, most of whom were condemned to a life of menial tasks, trying to survive in an ignorant and unforgiving society, but it most certainly must run into tens of thousands. It has been an instance of wholesale moral and, in many cases, physical destruction, and a downright 'holocaust' in every sense of the word.

The Missionary Position

The Congregation of Christian Brothers, founded in Waterford, in southern Ireland, in 1802, successfully sued the commission to prevent accused members being named in the report, but agreed to pay almost $200 million in reparations and for counseling services to the victims in Ireland. The congregation has also been involved in allegations of sexual abuse in Australia in the 1970s, at St. Alipius Primary School, and at St. Patrick's College in Ballarat, an old gold-mining town in Victoria, which earned the reputation as the worst of Australia's thirty-two dioceses for sexual abuse. following a police investigation into a pedophile ring among clergy which the Australian Catholic Church had allowed to flourish for two decades. The former Archbishop of Sidney, George Pell, an Oxford University philosophy graduate who was named cardinal in October 2003, had himself been accused the previous year of sexually abusing a 12-year-old boy at a Catholic youth camp while a seminarian in 1961, (an allegation he denied). He had been an assistant priest in Swan Hill in the Ballarat diocese in 1971, knew several of the priests and Christian Brothers later found guilty of systematically sodomizing young boys, but denied knowing about the pedophile network, although he admitted "hearing rumors" when one of

Without Grace or Favor

the most prolific offenders, Fr. Gerald Ridsdale, returned to Ballarat from treatment in the US in 1990. Ridsdale was sentenced to a minimum of 15 years in 1994, after pleading guilty to 46 counts of sexual offences committed over two decades, while his ultra-conservative former friend and colleague, George Pell, spoke out on controversial issues as he rose through the ranks of the Catholic Church. He has criticized President Barack Obama for his "anti-life voting record" in the US Senate, describing the President's policies on life-issues, such as the rights of gay couples, as "very, very bad indeed." He has also characterized Islam as an "intolerant religion" with a "severely-limited capacity for far-reaching renovation," and was a strong supporter of retired Pope Benedict's views on the use of artificial contraception to combat HIV/AIDS.

The Christian Brothers spent A$200,000 defending sexually abusive members later convicted of being part of the Ballarat network, one of several in Australia that had remained active because known sexual predators were moved from parish to parish for decades to protect the reputation of the Australian Catholic Church and conceal the truth from the lay authorities. A familiar pattern occurred in the US and Ireland where the leader of the Irish Catholic Church, Cardinal Sean Brady, had expressed his "profound sorrow" for what had taken place in the Catholic-run institutions. He described the Ryan Report, in May 2009, as a "shameful catalogue of cruelty" and called for those responsible to be "held to account."

Three years later this ecclesiastical prince of the Church faced calls for his own resignation for his handling of sexual abuse allegations in the mid-1970s, following a BBC documentary, *The Shame of the Catholic Church*, broadcast on 1 May 2012, when 51-year-old Brendan Boland, a victim of a notorious serial sex abuser, the late Fr. Brendan Smyth, claimed he had passed information about Smyth's crimes to a Church inquiry team, which included Fr. Brady as official notary, and had provided a list of six other children who were preyed upon by Smyth, but continued to be abused when the committee, comprising three priests, completed its work but failed to pass on the information to the victims' parents or the civil authorities.

A report on this low-level inquiry, which took place behind closed doors at the parochial house in Ballyjamesduff, County Cavan, in late-March/April 1975, was passed to the late Bishop of Kilmore, Francis McKiernan, who passed it on to Fr. Kevin Smith, the abbot of nearby Kilnacrott Abbey, where Smyth was based, but nothing was done to prevent Smyth, a member of the Norbertine Order, abusing again. In fact, there was awareness of Smyth's pedophile activities among the Norbertines prior to 1975, according to a UTV documentary, *Suffer the Children*, broadcast in September 1994, in which the head of the Kilnacrott monastery admitted to journalist, Chris Moore, that Smyth's behavior had "perplexed and troubled" the community for years, but it had been hoped that a combination of God's grace, Smyth's intelligence and "various treatments" would enable the seriously disturbed and predatory priest, who had exploited the relationship of trust between people and clergy in rural Ireland, to "overcome the compulsive nature of his disorder."

Smyth's treatment included being sent, on two occasions, to parishes in the US, including Langdon, North Dakota. It has been claimed that the Catholic Church authorities in the US were not informed about his "propensity to molest children," and only learned about the predator in their midst in 1994, when told by Chris Moore, as part of his documentary research and subsequent book, *Betrayal of Trust*. Moore admits having difficulty believing these denials, and those with whom he spoke, Bishop James Sullivan and Vicar General, Fr Wendelin Vetter, had difficulty explaining how "one of the world's largest employers could move staff all around the globe without having in place some kind of personal system which would indicate to everyone concerned with the supply of priests the individual's record of employment," which, in Smyth's case, included allegations that he had molested children. In 1994 Smyth was jailed in the North of Ireland, and later in the Irish Republic, for sexually abusing and indecently assaulting over 100 children in parishes in Belfast, Dublin and North Dakota over four decades. He died, aged 70, of a heart attack in the exercise yard of the Curragh Prison, about 30 miles west of Dublin, on a Friday evening in August 1997, one month into a 12 year sentence, and was buried secretly under slabs of concrete in the grounds Kilnacrott Abbey

The sexually promiscuous criminal careers of men like Smyth, and another notorious Irish pedophile priest, Fr. Sean Fortune, who committed suicide behind steel-shuttered windows of a small terraced house in New Ross, County Wexford, in March 1999, while awaiting trial on sixty-six charges of abusing twenty-nine boys, and the response of the Church's hierarchy in Ireland and Rome, has seriously weakened the position of the Irish Catholic Church in what used to be one of Europe's most Catholic countries, where the role of the Church's "special position in society" is actually acknowledged in the 1937 Irish Constitution.

Like any other global organization with serious criminal and disciplinary issues at grass roots level, the bishops, basically middle-management level employees, have been used as a 'firebreak' to prevent the Curia being consumed in the combustible fire-storm demand by victims for retribution. They have been the Vatican's willing fall-guys, rightly condemned for facilitating predatory priests by moving them, anonymously, from parish to parish. This practice was used extensively, and if it wasn't officially sanctioned, it was certainly known to senior CDF officials like Cardinal Ratzinger and his predecessors, and tacitly accepted as the norm, rather than the exception. And where local disgrace finally proved too difficult or costly to justify or defend, some senior 'executives' were forced to resign - men like Boston's Archbishop Bernard Francis Law, who stepped down in December 2002, after being accused of actively participating in the cover-up of child molestation.

When official documents revealed that Archbishop Law had confirmed that the 'normal practice' was to seek therapeutic and psychological treatment in residential centers for priests accused of abuse before returning them to their priestly duties, rather than reporting the alleged offenders to the civil authorities, he lost the support of many influential civil and business leaders among the archdiocese I.5 million Catholics. Next to the State of Massachusetts, the Boston diocese was the biggest provider of social services in the region, and as donations to the Church collapsed, Archbishop Law packed his bags and headed for Rome. Once there, Pope John Paul II, on the recommendation of Cardinal Ratzinger, appointed him Archpriest Emeritus of one of Rome's great churches, the Basilica di Santa Maria Maggiore, built, restored, redecorated and extended by various pontiffs from 432 to the mid-18th century. Cardinal Law also participated in the 2005 papal conclave that elected Joseph Ratzinger to succeed John Paul II.

Along with other 'princes of the Church' Law served on many influential Curia committees, including the Pontifical Council for the Family, and the Congregation for Institutes of Consecrated Life and Societies of Apostolic Life, both of which have a direct influence on clerical behavior in relation to lay members of the Catholic Church, and the lives of ordinary decent Catholics. Cardinal Law, as head the Church of Santa Susanna, on Rome's Quirinal Hill, known locally as the 'American Church' because it administers to US Catholics visiting or resident in the eternal city, was also an honored guest at diplomatic functions within the welcoming safe haven of the Vatican, until Curia membership and conclave participation rights ended in November 2011, when he reached his 80th birthday.

The financial cost to the Roman Catholic Church, in terms of diminished donations on the one hand, and compensation claims on the other, is almost impossible to calculate because of the secretive nature of proceedings and agreements, often bound by clauses of confidentiality. Estimates range from anywhere between $2 and $8 billion, and counting, in the US and Ireland alone since victims began to speak out for the first time in the early 1970s, and publicly challenge the authority of an institution which had expected them to suffer in silence. In July 2008, the Canadian Prime Minister, Stephen Harper, apologized for the abuses of the Aboriginal population in the country's Indian Residential Schools system, of which 60 percent were administered by the Catholic Church, and which included compulsory sterilization in Alberta and British Columbia in the 1920s and 1930s. The mortality rate - as a result of neglect, over-crowding, poor sanitation, and the lack of proper medical care - was described as "cultural genocide" in several reports, and was calculated, from the incomplete medical records available, as well in excess of 50,000 nationwide when the final school closed in 1996.

There is no documentation of abuse from counties like Spain, with 70 percent of the 47,190,493 population claiming allegiance to the Catholic Church, according to the statistics provided by an April 2011 Centro de Investigaciones Sociologicas (CIS), from Italy, where 91.6 percent regard themselves as Catholic from a population of 60,813 326, according to the country's Instituto Nazionale di Statistica (INSTAT), in October

2011, or from the devoutly-religious Poland, where over 80 percent of the country's 38,500,000 citizens profess allegiance to the Church of Rome, for political as well as spiritual reasons, and who knows the extent of what has been happening in Africa, where Irish Catholic missionaries have been an evangelical presence for decades, in Central America, with a huge Catholic constituency among a largely-impoverished population in excess of 42 million, or in Latin America, where 70 percent of the estimated 570 million people consider themselves Catholic

In order to maintain its reputation in those countries and continents where the behavior of sexually deviant clergy has yet to be scrutinized, the Church has been playing the role of victim. During Good Friday prayers in 2011 in St Peter's Basilica, the Italian priest, Fr. Raniero Cantalamessa, a member of the 16th century Order of Friars Minor Capuchin, who has served as Preacher to the Papal Household under John Paul II and Benedict XVI, suggested that the allegations of sexual abuse by predatory clergy, and criticism of the ham-fisted attempts at a cover-up by the Vatican authorities, were simply manifestations of anti-Catholicism. He expressed his "indignation" at the "violent and concentric attacks [and] the use of stereotypes" and suggested that the "passing from personal responsibility and guilt to a collective guilt" bore similarities to the "more shameful aspects of anti-Semitism."

A Rogue Institution?

This is what is known about the disappearance in 1983 of Emanuela Orlandi, the 15-year-old, secondary school student and daughter of Ercole Orlandi, an employee of the Vatican Bank, the Instituto per le Opere di Religione (IOR), headed by Archbishop Paul Marcinkus, and which, as the largest shareholder, had been involved in the 1982 collapse of the Banco Ambrosiano.

The teenager was a member of the choir of Saint Anne in Vatican, the 16th century parish church of the Vicariate of the Vatican City. On Wednesday afternoon, 22 June 1983, she left her family's Vatican City apartment to travel by bus to music lessons at the Tommaso Ludovico Da Vittoria School, part the Catholic Church's ecclesiastical academic institutes of higher education dedicated to the study of religious music, the Pontificio Instituto de Musica Sagrada, established by the Holy See on the instruction of Pope Pius X in 1910. She arrived late for her 7pm class, claiming to have been speaking to her sister about a job offer as an Avon Cosmetics representative. She discussed the Avon job with a girlfriend after class, and a short time later was last seen at a bus stop near the school, getting into a large, dark-colored BMW car.

Her father's association immediately led to speculation in sections of the Italian media that the American-born Marcinkus, a friend of Banco Ambrosiano chairman, Roberto Calvi, who had been found hanged beneath Blackfriars Bridge in central London, on 17 July 1982, had arranged the abduction of Miss Orlandi to prevent her father disclosing evidence of the extent of financial corruption inside the IOR that he had stumbled upon in the course of his clerical duties.

Three decades later, in an interview with the Turin-based, *La Stampa,* newspaper, in May 2012, the Catholic Church's leading exorcist, Fr. Gabriel Amorth, suggested that the teenager's disappearance was a "sexually-motivated crime," adding that this had previously been admitted by a Vatican archivist, the late Monsignor Simeone Duca, who claimed he had been asked to obtain young girls, with the help of the Vatican gendarmerie, for Vatican sex parties: "I believe Emanuela ended up in this circle, that this was a case of sexual exploitation, which led to murder and the then hiding of her body. Also involved are diplomatic staff of a foreign embassy to the Holy See." When Fr. Amorth (who had previously denounced J.K. Rowling's *Harry Potter* series as the "work of the Devil") made his claim last year, there was widespread speculation in the Italian media that the schoolgirl had been kidnapped and murdered by the Banda della Magliana, a loose alliance of hardcore gangsters, allegedly with links to senior members of the Italian Arma dei Carabinieri, and the country's Military Intelligence and Security Service (SISMI), that had been active in Rome for almost two decades. The Banda della Magliana was headed by Enrico 'Renatino' De Pedis, who was gunned down during an internecine feud in Camp de' Fiori ('the field of flowers') near Rome's Piazza Navone in 1990, and was buried in the nearby Basilica of Saint'Apollinare, next to the music school where Emanuela Orlandi was last seen. The burial was arranged by the late Vicar-General of Rome, Cardinal Ugo Poletti, who was also a member of the clandestine Masonic lodge, Propaganda Due (P2), having been initiated into the Brotherhood on 17 February 1969.

Headed by Italian financier and 'venerable grand master' Licio Gelli, P2 set out to influence the course of Italian history, recruiting leading industrialists, senior politicians, members of the armed forces and the intelligence community, intellectuals and journalists, to promote a 'Plan for Democratic Rebirth' which, in reality, had nothing to do with democracy. It called for a round-up of 'troublesome' left-wing activists and others who might protest against the 'New Order,' the suspension of trade unions and other basic democratic rights in a free society, and a new Italian constitution.

The Vatican claimed Cardinal Poletti gave permission for the convicted Mafioso to be interred in the crypt of the 7th century Arian church next to 'illustrious' prelates, because he was a "repentant sinner" who had been "involved in charitable works on behalf of the Church," but this failed to end speculation that the marble tomb also concealed the body of Emanuela Orlandi. This was fuelled by claims, made in a series of anonymous telephone calls to Agence France-Presse, and the Italian news agency ANSA, and by former Magliana gang member, Antonio Mancini, in an interview with the Rome daily, *il Fatto Quotidiano,* in mid-2011, who claimed that De Pedis drove the dark-green BMW involved in the abduction, and that the teenager had been kidnapped after senior Mafia figures had lost "more than $200 million" they had been laundering through the IOR when Banco Ambrosiano, Italy's largest private bank, collapsed. In addition there was speculation in sections of the Italian media that the Magliana crime boss had privately loaned the Vatican a huge sum of money "off the books" that had been used to fund the Polish trade union, *Solidarnosc*, and had also not been repaid, and that the disappearance and death of the teenager was both "a pay-back and a warning" to others who might be thinking of whistle-blowing.

In May 2012, five years after of what Pietro Orlandi has described as "embarrassing silence" since speculation about the location of his sister's body began, the Vatican, through the Vicariate of Rome and despite objections from Opus Dei which runs the basilica, finally gave the Italian police and investigating magistrates permission to enter the Saint' Appollinare crypt, open the tomb and remove the contents to Rome's La Sapienza University mortuary for forensic analysis. The Vatican was quick to claim credit for this development, with spokesman Fr. Federico Lombardi describing the inspection of the crypt a "positive development." The New York-based broadcaster, ABC News, described the body of crime boss De Pedis as being in "relatively good condition, dressed in a dark suit and black tie, with no trace of any other remains in the coffin." Vittorio Rizzo, the head of Rome crime squad, told Italian television on 15 May that about 200 boxes of unidentified bones had been found in the crypt, but all appeared to date from pre-Napoleonic times.

The Orlandi cold-case file was reopened in 2010, and the current investigation has focused on links between the IOR, and the criminal underworld. Immediately after the abduction, while Italian police were still investigating the 1981 assassination attempt on Pope John Paul II in Saint Peter's Square, there were claims that the young girl had been taken in order to secure the release of the gunman, Mehmet Ali Agra, a member of an ultra-right Turkish group called the Grey Wolves, which had allegedly carried out the failed assassination attempt on the orders of Bulgaria's Committee for State Security (CSS) 1st Directorate, acting on behalf of the KGB. While this speculation - fuelled by the late, right-wing, conspiracy theorist and propagandist, Clair Sterling - proved to be nothing more than a time-wasting distraction, claims that Emanuela Orlandi had been kidnapped on the orders of Paul Marcinkus persisted but remained unproven. Giancarlo Capaldo, the senior prosecutor investigating the case now believes he has uncovered evidence that serving members of the Curia "knew more than they were saying" about the case, and was quoted in Rome's, *Corriere della Sera*, saying "there are people still alive and still inside the Vatican, who know the truth." Not surprisingly the Vatican has rejected Capaldo's allegations, claiming "all that is known has been divulged." Cardinal Giovanni Battista Re, who was *Sostituto* ('Commissioner') for General Affairs in the Vatican's Secretariat of State, a key position under the Cardinal Secretary of State, Agostino Casaroli, at the time, also told Italy's oldest and once one of its most reputable daily newspapers (until compromised by P2's editorial influence) that "if someone on the inside had known anything they would have talked by now." He claimed that all members of the Curia were "interested in clarifying the matter, but unfortunately were not able to find out anything about it."

Sabrina Minardi, former mistress of Erico De Pedis, provided the Italian investigators with her version of events, published in Italy's largest circulation, center-left newspaper, *La Republica,* on 23 June 2008, claiming Emanuela Orlandi was the victim of a "power struggle" and had been "snatched on the orders of Marcinkus, in order to "send a message" to senior Vatican officials. De Pedis had carried out the abduction in return for the archbishop's help in laundering proceeds from other kidnappings undertaken by the Magliana gang. The ransom cash had been delivered to the archbishop's apartment in Louis Vutton bags, according to Minardi, claiming she knew the apartment because she had previously taken young girls there on Marcinkus's orders. *La Republica* suggests that although investigators were "cautious" about Minardi's testimony, they were "impressed by the accuracy of some details." If a link can be proved between the disappearance of Emanuela Orlandi, and Archbishop Marcinkus, it will reopen one of the Vatican's most corrosive financial corruption scandals.

Paul Marcinkus, the Illinois-born son of a Russian immigrant, who had taken Holy Orders in Chicago in May 1947, studied Canon Law at Rome's Georgian University in 1950, and spent eight years as secretary in the apostolic nunciatures in Bolivia and Canada, before returning to Rome where he briefly acted as English translator for Pope Pius VI, before being appointed president of the IOR in 1971. He was protected by the Vatican's right to diplomatic immunity, under the 1961 Vienna Convention on Diplomatic Relations, from questioning by Italian and US financial officials into his business relationship with 'God's banker' and P2 member, Roberto Calvi, following the collapse of Banco Ambrosiano, and into his association with Mafia-connected Sicilian banker and convicted fraudster, Michele Sindona, who died in Voghera Prison, in Lombardy, northern Italy, on 22 March 1986, after drinking coffee laced with cyanide.

Sindona, a friend of the Archbishop of Milan, Giovanni Battista Montini, later Pope Paul VI, and a member of P2, was serving a twenty-five years sentence for the murder of Italian lawyer, Giorgio Ambrosoli, who had been appointed liquidator of Banca Privata Italiana (BPI) one of several Italian banks, controlled by Sindona, that had been in the money-laundering business for only two months before being placed in compulsory liquidation, on 27 September 1974. Ambrosoli had provided US financial regulators with evidence which helped convict Sindona for his role in the "obscure circumstances" that led to the collapse of the New York-based, Franklin National Bank, the 20th largest bank in the US, in October 1974, and was under no illusions about the dangers he faced following his appointment as liquidator. According to author, Rupert Cornwell, the 45-years old lawyer wrote in a letter to his wife in 1975: "Whatever happens, I'll certainly pay a high price for taking this job. But I knew that before taking it on and I'm not complaining, because it has been a unique chance for me to do something for the country (...) This job gives me an enormous power, but I've worked only in the country's interests, obviously making only enemies for myself."

He died on 11 July 1979, shot at point-blank range outside the Milan building where he lived, a standard underworld 'contract killing' commissioned by Michele Sindona. The fee for this cold-blooded execution was $100,000, transferred from Sindona's Banca del Gottardo account into the Geneva-based Credit Suisse account of the shooter, William Arico. Ambrosoli's low-key funeral took place three days later, attended by only a handful of mourners. There was no official state acknowledgement of what he had given his life to accomplish, and no word from the Vatican.

The Root of All Evil

Following the collapse of Banco Ambrosiano and the disappearance of $1.3 billion in loans to several dummy companies in Latin America that had been provided with bogus IOR letters of credit, the Vatican agreed to pay $250 million to Ambrosiano's creditors. It continued to deny any wrongdoing in the scandal which remains shrouded in secrecy and deceit. Indeed, penance is not high on the Vatican's list of virtues. Paul Marcinkus's successor at the IOR, Monsignor Angelo Caloia, expanded the bank's money-laundering activities, with secret accounts opened for non-existent relief and charitable organizations. According to the Hamburg-based, weekly news magazine, *Der Spiegal,* Caloia would bring "suitcases into the Vatican full of donations from Italian companies in the form of cash and securities." The origins of the money would then be obscured using accounts such as one with the number 001-3-14772-C, owned by the nonexistent 'Cardinal Spellman Foundation'. Monsignor Caloia, a former president of the Mediocredito Lombardo, had been nominated for the IOR vacancy when Marcinkus left Rome for a parish in Illinois, by four council members of the Catholic, Milan-based, Group for Culture, Ethics and Finance (GCEF), which included Phillippe De Weck, expresident of the Union de Banques Suisse, who was close to Opus Dei and was Caloia's principal promoter.

In 2009, following the discovery of more than 4,000 documents containing evidence of the IOR's continuing money-laundering activities, which had been collected and hidden by the Vatican's financial expert, Renato Dardozzi, prior to his death in 2003, together with a hand-written note asking that the papers be published "so that everyone can learn what has happened here," Pope Benedict replaced Caloia with the Italian economist and banker, Ettore Gotti Tedeschi. An experienced industrialist and financial strategist, Tedeschi, a lay member of Opus Dei, was regarded as an "interfering outsider" by a powerful cabal of cardinals within the Curia. He was tasked with making the IOR eligible to be included in the Paris-based Organization for Economic Co-operation and Development (OECD) 'White List' of global financial institutions not involved in money-laundering or other nefarious financial practices. Such good intentions, however, were far from the murky realities of Vatican banking. In 2009, the year that Gotti Tedeschi took charge, the IOR set up a 'sweep facility account' with the Milan-based branch of the American bank, JP Morgan, which was used to transfer funds on a daily basis to another IOR cash account at the JP Morgan branch in Frankfurt, Germany.

Sweep accounts are used to manage a steady cash flow between financial institutions or private investors, and are a means to avoid paying interest on business checking accounts by being automatically swept clean and returned to zero at the end of each day. The Vatican claimed account number 1365 was primarily used to handle securities transactions. In September 2010, Italian prosecutors seized $30 million after the Vatican failed to declare the destination of several large transfers when management at the Rome branch of the Credito Artigiano Spa informed the Bank of Italy about possible violations of international anti-money laundering regulations. Most of the cash, about $20 million, was to be transferred to JP Morgan in Frankfurt, the remainder was destined for Banca del Fucino. The Vatican expressed "astonishment" when an Italian court rejected an application to have the funds returned, and at what the prosecutors called "a deliberate failure to observe the anti-laundering laws with the aim of hiding the ownership, destination and origin of the capital" - including a withdrawal of $1 million from a Vatican bank account at Intesa San Paolo Bank, without complying with the bank's request for details of the money's final destination, and also what was referred to as "suspicious transactions," in 2009, from another Vatican cash account with Unicredit Bank, using a false identity.

The Vatican professed "utmost confidence" in the IOR's senior management, including Signore Tedeschi, who was also an advisor to Italy's finance minister, Giulio Tremonti, during this period. This confidence was short-lived, however, and in May 2010, Tedeschi was sacked for failing to "carry out duties of primary importance." The Vatican refused to elaborate of this brief, vaguely-worded statement, and Tedeschi, also declined to comment, telling journalists "I'd rather say nothing, otherwise I'd say ugly things."

The following month, shortly after Tedeschi left his home on Via Giuseppe Verdi, in the old quarters of Piacenza in northern Italy, to travel by the high-speed ETR 500 on his daily commute to Rome, he was detained by four members of the Carabinieri, the national military police. His home and two offices in Milan were searched simultaneously, and two computers, two filing cabinets, a planner and a briefcase with documents Tedeschi was taking to Rome at the request of a confident of Pope Benedict, were confiscated. The Carabinieri were investigating alleged irregularities in a contract for 12 Agusta Westland helicopters that Italian arms manufacturer, Finmeccanica, had delivered to India, which involved Fincomsumo Banca SpA, the Italian subsidiary of the Spanish bank, Santander, and alleged illegal payments the company made to the multi-ideological regional and federalist

Italian political party, Lega Nord.

Among the confidential files confiscated were papers relating to the money laundering activities of the IOR in other areas, including details of anonymous and falsely-registered cash accounts, and copies of written and electronic communications between individuals and institutions - a detail money-trail showing how the IOR officials circumvented European and OECD money-laundering regulations. Several high-ranking members of the Curia regarded the IOR not as an Institution for Religious Works but as "something akin to a trust company for clandestine monetary transactions that is not only used by the Church, but also, allegedly, by the Mafia, corrupt politicians and companies" according to *Der Spiegel*, which claimed that in one of the confiscated memos seized in the Carabinieri raids, Tedeschi had written "I've seen things in the Vatican that scare me."

Tedeschi accused Cardinal Tarcisco Pietro Bertone, the Vatican's Secretary of State, and a man well-versed in ecclesiastical politics, having served in several influential posts including *Camerlengo* ('Chamberlain') of the Papal household, and Secretary of the CDF, from 1995 to 2002, under Cardinal Ratzinger, of being the "malignant influence" inside the Curia who had done everything possible to keep the IOR's accounts hidden from the Italian financial authorities, reportedly complaining in a confidential memo: "If we continue with Bertone's line, we will never get off the (OECD) Black List." The IOR's private, confidential and commercial documentation, and 33,000 accounts with total deposits of $7.6 billion, are housed in the bank's headquarters next to the Apostolic Palace, the Pope's official residence, in St .Peter's Square. The first task of Papal spokesman, Federico Lombardi, who took charge of the Vatican Press Office, in July 2006, when Pope Benedict appointed him to replace Opus Dei numerary, Joaquin Navarro Valls, was to call upon the Italian prosecutors to return confidential financial material to the IOR and respect the "sovereign rights of the Holy See."

The IOR, since its founding by Pope Pius XII in 1942, is listed among the Holy See's departments in the annual directory of the Holy See, the *Annuario Pontificio*, and has achieved an inevitable reputation as a shadowy, off-shore tax-haven through which illicit finds are laundered with anonymity guaranteed. The stench of corruption was still lingering when inspectors from Moneyval - the monitoring mechanism of the Council of Europe, which provides information to organizations such as the Financial Action Task Force (FATF) to determine if a national financial institution should be listed on a FAFT 'Black' or 'Grey' list of countries that fail to meet financial propriety in its private and commercial dealings - visited the Vatican on several occasions in 2011 and early 2012. Three years ago the IOR had requested a positive Moneyval evaluation, and the Vatican had drafted new financial transparency regulations, which it claimed met international standards on money-laundering and terrorism financing. However, Moneyval (officially known as The Committee of Experts on the Evaluation of Anti-Money Laundering Measures and the Financing of Terror) was not impressed. In

July 2012, it issued its report which sharply criticized IOR management, and gave it a negative rating of "partially compliant" or "non compliant" on seven out of sixteen of its most important financial transparency-related assessment criteria, including inadequate reporting of suspicious transactions, lack of supervision and monitoring, and insufficient "customer due diligence." The report strongly recommended that IOR management should be "independently supervised by a prudential supervisor in the near future."

'Res Ipsa Loquitur'

Four deaths in the late 1970s have three things in common: the shadowy presence of Paul Marcinkus, as he stalked the corridors of the medieval defensive tower, known as 'Niccolo V', which served as IOR headquarters; the lingering malignant influence of P2 inside and outside the Vatican; and the secretive, ultra-orthodox Catholic middle-class organization, Opus Dei. The latter shared the same paymasters as the 'black lodge' - Roberto Calvi and the Spanish businessman, Jose Ruiz Mateos - as it developed from an obscure sect, founded in Madrid in 1928 by Fr. St. Josemaria Escriva, to remind the laity of the "universal call to holiness" to be achieved "through work and ordinary life," as well as by spiritual and penitent practices, such as wearing "instruments of mortification" and a 'Cilice' - a coarse, sackcloth garment next to the skin to induce discomfort and pain - as a sign of repentance and atonement.

Opus Dei ('Work of God') supported the fascist regime of Spain's General Francisco Franco, and repressive military dictatorships in predominantly Catholic Central and Latin America countries, including General Augusto Pinochet in Chile in the 1970s, while ignoring the activities of right-wing death squads, and those thousands who were 'disappeared' by security forces and intelligence agencies throughout the Americas. The organization received the approval of Pope Pius XII in 1950, and since then, according to Canadian journalist, Robert Hutchison, has "forged an unholy alliance with the Mafia, secular pawnbrokers and highly placed prelates" while the organization's governing authority, the Prelate, currently headed by Javier Echevarrie, runs "an immense intelligence network and a vast multinational conglomerate" preparing for Christianity's final showdown with radical Islam.

The murder of lawyer, Giorgio Ambrosoli, was a 'standard' cold-blooded execution, as was that of journalist, Carmine 'Mino' Pecorelli, gunned down in Rome's Prati district, on 20 March 1979, while investigating Marcinkus, the IOR, and links to organized crime. Pecorelli was editor of a 'scurrilous' and sometimes profane magazine called, *Osservatore Politico,* who had "excellent [Italian] secret service contacts" according to Philip Willan, and whose reporting technique was similar to that practiced by the intelligence community - "reveal an awkward truth and then scoff at it as though it was untrue." Pecorelli's name appeared on a list of P2 members, and one example of his journalism was an article on P2's Licio Gelli, which he published on 2 January 1979, less than three months before his death. Entitled 'Twice a Partisan', the piece began by criticizing suggestions in the mainstream media that P2 members, by swearing allegiance to Freemasonry, had put themselves at the service of the Central Intelligence Agency (CIA) in order to prevent the Italian Communist Party achieving power through democratic means. It trepeated, in detail, the charges against Gelli, whom he described as an "ex-Nazi, agent of the Argentinean secret service, personal friend of Lopez Rega, and founder of the AAA death squads in Latin America, linked to the CIA (...) and to American hawks." Then he contradicted the allegations with anecdotal details of Gelli's collaboration with the Italian *Resistenza Partigiana* during WWII, including testimony from Partisan leader, Italo Carobbi. He finally concluded by stating that it is "not a fascist, pro-American and coup-plotting Gelli that emerges but a Venerable Master who is a sincere democrat and ex-partisan." His parting shot, according to Willan's excellent book, *The Puppetmasters*, was to mention Gelli's well-known "relationship with the People's Republic of Ceausescu."

Paul Marcinkus could expect this type of embarrassing journalistic treatment from the pen of Pecorelli as the scandal surrounding the IOR and Banco Ambrosiano widened, until crime boss, Danilo Abbruciati, commissioned former child actor, Valerio Fioravanti, a member of the far-right *Nuclei Armati Rivoluzionari* (who would be convicted, in 1988, of planning the 2 August 1980 Bologna train station bombing, in which 85 people died and over 200 were injured) to take care of the troublesome journalist. Abbruciati was also a leading member of the Banda della Magliana, which was beginning to emerge as part of a sinister underworld alliance of right-wing, fascist terrorists and gangsters, increasingly involved in assassinations, drug trafficking, money laundering, and abduction for profit or political leverage

The death of Cardinal Egidio Vagnozzi, four months later, should have been cause for concern, not least for those suspicious of coincidences. A graduate of Rome's Pontifical Lateran University, he had been a staff member of the apostolic delegation to the US in 1932, served as counselor at the apostolic nunciature in Portugal during WWII, and later as a member of the official papal delegation to establish diplomatic relations with India, before serving as charge d'affaires at the Vatican's mission in New Delhi in 1948. The following year he was appointed Papal Nuncio in the Philippines, and in 1958 he returned to the US as Apostolic Delegate. From 1968 until his death, this experienced diplomat served as head of the Vatican's Prefecture of Economic Affairs, where he became increasingly concerned with Opus Dei's efforts to take over at the IOR, and the organization's growing influence in Vatican business matters, both religious and secular. He distrusted Paul Marcinkus, and confided in Secretary of State, the late Cardinal Agostino Casaroli, the Vatican's 'spymaster' under five different Popes. Responsible for the Holy See's response to the plight of practicing Catholics in the Warsaw Pact nations in the late 1960s, and a man Hutchinson describes as a "master of ambivalence," Casaroli gave Vagnozzi "only a minimum of support." He did, however, back his proposal to call an extraordinary meeting attended by more than 100 cardinals, held on 5 November 1979, where Vagnozzi outlined his concerns about the "near state of collapse" of the Vatican's finances. This was the last major meeting Vagnozzi presided over. A short time later he was dead, presumably of natural causes, although without an autopsy or death certificate, only a few senior Vatican officials know the truth, and know the whereabouts of a confidential dossier Vagnozzi had assembled on Marcinkus, which disappeared from among his private papers after his death.

Paul Marcinkus served as president of the IOR until 1989, and then left Rome for the Archdiocese of Chicago, after being assured by the US Department of Justice (DoJ) of immunity from prosecution in connection with the delivery of $14.5 million in counterfeit US bonds to the Vatican shortly after he took charge at the IOR. His name had been found on official IOR notepaper by the DoJ's Organized Crime and Racketeering Section (OCRS), during an investigation headed by federal prosecutor, William Aronwald, and OCRS boss, Bill Lynch, into attempts to 'launder' $950 million worth of negotiable, secondary market securities.

Two years before Marcinkus left for the US, warrants for his arrest and for two civilian IOR officials had been issued by Italian prosecutors in Milan, accusing them of being accessories before the fact to the fraudulent collapse of the Banco Ambrosiano. Despite a 1982 Italian Constitutional Court ruling stating that the Vatican State's treaty with the Italian Republic precluded any "interference" by the Italian authorities in the affairs of the Holy See, prosecutors in Rome were still hoping to question Marcinkus when he finally retired to Phoenix, Arizona, where he was found dead, of natural causes, on 21 February 2006, according to a spokesperson for the Phoenix Catholic Diocese. Vatican sources claimed that Marcinkus had been sent back to the US to avoid confrontation with the Italian authorities, and despite his innocence he had agreed to "take the fall" to protect the real culprit, Bishop Pavol Hnilica, who had been charged in 1992 by Rome investigating magistrate, Dr Mario Almerighi, with attempting to purchase personal papers belonging to fugitive Banco Ambrosiano chairman, Roberto Calvi, last seen in the banker's possession at the Chelsea Cloisters apartment complex on Sloan Avenue, London, shortly before he was found dangling beneath London's Blackfriars Bridge.

In March 1993, Bishop Hnilica was convicted of conspiring to pay $1.5 million for the confidential documents, in an attempt to distance the Papacy and officials at the IOR from clandestine links to the collapse of Banco Ambrosiano. His co-defendants were Rome narcotics trafficker, Guilio Lena, and Sardinian property dealer, Flavio Mario Carboni, who had arranged for Calvi's flight from Italian justice, via Switzerland, in June 1982, and who has been described as the "on-the-ground fixer" of the multi-layered conspiracy known as Operation *SCIV* (the initials of the Vatican City state). Within months the verdict was overturned because of "faulty legal procedure" but the whole affair serves to illustrate the criminal enterprises of the men whom Marcinkus befriended and whose lifestyles he facilitated.

Operation *SCIV* began in the mid-1980s when Carboni contacted Bishop Hnilica and offered to obtain the documents in Calvi's black briefcase, which had been bought from "unknown vendors on a dark night" by Senator Giorgio Pinaso, the founder of the Italian fascist party, Movimento Fascismo e Liberta (MFL). Several documents allegedly implicated ranking Vatican officials in potentially embarrassing 'black operations', which included opening numerous bank accounts in Central and Latin America on behalf of the Roman Catholic Church "for the purpose of halting, above all, the penetration and expansion of Marxist and related ideologies" and, according to author, David Yallop, a letter reminding Pope John XII that the Church had provided the means to supply arms to right-wing regimes "to help them combat our common enemy."

Bishop Hnilica, born in the archdiocese of Trnava, in the Slovak region of the former central European Republic of Czechoslovakia, was a secretly-ordained Jesuit priest who had been appointed bishop of the non-existent diocese of Rusado by Pope Paul VI, and a man well-versed in clandestine Vatican intrigue. Having moved to Rome at the height of the Cold War, he became Pope John XII's personal adviser on Eastern European affairs, taking charge of an organization called Pro Fratribus, which smuggled funds and bibles into several Warsaw Pact, hard-line, communist states, and assisted Catholics threatened with persecution by the authorities.

The Vatican's Secretary of State, Cardinal Casaroli, authorized Hnilica to negotiate with Carboni, and at a meeting in January 1985 Carboni provided two original letters written by Calvi. The first, dated 30 May 1982, was to Cardinal Pietro Palazzini, a friend of Opus Dei founder, Fr Josemaria Escriva, and his successor Bishop Echevarria Rodriguez, to whom Calvi had appealed for help as his financial world crumbled around him before he fled Italy. The second letter, dated 6 June 1982, was to Msgr. Hilary Franco, another intercessor within the Curia on behalf of Opus Dei, who had agreed to act as Calvi's intermediary with the IOR and Opus Dei, according to Robert Hutchinson. It was described by the journalist as a "somewhat scissored document" referring to contact with Paul Marcinkus. According to the indictment drawn up by magistrate Almerighi, which provides the basis for Hutchinson's narrative, another of Pope John Paul II's close political advisers, Fr. Virgilio Rotondi, who had attended the meeting on behalf of Hnilica, gave Carboni a check for approximately $250,000.

At this point Carboni enlisted the help of Guilio Lena, who had funded the purchase of several documents. In May 1985, Lena gave Hnilica another undated letter, with the name of the recipient re-dated, signed by Calvi, and criticizing Gelli and Roman lawyer, Umberto Ortolani, a member of the inner council of the Knights of Malta, and proprietor of Banco Financiero

Sudamericano (BaFiSud), a small Montevideo bank that had been used by Calvi to channel funds to Central and Latin America. In the letter, a copy of which was included in Almerighi's indictment, Calvi describes both men as "agents of the Devil" adding: "Since I am abandoned and betrayed by those I regarded as my most reliable allies, I cannot help but remember the operations I undertook on behalf of the representatives of St. Peter," and a reference to "warships and other military equipment to be used to counter subversive activities of well-organized Communist forces" in Argentina, Colombia, Peru and Nicaragua. He also asked to be "repaid the $100 million that I furnished at the express wish of the Vatican in favor of Solidarity" and $175 million that had been "used to organize financial centers and political power" in five Latin American countries.

Details of this rather bizarre affair only came to light two years later, when Guilio Lena was questioned in connection with the seizure of 1,800 kilograms of Lebanese hashish, by Italian Coastguard, on a Spanish-registered yacht. In a search of his property in the Alban Hills, police officers found evidence of the drug trafficker's dealings with Bishop Hnilica. A subsequent search of the offices of Pro Fratribus, ordered by the investigating magistrate, Almerighi, uncovered a copy of a letter from Hnilica to Casaroli explaining the ongoing negotiations to acquire Calvi's stolen papers, and a reply from the Vatican's Secretary of State confirming that Pope John Paul II had been informed, and which also appeared to distance the Holy See from the subterfuge while at the same time warning Hnilica to "proceed with caution." Also found was an Italian military intelligence SISMI file on Carboni, confirming that SISMI had provided a false passport for Calvi, which saw the fugitive safely through British security at London's Gatwick Airport.

Italian military intelligence had been involved for decades with the Catholic Church, the Italian Christian Democrat Party, the CIA, the Mafia and right-wing terrorists, in a bloody covert campaign to destroy the Italian Communist Party, and the presence of the SISMI file on Carboni suggests Pro Fratribus had been a manipulative, shadowy influence behind the whole debacle. In his final report, magistrate Almerighi concluded that the affair suited those who found it expedient to maintain that Calvi was the principal defrauder of the IOR, and undermined the banker's repeated allegation that the IOR was controlled by Opus Dei. This fails to explain, however, why the IOR refused to cover the two checks Hnilica had given to Lena, and only makes sense if senior staff at the bank already knew the contents of Calvi's briefcase, and that the object of this multi-layered subterfuge was to damage high-ranking Curia members. In particular it targeted Cardinal Casaroli, who was regarded as an accomplished diplomat having successfully negotiated on behalf of the Vatican with a number of hard-line, Warsaw Pact communist regimes, and had chaired several sessions of the Organization for Security and Co-operation in Europe (OSCE) in Helsinki in 1975, where an accord was signed by the US, Canada, the Warsaw Pact and western European states (with the exception of Albania and Andorra) to improve relations between the

Communist bloc and the West. However, while the persecution of Catholics behind the Iron Curtain remained a "political threat" to the influence of the Vatican during the Cold War, Pope John Paul II regarded Cardinal Casaroli as an "irreplaceable asset" against the USSR. That said, Casaroli was less of a hardliner than many in the Curia, especially those close to Opus Dei, whose right-wing political credentials and fundamentalist spiritual beliefs made it anathema to have any dealings with the 'Godless' Soviets or their heathen allies anywhere.

The timing of Operation *SCIV* is interesting, as it was initiated and allowed to run into difficulties at a time when the investigation into the death of Roberto Calvi was ongoing, but no longer a priority, for Scotland Yard. An inquest jury in London, on 23 July 1982, had returned a suicide verdict, but this was overturned the following year when a second jury reached an 'open' verdict, suggesting the banker's death was 'suspicious', but was unable, legally, to take the matter any further. Six years later Operation *SCIV* was uncovered by magistrate Almerighi, and finally, in October 1992, forensic experts appointed by Italian magistrates concluded that Calvi had indeed been murdered, having found no evidence of injuries usually associated with a suicide death by hanging, and that his hands had never touched the stones, used to weigh down the body, which were found in the pockets of his well-tailored clothes.

A convicted Mafia drug trafficker, Francesco Marino Mannoia, has claimed that Calvi was executed by a member of the Altafonte clan, on the orders of the ruling 'Cupola,' the Sicilian Mafia Commission, which decides on issues of mutual importance to the cartels, or settles internecine disputes. Sicilian mafia clans had invested "tens of millions of dollars" in Banco Ambrosiano and Calvi's knowledge following the bank's collapse had made him "untrustworthy." Paul Marcinkus moved in the same circles as Sindona, Gelli and Calvi, and shared the same criminal knowledge as the murdered men, and while diplomatic immunity was no guarantee that he would not eventually decide to talk to the authorities in the United States or Italy, he retained the trust of the Cupola, which says much about the stature of the man among his peers.

"I love the old way best, the simple way of poison." (Euripides)

There is a certain symmetry to all of this. Although Propaganda Due, the "state within a state," ceased to exist as a Masonic entity in 1976 when the Grand Orient of Italy expelled the 'black lodge', the British author, David Yallop, believes the residual evil of P2, and the increasingly dominant influence of Opus Dei in the internal affairs of the Curia, contributed to the fourth controversial death of the late 1970s, that of Albino Luciani, at the age of sixty-five, whose body was found in the papal apartments on the top-floor of the Apostolic Palace, on 29 September 1978, thirty-three days after he had been elected to serve as Pope John Paul 1.

The son of a bricklayer, and a graduate in theology from the Pontifical Gregorian University, who had served as Bishop of Vittorio Veneto, the diocese in northern Italy where he was born, and as Patriarch of Venice since February 1970, Albino Luciani was elected Bishop of Rome, on 25 August 1978, by secret ballot on the fourth count at the papal conclave in the Sistine Chapel, called following the death of Pope Pius VI, at Castel Gandolfo, the papal summer residence in the Alban Hills. The Vatican's incompetent handling of Pope John Paul's death - such as uncertainty about how, and by whom, the body was found, and whether an autopsy would be carried out and a death certificate issued - contributed, in no small measure, to the controversy surrounding the incident. David Yallop's theory of murder is outlined in considerable detail in his book, *In God's Name*, and was, unsurprisingly, dismissed by the Vatican as "fanciful and absurd." Yallop claims that the "smiling Pope" was murdered because he planned to reform the Church from the top down, dismiss senior members of the Curia who were also members of the Freemason Brotherhood (contrary to the laws of the Church), and tackle financial corruption and money laundering facilities provided to the Mafia by Paul Marcinkus, who would later be promoted (rather than dismissed) by Luciani's successor, Pope John Paul II, making the recalcitrant American archbishop one of the most-powerful men in the Roman Catholic Church.

The evening before his death, Pope John Paul I dined with his private secretaries, Fr. Diego Lorenzi, who had worked with him for several years in Milan, and Fr. John Magee, who had been appointed to the Pope's staff following his election. While the three men discussed the convulsive nature of Italian political affairs, elsewhere, two senior members of the Curia, Archbishop Marcinkus, and Secretary of State, Cardinal Jean-Marie Villot, were concerned about forthcoming internal changes which would impact their positions within the Vatican hierarchy, according to Yallop. The former had learned of the newly-elected Pope's determination to rid the IOR of corrupt practices, while the latter studied, with concern, "the list of appointments, resignations to be asked for, and transfers" which he had been given earlier that evening. The Pope died sometime between his final meal, and dawn the following day. His body was found by a nun, Sister Vincenza, shortly after 4.45am when she returned to his study to collect a flask of coffee she had served 15 minutes earlier and found it untouched. Sister Vincenza had worked for Albino Luciani for almost twenty years, since his appointment as Patriarch of Venice by Pope Paul VI in December 1969, and was familiar with his habits. She entered his bedroom when there was no response, and found him seated upright in his bed, wearing reading glasses and holding several sheets of paper. She checked his pulse, then immediately called Fr. Lorenzi and several other nuns who also served the Pope.

The controversy begins here. An ANSA report quoted the Pope's younger brother, Eduardo Luciani, who confirmed Sister Vincenza's account of how the body was found. However, the official Vatican announcement, issued shortly after 8.30am, differs sharply, stating that Fr. Magee had entered the Pope's bedroom at 5.30am, when he failed to appear for morning prayers in his private chapel, and "found him dead in bed with the lights on, as if he were reading" while Vatican spokesman, Fr. Romeo Panciroli, categorically denied the ANSA dispatch as being "without any foundation in fact." After failing to agree on the time Luciani's body was discovered, and by whom, the allegations, suggestions, and contradictions multiply. Yallop claims the Pope's personal effects, including slippers and glasses, were removed by Cardinal Villot, to cover-up evidence of poisoning, while British author, John Cornwell, a former seminarian who abandoned the Catholic faith after post-graduate studies at Christ's College Cambridge in the mid-1960s, before re-affirming his spiritual roots two decades later, claims in his book, *A Thief in the Night*, that Pope John Paul died of a pulmonary embolism "possible brought on by overwork." He suggests that the Pope had died at his desk at 9.30pm or even later, and his body was found by Don Diego and Pat Magee, who moved it to the bedroom, and placed it upright to suggest he died of a heart attack while reading, in order to cover-up serious health problems, including chest pains and a coughing fit, consistent with imminent pulmonary embolism, for which Luciani had continuously refused medical treatment. Both Diego and Magee denied Cornwell's account, including claims that the body was extremely cold and rigor mortis had set in by the time it was found, despite high temperatures in Rome that autumn, which, Cornwell suggests, was behind the decision to embalm the Pope as soon as possible, a procedure which began that evening at 7pm, while Yallop claims the embalmers were called at 5am, and least 30 minutes before the Vatican's official time of discovery.

Yallop's suggestion that Pope John Paul was murdered, and that the alleged homicide primarily benefited Paul Marcinkus, and his corrupt Masonic religious and lay colleagues, is supported by the French theologian, Abbe George de Nantes, whose account is based on interviews with friends and colleagues who knew Luciani before and after his election. Abbe de Nantes, is a traditionalist and founder of the Catholic League of Counter Reformation, and despite his hardcore differences with the Vatican on what he considered fundamental teachings of the Church, including Luciani's "liberal views on artificial birth control," his narrative is a genuine attempt to discover the truth. Robert Hutchinson agrees with David Yallop and De Nantes, stating that Pope John Paul "was unlikely to have died from natural causes and - in spite of all that has been written and said on the subject - the indications are strong that a cover-up of the real cause of death was engineered by a Vatican clique convinced it was acting to protect the Church and her sacred teachings." He also describes the "scrambling that followed for his succession" to maintain the pre-Luciani status quo at the IOR and among Curia traditionalists, as a "minutely-prepared coup d'etat."

A Scandal That Just Keeps Giving

"Never has the sense of disorientation in the Catholic Church reached these levels of systemic disorder," wrote historian, Alberto Melloni, in *Corriere della Sera*, in May, 2012, following the arrest of Pope Benedict's personal valet, Paolo Gabriele, by members of the Corpo di Vigilenza (CdV), the Vatican's police force, when he arrived for work at the papal apartments in the Apostolic Palace behind St. Peter's Square. Described as a "devout Catholic" who was "intensely loyal" to the Pope for whom he worked since 2006, he was taken into custody one month after a three-strong Vatican commission - headed by the President Emeritus of the Pontifical Council for Legislative Texts, Spanish Cardinal Julian Herranz, a member of Opus Dei, and colleagues Cardinal Josef Tomko, Prefect Emeritus of the Congregation for the Evangelization of Peoples, and Cardinal Salvatore De Giorgi, Archbishop Emeritus of Palermo - was given "full pontifical mandate" to work with the CdV following the publication of confidential, private documents detailing a power struggle and bitter personal feuds at the highest level within the Curia. Among the files recovered from 'Paoletto' Gabriele's home were copies of personal letters from the former deputy governor of Vatican City, Archbishop Carlo Maria Vigano, to Pope Benedict, and the Vatican's Secretary of State, Cardinal Tarcisio Bertone, in which he asked not to be appointed as papal nuncio to the US. In his letter Cardinal Bertone - who resigned his position, along with other heads of Curia departments, when the Holy See became vacant with the resignation of Pope Benedict, on 28 February 2013 - also accused senior Vatican officials of "nepotism" and claimed contracts were awarded to favored Italian companies at inflated prices.

The allegations were described as "absolutely without foundation or plausibility" by the Vatican's 'spin doctor', Fr. Lombardi, who then threatened legal action against the Italian broadcaster, La 7, while Italian media sources, well-versed in Vatican intrigue, claimed Gabriele would not have "masterminded the leak," pointing out that there was no personal or financial motive involved, and possession of the "Vatican State's secrets" proved very little, except their unauthorized removal from the Pope's apartments. Paolo Rodari, a specialist on papal affairs, quoted on the Italian online news site, *World of Technology*, claimed that the Pope's valet had been made a scapegoat, and while some of the documents found in his possession were from the Pope's personal correspondence, most of the leaked papers, including the copy of Bertone's letter to Benedict, "had come from the Secretary of State's office, and he [Gabriele] would not have access to those."

Once again the influence of Opus Dei shrouds Vatican affairs. Cardinal Julian Harranz, a graduate of the University of Barcelona, and professor of Canon Law at the University of Navarra, before moving to Rome in 1960, and serving as president of the Vatican's Pontifical Council for the Interpretation of Legislative Texts, from 1994 to 2007, is one of two Opus

Dei cardinals in the Curia, the other being the Archbishop of Lima, Juan Luis Cipriani (who subscribes to the notion that homosexuality is a "curable disease" and has campaigned against same-sex marriage legislation in Spain and elsewhere). Many of the leaked documents referred to in the La 7 report appeared to discredit Cardinal Bertone's efforts to tackle cronyism and to improve transparency within the IOR. These latest allegations of Vatican corruption may also have been part of a power struggle to topple Bertone, who was arguably the most powerful man in the Curia, in anticipation of Pope Benedict's abdication or death. "Totally unexpected" was the comment most commonly used by Vatican correspondents to describe Benedict's retirement. The last Pope to "step down from the Cross" was Gregory XII, who was forced out of office in 1417, in order to heal a schism when two men claimed to be the "one true successor to St. Peter." Benedict was visibly weakening, however, and there are those who take account of such changes, and plan accordingly. Opus Dei failed, however, to influence the election of Benedict's successor, the Argentinean Jesuit priest, Jorge Bergoglio, who chose the papal name, Francis I - a man described by colleagues as a capable administrator and "friend of the poor," but a conservative on important issues like abortion, contraception and gay relationships.

The Italian media has claimed that the Harranz commission had concluded that at least five others, apart from Gabriele, were part of the 'Vatican leaks plot', while Cardinal Bertone tried to distance himself from the affair, describing the whole sorry mess as a "ferocious and targeted campaign" against Benedict's papacy. Not all the purloined papers were found in Gabriele's apartment. Some were leaked to journalist, Gianluigi Nuzzi, and used in his latest book, *Sua Santita* ('His Holiness'), which includes details of Benedict's personal correspondence with the former head of the IOR, Gotti Tedeschi, and claims that hypocrisy within the Vatican, including how sexual abuse cases have been handled, "goes unchallenged and scandals multiply." Nuzzi is an experienced journalist on Vatican affairs, despite suggestions by the Catholic media that his knowledge is "scant." He has collaborated with several Italian newspapers, including *Corriere della Sera*, the conservative, Milan-based, daily magazine, *il Giornale,* and the right-wing, weekly news magazine, *Panorama*, owned by Fininvest, the financial holding company of the former Italian prime minister, Silvio Berlusconi, who, despite controversy and multiple court cases throughout his political career, remains a powerful, populist influence in Italian politics, heading a right-wing coalition which won 125 seats in the Chamber of Deputies, and 117 seats in the Senate in the February 2013 general election.

Nuzzi says he was approached by "sources inside the Vatican" who provided him with the documents, many of them uncomplimentary to Tarcisio Bertone, which are the basis of his book. Also included was a 2010 memo to Pope Benedict from Cardinal Velasio De Paolis, the head of a Vatican delegation to the Legion of Christ and its lay affiliate, Regnum Christi, warning that the situation facing the religious order, including the scandal over its deceased pedophile founder, Fr Marcial Maciel, "while not grave is serious and pressing." To those who suffered at the hands of the Mexican priest, the matter is probably the gravest and most serious thing that has happened to them in their lives, and De Paolis's memo brings to mind previous suggestions that the close relationship between Maciel and Benedict's predecessor, Pope John Paul II, contributed to the CDF's lackadaisical attitude and commitment when sexual abuse allegations where first made against Maciel in the late 1970s.

Cardinal De Paolis was named as president of the Prefecture for the Economic Affairs of the Holy See in April 2008, and has been an outspoken critic of the best-selling novels of Dan Brown, accusing the American author of "turning the gospels upside down and poisoning the faith," adding that Brown's fiction "wounds common religious feelings." An interesting outburst, coming at a time when young boys and girls were being raped and sodomized by "men of the cloth," and who were being ignored by those anonymous dark-robed prelates who move in clusters through the Vatican and its environs like a murder of crows.

The overworked Vatican spokesman, Fr. Federico Lombardi, has described Nuzzi's latest book as an "objectively defamatory" work that "clearly assumes characters of a criminal act" and warned that the Curia, working with the Italian authorities and international agencies, would seek co-operation in the "quest for justice" - a damage-limitation legal threat, couched in language designed to dissuade English-language publishers from purchasing the translation rights.

The treatment of the unfortunate Paolo Gabriele served as an example of the Vatican's intentions. A 35-page indictment, issued by a Rome magistrate. on 13 August 2012, ordered that the former valet should stand trial for the theft and "unauthorized dissemination" of some of the private papers taken from the Pope's apartments. Also named on the charge sheet was a second Vatican employee, Claudio Sciarpelletti, a computer expert who was accused of aiding and abetting Gabriele after an envelope allegedly containing sensitive material was found on his desk. Sciarpelletti's detention was a distraction. He was not an important accomplice, and spent only 24 hours in CdV custody. The indictment against Gabriele, however, included a charge of aggravated theft relating to a check for $123,000 made out to Benedict, a golden nugget, and a 16th century translation of Virgil's *Aeneid*. When questioned by the Vatican's commission of inquiry following his arrest last May, Gabriele told Cardinal Harranz and his colleagues that he wanted to "expose and expunge the Church of evil and corruption." He claimed the Holy Father was not "adequately informed" - presumably by men like Bertone and Harranz - and having seen evil and corruption everywhere he had finally "reached a point of degeneration" and could no longer control himself. He described himself as an "infiltrator acting on behalf of the Holy Spirit" and believed that leaking the documents to the media would "shock the Church into returning to the right track." He described the theft of the items unrelated to his quest for justice as a "consequence of the degeneration of my disorder." Unfortunately, the 'Holy Spirit' cannot be subpoenaed to testify, and divine intervention, or inspiration, was unlikely to be accepted as a mitigating circumstance. And while in this case, at least, the butler admits he did it, he was most likely the 'fall guy' in a campaign to discredit some powerful individuals in the Curia with access to the Pope, similar to Operation *SCIV*, which undermined the influence and judgment of Cardinal Caseroli.

Paolo Gabriele's trial began on 2 October 2012 in the small, wood-paneled courtroom in a palazzo behind St. Peter's Basilica, a corner of the Vatican which is off-limits to the general public. After four days of hearings and two hours deliberation, Judge Guiseppe Dalla Torre, one of three judges who heard the case, pronounced the impassive butler guilty as charged and sentenced him to 18 months house arrest. Gabriele's lawyer, Christiana Arru, told the court that only photocopies, not original documents, were taken, disputing the testimony of the Pope's private secretary, Monsignor Georg Ganswein, who claimed he had seen "original letters" among the 82 boxes of documents seized by gendarmes from the butler's home, including encoded diplomatic communiqués from the Secretariat of State to papal nuncios around the world, and papers which bore Benedict's signature, on which "to be destroyed" had been written in German.

One of the unexpected consequences of the trial was Gabriele's disclosure of the harsh and disorientating conditions in which he was initially held - a tiny room less than two meters wide at gendarme headquarters, where the overhead lights burned for 24 hours for the first 15-20 days, leaving the prisoner depressed, and damaging his vision. Fr. Lombardi claimed that Gabriele had been held under "suicide watch" and his incarceration "conformed to international standards," although no evidence was presented to suggest the devout Catholic manservant was suicidal. Lombardi wasn't questioned on the matter by any of the restricted number of carefully-selected religious correspondents allowed to attend the trial, who were no doubt anxious to be allowed to return the following day to continue reporting on the charade.

"No one believes Gabriele was a lone whistleblower," says journalist and author, Marco Politi. The Vatican wanted to "close this case rapidly, so the trial was political and the sentence was mild to put an end to the matter." The judge did not investigate Gabriele's contacts outside the Papal State, and blocked him when he said the Pope had been asking about things he [Benedict] should have known about. Speaking to local journalists, Politi said the scandal had done "enormous damage [by] shedding light on corruption, conflicts between Benedict's secretary of state and senior cardinals and clashes over the need for transparency at the Vatican bank." Only Opus Dei emerges from these affairs more influential within the Curia, unscathed, and with its anonymity intact. This uncompromising, fundamentalist Catholic movement was once compared to the clandestine Freemason Brotherhood by the Austrian-born Superior General of the Society of Jesus, Fr. Wlodimir Ledochowski, prior to his death in the early 1940s, a man described in the *New York Times*, on 10 December 1942 (in an obituary actually published three days before he died), as "one of the two or three greatest heads of the Jesuit Order." Ledochowski's warning fell on deaf ears, and since then the influence of the Jesuits has waned, despite the election of Jorge Bergoglio to fill the vacancy left by Benedict, while Opus Dei is now the most powerful organization within the Roman Catholic Church, and still the most secretive.

The Vatican is a foreign place. Things are done differently there. What passes for an exercise in democracy - the papal conclave of succession - is based on a system introduced by Pope Gregory X in 1274, who was chosen in 1271 after an election which lasted for four years. Some changes have taken place since then. The electorate is limited to cardinals under 80 years of age, and a two-thirds majority is required to elect the "Vicar of Christ" - a traditional term, with several semantic variants, referring to the pastoral duty of the Holy Father, the Bishop of Rome. And that's as far as democracy goes in the Papal State. A secret process, taking place behind the imposing facade of the Sistine Chapel, while the faithful obediently stand and wait in St. Peter's Square until white smoke signals the election of a new pope, and then they applaud. It's the traditional greeting, and the Roman Catholic Church is steeped in tradition, which includes the systemic cover-up, for hundreds of years, of the physical and sexual abuse of minors. Without clear and precise instruction from the Roman Curia and the CDF, the bishops have been blamed for the failure to take responsibility for the deviants who have taken Holy Orders and have then betrayed the trust of the faithful. And, in so many well-documented cases, there has been no repentance, and a total lack of concern for the young lives and the families they have destroyed. Papal infallibility is a dogma of the Catholic Church. At a lower level this spiritual hubris has been used by rank-and-file clerical abusers to place themselves outside and above temporal law, convincing themselves, and attempting to convince others, that they are answerable only to a "higher authority" for the "sins of the flesh" - that forgiveness and repentance is for the confessional, and absolution is only for God.

The Catholic Church is being forced to face up to the fact that the global view of this state of affairs is changing, changing slowly. Priests have been found guilty before juries of their peers and have served time, or are currently incarcerated. In July 2012, in Philadelphia Common Pleas Court, Msgr. William Lynn, the former secretary for the clergy in the archdiocese of Philadelphia, and senior aide to Cardinal Anthony Bevilacqua, was sentenced to three-to-six years, by Judge M. Teresa Sarmina, for protecting "monsters in clerical garb who molested children"- the highest-ranking clergyman convicted in the US Catholic Church sexual abuse scandals. Lynn, described as a "master of deception" by lead prosecutor, Assistant DA, Patrick Blessington, oversaw the work of 800 priests, and covered-up criminal and predatory allegations by transferring priests to unsuspecting parishes.

The case has been followed closely in the Vatican, among officials in the CDF and the Office of the Secretary of State. However, the failure of the IOR to be recognized as a legitimate, transparent, financial institution is probably more damaging, in the long term, than the child abuse scandals, because the Catholic Church needs the cash. Unfortunately, for the victims of predatory clerics and complacent bishops who facilitate their crimes, it's as simple and as complicated as that.

BIBLIOGRAPHY
Berry, Jason and Renner, Gerald. *Vows of Silence*. New York: Free Press, 2004
Cornwell, John. *A Thief in the Night*. London: Penguin Books Ltd, 1990.
Cornwell, Rupert. *God's Banker*. London: Unwin Hyman Ltd., 1984.
Dawkins, Richard. *The God Delusion*. London: Transworld Publishers, 2006.
Doyle, Paddy. *The God Squad*. London: Corgi Books, 1989.
Follain, John. *City of Secrets*. New York: HarperCollins, 2003.
Hutchinson, Robert. *Their Kingdom Come*. London: Corgi Books, 1997.
Marinelli, Luigi. *Shroud of Secrecy*. Toronto: Key Porter Books, 2000.
Mooney, Tom. *All the Bishops' Men*. Cork: The Collins Press, 2011.
Moore, Chris. *Betrayal of Trust*. Dublin: Marino Books, 1995.
O'Connor, Alison. *A Message from Heaven*. Dingle: Brandon Books, 2000.
Rafferty, Mary and O'Sullivan, Eoin. *Suffer the Little Children*. Dublin: New Island Books, 1999.
Robinson, Geoffrey. *The Case of the Pope*. London: Penguin Book, 2010.
Saunders, Frances Stoner. *The Woman Who Shot Mussolini*. London: Faber & Faber, 2010.
Short, Martin. *Inside the Brotherhood*. London: Grafton Books, 1989.
Tornielli, Andrea. *Benedicto XVI: El Custodio dela Fe*. Madrid: Aguilar Publications, 2005.
Touher, Patrick. *Fear of the Collar*. Dublin: O'Brien Press, 1991.
Tyrrell, Peter. *Founded on Fear*. Dublin: Irish Academic Press, 2006.
Walsh, Martin. *The Secret World of Opus Dei*. London: Grafton Books, 1989.
Willan, Philip. *Puppetmasters*. San Jose: Authors Choice Press, 2002.
Yallop, David. *The Power and the Glory*. London: Constable, 2007.
Yallop, David. *Beyond Belief*. London: Constable, 2010.
Yallop, David. *In God's Name*. London: Jonathan Cape, 1984.

NEWSPAPERS & MAGAZINES
Age (www.theage.au)
Baltimore Sun (www.baltimoresun.com)
Der Spiegel (www.spiegel.de)
Globe and Mail (www.globaadvisor.com)
Irish Independent (www.independent.ie)
La Repubblica (www.repubblica.it)

La Stampa (www.lastampa.it)
New York Times (www.nytimes.com)
Philadelphia Inquirer (www.philly.com)

ONLINE OFFICIAL REPORTS & OTHER SOURCES
ABC News (www.abcnews.go.uk)
Canadian Encyclopedia (www.thecanadianencyclopedia.com)
Catholic News Agency (www.catholicnewsagency.com)
Ferns Report (www.bishop-accountability.org/ferns/)
Legion of Christ (www.legionariesofchrist.org/eng/articulos)
Magdalene Laundries Report (www.justice.ie/JELR/Pages/MagdalenRpt2013)
Mea Maxima Culpa, (dir. Alex Gibney) Dublin: Element Pictures, 2013.
National Catholic Register (www.ncregister.com)
Online Catholic News (www.catholicculture.org)
Ryan Report (www.childabusecommission.ie)
UN Resolution 263, session 54, 25 March 2000 (www.undemocracy.com/a-res-54-263)
World Aeronautical Press Agency (www.avionews.com)
World of Technology (www.worldoftechnology.it)

CHAPTER SEVEN

THE BUTCHER'S APRON

"War is not its own end, except in some catastrophic slide into absolute damnation. It's peace that's wanted. Some better peace than the one you started with."
Lois McMaster Bujold, *The Vor Game*

Unclenched Fists

Somewhere in England, in spring 2007, Peter Keeley, a convicted petty thief from Newry, County Down, in the North of Ireland, now living in unnecessary anonymity in a London suburb because of what he claims are 'credible' threats by persons unknown - shadows from his clandestine past - saw a published photograph of Jonathan Evans, the newly-appointed director-general of the British Security Service, MI5, and thought he recognized 'Bob', his intelligence handler when Evans was based in Belfast in the late 1980s, and Keeley, using the name 'Kevin Fulton', was a Force Research Unit (FRU) agent inside the Provisional IRA.

Peter Keeley is one of the 'abandoned' spies, flotsam from the 'dirty war' in the North of Ireland, washed ashore and beached by the peace process. He's a sad figure of a man whose only remaining task is to propagate the myth that he and several others like him made a difference, when in actual fact the only remaining legacy of British covert operations during the 'Troubles' is a rather impressive body count.

The myth-making would not be possible to the degree with which it has imposed itself on the history of the conflict without the help of complacent journalists who convinced themselves they were part of a secretive cabal, a privileged few given access to what they were told was the 'bigger picture', rather than gullible hacks whose 'penmanship' wouldn't matter a damn if the British Ministry of Defense (MoD) in Whitehall had honored its agreement with its former employees and provided them with new identities, relocation and financial security. However, there are honorable exceptions among members of the 'fourth estate', and Keeley's credibility has been challenged and found wanting on several occasions while Evans (who retired last April) was in charges at Thames House in central London This hasn't done his claim for compensation, or those of his colleagues, any favors, however righteous their grievances with the MoD may be. After all, the Ministry employed these men when the going was tough during the long war with the Provos, and abandoned them, so they claim, when peace became the only option.

This wasn't always the case. There was a time when Keeley, as Fulton, wearing a balaclava and 'shades', sometimes in silhouette for full dramatic effect, appeared quite regularly on British television, including the BBC World Service's 30-minute Hardtalk program, to expand on what he claimed was yet another example of duplicity and hardcore brutality on the part of the Provos, and how the organization couldn't, or shouldn't, be trusted in war or peace. These appearances often coincided with sensitive, top-level talks involving the political leadership of the Republican Movement and senior representatives from London and Dublin, with officials from the Clinton administration in the background, urging the protagonists to reach a compromise on what the international media described as "old hatreds." Eventually, the process resulted in the Belfast Agreement, two inter-related documents, both signed on Good Friday, 10 April 1998.

One of the documents was a multi-party agreement involving most of the political parties in the North, with the exception of the Democratic Unionists, led by Dr Ian Paisley. This agreement was approved by the vast majority in a referendum six weeks later, and ratified by the Irish Government on the same day, 23 May 1998. Doing so involved an amendment whereby the Irish Constitution relinquished a decades-old claim of jurisdiction over the North. The present 'constitutional status' of the North within the United Kingdom, and the region's joint executive, power-sharing system of government, is based on the Belfast Agreement. And it has worked surprisingly well, with the two political parties from opposite ends of the political spectrum, the anti-agreement DUP and Sinn Fein - often referred to as the "political wing of the IRA" - sharing power, based on their respective electoral mandates and genuine mutual respect. It produced a rare and wonderful image of the hard-line, fundamentalist, Protestant preacher, Reverend Paisley, founder of the DUP, the administration's First Minister, sharing a joke on the steps of Stormont Castle with his deputy, Martin McGuinness, a former IRA volunteer in Derry City in the early 1970s, and later a member of the Provisional's Northern Command, which was responsible for military operations in the 'war zone.'

And that was the 'unofficial' end of Operation *Banner,* which began with the deployment of 250 British soldiers in the Lower Falls area of Belfast, in August 1969, to prevent sectarian violence when nationalist areas were attacked, trashed and petrol-bombed by loyalist mobs. The scaling down of the military presence on the streets, the closure of bases, and the demolition of a network of surveillance sites along the border with the Irish Republic continued for several years until *Banner* officially ended on 31 July 2007, with the lowering of the colors of the 39th Brigade inside Thiepval Barracks, Lisburn, the operational headquarters of the British Army in Northern Ireland for thirty-eight years.

Despite being one of the best-documented, post-WWII conflicts in British military history, the exact number of combatant fatalities in not known. According to the University of Ulster's CAIN project, the Provisional IRA was responsible for the deaths of 1,824 people, a figure representing 48.6 percent of the total. This included 928 members of the British Armed Forces, comprising the British Army - including the locally-recruited Ulster Defense Regiment (UDR) - the Territorial Army, the Royal Irish Regiment (an amalgamation of the Royal Irish Rangers and the UDR, formed in 1992), four Royal Air Force (RAF) officers killed in attacks in Germany and the Netherlands, one member of the Royal Navy, and 272 members of the Royal Ulster Constabulary (RUC). The IRA lost 276 volunteers, including 103 killed in premature explosions by their own devices (105 according to an RUC 1993 report), and 11 on hunger strikes in Irish and British prisons.

According to *Lost Lives*, a reference work published in 2004 by four journalists who covered the Troubles, the Provos were responsible for the deaths of 1,781, including 944 members of the security forces, while 294 Provisional IRA volunteers died, around 150 killed by the British Army, and approximately 50 by the RUC, UDR and loyalist paramilitaries, with the remainder dying in self-inflicted accidents while handling unstable explosives. The Irish Republican Movement's newspaper, *An Phoblacht*, gives a figure of 341 republican dead, which includes between 50 and 60 Sinn Fein members. At least 1,854 civilians, the majority of whom were deliberately targeted, died during the 38 year conflict, and almost 30,000 were injured, many suffering serious physical and psychological damage.

The first soldier to die was Private Robert Curtis, aged 20, shot on 6 February 1971, by an IRA sniper while on foot patrol on the New Lodge Road in Belfast. Lance Bombardier Stephen Restorick was the last soldier to die, killed while manning a vehicle check point near the village of Bessbrook, County Armagh. The British Army claims to have killed 301 people, including 138 nationalist civilians and 20 loyalists, but these figures don't take into account the deaths of republicans murdered by loyalist gunmen - trained, armed and managed by the FRU. The number of all services (Army, Navy and RAF) casualties is also disputed. The MoD figure is 763, but in a letter to the London-based, *Daily Telegraph*, newspaper (the preferred daily publication of the MoD top brass) in 2000, a former Army medic, Sergeant John Black, claimed that almost 70 soldiers killed by the IRA, during undercover operations or in friendly fire incidents, are not listed as official casualties. One example is the death of SAS officer, Captain Julian Ball. The MoD claims he died in a traffic accident while stationed in the Gulf. He was actually shot dead in an IRA ambush, and was quietly buried in the Scottish capital, Edinburgh.

An internal MoD analysis, written by three senior officers, and released under the Freedom of Information Act, suggests that the British political and military establishment is in denial about the conflict and its legacy - similar to the trauma experienced in the United States following the withdrawal from Vietnam. General Sir Michael David Jackson is the only identified 'author' of the MoD's post-conflict analysis. Jackson is a man who knows a thing or two about revisionist history, even if this 'need to know' account was only intended for those "who require the information in the course of their official duties." Originally commissioned into the Intelligence Corps (Int. Corps) in 1963 at the age of 19, Jackson later transferred to the Parachute Regiment and was on the ground in Derry City, on 30 January 1972, as adjutant to senior command, when unarmed civil-rights demonstrators were shot dead by the members of the Parachute Regiment. Despite knowing the truth of what happened that destructive afternoon, Jackson accepted Lord Justice Widgery's highly-selective and blatantly dishonest account of the murderous behavior of the 1st Battalion.

He said nothing at all, as far as we know, until twice called to testify before a second tribunal of inquiry, almost 30 years later, shortly before the former Supreme Court Justice, Lord Saville, produced his report, stating that the soldiers had "lost control" and had "caused the deaths of 13 people and injury to a similar number, none of whom posed a threat of causing death or serious injury." The Army had fatally shot fleeing civilians and those who tried to aid the wounded, none of whom had been warned by the British soldiers that they were about to open fire, and that "contrary to previously established belief none of the soldiers fired in response to attacks by petrol bombers or stone throwers." Gen. Jackson, who had been appointed Chief of the General Staff (CGS) the professional head of the British Army, in 2003, mumbled an apology and reluctantly admitted that the Paras had "killed without justification."

Too little, and far too late from a soldier who was untroubled by the truth and would have allowed Widgery's version of events to become the official history of the Paras' murderous charge into the Bogside, had former Labour prime minister, Tony Blair, not convened the Saville Tribunal. So it is not surprising that Sir Mike, as he likes to be called, was the senior and most experienced officer of the three chosen by the MoD, under the direction of his CGS successor, Sir Richard Dannatt, to analyze *Banner* and produce a report under Army Code 71842. The only lesson the British Army appears to have learned from the events on 'Bloody Sunday', according to the analysis, is not to use armored vehicles when mounting an arrest operation in a built-up area. Incredibly, Bloody Sunday, and an illegal three-day curfew in the Lower Falls in mid-1970, are the only two examples of "poor military decision-making" mentioned in the document.

The authors appear to be linguistically challenged when it comes to defining exactly what the military was involved in. Operation *Banner* is described as a "peace mission," but there is also reference to the conflict as a "working-class war" between republicans and loyalists, to "the Troubles" and to an "insurgency campaign" waged by republicans, while the tactical military decisions which produced these results are described as "war winners" and high-level discussions as "war-gaming" - hardly the language of a peace mission.

The Provisional IRA is described as a "professional, dedicated, highly-skilled and resilient force" and one of the "most effective terrorist organizations in history" while loyalist paramilitary groups, and republican splinter organizations are described as "little more than a collection of gangsters." A quarter-of-a-million British soldiers served in the Northern Ireland, 10,000 on foot and in mobile patrol across the province on any given day in the 1970s. The worst year for the British Army was 1972, when the Provos responded to Bloody Sunday and Operation *Motorman* (re-taking the 'no-go' areas of Derry and Belfast) by killing 102 soldiers. The British Army "did not 'win' in any recognisable way," according to Israeli military theorist, Martin Levi van Creveld (the author of 17 books on military history and strategy) but had "shown the IRA that it could not achieve its ends through violence."

The MoD's analysis was obtained by the Pat Finucane Centre (PFC), a Belfast-based legal and human rights organization named after the Belfast solicitor, Patrick Finucane, who was shot dead by loyalist gunmen on 12 February 1989. The killing was one of the most controversial of the Troubles, a catalyst which finally focused international attention, at the United Nations in New York and on Capitol Hill in Washington, DC, on allegations of collusion between the security forces and loyalist paramilitary groups, previously dismissed in the mainstream media, at home and abroad, as republican propaganda. The PFC described the MoD's analysis as betraying a "profoundly colonial mindset towards the conflict here and those involved it" in which "loyalist violence and the links between loyalist paramilitaries and the State" have been "airbrushed out of this military history." Nowhere in this 100-page document is there any mention of the Military Reconnaissance Force (MRF), the 14th Field Security and Intelligence Company (14FSIC), or the FRU.

A Terrible Beauty

Almost from the beginning of the Troubles there was no real attempt to convince the minority nationalist/republican community - hundreds of whom had been burned out of their homes on the fringes of the Falls, while several thousand had fled in fear before the troops arrived in August 1971 - that things would change. The Unionist sectarian administration, uncompromising political masters for almost 50 years, was having none of it. Despite the well-marketed photo opportunities of soldiers sharing tea and biscuits with mothers, wives, sisters and girlfriends (the men folk are conspicuously absent in many of the photographs) the British Army's urban deployment strategists took their cue from the sectarian RUC, and regarded the nationalist districts of Belfast as hostile. The illegal 3-day military curfew on the Lower Falls in July 1970 began with troops from the Black Watch Regiment and the Life Guards, under the command of Army GOC, Lieutenant-General Sir Ian Freeland, moving into the area to conduct a weapons search and developed into a series of gun battles with the Official IRA, in which more than 70 people, including 15 soldiers, were wounded. In the following month, Operation *Demetrius* -

the mass arrest and internment of 342 people suspected of being involved with either the Official or Provisional IRA, during which eleven civilians were shot dead by the Paras in the Ballymurphy area of Belfast, while eight others also died across the North between the 9 and 13 August - finally put an end to the hopeless illusion that *Banner* was a peace-keeping operation.

Internment failed to end the low-intensity violence and civil rights protests. However, even today it is difficult to understand what the MRF was supposed to achieve - except make matters worse - when a decision was taken by senior British officers to expand operations from clandestine surveillance to the "destruction of armed groups and their supporters," as defined by Brigadier Frank Kitson, the Army's counterinsurgency expert. Perhaps the decision to send plainclothes military patrols in unmarked civilian vehicles into the republican heartland of West Belfast to carry out drive-by shootings was nothing more than a revengeful response to the bloody failure of the covert *Four Square Laundry* and *Lipstick* reconnaissance operations.

Four Square Laundry was a simple yet sophisticated operation, based at Palace Barracks and under the control of General Sir Harry Tuzo. It took several months for the Provos (the only republican armed group still active), with the help of a double-agent working for the MRF, to uncover what was going on. A former IRA Chief of Staff, Sean Mac Stiofain, later described it as "an application of the principle that any rounds-man's business is excellent cover for this kind of work," and because laundry vans are usually large "there is a good excuse to have a vehicle capable of holding several men and their equipment." The green Morris van used by the MRF, with the white FOUR SQUARE lettering stenciled on the side, consisted of a driver, a female helper, and two 22 SAS Regiment (Special Air Service/Regular Army) troopers, concealed in a compartment beneath the roof who took photographs of houses, residents, streets and vehicles when the van toured the nationalist housing estates, collecting laundry at a cheaper rate than its legitimate competitors. Back at Palace Barracks the clothes were forensically examined for traces of blood, firearms and explosives residue, while laundry lists were compared to previous collections which might indicate the presence of a man in a house where none was supposedly resident, before 'the wash' was sent to be cleaned by another laundry under contract to the British Army, and then returned to the customer.

On 2 October 1972, at 11.15am, as the laundry van drove through Juniper Street approaching the Twinbrook Estate, a blue Ford car containing two members of an IRA Active Service Unit (ASU) ambushed the vehicle, killing the two SAS observers and the driver, Sapper Ted Stuart, seconded to the MRF from the SAS. The female member of the operation, Corporal Sarah Warke, belonging to the Women's Royal Army Corps (WRAC), escaped into a nearby house, claiming loyalist gunmen were trying to kill her, and was later taken from the scene by plainclothes RUC Special Branch officers. Stuart and Warke had posed as brother and sister, and shared a flat on the Antrim Road near the Four Square Laundry office, above an evangelical bookshop on College Square East, in the city center. Eighteen months later Cpl. Warke was awarded the Military Medal, 'in absentia', for her part in the FSL operation,

Within hours of hitting the laundry van, another IRA ASU raided the Gemini Heath Studios on the Antim Road, one of two massage parlors (the other in the hardline, loyalist dominated East Belfast, across the River Lagan) being run by the MRF, killing another two undercover agents. The exact function of the massage parlors, which advertised their services in the pro- unionist *Belfast Telegraph*, has never been fully established. The *Scottish Daily Mail* of 8 October 1972 suggested that cameras behind two-way mirrors were used to record clients in compromising situations, and "blackmail them afterwards to spy on the IRA." This is speculation, encouraged by the British Army's Lisburn HQ-based press office as part of the propaganda war. Nationalists read the *Irish News* not the *Telegraph*, and were unlikely to use the services of the "very attractive masseuses" on the Antrim Road (which would have meant a wide detour to avoid the hardline loyalist Shankill Road enclave) let alone travel across town at the height of the IRA's economic bombing campaign into East Belfast, where death, not sexual release, was a more likely option. If blackmail for low-grade intelligence was the object of the exercise, the targets were probably local unionist councilors, businessmen, or individuals with connections to the loyalist paramilitary, Ulster Volunteer Force (UVF). The MoD admitted one soldier died that day, the IRA claimed five undercover operatives were killed. The difference for this single incident explains why Sgt. Black decided to write to the *Daily Telegraph*, one man's attempt to put the record straight. And that was the end of the MRF's clandestine surveillance.

The unit had also been involved in several drive-by shootings in 1972, one of which had ended with the arrest, by a uniformed RUC patrol, of two plainclothes soldiers in an unmarked car, in possession of a Thompson submachine gun, a weapon associated with the IRA (in literature and song) in previous campaigns. One former Army NCO and member of the MRF, speaking to the French journalist, Roger Faligot, explained how he was posted away from his battalion to join the MRF, based at the 39th Infantry Brigade's Lisburn HQ. There, along with other senior NCOs, junior officers and members of the WRAC, he was instructed in the use of Russian AK47 assault rifles, the US-manufactured, gas-operated, selected-fire Armalite AR-18, and Thompson submachine guns. He pointed out that "all these weapons are favored by the Provos. I leave it to your imagination why Brigadier Kitson thought this was necessary, as these weapons were not standard issue for the British Army. We use the Browning pistol and the Sterling submachine gun only."

This twelve-year veteran provided details of several drive-by shootings, including the murder of Patrick McVeigh, in Riversdale Park, Andersonstown, on 12 May, and the wounding, a month later, of three taxi-drivers, who were standing near their vehicles, on the Glen Road, in the same

The Butcher's Apron

area, by shots fired from a blue Ford Cortina, which sped off down the Falls towards the city center. Another victim was 19-year-old Daniel Rooney, shot dead while walking with a friend along St James Crescent, off the Falls Road, on 27 September. Following this killing, the O/C of the 3rd Battalion Royal Green Jackets, Lt-Colonel Robin Evelegh, told the BBC (without fear of contradiction) that Rooney (who had no paramilitary connections) was a "notorious IRA sniper" who had got what he deserved. He admitted that "plain clothes patrols do operate" in nationalist areas of the city, "but their work is reconnaissance to know what the IRA is doing."

After the FSL fiasco it was only a matter of time before Gen. Tuzo realized the counter-productive nature of MRF operations and shut down the unit. But the Army's low intensity campaign of terror had wiped out any semblance of optimism that remained among the local nationalist population, or any benefit of the doubt that the British military presence might bring some sort of peace. After Ballymurphy, Bloody Sunday, and the clandestine MRF operations, the British Army was recognized as part of the problem. For many young men and women there was no choice but to take on the British on the ground. And the 'long war' was only three years old.

It was now the turn of the SAS, working alongside 14FSIC, to fill the murderous vacuum left by the MRF. Prior to the Troubles the SAS was the only British Army regiment with a history of intelligence and counterinsurgency. Founded in Egypt in 1941 by Captain David Stirling, of the Scots Guards, the SAS had been deployed in North Africa against Field Marshal Erwin Rommel's Afrika Korps; during the Malayan Emergency (with Commonwealth forces) from June 1948 to July 1960; and in Malaysia from 1962 to 1966 (where Frank Kitson earned his stripes). The SAS had also been deployed in the southern Oman province of Dhofar, from 1962 to 1976, to support the absolute monarch, Sultan Qaboos bin Said al Said, who had been educated in the art of warfare at Royal Military Academy, located in the small town of Sandhurst, about 34 miles from central London, and who had served in the Cameronians (Scottish Rifles) before returning home to overthrow his father, Said bin Taimur, in a palace coup in 1970.

The SAS slipped into Ireland after the Falls curfew from its base in the cathedral city of Hereford, on the River Wye, about 12 miles from the border with Wales, attached to the 39th Infantry Brigade, following six weeks special training at an Army base in Honiton, East Devon. The forty-five SAS troopers were joined by members of the Army's Intelligence Corp based (until 1997) at Templer Barracks, in Ashford, Kent, and the WRAC. The history of this group of 'anonymous' military personnel is not only one of intelligence gathering, but of wanton human rights abuses which included torture, kidnapping, and murder, according to Raymond Murray, a Catholic priest and human rights campaigner who, with colleague Fr. Denis Faul, co-authored more than thirty-three books, pamphlets and leaflets on the violations of human rights, and the part played by SAS 'deep interrogation' experts during questioning of alleged republican suspects at 8 Infantry Brigade HQ,

Ballykelly Barracks, near Derry City in 1971. The in-depth interrogation techniques employed on 14 detainees, who became known as the 'Hooded Men', included sensory deprivation and waterboarding. It was later condemned by the Strasbourg-based European Court of Human Rights (ECtHR) in a case brought by the Irish Government against HMG, under Article 3 of the European Convention on Human Rights, which prohibits torture and the "inhuman and degrading treatment and punishment" of prisoners, without exception or limitation. Hundreds of other republican detainees held after the introduction of internment at Palace Barracks in Holywood County Down, at Girdwood Barracks in Belfast, and at Gough Barracks in Armagh City, were also subjected to beatings, sleep deprivation, intense 'white noise' disorientation, and were made to stand spread-eagled against walls for extended periods by soldiers and RUC Special Branch officers. This cruel and abusive treatment of prisoners, as BBC journalist, Peter Taylor, points out in *Beating the Terrorists?*, was not only illegal under British and European human rights legislation:

> but politically counter-productive because it destroys confidence in the police without which law and order can never be effectively restored, Further, on a purely practical level, dangerous men may have gone free because they were beaten up in police custody and their statements therefore rejected in court. Finally, even if the end were to justify the means, the end has not been achieved. The IRA has not been defeated.

The most secret phase of the SAS deployment was its role with units like the MRF, including the FSL operation - an episode which SAS historians and the MoD have officially forgotten. In this period, from 1972 to 1976, the SAS worked closely with 14FSIC, which moved into the operations block left vacant by the MRF at Palace Barracks, which was so secretive, according to self-laudatory and proud former operative, James Rennie, that the true identities of its members, who had successfully completed the "physically, emotionally and intellectually demanding" selection process, were unknown "even to each other." No doubt the training helped the 'Ruperts' (Army slang for junior officers) cope with the emotional stress of 14FSIC's role in the Dublin/Monaghan no-warning car-bombings, in May 1974, in which 33 people died and hundreds were injured - the highest number of fatalities in a single operation during Operation *Banner* - as well as the Miami Showband massacre, and a series of cross-border kidnappings and assassinations.

One of the elite regiment's highly-trained troopers - enlisted and commissioned 'regulars' who volunteered for 'Special Ops' for 18-38 months before being transferred back to their parent regiment - was the late Capt. Juilian Ball, ex-Para, SAS and King's Own Scottish Borderers. Bell was in charge of 14FSIC's 3 Brigade, under the operative name 4 Field Survey Troop. His second-in-command was Captain Robert Nairac from the Grenadier

Guards, who acted as liaison with the SAS and with the 'gangsters' of the UVF, known locally as the 'Glenanne Gang', a name derived from a farm suspected of being used by the UVF as an arms dump and bomb-making site, in the parish of Glenanne, near Markethill, County Armagh, owned by an RUC reserve officer, James Mitchell. Information confirming that the farm had been used by the loyalist organization as an operational base, weapons depot and training facility was later published in an interim report by the Irish Senate into the bombing of Kay's Tavern in Dundalk, in December 1975, and was based on sworn statements by former RUC officer, John Weir, a member of the Special Patrol Group (SPG) who had joined the Glenanne Gang while stationed at Lisanelly Army Base in Omagh. Weir admitted being involved in the March 1976 bomb and shooting attack on Tully's Bar in Belleeks, County Armagh, and the attempted cross-border bombing of Renaghan's Bar in Clontibret, County Monaghan. He later served 15 years following his conviction, with fellow RUC SPG officer, William McCaughey, for the 1977 killing of a civilian, William Strathearn, a chemist shot dead in his small shop in Ahoghill, County Antrim.

The Glenanne Gang (also called *The Committee*, by journalist, Sean McPhilemy, in his book of the same name) was headed by Robin Jackson, one of the most ruthless psychopaths in the history of the Troubles. That's saying something considering the activities of the 'Shankill Butchers' led by a fanatical loyalist called Lenny Murphy, whose sectarian murder spree involved the kidnapping, torture and savage killings of more than thirty people. Most of the Shankill-based killers were eventually caught and convicted in 1979 to the longest combined sentences in British legal history for what Lord Justice O'Donnell described as a "lasting monument to blind sectarian bigotry." Murphy died on the streets he stalked, on 16 November 1982, when two IRA gunmen armed with a 9mm sub-machine gun and a .38 Special revolver emerged from the rear of a blue Morris Marine van as Murphy parked his mustard-colored Rover near his girlfriend's home in the Glencairn housing estate. The assassination took place deep in loyalist territory (in Belfast, topography is important) and the IRA's statement of responsibility mentioned Murphy's feud with the UVF, which suggests that the loyalist group might have "cleared the streets" to facilitate Murphy's execution by the Provos, who had been hunting him for several years.

Apart from Robin 'Jackal' Jackson, the Glenanne Gang - responsible for between 85 and 100 killings, between 1972 and 1976, in an estimated 54 bombing and shooting operations - consisted of thirty-four men and two women. The hardcore membership included several UDR soldiers - Captain William Hanna, Cpt. John Irwin, Sgt. James McDonnell, and Lance Cpl. Thomas Crozier - all of whom served with the regiment's C Company, 11th Battalion - three members of the RUC SPC, two regular RUC officers, including Sgt Gary Armstrong, and one police reservist. The UDR was the locally-recruited infantry regiment, which replaced the RUC B Specials, a sectarian militia that had acted as the military wing of the ruling Unionist Party since the founding of the Northern Ireland state in 1922. The sectarian state's existence was based on a blood covenant organized by Dublin-born Sir Edward Carson a decade earlier, which bound its signatories to resist Home Rule (from Dublin) by "all means necessary," including the *Special Powers Act*, much admired and copied by the South Africa National Party leader, Hendrik Verwoerd, during his period as prime minister of the brutally-repressive apartheid regime, from September 1958 until his assassination in September 1966.

The UDR became operational in 1970, and within two years this overwhelmingly loyalist/unionist regiment was the largest in the British Army, with its arsenal providing much of the firepower for the loyalist assassins. The UDR was disbanded in 1992, and those who remained full-time amalgamated with the Royal Irish Regiment to become the Royal Irish Rangers. The decision was for "purely military reasons" according to the MoD. However, even the mainstream British media conceded that the UDR had an "image problem," implying the change was some sort of "cosmetic make-over" given the fact that dozens of members had been involved in lawlessness ranging from assault to bombings, abduction and murder.

Jackson, along with UDR Capt. Billy Hanna (whom former Lisburn HQ-based British Army PsyOps officer, Colin Wallace, has claimed organized the Dublin/Monaghan car-bombings) was controlled by 14FSIC's Capt. Robert Nairac, according to a Yorkshire Television program, *Hidden Hand: The Forgotten Massacre*, broadcast in 1993. Nairac was reporting back to his O/C Capt. Julian Ball, which raises one of the many still unanswered questions about how the British political and military establishment fought the 'dirty war' in Ireland: who was Ball taking to?

The British Army GOC (General Officer Commanding) and Director of Operations in the North of Ireland from 1973 to 1975 - during which the Glenanne Gang carried out more than 40 operations including the Dublin/Monaghan bombings, the cross-border murder of IRA volunteer John Francis Green, and the Miami Showband killings -was Gen. Sir Frank King, who went on to command NATO's Northern Army Group, and the British Army on the Rhine. During his period in charge in Ireland, IRA bombing and shooting incidents decreased from approximately 12,000 annually to 2,500; however, the number of covert killings involving British military intelligence personnel increased. When King died in March 1998, he took to the grave what he knew about 14FSIC and its links to the Army's 'proxy' assassins. Maybe he knew nothing at all, and if that's the case he certainly wasn't, as the London-based *Times* described him in a laudatory obituary, "one of the best and most successful" director of operations, unless ignorance of what those under your command are doing is the mark of a successful leader of men. Surely, on a convivial evening in an officers' mess on a military base somewhere in the UK, someone would have talked?

Tory prime minister, David Cameron, apologized for Bloody Sunday, in a special session of the House of Commons, on 15 June 2011, because Lord Widgery's account was no longer credible. Too many crass contradictions.

Too many eye-witness accounts. Too many photographs. Too much 8mm and 16mm film and VTR footage in foreign newsrooms. If it wasn't Cameron, it might have been his Labour Party predecessor, Gordon Brown, or Tony Blair before him, had Lord Saville reported earlier. But someday a British prime minister may have to stand before the dispatch box in the House of Commons and apologize for the part played by British agents in the Dublin/Monaghan bombings, if a full and truthful report, with access to the still highly-classified MoD files, is ever published.

Maybe, or maybe not. Because what we are dealing with here is the brutal fact that men working for the government of one EU member state, deliberately contrived to kill and maim innocent civilians on the capital city streets of another.

A "Most Disturbing Story."

At 5.12pm, on 17 May 1974, an "arrogant and impatient" man reversed a green Hillman Avenger car into a parking space outside the Welcome Inn public house on Parnell Street in Dublin. The car was one of three hijacked in Belfast earlier that day. At approximately the same time on Talbot Street, which runs from the Dublin's main thoroughfare, O'Connell Street, to one of the city's busy railway stations on Amiens Street, a metallic-blue Ford Escort parked outside O'Neill's Shoe Shop, while across the River Liffey, on the south-side of the city, a blue Austin Maxi 1800 was parked on South Leinster Street, outside the walled playing fields of Trinity College. It was a sunny Friday afternoon, and the streets were crowded with the city's citizens and tourists when the three car-bombs exploded without warning within 90 seconds of each other, about 18 minutes after they had been parked on streets chosen for the maximum effect, in terms of physical casualties and psychological terror. Twenty-six people died (including a French student in town to attend a two-week English course, an Italian citizen killed at his brother's fish-and-chip shop, the Venezian Cafe, when the first bomb exploded, along with four members of the O'Brien family). About 90 minutes later, a green Hillman Minx, reported stolen from Portadown at 4.30pm according to the RUC, exploded outside Grechen's Pub, on North Road, Monaghan Town, while customers were watching 'breaking news' footage from the Dublin explosions on RTE, the national broadcasting station. Seven people died in this attack, (including a mother of four children working part-time in the pub's restaurant). Nineteen of the victims caught in the four bombings were female, ages ranging from 4 months to 80 years. In total more than 300 people were injured. An official report by the Irish Government's Joint Committee on Justice, Defense and Equality (JCJDC), chaired by retired Supreme Court Justice, Henry Barron, was published in December 2003, and described the bombings as "an act of international terrorism" - an unambiguous accusation, based on the available evidence, that agents of a foreign state were involved in these ruthless acts of terror.

The British Government refused repeated requests from Dublin to release official defense and intelligence files relating to the attack. At one point, Dr. John Reid, who had served as Secretary of State for Northern Ireland in the Blair administration from June 2003 to May 2005, sent a 16-page explanation to Dublin, claiming that release of the material could damage the security of the United Kingdom. In his report Justice Barron states that a suggestion that the British security forces could have been involved in the bombings is "neither fanciful or absurd, given the number of instances in which similar illegal activity has been proven." However, the lack of cooperation from London meant there was insufficient data to indict British Army personnel. The UVF, which claimed responsibility, had the capability, but "this does not rule out the involvement of individual RUC, UDR or British Army members," the report states.

The Monaghan bombing, according to Barron, "had all the hallmarks of a standard loyalist operation" requiring no assistance. However, it was "likely that members of the UDR and the RUC" either helped prepare the four car-bombs at the Glenanne farm "or were aware of these preparation," and while the possibility exists that the involvement of Army and RUC officers "was covered-up at the highest level," it is unlikely that such decisions "would ever have been committed to writing."

There was no paper trail, though the chain of command and responsibility runs from 14FSIC's base at Bessbrook to Lisburn HQNI, and the Intelligence and Security Group (ISC), an 'elite' cabal of officers controlling the Army's "more shadowy teams," including men like Nairac, and from there to the Defense Intelligence Desk, at MoD HQ on Northumberland Avenue, in Whitehall, (since renamed Special Forces Section at Room RM/3/67), and finally to the Joint Intelligence Committee (JIC), which has been part of the British Cabinet Office since 1957, with representation from MI6, MI5, the Cheltenham-based, SIGINT agency, GCHQ, and Defense Intelligence. The JIC is responsible for the overall direction and management of UK national security operations, and providing the PM and relevant Cabinet ministers with advice on intelligence-gathering methodology, analysis and priority tasks. It all looks grand on official documentation, but in reality, especially in relation to the war in Ireland and how it was being fought, its deliberations were banal and wholly irrelevant. Despite the mantras of denial, references to "rogue elements" and "bad apples," those Knights of the British Empire, men honored by Queen Elizabeth II for their services, who chaired the JIC from 1970 to 1993, knew what was happening in Ireland during their watch, including 'off the books' operations, and did nothing at all.

On the specific allegations of British security forces collusion, the (often ambiguous) Barron report states that there is no evidence (presumably that the judge was been allowed to see) that any branch of the British military or intelligence establishment, active in the North of Ireland in the mid-1970s, "knew in advance the bombings were about to take place." Secretary of State Dr. John Reid's denial had been accepted by the inquiry, based, it appears, on nothing more than the false premise that politician's don't lie. Barron then goes on to say that if they did know (without saying who exactly he is referring to - generals perhaps, spy bosses, or their political masters?) there are probably no official records: "Such knowledge would not have been written down, or if it had been, would not be in any files made available to the Secretary of State [and] there is evidence that the Secretary of State of the day [Merlyn Rees, appointed by Labour PM Harold Wilson, on 5 March 1974] was not fully informed on matters of which he should have been made aware." And on that basis, as far as Barron is concerned, John Reid probably knew nothing. Having cut off the paper trail at street-level, the report then disappears down the rabbit hole, explaining that the security forces in the North had "good intelligence" to know who was responsible within a short time of the bombings taking place, giving, as an example, "unknown information" that led British intelligence sources to tell their Irish Army counterparts that at least two of the bombers had been arrested on 26 May and detained, "unfortunately the inquiry was unable to discover the nature of this and other intelligence" available to the security forces in the North at the time. However, a number of those suspected of the bombings were "reliably said to have had relationships with British Intelligence and/or RUC Special Branch." It is reasonable to assume, therefore, that "exchanges of information" took place , and that the "assistance provided to the Garda investigation team by the security forces in Northern Ireland was affected by the reluctance to compromise those relationships, in the interests of securing further information for the future." Exactly what Barron is talking about here is anybody's guess. Nairac discussing with his UVF 'brothers in arms' about the next no-warning bombing of civilians or cross-border assassination?

The report concludes that there is "deep suspicion" that the relationship between the loyalist bombers and the agents of the Crown hampered the investigation into the bombing (but not that it could have prevented the bombings) and there are "grounds for suspecting that the bombers may have had assistance from members of the security forces." However, "unless further information comes to hand, such involvement must remain a suspicion. It is not proven."

To give the venerable judge his due, he attached the full transcript of Yorkshire Television's documentary about the bombings to his report, and even after almost two decades there is a sense of righteous indignation at the cold indifference of the British military and intelligence establishment to the broken lives and to the price paid for a heartless counterinsurgency strategy of terror, by running pseudo gangs to crank up the fear.

The Yorkshire TV program begins with an account of the bombings, the casualties and the physical damage done, interviews with those who witnessed and survived the terror, and images of the carnage and devastation, then refers to the Garda Siochana investigation as the "biggest murder hunt in their history." According to narrator, Philip Tibenham, the Irish police, unusual in such cases, had "formally co-operated" with the program makers, and in a series of briefings had "revealed the contents of many classified files, eyewitness statements, forensic reports and released official photographs." Three former police commissioners and several retired senior officers were also interviewed, and although they did not wish to be identified on camera, allowed the verbatim use of their statements.

All the witnesses who claimed to have seen the car bombs in Dublin and Monaghan were shown official police photos at an early stage of the Garda investigation, and the result was a list of eight identified suspects, all of whom were members of the mid-Ulster UVF, based in Portadown, County Armagh. These eyewitnesses were contacted by the program's researchers, and two of the eight suspects were identified as the drivers of cars containing the bombs, one to Dublin and the vehicle parked in Monaghan. In both cases, the Garda had three separate eyewitnesses who identified the drivers from official photos. One Garda officer, who was part of the investigation team, described the positive identifications as "good strong evidence" which could have been used in court.

The list of suspects was extended to twelve following an analysis of information from Garda sources north of the border (presumably HUMINT assets within the nationalist community). According to the program, Garda files named William 'Frenchie' Marchant, the leader of the Belfast hijackers, Billy Fulton, the quartermaster in charge of the explosives for both operations, the Portadown UVF leader, Billy Hanna, his second-in-command, Harris Boyle, and a loyalist killer known as the 'Jackal' who wasn't named for legal reasons. The program also identified four planners - Robert McConnell, a farmer from South Armagh - adding that "all four were former or serving members of the British Army's biggest regiment, the UDR."

At the early stages of the Garda investigation there was good co-operation with the RUC, and, with an ever-growing list of suspects, the Irish police sought to interview the individuals and, if necessary, have them taken into custody. However, the "trail ran cold" at RUC Headquarters in East Belfast. The Irish police were not permitted to speak with the suspects, or the owners of the hijacked cars, even in the presence of RUC officers. In the end "all they could do was hand over their information and wait. They were to be disappointed."

Garda Chief Superintendent, John Paul McMahon, who headed the Monaghan investigation, states in his final report that they were "greatly hampered by reason of the fact that no direct enquiries could be made in the area where the crime originated. There was no access to potential witnesses in Northern Ireland and there was also the disadvantage of not having to be able to interrogate likely suspects and put them on identification parades." Garda Chief Supt. John Joy, who was in charge in Dublin, states in his final report that the RUC were conducting inquiries and the "results of the investigation will be reported," however, the RUC never reported back. According to the documentary, two RUC Special Branch officers were detailed to find out more about the bombings, and reported back to RUC HQ with a list of UVF suspects which tallied with the Garda's list, but they were never asked to interview or arrest anybody. The Irish detectives were "isolated in the North" and could only report back to their political masters in the hope that the Irish Government would take up the issue. Eventually, the Garda investigation had nowhere else to go, and "after only three months it was quietly wound down." Apart from the Garda and RUC combined lists of twenty suspects, the program makers spoke with contacts in loyalist circles and produced a similar number of names. They also confirmed that the bombings were planned in the Killycomaine Estate in Portadown, a "haven for loyalist paramilitaries" in 1974 where many acts of terrorism were planned by the UVF's mid-Ulster brigade.

The program then focused on the capability of the UVF to bomb Dublin, and introduced Capt. Fred Holroyd, a former Army Intelligence and MI6 agent, who worked undercover in Portadown in 1974. According to Holroyd, loyalist bombing capability was "pretty limited" at the time:

> they mainly used Double Diamond kegs, beer kegs, filled with explosives with a black powder fuse on, then they light the black powder fuse, disappear, and this thing would burn down. The detonator would go off, and the bomb would go off. They weren't as sophisticated as the IRA, who had electrical detonators, trembler devices and all sorts of other very sophisticated bits of equipment, anti-handling devices. I mean they [the UVF] were pretty primitive basically.

The narrator, Philip Tibenham, then pointed out that the Dublin operation was anything but primitive. It involved the use of "sophisticated timing devices to detonate three car bombs within ninety seconds of each other." If the UVF did bomb the Irish capital, he asked, "where did they get their new-found expertise?"

Yorkshire Television commissioned two leading forensic experts to examine all the technical information relating to the Dublin operation, including previously unreleased official Gardai forensic analysis. One of those was Lt.Col. George Styles, a former bomb disposal expert who was awarded the George Cross for service in the North of Ireland from 1969 to 1972, and was later appointed head of the Royal Army Ordnance Corps (RAOC) worldwide.

Lt. Col. Styles' expertise in the area of explosives, bombs and IEDs is beyond reproach. He served with the King's Yorkshire Light Infantry in the Malayan Emergency - a guerrilla war fought between Commonwealth forces and the Malayan National Liberation Army, the military wing of the Malayan Communist Party, from June 1948 to July 1960. Mentioned in dispatches (for gallant and meritorious action) he returned to England and obtained an engineering degree from the MoD's Royal Military College of

Science, based in the Vale of White Horse in southwest Oxfordshire, before returning to the Malaysian jungle to take charge of the 28th Commonwealth Brigade Ordnance Field Park Regiment, based at Taiping in the northern Perak region. He later served with the 1st British Corps of the British Army of the Rhine, before being posted to the North of Ireland with the first deployment, serving as O/C of the Explosive Ordnance and Disposal Teams (EODS). In his book, *Bombs Have No Pity*, he describes defusing an IRA bomb in November 1971, left in the telephone booth in the bar of the Europa Hotel in Belfast, the main watering-hole for journalists, local and foreign, covering the early years of the Irish Troubles. A similar IED had killed a colleague, and Styles was aware that the 4lb bomb was equipped with an anti-handling device with micro-switches that would detonate if the container was moved. Styles built a mock-up of the bomb to plan how to defuse the device, and then spent seven hours, with two colleagues, disabling the electrical circuits before the device could be removed from the cramped space. Two days later there was a second bomb alarm at the Europa - which had now become the "most bombed hotel in the world" having been targeted 28 times by the Provos without fatalities. On this occasion a 12lb device with extra multi-colored wiring, decoy micro-switches and redundant electrical circuits, took almost nine hours to disarm. This was the level of knowledge Styles brought to the issue and, disturbingly for the British, the level of Provo knowledge to which Holroyd referred.

Interviewed by the program's producer, Glyn Middleton, Lt. Col. Styles (who died on 1 August 2006, and whose RAOC uniform is on permanent display at the Imperial War Museum, London) explained that to build one car-bomb a "fair amount" of training and expertise is required but

> to get three to go off all at the same time, you've got to have some pretty good technicians organizing the timing mechanisms for instance. The organization of getting three cars into the centre of a city all going off at roughly at the same time, that smacks of some pretty good administrative ability and whatever organization therefore was behind this outrage, you might say they were not low down on the learning curve, they were high up on it.

Asked about the likelihood that the UVF could have carried out such a complex operation, Styles said he had "no high regard" for their skills in 1974, and in his opinion they were not at a level "that would equate to the sort of techniques" that were used in Dublin. The loyalists had no history of synchronized car-bombing, according to Styles, and the operation in the Irish capital was "outside their field of technology."

The Irish Army's most experienced bomb disposal officer, Commandant Patrick Trears, described the attack as a "very sophisticated, very military-type operation. The terrorist group had to be well-trained to carry this out, smoothly and without a flaw." The bombs contained 400lbs of explosives, which detonated so effectively that there was no residue traces to suggest the source. The fact that all the ingredients of the bombs exploded and were expended indicated, according to Cmd. Trears, that "the mix was consistent and that the expertise of the people that made up the mix was at a pretty sophisticated level. From a military point of view, it would have been considered a hundred percent successful." He supported Styles's assessment that the UVF could not have carried out the attacks without the assistance of "some other experienced people." That was also the view of former Garda Commissioner, Eamon Doherty, who added, "I didn't think at the time and I don't think now that any loyalist group could have done this on their own in 1974 (...) If they did participate in this operation, they must have been helped."

Asked by Middleton about the level of infiltration, Holroyd confirmed that the mid-Ulster UVF "belonged" to Int. Corps, and the organization was "running the leaders" as informers. In return for information, the UVF was allowed to carry on its campaign of terror unchecked. Despite his official designation as the British Army's Int. Corps officer for the area, Holroyd was not ordered to investigate the known local connections to the bombings: "I was never asked once by anybody to question my sources or to try and find out any information about this whatsoever. At the time, and immediately afterwards, there was just no interest at all. It was only quite some time after that my Special Branch colleague told me in fact who the Portadown men who were involved in this were, and where the cars had come from." Holroyd's official diary and intelligence notebooks, compiled during his posting in Portadown in 1974, reveal that the loyalist organization had 124 members, with 20 percent active, and they were being monitored by the Int. Corps and RUC Special Branch. On several occasions during March and April that year, William Hanna conducted bomb-making sessions, Billy Fulton is recorded as collecting illegal fertilizer for explosives in May, and the notebooks list six of the eight suspects identified by eyewitnesses, two of whom were paid informers

Black Propaganda & PsyOps

The Yorkshire TV program also interviewed Colin Wallace, describing him as a senior British Army information officer, working at Lisburn NIHQ. Wallace was a local man from Randalstown, County Antrim. A member of the Territorial Army Volunteer Reserve (TAVR) and the UDR, he was actually a civil servant, a press officer with the equivalent military rank of captain, working with the Information Policy Department (IPD) under Major Tony Staughton. The IPD had been established in September 1971, one month after Operation *Demetrius*, and was initially headed by Col. Maurice Tugwell, an intelligence officer who had served in Palestine, Malaya, Cyprus, and Kenya. Tugwell's job, according to the late Richard

Clutterbuck, a former Army officer and one of the MoD counterinsurgency 'experts' (based on his experience in anti-colonial conflicts as the British Empire fell apart following WWII), was "not merely to react to the media, or events, but to take a positive initiative in presenting the news to the best advantage of the security forces." Before he left Lisburn in March 1973 and transferred to Iran as instructor at the Imperial Armed Forces College, Tugwell worked closely with Wallace, and together they were responsible for some of the "horror stories" of the early 1970s that appeared in the British press, according to media specialist and author, Liz Curtis.

Following Operation *Demetrius*, Tugwell and his staff "made it their business to talk to journalists confidentially." Even reporters cautious of the official line, like the *Independent* newspaper's current Middle East correspondent, Robert Fisk, were initially convinced by the IPD's private one-on-one briefings. In an article for the *Times* (for whom he worked at the time) published on 26 June 1974, Fisk wrote that the IRA's command structure had been "severely fractured by the information gained during deep-interrogation. The interrogation methods themselves they would say, were harmless." This, of course, was completely untrue, as the case of the 'Hooded Men' later proved. And *Demetrius*, based on outdated RUC Special Branch intelligence, was also a total failure. Within months most of those lifted were released. The IRA's command structure wasn't touched, and hundreds of young men and women, many previously ambivalent to what was happening in their communities across the North, volunteered to join the resistance.

Tugwell repeated the lies in an article published in Canada in early 1973, entitled "Revolutionary Propaganda and the Role of the Information Services in Counter-Insurgency Operations," which was quoted in the *Times* stating that "Interrogation methods used by the security forces in 1971 brought in a mass of valuable intelligence. These methods, combined with the internment of known terrorists, threatened to destroy the IRA (...) None of those interrogated by these methods suffered any injury or ill-effects."

Black propaganda and covert action increased once the failure of internment had been analyzed by the MoD's counterinsurgency specialists. The British Army senior staff realized that RUC Special Branch intelligence was an unreliable source, and MI5 was called in to sort out the mess. Frank Howard Smith, a Bletchley Park WWII veteran (who would later become head of the Security Service) arrived at Lisburn and set up a PsyOps Unit, basically an extension of the IPD, and established close liaison practices between IPD/PsyOps, the Int. Corps and MI5, with the RUC Special Branch effectively 'out of the loop' because of the force's political and personal links with the unionist/loyalist community.

Homosexuality was illegal in Northern Ireland, and provided excellent opportunities for compromise and blackmail. MI5 targeted unionist members of the gay community in order to build up an intelligence data base on loyalist paramilitary organizations and grassroots politicians, while Colin

Wallace was involved in a parallel black propaganda operation, intended to isolate politicians at local level who seemed to be turning away from paramilitary activity. Wallace would later be dismissed from the Army, and was "neutralized by MI5," according to Holroyd, because of what he knew about various MI5 plots, including *Clockwork Orange*, a disinformation campaign hatched by right-wing members of the security forces in the North which targeted mainly British Labour Party MPs, including the prime minister, Harold Wilson. The frequently-used methodology was known in the trade as "placing a story and bringing it home" also involved briefing foreign journalists, and providing false documents to discredit the targeted individuals. Foreign news reports then provided 'published sources' for reports reproduced in the British press.

Wallace was framed after attempting to stop child abuse at the Kincora Boys' Home in East Belfast, which was frequently visited by several Ulster Unionist Party (UUP) officials. The pedophile ring was headed by staff member William McGrath, who was also the leader of a small loyalist paramilitary group called 'Tara.' He was blackmailed by MI5 to provide intelligence on other loyalist groups, according to Martin Dillon. Wallace was believed to be the source of information leaked to the press about Tara, after he resigned from the Civil Service (and the IPD) in 1975. Five years later, having moved to the UK, he was found guilty of the manslaughter of an antique dealer, whose body was found in the River Arun, in West Sussex, and he served six years of a ten year sentence. The conviction was quashed after a Home Office pathologist, Dr. Ian West, who had carried out two contradictory post-mortems on the victim (returning verdicts of accidental and non-accidental drowning) admitted during an appeal hearing that some of the evidence used to convict Wallace had been provided "by an American security source."

After his release Wallace produced handwritten contemporaneous notes of meetings he had with other members involved in *Clockwork Orange*, that were authenticated by a former MI6 officer and independent forensic scientist, Dr. Julius Grant, described as "arguably the world's most respected forensic scientist in his particular area of expertise." An inquiry, chaired by Sir David Calcutt, QC, later confirmed that members of MI5 had manipulated disciplinary proceedings against Wallace, and that Parliament had been "deliberately misled" over his work in the North of Ireland, admitting that he had been involved in disinformation and black propaganda operations on behalf of the security forces, and that he had been "authorized" by senior officers to "occasionally provide classified information to journalists."

Colin Wallace provided the Barron Inquiry with copies of two letters sent to Major Tony Staughton, before he was 'posted out' of the North. On 14 August 1975, he had written:

> There is good evidence the Dublin bombings in May last year were a reprisal for the Irish government's role in bringing about the [power sharing] Executive [based on an agreement reached on 21 November 1973, for an elected

78-member Assembly, which collapsed due to unionist opposition and a loyalist general strike in May 1974]. According to one of Craig's people [Craig Smellie, the top MI6 officer in the North] some of those involved (...) were closely working with SB [RUC Special Branch] and Int [Corps] at the time. Craig's people believe the sectarian assassinations were designed to destroy Rees's attempt to negotiate a ceasefire, and the targets were identified for both sides by Int/SB. They also believe some very senior RUC officers were involved with this group. In short, it would appear that loyalist paramilitaries and Int/SB have formed some sort of pseudo-gangs in an attempt to fight a war of attrition by getting paramilitaries on both sides to kill each other and, at the same time, prevent any future political initiative such as Sunningdale."

In a letter, dated 20 September 1975, Wallace claims MI5 was "trying to create a split within the UVF because they wanted the more politically-minded ones ousted. I believe much of the violence generated during the latter part of last year was caused by some of the new [Int. Corps] people deliberately stirring up conflict. As you know, we have never been allowed to target either the breakaway UVF, nor the UFF [Ulster Freedom Fighters] during the past year, yet they have killed more people than the IRA."

Researchers working on the *Forgotten Massacre* submitted both Wallace's letters and Holroyd's notebooks for analysis to a leading forensic scientist who confirmed they had been written in 1974 and 1975. Wallace explained on camera that one of the difficulties with the Dublin/ Monaghan bombings was "that there was really no follow-up, no major offensive, no major determination to find out whether these people had been responsible or not." Wallace was concerned at this lack of interest because it was "a departure from the normal procedure" adding that working with the loyalists were members of a "special duties team" who were then linked to SAS personnel.

This group of SAS-trained covert soldiers were based at a stately home in Castledillon, Country Armagh, described by Holroyd as a "remarkable little place, set behind an ordinary regiment of engineers in a compound of its own, guarded by civilian MoD police." It was made up of several wooden huts, and on one occasion when Holroyd was there he was shown a gun locker "with all their spare barrels so they could use weapons and then change the barrels and claim that they'd never shot people." He was also shown their communications equipment, which he suspected "went straight through to [SAS HQ] Hereford, and the MoD" [in Whitehall, London], and claimed that the group was "supported separately from regular uniformed Army people" and only the SAS "can sponsor anything like that." The group's code name was 'Four Field Survey Troop'.

Referring to a British Army manual, *Land Operations: Counter Revolutionary Operations, Part I: Principles and General Aspects,* which states that the SAS is "particularly suited" to work with "friendly guerrilla forces operating against a common enemy," the program reminded viewers that the friendly guerrilla forces, in this case, were loyalist terrorists. Wallace explained that the loyalists "worked willingly" with the intelligence community because they felt they were doing the same job as the British Army in trying to defeat the IRA, adding that certain officers based at Army HQ believed some of the explosives used were sourced by the security forces "which could mean from the RUC, the UDR or the Army" and that the planning and some of the organizing had been done "with the assistance of people who were working within the security community."

Dublin was vulnerable. There had been four car-bombings in the city center between 26 November 1972 (the end of the bloodiest year for the security forces north of the border since partition in 1922) and 20 January 1973, in which a total of three civilians died and 180 were injured. There was a specific political agenda to the bombs on Friday evening, 1 December 1972, which were hidden in vehicles hired in Belfast by an individual using a stolen British driving license. These were timed to influence the passage of amendments to the Dublin Government's *Offences Against the State Act,* which was being opposed by the cross-party majority of parliamentarians in the Dail until news of the deaths downtown reached Leinster House. Referring to allegations that British intelligence was responsible, the Barron Report mentions an anonymous letter sent to the *Irish Times,* and published six days later, which claimed that five members of the British Armed Forces were involved in this attack, and had left Dublin "not by car or train to Ulster but by plane to Heathrow." The Irish Prime Minister, Jack Lynch, in a 1973 RTE interview after he left office following his party's defeat in that year's general election, also suspected British agents had a role. While admitting there was no specific evidence "a lot of people in Ireland believe that many of these unexplained activists and actions [including the anti-personnel explosion at 3.18pm on 20 January 1973, when the city center was more crowded than usual with visitors in town for that afternoon's international rugby match between Ireland and the New Zealand 'All Blacks'] could well be related to British Intelligence."

Why bomb Dublin in 1974? There was no military or counterinsurgency advantage to be gained by allowing, encouraging, or assisting 'friendly guerrillas' to target and kill innocent people in the Irish capital? The Provos weren't based in the Irish Republic. The Republican Movement's only 'official' presence in the capital was a building on Parnell Square which housed some Sinn Fein offices, the weekly newspaper, *An Phoblact,* and a bookshop. It wasn't close enough to suffer even superficial damage from the first blast. Revenge for the IRA's economic bombing of Belfast and Derry, or to "keep the loyalists on side," suggested some local commentators. If that was so, it had the coward's touch. Dublin, unlike Belfast, was not clogged with military and police personnel, security barriers in the city centre, 'brick formation' foot-patrols moving through the streets, reinforced RUC Land Rovers and Army APC mobile patrols (with citizens being stared at through the sights of passing 7.62mm SLRs). There were no roof-top military observation posts or VCPs (vehicle check points) around the next corner. Dublin was open for business, and for the loyalists it didn't really matter what the target was, as long as the bang was loud enough and the casualties were plenty.

South of the Border

There's no doubt that Gen. King (one of the 'regular' uniformed Army officers) was briefed on the death of John Francis Green, O/C of the IRA's 2nd Battalion, who was shot dead on a bleak January night in 1975, in a remote farmhouse, one mile south of the border on the slopes of Mullyash Mountain, County Monaghan. Green was high on the Army's 'most wanted' list having embarrassed the authorities by escaping from Long Kesh internment camp, the former RAF base, about seven miles southwest of Belfast, three years earlier, dressed as a Roman Catholic priest. The killing, which was claimed by the UVF in the June edition of its monthly magazine, *Combat*, took place three weeks into an IRA ceasefire, during ongoing discussions on how a lasting peace might be achieved between representatives of the Republican Movement and the British Government, with a group of Protestant clergymen acting as unofficial intermediaries. Because of the efficiency of the killing, the location and the timing, there were allegations that Green's death was the work of a British Army assassination squad. Statements of this nature were generally dismissed as "Republican propaganda" by the British, Irish, and international media, especially in the United States, where HMG ran an efficient and effective propaganda service.

It wasn't until 1984, when a series of articles published in the London-based weekly magazine, *New Statesman*, by investigative journalist Duncan Campbell, based on several interviews with Fred Holroyd, who turned whistle-blower after falling foul of what he claimed was bitter inter-service rivalry among the various elements of Britain's counter-insurgency apparatus. Holroyd told Campbell that during a routine meeting with Capt. Nairac in Portadown in mid-1975, the 14FSIC officer had shown him a Polaroid color photograph of John Francis Green, a married man with three children, lying in a pool of blood on the farmhouse floor. Nairac described how he had traveled to Castleblaney with two other men, drove down a country lane and watched the farmhouse until the owner left to milk a neighbor's cow. He described watching Green through the window before kicking open the door and repeatedly shooting the IRA officer. A post-mortem later revealed that Green had been shot six times in the head at close range. Forensic tests later established that two guns were used, a Spanish-made, Star BM 9mm single-action, semi-automatic pistol, and a 9mm Lugar PO8 pistol both of which were later linked to several more 14FSIC/UDR/UVF killings between 1972 and 1976. A Gardai team which traveled from Dublin to head the investigation included a crime scene photographer, using standard black and white film. None of the Irish police officers were equipped to take Polaroid photographs.

During his maiden speech in the House of Commons on 7 July 1987, Labour MP, Ken Livingstone, raised the Green killing, Holroyd's allegations about the role of undercover British Army/UVF death squads, and the former Military Intelligence officer's mistreatment when he tried to expose MI5's part in the 'dirty war' in Ireland. To the visible discomfort of Tory MPs on the benches opposite, Mr. Livingstone stated that Holroyd had been

> shuffled to one side by the expedient method of being taken to a mental hospital and being basically declared unfit for duty. During the month he spent in the British mental hospital, the three tests that were administered to him were successfully passed. What is particularly disturbing is that what looked at the time like a random act of maniacal violence and sectarian killing now begins to take on a much more sinister stance. It begins to emerge that Captain Robert Nairac is quite likely the person who organized the killing of the three Miami Showband musicians. The evidence for the allegation is forensic and members of the UDR are prepared to say that they were members of the UVF gang who actually undertook the murder of the Miami Showband musicians. The evidence is quite clear. The same gun that was used by Capt. Nairac on his cross-border trip to assassinate John Francis Green was used in the Miami Showband massacre.

Within days of Ken Livingstone's speech, made under parliamentary privilege, the MoD sought to undermine the newly-elected Labour MP's allegations. Officials from the Cabinet Office approached Belfast-based journalist, Chris Ryder, the Newry-born correspondent for the *Sunday Times*, offering a copy of the polaroid photograph Nairac had passed to Holroyd with the suggestion that it had been taken by an Irish Garda photographer, and which proved that Holroyd's - and Livingstone's - allegations were untrue. To its credit the *Sunday Times* rejected the story recognizing it for what it was - HMG officially sourced 'black propaganda'. The same could not be said for the London-based, *Independent*, newspaper, which ran a full-page, "exclusive" expose, a few months later by its Northern Ireland correspondent, David McKittrick, which included the Polaroid photograph with the suggestion that it had been taken by the Irish police and passed to the RUC who had made it available to the newspaper, and that possession did not implicate Cpt. Nairac or British military intelligence personnel in assassinations south of the border. And the campaign to discredit Holroyd worked until RUC SPG officer, John Weir, in his 1990 sworn statement, identified Green's killers as Glennanne Gang boss, Robin Jackson, UDR 2nd Battalion Cpl, Robert O'Connell, who was being run by Nairac and also had links to the RUC Special Branch, and UDR part-time soldier and UVF member, Harris Boyle, who blew himself up during the Miami Showband killings.

If there was a military objective, behind the killing of John Francis Green, an intelligence officer with the IRA's North Armgh Brigade, the same could not be said for the Miami Showband members. The facts are straightforward. The six-piece band were returning to Dublin from a gig in Banbridge, County Down, on 31 July 1975, when their Volkswagen T2 minibus was pulled over by 10 men in British Army uniforms at a VCP just outside Newry. The musicians were ordered out. Two of the 'soldiers' placed a 10lb bomb on the bus which exploded prematurely, killing both of them. The other armed men then opened fire, killing three musicians and seriously wounding the band's bass guitarist. A least four of the gunmen were members of the UDR. The plan, according to journalist, Martin Dillon, was to conceal the bomb, set the timer, send the band on its way and have the bomb explode as the minibus crossed the border. The Army's IPD in Lisburn could then claim that the musicians were republican sympathizers, smuggling explosives for the IRA. The only flaw in this hypothesis is the direction the band was traveling. The IRA had no reason to move explosives south. If the 'friendly guerrillas' and their 14FSIC handlers had bothered to think it through, the van should have been stopped heading in the opposite direction, and the bomb timed to explode outside the dance-hall in Banbridge. The two men who died when they set off the bomb while closing the rear doors of the minibus were both members of the UDR and the Glenanne Gang, and the man in charge of this brief episode in brutality was Robin Jackson, the tout being run by Capt. Bob Nairac.

Less than two years later Nairac was dead, the fifth 14FSIC fatality. Two had died while on undercover surveillance in Belfast and Derry, and two were killed by a nervous RUC patrol in a 'friendly fire' incident near Markethill, County Armagh, in March 1974. Commissioned into the Grenadier Guards, the infantry regiment with which he is listed among the fallen, Nairac was on his fourth tour of duty, based at Bessbrook, as liaison officer between his covert unit, the RUC, and the 3rd Infantry Brigade, headquartered in the Kitchen Hill Factory in Lurgan. On 14 May 1977, claiming to be a motor mechanic from the republican Ardoyne area of Belfast, he was captured by the IRA in the carpark of the 'The Three Steps' public house in Drumintee, South Armagh, and taken across the border to Ravensdale Woods, in County Louth, where he was interrogated, executed, and secretly buried. He is one of seven remaining IRA victims whose graves have not been found. In his book, *Ghost Forces*, Ken Connor, a former 23-year SAS veteran involved in setting up 14FSIC, states that had Nairac been a member of the SAS "he would not have been allowed to operate in the way he did. Before his death we had been very concerned at the lack of checks on his activities. No one seemed to know who his boss was, and he appeared to have been allowed to get out of control, deciding himself what tasks he would do."

Nairac was awarded the George Cross for gallantry. But the citation for services rendered doesn't mention that this recipient of the UK's second highest military/civil decoration was one of Craig Smellie's 'people' - a group of SAS troopers including Fred Holroyd, Bernard Dearsley, and Julian Ball, who was described by an Army officer in a *New Statesman* article as an "irresponsible cowboy." Smellie was an MI6 officer based at Army NIHQ from 1973 to 1975, who was responsible for funding covert operations through a series of bank robberies on both sides of the border. He was also responsible for recruiting the 'Badger', the code-name for John McCoy, an Irish police officer based at Monaghan Garda station, who provided information on the movements of republicans to MI6. After a "brief but fierce battle" for intelligence primacy between Box 500 (MI5) and Box 600 (MI6) Smellie left Ireland in 1975 to become MI6 Chief of Station in Athens, and was replaced by MI5 officer, Ian Cameron.

The Badger gave Smellie details of Garda activity, and was able to use his position to clear certain areas of police and Irish Army personnel deployed along the border at crucial times to allow 14FSIC and loyalist death squads to cross into the Republic, and carry out two murders, an abduction and several covert surveillance missions. All the members of Smellie's clandestine group are dead, (including Smellie in 1981, according to the *New Statesman*) except Holroyd, who distanced himself from the illegal covert activity and turned whistle-blower, providing details of the Badger's relationship with Smellie, and describing the SAS as the "spearhead of Kitson's counterinsurgency policy, and the lever used by more ruthless operators than those who employed me to implement their policies."

It wasn't until mid-December 2011 that an official account of the Miami Showband murders was released by the Police Service of Northern Ireland (PSNI) cold-case squad, the Historical Enquiries Team (HET). Apart from confirming what was already known, the HET report states that after the killings, Robin Jackson was told by a senior RUC officer to "lie low" because his fingerprints had been found on the silencer attached to the Lugar PO8, the same gun used in the killing of John Francis Green. And the report concludes by stating the obvious, that the murders raised "disturbing questions about collusive and corrupt behavior" but detectives found no means "to assuage or rebut these concerns and that is a deeply troubling matter."

The Kingsmill Massacre

There was one particularly brutal incident in the mid-1970s, known as the 'Kingsmill Massacre', that underlined how far 14FSIC was prepared to go to implement Kitson's counterinsurgency strategy. On 5 January 1976, a red Ford Transit minibus, containing textiles workers traveling home from Glenanne to Bessbrook, was stopped by armed men. The ten passengers and the driver were ordered from the vehicle and shot dead. All were members of the unionist community, four were members of the Orange Order, a

Protestant fraternal organization, which annually celebrates the victory of the Dutch-born William of Orange over the Catholic King James II at the Battle of the Boyne in 1690. The Orange Order, with its annual raucous displays of sectarian triumphalism, had played a key role for several years in the late 1960s, calling on its members to oppose the Civil Rights Movement and provoking violence at peaceful civil rights demonstrations and marches which eventually led to the deployment of British troops on the streets.

Responsibility for the Kingsmill killings was claimed by a group calling itself the South Armagh Republican Action Force, who stated that their action was in retaliation for the murders of six members of the Reavey and O'Dowd families the previous evening, and a response to dozens of other killings carried out by the Glenanne Gang in an area known as the 'Murder Triangle'. The group also said there would be "no further action on our part" if the UVF stopped their sectarian attacks. An official Provisional IRA statement, dated 17 January, denied that the killings had been ordered at leadership level, pointing out that the IRA had never initiated sectarian killings, but "if the loyalist elements responsible for over 300 sectarian assassinations in the past four years stop such killing now, then the question of retaliation from whatever source does not arise." A PSNI cold-case HET investigation produced a report in 2011 which stated that intelligence at the time suggested that the men responsible for the Kinsgmill killings, while being locally-based members of the IRA, "were not well-disposed towards the organization's leadership." An IRA informer, Sean O'Callaghan, (who had worked as an adviser to Ulster Unionist Party during the cease-fire negotiations on issues such as IRA decommissioning) has claimed that the killings were "sanctioned" by two senior IRA officers, without consulting the Army Council. Several senior members of the republican community in the area were interviewed by *Daily Telegraph* journalist, Toby Harnden, for his book, *Bandit Country*, and condemned the attack, describing it as "dishonorable" though there had been a general consensus that "something had to be done." At that time the 14FSIC connection with the Glenanne Gang was an unknown factor. What was known to local people, and this included IRA members, was that the security forces were doing nothing at all to prevent the UVF killing non-combatant nationalists.

There is a brief reference to the Murder Triangle killings in Gen. Jackson's analysis. Paragraph 234 states:

> Sectarian killing had become common, but a particularly vicious feud erupted in County Armagh between South Armagh PIRA and North Armagh UVF. The two organizations probably numbered less than 30 terrorists each. Between 19 December 1975 and 12 January 1976 over 40 people were killed and over 100 wounded. The main effect of this feud was to raise tension and the perception of the political need to be doing something. The

last vestiges of the Sunningdale Agreement died quietly and the bulk of the population tacitly accepted Direct Rule from Whitehall, which lasted until the signing of the Good Friday Agreement in 1998.

Relatives of the victims of the O'Dowd and Reavey families, and five people who died in two coordinated UVF no-warning bombings at Kay's Tavern in Dundalk, in the Irish Republic, and at Donnelly's Bar, Silverbridge, South Armagh, on 19 December 1975, demanded a retraction from the MoD. In a statement they "totally reject" the description of events as a "feud," pointing out that the Glenanne Gang was made up of members of the British Army, the RUC and loyalist paramilitaries run by the Int. Corps and/or RUC Special Branch. The ballistic histories of the weapons used in various attacks

> allow us to state with absolute certainty that these incidents were linked to other loyalist attacks. The main instigators of theses attacks were serving RUC officers and UDR members [and] were carried out while the individuals were on duty, and/or were using official RUC and UDR uniforms and RUC vehicles. Access to police and army radios facilitated escape while some of the murders carried out by this gang were on occasion investigated by RUC officers linked to the very same gang.

The statement was a far more cogent analysis than the MoD's self-serving revisionism - which will be standard text for future studies of the Troubles for cadets at Sandhurst - and may explain why the British Army has never learned from past experiences in Ireland. The bereaved no longer regarded the incidents, in which their relatives were among "at least 120 deaths" attributed to the Glenanne Gang, as "loyalist attacks" but as part of a 'dirty war' being run by the security forces "aimed at terrorizing the nationalist community into isolating the IRA." The extent to which the security forces were aware of these activities, the degree to which the soldiers and police officers were central to this campaign, and the "appalling response of the criminal justice system," provided ample reason to believe the killings and the bombings were "officially sanctioned."

Several of the relatives met ex-RUC SPG officer, William McCaughey, a former member of the Glenanne Gang, in 2001, and asked him why there was no retaliation for the Kingsmill killings. They were told that a plan to attack a nationalist primary school in Beleek, and kill thirty children and their teachers, proposed by an unidentified UDR member, was abandoned because the UVF leadership in Belfast suspected British Military Intelligence was behind the plan, and it could lead to civil war. In a statement following the meeting the relatives said that they were "prepared to accept that this plan may have been regarded as morally unacceptable to the UVF, however, the plan was instigated by Military Intelligence, and was therefore part of a wider agenda that has never been investigated." The PSNI Chief Constable, Sir Huge Orde, when he met with relatives on 18 August 2004, confirmed that McCaughey had never been questioned about the plan to target schoolchildren.

There was no response from the MoD to the relatives' statement. And none should be expected. After dreadful deeds in anti-colonial struggles in places that never made headlines, a few more dead in County Armagh are worthy of only a brief, disingenuous mention in the official military narrative. And even that had to be less than the whole truth, a revisionist version to preserve the myth that the British were there to "hold the line" between two communities on the verge of outright sectarian conflict.

Showing Them the Folly of Their Ways

Almost all the journeys made by British forces south of the border ended in death. That was the nature of the journeys. So when highly-trained SAS troopers 'strayed' across the border because they were unable to read maps properly (a basic requirement for those involved in covert operations) it was the responsibility of the British ambassador in Dublin to sort out the mess with the Irish authorities.

At about 10.40pm on 5 May 1976, four days after the body of a forestry worker, Seamus Ludlow, was found in a field near Dundalk, two SAS soldiers in civilian clothes were stopped at a joint Irish Army/Garda VCP on the Flagstaff Road between Newry and Omeath, about a half-mile inside the Irish Republic. They were armed with Browning pistols and two Sterling submachine guns. They claimed they had misread a map while "off-duty test-driving" their Triumph 2000. Four hours later seven more plainclothes SAS men were arrested in two cars at the same checkpoint, out looking for their colleagues, and they too claimed a map-reading error. They were also heavily armed, the weaponry including a pump-action shotgun and a double-edged, acutely-tapered dagger, used for the 'silent kill' - standard SAS-issue since WWII.The following day, after being questioned in connection with the Dublin/Monaghan bombings, all eight appeared at the Special Criminal Court in Dublin, charged with possession of illegal firearms with intent to endanger life. They were bailed and allowed to return to their base at Mahon Road Barracks in Portadown. The British Foreign and Commonwealth Office (FCO) in Whitehall immediately set out to minimize the damage, with the UK ambassador to Ireland, Sir Arthur Galsworthy, a former Oxford-educated Army officer, warning his colleagues in a classified telex, on 7 May, that "one aspect of the defense that will need careful handling is the inclusion of a shotgun and what has been described as a dagger among the weapons carried."

Several confidential meetings followed between senior FCO, MoD, and Northern Ireland Office (NIO) officials, one of which discussed a "10 mile buffer zone" along the border - effectively a no-go area for all British military personnel and, presumably, only in South Armagh, an area disparagingly referred to in the UK media as "bandit country." On 14 May, Ambassador Galsworthy informed London that he had "warned" the Irish Foreign Minister, Garret FitzGerald, of the "appalling consequences that would follow if the case resulted in prison sentences." Galsworthy wasn't bluffing. In a letter from a senior FCO mandarin, GW Harding, to a colleague, TF Brenchey, at the Cabinet Office, dated 18 May, and released in 2005 under the 30-year rule, Harding wrote that if the SAS men are imprisoned, the Prime Minister, Harold Wilson, might wish to consider "drastic measures to bring home our displeasure" to the Irish Government, including "an embargo on trade, a ban on remittances, withdrawal of social security benefits from Irish citizens [living in the UK], prohibition or limitation of Irish immigration and the ending of voting rights of Irish citizens living in this country."

The IRA followed these developments closely. Watched the comings and goings of the British ambassador to the Irish Foreign Affairs Ministry in central Dublin, and waited. In July 1976 Galsworthy was replaced by Christopher Ewart-Biggs, a veteran diplomatic troubleshooter, hand-picked by the new Labour PM, James Callaghan, to co-ordinate Anglo-Irish policy, which was going through a rough period following the cross-border incursions of loyalist paramiliaries and security forces personnel. Ewart-Biggs was also Oxford-educated, served with the Royal West Kent Regiment in the North African western desert campaign during WWII, losing his right eye in the first battle of El Alamein against Rommel's Afrika Corps in 1942, and as a result wore a distinctive, tinted monocle over a glass eye. He joined MI6 – under Foreign Office diplomatic cover - in the late 1940s. While posted in Lebanon in 1950 he attended the Middle East Centre for Arab Studies (MECAS), the British FCO-funded college located in the small village of Shemlane, about 10 miles from the capital, Beirut - referred to locally as the "English spy school" - whose 'graduates' include the MI6/KGB double agent, George Blake.

Ewart-Biggs served as political officer in Bahrain, Qatar, and Manila. He was stationed in Algiers in the early 1960s during the Front de Liberation Nationale (FLN) War of Independence against the French, attracting the attention of the French counterintelligence service, Direction de Surveillance du Territoire (DST), who believed he was passing information on French military capabilities to the FLN. Diplomatic postings at the British embassies in Brussels and Paris followed, before he moved to Ireland. On 21 July, two weeks after he had presented his credentials to the Irish President, Cearbhail O'Dalaigh, at Aras an Uachtarain in Dublin's Phoenix Park, he left his official residence in Sandycove, a south-side seaside resort, accompanied by Brian Cubban, the Permanent Under Secretary of State at the NIO, and Mr. Cubban's secretary, Judith Cook, escorted by Irish Special Branch officers and heading for yet another meeting with Dr. Fitzgerald, to be briefed personally on the Irish Government's annoyance - and diplomatic difficulties - with the illegal SAS incursions. To reach Dublin city center the two cars had to turn left immediately after leaving the residence. However, within 200 yards of the perimeter a massive landmine was detonated by remote control beneath the ambassador's vehicle by an IRA unit, which immediately left the area in a Ford Cortina, heading north back across the border to South Armagh.

Judith Cook died at the scene, Christopher Ewart-Biggs died later in hospital, and Brian Cubban was seriously injured. In an interview in the *Sunday Independent* newspaper two months later, three senior IRA officers claimed responsibility on behalf of the organization; "We make no apology for it. He was sent here to co-ordinate British intelligence activities, and was assassinated because of that, and in retaliation for the murder of Peter Cleary [an IRA Staff Captain, 1st Battalion, South Armagh, shot dead while in SAS custody on 15 April 1976] and for the activities of the SAS in South Armagh."

An inquiry into security for British diplomatic staff was ordered by the Foreign Office, to be headed by Sir Richard Sykes, ambassador in The Hague. Apart from being a colleague of Ewart-Biggs he was also an Oxford-educated friend, who served with the Royal Corps of Signals during WWII, and later as a member of the FCO diplomatic staff working in Peking, Brussels and Santiago, as well as heading the FCO's Defence Policy Department in Whitehall. At 9am on Thursday, 22 March 1979, as he was about to step into his Rolls Royce outside his official residence at 12 Westeinde, in the Dutch capital, for the 5-minute drive to the British Embassy on Lange Voorhout, he was shot dead by an IRA gunman using a 9mm automatic pistol. His Dutch-born, 19-year-old footman, Karel Straub, also died at the scene, shot by a second assassin using a 7.62 pistol. The shooters then turned back the way they came, crossing the small cobbled-stone square in front of the neo-classical St. Theresia of Avila Catholic Church, walking down a narrow laneway and exiting into Laan, then turned left and passed the police station at the corner of Jan Hendrikstraat. The two men, smartly dressed, walked briskly but without attracting the attention of passers-by, headed downtown and disappeared.

Almost all ranking British intelligence and security officers, serving and retired, attended the slain ambassador's funeral, including MI6 directors, Sir John Rennie and Sir Maurice Oldfield, MI5 director Howard Smith, Cabinet Office security coordinator, Sir Clive Rose, Cabinet Office policy adviser (and former WWII Special Operations Executive director) Sir Francis Richards, and Cabinet Office intelligence coordinator, Sir Antony Duff.

One week after Sykes died the Brussels-based French-language daily newspaper, *Le Soir,* published an article by Rene Haquin, a respected journalist specializing in security matters, in which he claimed that Sykes had been active in investigating a "secondary-supply IRA arms-trafficking network via Antwerp and Rotterdam." In this task he was assisted by Paul Holmer, under diplomatic cover with the UK's NATO mission in Brussels, who was responsible for monitoring IRA supply lines from West Germany. The focus of this article was confirmed by an IRA Army Council representative in an interview with journalist, Ed Moloney, published in the September 1979 issue of *Magill,* a Dublin-based weekly current affairs magazine: "Last Spring we executed Sir Richard Sykes. He was involved in intelligence gathering against our organization, but he was also a leading propagandist in the same way as Peter Jay in Washington. Sykes was also the man who conducted the investigation into our attack on the British ambassador to Dublin (...) Sykes was a very important person."

The eight SAS troopers whose map-reading 'errors' had led to this particular cycle of death in the intelligence war, had stood trial before the Special Criminal Court, in March 1977. They were cleared on charges of possession with intent to endanger life, and each was given a minimum fine on lesser charges. Speaking after the court hearing the British ambassador, Robert Haydon, said HMG was "very happy" the soldiers had been acquitted of any ill-intent in the Irish Republic, adding "we imagine that the fine was more or less mandatory and the Ministry of Defense will pay." None of the victims' relatives of SAS violence, on both sides of the Irish border, were impressed by how the case was handled by Irish officials, or the ambassador's glib dismissal of the SAS threat.

An internal assessment of the intelligence options following Sykes death, presented to the JIC and the newly-elected Conservative Cabinet under Prime Minister, Margaret Thatcher, resulted in two covert operations in West Germany, code-named *Scream* and *Ward,* run by MI5 and MI6, approved by JIC chairman, Sir Antony Duff, and enthusiastically supported by Downing Street where Mrs. Thatcher, unlike her Labour predecessors, had always maintained an interest in intelligence matters. Even in opposition, she had been receiving regular briefings from the former MI6 boss, Maurice Oldfield, whom she later appointed Coordinator of Intelligence in Northern Ireland.

Operation *Scream* involved the British Army's Intelligence and Security Group (ISG), headed by Lt. Col. Small. The aim was to cultivate individuals within the Irish community in West Germany, several of whom, according to the ISG, had 'volunteered' information about republican activists and sympathizers. Problems with the credibility of the informers, and concern that *Scream* hadn't the approval of the West German authorities, led to Operation *Ward,* basically the same line-up under another name, but this time with the Germans onside. The chairman of the *Ward* Control Group was MI6 officer, Michael Moores, and members included MI5 F Branch boss, John Deverell (who would later be among 25 senior MI5, Int. Corps and RUC intelligence personnel to die in the Chinook Mk2 helicopter crash on the Mull of Kintyre, in June 1994), R.C Cullen, MI6 head of security at the British Services Security Organization (BSSO), and Lt. Col. Small. The *Ward* Group met every eight weeks at the Rheindahlan Barracks, British Forces HQ, in Monchengladbach, to discuss operations, monitor progress and analyze results. Despite this display of high-ranking intelligence talent, after almost four years *Scream/Ward* failed to produce any intelligence of value. A 1993 BSSO internal report stated that out of sixteen agents recruited, "only two could be said to be active, in the sense of reporting anything at all." One agent was dropped by his handler for habitual lying, two more were arrested by West German police for working illegally, and others came under suspicion from the closely-knit Irish Diaspora, which dramatically reduced their worth as informers.

MI6 was willing to bring the West Germans on board because of the possibility that people "subject to German jurisdiction" might be targeted, and Operation *Ward* was packaged simply as an exercise to pre-empt IRA strikes against British military personnel stationed in West Germany, but MI5 wanted more, and eventually the situation became so complicated that the Security Service decided to disengage. To make matters worse the IRA obtained several classified documents, detailing *Ward*'s line-up and methodology which were then selectively released to the British and German media, with details of their origin and routing obscured, suggesting the IRA had run a successful counter-operation. The London-based, *Independent,* summed up the feelings of many, stating that the disclosures left the Thatcher administration "facing the most serious leak of information in its 20 year war against the IRA."

Behind the Wire

For decades, prisons and detention centers have been military academies for the IRA, an opportunity to analyze the campaign and redefine the art of resistance, from Frongoch Internment Camp in the rough moorland countryside of Merionethshire in north Wales, (where 1,800 IRA prisoners were held following the 1916 Easter Rising in Dublin) to the corrugated iron-roofed Nissan huts of RAF Long Kesh, where many of the 342 men lifted in Operation *Demetrius* in August 1971 were held.

There was always something to learn, even in English penal facilities like HM Prison Wandsworth, in southwest London, where an IRA volunteer on remand became friendly with Michael Bettany, a former MI5 agent serving a 23 year sentence after being found guilty of treason, on 16 April 1984, following a trial held 'in camera' at the Old Bailey, London, before a jury vetted by MI5. Bettaney's case was handled by Scotland Yard Special Branch Detective Superintendent, John Wescott, who was a frequent visitor to the Irish Garda HQ in the Phoenix Park, Dublin. His lawyer was Larry Grant, former chairman of the National Council of Civil Liberties (NCCL), and prominent on MI5's blacklist of lawyers whose previous clients included the 'renegade' CIA spy, Philip Agee.

Bettaney had joined the Security Service in autumn 1975, after being 'talent spotted' as potential MI5 material while studying at Pembroke College, Oxford. After basic training he worked in F Branch, "studying files on British communism" before being posted to the North of Ireland. He was based at Thiepval Barrack, in an office on the first floor known as the 'Box 500 suite' and one of his cover names was 'Mr. Edmond'. He often met politicians and senior RUC officers in the bar of a hotel near Holywood on the shores of Belfast Lough, and at a small restaurant in Hillsborough near the NIO, introducing himself as a Home Office civil servant.

Bettaney's security clearance gave him access to the computer database, codenamed *Crucible*, holding personal files on tens of thousands of people in the North, including pictures of alleged republican activists, maps of where they lived and details of their families and friends. A second computer system known as *Vengeful* held details of all licensed vehicles and a tracking system, and was linked to the Northern Ireland driver and vehicle licensing agency. Both systems provided total cover. The information was graded, with low-level data available to the front-line battalions, while the classified, sensitive material could only be accessed at brigade headquarters level by 14FSIC, MI5 and RUC Special Branch. As a senior MI5 F Branch officer, Bettaney had access to every RUC Special Branch and Military Intelligence 'source' report.

He was recalled to London in 1980, transferred to MI5 Section K, dealing with the activities of the KGB in London, and at some point while working at Gower Street HQ, he decided to offer his services to the Soviet agency, posting a letter to Arkady Gouk, a KGB agent under diplomatic cover, living in Holland Park, London. The letter contained classified details of the expulsion of three KGB officers from Ireland - Gennady Saline, (codenamed *Silver*), First Secretary and press attaché at the USSR Embassy in Dublin, a junior diplomat, Victor Lipassov and his wife Evotokia, who was also suspected of being a Soviet spy. Mr. Gouk, believing Bettaney was an MI5 'walk in', did not respond and after Bettaney persisted in trying to make contact, Scotland Yard Special Branch, acting on a tip-off (probably from the KGB), arrested him on 16 September 1983, three days before he was due to fly to Vienna with 50 files detailing MI5's 'order of battle' in the UK.

Bettaney was described as "puerile, self-opinionated and dangerous" by the trial judge, and held for one year in solitary confinement following his conviction. In mid-1985 an unsigned letter, believed to be from Bettaney, was received by the *Irish News* daily newspaper in Belfast, claiming that MI5 was behind the murders of Miriam Daly, a Queen's University lecturer, and John Turnley, a former member of the National H-Block Committee, both of whom had campaigned for political status for republican prisoners during the 1981 hunger strike. They were also members of the Irish Republican Socialist Party (IRSP), the political wing of the republican splinter group, the Irish National Liberation Army (INLA), which had claimed responsibility for the death of Tory MP, Airey Neave, killed by a bomb fitted with a mercury tilt switch attached to his Vauxhall Cavalier car, which exploded as he left the House of Commons car-park, on 30 March 1979. A former WWII veteran, Colditz PoW, and war-time member of the British Directorate of Military Intelligence (MI9), at the time of his death Neave was a close personal friend of Margaret Thatcher, her campaign manager during her successful bid for Tory Party leadership, and head of her private office since 1975. One month after his death the Tories won the general election, and

Airey Neave, had he lived, had been Thatcher's likely choice to coordinate the intelligence services in the North of Ireland. The newly-elected PM was bitter about Neave's death, and her premiership, during three terms in office, would be marked by a series of uncompromising confrontations with Irish republicanism. Within weeks of her election she held meetings with the directors of MI5 and MI6, Howard Smith and Arthur Franks, who briefed her on the intelligence situation in Ireland, and the full extent of intelligence penetration. The briefings, according to *Magill* (June 1979) was "not specific in terms of actual cases, but highly-detailed in explaining the basic 'modus operandi' of MI5 and MI6 operations."

What lay ahead in the North of Ireland was brought home to her three months later, on 27 August, when the IRA attacked a military convoy at Narrow Water, near Warrenpoint, County Down, resulting in the British Army's greatest single loss of life during Operation *Banner*. Six soldiers, members of the 2nd Battalion Parachute Regiment, died when a 500lb bomb, hidden in straw bales on a trailer parked in a lay-by on the A2 opposite Narrow Water Castle, exploded at 4.40pm when a convoy of two, four-ton trucks and a Landrover drove past, having left Ballykinlar Barracks to take the scenic coastal road skirting the Mountains of Mourne to Newry - the route chosen only 10 minutes before departure, for security reasons. The remaining soldiers took cover behind a stone wall near a gate-lodge on the opposite side of the road to wait for reinforcements and assess the situation. This was exactly what the Provos expected would happen. Almost simultaneously with the arrival of a Wessex helicopter carrying the O/C of the Bessbrook-based 1st Battalion Queen's Own Highlanders, Lt. Col. David Blair, a second 1.000lb bomb embedded in the gate lodge wall exploded, killing 12 soldiers including Lt. Col. Blair, whose vaporized body was identified by his epaulettes, one of which was presented to PM Thatcher by Brig. David Calthrop Thorne, during a security briefing, to "illustrate the human factor" of the attack, according to Thorne's obituary in the *Guardian* newspaper.

Meanwhile, in HMP Wandsworth, one of the largest men's prisons in Europe, and the site of 135 executions between 1878 and 1961, when it was still lawful to be hung by the neck for crimes such as treason, Bettaney and a remanded IRA bomber spoke for at least one hour each week "unguarded and unsupervised" in the prison chapel, according to journalist, Nicholas Davies. For obvious reasons, there is no record of the conversations, but it seems likely that Bettaney, now in total conflict with the British state, had found an enthusiastic recipient for his secrets, including details of the MI5 and Force Research Unit (FRU) agents network in the North. When Bettaney was recalled to London, according to Davies, he knew the identities of all IRA informers and agents working for the intelligence services at the time, and this included the FRU, which Davies claims was set up in 1979 specifically to collate information on behalf of the Army.

However, the FRU was not a passive intelligence-gathering organization, but was designed to be "hard and aggressive, to carry the

The Butcher's Apron

undercover war raging on the streets of Belfast to the enemy within, the Provos." The FRU was not listed in any MoD literature. Based at Thiepval Barracks with its own classified budget, the FRU was represented on the Tasking Co-ordination Group (TCG) alongside MI5, the SAS, RUC Special Branch and the regular Army. As its name indicates, the TCG managed all security and intelligence operations in the North, including facilitating FRU requests for 'restriction orders' to cover specific areas at a specific time, to allow operations to take place without being inadvertently interrupted by an RUC or Army patrol. On nearly every occasion prior to FRU clandestine operations, intelligence was routed from street level to the top, from the FRU to the TCG and the Coordinator of Intelligence Northern Ireland (CINI), to the JIC in London, and eventually, to Downing Street and the private office of PM Thatcher.

In 1979/1980, when the FRU was mandated to conduct its murderous campaign, this line-up included the head of the FRU, Brig. Gordon Kerr, the RUC Chief Constable, Ronnie Flanagan, the RUC Special Branch boss, Bob Fitzsimmons, and MI5's chief-of-station, John Deverell, at TCG level, CINI ex-MI6 director Maurice Oldfield, who was replaced following his death in 1981 by Francis 'Brooks' Richards, and the JIC, chaired by Antony Duff. The intelligence would also have been routed (for political consideration, not for operational decision-making) to the Northern Ireland Secretary of State, Humphrey Atkins, and the Permanent Secretary NIO, Sir Philip Woodfield, who had represented HMG, along with senior MI6 officer, Frank Fenwick Steel, in secret talks with IRA representatives in June 1972, the first meeting between both sides. This had led to a 'bilateral truce' that collapsed within weeks when the IRA responded to loyalist violence in Belfast after the British Army failed to intervene.

The FRU intelligence product was reviewed in London by the senior echelon of Britain's political, military and intelligence establishment, all of whom were aware that the FRU was running loyalist agents, who were acting as 'proxy assassins' on behalf of the British state. But because nothing was done at senior level to prevent the sectarian killings, the only logical conclusion is that these murders were sanctioned - part of some senseless strategy to punish and terrorize the nationalist community.

The liaison between Bettaney and the IRA prisoner alarmed MI5 and the FRU, and talks were held to decide if agents should be pulled, and what measures should be taken to ensure informants' safety. When the IRA failed to respond a decision was taken to leave everybody in place, an assumption - which would later prove fatal for security forces personnel - that the Provos knew nothing, including of the presence within their ranks of *Stakeknife*, the codename given to Freddie Scappaticci, a Belfast-based member who had been turned by the Int. Corps and was now working for the FRU. It has been claimed that Scappaticci was in charge of the IRA's internal security unit and, according to former IRA intelligence officer, Eamon Collins, he had been responsible for more than forty murders over a period spanning two decades. Many of those killed were Army and RUC Special Branch low-level informants whom 'Scap' executed as part of his job and to protect his cover. We have, therefore, the rather bizarre situation of an FRU agent inside the IRA - described as the "jewel in the Crown" and the "most important agent ever inside the IRA" by the British media - killing other police and military HUMINT sources, and being paid the yearly sum of approximately $100,000, through a secret Gibraltar bank account, to do so. .

The FRU's home base was Repton Manor, a medieval building within Templar Barracks, a large military establishment in Ashford, Kent. Successful applicants included men and women from all three uniformed regular services - Army, Royal Navy and Royal Air Force (RAF) – as well as the SAS and the Int. Corps. They were subjected to an intense two-month training schedule involving all the basics for undercover, counter-insurgency tasks, such as small-arms proficiency, car-drill (including how to use the vehicle as a weapon to avoid capture) close-quarter combat, assault course and long-distance endurance, as well as how to handle agents, pick up and drop off information in public, carry out surveillance on foot or from a vehicle without attracting attention, and how to resist interrogation in rooms soundproofed and filled with 'white noise' and other disorientation techniques.

The massive resources available to the FRU created friction with the RUC Special Branch, whose role in intelligence gathering was diminished in favor of what some officers called the "English policy," and there were those within the force who believed that several of Scappaticci's victims, mainly touts for the RUC Special Branch, were betrayed by the FRU. Reducing the capability of the opposition's clandestine network prevented operational overlap, helped the West Belfast builder enhance his reputation for ruthlessness and efficiency, and maintain his cover. But there is no indication, in any of the literature available, that Scappaticci ever provided an ounce of intelligence that helped save lives or prevent IRA operations. He was little more than a 'fixer,' cleaning up some of the mess created by his handlers.

In the North of Ireland the FRU had between 50 and 80 officers, including field agents and handlers, scattered across the province, and support staff processing and analyzing the intelligence 'take'. The FRU operated from 1980 until 1992, when its name was changed (for operational and political reasons) to the Joint Services Group (JSG) during the course of three inquiries into allegations of collusion between the security forces and loyalist assassins, carried out by Sir John Stevens, who was Chief Constable of Northumbria Police when he began his investigation in 1990, and Chief Constable at Scotland Yard when he ended it in 2003.

The name-change, a tried and tested technique frequently used by the MoD during the Troubles to confuse, followed the arrest and trial of the FRU's most productive agent, Brian Nelson, an intelligence officer with the largest loyalist paramilitary organization, the Ulster Defense Association (UDA) which ran death squads under the *nom-de-guerre,* Ulster Freedom

Fighters (UFF). It targeted nationalists and republican political activists using intelligence from P-files provided by Nelson's FRU handlers, and weapons smuggled into the province from South Africa, an operation which could not have taken place without the clandestine cooperation of the securocrats in MI5, who were now running the war in the shadows in the North.

Brian Nelson was a borderline psychopath, an attribute which made him ideal agent material for what the FRU was planning. A convicted felon, Nelson had already served three years of a 7-year sentence handed down in February 1974, for his part in the abduction and electrocution of a registered blind man, Gerald Higgins, at a UDA drinking club on Belfast's Wilton Street. In 1965 Nelson, aged 17, had joined the Black Watch Regiment and claimed never to have left or been discharged from the Army, even while running with the UDA in the early 1970s, or following his conviction in connection with the death of Gerry Higgins. When he was released he moved to West Germany, and worked in the building trade in Munich. Meanwhile, back home in Belfast the lethal presence of the FRU was being considered and signed-off by the British Army's Commander of Land Forces, Major General James Glover, and Nelson was suggested as a useful asset because of his UDA credentials. According to Davies, MI5 asked MI6 to trace Nelson. The request was passed to the West German security service, Bundesamt fur Verfassungsschutz (BfV), and within 48 hours the FRU had Nelson's address and phone number. Contact was initially made by MI5, and at a meeting with two Int. Corps officers in Munich, Nelson was offered a job as a taxi-driver, a 'family-size' house, a weekly $500 retainer, and a mid-size, Mazda Capella car. He returned to Belfast, worked as a freelance driver with Woodvale Taxis, 'rejoined' the UDA as an intelligence officer, and according to Brig. Arundell Leakey, British Army Director of Operations - in a sworn affidavit supporting an MoD injunction to prevent publication of a book by one of Nelson's FRU handlers - Nelson "offered his services to the Army as an agent in 1983."

Arming the Sons of Ulster

Some statistics are damned lies, others, stripped of political spin, can provide a concise and accurate account of a specific situation. Between January 1982 and December 1987, a six-year period prior to the glory days of the FRU and the arrival of an arms shipment from South Africa, loyalist organizations killed 71 people, 49 of which were clearly sectarian/political murders, according to Professor Bill Rolston. In the six years following the shipment, from January 1988 to September 1994 (when the IRA's first ceasefire came into force), the loyalists killed 229 people, 207 of which were sectarian/political murders. Prof Rolston, in his excellent book, *Unfinished Business*, believes Nelson (who would die an unrepentant assassin in south Wales in April 2003) was directly involved in 15 murders, 15 attempted murders and 62 conspiracies to murder.

The re-arming of the loyalist death squads has been described as "one of the biggest and least-publicized security scandals" of the Troubles. A good point to begin addressing the issue is the visit home in 1985 by a former merchant seaman, Richard Wright, originally from Portadown, who had emigrated to South Africa. Wright was an agent for the South African state-owned arms company, Armscor, which had been established in 1968 and tasked by the apartheid regime with making the country self-sufficient in military hardware, by whatever means necessary, in defiance of the 1963 United Nations international arms embargo. High on Armscor's wish-list was a missile system which could be used in the bush campaigns in Namibia and Angola. Israel, which had also defied the UN ban on intellectual property relating to arms production, and supplied Pretoria with blueprints for ships, missiles, and small arms (which had made South Africa one of the world's top ten arms exporters by the mid-1980s), was keen to get its hands on plans for an advanced, man-portable, self-propelled, surface-to-air missile system, known as *Starstreak,* being developed by Short Brothers in Belfast.

Dick Wright was also related to Alan Wright, leader of the Ulster Clubs (a network of unionist political and evangelical organizations) and co-founder of Ulster Resistance, a loyalist paramilitary coordination group. The man from Armscor offered the loyalists weapons worth $500,000, but missile parts or plans were an "acceptable alternative" to cash. The UDA leader, John McMichael. decided to send the organization's intelligence officer, Brian Nelson, to investigate the possibility of doing business with the South Africans. Nelson traveled to Pretoria, via London over the weekend 7/8 June 1985.

The conditions of the deals being offered became more attractive after Wright had taken Nelson on a tour of Armscor facilities. The FRU agent offered to supply plans or parts for *Starstreak,* and if possible a complete Shorts missile system in return for a substantial arms shipment and $2 million. In 1992, the British magazine, *Private Eye,* claimed that Nelson's visit had been cleared by both the MoD and an unnamed HMG minister, and that part of the Director of Public Prosecution (DPP) leniency deal agreed to with Nelson, prior to his subsequent trial in Belfast, was that "no mention would be made of his visit to SA, or the government minister who signed-off on it."

The UDA had hit the mother-lode. In June 1987, the equivalent of $500,000 was raised by means of an armed robbery on the Northern Bank in Portadown which was used to buy even more weapons than the UDA could handle, so the UVF and Ulster Resistance were brought on board. A secret communications channel was set up to coordinate distribution. Nelson made five trips to South Africa, according to ex-FRU agent, Ian Hurst, meeting representatives of the apartheid regime and MI5 in London each time before flying to Johannesburg. He personally delivered Armscor manuals to the Sidney Street, West Belfast, home of UDA boss Tommy Lyttle, an RUC Special Branch informant, who careful selected the weapons he wanted.

The deal was finalized in December 1987, and Joseph Fawzi, a Lebanese trader employed by Douglas Bernhardt, a South African

National Intelligence Service (NIS) agent working with Armscor, dispatched a large shipment to Ireland, approximately 200 Czech-manufactured Vz.58 7.62mm, assault rifles (originally used by the Palestinian Liberation Organization during the Lebanese war in the early 1980s, confiscated by the Israeli Defense Forces and sold on to Armscor), 94 Browning 9mm pistols (holding 13 rounds, twelve in the clip, one in the barrel on reload), 450 Soviet-manufactured RGD-5 fragmentation grenades, 4 RPG rocket launchers and 62 warheads, and 30,000 rounds of assorted ammunition. At each stage in the proceedings Nelson had informed his FRU handler, Nicholas Nickleson, of every detail, including the lethal cargo's estimated time of arrival at Belfast docks from Lebanon, in January 1988. Nelson also claims, in his prison journal, that his handler told him the weapons had been allowed in, not as a result of some error or oversight on the part of the British military authorities, but because of the "deep suspicion the seizure would have been aroused, to protect me it had been decided to let the first shipment into the country untouched."

The loyalists lost about two-thirds of their dark materials of war during the course of the year. Enough remained, however, from a second smaller shipment to make a difference on the streets. One of those arrested in connection with the gun-running during RUC raids was Ulster Resistance chairman, Noel Lyttle, a Belfast civil servant, former member of the UDR, and associate of the DUP leadership, who had stood as candidate for the party at local elections. With these types of connections Lyttle was soon released without charge. He would spend longer behind bars, however, following his arrest by the French police in Paris in April 1989, when the South Africans, who had helped set up the 1988 shipment, renewed interest in an arms-for-technology deal. In October 1988, Ulster Resistance managed to steal a *Javelin* SAM aiming system (less desirable than *Starstreak* that superseded it, but nonetheless useful for research purposes), and three Ulster Resistance men traveled to the French capital to negotiate with the South Africans, who had already made a substantial cash down-payment. This time the loyalists were offering not only the missile component but expertise in how to use the weapon. One of the men who traveled with Lyttle and James King was Samuel Quinn, a senior NCO with the Territorial Army's Ulster Air Defense Regiment (UADR) who trained recruits in the use of the *Blowpipe* missile (which was replaced by the more advanced *Javelin*). One of the weapons being offered to the South Africans was a 'dummy' *Blowpipe*, stolen from the TA base in Newtownards, where Quinn served.

The three men were arrested in the company of US arms dealer, Douglas Bernhardt, and a South African diplomat, Daniel Storm. A diplomatic row blew up between France and the UK after Storm was expelled from France. The British authorities claimed they were unaware of the clandestine activities of the principals involved, despite the fact that Bernhardt, a South African-born, naturalized American married to an Englishwoman, had been operating a sporting gun dealership, Field Arms, in Mayfair, since the mid-1980s, and to do so he had to be registered with all the necessary licensing and trade departments in London. Bernhardt would have been known to Scotland Yard and MI5, because of the nature of the business. MI5 also knew that he was the US arms dealer involved with the January 1988 weapons shipment, that Dirk Wright had been employed as a marketing executive by Field Arms, and that Noel Lyttle, questioned in Belfast by the RUC, had admitted knowing Wright as an Armscor agent "for quite a few years."

The Swiss authorities began an investigation into Bernhardt's Geneva-based, container leasing company, Agencia Utica, in connection with the 1988 arms shipment from Lebanon to Belfast. The British made no extradition request for Bernhardt, or the three loyalists, all of whom were eventually released on bail and quietly left French jurisdiction. The Home Office responded to the allegations of contacts between the South African regime and Ulster loyalists by expelling three South Africa embassy personnel, the First Secretary, Jan Castleyn, Sgt. Mark Brunwer, who was not on the accredited diplomatic list and was described in the press as a "technical officer," and Etienne Fourie, an accredited journalist who had worked in Belfast as a South African news correspondent in the 1970s, and was listed by MI6, and in the FCO's diplomatic files, as a "covert asset" at the embassy because of his South African intelligence connections.

Bad Day in Belfast

During a speech in the House of Commons on 17 January 1989, Douglas Hogg, a junior Home Office minister in the Thatcher administration, suggested that certain Northern Irish solicitors were "unduly sympathetic" to republicans in RUC custody. Hogg had returned from Belfast the previous month where he had been briefed at RUC HQ on the security situation by Chief Constable John Hermon, and senior RUC Special Branch officers. His remark cause a storm of protest but the Home Office issued a statement saying the minister "stood by his statement" despite suggestions that it would put "the lives of certain solicitors" at risk. At the time that Hogg made his allegation, the Home Office almost certainly knew, from MI5 briefings, that the UDA had planned to assassinate Belfast solicitor, Patrick Finucane. The issue had also been raised at Downing Street meetings of the JIC, and was known to senior members of the Cabinet, including Prime Minister Thatcher. Short of signing a death warrant, Hogg's statement could not have been more of an encouragement for the UDA gunmen. Hogg denied this was his intention, and there's no reason to doubt his denial, but for an Eton and Oxford-educated, supposedly intelligent barrister, it was an act of crass stupidity. One again a British politician had displayed an appalling level of ignorance about the situation on the ground in Belfast, and his words contributed, however unintentionally, to the death of a man whose only 'crime' was to practice his profession to the best of his ability.

Within hours of Hogg's speech, Tommy 'Tucker' Lyttle met his RUC Special Branch handler. Hogg's comments were discussed, and according to Lyttle, his handler suggested "whacking" Finucane. Lyttle ordered Nelson to prepare an intelligence file, unaware that Nelson was already targeting the solicitor, according to two FRU reports passed to MI5. When Nelson reported back to his FRU handler that Lyttle was also planning a hit on Finucane, the FRU responded by compiling a dossier which included photographs of the Finucane family home on Fortwilliam Avenue, off the city's Antrim Road, and detailed maps of the area. On one occasion, according to journalist, Greg Harkin, an FRU officer and Nelson posed as window cleaners and offered their 'services' to a neighbor in order to check the rear of Finucane's property.

Sunday, 12 February 1989, was cold and overcast. At approximately 7.30pm two UDA gunman crashed through the front door and into the large kitchen where the Finucane family were about to have dinner, and shot the solicitor 14 times in front of his three children, and his wife, Geraldine, who was wounded in the attack. The shooter was Ken Barrett, later described by an RUC officer as "one of the most cold-blooded killers" he had ever met. Barrett, and a still unidentified 'back-up' left the scene in a taxi driven by a third man that had been hijacked earlier in Glencairn, and was later found abandoned at the junction of Ballygomartin and Forthriver, in a loyalist area of the city. Barrett had been an RUC Special Branch tout inside the UDA since the late 1980s. The weapons used were supplied by UDA quartermaster, William Stobie. He had been told to take some 'gear' to a UDA club on the Highfied Estate, where he met Barrett and UFF commander, Eric McKee. Also present was Jim Spence, a UDA commander who assured the hit team that their escape route across town had been cleared by his RUC Special Branch handlers. Strobie was also an RUC Special Branch tout and, as part of standard procedure in this relationship, he had called his handler after handing over the weapons to Barrett. Indeed, on the day he died it's difficult to find any RUC Special Branch officer who was unaware that the Finucane 'hit' was going down, or did anything to stop it. Most, in fact, were quite happy to be rid of the 'troublesome' solicitor, and had expressed such sentiments to republican suspects in police custody.

At the time of his death Pat Finucane was representing (among others) the family of Gervaise McKerr, one of three unarmed men shot dead by an SAS-trained RUC HMSU (Headquarters Mobile Support Unit) at a VCP near Craigavon, in South Armagh, in November 1982. Within a four-week period the undercover RUC unit shot dead four more unarmed suspects in the area. In May 1984, amid accusations that the police were now operating a shoot-to-kill policy, the Deputy Chief Constable of Greater Manchester Police (GMC), John Stalker, was called in to investigate.

From the beginning the senior ranks of the RUC, including Chief Con. John Hermon, and Special Branch boss, Trevor Forbes, were openly hostile to Stalker, while behind his back rank-and-file officers called the Manchester policeman a "fucking Fenien" (a derisive reference to the 19th century Irish revolutionary brotherhood).

In his account of the investigation Stalker states that his team of English detectives were told that shortly before the Armagh killings an informer had told the RUC Special Branch that four of the suspects had been involved in an IRA landmine attack on an armored RUC patrol at Oxford Island, near Lurgan, in which three police officers had died. RUC Special Branch denied Stalker access to the intelligence file on the landmine attack. This was typical of the obstruction that the Stalker inquiry faced. Special Branch officers also told members of the HMSU that the Official Secrets Act allowed them to lie to investigating officers, and in court, to protect the lives of informants. The RUC Criminal Investigation Department (CID) inquiry into the killings was "slipshod and in some aspects woefully incomplete" and several officers were "amateur and inefficient" or were "deliberately inept."

In two incidents Special Branch had targeted the victims, briefed the HMSU officers, and after the shootings they had removed the men, guns and cars from the crime scene before the CID were allowed access. Cover stories were provided, and they decided "at what point the CID were allowed to commence the official investigation of what had occurred, what was evidence and who was a fugitive terrorist." Stalker states that in all his years as a police officer he had never experienced "such an influence over an entire police force by one small section." Low-ranking Special Branch officers would tell senior CID officers how to conduct themselves, and the "power of the Special Branch pervaded the RUC at all levels." Not surprisingly one of the priority demands of Sinn Fein, during peace negotiations more than a decade later, was disbandment of the Special Branch. The Independent Commission for Policing in Northern Ireland (ICPNI), chaired by Conservative politician and former Hong Kong governor, Chris Patten, agreed, describing the Special Branch as a "force within a force," recommending the early retirement or transfer of its officers to other branches of the reconstituted and redefined Police Force of Northern Ireland (PSNI).

It was Stalker's investigation into the death of an innocent teenager, Michael Tighe, aged 17, shot by HMSU personnel when he inadvertently walked into a hayshed under surveillance, that led to the political establishment in London deciding to shut down the shoot-to-kill inquiry. The hayshed, suspected of being an IRA arms dump, was bugged by MI5 and the device was transmitting when Tighe was shot. John Hermon had one copy of the audiotape, which included conversations between the RUC officers involved in the stakeout, another copy was in the possession of MI5, and Stalker was refused access to both. In his book he describes the murder of Tighe as "the act of a Central American assassination squad - truly a police force out of control. The cover stories, the lies, the obstruction were insignificant when placed alongside possible state murder. I expected others to think the same. I was mistaken."

What they were actually thinking in London was how to destroy Stalker's credibility. Within weeks of obtaining a court order instructing Chief Con. Hermon to hand over all the evidence on the hayshed case, including a transcript of the audiotape - which the RUC boss now claimed had been destroyed - Stalker was "removed forever" from the shoot-to-kill inquiry in March 1986, after being accused of improper association with criminal elements in Manchester, and suspended, while his replacement, the Chief Constable of West Yorkshire, Colin Sampson, investigated allegations into Stalker's off-duty behavior and completed his shoot-to-kill inquiry. Sampson's report, three months later, criticized Stalker for a "less than excellent standard of professional performance" but produced no evidence to warrant his suspension. However, Stalker's relationship with two key colleagues at GMP, Chief Con. James Anderton, and CID boss, Detective Chief Supt. Peter Topping, who had investigated his [Stalker's] friends and alleged misdemeanors over a nine-month period, was irreparably damaged. Stalker resigned, the victim of a vendetta to protect the state, the reputation of RUC Chef Con. John Hermon, and to maintain the wall of silence surrounding the murderous behavior of the RUC Special Branch. And it cost the British Government approximately $15 million in legal fees and damages paid out in mid-1995 to Peter Taylor, a Manchester businessman who successfully sued GMP for malicious prosecution as part of a campaign to discredit his friend, John Stalker.

During a debate, on 14 February 1996, in the House of Commons on new powers for the nominally independent Police Complaints Authority, reference was made to joint operations between the police and MI5. Tory MP, Rupert Allason, reminded colleagues of the Stalker affair, and Colin Sampson's subsequent recommendation that two MI5 officers should be prosecuted for perverting the course of justice. This was rejected by the Crown Prosecution Service (CPS) "quite properly" according to Allason, because it was "not in the public interest to proceed with those prosecutions." This sums up HMG's attitude to capital crimes and 'misdemeanors' committed by MI5 during the Troubles. It has never been in the British Government's interest to publicly chastise, let alone prosecute, MI5 officers for criminal conduct in Ireland, and knowing this allowed MI5 securocrats to continue their nefarious activities, including attempts to undermine the peace process in the 1990s.

"Neither deal falsely, nor lie to one another" (Leviticus 19:11)

We are the sum of our experiences, of what has been learned along the way. For those of us who covered the Troubles, and were aware of the security forces collusion with the loyalists from local sources, including relatives of the victims, it was difficult to stomach the hypocrisy of men like Secretary of State for Northern Ireland, Tom King, who called on the RUC and MI5 to bring the perpetrators of the "awful cycle of violence" to justice.

Mr. King wasn't a stupid man. He was well-briefed before he took the job. He knew what was taking place on the streets of the city, and the covert conspiracies to eliminate the 'opposition'. All Mr. King had to do was issue a directive from the comfort of his well-appointed office at Stormont

Castle to call off the dogs of war and the awful cycle of violence would have ended. Other members of the British Government also knew exactly what was happening in Ireland. The Home Office, for example, was a recipient of information from MI5 representatives who were present in the same office as the FRU's Operations Officer at Thiepval Barracks. All dealings with Nelson were written up by his FRU handlers in a *Military Intelligence Source Report* (MISR), which was routed to the FRU's O/C Brig. Kerr and the TCG. It was also read by the MI5 duty officer. FRU handlers provided *Contact Reports* to backroom staff for analysis, which contained as much low-grade information as possible about Provisional activists, to be filed away for future reference.

The day after Pat Finucane's death, Colin Haddick, president of the Law Society of Northern Ireland, accused the unrepentant Douglas Hogg of 'encouraging' the proxy assassins of the State to murder Patrick Finucane:

> We are on record at the time Mr. Hogg made the statement of having expressed our disbelief at what he said. If Mr. Hogg had specific cause for concern about solicitors generally or as individuals, there are well-known channels through which he could have had such matters investigated. Let me add that the Law Society has never once been asked to investigate the conduct of any solicitor. What Mr. Hogg has done is to create an excuse for terrorist organizations to carry out murders, something which was not available to them before.

For six months the authorities in Belfast and London resisted calls for an official inquiry into Mr. Finucane's murder, and repeatedly dismissed allegations of collusion, saying there was no evidence, and that the lives of soldiers and policemen would be put at risk if 'confidential information' was leaked to the Provos. And then the UDA made a fatal error which completely undermined the official line. In order to justify the murder of Loughlin Maginn, shot dead by the UFF at his home near Rathfriland, County Down, on 25 August 1989, whom the loyalists falsely claimed was an IRA intelligence officer, the UDA published security documents to prove their allegation, and an RUC surveillance video provided by Brian Nelson's FRU handlers. Eventually the RUC Chief Constable, Hugh Annesley, a Dublin-born, senior British police officer (and graduate of the FBI National Executive Institute in the US) who had replaced John Hermon the previous June, was left with no choice but to order an official inquiry, to be handled by the deputy Chief Constable of Cambridgeshire Constabulary, John Stevens.

It's not known if John Stevens read John Stalker's account of his experiences in the North, but if the Cambridgeshire police officer assumed he would have the cooperation of the authorities in Belfast to conduct his investigation in a proper and diligent manner, he was quickly educated in the harsh realities of exactly where he was and what he was dealing with. Within months his team of detectives had issued warrants for the arrests of more than 30 loyalists, including Brian Nelson. On 11 January 1990, the evening before he was due to be taken into custody, Nelson, with the assistance of his FRU handlers, fled to England, while in Carrickfergus RUC station the offices used by the inquiry team was gutted by fire, deliberately started by members of the British Army's 'Covert Methods of Entry' squad, which seriously damaged hardcopy files, according to a November 1999 report in the *Sunday Times*. Nelson was finally arrested by Scotland Yard officers and returned to Belfast to stand trial on thirty-five counts, including murder and conspiracy to murder. Brig. Gordon Kerr, identified in trial transcripts as 'Colonel J', gave evidence, claiming Nelson had saved dozens of lives, testimony presumably based on briefings with one of Nelson's FRU handlers, Captain Margaret Walshaw, whom Nelson refers to as 'Mags' in his prison journal account of an arms theft:

> Mags informed me that she had been instructed by the boss [Brig. Kerr] to tell me that a substantial amount of weapons had been stolen from the armory at Palace Barracks, the police and she strongly suspected the UDA to have been involved (...) She told me that the person who had taken the weapons [including the gun later used in the murder of Patrick Finucane] was a UDR sergeant called Fletcher who lived in the Woodvale area. He was known to frequent [UDA] drinking clubs in that area, also used by Eric McKee [the UFF commander] and the boss reckons that Eric McKee has a hand in it somewhere.

The former NI Secretary, Tom King, also testified on Nelson's behalf. Eventually, after several meetings between the prosecution, MoD lawyers and defense counsel, fifteen of the most serious charges were dropped after the defendant agreed to plead guilty to conspiracy to murder, possession of weapons, and possession of classified documents. Nelson was sentenced to ten years, and was released and relocated to South Wales in 1996. No member of the FRU or the RUC Special Branch were questioned, arrested or charged with any offence.

The Stevens report does not name one individual whose life had been saved as a result of Nelson's activity. During a crowded press conference, on 7 May 1990 at RUC HQ in East Belfast, Stevens told journalists that he had been "able to draw firm conclusions that members of the security forces have passed information to paramilitaries. However, I must make it clear it is restricted to a small number of individuals, who have gravely abused their positions of trust. This abuse is not widespread or institutionalized." No RUC officers were involved with Ulster Resistance, there was no evidence that Special Branch officers had facilitated loyalist death squads, and he had no comment when asked about the mysterious fire at his Carrickfergus offices.

This RUC-friendly version of the investigation raised questions that Stevens was unwilling or unable to answer, and following Nelson's conviction he was asked by the Director of Public Prosecutions (DPPNI) in Belfast to look into matters raised, including leaks, during the course of his inquiry, and the tip-off that brought journalists sympathetic to the government's position to the province to cover the raids and arrests of loyalist paramilitaries twenty-four hours before they took place, but allowed Brian Nelson's FRU handlers time to move him to the mainland. He was also told to include Patrick Finucane's murder in his inquiries, following a growing international campaign, and calls for the UN Human Rights Commission (UNHRC) to intervene.

A police inquiry was now underway, headed on a day-to-day basis by Stevens' deputy at Scotland Yard, Hugh Orde (who would later take charge of the PSNI). In June 1999, William Stobie was arrested. The sole evidence against him was a statement given to the police by former journalist and NIO press officer, Neil Mulholland, about Stobie's logistics role in Finucane's murder. In November 2001, the case against him at Belfast Crown Court collapsed. Later, in two television interviews for Channel 4 and UTV, Stobie admitted working for RUC Special Branch, claimed he told his police handler about the murder plot when he was asked to provide the weapons, and supported calls for an independent inquiry into the solicitor's assassination.

Within weeks Stobie was dead, shot by a loyalist gunman at 6.30am on 12 December, as he left his home at Forthriver Road. Ken Barrett relocated to England. He was arrested, in May 2003, at a 'safe house' in Eastbourne, Sussex. During his trial at Belfast Crown Court in October 2004, he pleaded guilty to a series of charges, including the murder of Patrick Finucane, the attempted murder of Geraldine Finucane, possessing weapons, UFF membership, and the theft of standard-issue British Army weapons in 1987. He also admitted working for the RUC Special Branch since 1991. He was sentenced to 22 years, and served 18 months in Maghaberry Prison before being released, following a hearing of the Sentence Review Board, on 23 May 2006, under the terms of the Belfast Agreement, which allowed for the release of those convicted of paramilitary crimes to qualify for early release. Within hours Barrett had left Northern Ireland, accompanied by several FRU agents, relocated abroad, and provided with a new identity.

The speed of his departure suggested that the MoD was busy tidying up loose ends. By this stage two of Barrett's associates, Brian Nelson and William Stobie, were dead. Nelson's handlers, including Capt. Walshaw, had long since been recalled to Repton Manor, and Brig. Kerr had been appointed military attaché in Hong Kong. The only one obstacle remaining before the British Government and the MoD could close this sordid chapter in British military history was how to deal with an independently-minded Commonwealth judge.

The Man from Ontario

In 2003 retired Canadian Supreme Court Judge, Peter deCarteret Cory, was asked by London and Dublin to analyze the evidence in six cases of alleged collusion, four involving loyalist paramilitaries with the security forces in the North, and two involving the IRA with the Garda Siochana in the Irish Republic. The British and Irish governments agreed to act on the recommendations of the *Cory Collusion Report*, and in the four northern cases, including the murder of Patrick Finucane, Judge Cory recommended public inquiries.

One of two cases in the South involved the deaths of Lord Justice Maurice Gibson and his wife, Cecily, in a remotely-detonated car-bomb explosion on 25 April 1987, shortly after they had crossed the border in South Armagh, en route to Belfast following a Spanish holiday. Neither the British Army nor the RUC regularly patrolled close to the border, despite the high-tech, hilltop observation towers which were serviced by helicopters from Bessbrook. The towers were derisively referred to as the 'Maginot Line' by SAS troopers, according to Harnden, because they allowed a "siege mentality to develop," involved a lot of material and manpower, and achieved "the square-foot of fuck all." The IRA had conducted a topographical 'dead ground study' to include the new man-made features, and had worked out that on a clear day, the towers could cover no more than 35 percent of the land area. When the weather closed in this was reduced considerably. Judge Cory found no evidence of IRA/Garda collusion in the Gibson attack.

However, in the second case, the deaths of two senior RUC officers, Chief Supt. Harry Breen and Supt. Robert Buchanan, who died in an IRA ambush near the border at Jonesborough, South Armagh, shortly after meeting with Garda representatives in Dundalk, Cory recommended a public inquiry. The Dublin Government set up the Smithwick Tribunal, which has become a soapbox for abandoned FRU spies, like Keeley and Hurst, to express their grievances, and also, unwittingly, one of the more interesting forums for discussion on how the IRA, technically and militarily, successfully waged the long war.

The British Government reneged on its promise of an inquiry into Pat Finucane's murder, which surprised few republicans (having had some experience of dealing with "perfidious Albion") but came as something of a shock to Judge Cory. On 7 June 2005, the UK *Inquiries Act* (2005), replacing the 1921 *Tribunals of Inquiry (Evidence Act)*, was passed, severely limiting the scope of the independent inquiries proposed in his report. In a letter to Baroness Ashton, the minister responsible for constitutional affairs, Lord Saville, who chaired the Bloody Sunday inquiry, said he would "not be prepared to be appointed as a member" and be "subjected to provisions of this kind." Before the *Inquiries Act* became law in the UK, Judge Cory told US Congressional hearings into human rights in the North of Ireland that the changes "make a meaningful inquiry impossible" because HMG ministers in charge at the MoD and the Home Office (which has political responsibility for MI5) "would have the authority to thwart the efforts of the inquiry at every step." Judge Cory also advised all "self-respecting Canadian judges" to decline an appointment. His concerns were borne out when a British official confirmed to the UN Commission on Human Rights that most of the witnesses called to testify at any inquiry into collusion would be required to give evidence in private because of "security considerations."

Suspect Devices

At the height of the IRA's economic bombing campaign in the North of Ireland there was always a senior British political representative available, after yet another street echoed to the sound of falling masonry and broken glass, to "reassure the public" that the Provos "would not bomb their way to the conference table." It became one of the over-used clichés of the long war, despite both Cabinet ministers and senior MoD officials knowing that their own military option had failed. It was what unionist politicians, and the media wanted to hear, and used frequently because there was really nothing else to say. As long as the destructive campaign was confined to the North, the cost in material terms was manageable, despite the Government having to pick up the tab because the insurance companies had cancelled bomb damage coverage for the province in the early 1970s.

The Provos may not have arrived at the conference table covered in dust and debris, but after Margaret Thatcher had narrowly escaped assassination during the Conservative Party's annual conference in Brighton, on 12 October 1984, when the bomb, fitted with a time-delay unit manufactured from a VTR component, and hidden behind the bath in Room 629 of the Grand Hotel (where IRA member Patrick McGee, using the name "Roy Walsh" had stayed the previous month), exploded at 2.51am, killing five people, including Tory MP, Anthony Berry, and Roberta Wakeman, the wife of the Parliamentary Treasury Secretary, John Wakeham, it began to dawn on the unelected mandarins in positions of influence that matter in Whitehall, that some accommodation would have to be reached with the IRA or this thing could go on, if not forever, at least well into the 21st century.

Following the Brighton bombing, the IRA changed its tactics on the mainland. According to statistics produced by Queen's University academic, Mike Tomlinson, between 1984 and 1989

> only two incidents were recorded by the Home Office involving injury or loss of life. From 1989, the number of incidents grew rapidly so that by 1992 and 1993, there was on average one bombing per week. IRA actions disrupted commuter traffic (in England) on 1,060 occasions in 1992. The British Transport Police dealt with 1,850 bomb threats and explosive devices in 1992, and 1,143 last year [1993].

A back-channel between senior MI6 officer, Michael Oatley, and Sinn Fein's Martin McGuinness, in the early 1980s, had shown that the Republican Movement was willing to talk, and had something to say that was worth listening to. HMG has given the 'face-saving' impression that the IRA had no choice but to call a ceasefire in August 1994. The truth is more pragmatic. Both sides who occupied the battleground, the British Army and the Provisional IRA (the 'gangsters' no longer mattered at this stage), had realized for several years that a military victory was no longer an option. The Provos had achieved all that was required. They didn't have to win the war, they had to remain undefeated. And by the late-1980s there was a fairly solid political base to exploit what had been gained. However, it would take longer for the British political establishment, and certainly MI5's securocrats, to recognize the stalemate.

The bombs that mattered exploded in England in the early 1990s and there was no intelligence to warn of their arrival on the UK mainland. The Provo ASUs abroad operated autonomously, acting on their own initiative for security reasons until they ran out of space and time. The average 'shelf-life' of an ASU in England was estimated at between four to six months, and they were reliant on locally-available resources. But the big bombs, the 'spectaculars' which rocked the complacent, post-Thatcher Conservative administration, were originally sourced in South Armagh.

The IRA's most intensive campaign on the mainland targeted Tory politicians, serving military personnel and retired senior officers, high-profile financial institutions, and establishments linked to the ruling political classes. Conservative MP, Ian Gow, a former private secretary to PM Thatcher, was assassinated, on 30 July 1990, when a 4lb Semtex bomb exploded at 8.40am beneath his car in the driveway of his home in Hankham, East Sussex. In quick succession there were attacks on the homes of the retired Governor of Gibraltar, Sir Peter Terry, who headed the overseas territory administration when three unarmed IRA members were killed by the SAS in 1988; of former Para and ex-O/C in Northern Ireland Gen. Farrar-Hockley, and that of ex-Cabinet Secretary, Robert Armstrong, who had served in the Thatcher administration from 1979 to 1987, and was fully briefed on the war being waged in the shadows by 14FSIC and the FRU. Earlier that year - 1990 - a device had exploded near the speaker's lectern at the Royal Overseas League in central London, shortly before a conference on terrorism with guest speaker, Cabinet minister William Waldegrave, was due to begin, and at 8.39pm, on 25 June 1990, the Carlton Club on St James's Street in the heart of the capital, described as the "oldest and most elite" of the private Conservative clubs, was bombed, injuring more than 20 people, one of whom, Lord Kaberry, died of his injuries. This was a well-planned, focused, IRA response to the 'small lives' being lost on the streets of Belfast and elsewhere, and the campaign intensified in 1991.

Security was at an unprecedented level in Whitehall as a result of the UN-authorized response to the Iraqi invasion of Kuwait, codenamed

Operation *Desert Storm,* when Prime Minister John Major (who had succeeded Mrs. Thatcher in November 1990) chaired a meeting, on 7 February 1991, of his War Cabinet, which included Home Office, Defense, and FCO ministers, and Chiefs of Staff of the Armed Forces. As the meeting was about to begin a salvo of IRA 'Mark 10' mortars, each weighing about 140lbs, with a 40lb Semtex explosives payload, were launched from a van parked at the junction of Horse Guards Avenue, near the MoD HQ and about 200 yards from Downing Street. Two shells landed near the FCO offices on King Charles Street, and failed to explode, but the third detonated in the rear garden of No.10, about 30 yards from the room where the meeting was taking place. Bomb-proof netting on the windows prevented serious injuries from flying glass, however, some explosives forensic analysts believe that had the missile hit the PM's residence, it was "quite probable" that most those present at the meeting would have died. Several minutes after the attack, at 10.08am, the Ford Transit van, which had been fitted out at a rented garage, was destroyed when a pre-set incendiary device exploded. The attack was a warning to the British Government that the Provos were operating on a previously unknown and totally unexpected scale, and had set up a secure, fully-equipped, light-engineering plant on the mainland. Previous bombs had been manufactured in South Armagh and smuggled into England. The Provos were now tooled-up, close to home and dangerous, ready to sustain a long campaign.

The daily disruption caused by attacks on the rail and underground transport network, and incendiary devices in London and Manchester, was beginning to be felt financially, with business executives complaining about the inability of Scotland Yard and MI5 to come to grips with the bombers. This growing dissatisfaction could no longer be explained away when a massive bomb exploded at the Baltic Exchange offices, at 30 St Mary Axe in the City of London, the heavily-fortified financial square mile in the capital, at 9.20pm, on 10 April 1992, deliberately timed as the first results of the General Election were coming in 'live' on all the major broadcasting networks. Several hours later another large bomb exploded underneath the A40 flyover at Staples Corner, one of the North London access routes to Heathrow International Airport.

The Baltic Exchange bomb unfortunately killed three people when the building wasn't cleared on time, despite a telephoned warning. It cost an estimated $1.5 to $2 billion worth of damage to property and business, and with the threat of further attacks on this scale there was a major financial crisis in the insurance industry, with threats of firms relocating to Frankfurt or Geneva unless the incoming Conservative administration came to grips with the situation.

In April 1993 the IRA once again detonated a huge truck-bomb in the City of London at Bishopsgate. Despite a coded warning a journalist died in the explosion, which almost destroyed the 15th century St. Ethelburga's Church, badly damaged Liverpool Street railway station, and left insurers with another bill in excess of $1 billion. The payments were now so large that Lloyd's of London was seriously worried about the costs of a sustained bombing campaign. The crises in industry had increased, despite the Pool Reassurance Company Limited measure, known as 'Pool Re', set up following the Baltic Exchange bomb, and similar to the Northern Ireland Overriding Exclusion clause, which left business and property owners largely uninsured for damage caused by IRA attacks. Financial and physical damage on this scale was no longer sustainable. In two years the Provos had used more explosives in London than in the previous twenty years in the North, despite all the resources available to the covert units of the Int. Corps, RUC Special Branch, MI5, and the Royal Signals Corps, working with the Cheltenham-based SIGINT establishment, GCHQ, which had been monitoring and analyzing IRA communications for more than two decades. At the height of the campaign the Dublin-based magazine, *Phoenix,* described the IRA campaign as "hydra-headed." Following a setback, when volunteers and equipment were captured, another ASU revealed itself. In addition "they are now operating on twin levels, with an apparently coordinated interplay between the spectaculars and the day-to-day potboilers." Such was the intensity of the campaign that Londoners were becoming familiar which what passed as 'normal life' in Belfast - armed police manning VCPs, scanners and hand-baggage searches, low-flying helicopters, and screaming fire appliances, ambulances and police cars racing to the next probable incident.

Another tactical switch. This time the target was Heathrow Airport, 14 miles west of central London. The IRA's siege began at 5.56pm, on Thursday, 9 March 1994, and ended four days later when the third busiest airport in the world was brought to a complete standstill. The operation, which caused no casualties and very little physical damage, was regarded by political commentators and academic security experts as a major coup for the Provos. It was also a serious embarrassment for MI5 and its recently appointed female director general, Stella Rimington, because the agency's threat assessment specialists had failed to consider 'off-site' attacks. Commander David Tucker, head of Scotland Yard's anti-terrorist squad, confirmed that 12 missiles had been fired from launchers outside the airport's 10 mile perimeter, but they had failed to explode due to a "consistent mechanical defect." The IRA, in fact, had deliberately defused the missiles to achieve maximum publicity and minimum casualties, underlining the specialist skills of the ASUs now operating in Britain, and the elaborate logistics required to support such attacks. The missiles and launchers were manufactured and assembled by a 'technical unit' at a secure London-based, light-engineering plant. The Nissan Micra from which the first salvo was fired from the car-park of the Excelsior Hotel, had been stolen four days before the attack, while the launcher, five steel tubes, a half-inch thick with a 6-inch bore and approximately 18 inches long, was welded to the rear chassis. The launcher, concealed in an area of unsighted 'dead ground' near Heathrow's southern perimeter from which the third salvo was fired at 8.00am on Sunday, was "probably constructed by IRA engineers with operational experience against Army patrols in South Armagh," according to Scotland Yard sources. The RUC supplied another piece of the puzzle on 15 March, when Chief Supt. Terry Houston confirmed that the Provos had developed a new light-sensitive detonator by adapting US-made "photoflash slave units." The small, cordless device could be triggered by a flashgun from 750 yards, and both Scotland Yard and MI5 refused to comment on reports that it had been used in several attacks in London and during the siege of Heathrow.

That was the final, high-profile, pre-1994 ceasefire attack on the mainland. Five months later the IRA announced a "cessation of hostilities," and for the next 18 months the Republican Movement waited for the Tory Government to appoint representatives to negotiate directly. However, PM John Major had no political room to maneuver, relying on Unionist MPs in the Commons - bitterly opposed to negotiations with 'terrorists' - to maintain a parliamentary majority against the rising tide of New Labour. Patience ran out on 9 February 1996, and the Provos returned to London, exploding a massive bomb at Canary Wharf in Docklands, causing in excess of $2.2 billion in business and property damage. Eight months later, at 3.35pm on 7 October, a car-bomb exploded inside the Army's 'secure' Thiepval Barracks HQ, outside Lisburn,. Within minutes, while victims of this blast were being treated at the base's medical facility, a second bomb exploded. It was a major security breach and a huge embarrassment for the MoD. More significantly, there was a total lack of intelligence to prevent such an attack. Once again the HUMINT and SIGINT network had failed when high-grade 'product' was required.

One soldier died in the Thiepval attack, and twenty one were seriously injured. It was the first IRA attack in the North since August 1994, and PM Major publicly blamed Sinn Fein leader, Gerry Adams MP, for the "cold-blooded killing" despite being fully-briefed by MI5 on the Sinn Fein leadership's efforts to broker another ceasefire. The Thiepval attack took place less that a month before a meeting of the IRA's annual convention, held secretly in the Irish Republic, and was carried out by a special unit headed by a Northern Command intelligence officer, who supported the Adams/ McGuinness peace initiative and had "loyally policed the ceasefire" according to journalist, Ed Maloney. During what was a "temporary breakdown" a limited and focused return to violence was tolerated, designed to remind the British of what had been gained during the 18 month truce, and what could be lost. The limited campaign prevented a split in the Republican Movement, something which many commentators were predicting, based on historical precedent and not without good reason. But Adams and McGuinness persisted, supported by men like Gerry Kelly, the former IRA volunteer who had headed the unit which had bombed the Old Bailey and New Scotland Yard in March 1973, and had served twenty years before escaping from the "most secure prison in Europe," HMP Maze, with 37 other republican prisoners in September 1983, including Brendan 'Bik' McFarlane, the IRA

O/C in the H-Blocks during the 1981 hunger strike in which Bobby Sands MP, and nine other men (including a member of the INLA) died. Among IRA hardliners the credentials of these two men were beyond question, and helped convince IRA volunteers in local ASUs that in every "war of the flea" there comes a time when a political rather than a military decision is the right one to make.

Has Peace Broken Out?

To give credit where it's due: Tony Blair's decision, after the Labour Party won the May 1997 general election, to talk directly to the Sinn Fein leadership without the naive Conservative/Unionist precondition of IRA decommissioning, was a key factor in the renewed ceasefire, announced two months later, and in the final political solution to the Troubles. It means nothing, of course, to the relatives of the hundreds of thousands of Iraqis who have lost their lives as a result of Blair's worst policy decision of his political career, but his persistence and patience during the peace process dealing with republican sensitivities and loyalist intransigence, in which he was supported every step of the way by US president, Bill Clinton, and successive Irish prime ministers, cannot be underestimated or overstated.

For the MI5 securocrats, however, the peace process was a challenge. Something to be subtly undermined. But to destroy the process it was necessary to destroy the credibility of Sinn Fein, and MI5's efforts ranged to the sublime to the stupidly inept.

In 1995 President Bill Clinton appointed former Democratic Senator, George Mitchell, as US Special Envoy for Northern Ireland, to underline Washington's support for the peace process. The appointment fulfilled a promise Clinton had made to Irish American voters while campaigning for president in 1992, and infuriated members of Prime Minister Major's Cabinet, who regarded it as an "unwarranted interference in British domestic politics." George Mitchell had served as Senate Majority Leader from 1989 to 1995, and he was more than a token envoy. He represented an American president with a deep personal interest in events, who would not be distracted by the 'sensitivities' of the British Tories, a commitment he underlined during his first visit to Belfast in 1995, when his convoy detoured down the Falls and Mr. Clinton stepped out of his limousine to shake hands with Gerry Adams. If Mitchell's appointment angered the Tory leadership, the photograph of Clinton and Adams standing together in the heartland of republican resistance sent many Conservatives, and the London-based tabloid press, into an apoplectic fit

Senator Mitchell set up a commission that established a series of principles of non-violence to which all parties in the North had to agree, and later chaired negotiations which led to the signing of the April 1998 Good Friday Agreement (GFA). Later that year he was awarded the Liberty Medal, an annual award administered by the US National Constitutional Center to recognize "leadership in the pursuit of freedom." In his acceptance speech at the NCC in Philadelphia, he stated, "I believe there's no such thing as a conflict which can't be ended. They're created and sustained by human beings. They can be ended by human beings. No matter how ancient the conflict, no matter how hateful, no matter how hurtful, peace can prevail. But only if those who stand for peace and justice are supported and encouraged, while those who do not are opposed and condemned."

There were times when it might not have come to this. MI5 hadn't signed up to the 'Mitchell Principles', didn't believe in conflict resolution except on its own terms, and even before the first ceasefire announcement in August 1994, the organization had set out to undermine the process, using the media in a desperate attempt to generate hostile opinion.

In a *Mail on Sunday* report, on 10 July 1994, the paper claimed that one of the men convicted of the assassination of Lord Mountbatten - who died, with three others, including 83-year-old Lady Brabourne and two teenage boys, on 27 August 1979, when a bomb planted by the IRA on his fishing boat, the *Shadow V* at Mullaghmore, in County Sligo, was detonated by remote-control only hours before the Narrow Water ambush - had been secretly released from Dublin's Mountjoy Jail to help negotiate peace. The prisoner's movements were being "closely monitored by MI5," according to the newspaper. Two days later the Dublin Government described the story as "absolute nonsense," while the *Daily Telegraph,* a newspaper with a strong subscription-base among commissioned military personnel, and often regarded as a reliable conduit of FCO/MI6 opinion, reported that the convicted bomber had "never been influential" in Republican circles, and had "distanced himself" from the IRA.

The *Independent,* on 20 July, ran a story in which Said Muibar, described as one of Colonel Gaddafi's senior lieutenants, claimed much of the information which Libyan officials had given to FCO and MI6 representatives the previous year about his country's relationship with the IRA, was "completely bogus." While in itself not especially damaging to the peace process, the story linked the IRA with the Libyan dictator, regarded in the West as one of the most hated and dangerous leaders in North Africa. Next it was the turn of the Iranians, with the *Sunday Times,* on 21 August, reporting on its front page claims made by Mir Ali Montazam, former First Secretary at the Iranian Embassy in London, that Tehran had paid $30 million to the IRA through Channel Island bank accounts. Montazan admitted, on page two, that he had no direct knowledge of the funding, and his allegations were based on "snippets of gossip" picked up at the embassy in the late 1980s.

The *Sunday Times* also recycled a story, previously published in the *Sun,* and *Sunday Express,* claiming that an IRA sniper, responsible for killing nine British Army and RUC personnel using a US-manufactured specialist weapon, had been arrested in Dublin. Earlier versions had described this mysterious figure as a "former British Army serviceman who had served in

The Butcher's Apron

the Falklands" and an "American mercenary." Nothing more was heard of this individual, however, the story tried to exploit the US 'connection' to the final British Army casualty of Operation *Banner*, L/Bdr Restorick, shot at 6.21pm on 12 February 1997, by an IRA sniper using a Barrett M90, bolt-action, bullpup-configured rifle, manufactured at the Barrett Firearms factory in Murfreesboro, Tennessee, fitted with a Vari-X telescopic sight manufactured by Leupold & Stevens in Beaverton, Oregon, and capable of accurately firing a .50 caliber round at three times the speed of sound, at a target at distances in excess of one mile.

When the ceasefire was reinstated in 1996, MI5 focused on Gerry Kelly, who had been part of the back-channel negotiations, with Martin McGuinness, between 1990 and 1993, details of which were published by Sinn Fein in a booklet, *Setting the Record Straight*, in January 1994. Kelly had been active in promoting the peace process during talks in South Africa with senior ANC officials, including the former president, Thabo Mbeki. The relationship between the African National Congress (ANC) and Sinn Fein was close and decades old, and the Provisionals had helped carry out one of the largest economic bombing attacks against the South African apartheid regime in the early 1980s, according to Kader Asmal, a law professor for more than two decades at Trinity College, Dublin before he returned to South Africa, where he was appointed minister for education after the 1999 general election.

The target was the Sasol oil refinery in Sasolburg, near Johannesburg. The town was established in 1954 to provide housing and other facilities for the refinery workers. Sasol (formerly the South African Coal, Oil and Gas Company) refined oil from the extensive coal reserves in the region, and from the mid-1960s to the early 1980s, as a result of international trade embargoes against the apartheid regime, the secure operation of the pilot plant, Sasol 1, was an economic priority for the ruling National Party.

In his memoirs, *Politics in my Blood*, Prof. Asmal writes that he was approached by senior officials from Umkhonto we Sizwe (MK) - the military wing of the ANC - in the late 1970s to help arrange the "delicate task" of training MK activists in Ireland without attracting the attention of MI5, which maintained 24-hour surveillance on the ANC offices in London. Asmal met with Michael O'Riordan, General Secretary of the Communist Party of Ireland (CPI), whom he describes as a "man of great integrity whom I trusted to keep a secret." O'Riordan contacted Gerry Adams, and it was arranged that two IRA specialists would meet with the MK personnel in Dublin and take them to a safe-house for two weeks intensive training in the use of explosives. According to Asmal the "expertise the MK cadres obtained was duly imparted in the ANC [training] camps in Angola." Some time later Prof. Asmal was again used as a conduit between the MK and the IRA, who wanted two Provo surveillance experts to travel to SA to carry out reconnaissance and study the feasibility of attacking the Stasol facility. Once again a meeting was arranged in Dublin, and the IRA volunteers, according to

Prof. Asmal, "laid the ground for one of the most dramatic operations carried out by MK personnel." This "daring act of military insurgency" caused "relatively superficial damage" to the refinery, but in propaganda terms "its effect on the morale of the liberation movement was inestimable." Prof. Asmal, who died in 2010, described himself as a "strong believer in Irish independence and in a united Ireland" but added that he was "never an IRA supporter." Whatever his political sensitivities while teaching at Trinity, he had no qualms about approaching the Provos seeking assistance for the MK's military campaign against the apartheid regime.

Gerry Kelly's militant credentials were beyond reproach, so MI5 decided to smear him personally by claiming he was involved in a sexual relationship with a senior member of Senator Mitchell's staff. There was no truth in the allegation, and it was treated, in Washington and Belfast, with the contempt it deserved.

"Worse than Watergate?"

Another MI5 scheme involved a directional audio bug, later found beneath the floorboards in Sinn Fein's head office in Andersonstown. Former Secretary of State, Mo Mowlam, was forced to apologize when a similar device and signal transmitter was discovered in one of the cars used by Adams and McGuinness to travel to secret talks with the IRA to discuss the contentious issue of decommissioning.

The most serious challenge mounted to the Republican Movement's commitment to peace was an operation codenamed *Torsion*. It began on 4 October 2002, when PSNI officers, including members of the CID and technical support units, carried out pre-dawn raids on homes in North and West Belfast, seizing computer files and hundreds of hardcopy documents. Several hours later, in a blaze of pre-arranged publicity, a PSNI convoy of grey, armor-plated Land Rovers arrived at the Parliament Buildings, Stormont, to carry out raids on the office of Sinn Fein's head of administration, Denis Donaldson. Two CD-ROMs and other files were confiscated, and Mr. Donaldson and his son-in-law were charged with possession of material likely to be of use to terrorists [the IRA], while a civil servant, William Mackessey, was charged with collecting information on the security forces. Two days later, at Laganside Magistrates' Court, the Sinn Fein president, Gerry Adams MP, described the police raids and the ensuing publicity as "spin and political theatre." He denied that Sinn Fein had been involved in a clandestine intelligence-gathering operation. David Trimble, the Unionist First Minister, anxious to retain some credibility with hardline loyalists, rushed to judgment and described the affair as "worse than Watergate." One week later, on 14 October, the Northern Ireland Secretary, Dr John Reid, announced the "indefinite suspension" of the power-sharing Executive. And in the right-wing British broadsheets, 'special correspondents' suggested this was the end of the peace process because Sinn Fein was an "untrustworthy partner" with which to share power.

However, following the unexpected collapse, at Belfast Crown Court, of the trial of the alleged republican spy-ring accused, two months later, after Mr. Justice Hart was told by the DPP that "with regard to the materials placed before him [the PSNI report] it was no longer in the public interest" to proceed with the case, a series of bizarre revelations began which later confirmed that as far as the securocrats within MI5 were concerned, the covert war to cripple the Republican Movement continued, despite all that had been gained to achieve a degree of political stability.

Speculation that the trial of the 'Stormont 3' had collapsed to protect the identity of an MI5 'intelligence asset' within Sinn Fein ended, on 15 December, when Denis Donaldson admitted to a senior Sinn Fein official that he had been working for British intelligence for twenty years, and that he had been visited by the PSNI the previous weekend and warned that his cover was about to be blown. At a packed press conference in Dublin the following day, Gerry Adams told journalists: "The fact is that there was no Sinn Fein spy-ring at Stormont." He pointed out that "the collapse of the political institutions was a direct result of the actions of some of those who run the intelligence and policing system. The fact is that a key person at the centre of these events was a Sinn Fein member who was a British agent. This is the responsibility of the British Government."

Several hours later, in a statement recorded in a Dublin hotel room and broadcast on the Irish state radio and television network, RTE, Donaldson said he was used by the PSNI Special Branch to bring down the political institutions:

> I was a British agent at the time. I was recruited in the 1980s after compromising myself during a vulnerable period in my life. Since then I have worked for British intelligence and the RUC/PSNI Special Branch. Over that period I was paid money. My last two contacts with Special Branch were as follows -- two days before my arrest in October 2002, and on Thursday night. I was not involved in any republican spy-ring in Stormont. The so-called 'Stormontgate' affair was a scam and a fiction. It never existed. It was created by Special Branch.

Denis Donaldson was a highly-regarded republican activist who had played an important part in Sinn Fein's strategy and political development. He was a former member of the IRA who became a full-time Sinn Fein official in the mid-1980s. In 1987, already working for RUC Special Branch, he was part of a Sinn Fein delegation that flew to Lebanon in an attempt to secure the release of Belfast-born Brian Keenan, an Islamic Jihad hostage being held in Beirut. He later became increasingly involved in the political process as a key aide to Gerry Adams. In the late 1980s MI5 took charge of running Donaldson. He helped organize the first US trips by Adams and Martin McGuinness during the Clinton administration, and regularly met US State Department officials, acting as a 'diplomatic courier' between Washington and the Sinn Fein leadership in Belfast. As an MI5 agent he was in a position to provide information on the Clinton administration's strategy, summaries of classified US State Department briefing documents and contacts with Sinn Fein, to British Conservative ministers who were hostile to US interference in a domestic dispute. He also met influential members of the Irish American community, including senators, congressmen, business representatives and trade unionists who supported Sinn Fein's efforts to achieve a peaceful and permanent solution to the Troubles. It remains unclear - but it appears unlikely - that US Government officials were aware of Donaldson's covert role which, because of the nature of his contacts in Washington, included spying on US citizens for a foreign intelligence agency.

Of course it should never have come to this. Following the signing of the Belfast Agreement in 1998, a review of policing concluded that the unaccountable RUC Special Branch should be disbanded and its members transferred to other police departments, including CID. About 100 Special Branch officers resigned. Many were quickly recruited by MI5, and picked up where they had left off when MI5, in 2003 under director Eliza Manningham-Buller, was given primary responsibility over the PSNI for intelligence gathering in the North. The PSNI may have been involved at street-level in Operation *Torsion,* but MI5 was responsible for the Stormont spy-ring, and the subsequent damage and years of delay caused to the peace process.

Denis Donaldson paid with his life for his weakness and greed. He was expelled from Sinn Fein, and moved to County Donegal in the Irish Republic. In March 2006, he was tracked down by a journalist working for the Dublin-based tabloid, *Sunday World,* which published a photograph of the ex-undercover agent outside his remote, white-washed, slate-roof cottage in the Blue Stack Mountains, near the village of Glenties. In an interview Donaldson repeated his allegations that he had been "sacrificed" in a failed attempt by MI5 to preserve the failing political career of Unionist Party leader, David Trimble (a wholly undeserving winner of the 1988 Nobel Peace Prize) by blaming the collapse of the power-sharing executive on the Republican Movement. Shortly after 5pm, on 4 April 2006, Donaldson's body was found just inside the front door. He had died from a single gunshot wound to the chest. Within hours of his death being made public, the IRA, which had decommissioned its weapons the previous year under international supervision, denied having "any involvement whatsoever" in the killing, while Gerry Adams, on behalf of Sinn Fein, condemned the murder of his former aide.

The British and US mainstream media coverage suggested that Donaldson had fled to north-west Donegal "under threat from those he betrayed." This was quite a disingenuous account of the circumstances. The region where Donaldson was living has a long republican tradition, the cottage was owned by his brother-in-law and had been used by the IRA as a 'safe house' for volunteers. A BBC World Breaking News report, carried by several European broadcasting networks, stated that Donaldson had died a "traitor's death" implying that the IRA had been involved, while the *Independent* newspaper's correspondent, David McKittrick, wrote about the "long arm of Republican vengeance." The timing of Donaldson's death was largely ignored, coming two days before the British and Irish premiers, Blair and Ahern, were due to meet in Armagh City to put forward proposals for the return of devolved government at Stormont, three years after the Stormontgate affair. This would suggest that the murder was carried out by those opposed to the peace process, either a small group of republican dissidents, now calling themselves the Real IRA (RIRA), or elements within MI5. What Donaldson knew worked both ways. The Republican Movement could no longer be damaged by his secrets and lies, but MI5 agent handlers still had relevant careers to protect.

"Lies, Damned Lies..."

Perhaps it is true, as former US President Truman once said, that the only thing new in the world is the history we don't know. Maybe those former FRU agents thought the Troubles would last forever, that history would come later than their lifetimes. Men now trapped in the past, with no distance between who they were then, and who they are now. Having learned the fine art of deception, and lived the lie, it's hard to renege on old habits.

The world of abandoned spies is all about numbers. It's part of the myth they have created and insist we believe. But there's nothing to suggest we're missing something essential to the history of these times. The numbers are simply a distraction. Martin McGartland, who operated under the codename, *Agent Carol*, while providing information to the RUC Special Branch between 1987 and 1991, and was relocated to Cumbria, in north-east England, under the name 'Martin Ashe', boasts of "fifty dead men walking." Brig. Gordon Kerr, testifying at Belfast Crown Court, claims his man inside the UDA, Brian Nelson, saved more than thirty lives, while Peter Keeley, in his book, *Unsung Hero*, claims to have saved "dozens of lives as a secret agent inside the IRA." Without evidence, and there isn't any, these numbers mean nothing. But they help sell not just books but the merit of the securocrats' nefarious practices. The Smithwick Tribunal, probably the last of the independent inquiries into how the war in the shadows was waged, is likely to provide enough material for updated editions.

The MoD employed these men, and appears to have tidied up most of the loose ends. The only trail left is the one that leads to the door of 10 Downing Street, and into the heart of the British political establishment. That was why PM Cameron told Geraldine Finucane, on 14 October 2011, that there would be no independent inquiry into her husband's murder, as Canadian Judge, Peter Cory, had recommended. Cameron had been reminded by senior unelected mandarins who stalk the corridors of power in Whitehall, of the appalling consequences of such an inquiry. Finucane had died while a Conservative Cabinet, headed by the late Margaret Thatcher, was in power, and running the dirty war in Ireland. And when Geraldine Finucane later told journalists that she was brought to Downing Street to be "humiliated and insulted" and had been "let down by a disreputable government led by a dishonorable man," a red-faced Cameron sat in silence behind the front-door of his official residence. There was no official spokesman, or Tory Communications Office spin-doctor, to respond to the widow's bitter attack, because Cameron knew there was nothing left to lie about. After all, Brian Nelson was the FRU's most important asset during the Troubles, and his presence made a 'negative' difference for all the wrong reasons.

Just over a year later Geraldine Finucane was back in London, seated with her family in the public gallery of the House of Commons to hear David Cameron admit that "shocking levels of collusion" had been a key factor in the murder of her husband. The prime minister was speaking only hours after the publication of a 500-page review of the evidence carried out by Sir Desmond De Silva QC, a former UN Chief War Crimes Prosecutor in Sierra Leone, who found that the British Army and RUC Special Branch officers had advance notice of a series of UDA assassinations, but had done nothing to prevent them. The report states that employees of the security forces were involved in carrying out "serious violations of human rights" and had "actively furthered and facilitated" the murder of the Belfast solicitor.

There had been three UDA conspiracies to kill Pat Finucane - in 1981, 1985 and 1988/89 - that were known to the RUC Special Branch and/or MI5, but on none of these occasions was he warned of a threat to his life. However, important, but undeniably false, claims are made in paragraphs 84 and 87 of the 'Executive Summary and Principal Conclusions' - that the FRU "did not have foreknowledge" of the conspiracies because Nelson, having re-infiltrated the UDA, "failed to impart to his FRU handlers" plans to kill Finucane. Crucially, as far as HMG, the MoD and the official history of Operation *Banner* is concerned, De Silva found there was "no over-arching conspiracy" implying that the chain of command and knowledge of the widespread collusion, ended in Belfast, and that the first time the British Conservative Government knew of the threats to Mr. Finucane was the day after his death.

Geraldine Finucane described the report as "a sham, a whitewash and a confidence trick," pointing out that De Silva gives the benefit of the doubt to the State, its Cabinet and ministers, to the British Army and to the intelligence and security services, adding "at every turn dead witnesses have been blamed [Brian Nelson, William Stobie and Tommy Lyttle] and defunct agencies [the RUC Special Branch and the FRU] found wanting [while] serving personnel and active state departments appear to have been excused." She repeated her call for a full public inquiry, as Cory had originally recommended in his report on collusion allegations on both sides of the border.

Interviewed on RTE radio in Dublin the following day, Ed Maloney, one of the most experienced journalists to cover the Troubles, accused de Silva of deliberately covering-up the British Government's knowledge of the threats to three solicitors in the North. He claimed that two months before Pat Finucane died, the UDA 'brigadier' Tommy Lyttle, to whom Nelson had reported, had told him, in December 1988, that P.J. McGrory, Oliver Kelly and Mr. Finucane were being targeted by the UDA. Mr. McGrory had personally contacted the Irish Prime Minister, Charles Haughey, and Mr, Haughey had called the NIO, asking that extra security should be made available to protect the solicitors. If this is correct, and there is no reason to doubt Mr. Maloney's account, senior members of the Thatcher administration knew Mr. Finucane was at risk, and this fact alone strengthens the case for an independent public inquiry, something that is unlikely to happen during the lifetime of the current Con/Lib-Dem coalition.

"Where Dogs Bark at Helicopters"

When Judge Cory was commissioned by the Irish and British governments, in May 2002, to investigate six collusion killings, there was an assumption in Whitehall that whatever the outcome, if the data flow could be controlled for national security reasons, the damage could be limited. The Cory report into the Gibson killings was described by *Phoenix* magazine as a "classic of judicial investigation" that "convincingly refutes" claims that the IRA colluded with Irish police officers in targeting the couple, on the grounds that the Gibsons extensively revealed their travel plans, including booking their trip to Spain through a Belfast travel agency. He did, however, recommend a judicial inquiry into the deaths of RUC Chief. Supt Harry Breen and his colleague, Det. Supt. Robert Buchanan, because of "evidence that, if accepted, could be found to constitute collusion."

In his report, Cory states that 'Kevin Fulton', accompanied by a friend, delivered a statement on 9 September 2003, which reads:

> In 1979 I enlisted in the British Army. Within months of my posting I was recruited by a British intelligence agency to act as an agent. In this capacity I became a member of the Provisional IRA. On one occasion in the late 1980s, I was with my senior IRA commander and another individual in my car. I knew the other individual to be Garda B. I was introduced to Garda B. I knew that Garda B, who was stationed in Dundalk, was passing information to the Provisional IRA. I was in Dundalk on the day of the ambush of Superintendent Buchanan and Chief Superintendent Breen. I am aware that, after the ambush took place, my senior IRA commander was told by a member of PIRA that Garda B had telephoned to the Provisional IRA to tell then that officers Breen and

Buchanan were at Dundalk station. I should add that I know nothing about [the] murder of Lord Justice and Lady Gibson. I have read this statement and its contents are true and accurate.

In providing this statement Keeley appears to have convinced Judge Cory of his credibility, and that he had "made himself a threat and a target of some organizations." Which is surprising because Keeley had been called a 'Walter Mitty' figure by the former RUC Chief Constable, Sir Ronnie Flanagan, who was head of the RUC Special Branch, based in Armagh, and a member of the TCG for South Region, which covers the border area where Breen and Buchanan died. A Garda Crime and Security Intelligence Branch (also known as C3) briefing paper for the Irish Department of Foreign Affairs, describes Keeley as a "serial informer who is not to be trusted," with a "long history of fabricating evidence and selling it to various law enforcement agencies" who had cost Scotland Yard an estimated $2 million in wasted man-power after providing false information. Apparently neither Judge Cory nor his research assistants had bothered to read Keeley's book, a chronological account of his time in the IRA, in which he makes no mention of the Breen/Buchanan ambush, no mention of driving around South Armagh with a senior IRA commander or meeting Garda B. Chief Supt. Breen, head of the RUC's H Division covering County Down and County Armagh, who was the most senior police officer to die during the Troubles. It seems unusual that Keeley, a narcissist, full of his own importance, would not write up a role for himself in this high-profile killing. What he didn't put in the book he put in the hastily cobbled-together statement that he gave to Judge Cory.

Allegations of Garda collusion were also made by *Daily Telegraph* journalist, Toby Harnden, and his *Irish Times* colleague, Kevin Myers. In his book Harnden claims that a Garda stationed in Dundalk had tipped-off the IRA that Breen and Buchanan were due to attend a meeting with their Garda counterparts at 2pm, on 20 March 1989. The meeting had been arranged earlier that day and Buchanan, who was responsible for cross-border liaison, left Glengormley RUC station, Belfast, in his own car, a red Vauxhall Cavalier, drove to Corry Square RUC station in Newry to meet Breen, then headed for Dundalk, down the A1 dual carriageway. It was a trip Buchanan had made several times in his private car - which was a breach of basic security precautions - and the vehicle's make and registration was known to the local IRA.

The meeting took approximately 90 minutes. When the two RUC officers left Dundalk, and turned onto the Edenappa Road at 3.40pm, an IRA unit moved into place where the road is sheltered by trees from the Army's high-tech 'Romeo Two One' observation tower above Jonesborough village, less than a mile from the border. According to the *Cory Collusion Report,* the red Vauxhall Cavalier was flagged down by two IRA volunteer wearing British Army combat fatigues. Buchanan assumed he was approaching a VCP, and as he slowed down a beige Litace van, which had been following the RUC men along the Edenappa Road, pulled into a laneway leading to an empty house opposite Buchanan's car. Four IRA members in battle fatigues and armed with two .223 Armalite rifles, a Ruger Mini-14 and a 7.62 Short rifle, leapt from the van and opened fire. In an attempt to escape Buchanan backed into a stone wall before he died, still strapped in with his foot pressed on the accelerator. Although badly wounded, Chief Supt. Breen attempted to crawl from the car and was killed by a single shot to the back of the head. The IRA removed wallets, diaries and two briefcases from the trunk before leaving the area.

It was learned during the RUC CID investigation that the IRA had set up checkpoints on 'dead ground' just north of the border on the only four roads leading out of Dundalk. The ambush had been planned with "meticulous care" and had involved at least twenty IRA volunteers. RUC Chief Con. Sir John Hermon, at a press conference the following day, rejected press speculation about IRA/Garda collusion. Bob Buchanan was a lay preacher and a member of the Reformed Presbyterian Church. Hermon, in his book, *Holding the Line*, blamed Buchanan's belief in predestination for his failing to take basic security measures for the trip to Dundalk:

> There was no advance precautions, they just went. Bob Buchanan was a very devout Christian and he did not believe in taking precautions because God was in control (...) I still don't understand why no one spotted he was going down there so casually. By the time they left Dundalk the place was swarming with IRA men and there was no way they were going to get back.

False Flag 'High Tech' Terror

Keeley's credibility was key to Judge Cory recommending a judicial inquiry. It is also crucial in assessing the allegations he makes in his book, specifically the claim that he told his handlers, in 1991, that the IRA was developing a new method to detonate roadside bombs from a distance of one mile using a modified, photographic flash-gun to trigger Improvised Explosive Devices (IEDs). In 2006 the MoD claimed that Iraqi insurgents, using IEDs and infra-red 'trip wires' similar to those developed by the IRA twenty-five years earlier in South Armagh, had caused dozens of casualties among British troops stationed in Basra. The Chiefs of Staff might have been more circumspect had they been aware of the alleged role played by MI5 and the FRU in facilitating the IRA procurement of sophisticated, remote-control, infra-red triggers. The innovative technology developed by the Provos to deal with British anti-IED measures in the North had also been deployed against US military personnel in Baghdad, and had reached Iraq via Hezbollah in South Lebanon.

Keeley claims that he was introduced to a new FRU handler called 'Pete,' and a new MI5 handler who introduced himself as 'Bob,' during the period that Jonathan Evans - who retired as MI5 director in April 2013 - was based in Belfast, seconded to the NIO to provide management and logistical back-up for the FRU's covert operations. Sometime in the early 1990s a decision was taken at a top-level meeting in Belfast between all the key figures involved in the 'dirty war' to use Keeley to procure bomb-detonation equipment in the US for the IRA. Those present from MI5, the FRU and the TCG accepted that the IRA was going to develop this technology sooner or later, and the "radical solution" was to provide the Provos with the equipment they needed, the logic being that it was "better to know what the enemy was doing, so they could counter it" according to one of Keeley's FRU colleagues. The agent known as 'Bob' was fully briefed and dispatched to New York to liaise with the FBI, who agreed to co-operate in return for assistance in securing the deportation of a prominent Irish republican living in Queens. MI5 arranged for Keeley to stay at the Murray Hill Inn in Manhattan, the FBI procured the detonators, and the Irishman was deported.

Keeley's account was 'corroborated' by US investigative journalist, Matthew Teague, in the March 2006 issue of the Boston-based monthly magazine, *The Atlantic*. Teague, who refuses to use Fulton's real name, claims that FBI sources have confirmed Keeley's trip to the US, have receipts of Keeley's stay at the Murray Hill Inn "at the time he said he was there," and that he had access to Homeland Security's Immigration and Naturalization Service (INS) files which confirmed that the Irishman who lived in Queens had been deported "exactly the way Fulton describes, so everything sort of triangulates, it really happened." Teague suggests that several American politicians were prepared to raise the issue of FBI cooperation with Keeley's techno-buying trip to New York, and Keeley, in an interview with the London-based, *Independent on Sunday*, in mid-March 2006, claimed to have been "in touch with US political representatives" and was willing to travel to Washington and "appear before Congress if necessary."

If this issue is buried on Capitol Hill, a trip to Belfast Crown Court might be a productive option for Beltway journalists interested in the truth of the matter. This is where Keeley still plans to sue the MoD, his former employer, for failing to honor its pledge to provide him with a new identity and financial security, with several former FRU colleagues willing to support his claim. Matthew Teague may also be asked to corroborate the US connection from documentation and FBI sources he used in his investigation. A retired RUC Special Branch officer, George Skerritt, has also confirmed to the former PSNI Police Ombudsman, Nuala O'Loan, in a separate collusion inquiry, that Keeley had traveled to New York and the operation had been "overseen by a senior MI5 officer." However, Skerritt had been unable (or unwilling) to identify the agent in question.

The IRA wasted little time in adopting the latest technology procured in the US. On 27 March 1992, WPC Colleen McMurry was killed in a horizontal mortar attack on an RUC armored Land Rover traveling along Merchant's Quay in Newry. Her colleague, Constable Paul Slane, was seriously injured in the incident. Keeley claims that two days before the attack he warned his FRU and Special Branch handlers that the IRA planned to use "what we called a doodlebug" in the attack. But instead of trying to prevent the ambush, Special Branch allowed the IRA unit to enter Newry, set the device and leave the area. This is only one incident of several in which Keeley alleges that the FRU, MI5 and the RUC Special Branch colluded in the killing and maiming of their own officers, soldiers and undercover operatives in order to maintain the cover of key agents like *Stakeknife*, higher up the intelligence food-chain. On the other hand, he has repeatedly refused to comment on claims that he had been directly responsible for 11 murders, and was given *carte blanche* to kill by his handlers.

Indeed, if there were some sense of justice in all of this, we might have expected the abandoned spies to be a serious embarrassment for the MoD, but, so far, the military establishment has been successful in containing the damage. And as far as many mainstream media security analysts are concerned, all the MoD is guilty of is bad counter-insurgency management. But it says a lot about how British intelligence fought and lost the so-called dirty war that the MoD has to seek court injunctions, signed by senior staff officers, to prevent the publication of books like *Ten-Thirty-Three*, by Nicholas Davies, use Public Interest Immunity (PPI) certificates ('gagging orders') to prevent witness testimony, and if necessary issue a *D Notice*, warning editors that certain material might infringe national security. Of course none of this would matter if the media ignored these men who are guilty of nothing more, as far as they are concerned, than following orders on behalf of Queen and Country.

Men like Samuel Jay Rosenfeld, one of the more interesting individuals to emerge from the shadows. An English-born former para with the Israeli Defense Force (IDF), Rosenfeld spent 3 years in Ireland in the early 1990s working for the Joint Services Group (JSG), a unit attached to the Int. Corps. Claiming to be a businessman called 'Thomas Doheny', working for a timber-frame construction company, and tasked with compromising republican activists in the Fermanagh/South Tyrone area, Rosenfeld also claims he was a victim of inter-agency rivalry, similar to the bloody Box 500/Box 600 dispute in the mid-1970s which cost the lives of several MI6 informants. In June 2003 he wrote directly to Queen Elizabeth II in her capacity as supreme head of the British Armed Forces, accusing the "very institutions of the state" of engaging in a campaign of terror against her subjects and, in a reference to *Stakeknife*, he asked

> how many innocent lives were taken as a direct result of agents penetrating the IRA, subsequently becoming entrenched and hunting British agents out of its ranks? The obvious question here is how many agents lives were sacrificed to protect others, how many were murdered by other agents operating within the IRA, and who directed and sanctioned these killings.

With the letter Rosenfeld included photographs of the badly beaten bodies of three FRU/RUC Special Branch agents, Gregory Burns, John Dignam and Aidan Starrs, who were found on the South Armagh border, on 30 June 1992, whom he claims were "abandoned by the British Army" because Brig. Kerr "decided it wasn't worth spending money on relocation." The three men, who had used IRA weapons for personal purposes, were directly involved in the murder of a local woman, Margaret Perry, and the disposal of her body, and were themselves the victims of an IRA internal security unit, allegedly headed by *Stakeknife*, who was ordered by his FRU handlers to "deal with a possible security threat." Had the three men being arrested and charged with the murder of Margaret Perry, whose body was found in the woods on the Classiebawn Castle estate in County Sligo, in the Irish Republic, the damage and exposure of FRU operations would have reverberated from Dublin to Whitehall. *Stakeknife* 'exposed' Burns, Dignam and Starrs as informants, according to Rosenfeld, and the FRU agent was also aware that the more brutal the beatings, the easier it would be for Unionist and British politicians to accuse the IRA of excessive and dreadful abuse.

The Smithwick Tribunal

Almost none of the inquiries and special reviews, scattered awkwardly throughout the years of the Troubles, have lived up to the pre-investigation political hype, for one reason or several. Nonetheless, there was a sense of anticipation that something might be achieved when Judge Peter Smithwick called for order at the first public hearing of the collusion tribunal in Dublin's Blackhall Place Hearing Room, in April 2011, with a list of 213 witnesses, including several "outside jurisdiction" whose presence was expected, some more in hope than expectation. In his opening statement Judge Smithwick said the inquiry's legal team had already met three former IRA members, including the volunteer who had been in charge of the Edenappa Road ambush. The men had provided detailed accounts of what had happened and answered all questions without reservation.

On the docket it was about the deaths of Harry Breen and Bob Buchanan, but it was also about how the long war had been waged. Judge Cory had already stated that he believed the IRA could have killed both men without help for a rogue Garda, but in order to avoid accusations of a cover-up in the British media he had felt obliged to recommend a judicial review of the evidence and the allegations made by Keeley, and another discarded military spy, Ian Hurst, a Bolton-born, lance corporal in the Int. Corps who worked as a clerk at Thiepval Barracks, shuffling the classified paperwork generated by the FRU agent handlers.

One of 200 desk-bound support staff feeding scraps of information into the *Caister* computer system, Hurst, a Parachute Regiment reject using the name 'Martin Ingram' claimed to have 'Level One' security clearance which gave him access to the Int. Corps summaries used to brief the TCG. He is also the co-author, with journalist, Greg Harkin, of a book about Scappaticci called *Stakeknife*. Despite making no reference to the incident he was questioned privately, by Judge Smithwick, prior to the public hearings about the FRU agent's possible link to the deaths of the two senior RUC officers. When Hurst agreed to give evidence Scappaticci's lawyers unsuccessfully applied for financial support to represent their client, and to be allowed cross-examine Hurst if 'Scap' was named in connection with the Edenappa Road ambush, no matter how tenuous. The issue became relevant when Hurst appeared on a BBC *Panorama* program dealing with the alleged hacking of his computer on behalf of journalists working for the Rupert Murdoch-owned tabloid, *News of the World*, in order to find out if Hurst knew the European mainland whereabouts of Scappaticci, whose address was subject to a stringent High Court injunction, issued on behalf of the MoD, preventing its publication.

Although Hurst was speaking on the BBC about a crime perpetrated against him under the *Computer Misuse Act*, such is the paranoia among the MoD mandarins about Hurst (who has been the subject of several court injunctions and committal proceedings in relation to his book) that his appearance on national television, even when he was not talking about *Stakeknife*, prompted a letter from the Treasury Solicitor's Office warning him about the "consequences of public utterances." The injunctions are so pervasive that Hurst was not allowed to discuss the conditions or consequences with his elected MP, or provide details of the undertakings given by his lawyers to the MoD on his behalf. According to *Panorama*, the hacker who accessed Hurst's computer was a former FRU colleague, Philip Campbell-Smith, who used a Trojan virus to download emails, which were then sent by fax to the Dublin office of the newspaper's Irish edition editor, Alex Marunchak.

Smithwick Tribunal testimony ranged from claim and counter-claim by former Garda and RUC officers, to suggestions, allegations, contradictions, hearsay and lies. But as expected, it was the evidence of the abandoned FRU agents which was the most interesting and controversial. Ian Hurst claimed that the retired Metropolitan Police Commissioner, Sir John Stevens - whose three collusion inquiries had generated almost 3,000 pages, of which only a brief 3-page summary has been released - and his team of detectives were aware of Scappaticci's role as a British agent, and his relationship with alleged "rogue Gardai in the border region." In a statement submitted to the tribunal, he mentioned a meeting at Heathrow Airport with one of the English detectives during the investigation into the role of British agents inside the UDA, to discuss "a number of subjects relating to Scappaticci" including the death of alleged IRA informer, Tom Oliver, and UDA victim, Francisco Notarantonio. Hurst stated: "I told him I knew Scappaticci had meetings with rogue Gardai. I told him that I knew this from [a senior FRU officer]." Hurst also claimed that the IRA had planned to capture Breen and Buchanan to question them about cross-border operations and other security matters, rather than kill them. In his submitted statement, however, Keeley claimed that "British agents among the IRA men involved in the ambush had deliberately killed the two RUC officers" to prevent them revealing the identities of FRU and RUC Special Branch agents to an IRA interrogation team.

A colleague of the slain RUC officers, the UUP spokesman on the legacy of the Troubles, Colin Breen, supported Hurst's assessment of British intelligence operations, saying his analysis of the level of penetration "could only lead to a fairly damning conclusion in relation to this inquiry. If these figures are correct, it is logical to assume that the authorities must have had prior knowledge of this operation." With over two dozen IRA volunteers involved

> there must, at the very least, have been indications that something major was being planned by the Provos in the area. Given the number of potential intelligence streams it would appear inconceivable that these murders could not have been prevented. While I would concede that the specifics of the operation might not have been known at the time, there must have been enough information to cause the instigation of a spoiler operation by the security forces at the very least. Based on this testimony it is with a heavy heart that I conclude that Breen and Buchanan might have been saved.

The UUP politician wasn't questioned about the source of the information on which he based his analysis. It wasn't from the IRA or the loyalists, which leaves the Special Branch, whose openly-hostile relationship with MI5 and the FRU must surely undermine the credibility of what he was told, or from the former FRU agents, who have used Unionist politicians several times to highlight their grievances.

Testimony that the IRA learned of the RUC officers' presence in Dundalk, via a telephone call about 90 minutes before the ambush, was contradicted by two retired British Army officers. Brig. Ian Lisles, who spent most of his 14 years in the North stationed in South Armagh, told the tribunal it would have been "impossible for the IRA to mount the ambush in the time-scale suggested" by the two FRU agents. The IRA in the border region was "extremely professional and extremely risk adverse" and if there was a chance that an operation would not be a success from their point of view it would be cancelled. Their attitude was that they could always come back another day "because time was always on their side." In his experience the IRA "never did anything ad hoc. All their operations were well-planned and generally well-executed. The ambush would have taken considerable organization as several roads would have to have been covered, and it would have been impossible to do that in the time scale suggested - ideally they would have needed between 5-to-8 hours to mobilize weapons and men." Brig. Lisles also stated that the had seen the intelligence reports relating to the killings and there was "absolutely no information" that there had been a tip-off to the IRA from Dundalk.

Another retired officer, Brig. Mike Smith, a veteran of seven tours of duty ending in 1997, told Judge Smithwick he couldn't comment on RUC and Int. Corps claims of an "increase in radio traffic among known IRA members in South Armagh" around noon on the day of the ambush because he was not in the North at the time. He described the IRA as "among the most capable and experienced terror groups" and he did not believe that the operation was an attempt to kidnap the two RUC men, as Hurst had claimed. The scene of crime evidence indicated that the IRA was expecting a target to approach and it was "an operation to kill them." Brig. Smith pointed out that the "relatively small number of rounds fired during the ambush, just twenty-eight" showed that there was "controlled fire" and the pattern of fire "did not suggest an element of panic." Asked how long it would take to organize such an operation, he replied that as an experienced British Army officer he would not have liked to try to arrange such a major operation within two hours.

The testimony of retired Garda Chief Supt. Michael Staunton, based on 25 years combating the IRA along the border, supported the British Army officers' assessment. He did not believe the assassinations of Breen and Buchanan could have been carried out in 90 minutes. Visits by Chief Supt. Buchanan to Dundalk and other Garda stations in the Republic were "regular events" in the late 1980s, and his Northern-registered, red Vauxhall Cavalier would have been a "notable sight" when he used rural unapproved border-crossings, or parked outside Dundalk station. Even with good surveillance in place, Mr. Staunton said, it would be unlikely the IRA would have been able to mobilize an assassination unit, take weapons and other equipment out of hiding, and be on the right road at the right time to mount the ambush within the generally-accepted time-scale. Considerable planning would have gone into the operation and the IRA did not need collusion from a rogue police officer. He told Justin Dillon QC, acting for the tribunal, that Chief Supt. Buchanan did not take sufficient care, and should have been more aware of the security risks. Edenappa Road was a "no-go area controlled by the IRA" used only by local traffic and Staunton had thought that Buchanan would come to Dundalk "in a casual way and not in a way that exposed him to risks that I thought were unwise."

So how could the IRA indeed learn about the visit in time to mobilize and mount the ambush? One possible answer was by tapping the landline at Dundalk Garda station via the local telephone exchange. Suggestions that this had occurred were dismissed by telecom employees and retired Garda Inspector Chris Kelly, who had carried out an investigation into phone tapping at Dundalk following an article in *Phoenix*, but had "found no evidence" to support the magazine's claim that this was precisely what happened. He did admit that it was possible if someone had the technical expertise to carry it out, but this would have involved "cutting through airtight telecom wires, which would have set-off an alarm at the exchange."

But the IRA did have the expertise, according to Kings Own Scottish Borderers, Col. Clive Fairweather, 2nd O/C of the SAS during the 5-day Iranian Embassy siege in London in 1980. Fairweather had served in the North periodically between 1974 and the mid-1990s ceasefires, and is regarded by colleagues as the British Army's leading counterinsurgency expert after Gen. Sir Frank Kitson. Col. Fairweather has described the Provos as the most organized guerrilla force he had ever experienced, adding "the opposition [the IRA] monitored everything south of the border. They had all their men on the inside."

The technical expertise used by the IRA involved isolating the lines to be tapped in a specific circuit of twin cables. The standard piece of equipment required was an oscillator used to track a cable or wires inside a cable, and issued to telecom companies technicians and other communications providers. Training was available at Yarnfield, in Staffordshire, a technical facility, previously the General Post Office Engineering Department Central Training School, taken over by British Telecom in 1984, which instructs trainee technicians in this type of work, as well as overseas engineers and cadets from the Royal Corps of Signals, one of the MoD's combat support units, providing military telecommunications infrastructure worldwide.

Once the target lines were identified by faking faults on other lines, they were tracked to a purportedly secure and untraceable monitoring point via stand-alone, unguarded metal roadside connection cabinets, described by *Phoenix* as a "hotchpotch" of old and new wiring, abandoned lines and "jumpers connecting suburban subscribers' lines with main exchange cables." The cabinets could be opened with a spigot key, and the modus operandi was "marked with the cunning which was the basis of all IRA improvised communications interceptions." Two suitably-attired IRA engineers working on a roadside cabinet to transfer the tapped line to another cabinet would attract little attention, and as the magazine pointed out, while it may be politically and professionally difficult for the Irish police to admit the IRA tapped their phones, "the claim that it was not technically feasible is simply untrue."

Sometime during 1987 two IRA engineers climbed the traveling ladders on each side of the main distribution frame carrying the internal cables at Dundalk telephone exchange. In order to prevent the alarm going off when the air-pressured cable was cut they "heat-shrinked a repair sleeve and nozzle to the sliced cable with the identified wires" which were removed, and its paper and enamel insulation stripped. Copper wire was then attached "by means of a twist joint, crimped for a secure permanent electrical connection." It was then covered by an insulating paper sleeve, replaced inside the parent cable, and the cut away silk and cotton 'thatch' pulled tight "to create the impression that the cable had never been opened." What the magazine describes as the "mark of perfection" was the use of Denso tape, "a grey, oozing, two-inch wide water-protective fabric tape" used extensively by the Irish telecommunications company, Eircom. By "binding it tightly on the

The Butcher's Apron

internal cable and burying it in inches of dust" on top of the main distribution frame "it gave cover that ensured the tap would be extremely difficult to find." Using the same "cunning" the IRA had monitored RUC Special Branch HQ at Castlereagh in the 1990s, facilitated by tapping phone lines at Belfast East Exchange at Cluan Place, from where the RUC E Department's (Special Branch) designated private wires were routed.

Damage Limitation

During an eight week recess, from November 2011 to spring 2012, several meetings were held at Palace Barracks in Holywood, MI5's regional headquarters near Belfast, and at Thames House in central London, to analyze the testimony provided by witnesses to the Tribunal, as well as discuss ways to limit, or damage, the credibility of whatever conclusions the Dublin judge might reach. After months of written and oral testimony it was fairly obvious that whatever the IRA knew about the movements of Breen and Buchanen, the information could have been obtained from sources other than an informer in the Garda Siochana station in Dundalk. Indeed, it would have been surprising, not to say negligent, if the Provos hadn't tried to cultivate police officers with republican sympathies based along the border in order to obtain low-grade intelligence about local relationships with the RUC. But allegations of a connection with the Breen/Buchanan slayings appeared wide of the mark.

The first indication that things had changed at what was supposed to be the final session of hearings before Peter Smithwick declared the tribunal closed and focused on writing his report, came in early February 2012, when journalist,Toby Harnden, the tribunal's star witness, failed to appear, as agreed. Harnden was scheduled to be cross-examined about the claims he had made concerning Garda/IRA collusion, which were a key factor in the Dublin Government establishing the tribunal, despite Judge Cory's doubts - raised in his 2003 collusion report - about Harnden's "un-collaborated original statement" - saying the journalist had "put forward as matters of fact, allegations and off-the-record briefings" from anonymous British Army and MI5 sources, which were "founded on speculation and hypothesis." These allegations were then repeated, as fact, in the mainstream British and Irish media, creating a perverse situation in which the Dublin Government had no choice but to order an investigation, or be accused by the same media of trying to cover up Garda involvement in the killings of two ranking RUC officers. According to Judge Cory, Harden was prepared to discuss his sources, but was "vague about where or when" he had been briefed, and by whom. If he wasn't willing to be more forthright with the retired member of the Canadian judiciary in private, he was certainly not prepared to be so in public. Perhaps getting a tribunal up and running had been Harnden's intention. If so, he succeeded admirably.

Judge Smithwick refused to comment in detail on Harnden's refusal to appear, except to confirm that the dates had been chosen by the journalist himself, who is currently the *Daily Telegraph*'s New York-based US editor. Instead, the statement originally given by Brig. Ian Liles in private was read into the record, on 9 February, after the MoD had requested "three minor changes." In this written testimony Brig. Liles, who had worked as an intelligence officer with 3rd Brigade along the South Armagh border, confirmed that radio traffic between IRA members on the day Breen and Buchanan died, began between 11.30am and noon. He said there was a detailed analysis in the aftermath of the ambush, carried out by the Int. Corps, in which it was estimated that at least seventy IRA members had taken part, covering the three possible routes the RUC officers would have taken returning to Belfast. He described IRA security in South Armagh as "water tight" with "dickers" continually monitoring British Army activity on local roads, very likely unknown to each other. The volunteers involved in preparing and carrying out the ambush included "beaters" who would have searched the hedge-rows for British soldiers before retrieving weapons from "secure, environmentally-protected" arsenals, and "spotters" on the lookout for British foot and mobile patrols in the area, as well as those who had carried out the ambush.

After being given permission by the MoD, the ex-FRU agent, Ian Hurst, testified during the final week of April 2012, and claimed the ambush had been ordered by Sinn Fein's Martin McGuinness, the current deputy First Minister in the Northern Ireland Executive, who was the IRA O/C Northern Command at the time, and that the intention of the IRA was to abduct Breen and Buchanan, interrogate them, remove any classified material they might be carrying, and finally to execute them. He claimed to be aware of ten Int. Corps reports which named Garda Sgt. Owen Corrigan, stationed in Dundalk, as the source of IRA information, which was routed though his handler and Scappaticci's FRU handlers to Int. Corps and MI5. Hurst named another Dundalk-based police officer, Sgt. Leo Colton, as an IRA sympathizer. Along with Sgt. Finbarr Hickey, named in previous testimony, Colton became the third police officer to be accused of working with the Provos.

Within hours of Hurst's allegations about McGuinness, Sinn Fein issued a statement totally rejecting the ex-FRU agent's uncorroborated account, pointing out that Judge Smithwick had already criticized the "quality and nature of the evidence" provided by agents of the British security and intelligence apparatus which had "played a negative and malign role in the conflict, including widespread involvement in collusion."

Writing in the *Guardian*, Danny Morrison, ex-IRA Long Kesh internee and former editor of *An Phoblacht*, described Scappaticci's alleged role as "pure fantasy" pointing out that "territory is important in Ireland" and IRA ASU's in South Armagh would have "no need or desire" to consult anyone about the planned ambush, "least of all a Belfast man like Scap." Morrison, the author of several well-received novels based on the Troubles, also referred to the evidence given by a senior RUC Special Branch officer, identified only as 'Witness 62', who had told the tribunal that "no agent of the state who was recruited at the time was in any way involved in the shooting." Morrison rejected claims that the Provos were "riddled with spies" run by British agent-handlers as part of the "FRU-inspired myth that has become the accepted narrative" and in his account, based on his experiences in Belfast and his daily association with republican comrades and colleagues, he claimed that Scappaticci was a member of a "debrief unit" that questioned IRA volunteers "after certain operations in certain areas" but was "never briefed about upcoming operations" and was never a member of the IRA's Dundalk-based security unit (as Hurst, and others have claimed) nor could he "walk into a particular area and demand prior details of an operation or the head of an IRA volunteer on a plate."

By this stage, Peter Smithwick had been expected to wind up proceedings, and present an interim report of his finding by 31 May, despite the British authorities refusing to cooperate fully with his inquiry. Sources in Dublin believe that as much as 75 percent of the material presented to the tribunal has not been published, including correspondence between the tribunal and the British Home Office (on behalf of MI5), the MoD, New Scotland Yard, and the PSNI. Most of the civilian "outside jurisdiction" witnesses had been vetted by MI5, and their testimony was what MI5 wanted the tribunal to hear. The organization graded the intelligence, and decisions were then taken by anonymous officials with regard to what should be said and who should say it.

This became clear following a six-week adjournment with a new deadline set for 31 October 2012, when PSNI Ass. Chief Con. Drew Harris informed the tribunal that, after seven years of private and public hearings, "five new pieces of evidence" had been found concerning another Irish police officer not previously referred to, who had, allegedly, passed information to the IRA and was implicated in the deaths of Lord Justice Gibson and his wife This was followed within weeks by the disclosure that "more important new intelligence" had "manifested itself quite recently" and was "so sensitive" it could only be heard in private. PSNI Det. Chief Supt. Roy McComb provided Judge Smithwick with a brief summary of the intelligence, but he was under strict instructions from MI5 to stay within the narrow parameters of his brief, saying "decisions were made that the documentation should not be shared. I am afraid I can't assist you at this point as to who made the decision or when those decisions were made."

In order to consider fully the 'new' information, coupled with concerns about the deteriorating health of Mr. Corrigan, the Irish Minister for Justice and Defense, Alan Shatter, agreed to extend the deadline for the tribunal's final report to 31 July 2013. When he took office in March 2011, Mr. Shatter had hoped the tribunal would complete its business by the end of that year. Three deadlines have since come and gone, and a frustrated Judge Smithwick is still trying to come to terms with the disinformation, redacted testimony and deliberate subterfuge to which the British authorities have treated the tribunal, making it difficult to escape the conclusion that this was never about IRA/Garda collusion in the deaths of Breen and Buchanan. The IRA did not need Garda assistance to mount the ambush because they had information from several other sources. The Smithwick Tribunal was an opportunity for bitter men within MI5 to raise the issue of collusion between the Dublin politicians and the Provisional IRA, dating back to the late 1960s, when unarmed Belfast nationalists, who had formed local defense committees, had traveled to Dublin seeking help to defend their vulnerable communities faced with the threat of sectarian slaughter, after Ulster loyalist and RUC's reservist 'B Specials' attacked and destroyed nationalist homes along the Falls/Shankill interface. This led to the first collusion inquiry of the Troubles, and a report by Lord Hunt, a former British Army officer, that called for the B Specials to be disbanded, and replaced by the locally-recruited UDR, many of whose members would later play a murderous role in the 'dirty war.'

Operation *Banner* was the last major, all-services, 20th century deployment in which the British Army, its elite forces and clandestine units, unsuccessfully tried to adapt the tactics employed in anti-colonial struggles in Malaysia and Kenya, to a European urban environment. The MoD top brass, veterans of decades of triumphant and ceremonial soldering, were uncomfortable with their final assessment of how the war was fought, and tried to bury it.The MoD's report acknowledges that the British Army did not win militarily, but claims to have achieved a "desired end state" by making it clear to the Provisional IRA that they too could not win through violence. The point which the military analysts failed to recognize, however, is that the Provos did not have to win this war, they simply had to remain undefeated.

The institutionalized sectarianism of the RUC was a major factor in the escalation of violence, while the covert campaign waged by the British intelligence and security services which involved black propaganda, abduction, torture and murder, directly or by proxy, generated a level of hatred and distrust that still resonates, and has already been redacted from the official, taught history of the period. Much of what happened during the Troubles has also been fictionalized, and much of what has been written is reinforced by tired clichés and stereotypes, with British forces being portrayed as 'honest' brokers, while religion is used as a convenient means of classifying the violence without having to explain the complex political and historical background, effectively reducing what was initially a non-violent civil rights struggle to change a wholly unjust, bigoted and corrupt political system, to the level of a mindless sectarian conflict rooted in several centuries of history.

It is now 15 years since the GFA, yet this distorted view continues in contemporary Troubles fiction. Speaking at the annual Hay-on-Wye literary festival in Wales in June 2005, the former Goldsmiths College, and Lancaster University head of creative writing studies, award-winning author, Dr Linda Anderson, described the conflict as "one of the most over-narrativised" and explained that "factual inaccuracy in novels using real events have consequences in the real world" because they "reinforce media bias instead of giving a fresh vision and understanding." Judge Peter Smithwick has the opportunity of providing what may be the final official narrative, once he distinguishes between testimony designed to deceive and perpetuate the lies, and that which provides some fresh insight and understanding of how the war was fought.

BIBLIOGRAPHY
Asmal, Kader. *Politics in my Blood*. Johannesburg: Jacana Media Ltd. 2010.
Barzilay, David. *The British Army in Ulster* (Volumes 1-IV). Belfast: Century Books, 1973/81.
Collins, Eamon and McGovern, Mick. *Killing Rage*. London: Granta Books, 1998.
Connor, Ken. *Ghost Force*. London: Cassell & Co., 1998.
Curtis, Liz. *Ireland: the Propaganda War*. London: Pluto Press,1984.
Davies, Nicholas. *Ten-Thirty-Three*. Edinburgh: Mainstream Publishing, 1999
Dillon, Martin. *The Shankhill Butchers*. London: Arrow Books,1990.
Dillon, Martin. *The Dirty War*. London: Arrow Books, 1990.
Faligot, Roger. *The Kitson Experiment*. Dingle/London: Brandon/Zed Press 1983.
Foot, Paul. *Who Framed Colin Wallace?* Macmillan,1989.
Geraghty, Tony. *The Irish War*. London: HarperCollins 1998.
Harnden, Toby. *Bandit Country*. London: Coronet Books, 2000.
Hermon, John. *Holding the Line*. Dublin: Gill & Macmillan, 1997.
Holland, Jack and Phoenix, Susan. *Phoenix: Policing the Shadows*. London: Coronet Books, 1996.
Holroyd, Fred (with Burbridge, Nick). *War Without Honour* Hull: Medium Publishing, 1989.
Ingram, Martin and Harkin, Greg. *Stakeknife*. Dublin: The O'Brien Press, 2004.
Kitson,Frank. *Low Intensity Operations*. London: Faber and Faber, 1991.
Larkin, Paul. *A Very British Jihad*. Belfast: Beyond the Pale Publications, 2004.
McKittrick,David, Kelters, Seamus, Feeney Brian and Thornton, Chris. *Lost Lives*. Edinburgh: Mainstream Publishing, second revised edition, June 2004
McPhilemy, Sean. *The Committee*. Colorado: Roberts Rineharts Publishers,1998.
Mullan, Don. *The Dublin & Monaghan Bombings*. Dublin: Wolfhound Press, 2000.
Murray, Raymond. *The SAS in Ireland*. Dublin: The Mercier Press, 1990.
O'Mahony, Sean. *Frongoch*. Dublin: FDR Teoranta,1987.
Pincher, Chapman. *Too Secret Too Long*. London: Sidgwick & Jackson, 1984.

Rolston, Bill (with Gilmartin, Mairead), *Unfinished Business*. Belfast: Beyond the Pale Publications, 2000.
Schmidt, Olivier (ed.) *The Intelligence Files*. Atlanta: Clarity Press, 2005.
Short, Martin. *Inside the Brotherhood*. London: Grafton Books. 1989
Stalker, John. *Stalker*. London: Harrap. 1998.
Styles, George. *Bombs Have No Pity*. London: Luscombe, 1975.
Sutton, Malcolm. *An Index of Deaths from the Conflict in Ireland 1969-1993*. Belfast: Beyond the Pale
Publications, 1994.
Taber, Robert. *The War of the Flea*. St. Albans: Paladin, 1969.
Taylor, Peter. *Beating the Terrorists?* London: Penguin Books, 1980.
Urban, Mark. *Big Boys' Rules*. London: Faber and Faber, 1992.

NEWSPAPERS & MAGAZINES,
Andersonstown News (www.belfastmedia.com
The Atlantic (www.theatlantic.com)
An Phoblacht (www.anphoblacht.com)
Belfast Telegraph (www.belfasttelegraph.co.uk)
Daily Mail (www.dailymail.co.uk)
Daily Telegraph (www.telegraph.co.uk)
Guardian (www.guardian.co.uk)
Intelligence (ADI) Paris, France
*Independent (*www.independent.co.uk)
Irish News (www.irishnews.com)
Irish Times (www.irishtimes.com)
Lobster Magazine (editor Robin Ramsay), Hull, UK,
Lobster Magazine (editor Stephen Dorril) Holmfirth, West Yorkshire, UK,
Magill (www.magill.ie)
Observer (www.observer.guardian.co.uk)
Phoenix (www.thephoenix.ie)
Sunday Business Post (www.businesspost.ie)
Sunday Tribune (www.sundaytribune.ie)
Sunday Times (www.thesundaytimes.co.uk)
Times (www.thetimes.co.uk)

BRITISH & IRISH PARLIAMENTARY & DEPARTMENTAL REPORTS
De Silva Report (www.patfinucanereview.org)
Hansard Parliamentary Debates, Vol 118, The Stationary Office (London) 1987
The Report of the Bloody Sunday Inquiry, chaired by the Rt. Hon. Lord Saville of Newdigate,
published on 15 June 2010.
Official British Parliamentary Reports (www.theyworkforyou.com)
Operation Banner: An Analysis of Military Operations in Northern Ireland,

Ministry of Defence, London, 2006.
25 Years on: The Costs of War and the Dividends of Peace, Mike Tomlinson, Foram Eacnamaiochta Iarthar Bheal Feirste, 1994
Setting the Record Straight, Sinn Fein Publications, Dublin 1994 (available as pdf.download at www.sinnfein.ie/files/2009/settingtherecordstraight/pdf)
Smithwick Tribunal (www.smithwicktribunal.ie)

INDEX

14 Field Security and Intelligence Company (14FSIC) 282, 285, 286, 288, 290, 300, 302-304, 311, 327
39th Infantry Brigade 279, 284, 285
4 Field Survey Troop 286

A

Adams, Gerry 330, 331, 333-336
Aeroflot 221, 222
Aerospatiale/DaimlerChrysler AG 26, 133
African Defence Systems (ASD) 116
African Union (AU) 150
Afrikaner WeestandsBeweging (AWB) 122
Aitken, Jonathan William Patrick 138, 139
al-Aqsa Martyrs' Brigades 51
Al-Fatah Movement 25-30, 34-36, 50
al-Masri, Abu Hamza 73, 74, 87
al-Masri, Abu Ubaida 100
Al-Muhajiroun (The Emigrants) 74, 75, 104
Al-Mustansiriya University's Department of Community Medicine (DCM) 187
al-Qassam Brigades 50, 53, 54
Albert Schweitzer College (Switzerland) 204
Algerian Socialist Forces Front (FFS) 64, 65
All-Union Pioneer Organization 227
Amalgamated Banks of South Africa (ABSA) 132-134
American Express Travel Section 206, 227, 229, 230
American Friends of the Anti-Bolshevik Bloc of Nations 228
American Israel Public Affairs Committee (AIPAC) 25, 40
American Israeli Cooperative Enterprise (AICE) 18
Amtorg Trading Corporation 221
Anderson, Jeff 352
Angleton, James Jesus 206, 226, 229, 230
Annesley, Hugh Norman 322

Anti-Terrorist Alert Center (ATAC) 44
Apology for the Christians 245
Arafat, Yasser 25, 34, 40, 42, 45, 46, 49
Arma dei Carabinieri 257, 261, 262
Armaments Acquisition Council (AAC) 143
Armaments Corporation of South Africa (ARMSCOR) 118, 131-134, 141, 316-318
Armed Islamic Group (GIA) 63, 65, 66, 68, 74
Artane Industrial School 248
Asset Forfeiture Bureau (AFB) 135
Association of Chief Police Officers (ACPO) 84
Athenagoras of Athens 245
Atomic Energy Commission (AEC) 23-24
Atsugi Naval Air Facility 204, 210
Attwood, William Hollingsworth 234,
Audiencia Nacional (Spanish Judiciary Criminal Chamber) 81
Aurelius, Marcus 245
Azanian People's Organisation (AZAPO) 129

B

Ba'ath Party 156, 166, 180, 187, 193
BAE Systems 111, 118, 120, 132
Bagley, Peter 224-226,
Baker, Norman John 165-172, 199, 214, 236
Ball, Julian 280, 286, 288, 303
Ballykinlar Barracks 312
Banca del Fucino 261
Banca del Gottardo 260
Banca Privata Italiana (BPI) 259
Banco Ambrosiano 256, 258-260, 264-265, 268
Banco Financiero Sudamericano 266
Banda della Magliana 257, 264
Bank of Italy 261

Index

Barak, Ehud 37, 46, 54
Barrett, Ken 319, 324, 333
Barron, Henry 289-291, 297, 299,
Bechtel Corporation 180, 198
Begin, Menachem 17, 19, 29, 33-35, 37, 49
Belhadj, Ali 63,
Belkheir, Larbi 64
Ben Gurion, David 18-19, 21-22, 25, 33, 79
Bendjedid, Chadi 63- 64
Benedict XV (Giacomo Paolo Giovanni Battista della Chiesa) 246
Benedict XVI (Joseph Aloisius Ratzinger)238, 239, 256
Bergoglio, Jorge Mario 272, 275
Berlusconi, Silvio 272
Bernard of Clairvaux 246,
Bertone, Tarcisco, Pietro 262, 271, 272, 273
Bethesda Naval Hospital 209
Bettaney, Michael John 310-313
Bin Laden, Osama 62, 72, 158-160, 166, 194, 197
Binnenlandse Veiligheidsdienst (BVD) 203, 219, 220-223, 229
Black Economic Empowerment (BEE) 144
Black September 27-28, 38
Black, John 280, 284
Blair, Anthony Charles Lynton 'Tony' 10, 47, 60, 67, 78, 81, 84, 89, 96, 138, 140, 146-147, 153, 156, 158-169, 172-175, 177-187, 189-199, 281, 289-290, 312, 331, 337
Blix, Hans Martin 195, 197
Bloody Sunday (Derry City, 30 January 1972) 9, 86, 185, 281-282, 285, 288, 325, 354
Boyce, Michael Cecil 164-165, 184, 196
Brady, Sean Baptist 253
Breen, Henry Alexander 'Harry' 325, 339-341, 344-347, 349-350, 352
Bremer, Lewis Paul 'Jerry' 180, 190, 193
British Aerospace 120,
British Military Intelligence Corps (Int. Corps) 281, 295-296, 298, 305, 309, 313-315, 329, 343-344, 347, 350
British Ministry of Defense (MoD) 86, 132, 137, 153, 167-169, 171, 176, 179, 181-184, 186, 194, 196, 278-284, 286, 288-290, 293, 296, 298, 301, 305-306, 313-316, 323-326, 328, 330, 337-338, 341-343, 345, 348, 350-352

British Secret Intelligence Service (MI6) 31, 61, 71, 76, 77, 80, 88-91, 93, 98, 102, 105, 106, 130-132, 138, 151, 154, 158-159, 164, 166-169, 174, 180, 186-187, 189, 192-193, 199, 213, 226, 293, 297-298, 303, 307-310, 312-313, 315, 318, 327, 332, 343,
British Security Service (MI5) 61, 71, 73, 74, 77, 79, 80, 87- 94, 96-107, 109, 132, 159, 168, 186, 187, 198, 199, 220, 278, 290, 296, 297, 298, 301, 303, 308- 313, 315, 316, 318-322, 326-338, 341-343, 346, 349, 350, 351, 352
British Security Service Organisation (BSSO) 309
Brown, Gordon James 97, 185, 186, 194, 210, 273, 284, 289
Buchanan, Robert James 'Bob' 236, 325, 339-341, 344-347, 349-350, 352
Buitenland Inlichtingendienst (BID) 203, 213, 223
Bureau of Scientific Relations (Lekem) 24, 44, 80
Bureau van Nationale Veiligheid (BNV) 220
Bush, George Herbert Walker 10, 41, 46, 49, 60,
Bush, George Walker 68, 74, 82, 101, 140, 147, 153-158, 160, 161, 162, 163, 164, 167, 173, 178-180, 186, 188, 189, 191-196, 198, 199, 242, 244, 280, 283,
Bush, Neil Mallon 224, 244

C

Cabinet Office Briefing Room A (COBRA) 98, 180, 199
CAIN (Conflict Archive on the Internet) 280
Calvi, Roberto 256, 259, 263, 265-268
Cameron, David William Donald 199, 288, 289, 337-338
Campbell, Alistair John 163, 164, 165, 169, 172, 192, 197
Cantalamessa, Raniero 256
Carboni, Flavio Mario 265-267
Carobbi, Italo 264
Casaroli, Agostino 258, 264, 265, 266, 267, 268
Catholic League of Counter Reformation 270
Center for International Emergency Disaster

and Refugee Studies (CIEDRS) 187
Center for the Preservation of Modern
   History (CPMH) 209
Central Intelligence Agency (CIA) 10, 15,
   18-19, 24, 25, 31, 35, 38, 71-72, 76-77,
   88, 97, 101, 141, 154-155, 159, 167-
   168, 170-172, 181, 187, 196, 203-207,
   209-210, 212-214, 217, 219-231, 233,
   235, 264, 267, 310
Centrale Veiligheidsdienst (CVD) 220
Centre for Economic Diplomacy in Africa
   (CEDIA) 130
Centre for Research on the Epidemiology of
   Disasters (CRED) 188
Centro de Investigaciones Sociologicas
   (CIS) 255
Centro Nacional de Inteligencia (CNI)
Chalabi, Ahmed 161, 162, 192, 196
Chilcot, John 164, 167, 181, 185-186, 188,
   190, 194-199
Cipriani, Juan Luis 272
Clinton, William Jefferson 'Bill' 41, 45, 66,
   72, 140, 153, 279, 331, 336,
Clutterbuck, Richard 296
Coalition Information Centre (CIC) 163,
   165, 166
Coalition Provisional Authority (CPA) 190,
   193
Colby, William Egan 230, 231
Colton, Leo 350
Commission of Inquiry into Child Abuse
   (CICA) 248
Committee of Intelligence and Security
   Service (CISSA) 150
Conference for a Democratic South Africa
   (CODESA) 141
Congregation for the Doctrine of the Faith
   (CDF) 239, 242, 245, 254, 262, 273,
   275, 276
Congregation of Christian Brothers 248, 252
Congregation for the Evangelization of
   Peoples 271
Congress of South African Trade Unions
   (COSATU) 125, 127, 135, 141, 149
Congress of the People (COPE) 136
Corpo di Vigilenza (CdV) 271, 273
Corrigan, Owen 350, 351
Cory Collusion Report 325, 340
Cory, Peter deCarteret 325, 326, 337, 338,
   339, 340, 341, 344, 349

Council for the Public Affairs of the Church
   241
Council on Foreign Relations (CFR) 51
Credit Suisse 260
Credit Suisse First Boston (CSFB) 145
Credito Artigiano Spa 261
Crichton, Jack Alston 214
Criminal Intelligence Department (CID)320,
   321, 334, 336, 341
Crown Prosecution Service (CPS) 94, 95,
   100, 101, 107, 238, 239, 321
Cubban, Brian 307, 308
Curtis, Robert 280
Cwele, Sheryl 149,
Cwele, Siyabonga 149, 151

D

da Pisa, Bernardo 246
De Silva, Desmond 338, 339
Dallas Police Department (DPD) 203, 214
Damiani, Petrus 246
Data Protection Act (1998) 187
Dawkins, Clinton Richard 238, 239
Dayan, Moshe 20, 23, 26, 33
De Booy, Mr 229, 230
De Lille, Patricia 119, 130, 145
de Menezes, Jean Charles 84, 85, 86, 94,
   95, 96
de Nantes, George 270
De Paolis, Velasio 272, 273
Dearlove, Richard Billing 164
Dearsley, Bernard 303
Decretum Gratiani 246
Defense Export Services
   Organization(DESO) 137, 147
Defense Intelligence Agency (DIA) 35
Defense Intelligence Staff (DIS) 80
Defense Policy Department (DPD) (Dallas
   Police Department)
Democratic Unionist Party (DUP) 279, 317
Denel (Pty) Ltd. 118
Department du Renseignement at de la
   Securite (DRS) 64-68
Department of Homeland Security (DHS)
   101, 122
Derby-Lewis, Clive 122
Dick, Cressida (Scotland Yard) 85, 95, 96
Direction et de la Surveillance du Territoire
   (DST) 65, 66, 73-75, 307
Direction Generale de la Securite Exterieure

Index

(DGSE) 65, 66, 75, 187
Directorate for Priority Crime Investigation (DPCI) 115, 118, 123, 134
Directorate of Serious Economic Offences (DSEO) 120
Directorate of Special Operations (DSO) 112, 114, 116, 117, 119, 123-125, 127, 130, 134, 135, 139, 143-144, 149
Dombey, Norman 168
Donaldson, Denis 334-337
du Citeaux, Arnold 246
Duff, Arthur Antony 308-309, 313
Dulles, Allan Welsh 219-221
Dutch Communist Party (CPN) 220

E

Echevarrie, Javier Rodriguez 263
EG&G Company 44
Egyptian General Intelligence Service (GIS) 26, 78
Einthoven, L. 219-221
Eitan, Rafael 'Raful' 24, 28, 35, 36
Empresa Nacional Bazan 142
Engelen, Dick 220
Epstein, Edward Jay 209
Escriva, St. Josemaria 263, 266
Eugenius III (Bernardo da Pisa) 246
European Convention of Human Rights (ECHR) 70, 76, 102, 182
European Court of Human Rights (ECtHR) 70, 182, 243, 245, 286
Evans, Jonathan 102, 278, 342
Evelegh, John Robin Garnet 285
Ewart-Biggs, Christopher 307, 308
Explosive Ordnance and Disposal Team (EODS) 294

F

Fafo Research Foundation 41
Fatah Revolutionary Council (FRC) 34, 35
Federal Bureau of Investigation (FBI) 24, 44, 62, 71, 72, 75, 87-88, 101, 103-104, 147, 160, 170, 205-206, 208, 214, 219, 221, 228, 235, 322, 342,
Feinstein, Andrew Josef 111, 119-121, 123, 126, 132, 136, 137, 143, 145,
Ferns Report 277
Financial Action Task Force (FATF) 262

Fincomsumo Banca SpA 261
Fininvest 272
Finmeccanica 261
Finucane, Geraldine 324, 337, 338
Finucane, Patrick 10, 282, 318, 319, 322, 324, 325, 338, 339
Fisher, Alice S. 147, 221
Forbes, Trevor 319
Force Research Unit (FRU) 11, 61, 68, 278, 280, 282, 312-317, 319, 322-325, 327, 337-338, 341-346, 350-351,
Foreign and Commonwealth Office (FCO) 71, 97, 132, 162, 163, 165, 169, 177, 178, 180, 189, 190, 192, 193, 306-308, 318, 328, 332
Foreign Corrupt Practices Act (FCPA) 140
Fortune, Sean 254
Foundation for Inter-religious and Intercultural Research and Dialogue (FIIRD) 244
Francis 1 (Bergoglio Jorge Mario) 272, 275
Franklin National Bank 259
Franks, Arthur 312
Freddie Scappaticci 313, 314, 345, 350, 351
Freeland, Ian Henry 282
Freemason Brotherhood 269, 274
Front de Liberation Nationale (FLN) 63, 65, 307
Futuristic Business Solutions (FBS) 145

G

Gabriele, Paolo 271, 272, 273, 274
Ganswein, Georg 274
Garda Crime and Security Intelligence Branch (G3)*C3* 340
Garda Siochana (Irish Police Force) 247, 250, 291, 325, 349
Gelli, Licio 10, 257, 264, 266, 268
General Communications Headquarters (GCHQ)
General Intelligence Directorate (GID) 76
General Intelligence Service (GIS) 26, 78
General Security Directorate (GSD) 34, 35
General Zionist Party (GZP) 56
German Frigate Consortium (GFC) 116, 136, 142, 145, 146
Gilligan, Andrew Paul 166, 169
Glaspie, April Catherine 154, 173
Glavnoye Razvedyvatel'noye Upravleniye

(GRU) 203, 212, 220-221, 229
Glenanne Gang 287, 288, 290, 302, 303, 304, 305
Golitsyn, Anatoli Mikhaylovich 224, 226, 227
Goloeb, Aleksej 222, 223
Gorizont Electronics Factory 204
Government Accounting Office (GAO) 23, 58
Government Communications Headquarters (GCHQ) 80, 88, 106, 174, 175, 187, 199, 290, 329
Gow, Ian Reginald 327
Grand Orient of Italy (Masonic organization) 268
Gratian, Flavius Gratianus Augustus 246
Green, John Francis 288, 300-303
Gregory X (Teobaldo Visconti) 275
Groer, Hans Hermann 240
Gromyko, Andre Andreyevich 222
Group for Culture, Ethics and Finance (GCEF) 260
Grupo Especial de Operaciones (Special Operations Group) 80
Gun, Katherine Teresa 190

H

Habash, George 27
Haddick, Colin 322
Haganah 18, 20, 23, 33
Hani, Chris 120, 121, 122, 141
Hanna, William 287, 295
Haraket al-Muqawamah al-Islamiyyah (Hamas) 40, 42, 50- 53
Harding, Luke 166, 167, 307
Harriman, William Averill 277
Hassaine, Reda 73, 74
Hayman, Andrew Christopher 93, 96, 101
Heath Special Investigative Unit (HSIU) 120,
Heath, William 132-133
Heli Trading 44
Helms, Richard McGarrah 205-206, 223,
Hermon, John Charles 318-322, 341
Heywood, Jeremy 199
Hickey, Finbarr 350
Hitchens, Christopher Eric 238-239
Hizb ut-Tahir (The Party of Liberation) 74
Hnilica, Pavol 265-267

Hogg, Douglas Martin 318, 322
Holroyd, Frederick John 293-297, 298, 300-301, 303
Hoon, Geoffrey, William 'Geoff' 159, 164, 166, 169, 172, 194
Hotel Torni (Helsinki) 204-205
House of Commons Foreign Affairs Select Committee (HCFASC) 200
House of Representatives Permanent Select Committee on Intelligence 235
House Select Committee on Assassinations (HSCA) 205, 217, 234
Human Rights Watch (HRW) 52, 155, 156
Hurst, Ian (aka 'Martin Ingram') 316, 325, 344-347, 350, 351,
Hutton, James Brian Edward 86, 168-170, 172, 181, 185

I

IDF General Reconnaissance Staff 26
Imperial Armed Forces College 296
Independent Police Complaints Commission (IPCC) 86, 94, 96
Indian Residential Schools (Canada) 255
Information Policy Department (IPD) 295, 296, 297, 302
Innocent III (Lotario dei Conti di Segni) 246
Institute for Accountability in South Africa (IASA) 133
Institute for Research: Middle East Policy (Irmep) 23
Institute for Security Studies (ISS) 115, 134,
Institute of the History of the Reformation (IHR) 244
Instituto Nazionale di Statistica (INSTAT) 255
Instituto per le Opere di Religione (IOR) 256-267, 269, 270, 272, 276
Intelligence and Security Committee (ISC) 89, 167, 172, 181, 290
Intelligence and Security Group (ISG) 290, 309
Inter-Services Intelligence (ISI) 31, 88, 90, 91, 97, 100, 104,
Internal Security Act (ISA) 149, 228
International Atomic Energy Agency (IAEA)34, 168
International Committee of the Red Cross (ICRC) 39, 188

Index

International Court of Justice (ICJ) 191
International Criminal Court (ICC) 165, 182, 196, 238
International Security Assistance Force (ISAF) 161
International Solidarity Movement (ISM) 47
International Trade Center (ITC) 117
Intesa San Paolo Bank 261
Iraq Body Count (IBC) Project 187, 188
Iraq Family Health Survey (IFHS) 188
Iraqi National Congress (INC) 70, 161, 192, 196,
Irgun Tzvai-Leumi 19
Irish National Liberation Army (INLA) 69, 311
Irish Republican Movement 280
Irish Republican Socialist Party (IRSP) 311
Islamic Salvation Front (FIS) 63-65
Isotopes and Radiation Enterprises Limited (ISORAD) 23
Israeli Air Force (IAF) 15-17, 26, 33, 34, 40, 53, 54
Israeli Atomic Energy Commission (IAEC) 23
Israeli Defense Forces (IDF) 317
Israeli Military Intelligence Directorate (Aman) 19, 23, 32, 33, 36
Israeli Police Force (IPF) 46
Italian Communist Party (ICP)
Italian Military Intelligence and Security Service (SISMI) 167, 257, 267

J

Jackson, Michael David 'Mike' 281
Jackson, Robert John 'Robin' 287
Jagan, Cheddi Berret 181
Jean-Marie Villot 269
John Paul 1 (Albino Luciani) 269
John Paul II (Karol Jozef Wojtyla) 239, 240, 241, 242, 247, 255, 256, 258, 266-269, 273
Johnson, Lyndon Baines 15, 233, 234,
Johnson, Priscilla 207, 209, 214, 217,
Joint Committee of Justice, Defense and Equality (JCJDE) 289
Joint Intelligence Committee (JIC) 89, 132, 163, 290, 309, 313, 318
Joint Services Group (JSG) 314, 343
Joint Standing Committee on Intelligence

(JSCI) 149, 150
Joint Terrorism Analysis Centre (JTAC) 80, 82
Jordanian General Intelligence Directorate (GID) 76
JP Morgan 261
Judicial Services Commission (JSC) 111

K

Kader, Asmal 333
Kampfgruppen der Arbeiterklasse (KdA) 213
Keeley, Peter (aka 'Kevin Fulton') 278, 279, 325, 337, 240-343
Kelly, David Christopher 347
Kennedy, John Fitzgerald (JFK) 43, 202, 203, 206, 209, 221, 229-236
Kennedy, Robert Francis 'Bobby' 234
Kerr, James Gordon ('Colonel J') 313, 322, 323, 324, 337, 344
Khan, Mohammad Sidique 59, 78, 90- 93, 95, 97, 102-106
King, Frank Douglas 288
King, Thomas Jeremy 321, 323,
Kissinger, Henry Alfred 9, 19, 33, 234
Kisvalter, George 224, 225, 226
Kitson, Frank Edward 181, 283, 285, 303, 348
Knights of Malta (Knights Hospitaller) 266
Komitet Gosudarstvennoy Bezopasnosti (KGB) 30, 203, 204, 206, 207, 209, 213, 217, 218, 220-230, 236, 258, 307, 311
Koza, Frank 174, 175
Kwiatkowski, Karen 157

L

Lane, Mark 234, 235
Law Society of Northern Ireland 322
Law, Bernard Francis 254
Ledochowski, Wlodimir 275
Legion of Christ 241, 242, 272
Leo IX (Bruno of Egisheim-Dagsburg) 246
Libby, Lewis 'Scooter' 162, 172, 173
Likud 17, 19, 37-38, 41-46, 49, 52, 54-55
Lindsay, Germaine 60, 92
Livingstone, Kenneth Robert 301
Lombardi, Federico 273, 274, 258, 262, 271

Understanding Shadows: The Corrupt Use of Intelligence

Lord Justice Widgery 281
Lorenzi, Diego 269
Luciani, Albino 268
Luciani, Eduardo 279, 270
Luns, Joseph Marie Antoine 222
Lynn, William J. 275
Lyttle, Tommy 'Tucker' 316-319, 338, 339

M

Maciel, Marcial Degollado 241, 242, 273
Madani, Abbassi 63
Magdalene Laundries (Ireland) 248, 249
Magee, John 269, 270
Maharaj Sathyandranath 'Mac' 114-116, 118, 122, 123, 141, 150
Mahon Road Barracks (Portadown) 306
Mailer, Norman Kingsley 208, 209, 214, 237
Malema, Julius 126, 127
Mamantov, Ilya 214
Mandela, Nelson Rolihlahla 113, 121-123, 127, 130, 133, 142, 145, 146, 148, 151
Manningham-Buller, Elizabeth 91, 92, 198, 336
Marchant, William 'Frenchie' 292
Marcinkus, Paul Casimir 10, 256, 258-260, 263-266, 268-270,
Marconi Electronic Systems 120
Marinelli, Luigi 246, 276
Mbeki, Thabo Mvuyelwa 114, 119-124, 126-131, 133, 135, 136, 141, 142, 145, 149, 333
McCain, John Sidney 15
McCaughey, William 287, 305, 306
McCone, John Alexander 205-207
McCoy, John (the 'Badger') 303
McGartland, Martin (aka 'Martin Ashe') 337
McGee, Patrick 326
McGuinness, James Martin 131, 279, 327, 330, 333-335, 350
McKiernan, Francis 253
McMillan, Priscilla ('nee' Johnson) 202, 209, 217
McVickar, John 207, 211, 217, 224, 225, 228
Meir, Golda 18, 23, 27, 33, 42, 57, 88
Metropolitan Police Special Branch 71, 95
Meyer, Christopher John Rome 60, 61, 128, 162-164, 190, 191, 199

Miami Showband 286, 288, 301-303
Middle East Centre for Arabic Studies (MECAS) 189, 307
Middleton, Glyn 294, 295
Milco International Incorporated (MII) 44
Military Reaction Force (MRF) 282-286
Miller, Judith 172, 173
Milsek Investment Trust (MIT) 117
Minderley Investments 117, 118
Ministerstvo Vnutrennikh Del (MVD) 204, 207, 208, 210, 211, 225
Ministry of Defence (MoD) 153
Mitchell, George John 56, 331, 332, 334
Mitchell, James 287,
Mitrokhin, Vasili Nikitich 222, 223
MK-ULTRA 223
Mo Shaik 141, 142, 150
MoD's Defense Intelligence Desk (Special Forces Section) 290
Modise, Joe 119-122, 132, 135, 143, 144
Mohammed, Omar Bakri 74, 160
Morris, James 39, 283, 287
Mosaddegh, Mohammad 154
Mosby, Aline 207
Mossad 9, 18, 19, 23-25, 27-30, 34, 35, 37, 38, 76, 85, 88, 141, 187
Mousa, Baha 182, 183
Moussaoui, Zacarias 74, 75
Movimento Fascismo e Liberta (MFL) 266
Murphy, Hugh Leonard 'Lenny 287
Murphy, Lawrence 244, 245
Muslim Brotherhood 50

N

Nairac, Robert Laurence 286, 288, 290, 291, 300-303
Nasser, Gamal Abdel 26, 28, 32, 181
National Abti-Corruption Forum (NACF) 134
National Communications Centre (NCC) 149, 310, 332
National Intelligence Agency (NIA) 125, 133, 149
National Intelligence Coordinating Committee (NICC) 128, 150
National Prosecuting Authority (NPA) 63, 115, 123-131, 134, 145,
National Religious Party (NRP) 45
National Security Agency (NSA)16, 44, 88,

Index

157, 227,
National Security Council (NSC) 25, 141, 161, 164
Naval Air Technical Training Center 174, 204
Near East and South Asia (NESA) directorate 157
Neave, Airey Middleton 311, 312
Nelson, Brian 314, 315, 316, 322, 323, 324, 337, 338, 339
Netanyahu, Benjamin 'Bibi' 41- 46, 49, 55, 56
Ngcakani, Zolile 125
Nixon, Richard Milhous 19, 33, 234
Norbertine Order 253
North American Newspaper Alliance (NANA) 217
North Yorkshire Police (NYP)
Norwegian Police Surveillance Agency (POT)
Nosenko, Yuri Ivanovich 223-226
Nuclear Materials and Equipment Corporation (NUMEC) 23-25
Nuclear Suppliers Group (NSG) 44, 239, 304

O

O'Callaghan, Sean 304
Oatley, Michael 131, 132, 133, 327
Obama, Barack Hussein 15, 253
Ochs, Philip David 236
Office of Naval Intelligence (ONI) 207
Office of Security and Counter-Terrorism (OSCT) 107
Office of Special Plans (OSP) 157
Office of Strategic Services (OSS) 214, 231
Official IRA (OIRA) 282
Oldfield, Maurice 308, 309, 313
Omar, Mullah Mohammed 160
Operation Ajax 154
Operation Banner 279, 281, 286, 312, 333, 338, 352, 354
Operation Bayonet 38
Operation Blue Star 70
Operation Clockwork Orange 297
Operation Crevice 88, 103, 104
Operation Demetrius 282, 295, 296, 310
Operation Desert Storm 34, 153, 155, 177, 328,
Operation Destroy Lucifer 125

Operation Enduring Freedom 160
Operation Gold 213
Operation Hot Winter 53
Operation Inferno 25
Operation Kratos 83, 95
Operation Lipstick 283
Operation Locked Garden 53
Operation Motorman 282
Operation Overt 100, 101
Operation Pathway 96, 97
Operation Rooster 26,
Operation SCIV 266, 268, 274
Operation Scream 309
Operation Silver 213, 311
Operation Stopwatch 52,
Operation Torsion 336
Operation Volga 94
Operation Ward 309, 310
Opus Dei 258, 260, 262-264, 266-268, 271, 272, 274, 275
Order of Friars Minor Capuchin 256
Organization for Economic Co-operation and Development (OECD) 137, 260, 262
Organization for Security and Co-operation in Europe (OSCE) 267,
Organized Crime and Racketeering Section (OCRS) 265
Orlandi, Emanuela 256, 257, 258, 259
Orlandi, Ercole 256
Oswald, Lee Harvey 10, 202, 203, 204, 205, 207, 209-213, 215,-219, 221, 224-226, 228-233

P

Paisley, Ian Richard Kyle 279
Palestinian Islamic Jihad (PIJ) 50
Palestinian Liberation Organization (PLO) 25, 317
Pan Africanist Congress of Azania (PAC) 119,
Panciroli, Romeo 270
Parachute Intervention Squadron of the National Gendarmerie (EPIGN) 63
Parkland General Hospital 203
Pat Finucane Centre (PFC) 282, 206, 210
Pecorelli, Carmine 'Mino' 263, 264
Pederson, Mai 172
Pell, George 252, 253

People's Progressive Party (PPP) Guyana 181
Peres, Shimon 41, 42, 43, 45
Philby, Harold Adrian 'Kim' 226
Pinaso, Giorgio 266
Pinochet, Augusto Jose Ramon 9, 238, 241, 263
Pius VI (Count Giovanni Angelo Braschi) 259, 269
Pius X 256
Plan for Democratic Rebirth 257
Police Service of Northern Ireland (PSNI)
Pontifical Council for Legislative Texts
Pontificio Instituto de Musica Sagrada
Popular Front for the Liberation of Palestine (PFLP) 27, 28, 31, 32, 43
Powell, Colin Luther 125, 149, 165, 166, 167, 178
Project Pinto 44
Propaganda Due (P2) 257, 258, 259, 263, 264, 268
Prosecutor's Management Information System (PROMIS) 170
Protection of State Information Bill (PSIB) 113-115, 118, 148-151
Protocols of the Elders of Zion 243
Prouty, Leroy Fletcher 231, 232
Provisional Irish Republican Army (PIRA / Provos) 304
Prusakova, Marina Nikolayevna ('nee' Oswald) 202, 204, 208, 209, 211- 218, 221, 225, 233
Public Interest Immunity (PII) 186
Public Interest Lawyers (PIL) 184
Putin, Vladimir Vladimirovich 46

Rega, Jose Lopez 264
Regnum Christi 241, 272
Regulation of Investigatory Powers Act (2000) 186
Reid, John 92, 93, 290
Reid, Richard Colvin 75, 79, 91
Rennie, James 286
Rennie, John Ogilvy 308
Research, Information and Communications unit (RIC) 107
Restorick, Stephen 280, 333
Richards, Francis 'Brooks' 308, 313
Ridsdale, Gerald 253
Rimington, Stella 329
Robertson, Geoffrey Ronald 238, 243
Rockefeller Report, 1975 223
Rokach, Livia 19, 56, 161
Romero, Oscar Arnulfo 246, 247
Romney, Willard Mitt 15
Rose, Clive 308,
Rosenfeld, Samual, Jay (aka 'Thomas Doheny') 343, 344
Rositzke, Harry 225
Royal Air Force (RAF) 280, 314
Royal Institute of International Affairs (RIIA) 159, 177
Royal Ulster Constabulary (RUC) 11, 85, 105, 280
Royal United Services Institute (RUSI) 98
RUC Criminal Investigations Division (CID) 320, 321
RUC Headquarters Mobile Support Unit (HMSU) 319, 320
Rumsfeld, Donald Henry 157, 158, 162, 180, 181, 182

R

Rabin, Yitzhak 33, 40-43
Raikin, Spas Theodore 228
Rankin, J. Lee 262, 266, 267, 275, 308, 309, 320, 349
Ratzinger, Joseph Aloisius 238, 239, 240, 242, 244-246, 254, 255, 262
Re, Giovanni Battista 258, 259
Red Diamond Trading Company 139, 140, 143, 144
Rees, Merlyn (Baron Merlyn-Rees) 291
Reformatory and Industrial Schools System (Ireland) 248

S

SAAB 118, 120, 136-38, 140, 143, 144
Sabra and Shatila refugee camps 35-37, 47
Sadat, Anwar 26, 32, 33, 49
Salafist Group for Preaching and Combat (GSPC) 68
Santander 261
Saudi General Intelligence Presidency (GIP) 88
South Africa Judicial Instiute (SAJI) 129
Save the Children (Sweden) 39
Saville Inquiry 86, 326
Saville, Mark Oliver (Baron Saville of

Index

Newdigate)185, 281, 289, 325
Sawers, Robert John 179, 180, 181, 193, 194
Scarlett, John McLeod 89, 90, 163, 169, 173, 174, 192, 193
Schonborn, Christoph Maria Michael 239-241
Schweiker, Richard Schultz 219, 326
Selebi, Jacob Sello 'Jackie' 124, 125, 127-130, 135, 142, 149
Serious Fraud Office (SFO) 119, 138
Seriti, Willie 111, 112
Servizio per le Informazioni a la Sicurezza Militare (SISMI) 167, 257, 267
Sexwale, Mosima Gabriel 'Tokyo' 122
Shaik, Chippy 116,143-145,
Shaik, Schabir 116, 117, 123, 141
Shame of the Catholic Church 253
Shamir, Yitzhak 19, 40, 41
Sharett, Moshe 15, 19, 21, 34, 56
Sharon, Ariel 21, 32, 34-37, 43, 44, 46, 49
Shroud of Secrecy 246
Sindona, Michele 10, 259, 260, 268
Sinn Fein ('We Ourselves') 131, 279, 280, 299, 320, 327, 330, 331, 333-336, 350
Sisulu, Max Vuyesile 148
Sisulu, Nontsikelelo Albertina 148
Sisulu, Walter Max Ulyate 121
Slovo, Joe 141, 122
Smellie, Craig Connel 298, 303
Smith, Howard 131
Smyth, Brendan Gerard 253, 254,
Society of Jesus 275
Sodano, Angelo 240- 242
South Africa Institute of International Affairs (Sodano SAIIA) 129,
South Africa Secret Service (SASS) 142, 149
South African Coal, Oil, and Gas Company (Sasol) 333
South African Communist Party (SACP) 121, 122, 125, 127, 140, 149
South African National Academy of Intelligence (SANAI) 149
South African National Defense Force (SANDF) 118
South African National Industrial Participation (SANIP) 143, 144
South African Navy (SAN) 116, 142, 145
South African Police Service (SAPS) 115, 125, 134

Spanish National Police Corps (NPC) 80
Special Air Service (SAS) 283
Special Immigration Appeals Commission (SIAC) 70, 71
Special Patrol Group (SPG) 287, 301, 305
SS Maasdam 203, 212, 214, 218, 229, 230
St Alipius Primary School 252
St Francis Police Department 244
St Joseph's Industrial School 248
St John›s School for the Deaf 243
St Michael›s Industrial School 248
St Patrick›s College 252
Stalker, John 319-322, 354
State Security Agency (SSA) 149
Staughton, Tony 295, 197
Steel, Frank Fenwick 313
Stephens, Mark Howard 238, 239
Stern Gang 19, 20
Stevens, John Arthur 314, 322, 324, 345
Stirling, David Archibald 285
Stone, William Oliver 210, 235
Storm, Daniel 317
Strategic Defence Procurement (SDP) 111-113, 118, 119, 121, 130-133, 136, 139, 141-145
Straw, John Whitaker 'Jack' 78, 79, 84, 159, 164, 166, 173, 312
Stuart, Ted 283
Styles, Stephen George 293, 294, 295
Suffer the Children 253
Sultan, Prince Bandar bin 145, 181
Swedish National Police Board (SNPB) 62
Sykes, Richard 308, 309

T

Tague, James 208-210
Tanweer, Shehzad 59, 87, 91, 92, 95, 103, 104, 105
Tasking Co-ordination Group (TCG) 313, 322, 340, 342, 345
Templer Barracks (Ashford, Kent, UK) 285
Terry, Peter David 327
Texas School Book Depository 203,
Thames Valley Police (TVP)95, 171
Thatcher, Margaret Hilda 98, 121, 137, 142, 143, 313, 318, 326-328, 338, 339,
Thiepval Barracks, Lisburn. (British Army NIHQ.) 279
Thomson-CSF 116, 117, 118, 143, 145

...am, Philip 291, 293
Tippit, J.D. 214, 232, 233, 235
Tommaso Ludovico Da Vittoria School 256
Tornielli, Andrea 240, 276
Travellers Aid Society (TAS) 228
TSS Chemicals Division 223
Tugwell, Maurice 295, 296
Turner, Stansfield M. 71, 139, 223,
Tutu, Desmond 114, 151
Tuzo, Harry Craufurd 283, 285
TyssenKrupp 145

U

UKUSA/ECHELON 175
Ulster Defense Association (UDA) 314, 315, 316, 318, 319, 322, 323, 337-339
Ulster Defense Regiment (UDR) 280, 287, 288, 292, 295, 299-302, 305, 317, 323, 352
Ulster Freedom Fighters (UFF) 298
Ulster Unionist Party (UUP) 297, 346
Ulster Volunteer Force (UVF) 284, 287, 290-295, 298, 300-305, 316,
Umkhonto we Sizwe (MK) Veterans Association 120, 121, 333
UN Committee Against Torture 249
Unicredit Bank 261
Union de Banques Suisse 260
Union of Black Journalists (UBJ) 113
United Nations Monitoring, Verification and Inspection Commission (UNMOVIC) 167, 169, 172, 195-198
United States Air Force (USAF) 34, 157, 178, 182, 229, 231
US Army Chemical Corps 223
US Department of Energy (DoE) 24
US Department of Justice (DoJ) 75, 139, 242, 265
US Marine Control Squadron 204
US National Intelligence Estimate (NIE) 167
USS Liberty 9, 15, 16, 17, 22, 25
Uthman, Omar (Abu Qatada) 77

V

Valencia, Rafael Guizar 241
Valls, Joaquin Navarro 262
van der Merwe, Willem

Vetter, Wendelin 254
Vorster, Balthazar Johannes 113

W

Wallace, John Colin 214, 288, 295, 296-299
Walshaw, Margaret 323, 324
Walus, Janusz 122
Warke, Sarah 283, 284
Warren Commission 202, 204-206, 208-215, 221, 228, 234, 235, 237
Warren, Earl 215
Weakland, Rembert G. 244
Weir, John Oliver 287, 301
Wescott, John 310
West Midlands Police (WMP) 100
Wilmshurst, Elizabeth 177, 178, 206
Wilson, Joseph 172
Wolfowitz, Paul 157, 191
Women›s Royal Army Corps (WRAC) 283
Woodfield, Philip 313
World Anti-Communist League (WACL) 228
World Trade Center (NY) 72, 73, 87, 119, 140
Wright, Alan 316

Y

Young Communist League (YCL) 121

Z

Zawahri, Ayman 72
Zionist Organization of America (ZOA) 23
Zuma, Jacob Gedleyihlekisa 111-117, 122, 124-130, 134-136, 141, 142, 148-150

FEB 2 0 2014